HISTORICAL DICTIONARIES OF RELIGIONS, PHILOSOPHIES, AND MOVEMENTS
Jon Woronoff, Series Editor

1. *Buddhism*, by Charles S. Prebish, 1993.
2. *Mormonism*, by Davis Bitton, 1994. *Out of print. See no. 32.*
3. *Ecumenical Christianity*, by Ans Joachim van der Bent, 1994.
4. *Terrorism*, by Sean Anderson and Stephen Sloan, 1995. *Out of print. See no. 41.*
5. *Sikhism*, by W. H. McLeod, 1995. *Out of print. See no. 59.*
6. *Feminism*, by Janet K. Boles and Diane Long Hoeveler, 1995. *Out of print. See no. 52.*
7. *Olympic Movement*, by Ian Buchanan and Bill Mallon, 1995. *Out of print. See no. 39.*
8. *Methodism*, by Charles Yrigoyen Jr. and Susan E. Warrick, 1996. *Out of print. See no. 57.*
9. *Orthodox Church*, by Michael Prokurat, Alexander Golitzin, and Michael D. Peterson, 1996.
10. *Organized Labor*, by James C. Docherty, 1996. *Out of print. See no. 50.*
11. *Civil Rights Movement*, by Ralph E. Luker, 1997.
12. *Catholicism*, by William J. Collinge, 1997.
13. *Hinduism*, by Bruce M. Sullivan, 1997.
14. *North American Environmentalism*, by Edward R. Wells and Alan M. Schwartz, 1997.
15. *Welfare State*, by Bent Greve, 1998. *Out of print. See no. 63.*
16. *Socialism*, by James C. Docherty, 1997. *Out of print. See no. 73.*
17. *Bahá'í Faith*, by Hugh C. Adamson and Philip Hainsworth, 1998. *Out of print. See no. 71.*
18. *Taoism*, by Julian F. Pas in cooperation with Man Kam Leung, 1998.
19. *Judaism*, by Norman Solomon, 1998. *Out of print. See no. 69.*
20. *Green Movement*, by Elim Papadakis, 1998. *Out of print. See no. 80.*
21. *Nietzscheanism*, by Carol Diethe, 1999. *Out of print. See no. 75.*
22. *Gay Liberation Movement*, by Ronald J. Hunt, 1999.
23. *Islamic Fundamentalist Movements in the Arab World, Iran, and Turkey*, by Ahmad S. Moussalli, 1999.

Historical Dictionary of the Baptists

Second Edition

William H. Brackney

*Historical Dictionaries of Religions,
Philosophies, and Movements, No. 94*

400th Anniversary Commemorative Edition, 1609–2009

The Scarecrow Press, Inc.
Lanham, Maryland • Toronto • Plymouth, UK
2009

SCARECROW PRESS, INC.

Published in the United States of America
by Scarecrow Press, Inc.
A wholly owned subsidiary of
The Rowman & Littlefield Publishing Group, Inc.
4501 Forbes Boulevard, Suite 200, Lanham, Maryland 20706
www.scarecrowpress.com

Estover Road
Plymouth PL6 7PY
United Kingdom

British Library Cataloguing in Publication Information Available

Library of Congress Cataloging-in-Publication Data
Brackney, William H.
 Historical dictionary of the Baptists / William H. Brackney. – 2nd ed.
  p. cm. — (Historical dictionaries of religions, philosophies, and movements ;
No. 94)
 Includes bibliographical references (p.   ).
 ISBN-13: 978-0-8108-5622-6 (cloth : alk. paper)
 ISBN-10: 0-8108-5622-0 (cloth : alk. paper)
 ISBN-13: 978-0-8108-6282-1 (ebook)
 ISBN-10: 0-8108-6282-4 (ebook)
 1. Baptists–Dictionaries. I. Title.
 BX6211.B73 2009
 286.03–dc22   2008044067

Dedicated to
Dr. Noel Christian Brackney
Gentleman, scholar, linguist,
who has traversed many Baptist trails

Contents

Editor's Foreword

Although relative newcomers to the Christian community, the Baptists have left an indelible mark as a movement, denomination, and tradition. Due to the Baptists' deep convictions and strong drive, this mark is bound to grow as more members join the fold. The expansion recently, at a time of relative stagnation among other groups, has been quite phenomenal—a growth that involves not only an increased number of churches and members but also an ability to reach into very different cultures, far removed from the home bases of Great Britain and North America and now including the rest of the Americas, other parts of Europe, Africa, and Asia. However, this expansion and the exceptional individualism of the members as well as the diversity of their groups make the Baptists difficult to define.

This second edition of the *Historical Dictionary of the Baptists* goes to great lengths to describe and explain the Baptists to others and to themselves as well. Few could expect as many entries on eminent Baptists, from the founders four centuries ago to those active today—to say nothing of the summaries of various groupings, conventions, and organizations or the résumés of Baptist activities around the world. There are also informative presentations of guiding principles, theological concepts, and church polity. This is rounded out with a chronology, list of abbreviations, and extensive bibliography.

It took William Brackney three decades to acquire this knowledge and the ability to present it cogently—very busy decades to judge by his curriculum vitae. He was a pastor of congregations as well as a teacher at various colleges and universities; he is presently principal and professor of historical theology at McMaster University in Hamilton, Ontario. Along the way, Dr. Brackney has also edited several journals, written a number of books and countless articles, and served as executive director of the American Baptist Historical Society and chair of the Study and Research Division of the Baptist World Alliance. This dictionary is not the least of his contributions and will certainly be appreciated by his students, colleagues, and fellow Baptists, as well as others for whom it will serve as a welcome tool.

Jon Woronoff
Series Editor

Preface

The 400th anniversary of the modern Baptist movement, 1609–2009, gives us an opportunity to remember those men and women, some famous and some lesser known, who contributed to the growth and defining moments of Baptist history. We are indebted to premier Baptist historian William H. Brackney for this scholarly historical dictionary of the Baptists. This is indeed a handbook of Baptist heritage and thought, a handy reference that reminds us of those great Baptist saints and events that have created Baptist identity today!

Scholars, students, pastors, and laity now have available in a single volume a dictionary of "who's who" and "what happened when" throughout Baptist history. Although it is a dictionary in the sense of defining terms and names of outstanding Baptists, it is more than a dictionary. It is a history of Baptists in alphabetical order! If you want a brief biography of John Smyth or Helen Barrett Montgomery, Billy Graham or E. Y. Mullins, Martin Luther King Jr. or John Diefenbaker—it is all in this volume, where you will find an accurate record of each one's ministry. If you need a description of a Baptist organization or event, it is here with fascinating details.

Baptists, like members of all denominations, continue to seek and redefine their identity. How can one do that without knowing the history and thought of our Baptist heritage and the people who shaped it? In a period of rapid growth, particularly in the Southern Hemisphere and "Two-thirds World," it is especially important for any religious movement to know its history and those who shaped it from the beginning to the present. When John Smyth and a congregation of less than 40 men and women were baptized as believers in 1609, they were looked down upon as an insignificant group of dissidents, sectarians, and refugees from England who had fled to Amsterdam. Who would have thought that this despised sectarian movement in 1609 would become in 2009 the largest Protestant Christian World Communion? According to the eminent Christian world statistician David Barrett, the Baptist World Alliance (BWA) alone represents a community of more than 100 million persons. There are 38 million baptized believers in the membership of the BWA. Since Baptists do not count children and families in their statistics—as do the Anglican World Communion, Lutheran World Federation, World Methodist Council, and World Alliance of Reformed Churches—missiologists conclude that groups practicing believer's baptism, such as Churches of Christ, Mennonites, Pentecostals, and so forth, really represent a worshipping community of at least two or three times their adult membership. (Note: The aforementioned BWA statistics do not include the millions of independent Baptists who are not BWA members, nor the 16 million members of the Southern Baptist Convention, who, due to internal conflict, withdrew from the BWA in 2004.) This dictionary contains many entries for groups beyond the BWA family.

Being one of the largest Protestant groups in the world demands a certain responsibility with respect to other Christian groups. Such responsibility requires that we know who we are and from whence we have come. The BWA continues to participate in theological conversations with other Christian groups such as Anglican, Lutheran, Methodist, Reformed, Catholic, and Orthodox. This volume will assist in giving background to such ecumenical conversations.

Missiologists remind us of the paradigm shift of the world Christian movement from the Northern Hemisphere to the South. This dictionary will help the new leadership of Baptists in the Southern Hemisphere know better who they are. Furthermore, students of Baptist history will welcome this volume because now in one place can be found the significant dates and facts of 400 years of Baptist history.

In his obituary of Karl Barth, Professor Jan Lochman mentioned the more than 20 volumes of *Church Dogmatics* and, paraphrasing he *New York Times*, said, "You don't have to read it all, but it is good to know that it is all there." In a similar way, a dictionary is usually not read all at once. Rather it is a reference work to inform and also give impetus for further study. We are grateful to Professor Brackney for his excellent research and outstanding scholarship that have given us a comprehensive international handbook of Baptist life and work. Baptist leaders and scholars will use it for years to come.

It is with enthusiasm that I recommend the *Historical Dictionary of the Baptists*, not only to Baptists, but to the larger Christian community.

Dr. Denton Lotz
General Secretary, Baptist World Alliance 1988–2007

Acknowledgments

The idea of this project began while I was executive director of the American Baptist Historical Society more than 20 years ago. I recognized the need for a concise, one-volume reference that reduced the voluminous accomplishment of Edward C. Starr's *Baptist Bibliography* (26 volumes) and updated the work in William Cathcart's 19th-century *Dictionary of the Baptists*. Under the guidelines for Scarecrow Press historical dictionaries, I have developed entries on topics, people, and geographical locations, as well as important themes and issues. In all, a search for as much accuracy and appropriate detail as possible has characterized the formation of this second edition. There is nothing else available with many of the details I was able to recover, and it is my hope that this historical dictionary will continue to make a useful contribution to religious studies.

Most dictionaries are the work of scores, if not hundreds, of contributors. This book is different because it bears the name of one author who has indirectly depended upon the work and advice of many authorities and sources.

Among those I especially want to thank are Denton Lotz, BWA general secretary, for access to Baptist World Alliance data; Betty Layton and Patricia Williams of the American Baptist Churches, USA, in Valley Forge, Pennsylvania; Frederick S. Downs, retired American Baptist missionary in Massachusetts; Keith Clements, John Nicholson, Roger Hayden, Karl Heinz Walter, Keith Jones, and Regina Claas, for details pertaining to British and European Baptists; Ken R. Manley in Melbourne, Thorwald Lorenzen and Rod Benson in New South Wales, and Noel Vose and Richard Moore in Western Australia, for assistance with Australian Baptists; Patricia Townsend at Acadia University Archives; Charles Hartman, pastor at Swansea Baptist Church; Kenneth Chroniger at Alfred Station Seventh Day Baptist Church; Diane Magnuson at

Bethel Theological Seminary; Patricia Passig and Jeff Straub at Central Baptist Seminary, St. Paul, Minnesota; Bill Summers at Southern Baptist Library and Archives; Melinda Gilpin at the Warren Harding Home in Ohio; Deborah Dempsey at First Baptist Church in Ottawa, Ontario; Dean Noakes at Hanover, Ontario Baptist Church; Ashley Smith at Colgate Rochester; Sandra Dugal at Kalamazoo College; Stanley Lemmons at First Baptist Church in America; Diana Yount at Andover Newton Theological School; James R. C. Perkin in Wolfville, Nova Scotia; and J. Daniel Gibson, at Pereau Baptist Church, Canning, Nova Scotia.

A large word of gratitude must be expressed to various friends far and wide: Marion Dorey, Acadia Divinity College; Ruby Burke and Nina Niebower, Baptist World Alliance; and Beverlee Everett and Ben Chan, American Baptist Churches, USA. A generous travel grant from the Herbert and Joy Reynolds Excellence Fund at Baylor University underwrote some of my travel and research costs. On a personal note, my wife, Kitty, has provided patience and encouragement for every stage of this project, especially the almost daily appearance of pieces of the mosaic, which she has always placed in the larger picture.

Finally, I wish to thank my graduate assistant, Borden Scott at Acadia for his expertise at the final stage, and Andrew Yoder at Scarecrow Press for supervising final production of the second edition.

William H. Brackney
Wallbrook Mountain, Nova Scotia
30 January 2008

Reader's Note

For convenience and uniformity, geographical entries include the majority of countries in the world as of 2005 and, for the most part, the statistical data is stated as of 2005–2006. A statistical note is made only for major Baptist groups in a country. Biographical entry selection is based upon a master list of Baptist leaders of all persuasions, and priority is given to suggestions from international leaders and to the selection of persons in roles not included in other reference works. Users of the dictionary should recognize that abbreviations have been kept to a minimum. Generally, organizational abbreviations are used only within the entry where the organization appears. When the terminology "American" is used in the biographical entries, it has two meanings: in discussions of events prior to 1845, it designates generically a Baptist minister in any region of the United States; in contexts after 1845, "American" denotes a minister or leader related to the American Baptist Churches or its predecessors.

Cross references are indicated by bold face type. "See also" references indicate entries of related interest.

List of Acronyms and Abbreviations

AABF	All Africa Baptist Fellowship
ABA	American Baptist Association
ABC	American Baptist Convention
ABCUSA	American Baptist Churches in the U.S.A.
ABE	American Baptist Evangelicals
ABEC	American Baptist Educational Commission
ABES	American Baptist Education Society
ABF	Asian Baptist Federation
ABFMS	American Baptist Foreign Mission Society
ABFrMs	American Baptist Free Mission Society
ABHMS	American Baptist Home Mission Society
ABHS	American Baptist Historical Society
ABMU	American Baptist Missionary Union
ABPS	American Baptist Publication Society
ABWE	Association of Baptists for World Evangelism
AGM	Amazing Grace Missions
ANBC	American National Baptist Convention
AUBA	African United Baptist Association
AUCECB	All-Union Council of Evangelical Christians-Baptists
BBF	Baptist Bible Fellowship
BBFM	Baptist Board of Foreign Missions
BBUA	Baptist Bible Union of America
BC	Baptist Congress
BCE	Baptist Center for Ethics
BCOQ	Baptist Convention of Ontario and Quebec
BCWM	Baptist Council on World Mission
BFM	Baptist Faith and Message
BFaM	Baptist Faith Missions
BFMC	Baptist Foreign Missionary Convention

BGC	Baptist General Conference
BGTS	Baptist General Tract Society
BHMS	Baptist Home Mission Society
BIMI	Baptist International Missions, Inc.
BJA	Baptist Jubilee Advance
BJCPA	Baptist Joint Committee on Public Affairs
BMA	Baptist Missionary Association of America
BMM	Baptist Mid-Missions
BMS	Baptist Missionary Society
BPFNA	Baptist Peace Fellowship of North America
BRF	Baptist Revival Fellowship
BRG	Baptist Renewal Group
BSSB	Sunday School Board, Southern Baptist Convention
BU	Baptist Union of Great Britain and Ireland
BUA	Baptist Union of Australia
BWA	Baptist World Alliance
BWM	Baptist World Mission
CaBF	Caribbean Baptist Fellowship
CBA	Conservative Baptist Association of America
CBCNEI	Council of Baptist Churches of Northeast India
CBF	Cooperative Baptist Fellowship
CBFMS	Conservative Baptist Foreign Mission Society
CCF	Canadian Commonwealth Federation
EBC	European Baptist Convention
EBF	European Baptist Federation
EBM	Evangelical Baptist Missions
FBB	Fellowship of British Baptists
FBHM	Fellowship of Baptists for Home Mission
FEBC	Fellowship of Evangelical Baptist Churches in Canada
FMB	Foreign Mission Board, Southern Baptist Convention
FWB	Freewill Baptists
GAGB	General Association of General Baptists
GARBC	General Association of Regular Baptist Churches
GMC	General Missionary Convention
IMB	International Mission Board, Southern Baptist Convention
KJV	King James Version
L&T	Literary and theological

LBF	Liberty Baptist Fellowship
LBFMC	Lott Carey Baptist Foreign Mission Convention
MBMS	Massachusetts Baptist Missionary Society
NAACP	National Association for the Advancement of Colored People
NABC	North American Baptist Conference
NABF	North American Baptist Fellowship
NBC	Northern Baptist Convention
NBCA	National Baptist Convention of America
NBCUSA	National Baptist Convention of the United States of America
NBMCA	National Baptist Missionary Convention of America
PBA	Philadelphia Baptist Association
PNBC	Progressive National Baptist Convention
RBA	Reformed Baptist Alliance
RSV	Revised Standard Version
RUEBU	Russian-Ukrainian Evangelical Baptist Union
RWF	Roger Williams Fellowship
SB	Strict Baptists
SBC	Southern Baptist Convention
SBF	Southwide Baptist Fellowship
SBTS	Southern Baptist Theological Seminary
SCOR	Study Commission on Relationships
SDA	Seventh-day Adventist
SDB	Seventh Day Baptist
TBC	Texas Baptists Committed
WABHMS	Woman's American Baptist Home Mission Society
WBF	World Baptist Fellowship
WCC	World Council of Churches
WMU	Women's Missionary Union

Chronology

1606 John Smyth separated from the Church of England

1609 Smyth baptizes himself and others: initiates first Baptist Congregation

1612 First General Baptist congregation met at Spitalfields, London; Thomas Helwys published *The Mistery of Iniquity*

1614 Leonard Busher published a tract advocating religious toleration and baptism by immersion

1626 London area churches associated and had correspondence with Mennonites

1633 Howell Vaughan gathered first congregation in Wales

1638–1639 First Particular Baptist Church emerged in London; first congregation in America founded at Providence, Rhode Island

1640 Dorothy Hazzard was instrumental in founding Broadmead Church, Bristol; Richard Blunt began practice among English Separatists of believer's baptism by immersion

1642 Great Debate at Southwark occurred between Baptists and Anglicans

1644 *First London Confession of Faith* published by Particular Baptists; John Denne imprisoned for itinerant preaching at Cambridge

1654 General Baptist Assembly commenced; Henry Dunster forced to resign as president of Harvard College

1660 John Bunyan imprisoned under the Conventicle Act

1661 Uprising of Fifth Monarchists led by Thomas Venner

1663 John Clarke enabled the colonial charter of Rhode Island

1670 General Six Principle Baptists held association meeting in New England

1671 First Seventh Day Baptist congregation established in America

1678 John Bunyan published *A Pilgrim's Progress*

1679 Edward Terrill Trust laid foundation for Bristol Academy

1689 Act of Toleration passed

1691 Benjamin Keach introduced first Baptist hymnal

1700 First Baptist settlers noted in Virginia

1702 General Baptists supported mission in Carolina Colony

1707 Philadelphia Baptist Association held first meeting

1714 Hanover Coffeehouse ministerial society founded in London

1717 Particular Baptist Fund established in England

1719 German Baptist Brethren emigrated to Pennsylvania

1725 General Baptist Fund established in England

1728 German Seventh Day Baptist Church formed at Germantown, Pennsylvania

1738 Thomas Crosby published first Baptist history

1740 New Light movement began among New England churches

1742 Philadelphia Confession of Faith issued; it was published by Benjamin Franklin

1752 London Baptist Education Society founded

1756 Isaac Eaton founded academy at Hopewell, New Jersey

1764 College of Rhode Island founded by Philadelphia Baptists

1765 Ebenezer Moulton formed first congregation in Canada

1774 Isaac Backus presented case for religious liberty to U.S. Continental Congress

1776   Henry Alline began itinerant preaching in Nova Scotia

1777   Isaac Backus published history of Baptists in America

1781   Benjamin Randal organized Freewill Baptist Connection; Elhanan Winchester of Philadelphia declared himself a Universalist

1785   Joseph Hughes of London proposed the Sunday School Society

1787   Virginia Baptists opposed slavery

1792   Baptist Missionary Society founded at Kettering; David George established first Baptist congregation in Africa

1797   Home Missionary Society formed in England

1798   First Baptist church in Asia organized at Serampore, India

1799   New Connexion of General Baptists (U.K.) formed

1800   Mary Webb formed first missionary society among Baptists in United States

1801   *Georgia Analytical Repository* first published, oldest Baptist paper in United States

1802   Massachusetts Baptist Missionary Society founded

1804   Baptists joined in forming British and Foreign Bible Society; Northern Baptist Education Society formed in England

1808   David Barrow published first antislavery tract among Baptists

1810   Baptist Theological Institution at Stepney established

1812   William Staughton began theological school in his Philadelphia home

1813   Adoniram and Ann Judson commenced mission in Burma; Baptist Union of Great Britain formed; Baptist Irish Society founded; David Benedict's history of Baptists appeared in United States

1814   General Baptist Missionary Convention (U.S.) held first meeting

1815   African Missionary Society of Richmond (Virginia) formed

1817   John Mason Peck and James Welch appointed missionaries to western United States

1819 First Baptist congregation in France established

1820 Brethren in Christ formed in Lancaster, Pennsylvania, with Baptist practices

1821 United States Congress chartered Columbian College in Washington, D.C., a national Baptist university; Lott Carey planted first congregation in Liberia

1823 Alexander Campbell began publication of *Christian Baptist*

1824 Baptist General Tract Society formed in Washington, D.C.

1825 First Baptist post-undergraduate theological seminary in United States opened at Newton, Massachusetts

1826 London University founded by Baptist advocacy; Daniel Parker published theory of "two seeds"

1827 Antimasonic controversy divided Baptists in United States

1831 John Winebrenner organized Church of God, with Baptist principles; first Baptist congregation in Australia founded

1832 American Baptist Home Mission Society formed; William Knibb spoke against slavery in British Empire

1833 First issue of *Gospel Herald* circulated among English Baptists

1834 J. G. Oncken formed first congregation in Hamburg, Germany; Providence, Ohio Association formed by black churches

1835 Chemung (New York) disfellowshiped others who supported mission work; William Dean commenced mission work among the Chinese; first issue of the *Gospel Standard* circulated among English Baptists

1838 Acadia University chartered in Nova Scotia; Canada Baptist College opened in Montreal

1839 Julius Köbner formed church at Copenhagen, Denmark

1840 American Baptist Missionary Convention formed of black churches

1842   Adventist movement coalesced around preaching of William Miller, a New York local Baptist preacher

1843   American Baptist Free Mission Society founded

1844   Triennial Convention held final meeting

1845   Southern Baptist Convention formed

1846   American Baptist Missionary Union organized; Ruby Bixby, a Freewill Baptist, licensed to the ministry

1848   First Baptist church in Sweden formed

1851   Landmarkist movement began in United States with Cotton Grove Resolutions; first Baptist congregation established in New Zealand; German Baptist Conference in America formed

1853   Jonathan Goble commenced mission work in Japan

1856   Charles Spurgeon's Pastor's College opened in London

1858   Gottfried A. Alf began first church in Poland

1861   Metropolitan Tabernacle opened in London

1863   Southern Baptist Sunday School Board formed

1864   First baptism in Russia recorded

1865   Letter from Baptist Missionary Society sparked Morant Bay Uprising in Jamaica

1870   General Association of General Baptists founded in United States

1871   Southern Baptists began missions in Italy

1877   Women's American Baptist Home Mission Societies founded in United States

1878   At Ongole, India, 2,222 baptized in single day

1879   Baptist missions in Spain began; Baptist General Conference of America (Swedish) organized

1880 Seminary at Hamburg, Germany, opened

1882 Baptist Congress held first meeting

1884 Great revival occurred in Belgian Congo; first Baptist congregation established in Mexico

1886 Pentecost on the Congo began at Banza Manteke

1887 McMaster University chartered in Canada

1888 American Baptist Education Society founded; Women's Missionary Union founded by Southern Baptists; Reformed Baptists in Canada adopted holiness theology

1890 University of Chicago reopened with support of John D. Rockefeller

1891 First railroad chapel car put in service in United States; Baptist Young People's Union of America organized

1894 Fortress Monroe Conference held

1895 National Baptist Convention in the United States formed; Irish Baptist Union reorganized and separated from British Baptists

1896 Sir Charles Tupper, a Baptist, became prime minister of Canada

1905 Baptist World Alliance formed

1907 Northern Baptist Convention (U.S.) organized; Colored Primitive Baptists organized

1908 Southwestern Baptist Theological Seminary separated from Baylor University

1911 Free Baptists merged with Northern Baptist Convention

1915 National Baptist Convention of America founded

1918 First woman pastor appointed in Baptist Union of Great Britain

1919 New World Movement began among Northern Baptists

1920 London Conference of European Baptists held; Helen Barrett Montgomery became first woman president of Northern Baptist Convention; Baptist Seminary at Budapest, Hungary, opened; Baptist Mid-Missions founded in United States; Warren G. Harding of Ohio elected president of the United States, the first Baptist to hold the office

1924　American Baptist Association formed

1928　Association of Baptists for World Evangelism founded; Evangelical Baptist Missions founded

1933　General Association of Regular Baptist Churches (U.S.) formed

1939　American Baptist Bill of Rights issued

1943　Conservative Baptist Foreign Mission Society founded

1944　Baptist Federation of Canada formed; All Union Council of Evangelicals-Baptists formed in the Soviet Union

1945　Harry S. Truman, a Southern Baptist, became president of the United States

1946　Baptist Joint Committee on Public Affairs formed in United States

1948　Baptists participated in World Council of Churches

1949　European Baptist Federation organized; Baptist Theological Seminary opened at Rüschlikon, Switzerland; missionaries and workers in Bolivia martyred

1950　Baptist Bible Fellowship formed in United States

1957　John Diefenbaker, a Baptist, became prime minister of Canada

1959　Baptist Jubilee Advance commenced

1961　Progressive National Baptist Convention founded in United States

1968　Crusade of the Americas began

1976　James E. "Jimmy" Carter, a Southern Baptist, elected president of the United States

1977　Liberty Baptist Fellowship founded in United States

1991 Cooperative Baptist Fellowship organized in United States

1992 Two Southern Baptists, William J. Clinton and Albert Gore, elected president and vice president, respectively, of the United States

1993 Tadeusz Zielinski, a Baptist of Katowice, Poland, elected member of Polish National Parliament

1995 Baptists and Orthodox Churches engaged in international dialogue

1996 Baptist World Alliance published report *Baptists against Racism*

1997 Baptists in Belarus outlawed by government

1998 Baptists in the Republic of the Congo, Liberia, and Sierra Leone suffered persecution and displacement from homes

2000 Southern Baptists adopted a new version of the Baptist Faith and Message

2004 Southern Baptist Convention withdrew membership from the Baptist World Alliance

2005 Baptist World Alliance celebrated centenary in Birmingham, England

2007 Former U.S. vice president Albert Gore, a Baptist, won Nobel Prize for Peace

2008 Baptist groups from Canada and United States met in Atlanta, Georgia, as a New Covenant is proposed to 16,000 in attendance

2009 Worldwide Baptist community celebrated 400th anniversary of founding of first Baptist congregation

Introduction

Baptists occupy a large segment of Christianity worldwide, surpassed only by Roman Catholic and Orthodox groups. Essentially an outgrowth of the Puritan Reformation in England, Baptists have spread their principles to every continent and nation in the world. While the primary language of discourse and publication is English, Baptists now represent the many languages of Europe, Asia, and Africa. Their growing edge numerically is in the Southern Hemisphere (Africa and Latin America), while the largest numbers of Baptists are found in the United States and Asia, respectively.

There is great variety among Baptists. They have produced divergent opinions and organizations on the basis of theology, ethnicity, race, polity, and leadership distinctives. At the heart of being Baptist is an unflinching commitment to the local congregation as the visible manifestation of the people of God. Yet, Baptists also build relationships with others of like faith and order by what they refer to as the "associational principle." They have no ecclesiastical hierarchies, nor do they observe the sacraments as means of grace; Baptists hold uniformly to the separation of church and state and individual accountability before God, which they call "soul liberty." They are evangelical and mostly missionary, by which Baptists hold to a need to share the gospel of Christ with unbelievers.

One of the problems Baptist historians have faced is whether Baptists are a movement, a denomination, or a tradition. In some ways, they are all three. It takes all of Baptist history to comprehend their full meaning.

A NEW RELIGIOUS MOVEMENT

Where did Baptists come from? The most plausible explanation is that Baptists were a religious sect or movement within the broad sweep of the English Reformation. They were part of a trend called Nonconformity or, to use a related term, "dissenters." By Michael Watts's definition of dissenters as persons of "devotion, discipline, individualists and humble people," Baptists qualified well as a movement of persons and organized groups (congregations) who adhered to a consistent set of ideas with an action program to alter the social order. That is, early Baptists created confessional statements of their principles, propagated their faith through worship and education, practiced certain rites like believer's baptism, and sought to win converts to their religious ideals. In the strictest sense of the term "movement," the General Baptists, the Particular Baptists, and possibly the Seventh Day Baptists were differentiated religious movements.

If one searches for the ultimate beginning of the Baptists as a movement, it must be the gradual conversion of an Anglican priest and an Anglican lawyer, John Smyth and Thomas Helwys, respectively. Smyth began his pilgrimage as a Cambridge University graduate who tried the priesthood, then moved to radical Puritanism, then Separatism, and finally, searching his Bible, a Baptistic position. Smyth met Helwys at some point in Gainsborough, England, and brought him along the ideological continuum as well. From this root sprang theological conviction, flight into exile (in Amsterdam), differentiation of belief, and schism within the first congregation. When the small group under Helwys's leadership returned to England in 1611, they became the first Baptist congregation on English soil, the second in point of history. Smyth and his branch remained in Amsterdam and were slowly absorbed into the Dutch Mennonite community.

Influenced by Anabaptist communities and the Puritan Separatist tradition among a growing number of Christians in and around London, then other cities such as Bristol, the original two Baptist movements marked their pilgrimage with a consistent set of affirmations, including individual accountability before God; the authority of Scripture; the Lordship of Christ; and the necessity of a Christian experience, a church composed of believers, believer's baptism, and religious liberty. All of these traits may be found in earlier forms of dissent and among the Anabaptists, but not altogether as would be the case with the self-conscious Baptists.

The General Baptists, so called for their understanding of the work of Christ as it applied to all persons, were the first identifiable movement of Baptists, and they appeared about 1612. Next in time, a second grouping of Baptists arose from among those Separatists in the congregation first formed by Henry Jacob in 1613; by the 1630s, this group began to wrestle with the nature of the church and the issue of baptism. Under the leadership of John Spilsbury, they became, about 1640, the Particular Baptist movement, due to their belief that Christ's atonement applied to the elect of God. There were also other branches and patterns as variegated as the liberty to interpret Scripture: Seventh Day Baptists, Leg of Mutton Baptists, and so forth. England was their cradle, then Wales and Scotland, and the American colonies.

Baptists were, then, at their beginning a collection of English-speaking Christians who stressed Christian experience over doctrinal subtleties, who derived their beliefs and practices from the words of Scripture, and who professed a fairly universal need to share their faith. They were differentiated by their group origins, their theological perspectives on the breadth of the application of the work of Christ, and their positions on issues of polity and order.

Demographically, who were these Baptists and their descendants? In his survey of 1707, Marius D'Assigny, an educated Anglican divine, observed of the English Baptist community that they included mostly mechanics and tradesmen: "butchers, tallow-chandlers, peddlers, tinkers, taylors, tinmen"; in short, "men of all trades and employments."[1] Occasionally, there were to be found physicians, lawyers, military officers, and politicians, and in the early American experience, numerous subsistence farmers. The Baptist ministry contained a surprising number of university- and academy-trained people in the English context, and this trend continued in the American colonial development. For the most part, Baptists were uncomfortable in the formal religious atmospheres of establishment Christianity and probably were not invited into many elite social circles. In 17th-century England and Wales, Baptists could be described by their social betters as uncouth and of the "meaner sort."

In Britain, varieties of Baptists grew up from mostly Calvinistic types, theologically speaking, to several sorts of "Arminian" groups like General Baptists and New Connexion Baptists. In England, the Strict, or Evangelical, Baptists, who underwent several permutations, occupied a stiff Calvinistic tradition. Andrew Fuller and William Carey marked a new course among evangelical Calvinists in Britain, who would send missionaries to every continent. In Scotland, Baptists also differentiated among McLeanites, Glasites, Scotch Baptists, Haldanites, and Sandemanians.

THE EMERGING TRADITION

Baptists emigrated to the various British colonies for the same reason most other colonists did: improved economic opportunity, escape from an undesirable past, and religious freedom. They came as individuals without a congregation, as persons of another religious persuasion, and as entire immigrant congregations. In the North American context, Roger Williams went to Massachusetts Bay as a Puritan teacher and under the influence of a woman coreligionist, converted to Baptistic principles in exile in Rhode Island. There were members of the Swansea congregation of John Myles, who transplanted themselves to Rehoboth, Massachusetts Bay Colony. And there were people like Elias Keach, who fled from his father's reputation and found himself in eastern Pennsylvania, and others like William Staughton, who shed youthful indiscretions to build a new life in the newly independent United States. There were three Baptist entry points to the American colonies, in order of frequency: Massachusetts, the Delaware Valley, and the southern tidewater region. Most went to New England and the heart of the fragile colonial American Baptist movement was to be found there before 1700. Baptists found in New England a Congregational intolerance in some ways more oppressive than in England. In Pennsylvania and the Jerseys, there was more freedom in the latter decades of the 17th century. Thus, several individuals emigrated to the Middle Colonies and started congregations there with transplanted New England names. In the South, it was difficult for Baptists, who culturally irritated the Scotch-Irish Presbyterians and angered the solidly Anglican upper classes of colonial society. One historian's view of Baptists in New England is probably valid for the overall colonial experience: "The rank and file of the Baptists were honest, hard-working plowmen, artisans, mechanics, and day-laborers."[2] A few were chimneysweeps; fewer were elected selectmen. To their credit, some Baptists tenaciously pioneered despite real persecution. By 1750, the foundations had been laid in each colonial region, and a rudimentary associational life had grown among the congregations.

Baptists thrived in an unusual way as an identifiable religious community in the United States. Along the eastern seaboard and later on the frontier, Baptist life was characterized by flexible organization and differences of opinion. It is overemphasizing the issue to indicate there was only one primary schism—over the institution of slavery. There were actually multiple points of sharp difference that oriented Baptists into at least three kinds or types of groupings: regional, theological, and racial/ethnic.

The first American differentiation came with regionalization. New England Baptists were organized according to a pattern of towns and villages, and their polity tended to reflect a kind of familial elitism. Calvinistic theology and democratic idealism merely buttressed the social reality of the New England way in the settled villages of Massachusetts, Connecticut, and Rhode Island. A kind of regional differentiation is evident in upcountry New England—New Hampshire, Vermont, and Maine—where the Freewill Baptists identified with a frontier sect orientation rather than as well-boundaried Calvinistic communities. In the Middle Colonies, Baptists tended to follow the New England pattern because of their roots, although a kind of ethnic diversification occurred in the early 18th century when Welsh Baptists moved into the region and had a profound influence on the polity and experience of Baptists in the Delaware Valley. In the South, a distinctly regional ethos emerged, built of mostly frontier small congregations and rugged individualism, expressed in religious enthusiasm and rural culture. Later in the 18th century, Canadian Baptists as an outgrowth of New England and frontier New York American Baptists, formed a distinct regional movement.

A second type of differentiation occurred along theological lines. Historic emphases—Bible, mission, church—became points of departure. Differing biblical interpretation of culture was at the base of the slavery debate, the choice of an authorized edition of the Bible, and, of course, the literalist/historical critical battles of the later fundamentalist era. Many Baptists came to disagree sharply over what the authority of Scripture actually meant. Debates over missionary methods stemmed from the earliest differences over election versus freewill and inclusivity. Groups like Primitive Baptists, Freewill Baptists, Separate Baptists, and Conservative Baptists exhibit this ongoing differentiation. The doctrine of the church was the main issue in creedalism, gospel missionism, and ecumenism. Whole segments of the Baptist family have hived off into new forms of the tradition, like Gospel Standard Baptists, Regular Baptists, Bible Baptists, and Fellowship Baptists, basically because they have well-defined views on who constitutes the church and what the role of the church in the world should be.

Baptists in the United States, predominantly a white movement at the beginning of the 19th century, witnessed delineation according to race/ethnicity diversity in all three sections and the Canadian provinces. Black Baptists in the northern states comprised segregated communities and associations in the antebellum period. Because of their slave status in the South, blacks naturally organized their own associative patterns, which after the Civil War would become the nexus of denominations. In the middle states, New England, and the Great Lakes region, attempts were made to blend blacks and whites in congregations; however, racial separatism remained the preferred pattern until the 1960s. This was also seen in the Canadian context where the early Baptist communities of Nova Scotia and New Brunswick, and later southwestern Ontario, virtually shut out the free black communities in the 19th century. David George, a pioneer Baptist preacher in Canada and a black loyalist, ultimately found refuge of sorts in Sierra Leone, West Africa. This racial categorization continued with Asians and Latinos in both the United States and Canada.

Related to racial differentiation is the noticeable categorization according to ethnicity. In the 17th century, there were the Welsh Baptists, who emigrated to America beginning in 1663 and continued in many cases to maintain Welsh communities. As non-British Christians moved into the Baptist family, either by evangelism or denominational conversion, there was a strong ethnicity that maintained its separateness from the mainstream. Ultimately, what began as conferences of German, Swedish, Danish, or Norwegian churches became smaller denominations in their own rights, to use Robert Torbet's analysis. In Canada, the groups included French, Ukrainian, Korean, Portuguese, and Polish Baptists, to mention a few. What happened in the Baptist family was not unlike the same ethnic experience that occurred among Methodists, Lutherans, and the Reformed churches in the United States and Canada.

Baptists were to be found in other British colonies as well. Early in the histories of Australia and New Zealand, Baptist people emigrated as mariners, farmers, miners, tradesmen, teachers, and convicts. Like the Baptists headed for America, they emigrated for the hope of an improved socioeconomic opportunity. Most were not self-consciously Baptist, but because of their individual spiritual needs, they did coalesce into familiar religious communities.

Outside the British homeland and North America, the Baptist movement grew as the result of intense and intentional evangelization and inculturation. Following the example of William Carey, the first missionary organizations set the patterns for others in commissioning full-time translators, evangelists, church planters, teachers, and special workers such as printers, doctors, nurses, women's workers, agricultural specialists, and administrators. As the fields of work matured, indigenous leaders filled the ranks and the missionary forces moved on to subdue another field in the cause of the gospel. In Australasia, they began work first in India, then Siam, China, and the East Indies. British missionaries planted the first congregation in Australia in the 1830s. In Africa, Baptist work began in Liberia, Sierra Leone, and the Congo, then in southern Africa and coastal regions. In Latin America, Brazil, Argentina, Chile, and Bolivia headed the early list, with Mexico, Venezuela, and Colombia opening missions later. Very early in Baptist missions, the West Indies witnessed evangelization in Jamaica, Haiti, the Bahamas, and Trinidad. In Europe, the Baptist witness spread from Germany to Eastern Europe and Scandinavia. In the later 19th century, energetic missionary efforts were produced in Russia and Italy. The pioneers of Baptist missions were the British Baptists and American Baptists; the most extensive investment and influence in Baptist world mission has been made by the Foreign Mission Board of the Southern Baptist Convention in the United States.

Beyond the transatlantic experience, ethnic divisions in the Baptist tradition mirror the experience in North America. Ethnic differentiation is found in Ireland, Poland, Russia (U.S.S.R.) and its successor Asian states, the Balkan states, Africa, India, and the Far East. Entire organizations denoting the same geographical territory have grown up side by side in the Baptist world. Sometimes this has led to a modicum of cooperation, but often much adversity and competition has resulted. Unfortunately, the mission fields have not resolved this problem but have perpetuated it.

Wherever Baptist church life has been found outside its native cultures, there have been some identifiable characteristics. First is an advocacy of religious liberty, which has led to changes in public policy and laws in places such as Burma, Germany, Sweden, and Bolivia, to mention a few. Next is the development of a strong organizational support, generally referred to as the association. This pattern has allowed for support from the sending body and has served as a training laboratory for indigenous leadership. Third, Baptists have expended large efforts on the creation of enduring institutions such as schools, colleges, publishing houses, theological seminaries, hospitals, homes, camps, and retreat centers. Over the years, as leadership has evolved to local control, the institutions have passed into other administrations as well, including public and private models, leading to a uniquely indigenized international denominational culture.

Historically speaking, then, Baptists are a movement, a denomination, and a tradition. In the beginning stages, in any given location, whether during the 17th or 20th century, Baptists have behaved like a movement of spiritual renewal and awakening. Following evangelization and organizational development (local congregations and associations), a sense of coordinated, integrated institutional life has emerged, denoting the appearance of a denominational type. Ironically, for those who desire the continuation of the movement in its informal stage, it is often governments that require at least some level of denominational recognition, as in the instance of Baptist churches in the Soviet or Chinese contexts who were (and are!) required to register their religious organizational status. Finally, the term "tradition" is the only adequate vehicle that seems appropriate to describe the acceptance of Baptist principles given the proliferation of so many parts of the Baptist family who are loath to recognize even their own heritage. The Baptist tradition includes such time-worn characteristics as the rule of Scripture, Christian experience, believer's baptism by immersion, the authority of the local congregation to govern its own affairs, separation of church and state, and a genuine urgency to proclaim the kingdom of God. As non-Baptist observers have noted, the "baptistification" of North American culture has been a major feature of the 20th century.

BAPTISTS IN THE WORLD TODAY

Taken as a denominational category of Protestants or the Free Churches, Baptists numerically constitute one of the top five religious groups, active in almost every nation. Their actual numbers, from 35–38 million members, could be multiplied to 80–100 million, if families were counted as in the sacramental churches.

Generally speaking, Baptists are understood to be somewhere between Presbyterians and Pentecostals, an admixture of confessionalism and religious experience. They are less ethnically identifiable than Mennonites or Lutherans and less theologically or historically articulated than Methodists or the Reformed churches. Their closest kin are likely the Congregationalists and Disciples of Christ/Christian Churches. Baptists are evangelicals, despite their wide variety of theological statements and expressions.

Organizationally, the great numbers of Baptists worldwide belong to a convention or union, which evidences the associational principle. For many, this leads ultimately to a connection with the Baptist World Alliance, an entirely voluntary body with regional suborganizations in Europe, North America, Asia, Latin America, Africa, and the Caribbean. A smaller, disparate collection of Baptist associations and churches, mostly in Great Britain and North America, lies outside the mainstream, in defiance of collectives and conglomerates and illustrating the continuing need to be "dissenters."

No longer alone in most of their positions, Baptists advocate religious liberty, the authority of the Bible, the Lordship of Jesus Christ, local church ecclesiology, democratic decision making, a passion for witness, and religious experience. It is the peculiar combination of these character elements in the Baptist psyche, not any one uniquely, which gives the group its flavor. Where Baptists have engaged in ecumenical discussions, they have noticed their similarity to a wide range of other Christians, and likewise the larger Christian community has been shaped by Baptist emphases.

Baptist principles have influenced the form of governments and have given birth to significant leadership. The Constitution and Bill of Rights of the United States, for instance, were influenced by Baptist principles, as were many nations, notably Liberia, Canada, and Bolivia. Baptists can count among their ranks presidents, prime ministers, industrial barons, and scientists. Countless institutions worldwide owe their origins to Baptists who possessed an educational or care-giving vision.

Sometimes a sect; broadly speaking, a movement; historically, now a tradition; and for convenience sake, a denomination—the Baptist tradition has earned its place in history and Christian witness. Its character has ensured that it will continue to create history.

NOTES

1. Marius D'Assigny B. D., *An Antidote against the Pernicious Errors of the Anabaptists or of the Dipping Sect* (London: W. Taylor, 1707), X, 139.

2. William G. McLoughlin, *New England Dissent, 1630–1833: The Baptists and the Separation of Church and State* (Cambridge, MA: Harvard University Press, 1971), 1:77.

The Dictionary

– A –

ABERHART, WILLIAM (1878–1943). Canadian Baptist minister and political leader, born at Hibbert, Ontario. He was educated at Queen's University and initially pursued a school-teaching career in Brantford, Ontario, and later Calgary, Alberta. In 1915, Aberhart began to practice preaching at Westbourne Baptist Church in Calgary, and, owing to his prophetic and **dispensationalist** themes, he soon became the most popular **Bible** teacher in the city. As an unpaid lay minister at Westbourne, Aberhart formed in 1918 the Calgary Prophetic Bible Conference, which drew hundreds to his church on Thursday evenings. Although raised a Presbyterian, Aberhart was baptized in 1920 and built a prairie-wide following from Westbourne Church. In a famous Bible lesson, Aberhart compared Baptists to the apocalyptic church at Ephesus, "the least of the problem churches." In November 1925, he began broadcasting the "Back to the Bible" programs from radio station CFCN in Calgary, reaching thousands of loyal listeners. In 1926, he launched his Radio Sunday School, enrolling over 9,000 children. Eventually, Aberhart entered the political realm in the Great Depression and formed from his religious following a new political party, Social Credit, which sought relief for the thousands of destitute western Canadians. In a 1935 sweep of popularity, Aberhart was elected premier of Alberta, handing over to trusted associates the work at the Bible Institute and the church, although he returned regularly to preach. He was reelected premier in 1940 and died in office.

ABERNATHY, RALPH DAVID (1926–1990). American black Baptist minister and civil rights leader, born at Linden, Alabama. He was

1

educated at Alabama State College and Atlanta University, where he received the M.A. degree. Abernathy began his work as a college instructor in social sciences and quickly moved to the Baptist **ministry**, being ordained in 1948. He served two churches: First Baptist Church, Montgomery, Alabama (1951–1961), and West Hunter Street Baptist Church, Atlanta, Georgia (1961–1990). During the civil rights campaigns of the 1950s and 1960s, Abernathy joined **Martin Luther King Jr.** and became a national organizer and leader. In 1955 in Alabama, he led the bus boycott and organized the Montgomery Improvement Association. He was a founder of the Southern Christian Leadership Conference and served various offices in the organization, including president, 1968–1977. Abernathy sought national attention for the plight of the poor, and in 1968, he organized the Poor Peoples' Campaign, which set up "Resurrection City" on the Mall in Washington, D.C. Later in life, Abernathy spoke openly of King's personal shortcomings, but he never renounced his friendship with the slain civil rights leader. Five U.S. colleges awarded Abernathy honorary degrees, and he received the Peace Medal from the German Democratic Republic in 1971.

ADMONITION. *See* DISCIPLINE, CHURCH.

ADVENTISM. An emphasis among Christian churches upon the second coming or return of Jesus Christ. In the early church, Adventism was related to chiliasm (the doctrine of the thousand-year reign of Christ) and claimed in its following leaders such as Tertullian and Cyprian. From about the 5th century, the Augustinian synthesis held that the millennial kingdom was to be understood as the present age, the time span between the first and second advents of Christ. This "amillennial" interpretation prevailed among the main body of Christians for many centuries. Throughout the Middle Ages and Reformation era, however, a small number of minor sects held to a literal advent of **Christ** and his kingdom.

In the 17th century, the **Fifth Monarchy Movement** in England took up a form of Adventism and made it a political movement. In the 19th century in the United States, **William Miller**, a Baptist lay preacher, discovered what he believed to be key elements in the calculation of the timing of Christ's return, and he announced the date for 1843. Those who followed his teachings came to be called Adventists, and eventually a separate church was formed. Many Baptists followed Miller's teachings with interest and supported lectures and purchased the publications produced by the movement. Later in the 19th century, the Adventist tradition was joined to the Sabbatarian movement, particularly as taught by Ellen G. H. White (1827–1915), and the Seventh-day Adventist (SDA) movement was organized in 1860; smaller groups of Adventists remained aloof from the SDAs.

In the 20th century, most Baptists rejected the position of the Adventist tradition in its several forms and nomenclature. However, large numbers of Baptists do adhere to various eschatological positions on the details of a "rapture" of the church and the establishment of the millennial kingdom. Major North American spokesmen, such as **Elon Galusha, A. J. Gordon, Elmore Harris, Henry G. Weston,** and most leaders of the **fundamentalist** movement among Baptists, hold great interest in eschatological discussions.

AFRICAN UNITED BAPTIST ASSOCIATION (AUBA). Black Baptists were an integral part of the early heritage of Baptists in the Canadian Maritimes. The history of development from congregations to association is an important chapter in black Baptist life in North America. The first African congregations were established in the 1780s and 1790s in both New Brunswick and Nova Scotia by Regular Baptists. Halifax was a center of African Baptist development, commencing with a congregation that John Burton gathered in 1795. A possible plan to merge this congregation with the Granville Street Baptist congregation in 1827 was not realized, and a dispute emerged over which congregation was the first Baptist church in Halifax. Other African congregations existed at Digby and in the Windsor area. In the early 1830s, some of these churches applied for admission to the Nova Scotia Baptist Association but were refused admission, ostensibly because of disciplinary issues, but practically for racial reasons. Thus, in 1854, churches in Halifax, Hammonds Plains, Preston, Beech Hill, and the surrounding territory constituted an African Baptist Association. In 1867, a second African association was formed among the churches from Granville Mountain to Digby and Yarmouth.

Relations with the Nova Scotia white associations were strained in the later 19th century, with the white bodies often conducting missions among the African populations in spite of the African associations. After several years of assistance and cooperation, in 1884 the African Baptist Association in the Halifax region joined the Convention of Atlantic Baptist Churches as a member association. Over the next sixty years, a protracted discussion ensued about the amalgamation of the African congregations into the white associations versus continuing a region-wide black Baptist body of churches. With greater appreciation being paid to Nova Scotia's African heritage in the 1980s and 1990s by government and cultural institutions, the identity of the African United Baptist Association (AUBA) as a separate entity but in cooperation with the other associations and the Convention, came to define the relationship with other Baptists in the Atlantic Convention. Two important landmarks were ultimately reached: first, in 1982, the Cornwallis Street United Baptist Church in Halifax celebrated its 150th anniversary, signaling a rich heritage for African Baptists; second, the 2007 annual meeting of the Convention of Atlantic Baptist Churches focused on the need to build bridges with the AUBA and confessed its racist heritage and desire to find a new future of cooperation.

ALBANIA. The first Baptist witness in what is now Albania occurred in the 1840s as missionaries of the **Baptist Board of Foreign Missions** attempted to plant churches in the region. Missionary work was forbidden by governments and discouraged by state churches until the 1990s, when political change occurred. In 1992, Canadian Baptists under John Keith initiated the Albania Project with the support of the **European Baptist Federation** and were soon joined by **Southern Baptists**. Together they planted the first congregation in Tirana. The U.S. **Conservative Baptist** Foreign Mission Society also opened a mission to Albania in 1993, centered at Korce, and the U.S. **Baptist Bible Fellowship** opened a mission in Albania in 1995. As of 2006, the Baptist community included five congregations and about 250 members.

ALDERSON, JOHN (1738–1821). American Baptist minister who pioneered church development in what is now the state of West Virginia. Alderson was first **pastor** of the Lynville, Rockingham County, congregation, but moved west in 1777, settling at Jerrett's Fort on Wolf Creek. He pioneered a farm and was often described as carrying a gun while he plowed. Against opposition from Indian tribes and difficulties in supporting his family, Alderson preached in military forts and at farmsteads, eventually commencing what became (before 1780) the Greenbrier Church. In 1781, Alderson constituted this congregation, the first in the region, and he constructed the first Baptist meetinghouse in remote Indian country. His field of influence covered the extent of the southwestern Virginia frontier, and he was considered the apostle of mission-oriented Baptists after the turn of the 19th century.

ALGERIA. Country in which Baptist life has been greatly inhibited by changing geopolitical circumstances. In 1950, the **Evangelical Baptist Missions** began a mission in Algeria among the Berbers, La Mission Baptiste Evangélique, but it was expelled in 1970.

ALL AFRICA BAPTIST FELLOWSHIP (AABF). One of the six regional fellowships of the **Baptist World Alliance** (BWA), founded in 1982 at Nairobi, **Kenya**. The fellowship was the result of the Africa for Christ Campaign in 1982, supported by Baptists of the world to evangelize Africa. The purposes of the AABF are to promote education, Baptist faith and witness, mission, and **evangelism**, and to advance the objectives of the BWA.

ALLIANCE OF [SOUTHERN] BAPTISTS. Group of moderate political activists who, following the 1986 annual meeting of the **Southern Baptist Convention** in Atlanta, Georgia, gathered to assess the theological future of the Convention. In their opinion, the Convention had come under the control of **fundamentalists** who sought to purge the boards, agencies, and seminaries of those who did not agree with their position. On February 12, 1987, these activists organized the Southern Baptist Alliance to pursue objectives like freedom of individuals to interpret the Scriptures, freedom of the local church to determine its mission, support for cooperation with other Christian bodies, a servant leadership model, **theological education** based upon responsible scholarship and open inquiry, and actions to proclaim the "good news" of Jesus Christ. Individuals and churches were invited to join, upon contribution of $25.00 annually or $1.00 per resident member, respectively. The alliance, renamed in 1992 the Alliance of Baptists, is led by a 30-member board and includes numerous congregations mostly from the eastern seaboard former Southern Baptist constituency, plus several **American Baptist** congregations, that are also **Welcoming and Affirming** congregations. A new school, the Baptist Theological Seminary in Richmond, Virginia, is associated with the Alliance. Offices are in Washington, D.C., and the full-time administrator is Stan Hastey, formerly with the **Baptist Joint Committee on Public Affairs**. As of 2007, the alliance claimed 121 churches and was associated with the publication *Baptists Today* (1982–).

ALLINE, HENRY (1748–1784). American and Canadian New Light evangelist, born at Newport, Rhode Island. He emigrated to Falmouth, Nova Scotia, where he experienced a new birth spiritually. From 1776 to 1779, Alline preached around the Minas Basin region in the style of New Light evangelist George Whitefield (1703–1770). In 1779, Alline was ordained an evangelist by three Annapolis Valley churches. He itinerated widely in Nova Scotia and New Brunswick, establishing congregations and holding public outdoor meetings; he embodied the essence of the **Great Awakening** in the Maritimes, stressing hymn singing and strong, direct, extemporaneous preaching. He focused his efforts upon the rural regions around the Bay of Fundy, where New England Planters had settled and hardship was common, rejecting Calvinism in favor of an emphasis upon God's love. At the time of his death, Alline had broadened his mission to northern New England and was remarkably close to the ministry of **Benjamin Randal**. Most of the churches he founded in the Maritimes collapsed or became Baptist. Many of the early Baptist leaders in the region owed their spiritual pilgrimages to Alline, if not their perspective on **mission** and **ministry**. While never formally a Baptist, Alline had a profound impact upon early Canadian Baptists in stressing experiential religion and linking their roots with the Great Awakening.

ALL PEOPLES BAPTIST MISSION. An evangelical Baptist missionary agency formed in 1980 to facilitate church planting, **evan-**

gelism, and literature distribution. The mission has work in **El Salvador**, **Mexico**, and **Germany** and employs about 15 overseas personnel.

ALL UNION COUNCIL OF EVANGELICAL CHRISTIANS-BAPTISTS. *See* RUSSIA.

AMAZING GRACE MISSIONS (AGM). An American independent **fundamentalist** Baptist **missionary** agency founded in 1983 by James Gardner, an independent Baptist pastor in Indiana. Gardner continues to serve as president of AGM. The organization, which raises funds for various projects, administers a program of evangelism among regional fairs and farm shows across the United States, with 136 missionaries in its service as of 2007. Missionaries work primarily from mobile homes, strategically following fairs. The agency, headquartered at Dayton, Tennessee, also supports missions in **Nigeria**, the **Philippines**, **India**, and **Kenya**. Theologically, the doctrinal statement indicates affirmation of biblical inerrancy (King James Version only) and eternal security, while also espousing historically accurate notions about Baptist beliefs and history from a **Southern Baptist** orientation. An Internet blog, "The Journey," is maintained and connections with the *Sword of the Lord* are current.

AMERICAN BAPTIST ASSOCIATION (ABA). An international fellowship of **independent Baptist** churches primarily located in the southern and southwestern United States. Mostly as a reaction to the organization of the **Southern Baptist Convention** in the 1840s, **Landmark** Baptist theology swept through the churches of Texas, Arkansas, and Louisiana and focused on working through the local **associations**. In March 1924 at Texarkana, Texas, several of the major Landmarkist associations—the Baptist Missionary Association of Texas; the Mississippi Baptist Association; state associations of Arkansas, Oklahoma, Louisiana, Florida, Missouri; and the Old General Association—were merged into the American Baptist Missionary Association. The term "missionary" was later dropped, leaving the official title, American Baptist Association. Successive internal leadership disagreements in 1934, 1937, and 1949 led to a schism in the Association, which gave birth to the North American Baptist Association, later the **Baptist**

Missionary Association of America. Educational institutions of the ABA include Missionary Baptist College, Sheridan, Arkansas (1919–1934); Missionary Baptist Seminary, Little Rock, Arkansas; Texas Baptist Seminary, Henderson, Texas; Oklahoma Missionary Baptist College, Marlow, Oklahoma; and Florida Baptist Schools, Lakeland, Florida. There are institutes in 16 locations in the United States plus **India**, **Mexico**, the **Philippines**, **Korea**, and **Peru**. Doctrinally, the association is **fundamentalist**, holding to biblical inerrancy and that the only true churches are those that are local and practice believer's **baptism**. The periodical *Missionary Baptist Searchlight* (1937–) is published at Texarkana.

The association conducts a foreign mission program in over a dozen countries, including Mexico, **Canada**, **Japan**, India, the British Solomon Islands, **Honduras**, **Colombia**, **Costa Rica**, **Nicaragua**, **Germany**, the Philippines, Korea, and **Israel**.

As of 2006, there were 1,550 churches with 1,100,000 members affiliated with the ABA in the United States and overseas. *See also* MISSIONARY BAPTISTS.

AMERICAN BAPTIST BILL OF RIGHTS. With the rise of international totalitarian government regimes that threatened **religious liberty** and the overtures of the Franklin Roosevelt administration to recognize the Vatican diplomatically, three major groups in the United States joined forces to produce a proclamation for religious liberty. The American Baptist Bill of Rights was ratified in 1939 through the Joint Committee on Public Relations by the Northern Baptist Convention, the **Southern Baptist Convention**, and the **National Baptist Convention**, a total of more than 10 million persons being represented. The document, with style and terminology borrowed from the U.S. Constitution, contained affirmations of religious liberty, spirituality, the competency of the human soul, and free churches in a free state. Condemned were paternalism (state interference in philanthropic efforts), any unions of church and state, special favors to ecclesiastical bodies, and the preference of coercion over persuasion. *See also* BAPTIST JOINT COMMITTEE ON PUBLIC AFFAIRS.

AMERICAN BAPTIST CHURCHES IN THE U.S.A. (ABCUSA). The designation since 1973 of what was formerly known as the

Northern Baptist Convention (NBC, 1907–1950) and the American Baptist Convention (ABC, 1950–1972).

The taproot of American Baptist life is the First Baptist Church in Providence, Rhode Island, the oldest Baptist congregation in North America. By 1900, over 9,000 congregations belonged to this family of churches. Gradually in the late 17th century, **associations** of congregations were formed, giving a broader shape to the concept of a denomination. Later, in the 19th century, state organizations, called **conventions**, were formed, beginning in South Carolina in 1821, and these added to the growth of a denominational consciousness. In the same era in the 19th century, task-oriented societies emerged principally in New England to round out American Baptist organizational models.

Prior to the formation of a national convention in 1907, northern U.S. Baptist congregations generally cooperated in supporting a cluster of interlocking national **voluntary** societies. These societies included tasks such as foreign **missions**, home missions, publication, and **women's organizations**. In 1814, the first comprehensive organization was formed, the **General Missionary Convention of the Baptist Denomination in the United States of America for Foreign Missions** (GMC), to which the majority of northern congregations related. When, however, the GMC fragmented in 1845 over the issue of **slavery**, the Baptist churches of the North reverted to a society model of organization, supplemented by the regular associational system. From 1846 to 1907, the national organization was known as the **American Baptist Missionary Union** and related societies.

Although various interests contended for a national organization throughout the 19th century, the closest proximity to a unified organization were the annual anniversary meetings when all of the societies met in a single location and conducted their business. Finally, in May 1907, representatives of the state conventions, city societies, associations, and national societies gathered in Washington, D.C., at Calvary Baptist Church to form the NBC. Among the prime movers were W. C. Bitting (1857–1931), who became executive secretary of the Convention; A. J. Rowland (1840–1920); **Shailer Mathews**; **Henry L. Morehouse**; and Lathan A. Crandall (1850–1923).

The NBC operated through two boards and was visible in national meetings held in various cities across the northern and western

United States. The boards and related societies adopted policies for themselves that influenced regional and congregational life as well. The NBC joined the Federal Council of Churches in 1913 and successfully completed a merger with the **Free Baptist** General Conference in 1911.

In June 1949, amidst a flurry of rapid expansion among U.S. Baptists and the new design of the **Southern Baptist Convention** to enter northern fields, leaders of the NBC brought a proposal to their annual meeting at San Francisco to change the name to the ABC. The rationale was twofold: to recognize the historic nomenclature of most national American Baptist societies and to "hold the name in trust" for other Baptist bodies to consider joining the convention in a spirit of cooperative Protestantism.

Further modifications were made to the structure of the ABC in the 1950s and after. In 1955, the two women's societies were integrated into the respective national mission organizations. In 1968, a Study Commission on Denominational Structures was authorized, and in 1972, the ABC proposed that the entire denomination be revised to emphasize the local church and the interrelationships of regional and national organizations. The result was the ABCUSA, officially recognized on January 1, 1973. Subsequently, a Study Commission on Relationships (SCOR) in 1976 recommended the establishment of covenants of relationships between regional organizations and national boards, and that agreements are reached on the support system for the denomination's stewardship. SCOR also defined the new national board structures. A third reorganization plan that would have reduced the number of regional organizations and redrawn geographical boundaries, the Study of Administrative Areas and Relationships, was never formally adopted, but its driving impetus to reduce the number of regional organizations has slowly taken place, notably in the New England and Great Plains geographical areas.

Programmatically, American Baptists function through national boards for international and domestic ministries, plus a national benefit plan, men's and women's organizations, several commissions, and the oldest Baptist historical agency in North America. About three dozen regional organizations exist, covering all the United States, as do over a hundred associations. American Baptists operate fifteen colleges and eight seminaries in the United States and Puerto Rico, plus numerous hospitals and retirement homes.

The most **ecumenical** of Baptist bodies in the United States, ABCUSA has sought "associated" relationships with the **Progressive National Baptist Convention** (1961), the Church of the Brethren (1973), and various ethnically diverse bodies such as the **German**, Swedish, **Danish-Norwegian**, Slavic, and **Hispanic Baptist** groups. Formal discussions toward a possible merger with the Christian Church (Disciples of Christ) were conducted from 1947 to 1952 but failed to produce anything more than a common hymnal. About 40 percent of American Baptist local congregations are dually aligned with either African American Baptist bodies, the Southern Baptist Convention, or an ethnic Baptist conference. American Baptists are full members of the **Baptist World Alliance**, the World Council of Churches, the **Baptist Joint Committee on Public Affairs**, and the National Council of Churches of Christ in the United States of America.

In the 1990s, a serious debate arose among American Baptists over recognition of homosexuals: the caucus groups American Baptist Evangelicals and the Association of Welcoming and Affirming Baptists drew polarized positions. This division ultimately led to the withdrawal of the American Baptist Churches of the Pacific Southwest from the national program relationship, and expressions of deep concern from other regional organizations in 2000–2005. New coalitions of churches along the West Coast, notably the Evergreeen Association of Baptist Churches, were formed to accommodate the realignments over sexuality issues and the loss of the Pacific Southwest and other regional units.

The national headquarters of the ABCUSA was built in 1962 at Valley Forge, Pennsylvania, in a unique circular building designed by nationally renowned architect Vincent Kling. The building reflects the interrelated yet autonomous nature of the denomination's organizational history. From 1802 to 1991, the denominational periodical was the *American Baptist Magazine*, discontinued in 1992 due to falling subscriber interest and succeeded by an informal periodical, *American Baptists in Mission* (1992–). The **American Baptist Publication Society** (after 1922–1924, known to the public as Judson Press in honor of **Adoniram Judson**), the denomination's book publisher from 1824, continues to produce titles, though since 1986 it has been a limited list.

As of 2006, there were 5,800 churches and 1,418,403 members affiliated with the ABCUSA.

AMERICAN BAPTIST CONVENTION (ABC). *See* AMERICAN BAPTIST CHURCHES IN THE U.S.A.

AMERICAN BAPTIST EDUCATION SOCIETY (ABES). A **voluntary** membership organization founded in 1888 to advance the interests of Baptist higher education in the United States. Its predecessor organization was the **American Baptist Educational Commission**. Leaders of colleges, north and south, recognized the pressing financial needs as well as the growing competition of schools for the same sources of funding in the era. A strong impetus to a more coordinated effort was encouraged by Frederick Gates and **John D. Rockefeller**, who were developing plans with **William R. Harper** and others to establish a new Baptist university of national character. That institution became the revived University of Chicago, and the ABES became the principal conduit to channel funds from the Rockefellers to several institutions, especially Chicago. Annual meetings of the ABES featured addresses from leading Baptist educators, and the annual minutes contained a comprehensive listing of Baptist schools, colleges, seminaries, and academies across the United States. Schools from the South, notably Wake Forest College and Stephens College, were able to obtain funding through the ABES. With the formation of the Northern Baptist Convention in 1907, the ABES was superceded by the Northern (later American) Baptist Convention Board of Education. In 1944, the interests and assets of the society were assumed by the combined organization, the **American Baptist Board of Education and Publication**.

AMERICAN BAPTIST EDUCATIONAL COMMISSION (ABEC). Following the American Civil War, Baptists in the northern states increasingly recognized the need for a unified effort in establishing and maintaining educational institutions. Of immediate concern was the southern states mission of the American Baptist Home Mission Society and the schools that were planned or under way in various territories and states in the West. Sewall S. Cutting, a leading pastor in New York, was a prime mover in creating the ABEC in 1868 to serve as a medium of communication between institutions and a source of data for men of wealth who might become institutional benefactors. There was also hope that expertise could be given to newer schools that needed leaders and advice. There were regional advisory chapters set up by the ABEC, and conventions with institutional and denominational leaders present were held in Brooklyn, New York; Philadelphia, Pennsylvania; and Chicago, Illinois. After a few years, the ABEC became defunct, but not without raising the denominational awareness about Christian higher education. Its successor in many ways was the **American Baptist Education Society**.

AMERICAN BAPTIST EVANGELICALS (ABE). A voluntary association of individuals and congregations in the greater **American Baptist Churches** tradition who espouse conservative evangelical doctrines and ethical positions. Founded in 1992 at the Harmony Baptist Church in New Castle, Pennsylvania, the group has both national and regional manifestations. At the national level, members meet at the American Baptist Biennial Meeting for business, fellowship, and inspiration. In many of the regional bodies, chapters are organized and meet several times per year. At first mostly a northeastern U.S. phenomenon, there are about 1,000 members and 10,000–20,000 adherents in the **association**. Among the core elements of the group are the Lordship of Jesus Christ, biblical authority, Baptist heritage, and proclamation in love of the life-changing message of **Christ** to the lost world. Overall, there is a strong commitment to the implications of the authority of **Scripture**. In the ongoing debates in the denomination over the recognition of gay and lesbian lifestyles, ABE has often been understood as withholding support for alternative lifestyles from what they believe is clearly taught in the **Bible**. The association publishes a quarterly newsletter, *ABE Connections* (1992–).

AMERICAN BAPTIST FOREIGN MISSION SOCIETY (ABFMS). The corporate name of the oldest Baptist national overseas mission organization in the United States. The society was founded in 1814 as the **General Missionary Convention of the Baptist Denomination in the United States of America for Foreign Missions** (GMC), and the specific administration of **missions**

was conducted by the **Baptist Board of Foreign Missions** (BBFM) in the United States from 1814 to 1846. It was this aspect of the overall work of the GMC—supporting overseas missions of the growing Baptist community in the United States—that, 1826, became the single purpose of the society. In 1846, following the schism with the churches of the South from which the **Southern Baptist Convention** came, the BBFM became the **American Baptist Missionary Union** (1846–1905); in 1905, the name American Baptist Foreign Mission Society was adopted legally in recognition of its popular usage and congruity with other Northern Baptist societies.

The first field of the society was in **Burma** (1814), set up by the first missionaries, **Adoniram** and **Ann Judson**. Burma was followed by **Liberia** (1821), **Siam** (1833), **China** (1836), **India** (1836), Europe (1839), **Japan** (1873), **Congo** (1884), and the **Philippines** (1900). The Latin American missions of the **American Baptist Home Mission Society** were added in 1973; these included **Mexico** (1870), **Cuba** (1899), **El Salvador** (1911), and **Nicaragua** (1917). From 1817 to 1845, the ABFMS also conducted missions among American Indian tribes, with notable appointments like **John Mason Peck**, **Isaac McCoy**, and **James E. Welch** serving among Shawnee, Choctaw, Cherokee, and Pottawattamie tribes.

Missionary work over the years and contexts has included **evangelism**, church planting, **Scripture** translation, education, and health care. The first women missionaries were spouses of the early male appointments, the exception being **Charlotte White**, who was appointed to Burma in 1814. Single women were later the responsibility of the Woman's American Baptist Foreign Mission Society, founded in 1877. This society was integrated with the ABFMS in 1955.

With the formation of the Northern Baptist Convention in 1905, the ABFMS became an official national society of the denomination and participated in its budget and planning processes. Since 1973, the ABFMS has been integrated with the **American Baptist Churches** as the Board of International Ministries. It maintains missions or cooperates in work in 24 nations.

AMERICAN BAPTIST FREE MISSION SOCIETY (ABFrMS). A society formed by northern Baptists who wanted to take a strong stand against slaveholding.

In the late 1830s, increasing numbers of Baptist leaders in the northern United States became dissatisfied with the reluctance of the Baptist Triennial Convention to take a firm stand on the question of slaveholding. At Tremont Temple in Boston, Massachusetts, in May 1843, a group of ministers and writers, including Albert Post (1809–1887), John Duer (1823–1875), and **William H. Brisbane**, formed the American and Foreign Mission Society on the model of the American and Foreign Bible Society. In addition to being abolitionist, the society was **antimasonic**; supported temperance and opposed foreign immigration, oath taking, and honorary degrees—in short, the group held an ultraistic social and political agenda. By 1848, the society had changed its name to the American Baptist Free Mission Society, doubtless a response to the national election platform that year—"Free Soil." Leaders ventured into broader concerns, notably the establishment of an undergraduate school—the New York Central College—and support for missionary work in **Haiti**, Burma, Africa, **Japan**, upper **Canada**, and the western United States. The ABFrMS was first to establish a Baptist mission in Japan. Among the outstanding leaders of the society was **Nathan Brown**, a former missionary to Japan, who became corresponding secretary of the society in 1858. In 1872, the ABFrMS merged its interests with other Baptist bodies, notably the Consolidated American Baptist Missionary Convention and the **American Baptist Missionary Union**. Among several periodicals published by the society were *The Free Missionary* (Newton Centre, Massachusetts), *The Christian Reflector* (Worcester, Massachusetts), *The Christian Contributor* (Utica, New York), and the *American Baptist* (Utica and New York, New York). *See also* ANTISLAVERY, AMONG BAPTISTS.

AMERICAN BAPTIST HOME MISSION SOCIETY (ABHMS). The oldest of the national Baptist societies devoted to missionary work in the United States and its territories. The ABHMS was founded in 1832 at Mulberry Street Baptist Church at an adjourned session of the Baptist Triennial Convention in New York City. The two most influential promoters of home missions were **Jonathan Going** of Massachusetts and **John Mason Peck** of Illinois.

Home missions in an earlier generation had been conducted by associations, notably the Shaftsbury (Vermont) and **Philadelphia**

(Pennsylvania) Baptist Associations. In 1802, Baptists in Massachusetts formed a voluntary society, the Massachusetts Baptist Missionary Society, to aid destitute churches and plant new congregations in northern New England and western New York State. Eventually, with the expansion of settlements into the Ohio Valley, the task became immense and beyond the resources of these efforts. When the **General Missionary Convention of the Baptist Denomination in the United States** was formed in 1814, home missions were added to that agenda and missionaries were appointed to work in the Old Northwest, in the Mississippi Valley, and among Indian tribes. Home missions competed less than favorably with the Judson Mission in Burma, the Liberian Mission in Africa, and work in Europe. Thus, a new national society was formed to focus exclusively on home missions. Baptists followed the lead of Presbyterians and Congregationalists in this regard, as witnessed in the establishment in 1826 of the American Home Mission Society.

The ABHMS turned its attention to planting new churches, working with immigrants, and establishing Indian missions. Regionally, the society placed emphasis upon church planting in the upper South, the lower Ohio Valley, and the upper Mississippi Valley. Indians, new immigrants, and free blacks reflected focal points of the society's mission.

In 1844, a dispute arose in the management of ABHMS over whether a person sympathetic to slaveholding could be appointed by the Society. The issue, raised by the Georgia Baptist Convention, was a test case and the board of managers decided not to receive an application in which the question of slaveholding was at stake. The next year, Southern Baptist congregations organized their own convention with a domestic mission board, which served their interests regardless of political concerns.

The next major phase of the ABHMS's efforts focused on work among freedmen during and after the Civil War. The society adopted the position that the greatest need of the former slave population was leadership development. Hence, large sums were spent to start schools of every level to train ministers and upgrade the general population's educational attainment. Subscriptions for buildings were raised, and many educational missionaries were sent to the southern states.

The ABHMS was also involved in outreach beyond the national borders. As a natural outgrowth of missions in the Deep South, beginning in 1870, the ABHMS entered **Mexico** and in 1898 **Puerto Rico**. Eventually, missions were organized in **Cuba**, **El Salvador**, **Nicaragua**, and **Haiti**. In the 20th century, these fields were transferred to the **American Baptist Foreign Mission Society**.

When the Northern Baptist Convention was formed in 1907, the ABHMS became one of the cooperating national mission societies. It related to city **mission** societies and state **conventions**.

With denominational reorganization in 1968–1973, the ABHMS became the Board of National Ministries of the **American Baptist Churches in the U.S.A**. Presently the board conducts work in **evangelism** among urban mission centers and Native Americans, it addresses social concerns, and it operates various contract services such as church loans and homes and hospitals coordination. In 2004, the Board of National Ministries assumed the administration of Judson Press, formerly associated with the American Baptist Board of Education and Publication. With other American Baptist national agencies, the board is administratively located at Valley Forge, Pennsylvania. *See also* AMERICAN BAPTIST PUBLICATION SOCIETY.

AMERICAN BAPTIST MISSIONARY UNION (ABMU). Official name given in 1846 to the organization that followed the **General Missionary Convention** and **Baptist Board of Foreign Missions**, after the schism with the churches that created the **Southern Baptist Convention** and the Baptist congregations of the northern states. At its outset, the ABMU faced the challenges of a depleted membership, a rising debt, and a new structure. A new constitution allowed for a society-type membership that recognized proportional representation according to the magnitude of individual and congregational contributions. Eventually, three classes of membership evolved: life, honorary, and annual; this system characterized denominational funding in the North until the organization of the Northern Baptist Convention in 1905.

Mission policy under the ABMU changed dramatically. Indian **missions** in the United States were transferred to the **American Baptist Home Mission Society** in 1854–1866. Mission stations in **India** were retrenched in favor of entering **Japan** and upgrading work in

China after 1860. The union competed with the **American Baptist Free Mission Society** for support and mission assignments until it merged with that body in 1872. Expansion of fields occurred in 1884 with the takeover of the Livingston Inland Mission in the **Congo**, and in 1898, when the first missionaries were sent to the **Philippines**.

Because of the high interest of the churches in overseas missions, the ABMU in essence became the heart of a growing denomination and the centerpiece of annual mission and publication society meetings called anniversaries. This structure prevailed until 1905 when the NBC was organized and the ABMU became the **American Baptist Foreign Mission Society**, a name that the public had recognized for decades. *See also* AMERICAN BAPTIST FOREIGN MISSION SOCIETY.

AMERICAN BAPTIST PUBLICATION SOCIETY (ABPS). Founded originally in 1824 as the Baptist General Tract Society (BGTS), the ABPS was the second of the national Baptist **voluntary** societies. It was based on the model of the Religious Tract Society in Britain and the American Tract Society in New York, a Congregationalist and Presbyterian organization. Baptists who had entered the field of domestic and foreign missions earlier in the 1800s recognized the need for a printer and distributor of Christian literature. It was **Luther Rice** and **Noah Davis** who set up the BGTS in Washington, D.C., in proximity to the proposed national Baptist university and center of operations that Rice had envisioned for the Baptist movement in the nation's capital.

In 1840, the BGTS became the American Baptist Publication and Sunday School Society; in 1844, the words "Sunday School" were dropped with no lessening of the emphasis. Under the leadership of **John Mason Peck** and Benjamin Griffith (1821–1893), the society adopted an aggressive **colporterage** program in conjunction with the **American Baptist Home Mission Society**, which earned ABPS the reputation of being the leading educational agency in the Baptist family in the United States. Among the forward strides the ABPS is credited with are **Sunday School** Bible lessons in 1868, teacher and pupil booklets in 1870, a uniform lesson series in 1872, and graded lessons in 1909.

Another stream of activity that became part of the ABPS was the **American Baptist Education Society** (ABES), formed in 1888. The

ABES brought together institutions of higher education historically related to the northern Baptists, plus the potential for funding sources and planning by the churches and other societies. In 1944, with reorganization of the Northern Baptist Convention (NBC), the publication and education societies were merged into the American Baptist Board of Education and Publication. This entity, a recognized national board of the NBC, remains the corporate title, although the name American Baptist Educational Ministries was adopted in 1973 as part of the further reorganization of the **American Baptist Churches U.S.A.** Over the years of its work, the board has asssumed administrative oversight for the Commission on the Ministry; the American Baptist Assembly in Green Lake, Wisconsin; American Baptist Men; American Baptist Women; and the American Baptist Historical Society. Headquarters of the Board of Education and Publication are at Valley Forge, Pennsylvania. The publishing arm of the board has been known as Judson Press since 1922, honoring **Adoniram Judson**, the first American Baptist overseas missionary.

In the 1990s, the work of the Board of Education and Publication began to recede and did not recover. Beginning in the executive directorship of Daniel Weiss, Judson Printing, the manufacturing arm of Judson Press, ceased operations in the 1990s; professional staff reductions continued into the next decade and ultimately program initiatives and educational materials were reduced drastically. In 2002, owing to financial exigencies identified during the leadership of Dr. Jeanne Kim, the general board of the American Baptist Churches U.S.A. voted to dissolve the Board of Educational Ministries. By 2004, the Judson Press and discipleship ministries formerly associated with the Board of Educational Ministries were transferred to the Board of National Ministries, formerly the **American Baptist Home Mission Society**. *See also* AMERICAN BAPTIST EDUCATION SOCIETY.

AMERICAN NATIONAL BAPTIST CONVENTION (ANBC). One of the predecessor national black Baptist organizations in the United States, formed in August 1886 in St. Louis, Missouri. Its purpose was to devise means for the creation of a black national Baptist denomination, and its leaders sought to deliberate on great Baptist questions of the day. The Convention was largely the organizing genius of

William J. Simmons, its first president. Among the ANBC's achievements are the inclusion of black women in its ranks, a first for a black Baptist organization; the first statistical analysis of the black Baptist movement in the United States; and the calling together of diverse elements in the black Baptist family. The ANBC was often seen as the black equivalent of the **Baptist Congress**. Its work was carried out in the shadow of the foreign mission movement among blacks, the leadership favored integration with white organizations, and finally it lost its great leader, W. J. Simmons, in 1890. In 1895, at a national gathering in Atlanta, Georgia, the ANBC was merged to form the **National Baptist Convention of the United States of America**. *See also* LOTT CAREY BAPTIST FOREIGN MISSION CONVENTION.

ANABAPTIST. Beginning in the 16th century, groups of European Christian believers recovered the importance of believers' **baptism** as a prerequisite to church membership. Because this involved the re-baptism of persons baptized in the Catholic tradition as infants, the Greek preposition *ana* (meaning "re") was added to the baptist idea, making the term "anabaptist" applicable to those who called for a re-baptism. Among the clusters of Anabaptists were the Swiss Brethren of Zurich, who as of 1525 moved beyond the teachings of their mentor, Huldrych Zwingli (1484–1531), and practiced believers' baptism (Zwingli actually referred to them as "Catabaptists"). Other Anabaptists emerged in Poland, Westphalia, Bohemia, and the Netherlands, to mention major evidences. Eventually, the Anabaptist movement came to include the Mennonites, Brethren, Amish, and Hutterites as the principal surviving groups.

In the mid-20th-century North American context, Harold S. Bender (1897–1962), a professor at Mennonite/Biblical Seminary in the United States, proposed that what several of these groups had in common was their life of discipleship, and the term "anabaptist" came to be associated with a newly identified group in the era of the Protestant Reformation. In 1962, George H. Williams (1914–2000) at Harvard University coined the term "Radical Reformation" to include many of the Anabaptist types and others such as spiritualists, Waldensians, smaller churches of a Pietist kind, and some Unitarians. In a third round of nomenclature revision, Brethren historian Donald F. Durnbaugh (1927–2005) at Bethany Theological Seminary in the

United States used the term "believer's churches" to designate a wider variety of Anabaptists, including the Baptists, who held to a collection of ideals other than believer's baptism, such as the Lordship of Christ, the authority of the Word of God, a covenant of believers, **missionary** service, proclamation, and Christian unity. *See also* BELIEVER'S CHURCH.

ANABAPTIST KINSHIP THEORY. Hypothesis advanced by several Baptist historians that the origins of the Baptist movement are to be found in the Anabaptist movement of the 16th century. The kinship of ideas such as **religious liberty**, congregational governance, believers' **baptism**, radical discipleship, and **mission** suggests that whether there is any documentary evidence extant, the spiritual forbears of the Baptists are the Anabaptists. Some writers attempt to do literary analyses on confessional texts to demonstrate theological dependance, while others construct scenarios of possible personal relationships that connect the Dutch Anabaptists with English Separatists. The Anabaptist kinship theory generally produces an affinity for "sect-oriented" (to use Ernst Troeltsch's term) Christianity that eschews **ecumenism** and political engagement with other Protestant traditions and public issues. Among those writers in the Anabaptist kinship school of interpretation are **William R. Estep** of Southwestern Baptist Theological Seminary, James A. Mosteller (1915–1977) of Northern Baptist Theological Seminary and New Orleans Baptist Seminary, **Ernest Payne** of the Baptist Union, and **A. C. Underwood** of Rawdon College in Great Britain. *See also* PURITAN SEPARATIST HYPOTHESIS.

ANDERSON, MARTIN BREWER (1815–1890). Baptist minister and educator, born at Brunswick, Maine. Anderson was educated at Waterville College and Newton Theological Institution. He secured a teaching position at Waterville College in classics and mathematics and, later, rhetoric. In 1850, he became editor of the *New York Recorder*, a weekly Baptist journal. In 1853, he was elected the first president of the Baptist-related University of Rochester in upstate New York. During his long tenure in that office, Anderson emphasized the sciences and social sciences, making Rochester a first-rate institution. A prolific writer, Anderson served as president of the

Home and Foreign Mission Societies and advised **Matthew Vassar** on the establishment of the first American college for women.

ANGOLA. Four different Baptist groups established denominational presence in Angola. In 1878, missionaries of the **Baptist Missionary Society** (BMS) established a church at San Salvador, and the Igreja Evangelica Baptista, a national organization, was the result. In 1929, Portuguese missionaries began their work in the country. Canadian Baptists began assisting the BMS in 1954, and in 1968, **Southern Baptist** missionaries entered Angola and created the Convencão Baptista de Angola.

As of 2006, there were 315 churches and 31,000 members in the Convencão Baptista de Angola; 300 churches and 90,000 members in the Igreja Evangelica de Angola; and 30 churches and 18,075 members in the Igreja Baptista Livre em Angola.

ANGUILLA. Caribbean island with first Baptist mission established by the **Southern Baptist** Foreign Mission Societyin 1970. As of 2005, there were three churches with about 350 members affiliated with the mission.

ANGUS, JOSEPH (1816–1902). English Baptist minister, born in Northumberland. A prize-winning student in moral philosophy, Angus graduated from the University of Edinburgh and attended Stepney College in London. In 1837, he succeeded **John Rippon** as pastor at New Park Street Church in London. Two years later he became associated with the **Baptist Missionary Society**, later becoming its secretary (1839–1849). In that role, he urged the expansion of missionary work and visited many of the fields. In 1850, he was named principal of Stepney College and became a widely renowned educator among the Baptists and beyond. During his 44 years as principal, Angus improved the prospects of the college, in 1856 moving it from Stepney to Regent's Park where he negotiated a relationship with the University of London. He published a popular **Bible** handbook in 1854 and edited several biographical works. Having noted several inaccuracies in the King James text of the Bible, he was named to the panel of New Testament revisers that produced the English Revised Version. The library of Baptistiana at Regent's Park College, Oxford, is named in his honor.

ANTHONY, ALFRED WILLIAMS (1860–1939). Freewill Baptist minister and educator born at Providence, Rhode Island. Alfred was the son of a prominent Free Baptist minister and a descendant of Roger Williams. He graduated from Brown University and Cobb Divinity School, Bates College, and entered the pastoral ministry at Essex Street Freewill Baptist Church in Bangor, Maine. In 1887, Anthony was elected to the Fullonton Professorship of New Testament Criticism and Exegesis at Cobb Divinity School, Bates College. In order to prepare himself for an academic career, he took further studies at the University of Berlin under Adolf von Harnack (1851–1930) and Bernhard Weiss (1827–1918). Anthony wrote a useful study of the life of **Christ** (1899) and a history of Bates College (1936). After Cobb Divinity School was closed in 1908, Anthony gave himself to consummating the merger between **Free Baptists** and Northern Baptists. He extolled the virtues of greater **mission** opportunities, and he supported the Northern Baptist membership in the Federal Council of Churches. In 1918, he was elected secretary of the Home Missions Council, an affiliate of the Federal Council of Churches. To facilitate the merger among Baptists, Anthony served as corresponding secretary of the Free Baptist General Conference until his death in 1939.

ANTIGUA. Recipient of Baptist influence starting in the 1960s. The first to arrive were related to the **Baptist Missionary Association of America**; they started a congregation in 1960 at St. John's. In 1968, **Southern Baptists**, as an outgrowth of **missions** in Trinidad, began missionary work on both Antigua and **Barbuda** and established Central Baptist Church. The Antigua Barbuda Baptist Association was formed in 1980, with headquarters at St. John's, Antigua.

As of 2006, there were three churches and about 600 members affiliated with the Antigua Barbuda Baptist Association.

ANTIMASONRY. A movement that began in upstate New York in the 1820s and spread to the northeastern United States. In 1826, a Batavia, New York, stonemason named William Morgan (fl. 1825) was accused of exposing Masonic secrets; he was abducted by persons alleged to be Masons and supposedly killed. A propaganda crusade against the fraternity was launched, and scores of evangelical Christians rallied to the antimasonic political party and the concomitant religious crusade. Indeed, the enduring characteristics of Antimasonry were religiously motivated. Baptists participated in the movement by forming local **associations** and even disfellowshipping congregations that had Masonic members. An important epicenter of the Antimasonic fervor was in Chautauqua County, New York, where in 1829 a parallel associational body was formed to oppose membership in local lodges. Similar outbreaks of Antimasonic sentiment occurred in Vermont, Massachusetts, Ohio, and Pennsylvania. In many associations—and, later, the theologically **fundamentalistic** and **holiness** groups—Masonic membership was forbidden on the grounds that it was elitist, antidemocratic, promotive of infidelism, and unwholesomely blended biblical narrative with superstition and "Satanic" oaths. Despite the early aversion to Freemasonry among evangelicals, there are considerable numbers of Baptists, including clergy, in North America who maintain membership in Masonic lodges.

ANTI-MISSIONARY BAPTISTS. *See* PRIMITIVE BAPTISTS.

ANTISLAVERY, AMONG BAPTISTS. The antislavery movement was an important social concern among Baptists in the Western Hemisphere from the late 18th through the mid-19th century. While legal battles and debates raged in the legislatures of the United States and the British Parliament, actual application of antislavery principles led by Baptists occurred in **Jamaica**, **Liberia**, **Sierra Leone**, **Nova Scotia**, and **Haiti**.

The United States. In the late 18th century, Baptists in the United States began to agitate against the institution of slavery and in Britain after the turn of the century. Early in the 1780s, **Elhanan Winchester** openly opposed slaveholding. With the passage in 1787 of the (U.S.) Northwest Ordinance, slavery was forbidden in the Northwest Territory and the slave trade was abolished by 1807. In Pennsylvania, Virginia, and Kentucky, Baptists were stimulated to action. In Virginia, several prominent Baptist slaveholders manumitted their slaves, including **David Barrow**, who would become a prominent emancipator in Kentucky. **John Leland** offered a resolution in the Virginia General Committee in 1789, which called for an end to slavery. The same year, the **Philadelphia Baptist Association** supported the establishment of abolition societies and protection of the freedmen.

After 1790, the force of antislavery among Baptists shifted to Kentucky, where Baptist ministers advocated a clause in the state constitution abolishing slavery. In the Elkhorn (Kentucky) Association in 1792, a resolution opposing slavery was passed, and elsewhere several churches passed similar resolutions. At times, the opposition was strong, as when David Barrow was expelled from the North District Association in 1806. A movement called the Friends of Humanity Association began in Kentucky in 1807 and spread throughout the Ohio Valley as far as Missouri in support of abolition. Much of the Friends of Humanity fervor died about 1816–1817 as the colonization movement became a more popular alternative and as the right of a Baptist associational body to interfere in political and moral issues was questioned. When the American Antislavery Society was organized in 1830 by William Lloyd Garrison (1805–1879), a nominal Baptist himself, numerous Baptists in the northern states joined that segment of the abolitionist movement.

Still another form of antislavery expression in the United States was found in antislavery societies and missionary bodies. In New Hampshire, for instance, a state Baptist antislavery society was formed in 1838. When the debate over slaveholding in the General Missionary (Triennial) Convention proved frustrating for abolitionists, several prominent leaders formed the **American Baptist Free Mission Society** in 1843 and commissioned missionaries until after the Civil War. Among black Baptists, **associations** and small societies fostered antislavery sentiments in the free black communities.

Great Britain. While earlier writers had opposed slavery, British Baptists first expressed their opposition to the institution in the 1820s and with renewed effort in the 1830s. The presence of slavery in Jamaica focused the issue through publications of the **Baptist Missionary Society** and prompted **William Knibb** among others to advocate strongly for abolition. This campaign in 1832–1833 was considered influential in the Reform Legislation of 1833, which abolished slavery in the British Empire. One of the early actions of the reorganized **Baptist Union** in 1836 was to authorize a delegation to visit the Baptists of the United States to express, among other objectives, their antipathy to slaveholding. A similar delegation of English

General Baptists visited in 1848 to carry the same message. Predominantly, the Baptists of the United Kingdom lent their moral support to the northern cause during the American Civil War.

ARCHITECTURE, BAPTIST CHURCH. Reflects great variety and a sense of contextual evolution. In England, in the earliest years of **General** and **Particular Baptist** development, the meeting places were often in homes, similar to the Elizabethan "conventicles" of other Nonconformists. **Seventh Day Baptists** met in homes and sometimes rented halls. As congregations grew in size and regularity of meetings, some of the houses were modified to include sufficient space for 25 to 30 to assemble. An important modification was the provision for an indoor **baptistery**, such as at Tewksbury. Balconies were added as well as rooms to accommodate traveling preachers. The oldest-known structure designed as a Baptist meetinghouse was the Glass House on Broad Street in London, which was fitted with two tiers of galleries. Gradually, at the time of toleration, separate meetinghouses of this kind were constructed, mostly of brick or native stone. The interiors were simple, with box pews enclosing family units. Often families rented the pews, a means of providing for the overall upkeep of the meetinghouse. It became fashionable to elevate the pulpits of the 18th century, with a sounding board above to reflect the preacher's voice. Churches located in urban areas took advantage of interior space, while having rather simple unadorned exteriors, as in Broadmead, Bristol. Where there were large congregations, as in London, balconies were constructed for seating and frequent modifications were made. By the mid-18th century in Wales, the meetinghouses were a characteristic feature of the village and rural landscapes, again constructed of brick and stone. Many of these survive into the present era.

A watershed event in the history of Baptist church architecture in Britain was the construction of Bloomsbury Chapel by **Samuel Morton Peto** in 1848. He used his own funds to construct an impressive urban edifice that resembled a cross between a French Church of England building and a chapel; the result was a two-spired magnificent Victorian structure. Peto helped to form the Metropolitan Chapel Building Society, which assisted in the construction of many commodious churches in Great Britain in the 1850s. His style was imitated throughout many English and Scottish cities, notably in Bristol, Glasgow, and Manchester.

Educational architecture among British Baptist schools is especially varied. Stepney College housed an elaborate Greek revival building in London and similar facilities later at Regent's Park. At Oxford, a plain quadrangle of late Victorian Oxford style encloses the facilities of the Regent's Park College. Manchester Baptist College's campus was transformed into a Georgian brick-style enclosure when Northern Baptist College was completed in 1964. Spurgeon's College, originally housed in or near the Metropolitan Tabernacle, moved to Norwood Hill in 1923 to occupy an expanded Falklands Mansion on a bluff overlooking Croydon. Bristol Baptist College, which has moved several times, occupied until the 1990s a red brick building of columnar late-Victorian vintage in the style of Bristol University. South Wales Baptist College has been housed for most of the present century in a series of residences fronting a city street in Cardiff.

Early North American Baptist buildings were simple and, in contrast to their English and Welsh counterparts, were generally constructed of wood rather than stone. A simple rectangular building with pews occupying the majority of the floor space was common; the pews faced a pulpit and perhaps a choir area without adornments. Usually, there were no artistic windows and little more than a cross on the wall. The model for much of the 18th century must have been the New England Congregational meetinghouses, which also influenced the Middle Colonies, the South, and, later, the eastern Canadian provinces. **Freewill Baptists** built frame structures in remote areas of New England, which had plain, unpainted interiors with a woodstove situated in the middle of the box pews; similar church buildings were erected by the **Primitive Baptists** of the South and West. Among the Primitive and **Old Regular Baptists**, there are separate front doors for women and men, and the interiors may exhibit pictures of former pastors and elders. Examples of the white-frame style have survived at Ossippee and New Durham, New Hampshire; Cross Roads, Virginia; Horse Creek, North Carolina; Burtonsville, Maryland; and as far west as West Union, Oregon. Interesting modifications of the frame meetinghouse design can be seen at Imlaystown, New Jersey, and Hopewell, New Jersey. Fine brick versions are located at Pennypack (Lower Dublin), Pennsylvania, and Cohansey, New Jersey. In the Canadian Maritimes, surviving early frame meetinghouses are located in Pereaux and Billtown, Nova Scotia; and in Ontario at Peterborough, Charlotteville, and Strathaven.

The fine meetinghouse that **James Manning** constructed at Providence, Rhode Island, signaled a new era among Baptists in the American colonies. Completed in 1775, it towered above the city of Providence and carried a 185-foot steeple, which symbolized the emergence of Baptists as a social reality in the colonial/state capital. The Declaration of Independence was read from the steps of the meetinghouse on July 4, 1776. From the Providence design would emerge urban meetinghouses and church buildings in the South that demonstrated classical designs—Greek revival, Romanesque, and even experimental. The First Baptist Church of Charleston, South Carolina (1887), exemplified the Greek-revival style, and examples of Romanesque could be found at University Baptist, Baltimore, Maryland, and the Baptist Temple in Philadelphia. Earlier in Philadelphia, **William Staughton** had constructed in 1811, at considerable expense, a meetinghouse in the round, with the baptistery located in the center of the congregational seating under a dome! Robert Mills (1781–1855), a prominent public architect and the designer of the Washington Monument, designed this futuristic structure, inspired by a similar plan he had made in 1804 for the "Circular" Congregational Church in Charleston, South Carolina; the Sansom Street sanctuary seated 4,000 people and introduced the auditorium concept to the preaching service. Later in 1817–1820, Mills designed for First Baptist in Baltimore a landmark building known as "Round Top."

In the 19th century, the national denominational bodies needed commodious rooms and prestigious locations to hold the triennial assembly meetings, and this led to new meetinghouses constructed in the eastern seaboard cities: Boston, New York, Philadelphia, Baltimore, Richmond, and Charleston, though the last would have to wait until a southern convention was organized in order to serve as a suitable travel venue.

As the social status of urban congregations rose, Baptists kept pace with Presbyterians, Lutherans, and Congregationalists in the construction of church buildings and educational space. Generally, the greater portion of space was devoted to worship, with the basement or ground level providing a social hall or church school area. Great stained-glass windows portraying departed leaders or war veterans or depicting scenes from **Scripture** were commonly found. Pipe organs became commonplace in urban Baptist churches as music became widely available and choirs were organized after the mid-19th century. It was not uncommon to have woodcarved communion tables with silver chalices and plates, brass clocks, and candlestick holders in prominent view in the city churches. Gradually, by the late 19th century, the term "meetinghouse" was replaced by "church," and theologians took care to explain that Baptists still understood the church to be "people" rather than buildings, despite the popular connotation.

An interesting feature of the last two decades of the 19th century was the Baptist "temples." These downtown churches, primarily in the northern states, were spectacles of great preaching and music similar to the Methodist great halls. In many cities—Boston; Philadelphia; New York; Rochester, New York; Cleveland, Ohio; and Charleston, West Virginia—temples became center city buildings of multiple programs and Sunday spectacles. **Russell Conwell** in Philadelphia and **Edward Judson** in New York personified the need for such a room to receive the preaching services.

The **fundamentalist** movement had a pronounced impact upon Baptist architecture in North America. Electrifying pulpiteers like **J. Frank Norris** concentrated their ministries on large crowds at worship services and protracted meetings, and this naturally led to architectural modifications. Eschewing the use of stained glass, organs, and comfortable pews, the new "evangelists" built rather plain buildings with plenty of aisle room for respondents to come forward at the altar call. The remaining space was dedicated to **Sunday School** classes. Norris actually inveighed against Gothic architecture and criticized his fellow Baptists who worshipped in such structures as being elite and formalistic. His impact was felt in such groups as the **World Baptist Fellowship** and the **Baptist Bible Fellowship**.

Following World War II, there was a fairly rapid expansion of Baptist church building in North America, mostly in the suburbs. Typically, these structures lacked the resources of classical or Gothic tastes but instead were practical and fairly uniform. High-ceiling, exposed-beam "sanctuaries" replicated in a small way the concept of the tent of the Old Testament tabernacle. In most instances, the seating arrangement continued to consist of rows of pews facing the pulpit and communion table, with a center aisle.

Baptisteries in Baptist church buildings across the South and West frequently dominate the interior front, while in the northern United States and the Canadian provinces a simple cross on the wall behind the pulpit suffices. In the latter situations, the baptistery is hidden under the floor of the pulpit area.

Following the erection of the principal structure, which is usually used for worship, most building programs next turn to educational space. Typically designed for individual Sunday School classes and a common area for assemblies, this space is also used for community groups such as scouts or for senior citizens and church fellowship dinners. In churches where exterior property is limited, the basement area under the sanctuary serves these purposes.

In the 20th century as urban development limited church-yard space, parking space for automobiles became a determinant of the suitability of location for a congregation. Still, a historic building that is cherished by the community and the congregation can outweigh the need to move for more space. Edifices of this type can be found in Philadelphia; Boston; Washington, D.C.; Charleston, South Carolina; and San Francisco, California, for instance. In Canada, urban heritage buildings survive in Moncton and St. John, New Brunswick; Montreal, Quebec; Toronto, Peterborough, and Hamilton, Ontario; Calgary, Alberta; and Vancouver, British Columbia.

Related to North American Baptist church architecture is the design of educational buildings owned by Baptists. Often, the benefactors of colleges and universities imitated styles that they designed for their local churches. This pattern was seen in the eastern urban areas and, later, in Chicago, Toronto, and smaller cities such as Granville, Ohio, and Georgetown, Kentucky. Such structures constituted a statement that graphically depicted the emerging social status of Baptists.

The first buildings of an educational use in the Baptist community were those constructed by the Brown family for the College of Rhode Island in Providence. University Hall and Manning Hall were imitations of Harvard College and a modified Greek revival style. The first national university, Columbian College in Washington, D.C., embodied a bold vision of national leadership in the nation's capital, whose facilities bankrupted its trustees. "College Hill" in Washington, D.C. (later Meridian Hill Park), stood on a promontory of prized real estate value. Structures at Colgate University, Newton Theological Institution, and the University at Lewisburg in Pennsylvania were likewise designed to embody the New England college tradition—conservative, brick, and permanent, dominant motifs of their local landscapes. With the coming of **John D. Rockefeller**'s munificence, Baptist colleges imitated the Gothic style; this is illustrated in the University of Chicago (Illinois), Colgate Rochester Divinity School (New York), McMaster University (Ontario), and the University of Richmond (Virginia). Smaller schools in the Midwest and West constructed more functional structures closely resembling Victorian brick combination classroom and dormitory facilities found throughout the United States. Examples of this style are found at Franklin College in Indiana, Shurtleff College in Illinois, Sioux Falls College in South Dakota, Wake Forest College in North Carolina (the original campus now occupied by Southeastern Baptist Theological Seminary), and Southern Baptist Theological Seminary in Louisville, Kentucky.

AREA MINISTER. Terminology applied to regional ministers in the American Baptist, British Baptist, and Canadian Baptist traditions of the 20th century. Following the adoption of the "area" terminology, traveling ministers were appointed to relate to congregations in a geographical region comprising several associations. Usually accountable to the **executive minister**, area ministers serve as resources in program interpretation to churches, staff to associational programs, **pastors** to pastors, and missionary agents. Sometimes personnel work is part of the task, as when congregations are seeking new leadership.

Historically, area ministers have tasks similar to those of the "messengers" of ancient English **General Baptist** tradition and **association** missionaries in American and **Southern Baptist** polity. The first area, or general, superintendents in Britain were appointed in 1916. In the American Baptist family, persons holding specific program responsibilities, such as Christian education or rural ministry, began to assume oversight of certain regions; for instance, in 1948 the New

York Baptist Convention began designating areas and ministers to care for churches in those areas. Later, state convention "field secretaries" evolved to area ministers, particularly in the Midwest. The title "area minister" was in broad usage by 1967 among American Baptists. Southern Baptists made use of "area workers" following World War II, which evolved into associational missionaries or superintendents of **missions** (the latter had been employed in some states since the early 1900s). *See also* EXECUTIVE MINISTER.

ARGENTINA. Pablo Besson (1848–1932) was the founder of the permanent Baptist movement in Argentina, arriving in 1881 to start a church at Buenos Aires in 1883. In 1908, a national organization was organized, the Convención Evangelica Bautista de la República Argentina. U.S. **Southern Baptists**, who began their mission in 1901–1903, aware of the strategic location of Argentina, established the Seminario Internacional Teológico Bautista in Buenos Aires in 1953, to serve not only Argentina but also **Uruguay**, **Chile**, and **Paraguay**. The U.S. **Baptist General Conference** pioneered mission churches in 1955, resulting in Iglesias Bautistas Evangelicas del Norte America. The **Conservative Baptist** Foreign Mission Society established a mission in 1947, which relates to the General Association of Baptist Churches of Northwestern Argentina (1972) and the Evangelical Baptist Seminary of Argentina (1965) at Salta (formerly Tucuman). The **Baptist Bible Fellowship** has had a mission in Argentina since 1959, and the **Association of Baptists for World Evangelism** started a mission in 1978.

As of 2006, there were 530 churches and 90,000 members affiliated with the Convención Evangelica Bautista de Argentina. A theological school, Seminario Internacional Teológico Bautista, is located at Buenos Aires.

ARMENIA. At the political reorganization of the former Soviet Union in 1991, the Republic of Armenia emerged as a new state and with it the Baptist community. Formerly related to the All-Union Council of Evangelical Christians-Baptists, Baptists in Armenia formed Soiuz Evangelskikh Christian-Baptistov Armenii in 1992. This body of churches cooperates with the **European Baptist Federation** and the **Baptist World Alliance**.

As of 2006, there were 119 churches with 3,311 members affiliated with Soiuz Evangelskikh Christian-Baptistov Armenii. There are also missionaries present in Armenia from the U.S. **Baptist Missionary Association**.

ARMINIANISM, AMONG BAPTISTS. Strictly speaking, the term "Arminian" applies to those in the theological tradition of Jacobus Arminius (1560–1609), a Dutch Reformed pastor and theologian in the **Netherlands**. Arminius came to oppose the Calvinistic understanding of predestination and stressed the involvement of human response to God's gracious offer of salvation. Arminian thought was formally condemned at the Synod of Dort in 1618, and the Arminians (also called Remonstrants) were silenced in the Netherlands for a generation. The themes of Arminian thought, however, found their way into the Church of England and smaller evangelical sects like the **General Baptists** and, later, the Methodists. While there is no evidence of direct dependance of any Baptists upon Arminius, those in the General, Freewill, and **holiness** Baptist groups (Freewill, General) are frequently described as "Arminian" because of their emphases upon free grace, a free response to the gospel, and a view of Christ's atonement as unlimited in its effect upon humanity. Baptists with "high Calvinist" theological positions (e.g., **Strict Baptists**, **Primitive Baptists**, and **Reformed Baptists**) often take offense at Arminian groups or overly evangelistic emphases, claiming either a diminution of the sovereignty of God or the possibility of lapsing into Unitarian or Universalist theologies. In the past decade, a movement known as Open Theism has emerged among theologians in North America of an Arminian bent. Prominent among Open Theists is **Clark Pinnock**, a Canadian Baptist theologian. Roger Olson, a Baptist theology professor at Truett Seminary, Baylor University, is an ardent Arminian apologist. *See also* GENERAL BAPTISTS; PRIMITIVE BAPTISTS; STRICT BAPTISTS.

ARMITAGE, THOMAS (1819–1896). Baptist minister and historian, born in Pontefract, Yorkshire, England. Armitage preached his first sermon at 15 years old. He emigrated to the United States in 1838 and became a Methodist minister at Washington Street Methodist Church in Albany, New York. Disagreeing with the Methodists on doctrinal and **polity** issues, Armitage converted to Baptist principles in 1848, under the influence of **Jabez Swan**, and was baptized at Pearl Street Baptist Church in Albany. That year, he was called to the pastorate at Norfolk Street Baptist Church (later Fifth Avenue Baptist Church) in New York City, where he served until 1888. The day following Armitage's first Sunday at Norfolk Street Church, a fire destroyed the building and a new structure was soon erected at a cost of $30,000. Armitage also survived a vote of no confidence in 1853, which was rooted in 96 members' petition to obtain a new **pastor**. In 1865, he led in the construction of the Fifth Avenue Baptist Church, which became a city landmark. In 1886, he published a well-received history of the Baptists.

ARMSTRONG, ANNE WALKER (1850–1938). Southern Baptist denominational leader, born at Baltimore, Maryland. She was not formally educated but joined the Seventh Baptist Church in Baltimore, which was then served by the venerable **Richard Fuller**. Armstrong was much interested in children's education and taught the infant's class in her home church for 30 years. In the 1880s, Armstrong led in the establishment of the Women's Missionary Union and its auxiliary status with the **Southern Baptist Convention**. In 1899, she became corresponding secretary for the Women's Missionary Union, eventually refusing to take a salary. In 1888, she wrote letters to hundreds of missionary supporters, raising almost $3,000 to support **Charlotte Moon** in China. Armstrong was also active in missionary work among African Americans, providing funds to produce literature for their churches. In 1934, the Southern Baptist **Foreign Mission Board** established the Annie Armstrong Offering, an annual fundraising effort for foreign work.

ARNOLD, ELLEN (1858–1931). Australian Baptist overseas missionary, born at Aston, Warwickshire, England. Arnold was educated at Adelaide Teachers College and taught for a time in that city. She joined Flinders Street Baptist Church and was much influenced by its **pastor**, **Silas Mead**. In 1882, Arnold became the first appointee of the Australian Baptist Missionary Society and embarked for Faridpur, India. Taken ill, she returned in 1884 to Adelaide to recuperate and upon recovery made an extensive tour (the "Ellen Arnold Crusade") of the colonial states to raise awareness and support for the East Bengal mission. She recruited four other **women** who together were known as the "five barley loaves." Having administrative difficulties with her board, Arnold transferred in 1886 to the New South Wales Baptist Mission Society and pioneered its work at Comilla in East Bengal. Her final relocation in 1892 sent her to Pabna, where she worked tirelessly to establish schools and clinics, preach, and plant churches. Her centers were Ataikola and Bera. Arnold returned in 1930 as a volunteer and continued her work until her death. The primary force behind the creation of the East Bengal Baptist Union, Arnold was highly regarded in that region, later to become **Bangladesh**. The Baptists in Bangladesh celebrate Ellen Arnold Day, and there is a medical clinic at Ataikola named in her honor. In 1919, Arnold was awarded the Kaiser-I-Hind Medal for public service in India, but she declined the award.

ASHANTI. *See* GHANA.

ASHMORE, WILLIAM (1824–1909). American Baptist missionary, born at Putnam, Ohio. A graduate of Granville College and Western Baptist Theological Seminary, Ashmore first served the pastorate of First Baptist, Hamilton, Ohio. Under the appointment of the **American Baptist Missionary Union** to Bangkok, **Siam**, he conducted street preaching and mastered the Tie-chiu dialect. In 1858, Ashmore became a missionary in **Hong Kong** and, later, Swatow, **China**, where he spent the bulk of his career. In China, he developed an extensive Chinese staff and built a strong theological seminary at Swatow, plus a school to train women. He is best remembered for his advocacy of indigenous leadership in Baptist missionary work. The theological school in Swatow was named in his honor. In addition to numerous translations into Swatow, Ashmore published an outline of theology for Chinese students in 1902.

ASIAN BAPTIST FEDERATION (ABF). A regional organization of the **Baptist World Alliance** (BWA) founded in 1975. The ABF was organized to promote fellowship, cooperation, and service among its member unions/conventions in Asia and Oceania. Mission planning and relief programs are also included in the agenda, as is the promotion of the overall objectives of the BWA. Structurally, the ABF consists of a general council, an executive committee, and a congress that meets every five years in various cities throughout Asia. The ABF publishes the *Asian Baptist Digest* (1997–), formerly the *Asian Baptist News* (1972–1996).

ASPLAND, ROBERT (1782–1845). English Baptist, and, later, Unitarian, minister, born at Wicken, Cambridgeshire, England. Aspland was well educated at Bristol Baptist Academy and the University of Aberdeen, receiving the Ward Scholarship. He was baptized at the Devonshire Square Baptist Church and became **pastor** at the Baptist Chapel in Battersea in 1798. While a student at Bristol, Aspland developed unorthodox theological views and was known as the "boy preacher" for his communication skills. In 1799, he matriculated at Marischal College, but a year later was dropped from the rolls at Devonshire Square Church. In 1800, Aspland joined a firm manufacturing artist's colors and did supply preaching in London. In 1801, he was called to the General Baptist Church at Newport, Isle of Wight, but two years later became secretary to the South Unitarian Society. In 1805, Aspland became minister at the Gravel Pit, Hackney Church, and remained there for 40 years. He became essentially a Unitarian, organizing a minister's fund and the Christian Tract Society, but he also maintained personal relations and influence in the declining **General Baptist** community. His influence as a **liberal** thinker was greatly enhanced by his journal, *The Christian Reformer*, which he commenced and edited, 1815–1844.

ASPLUND, JOHN (1750–1807). American Baptist minister and editor, born in Sweden. Early in life, Asplund was involved in mercantile pursuits, without formal education. In 1775, he visited England and worked as a clerk. During the American Revolution, Asplund joined the British Navy, and while on duty near the American coast, he deserted ship. He settled in North Carolina, became a Baptist in 1782, and united with the Ballard's Bridge Church in Chowan County. Shortly thereafter, he moved to Southampton, Virginia, to be a **pastor** through 1785 and again from 1791 to 1794. Asplund returned to Europe in 1785 to make a survey of Dissenters and Baptists, visiting England, **Denmark**, **Germany**, **Finland**, Lapland, and the

United States, covering about 7,000 miles. He made a second tour in 1794 and covered over 10,000 miles. Each of his tours produced an edition of *The Baptist Annual Register*. Asplund's purpose was twofold: to conduct itinerant preaching and to collect materials to assist future historians. Asplund reckoned that his experience as a clerk placed him in a unique position to calculate the statistics of over 250 Baptist churches and ministers. He relocated to Maryland in the early 19th century and died in a drowning accident.

ASSEMBLY OF FREE GRACE GENERAL BAPTISTS. *See* GENERAL BAPTISTS.

ASSOCIATION OF BAPTISTS FOR WORLD EVANGELISM (ABWE). A U.S.-based mission-sending organization formed in reaction to policies of the **American Baptist Foreign Mission Society** (ABFMS) and the Northern Baptist Convention (NBC). In the 1920s, amidst the **fundamentalist** controversy, the leadership of the NBC urged upon its missionary agency, the ABFMS, a more open policy of nonconfessional personnel appointments. Moreover, one of the medical missionaries of the ABFMS, Dr. Raphael C. Thomas (1873–1956), then a missionary in the **Philippines**, was reprimanded for his open advocacy of more attention to evangelism, and this ultimately led to his resignation from service. His relatives and supporters in the United States—who were already coalescing around conservative evangelical issues in the NBC, such as a confession of faith and seminary education in the **evangelical** if not moderately fundamentalist tradition—assisted in the formation of a new missionary agency to carry forth Dr. Thomas's work and perhaps to expand to other fields. The original group of founders of ABWE included **Lucy W. Peabody** and Marguerite Treat Doane (1868–1954), daughter of **William Howard Doane.**

ABWE was founded in Philadelphia in 1927–1928, stressing historic Baptist principles and a voluntary association of supporters rather than a denominational body. The first field was in the Philippines, followed by **Peru**, **Brazil**, **Colombia**, and South **China** (to 1953), **Hong Kong**, **Chile**, **Japan**, and **Pakistan**, to name the major areas. The mission, which operates as a faith mission and primarily accepts designated gifts, sponsors a theological seminary at Manila and a **Bible** college in Iloilo in the Philippines, and Bible **colleges** in South America. Currently, ABWE sponsors 1,250 missionaries in 70 countries and relates to about 5,000 congregations in the United States and Canada. In addition, ABWE works with national Christians in over a dozen countries where Christian witness is restricted through the Global Access Partners. The official periodical of ABWE is *The Message*, and the headquarters are in Harrisburg, Pennsylvania. A separate organization of ABWE was created in the 1960s for Canadian supporters and is headquartered in London, Ontario.

ASSOCIATIONS, BAPTIST. Groups of Baptist churches formed for the purpose of mutual support, aid to destitute congregations, and advice on matters of order, **discipline**, expansion, and identity. Based upon a principle common to most Christian organizations, Baptists have almost from their beginnings associated in this way with other churches of like faith and order.

The Baptist association is not considered a superior body to the local congregation but rather an advisory body voluntarily covenanting with local churches for specific tasks. Delegates or messengers from local churches usually include the **pastor** and one lay representative, according to the relative size of the church. Annual meetings of delegates consist of business sessions, worship and preaching, and reports on the status of members congregations. Actions may be taken in the name of the association but are not binding on the local churches. Churches may be "**disfellowshipped**," that is, dropped from associational membership by vote of the delegates. Theological consensus was important in the 17th and 18th centuries, usually becoming the basis of effective associative relations.

In terms of size and numbers of participating churches, the association has evolved considerably. In the beginning, the association usually represented the distance of one day's travel by horse and buggy between points of greatest distance. As the Baptist movement expanded, the political unit of the county corresponded roughly to an association's geography. Size has ranged from 5 or 7 congregations in early days to 20 or 30 member churches in the 20th century.

The first associations among the English Baptists were formed in the 1620s. London Baptists, divided over relations with other Christians and the meaning of the magistracy, met informally and corresponded with the Dutch Mennonites. Later, the **Particular Baptists** of London formed an association, and they prepared and ratified the First London Confession of Faith in 1644. By the 1660s, Baptists in England and **Wales** had formed local and national associations and met regularly, at least once per year.

In the American colonies, the associational principle developed very early. **General Six Principle Baptist** congregations held yearly meetings in Rhode Island as early as the 1670s. In the Middle Colonies, Philadelphia churches met beginning in 1707. In New England, the **Five Principle** Calvinistic Baptist Association met from 1754, and in the South, the churches of Charleston formed an association in 1751. The Philadelphia (Pennsylvania), Warren (Rhode Island), and Charleston (South Carolina) associations became models for a rapidly expanding associational life in the United States.

The classic statement in an American context concerning the association was made by Benjamin Griffiths (1688–1768), a Philadelphia minister, who wrote in 1749 that the purposes of associations include the drafting of sound doctrine and the disowning of erroneous teachings, the sending of representatives for consultation, and the making of decisions to withdraw from defective or disorderly churches. Griffiths was careful to indicate that each congregation is independent in its authority and church power, the association being advisory and voluntary. Griffiths's statement has been referred to by both mainstream and **fundamentalist** Baptist groups in the United States.

Among Baptists in **Canada**, the first associations emerged in Nova Scotia and Upper Canada (the predecessor of modern Ontario). Missionaries from New York State and New England planted associations in the vicinity of Lakes Ontario and Erie. In Nova Scotia, the Danbury, Connecticut, Association was a specific model. Among churches in the Ottawa River Valley, English Baptist associational principles were witnessed in the formation of associations.

As Baptists spread forth, primarily from North America and Great Britain, the associational principle followed the establishment of congregations. In Europe, **J. G. Oncken** toured widely in the **German** states and Austria-Hungary and formed associations that frequently became national unions of Baptist churches. In Africa, missions to **Liberia**, the **Congo**, and **South Africa** produced associations of churches. In South Asia, Indian Baptists formed their associations early in the 19th century, and the missionary churches in **China** and **Japan** did likewise in the 1860s and 1870s. Latin American associations were built on American models, differing only as influenced by northern or southern U.S. Baptist missionaries. Generally, the formation of associations precedes the creation of national unions or conventions.

AUSTRALIA. The first Baptists in Australia came among the pioneer settlers from Great Britain; one of these was a convict named Richard Boots who arrived in 1788 and listed his religious affiliation as "Baptist." In 1831, John McKaeg (fl. 1818–1837) held the first Baptist service in a hotel in Sydney; two years later, John Saunders, a missionary of the **Baptist Missionary Society** (BMS), planted the Bathurst Street Church in Sydney, New South Wales, considered the mother congregation of Baptists in Australia. For a time in the 1840s, British Baptists considered making Australia an official field but declined in favor of unevangelized peoples. However, at the request of Australian leaders, the BMS did send several church planters. Various states had differing beginning points of Baptist mission work: in 1835, what is considered the earliest constituted church was planted at Hobart, Tasmania, in what is now Australia, although it survived only eight years; the first church in South Australia was established in Adelaide, following missionary beginnings with aboriginal peoples; about 1839, a congregation was gathered in Melbourne, Victoria; another at Moreton Bay, Queensland, in 1855; and in Western Australia, a church was formed at Perth in 1895.

More influenced by British than U.S. Baptists in its early development, Australian Baptist associational life emerged in 1858 in Victoria; South Australians organized an association in 1863 and then in 1872 with the **Particular Baptist** Association of Australia (New South Wales). Cooperation for **mission** occurred quite early with the establishment of an auxiliary to the BMS in South Australia in 1863, which evolved into separate mission societies in each colony/state. In 1913, the six organizations were drawn together as the Australian Baptist Mission (renamed in 1959 the Australian Baptist Missionary Society). The society began a mission in East Bengal at the time of its organization in 1867; from 1876 to 1880, it supported a mission in **Japan;** and since has conducted work in **India**, Bengal, **Pakistan,**

Papua, New Guinea, Irian Jaya, and individual appointments in cooperation with other Baptists in four African nations (**Zambia, Zimbabwe, Malawi, Mozambique**) and nine Asian nations (**Hong Kong, Thailand, Indonesia,** the **Philippines, Cambodia, Viet Nam, China, Singapore, Kazakstan**). In 2002, the Australian Baptist Mission Society took a new name, Global Interaction, and as of 2007, supported 140 missionaries in six nations and people groups in Africa and Asia, 225 short-term workers, and 40 home personnel. The national mission effort is the unifying factor for Australian Baptists and also includes the Australian Baptist World Aid and Relief Committee from 1975 (now called Baptist World Aid Australia).

In 1926, a national organization, the Baptist Union of Australia (BUA), was founded by delegates from among the state associations, largely building upon the cooperation of the Australian Baptist Foreign Mission. In the first decade of the BUA, a Federal Home Mission Board, an Educational Board, an Evangelism Board, a Young People's Board, and the Australian Baptist Ministerial Fund were formed. The original Board of Literature evolved in 1953 with the Educational Board to become the Board of Christian Education and Publication, imitating an American Baptist Convention structure. Clifford Press, named for English Baptist **John Clifford**, served the denomination from 1947 through the 1950s in providing literature for the churches. Under changing circumstances, however, the Educational Board was discontinued in 1975, the Board of Christian Education and Publication ended in 1983, and the publication of *The Australian Baptist* concluded in 1991, the latter a victim of lack of support. Aside from council meetings, a national Triennial Assembly met from 1926 through 1997 at strategic cities across the country. In the 1970s, the structure shifted from an assembly to a convention model, and then to a Baptist Family Celebration for the 1990s, culminating in the Baptist World Congress at Melbourne in January 2000. Presently, the Baptist Union of Australia National Council meets three times annually, with representatives from each state plus the international and national mission agencies. There are state Baptist unions in Victoria (1862), South Australia (1863), New South Wales (1868), Queensland (1877), Tasmania (1884), and Western Australia (1896). Each state body is independent, with its own regional conventions and general superintendents (appointed from the

1960s in most cases), resulting in a reality that the BUA is a less than fully effective national organization.

There are seven Australian Baptist theological or secondary schools that are under the auspices of their respective states, which include Victoria Baptist College (later Whitley College) in Melbourne (1891); Malyon College in Queensland (1904); Morling College, New South Wales (1916); Kings College, Kensington, New South Wales (1910); Carey Baptist Grammar School at Kew, New South Wales (1923); Burleigh College in South Australia (1952); Vose Baptist Theological College of Western Australia (1963); and the North Queensland College of Ministries (1986). An attempt at practical Christian training, particularly for women missionaries, commenced at the Victoria Baptist Training Institute from 1947 to 1968. Australian Baptists have also participated in **ecumenical** theological ventures, including Union College in South Australia from 1872 to 1886, and the Melbourne College of Divinity and the Sydney College of Divinity, both university-related ecumenical faculties on the contemporary scene. An independent Fundamentalist Baptist congregation, Lighthouse Baptist Church in Queensland, started the Australian Baptist College in 1997–1998.

In addition to the indigenous Baptist work in Australia, **Baptist Mid-Missions** from the United States established a work in Melbourne in 1968 and, later, at Croydon. In 1973, the Victoria Baptist Bible College emerged from this effort. Also in 1968, the **Baptist Bible Fellowship** established a mission, as did the **Association of Baptists for World Evangelism** in 1970. **Strict** and **Particular Baptists**, relating to that tradition from England, maintain three to four congregations and a small membership under 50 in the country. **Seventh Day Baptists** from New Zealand established a church at Bundaberg in 1975.

As of 2006, there were 945 churches/fellowships and 61,409 members associated with the BUA. The official periodical was the *Australian Baptist* (1913–1991), afterward the *National Baptist* (1987–2002) for a time, plus various state periodicals that continue. Other short-lived perioidicals include *On Being* (1975–1997), and *Anvil* (1968–1970).

AUSTRIA. Baptist development in the heart of the Austro-Hungarian Empire may be traced to missionary work by **J. G. Oncken**. In 1847, the first Austrians were baptized, and in 1851, Edward Millard began a long-term mission in Vienna that eventuated in the first congregation in 1869. A. Meereis was the first appointed pastor in 1879. In the 20th century, Arnold Köster, the pastor at Vienna, unified the Baptist work and suffered greatly during Nazi occupation. In 1953, the Bund der Baptistengemeinden in Österreich (Union of Baptist Churches in Austria) was created, and the Austrian churches assisted in the creation of the German Baptist Confession of 1977. In addition to the regular Baptist work, **Baptist Mid-Missions** from the United States established an independent mission in 1967, the **Conservative Baptist** Foreign Mission Society began its mission in 1970, and the **Baptist Bible Fellowship** opened a mission in 1984.

As of 2006, there were 22 churches and 1,389 members affiliated with the Bund der Baptistengemeinden in Österreich. A periodical, *Gemeindebrief* (*Church Notes*) (1950–) is associated with the Bund der Baptistengemeinden.

AUTONOMY OF THE LOCAL CHURCH. A much discussed facet of Baptistic identity that pertains to the local congregation. The terminology "autonomy of the local church" actually appeared as such first in the work of **E. Y. Mullins**, a **Southern Baptist** theologian, in 1898.

From the earliest development of English Baptist theological understanding of the church, Baptists have clearly articulated the freedom of a local congregation to determine its own affairs. A congregation is to be free from interference by government and from other ecclesiastical bodies. Early Baptists wrote of the independence of congregations, by which they meant that the gifts and authority of **Christ** were given to each congregation to manage its own affairs. At the same time, both the First and Second London Confessions of Faith also speak of the associational principle which relates individual congregations together. *See also* ASSOCIATIONS.

In the United States, the associational principle prevailed among the scattered communities of Baptist churches along the eastern seaboard. However, in the backcountry a frontier individualism developed by the third decade of the 19th century, which sought to protect the rights of the congregation. Referred to by some historians as "**local church protectionism**," this attitude was militantly expressed in the New Hampshire Confession of Faith (1832). A combination of New England protectionism, Western frontier ethos, and theological obscurantism (as illustrated in the antimission campaign) thus created an emphasis upon the prerogatives of the local church.

The **Landmarkist** movement carried forth the independence of the local church as one of its major assertions. Landmarkist writers such as **James M. Graves** and **James M. Pendleton** asserted that each local congregation was the "true church" and that nothing held power or authority over it or could interfere in its government. Churches were subject to the Lordship of **Christ** alone, making rules and exercising discipline under Christ's authority exclusively. A belligerent style of local church independence was revealed in Landmarkist literature, which caused much offense among other Baptists and within the larger paedo-Baptist Christian community. Because pastors often waged the debates over the rights of local churches, the Landmarkist position on this "doctrine" is seen as affirming a strong, authoritarian pastoral leadership that resists interference in its **ministry**.

In 1898, E. Y. Mullins in the southern United States wrote authoritatively on Baptist beliefs and described much of the theological basis of the idea of autonomy. In fact, the term "autonomy" is likely his addition to the Baptist vocabulary. He held that the government of each local church is democratic and autonomous, free and independent. But, lest his position be confused with Landmarkism, he also argued for cooperation as one of the highest privileges a church could enjoy.

In the present century, the doctrine of the autonomy of the local church has received much affirmation among **independent Baptists** and those who favor weak associational bodies. "Conventionism" is seen as an unwarranted interference in local church affairs, notably in decisions about distribution of funds, theological exclusivity, and selection of leadership. In 2007, the **Baptist World Alliance** held a Theological Colloquy in Elstal, Germany, on the subject of autonomy, owing to international concern for its implications in cooperative Baptist work. *See also* LOCAL CHURCH PROTECTIONISM; POLITY, BAPTIST.

AZERBAIJAN. Baptists have been in Azerbaijan since 1950. When the former Soviet Union collapsed in 1991–1992, Azerbaijan emerged as an independent state. Along with this political change, the Baptist community, fostered by Russian and Ukrainian Baptists and which had been part of the All-Union Council of Evangelical Christians-Baptists, formed the Soiuz Evangelskikh Christian-Baptistov Azerbaijana (Union of Evangelical Christians-Baptists of Azerbaijan) in 1992.

As of 2006, there were 50 churches with 3,000 members affiliated with Soiuz Evangelskikh Christian-Baptistov Azerbaijana.

– B –

BABCOCK, RUFUS (1798–1875). American Baptist minister and educator, born at Colebrook, Connecticut. Babcock graduated from Brown University and studied theology under **William Staughton** in Philadelphia. He was one of the first faculty members of Columbian College, Washington, D.C., and served pastorates in New York and Massachusetts. In 1833, he was elected president of Waterville College in Maine, where he served for four years before becoming **pastor** at Spruce Street Church in Philadelphia. Babcock was an avid supporter of religious **voluntarism**, serving with the **American Baptist Publication Society**, the American and Foreign Bible Society, and the American **Sunday School** Union. From 1841 to 1845, he was editor of the newspaper, *The Baptist Memorial*. Babcock also edited the published journal of the pioneer domestic missionary, **John Mason Peck**.

BACKUS, ISAAC (1724–1806). American Baptist **pastor** and historian, born at Norwich, Connecticut. Backus was one of the best-known and highly regarded ministers of the Revolutionary and Early National periods. Converted in 1741 during the **Great Awakening**, he began his **ministry** as a Congregationalist and soon joined the **Separate** or New Light movement. Backus was ordained at Middleborough, Massachusetts, where he served his first pastorate. He itinerated widely as an evangelist, and in 1756, he converted to Baptist principles and subsequently organized a Baptist congregation at Middleborough. Backus was a leading polemicist against taxation of **Nonconformists**, and in 1774, he served as the agent of the Warren

Baptist Association to the Continental Congress. His letter to the citizens of New England in 1777 moved many people to the cause of **religious liberty**. In 1789, Backus made a 3,000-mile tour of the middle and southern states, strengthening churches and gathering materials for a history of the Baptists. Using materials supplied by **Morgan Edwards** and his own notes, Backus published a major historical treatise on Baptists (1804) in which he recounted the struggles of the 17th century and particularly the role of **Roger Williams** in achieving religious liberty. In recent historiography, Backus's diaries were edited by **William G. McLoughlin** of Brown University, and Backus has survived as a major interpreter of 18th-century Baptist thought. *See also* SEPARATE BAPTISTS.

BAHAMAS. Early Baptist history in the Bahamas stems from the presence of several former slaves who began preaching and gathered churches: Frank Spence (1780), Prince Williams (1790), and, later, Thomas Rumer (1840). In 1833, missionaries appointed by the **Baptist Missionary Society** (BMS) in London arrived in the Bahamas and greatly aided the Baptist cause. In addition to **evangelism**, the BMS staff started Sabbath schools, temperance societies, and Bible societies; in 1929, the BMS withdrew from the islands. In 1892, the Bahamas Baptist Union was formed, uniting several islands of the Baptist community. In 1925–1930, two representatives of the **National Baptist Convention of the United States of America**, the Reverend J. R. Evans and Mrs. Jannie Morris of Miami, Florida, visited the Bahamas and organized women's home mission societies and young people's unions, relating to the U.S. body. In 1937, the Bahamas Baptist Missionary and Educational Convention emerged, bringing much needed support from the National Baptist Convention. U.S. **Southern Baptists** began vacation Bible school ministries in the Bahamas in 1949, out of which grew the Bahamas Baptist Institute in 1953, which was ultimately merged into the Bahamas Baptist College in 1965. There is also an **Independent Baptist** work in the Bahamas, related to **fundamentalist** Baptists in the southern United States.

As of 2006, there were 272 churches and 75,000 members relating to the Bahamas National Baptist Missionary and Education Convention. A school, Bahamas Baptist Community College, is located at Nassau.

BAKER, ROBERT ANDREW (1910–1992). Southern Baptist minister and church historian, born at St. Louis, Missouri. Baker was educated at a business college and in 1932 was appointed to the U.S. Secret Service, where he spent four years as an operative. Beginning in 1936, he continued his education at Baylor University, Southwestern Baptist Seminary, and ultimately at Yale University, where he studied with **Kenneth Scott Latourette** and Roland Bainton (1894–1984). From 1946 to 1952, Baker was pastor at Highland Baptist Church in Dallas, Texas. In 1952, he became professor of church history at Southwestern Seminary, succeeding his mentor, **William Wright Barnes.** Baker became one of the most influential scholars of his era in the **Southern Baptist** tradition. Among his published works are *Relations between Northern and Southern Baptists* (1948), *A Summary of Christian History* (1959), and *The Southern Baptist Convention and Its People, 1607–1972* (1974).

BALDWIN, THOMAS (1753–1826). Baptist **pastor**, born at Bozrah, Connecticut. Originally trained to practice law, Baldwin converted to Baptist principles in 1780 and was ordained an **evangelist** in Connecticut. Eventually, he served the church at Canaan and was called to Second Baptist Church, Boston, in 1790. In association with **Samuel Stillman** at First Baptist, Boston, Baldwin helped to make Boston an epicenter of New England Baptist life. He was active in promoting various **voluntary** associations, notably the Massachusetts Baptist Missionary Society, where he served as an officer and editor of their magazine, the oldest Baptist periodical in the United States in continuous circulation. In 1810, he published a series of letters on Baptist principles, considered by his contemporaries to be a preeminent statement of denominational beliefs. Baldwin was one of the chief promoters of establishing the Newton Theological Institution, based on the Andover Theological Seminary model of the Congregationalists. He was also the first president of the **Baptist Board of Foreign Missions.** Baldwin's book, *The Baptism of Believers Only* (1806), is considered a classic treatment of its subject.

BALTIMORE COMPROMISE. Name given to an important agreement struck between Baptist churches in the United States who differed on the question of slaveholding and missionary appointments. At the Tenth Triennial meeting of the **General Missionary Convention** (GMC), held in Baltimore, Maryland, in May 1841, the delegates wrestled with the moral and political questions that their respective sections exhibited. Northerners were increasingly interested in a strong stand against slaveholding and wanted it placed in the bylaws of the GMC. Southerners, on the other hand, felt that political considerations had no place in **evangelical** work and would tolerate no such retractions. Under the skillful leadership of GMC president **William Bullein Johnson** of South Carolina, the delegates agreed that the Convention had no right to interfere in political questions and that union was more important than sectional jealousies. The **Baptist Board of Foreign Missions**, actually responsible for the appointment of missionaries, affirmed the "Baltimore Compromise" in holding that all churches are independent communities and that they had delegated no power to individuals or **associations** to act for them. The Baltimore Compromise, then, held that issues of appointing slaveholders or countenancing slaveholding were inappropriate to hold as a criterion in the work of missions.

Between 1843 and 1845, however, pressure mounted in the northern Baptist churches as the American Baptist Free Missionary Society (ABFrMS) was formed as an **antislavery** body, and southerners looked for inviolable defenses against their pro-slavery position. When in 1844 the Acting Board of the GMC voted to refuse the appointment of a slaveholder to missionary work in a hypothetical question put to it by Alabama delegates, the Baltimore Compromise was broken and the steps toward a regional schism were taken. *See* SOUTHERN BAPTIST CONVENTION.

BAMPFIELD, FRANCIS (1615–1683). Seventh Day Baptist minister and author, born in Poltimore, Devon, England. Bampfield was educated at Wadham College, Oxford, and ordained a priest in the Church of England. He served initially in Dorsetshire, where he organized various charitable enterprises for the poor; later, he was a prebend in Exeter Cathedral. Bampfield moved to Sherborne, where he became a Puritan. In 1662, he was driven out by the Act of Uniformity, which required strict adherence to the Book of Common Prayer. A Royalist under Charles I, he was also a Trier under Oliver Cromwell (1599–1658). With the passage of the Act of Uniformity in 1662, Bampfield was imprisoned for up to nine years. During his incarceration, he arrived at Baptistic and Sabbatarian positions and preached in the jail, where he also gathered a congregation. Bampfield **baptized** himself in the River Salisbury. In 1676, he started a Seventh Day church at Bethnal Green in his home; in 1681, he hired Pinner's Hall in London to accommodate the crowds in attendance. Bampfield was arrested for conducting these services and sentenced to Newgate prison where he died. He published eight works, including a major study of the Sabbath and a defense of **religious liberty**.

BAND OF HOPE. Leading movement of children in the **temperance** crusade in early Victorian England. At a Temperance Society meeting at Leeds in 1847, Baptist minister Jabez Tunnicliff met Anne Jane Carlile, a prison worker, and the two agreed to begin the Band of Hope to attract children to the temperance cause. Most of those who joined the bands were from working-class families of a great variety of dissenting congregations. *See also* TEMPERANCE.

BANGLADESH. Region also known as East Bengal, where Baptist work can be traced from **William Carey**, who in 1793 began a mission in Bengal for the **Baptist Missionary Society** (BMS). Various American Baptist missionaries have passed through Bengal as well, beginning with **Adoniram Judson**. In the period of 1882–1931, **Ellen Arnold** of **Australia** established a firm foundation that led to the East Bengal Baptist Union. With the partition of East and West **Pakistan** from **India** in 1947, the Bengal Baptist Union was forced to make administrative arrangements in the new geopolitical situation. Temporarily, the West Dinajpur Baptist Union assumed leadership in the territory, but this proved inadequate. In 1955, the Bengal Baptist Union recognized the establishment of the Baptist Union of Pakistan, which encompassed the region of East Pakistan. In 1971, the Republic of Bangladesh was proclaimed amidst open military hostilities, and Baptists within the country, as well as missionary organizations, provided aid and leadership in the crisis. Eventually the Baptist Union of Pakistan became the Bangladesh Baptist Sangha, still historically related to the BMS. A second organization of churches, the Bangladesh Baptist Union, relates to the mission work of **Australia, New Zealand**, and **Southern Baptists**. The **Association of Baptists for World Evangelism** began a mission in East Pakistan (Bangladesh) in 1955.

As of 2006, there were 459 churches with 15,100 members affiliated with the Bangladesh Baptist Fellowship; 337 churches with 15,000 members affiliated with the Bangladesh Baptist Sangha; and 148 churches with 12,254 members affiliated with the Garo Baptist Convention. There are two Baptist-related schools in Bangladesh: J.N.B. Memorial Baptist Training Institute at Mymensingh and the College of Christian Theology in Bangladesh at Dacca.

BAPTISM. Primary rite among Baptists. According to the 18th-century British-American historian **Morgan Edwards**, baptism was their denominating article.

The Meaning of Baptism. From a Baptist perspective, baptism is a profession of faith, an initiatory act, a symbolic rite of cleansing, a transition rite to a new creation, and an act of obedience. Based on Romans 6, baptism is a picture of the gospel at work in one's experience: crucifixion with Christ, burial with Christ, and resurrection to new life in Christ. Only the mode of immersion signifies this aspect so vividly. From Matthew 28:19–20, Baptists believe it is incumbent upon every able believer to be baptized in the name of the Father, Son, and Holy Spirit. Just as Jesus submitted himself to the baptism of John (Matt. 3:13–17; John 1:26–34; Mark 1:9–13), so all believers must submit themselves to the example and command of Christ. Commonly in the **black Baptist** community, baptism signifies the transition from a "bastard people" to a new social creation (2 Cor. 5:17). In 2008, the government of Jordan invited the **Baptist World Alliance** to create a center among other Christian groups at the likely site of the baptism of Jesus at Bethany beyond Jordan in the Jordan River Valley.

For Baptists, believer's baptism precedes admission to the church. Having professed one's faith in **Christ** through the act of baptism, a person is initiated through a faithful experience into, first, the universal body of Christ and, second, into the local congregation, the visible manifestation of the Body of Christ. It was common for early confessions of faith to limit the enjoyment of the benefits of the church, particularly admission to the Lord's Supper, to baptized believers only.

The Issue of Believer's versus Paedo Baptism. In the first generation of Baptistic believers in England and, later, the **Netherlands**, believer's baptism was a key issue. Virtually the entire Christian community, except the Anabaptist sects, practiced infant, or paedo (meaning "child"), baptism as a **sacrament**. This had the dual significance of introducing children at the beginning of their lives to the Christian community as well as registering them in the social community, that is, giving the child a "Christian" name. **Anabaptists** in the early 16th century recovered the ancient practice of baptizing believers only, which in reality limited the act of baptism to adults. Later, **John Smyth** and a small group of English Separatists began to practice believer's baptism to reestablish a "true church of true believers." This was seen as a radical act because it called into question the long-standing sacrament of the churches, both Catholic and Protestant, and because it dismissed the social significance of paedobaptism. Baptists of all kinds in the English community of the 17th century held tenaciously to believer's baptism.

The Issue of Sacrament or Ordinance. Early Baptists recognized the value of the term "sacrament," but commonly did not use it with respect to baptism. Instead, the term "ordinance," meaning "teaching," was used to denote one of the two recognized scriptural rites of the church. Baptists universally have eschewed any concept of baptismal regeneration, preferring to understand baptism as a sign that pointed to deeper spiritual truths. In this regard, they bore the marks of the English Reformed tradition. In the 20th century, among British and American Baptist congregations, there is a renewed tendency to understand baptism as a sacrament, in part in response to the **ecumenical** dialogue.

The Issue of Mode. Early **General Baptists** in England doubtless followed the accepted baptismal mode of the English Separatist tradition: pouring or affusion. This changed, however, with the **Particular Baptists** in the 1640s. A congregation at Southwark, London, under the leadership of **John Spilsbury** sent Deacon Richard Blunt to discover the ways and means of believer's baptism among the Dutch Mennonites. In a congregation at Rhynsburg, Blunt began fraternal relations and witnessed the practice of baptism by immersion. This he brought back to England, and before 1644 it was the common understanding of Particular Baptists. General Baptists appeared to have adopted the immersion mode by 1650.

In the North American colonies, immersion became the standard from the 1670s. It was common to baptize in streams, rivers, or any "living waters," the latter phrase in contrast with "still waters" like those in a pond. Accounts survive well into the 19th century of winter baptisms where the ice had to be broken for immersion to take place. Similarly, in the early experiences of Canadian Baptists, New England practices regarding baptism were common.

The act of immersion consists of lowering the candidate into the water once, while reciting the trinitarian formula: "I baptize you in the name of the Father, the Son, and the Holy Spirit." In some smaller Baptist bodies in the United States, triune immersion, or three times into the water by the trinitarian formula, is used. Some early Baptists in England are reputed to have held candidates under water for several seconds, in order that a sense of new life and freedom would result. In colder climates in Great Britain and North America, stories abound of baptismal services during the winter months where the ice was broken on lakes to baptize candidates; at least one person is known to have died following a baptism in the winter, Ann Hart Reekie (d. 1863) of Tiverton, Ontario.

Global Generalizations. The practice of baptism in Europe follows the experience of British and American examples. For instance, **J. G. Oncken** was baptized by an American missionary, **Barnas Sears**. Oncken, in turn, practiced from his own experience as he preached conversion and believer's baptism in the Lutheran, Reformed, and Catholic locales of his missionary work. In **Sweden**, the scene of believer's baptism by immersion has become the hallmark of Baptists, thanks to a famous 1886 painting by Baron Gustaf Cederstrom, *The Baptists*, of a baptism at Lake Malaren, near Uppsala.

Extraordinary Issues. Generally, it is reserved to ministers (ordained or licensed), and also less frequently **deacons**, to baptize candidates. On unusual occasions, some people have baptized themselves. John Smyth read the new meaning of baptize in the New Testament and, finding no one acceptable, baptized himself and then his deacons. He rationalized this by arguing that he was ushering in a new order of the church, true believers, and that further baptisms would take their authority from Christ through his act. Later, under criticism from Mennonites, Smyth regretted this move and probably accepted another believer's baptism from the Waterlander Mennonites. Similarly, the eccentric **Seventh Day Baptist Francis Bampfield**, having arrived at Baptistic principles, baptized himself in the River Salisbury. In North America, **Roger Williams** deputed a follower to baptize Williams, and then Williams baptized others in his congregation.

William Carey introduced Baptistic baptismal practices to Asia. At Serampore, he built the Lall Bazaar Chapel, which included a **baptistery**. Carey's son, Felix (1786–1822), expanded the practice to eastern **India**, and **Adoniram Judson** introduced believer's baptism to **Burma**. Baptism became a prominent feature of Christian experience in northeastern India, as indicated in the village of Haimong in the Naga Hills, where a pool hollowed out of solid rock became a place of frequent baptisms from the 1870s and, ultimately, a shrine. As an outgrowth of missions in Siam, Baptist practices followed the Chinese community to China itself through **William Dean**, **J. Lewis Shuck**, and others. J. G. Oncken taught believer's baptism in his travels and reintroduced it to much of northern and eastern Europe (the Anabaptist sects doubtless practiced believer's baptism three centuries before). **David George** in **Sierra Leone** and **Lott Carey** were among the first to practice believer's baptism on the African continent in 1792 and 1821, respectively. *See also* BAPTISTERION, BAPTISTERY.

In the mission fields of North America, Latin America, Africa, and the Far East, believer's baptism by immersion is a distinguishing mark of Baptists. Often, a public spectacle of baptism signifies to the community that the candidates have in fact renounced former religious practices and embarked upon a new life. In 18th-century Philadelphia, Morgan Edwards regularly baptized new converts at a prominent site along the city's waterfront. In the next century, American Baptist evangelist **Jacob Knapp** in 1837 baptized 60 people in half an hour (probably the record) and frequently invited public officials, including the president of the United States, to his baptismal ceremonies. Noted Australian Baptist pastor-evangelist **Silas Mead** baptized 1,000 candidates in a little over two decades of ministry in the 1880s. The missionary context has been the backdrop for some of the largest numbers of baptisms: American Baptist missionary in India **John E. Clough**, with six ordained pastors at Velumpilly near Ongole, baptized 2,222 persons in one day; Henry Richards (1851–1928), a missionary of the **American Baptist Missionary Union** at Banza Manteke in the **Congo**, baptized over 1,000 converts in a few weeks in 1886; later, Chester J. Jump (1918–), also an American Baptist, baptized more than 10,000 candidates between 1951 and 1953 at Vanga in the Congo. Under the eye of the Marxist U.S.S.R. government of the era, Russian Baptists baptized 365 candidates in the river at Moscow in 1926. An interesting part of Baptist practices regarding baptism is "spontaneous baptism." Based upon the Apostle Philip's experience in Acts 8:36 where the Ethiopian said, "Here is water. What hinders me from being baptized?" Baptist ministers may invite any seekers to be baptized at the conclusion of a baptismal service. Because such baptisms lack preparation or catechism, they are referred to as "spontaneous baptisms." One such baptism occurred as recently as 2007 in Nova Scotia, Canada, at the New Minas Baptist Church.

BAPTIST (THE NAME). In the 16th century, those who rebaptized adherents were called either Catabaptists or **Anabaptists**, the former term used by Huldrych Zwingli (1484–1531) and the latter used elsewhere in Europe. In Western Europe, several terms became common, particularly among Mennonite groups, to describe "baptizing people": "Doopsgezinde" (Dutch for "baptism-minded people"), "Taufgesinnte" or "Taufer" (the German equivalent), and "Wiedertaufer" (Anabaptist). At the turn of the 17th century, the Englishman **John Smyth** described **believer's churches** as "churches of the apostolical constitution . . . primitive apostolique institution," and he himself was called a se-Baptist because he administered his own **baptism**. His close friend **Thomas Helwys** used the name "Church of Christ" in his confession of 1612, and others throughout the century used "Churches which are commonly (though falsely) called Anabaptist," "Congregations gathered according to the Primitive Pattern," "Christians baptized upon profession of their faith," and "Baptized believers." As yet, little evidence exists of a 17th-century English Baptist church of any kind prior to 1680 being referred to simply as "Baptist" (though the word appears in titles and for some isolated individuals beginning in the 1640s). The most common terminology appears to have been "Church of Christ," followed by a geographical identification. Among many **General Baptists**, the term "Baptized believers" was prevalent toward the end of the 18th century.

Two related terms were employed by disputants in the 17th century. Daniel Featley (1582–1645) called Baptists "Dippers" and John Tombes (1603–1676) referred to them as "Anti-paedo-baptists."

In the American colonies, the derogatory terms "anti-paedo-baptist" and "anabaptist" were used to designate many early dissenters from the Puritan and Anglican positions. Anti-paedo-baptists were those who waged the argument against the baptism of children; these folk were not always rebaptizers, as in the case of **Henry Dunster**, president of Harvard College. More often used was the catchall "anabaptist," which connected unfavorably with Münsterites and focused on the issue of rebaptism, perhaps the most repugnant issue the early Baptists advocated. Probably as a short, derogatory form of anabaptist, "baptist" was used to designate an array of people like Charles Chauncey (1592–1671), who understood the biblical mode of baptism to be immersion. The capitalized term "Baptist" seems to have emerged to designate the congregations at Boston, Newport, and Providence after the 1660s and perhaps under some influence from English Baptist and dissenting nomenclature.

The actual origin of the term "Baptist" is obscure. It may well have been intended as a shortened form of "anabaptist" or simply a colloquialism. The simple term had a biblical nuance to it, suggested by John the Baptist of the New Testament, though no one seems to have made that association directly. In any case, Edward Terrill (1634–1685) of Bristol referred to John Cann (fl. 1640) as a Baptist in about 1640; in 1654, William Britten (1608–?) used the word in his title *A Moderate Baptist*; Robert Pittiloh (fl. 1650–1680) in Scotland used it in his book *Hammer of Persecution* (1659); **John Bunyan** used the term in the 1670s; and it is found in the Orthodox Creed (1679). From these roots, the word made its way to North America and Europe. Clearly, from whatever source originally, the term "baptist" was in common usage at the beginning of the 18th century on both sides of the Atlantic. Of special note in the 19th century, the earliest Russian Baptists were referred to as "a union of believers, baptized Christians."

BAPTIST "BIBLE." *See* BIBLE.

BAPTIST BIBLE FELLOWSHIP (BBF). A loose coalition of independent Baptist churches located in the United States and Canada. The BBF was founded in 1950 by **pastors** and laymen who were disenchanted with the World Fundamental Baptist Missionary Fellowship, led by **J. Frank Norris**. The fellowship recognizes the basic tenets of Baptist **fundamentalism**, including biblical infallibility, substitutionary atonement, the literal resurrection of **Christ** and his premillennial bodily return, strong pastoral leadership, and autonomous local churches. An important facet of many BBF congregations is an aggressive **Sunday School** program, which is a primary evangelistic tool for the church. A newspaper, the *Baptist Bible Tribune* (1950–), is published.

In a loose association with great emphasis placed on local congregations, the national BBF is governed by a Committee of Forty-Five, with three functional committees: administration, education, and missionary work. Originally recognized, there was one school, the Baptist Bible College in Springfield, Missouri; now there are six approved institutions: Baptist Bible College East, Boston, Massachusetts; Pacific Coast Baptist Bible College, San Dimas, California; Baptist Christian College, Shreveport, Louisiana; Atlantic Baptist Bible College, Chester, Virginia; Spanish Baptist Bible Institute, Miami, Florida; Baptist Bible Graduate School of Theology, Springfield, Missouri. Currently, the BBF sponsors missionary work in 107 countries and has 853 missionaries.

As of 2006, there were 3,000 congregations with approximately 1.5 million members in the United States and 28 congregations in Canada affiliated with the Baptist Bible Fellowship.

BAPTIST BIBLE UNION OF AMERICA (BBUA). Group formed in 1923 consisting of Baptists from the northern United States, the **Southern Baptist Convention**, and central **Canada**. Under the influence of the World's Christian Fundamentals movement, in which some Baptists participated (1915–1920), these Baptists issued a manifesto and call to action to oppose modernism; subsequently, they organized themselves into the BBUA with this stated purpose: "to unite all Baptists who believe the Word of God." Leaders of the BBUA included **T. T. Shields** of Toronto, **J. C. Massee** of Minneapolis, and **J. Frank Norris** of Ft. Worth, Texas, and the vast majority of members of the union were **pastors**. In each of their respective convention relationships, the members pressed an agenda to have a statement of faith adopted as a standard of orthodoxy. In 1925, the BBUA issued its own set of articles of faith, which was widely disseminated in the major conventions and beyond.

The BBUA reached its peak of effectiveness in 1928, when its annual convention in Toronto included delegates from 18 states and five Canadian provinces; a dubious count claimed 50,000 members affiliated with the BBUA. One of the perceived weaknesses of the union was the avowed strategy not to separate from the respective denominational organizations; there were also conflicts over leadership and involvement in educational enterprises like Des Moines University in Iowa. Meetings of the BBUA were held in diverse northern cities such as Washington, D.C., Grand Rapids, Toronto, and Chicago; the last meeting was held at Chicago in 1930, with 35 delegates present. Supporters of the BBUA after 1930 gradually reorganized their efforts as Regular Baptists in Canada or as the **General Association of Regular Baptists** in the United States. Also noteworthy was the organization of a "chapter" of the BBUA in 1919 in England that was supported by Baptist Union ministers like J. W. Thirtle (editor of *The Christian*), C. T. Cook (Tollington Park), and F. E. Marsh (Weston-super-Mare). The BBUA in England was considered too belligerent for most Baptists, even those associated with Spurgeon's College.

BAPTIST BOARD OF FOREIGN MISSIONS (BBFM). The title given to the administrative and executive body relating to the **General Missionary Convention of the Baptist Denomination in the United States** (GMC). In 1814, at the organizational meetings of the GMC, a constitution was written that created a Baptist Board of Foreign Missions in the United States. Originally, the board was composed of 21 commissioners who were elected by the convention for a term of three years. The purpose of the board was to act for the GMC in setting policy and appointing missionaries in the name of the

GMC. Officers of the board included a president, two vice presidents, a secretary, and a treasurer. The first officers of the board were **Thomas Baldwin**, president; Henry Holcombe (1762–1824) and **William Rogers**, vice presidents; John Cauldwell (fl. 1815), treasurer; and **William Staughton**, corresponding secretary. Staughton, in his capacity, was in essence the first national denominational executive in **American Baptist** history. The first action of the board was to appoint **Adoniram Judson** as its first missionary and **Luther Rice** as its agent.

In 1820, the membership of the board was increased to 28, and more vice presidents were allowed in order to increase regional representation. The board also moved into the areas of **higher education** and domestic **missions**. In 1826, a reduction maneuver engineered by New England delegates led to the permanent location of the board in Boston and a limitation of its activities to foreign missions. In 1832, the size of the board was increased to 40 and in 1841, to 60, with vice presidents elected from every state convention. Because there was a consistent difficulty in securing sufficient leadership for the meetings of the board, in 1841 an "Acting Board" of 15 members was created of Boston local Baptist ministers and laymen. The Acting Board took strongly worded positions on controversial issues, notably the question of appointing slaveholders as missionaries. This caused friction among the southern Baptist members, few of whom ever made it to regular board meetings or those of the acting board.

Eventually, in 1845, the southern delegates to the GMC withdrew to form the **Southern Baptist Convention**, and the following year the GMC and the BBFM evolved organizationally into the **American Baptist Missionary Union**, a simple voluntary society. *See also* AMERICAN BAPTIST FOREIGN MISSION SOCIETY; BALTIMORE COMPROMISE.

BAPTIST CENTER FOR ETHICS (BCE). An issue-oriented ministry that seeks to provide resources to churches and faith groups on emerging ethical issues from an essentially theologically moderate **Southern Baptist** perspective. Based in Nashville, Tennessee, BCE was founded in 1991 by Robert Parham, a Southern Baptist missionary son who completed a doctorate in ethics at Baylor University. As director, Parham leads a small professional staff in researching and commenting upon current issues in environmental ethics, bioethics, peace and justice, and clergy professional areas of discussion, as well as advancing social change. The result of the work of BCE is produced in a popular newsletter, *EthicsDaily.com*, and enjoys the support of the national **Cooperative Baptist Fellowship** (CBF), the state Baptist organizations in Virginia and North Carolina, and several CBF state organizations. *See also* BAPTIST PEACE FELLOWSHIP OF NORTH AMERICA.

BAPTIST CONGRESS (BC). An organized forum for discussion of current issues and questions among Baptists in the United States from 1881 to 1915. Originally called the Baptist Autumnal Conference for Discussion of Current Issues, the BC was modeled after the Church of England, which held church congresses beginning in 1861. Elias H. Johnson (1841–1906) of Providence, Rhode Island, called upon 13 distinguished colleagues from the northeastern United States in November 1881 to voluntarily organize themselves into a committee for planning and implementation. The first public congress was held in Brooklyn, New York, November 14–16, 1882, with **George Dana Boardman Jr.** presiding. Subsequent meetings were held in Philadelphia, Indianapolis, Toronto, Richmond, New Haven, Providence, and Nashville. Presiding over the sessions were among the most distinguished Baptist clergy of the era, including **Henry G. Weston**, **Thomas Armitage**, **Walter Rauschenbusch**, and **Alvah Hovey**.

The purpose of the BC was not to advocate Baptist principles; rather, it was assumed that no denomination was infallible, including the Baptists, and papers were presented that carried a variety of topics and opinions. The BC earned a reputation for being a forum for **liberal** expression at a time when doctrinal purity and **Landmarkism** were popular expressions of local churches. Its annual programs featured papers on the deity of Christ, social Christianity, free speech, ethical issues, and the mystical element in Christianity, biblical criticism, and the use of noncanonical scriptures. Eventually, the larger interests of the Baptist community were drawn to the formation of the **Baptist World Alliance** (BWA), and after the first BWA congress in 1905, the BC became less popular as a gathering of Baptist leaders. Through the years of its existence, the BC published *Proceedings of the Baptist Congress* (1888–1912).

BAPTIST COUNCIL ON WORLD MISSION (BCWM). A consultative fellowship of those mission and national church bodies historically related to the **American Baptist Foreign Mission Society** (ABFMS). Beginning about 1957, various church organizations worldwide were invited to confer with the leaders of ABFMS and this evolved into a regular conciliar format in 1968. The purpose of the BCWM is to promote better understanding among mission partners, exchange leadership, consult about entering new fields, and cooperate with regional Christian bodies. Eighteen members comprise the BCWM, including church bodies in the Far East, **India**, Latin America, and Africa, plus the Board of International Ministries of the **American Baptist Churches in the U.S.A**. Current programs of the BCWM include student fellowships, third world missionaries, and regional stewardship conferences. Main offices for the BCWM are in Valley Forge, Pennsylvania.

BAPTISTERION, BAPTISTERY. The names variously given to the container of the water used in **baptism**. In Baptist practice, baptism most authentically occurs in "living waters" (meaning running water) in an outdoor setting. Among the early English Baptists, public baptisms were forbidden in rivers or ponds until after toleration. Prominent laymen sometimes constructed outdoor baptisterions on private property for the rite. Such a baptisterion survives at Rhual near Mold in North **Wales**. In North America, outdoor baptisms provided a spectacle, such as the site on the Schuylkill River in Philadelphia, where crowds came to witness 18th-century baptisms and the minister who appeared to be standing on the water (actually on a submersed rock for safety). A famous woodcut in **Morgan Edwards**'s *Materials Toward a History of Baptists in Pennsylvania* depicts the scene. At Haimong in northeastern India, a hollowed rock provided a natural setting for hundreds of 19th-century baptisms.

However, as the technology of heating water improved and the baptismal ceremony became part of a regular service and was required throughout the entire year (not to mention human convenience), provisions were made for indoor baptisms. Architecturally, these were called baptisterions. Often, groups of congregations would pool their resources to construct a common baptisterion, as was the case at the Horsley-down Church. In 1716, the Barbican

Church constructed a new baptisterion that was intended for the use of several congregations. The **Thomas Hollis** family paid for the construction and laid down specific rules about who should use it. A "license" was issued to appropriate ministers and a charge of two shillings per person was made (this included the use of changing rooms); a register of those baptized was also kept. These conditions offended the London ministers who responded by raising funds for the repair of the Horsley-down baptisterion, which had fallen into disrepair.

Early baptisterions were made to resemble stone-lined graves, approximately four to six feet deep. The baptisterion was filled with fresh water prior to the baptismal service. The officiant then called the candidates into the pool in waist-deep water and performed the baptism. Afterward, the candidate left the pool to change clothes and return to the congregation.

In many churches of the 19th century, the baptistery, as it came to be called in North America, was located in an inconspicuous place usually beneath the pulpit or under the floor. When not in use, it was not visible. Church **architecture** shifted in the United States in the 20th century to emphasize the public witness nature of the rite, and the baptistery was moved to an elevated or prominent position, usually behind or to the side of the pulpit or choir area. Many churches painted a river scene on the wall behind the baptistery to evoke an impression of the Jordan River baptism of Jesus Christ.

With travel to the Middle East more common, numbers of pastors have encouraged baptismal candidates to be baptized in the Jordan River at a location that the Israeli government has declared appropriate. For those who cannot make such a trip, water can be transported from the actual Jordan River and poured from a vial into a local church baptistery, adding to the poignancy of the rite.

Technology affected the use of the baptistery in other ways. In the mid-19th century, deacon **William Colgate** of New York City offered his friend **Pharcellus Church**, pastor at First Baptist Church, Rochester, New York, a pair of rubber pantaloons to wear underneath his baptismal robes. While the initial pair shrank under the lower water temperature, the concept caught on and most Baptist ministers today wear either waist boots or waterproof clothing for an expeditious transition to and from the baptistery.

BAPTIST FAITH AND MESSAGE (BFM). In the midst of the **fundamentalist** controversy and fears about the teaching of evolution theory in schools, the **Southern Baptist Convention** (SBC) in 1924 appointed a committee chaired by **E. Y. Mullins** to produce a statement of Baptist faith and message. Its stated concern was the rising tide of anti-supernaturalism of that era. The committee studied the New Hampshire Confession of Faith (1833) and added 10 new articles. This document was adopted at the 1925 session of the SBC as "The Baptist Faith and Message" and it served to define the doctrinal understanding of the SBC at large through the 1950s. Again in response to a crisis among theological teachers, in 1962 a committee was appointed by the SBC to update or modify appropriately the 1925 statement. Under the direction of Oklahoma Baptist pastor **Herschel H. Hobbs**, modest changes, mostly for clarification and elaboration, were made to the 1925 version, and the 1963 SBC unanimously adopted the new "Baptist Faith and Message" statement. From 1963, Southern Baptists in general were careful to define the statement as a guide, which was in no way mandatory, even upon SBC institutions. Several seminaries, including Southern Baptist Theological Seminary and New Orleans Baptist Theological Seminary had their own doctrinal statements.

In 1998, changes of major import began to emerge in the doctrinal identity of Southern Baptists. Following the lead of Southern Baptist conservative evangelicals who had been elected to the SBC presidency (Charles Stanley, **Adrian Rogers**, Jerry Vines, and **Paige Patterson**), an article on the family was added to the BFM in 1998. This material, more ethical than doctrinal, sought to address Southern Baptist responses to changing views of sexuality, marriage, and male-female relationships in the home and family. It asserted a definition of marriage: "the uniting of one man and one woman in covenant commitment for life." Further it stated, "A wife is to submit herself graciously to the servant leadership of her husband." The role of women was defined as follows: "She has the God-given responsibility to respect her husband and to serve as his helper in managing the household and nurturing the next generation." The next year, a blue ribbon committee was authorized by the SBC to review the BFM and make recommendations. This committee included 16 persons, notably Albert Mohler, Adrian Rogers, Richard Land, T. C. Pinckney, and Jerry Vines. The president of the SBC who appointed the committee was Paige Patterson, president of Southeastern Baptist Theological Seminary. The committee reported back in 2000 with a much redirected BFM that included the following substantive changes: (1) under Article I, "Scripture," the phraseology "Jesus Christ is the criterion by which the Bible is to be interpreted" from 1963 was removed and the words "without any mixture of error for its matter" were added; (2) in Article VII the additional statement was added: "While both men and women are gifted for service in the church, the office of pastor is limited to men as qualified by Scripture."

With the subsequent adoption of the BFM 2000 by the messengers to the Southern Baptist 2000 annual convention meeting, there was a new doctrinal basis for employment in all boards and agencies, the six seminaries, the many colleges, and the domestic and overseas missionary organizations, as well as the majority of the Baptist state conventions across the South. The only two state conventions that did not adopt the BFM 2000 were Virginia and Texas, where new coalitions of churches in those states formed new SBC-related conventions that did adopt the BFM 2000. SBC leadership has affirmed there is greater theological solidarity across the SBC as a result of this widespread adoption. However, the net impact of the BFM 2000 upon the dissenting churches and leadership was to cause numerous SBC national executives and missionaries to retire early, prompt several universities to sever ties with SBC organizations, and enlarge the membership in new national organizations such as the **Alliance of Baptists** and the **Cooperative Baptist Fellowship** to coordinate the work of theologically moderate to progressive Baptists in the South. Several new theological schools also emerged to meet the demand for moderate leadership.

BAPTIST FAITH MISSIONS (BFaM). Founded in 1922 as Amazon Valley Baptist Faith Missions to support the work of an **independent Baptist**, Eric Nelson (1862–1939), the pioneer Baptist missionary in the Amazon Valley of **Brazil**. Boyce Taylor (1870–1932), a **Southern Baptist** pastor in Murray, Kentucky, founded the organization, which eventually expanded fields to **Peru**. In 1941, H. H. Overby (1902–1994), Z. E. Clark (1887–1977), and a missionary, Joseph Brandon (d. 1970), reorganized the mission, dropping "Amazon

Valley" from the name. Still later, missionaries to **Korea**, **Kenya**, **Colombia**, **Honduras**, and primarily Brazil were added. At present, BFaM supports 11 missionaries; maintains offices in Ironton, Ohio; and publishes *Mission Sheets* (1941–). Mostly independent Baptist churches support the work.

BAPTIST FOREIGN MISSION CONVENTION OF THE UNITED STATES (BFMC). One of the predecessor organizations of **black Baptists** in the United States. It was organized at Montgomery, Alabama, in December 1880 to conduct missions in West Africa. The BFMC consisted mainly of southern black leaders. In 1886, the black convention was invited by the **American Baptist Missionary Union** to merge its overseas interests, but, owing to separatist feelings in the black community, the invitation was rejected. For 15 years, the BFMC represented the major organizing tendency among black Baptists along with the parallel **American National Baptist Convention**. In 1895, the BFMC was merged with other organizations in the formation of the **National Baptist Convention of the United States of America** to become the foreign missionary arm of black Baptists.

BAPTIST GENERAL CONFERENCE OF AMERICA (BGC). Organization formed in 1856 at Rock Island, Illinois, and formerly known as the Swedish Baptist Conference. The first Swedish Baptist congregation in the United States had also been organized at Rock Island, three years earlier, the result of the preaching of emigrant/pioneer **Gustav Palmquist**. The movement grew slowly in the states of Illinois, Iowa, Minnesota, and Wisconsin, and in addition to Palmquist, **Anders Wiberg** and **Fredrik O. Nilson** were active in promoting **evangelism** and church planting.

As part of its program to reach immigrant groups in the eastern cities, the **American Baptist Home Mission Society** (ABHMS) began support of Swedish missions in New York in 1867 in association with Mariner's Temple Baptist Church. Other missionaries in western states were supported by both the ABHMS and the **American Baptist Publication Society**. Like the German Conference, the Swedish Conference became loosely affiliated with the American Baptist movement and provided numerous congregations that were cross-listed in the statistics. Also, overseas missionaries of Swedish-American culture were appointed under the auspices of the **American Baptist Missionary Union** (later the American Baptist Foreign Mission Society) until 1944 when the BGC launched its own Foreign Mission Advance.

The early purposes of the BGC were missionary and cultural support. To meet the educational needs of the **ministry**, a theological school was started at Chicago in 1871, thereafter moving to St. Paul and Stromsberg, Nebraska, before being reorganized as a department of the Divinity School of the Baptist Union Theological School (later the University of Chicago) in 1888. A foreign mission society was organized in 1917, and provision was made for enlarged domestic mission work in that same year.

Following World War I, the Swedish Baptist Conference began to mature organizationally. When the Northern Baptist Convention (NBC) invited ethnic conferences to join a fund-raising crusade in 1919–1921 and, later, to belong to the NBC as associate members, the Swedish leadership declined, in part because of problems inherent in the **ecumenical** stance of the NBC Baptists and perceived theological **liberalism**. Separate organizations for **missions**, a strong school at Chicago under the direction of stalwart **Carl Gustaf Lagergran**, and the establishment of churches in every section of the United States suggested a new and separate identity for "Conference Baptists." The foreign mission program of the BGC, organized independently in 1944 as a final break with Northern Baptists, has included work in **India**, **China**, **Russia**, **Burma**, **Argentina**, **Brazil**, **Japan**, the **Philippines**, and **Ethiopia**. In 1914, an early interest in a mission to **Spain** had also been supported until it was transferred to the Southern Baptists in 1922.

In 1980, the BGC established its headquarters at Arlington Heights, Illinois. In St. Paul, Minnesota, Bethel College and Theological Seminary were established from the foundation laid at Chicago. Another institution, Adelphia College, was established in 1905 at Seattle, Washington, but closed in 1918 due to financial losses. The periodical of the BGC is the *Standard* (1853–).

In 1946, negotiations took place between the **Conservative Baptist Association** and the BGC; in another set of negotiations, the German Baptists also considered alignment with the Swedish

Conference. Neither discussion proved to be fruitful. Although separate organizationally, the BGC and the American Baptist Convention have continued some cooperation. Swedish Baptists have served in American Baptist executive roles, notably Wilber Larson (1911–1991) in home missions, Reuben Nelson (1905–1960) as general secretary, and Emmett Johnson (1928–) in evangelism. The BGC is also a member of the **Baptist World Alliance** and cooperates with the **Baptist Joint Committee on Public Affairs**.

As of 2007, 875 churches and 194,000 members were affiliated with the BGC.

BAPTIST GENERAL CONVENTION. *See* GENERAL MISSIONARY CONVENTION OF THE BAPTIST DENOMINATION IN THE UNITED STATES OF AMERICA FOR FOREIGN MISSIONS.

BAPTIST GENERAL TRACT SOCIETY (BGTS). *See* AMERICAN BAPTIST PUBLICATION SOCIETY.

BAPTIST HOME MISSION SOCIETY (BHMS). The oldest national domestic missionary organization among Baptists, founded in England in 1797. In 1796, John Saffery (1762–1825) and **William Steadman** made a preaching tour from Salisbury to Plymouth and reached audiences of several hundred hearers. This led to a concern for evangelism and church planting in the homeland, and the result was a second national **voluntary** society, the Baptist Society in London for the Encouragement and Support of Itinerant Preaching. Prominent early board members were **Abraham Booth**, **John Rippon**, William Smith, and Timothy Thomas (1811–1887). The purpose of the BHMS was to provide and send out after due examination such Calvinistic ministers of the Baptist persuasion as appeared to be qualified for itinerant preaching. Each of the full-time missionaries was paid 40 pounds per year, and in 1817, a plan for auxiliaries was put in place.

The BHMS's purposes and names changed over the course of its history: in 1817, it was called the Baptist Itinerant and Home Mission Society, and in 1822 simply the Baptist Home Mission Society. In 1834, the Baptist Irish Society was merged with BHMS, and in 1841, the first full-time secretary was hired, Stephen J. Davis (1805–1866) of Salter's Hall. In 1875, the **Baptist Union** took responsibility for home missions, and less active in terms of separate personnel, the BHMS became the Home Mission Fund in 1890. In 1912, the Ministerial Settlement and Sustentation Scheme was adopted, effectively carrying forth the program of the Home Mission Society. In 1970, the Baptist Home Work Scheme was again renamed the Baptist Home Mission Scheme. Several other agencies gradually eclipsed the focus of the Home Mission Society, including the Baptist Union Annuity Fund (1875), the Church Extension Fund (1893), and the Twentieth Century Fund (1899).

BAPTIST INTERNATIONAL MISSIONS, INC. (BIMI). An independent U.S. Baptist missionary organization founded in 1960 by 160 independent Baptist **pastors** primarily from across the southern United States. Based in Harrison, Tennessee, BIMI has a connection with Baptist pastors in the **Southwide Baptist Fellowship**, formerly associated with Lee Roberson. The agency specializes in **evangelism**, church planting, and Christian education within the United States, and it maintains 1,025 missionaries in 90 countries overseas (2007). One of the foci of BIMI is with U.S. military personnel around the world. Supported by 8,500 congregations in the U.S., the organization publishes *BIMI World*.

BAPTIST JOINT COMMITTEE ON PUBLIC AFFAIRS (BJCPA). An organization of six Baptist national organizations that seeks to maintain a united witness for **religious liberty** in the United States. In the 1930s, various Baptist groups were troubled at certain political and international events, including the rise of totalitarian dictatorships, the pilgrimage of Jewish people to the Middle East, plans of the government of **Romania** to close Baptist churches, the Japanese invasion of **China**, and the expressed design of the U.S. government to recognize the Vatican diplomatically. Throughout World War II, Southern, Northern, and National Baptists worked together in a structure called the Associated Committees on Public Affairs; in 1939, they issued the **American Baptist Bill of Rights**. These committees became in 1946 a permanent organization, the Baptist Joint Committee on Public Affairs.

Joseph M. Dawson (1879–1973), a social activist pastor and editor from Waco, Texas, was chosen executive director, with five Baptist groups coalescing in the BJCPA. Dawson advocated a variety of positions, including no U.S. ambassador for the Vatican, support for the United Nations, and consideration of human rights as a criterion in all U.S. foreign affairs. C. Emmanuel Carlson (1906–1976), dean of Bethel College in St. Paul, Minnesota, became Dawson's successor (1954–1971) and turned toward a more scholarly approach, providing resources for the Baptist community. The third director, James E. Wood Jr. (1922–), moved in the same direction from 1971 to 1980, having been a professor at Baylor University. In 1980, James M. Dunn (1932–), the director of the Christian Life Commission of the Baptist Convention of Texas, became director of the BJCPA and developed an activist approach, especially with respect to what was referred to as the "new Christian Right." The BJCPA has sponsored forums on religious liberty and **separation of church and state**, amicus curae briefs on U.S. Supreme Court cases, and a periodical, *Report from the Capital* (1946–), which provides watchdog service on concerns in the government that appear to have an impact upon separation of church and state. From 1959 to 1985, the Baptist Federation of **Canada** participated in various activities of the BJCPA where appropriate.

In 2005, the BJCPA changed its title to the Baptist Joint Committee on Religious Liberty. With its support base reorganized, its constituent members now include Alliance of Baptists; **American Baptist Churches in the U.S.A.**; **Baptist General Conference**; **Cooperative Baptist Fellowship**; **National Baptist Convention, U.S.A.**; **National Baptist Convention of America**; National Missionary Baptist Convention; **Progressive National Baptist Convention**; **Seventh Day Baptist** General Conference; and state Baptist conventions in Texas, Virginia, and North Carolina.

BAPTIST JOINT COMMITTEE ON RELIGIOUS LIBERTY. *See* BAPTIST JOINT COMMITTEE ON PUBLIC AFFAIRS.

BAPTIST JUBILEE ADVANCE (BJA). The official name given to the celebrations and activities associated with the 150th anniversary of Baptist organization in North America, 1814–1964. Representatives of several Baptist bodies first gathered in Chicago in 1955 to consider a joint celebration. A steering committee composed of delegates from the American Baptist Convention; **Southern Baptist Convention; National Baptist Convention, U.S.A.**; **National Baptist Convention of America; North American Baptist Conference; Baptist General Conference; Seventh Day Baptist** General Conference; and the Baptist Federation of Canada adopted a plan of action in **Bible** teaching, Baptist witness, **evangelism**, stewardship, church extension, world mission, and leadership training. The results of the year-long BJA celebrations in 1964 included better understanding of differences among Baptist groups; cooperation in several projects; a joint session of the American and Southern Baptist Conventions in Atlantic City, New Jersey, May 18, 1964; and the publication of a book, *Baptist Advance: The Achievements of the Baptists of North America for a Century and a Half* (1964).

BAPTIST MID-MISSIONS (BMM). An extensive Baptistic independent overseas **missionary** agency based in the United States. Formed in September 1920 as the General Council of Cooperating Baptist Missions of North America, the BMM was based on **fundamentalistic** principles and opposition to the modernism perceived to exist in the Northern Baptist Convention. The founders included a group of Baptist pastors from Ohio, Minnesota, and New York: A. H. Bond (fl. 1920–1925), Edwin S. Carman (fl. 1920–1930), and Alison De Nise (fl. 1920–1929). Their purpose was to reach the world for **Christ** and to awaken Baptist churches in the United States to the Great Commission (Matt. 28:19–20). The working name of the mission was Mid-Africa Mission, owing to the choice of the first field as French Equatorial Africa. The name "Baptist Mid-Missions" was introduced in 1952 to replace the cumbersome corporate title.

The first BMM missionaries appointed were **William Haas** and his wife, Genevieve; Rowena Becker (1883–1963); Arthur and Blanche Young (fl. 1920); and a Swedish preacher whom Haas recruited at Moody Bible Institute, Gust Pearson (1895–1989). The fact that William Haas had earlier worked with the Africa Inland Mission and the Heart of Africa Mission set the stage for a beginning thrust into Africa. Later, the number of fields of endeavor was expanded to include 37 countries and five types of domestic missions in the United States and **Canada**. The places of endeavor have included French Equatorial Africa, **Venezuela, Chad, Brazil, India, Haiti,**

Jamaica, Liberia, Czech Republic, France, Germany, Italy, the **Netherlands, China, Hong Kong, Indonesia, Japan, Peru, Dominican Republic, Honduras, West Indies, Congo, Australia, New Zealand,** United Kingdom, **Ivory Coast, Ghana, Bangladesh, Spain, Puerto Rico, Finland, Taiwan, Korea, Mexico, Ecuador,** and Canada (British Columbia, Quebec). Domestic ministries include migrants, Appalachia mountain villages, Native Americans, Alaska, and **evangelism** to Jewish people. Early in its history, BMM enjoyed the support of fundamentalist Baptist churches and groups in Canada, including **T. T. Shields** of Toronto, and the agency was separately organized in Canada in 1967. Over the years, BMM has often closely paralleled the work of the **Association of Baptists for World Evangelism**, a similar body representing both Baptistic identity and fundamentalistic theology. The international headquarters is located in Cleveland, Ohio, and the organization has published *Mid-African Mission* (1921–1925), *Mid-Missions Bulletin* (1925–1938), *Mid-Missions* (1938–1943), *Mid-Missions News* (1943–1954), and *Harvest* (1954–). As of 2006, BMM employed over 1,000 missionaries in 50 countries.

BAPTIST MISSIONARY ASSOCIATION OF AMERICA (BMA). Group formed in Little Rock, Arkansas, in May 1950 and called the North American Baptist Association until 1969. Partially a reaction to alleged violations of church sovereignty and authoritarian leadership in the **American Baptist Association**, the BMA coalesced around militant Baptist **fundamentalism**, including the verbal plenary inspiration of **Scripture**, literal creation, the virgin birth and deity of Jesus Christ, Christ's blood atonement, salvation by grace alone, and the personal, imminent return of Christ. Missionary Baptists, as they are called, oppose open communion, alien **baptism**, pulpit affiliation with unacceptable ministers, conventionism, and unionism. Interstate missionaries serve the BMA within the United States, and foreign missionaries are found in **Brazil**, Central America, **Korea**, the **Philippines**, **Australia**, the Commonwealth of Independent States (**Armenia**, **Azerbaijan**, **Belarus**, **Georgia**, Kazakhstan, Kyrgyzstan, Moldova, **Russia**, Tajikistan, **Ukraine**, and Uzbekistan; there is a special effort in these states), and the Cape Verde Islands. In 1956, the North American Theological Seminary was founded, to become in 1970 the Baptist Missionary Association Theological Seminary, at Jacksonville, Texas. The BMA publishes *The Gleaner* (1953–).

As of 2007, there were 1,384 churches and 234,110 members in the BMA; the BMA also supported 1,068 missionaries and workers in 55 countries, plus an additional 55 missionaries in North America.

BAPTIST MISSIONARY SOCIETY (BMS). The oldest foreign missionary sending agency in Baptist experience. The organization, chartered as the Particular Baptist Society for the Propagation of the Gospel among the Heathen (abbreviated BMS), was founded in Kettering, England, on October 2, 1792, by **William Carey**, **Andrew Fuller**, and ten other leaders, including **Samuel Pearce**, **John Ryland**, **William Staughton**, Abraham Greenwood (1749–1827), and Thomas Blundell (1752–1824). The founders desired an **evangelical** and **ecumenical** society, but realized the need for a particular constituency and chose to be specifically Baptist. The organization itself was a simple **voluntary** association that depended upon contributions from churches and individuals. Almost immediately the BMS organized auxiliary societies to itself, located throughout England and, later, the British Empire.

The first field of the BMS was **India**, established by William Carey in 1793. Next were **Ceylon** (1812), the West Indies (1813), **Cameroon** (1841), **Canada** (1843), **China** (1860), **Congo** (1877), Angola (1899), Mizoram (1901), **Bangladesh** (1971), **Nepal** (1954), and **Brazil** (1953). The focus of the BMS was broadened in 1843 when the BMS was merged with the Baptist Colonial Missionary Society, a group that fostered work in the province of Upper Canada (the predecessor of modern Ontario). This led to the BMS accepting limited responsibility for locations of British settlement.

The BMS had the advantage of outstanding leadership throughout most of its early history. The first secretary was the venerable Andrew Fuller, followed by James Hinton (d. 1823) and John Ryland (1815–1825). John Dyer (1817–1840) was the secretary who commenced an official office for the BMS in London in 1819 and presided over resolution of the schism that emerged among the Serampore missionaries, as they differed over terms of their support and lifestyle. **Joseph Angus** served 1840–1849 during a period of growth, succeeded by **Edward Bean Underhill**, 1849–1876. Underhill visited churches, restoring confidence, and reduced the BMS's debt, largely due to his association with the benefactor and, later, treasurer of the BMS, **Samuel Morton Peto**. Overseas, Underhill also spearheaded an expansion of the fields; in 1865, he became embroiled in a political uprising in **Jamaica**, due to his social advocacy of the poor. From 1876 to 1906, Alfred Henry Baynes served as secretary, one of his outstanding accomplishments being the amalgamation of the General Baptist Missionary Society (1816) with the BMS in 1891.

In many locations, the BMS has cooperated with both Baptists and other Christian groups in maintaining mission stations and various kinds of partnerships. Programmatically, its work is divided into five categories: church-based, partnership work, disaster relief, compassion ministries, and mission mobilization. As of 2007, BMS employed 150 full-time workers, 191 partner workers, 70 volunteers, and 131 short-term workers in 32 countries on four continents—in Europe: **Albania, Belgium**, **Bosnia**, **Bulgaria**, **Croatia, Czech Republic**, **France**, **Hungary**, **Italy**, and Kosova; in Asia and the Middle East: Bangladesh, China, Guinea, India, **Indonesia, Lebanon**, Nepal, and North Africa, **Sri Lanka**, and **Thailand**; in Latin America and the Carribean: Brazil, **Ecuador,** Jamaica, **Peru,** and **Trinidad**; in Africa: **Angola,** Democratic Republic of Congo, **South Africa**, **Uganda,** and **Zimbabwe.**

Over the years, the BMS has retained its independent organizational status, preferring to relate to the several British Baptist Unions and their congregations directly, rather than to become an auxiliary of a single union. Among the Welsh-speaking churches, BMS Cymru is a support chapter of the society. In the 1990s, the links have become closer with the English Baptist Union, and the BMS has relocated its headquarters to Baptist House at Didcot, Oxfordshire, which it shares with the **Baptist Union of Great Britain**. In 1999, facing a new millennium, the BMS experienced renewal in restyling itself as BMS World Mission, thus identifying with the leading global mission organizations. At that time, it commenced the BMS International Mission Centre, comprising the former Carey Hall and St. Andrew's Hall in the Selly Oak Colleges in Birmingham. *See also* BAPTIST UNION OF GREAT BRITAIN; PARTICULAR BAPTISTS.

BAPTIST MISSION TO FORGOTTEN PEOPLES. An **Independent Baptist** missionary organization that was founded in 1982 from among Independent Baptist churches in the southern United States. Headquartered in Jacksonville, Florida, the mission has a 10-member board that oversees the support of 140 missionaries in forty countries outside of North America (as of 2007). The words *forgotten peoples* refer to those who are overlooked by ethnic, social, vocational, or educational factors in the purview of other mission agencies. The organization produces a newsletter, the *BFMP Newsletter*.

BAPTIST MISSION UNION OF AMERICA. *See* FINNISH BAPTIST UNION OF AMERICA.

BAPTIST PEACE FELLOWSHIP OF NORTH AMERICA (BPFNA). An influential group among individuals, churches, and conventions of Baptists in the United States and Canada that focuses upon peace and justice issues. Baptists have long been concerned about peace, particularly in periods when the United States was engaged in military endeavors, like the Mexican War, the Spanish-American War, and the two world wars. In 1940, advocates of peace in the Northern Baptist Convention formed the Baptist Pacifist Fellowship, and in 1980 a newspaper, the *Baptist Peacemaker*, appeared from Deer Park Baptist Church in Louisville, Kentucky. In March 1984, leaders from north and south and Canada formed the Baptist Peace Fellowship of North America (BPFNA). The stated purpose of BPFNA was "to unite and enable Baptists to make peace in a warring world." The organization assumed publication of the *Baptist Peacemaker* and held biennial conferences in Canada and the United States, where inspirational speakers and specialists focus upon topics of peace and justice. Other activities include Peace Fellowship tours to underscore Baptist solidarity, for example, to the Soviet Union, Nicaragua, and Cuba. Ken Sehested, a Southern Baptist pastor from Tennessee, served as the first full-time staff member from 1984 to 2002, followed by Gary Percesepe (2004–2006), and Evelyn Hanneman (2006–). As of 2006, there were about 90 supporting churches and regional organizations from the United States and two congregations in Canada that identify with BPFNA. *See also* BAPTIST CENTER FOR ETHICS.

BAPTIST RENEWAL GROUP (BRG). A British Baptist fellowship of pastors that encouraged a broader theological outlook and **ecumenical** endeavor in the life of the **Baptist Union of Great Britain and Ireland** during the mid-20th century. Among its founders in 1968 were Paul Rowntree Clifford (Selly Oaks Colleges), Michael Taylor (Northern Baptist College), Alec Gilmore (West Worthing), and John Nicholson (North Cheshire Fellowship). These leaders saw positive action in the Baptist Union becoming part of the Ten Propositions movement that produced the Covenant for Unity. However, when the general synod of the Church of England did not approve the covenant, a Baptist Union effort in Christian unity was transformed into emphases on local ecumenical projects and sending representatives to key national and regional meetings with other denominations. During the polarizing discussions surrounding the 1971 Assembly address of **Michael Taylor** to the Baptist Union, BRG members stood with Taylor. At length, various publications detailing the Baptist heritage in intra-chuch cooperation came forth from BRG folk, including Alec Gilmore's *The Pattern of the Church* (1963) and Michael Taylor's *Baptists for Unity* (1968). Northern Baptist College in Manchester, where Taylor and Nicholson served on the faculty, became a center of ecumenical activity and education, as did Bristol Baptist College, in the 1990s and Regent's Park College, Oxford, while Ernest Payne was related to the school. As the influence of the BRG waned, one successor body was the 1980 Group, founded by Hugh Cross and John Nicholson who supported the Covenant for Unity.

BAPTIST REVIVAL FELLOWSHIP (BRF). A British Baptist renewal group that espoused **evangelical** principles throughout the mid-20th-century history of the **Baptist Union of Great Britain and Ireland** (BU). Founded in 1938 by a group of concerned pastors, including Theo Bamber (Peckham), Geoffrey King (East London), and Angus McMillan (Streatham), their agenda was to influence the BU toward a conservative evangelical stance and away from ecumenical trends. The first public meeting of the BRF was held in 1942 at Bloomsbury Chapel, London. In later years, the BRF was especially energized by the program of **ecumenical** engagement under Baptist Union General Secretaries **Ernest Payne** and **David S. Russell** in light of the numerical decline of the churches and membership in the 1950s–1970s. In 1971, the BRF stoutly opposed and criticized the BU's handling of the **Michael Taylor** address that seemed to underplay the divinity of Jesus Christ. Spurgeon's College and the Irish Baptist College were identified with the BRF, with Spurgeon's promoting an evangelical kind of ecumenism, and with the Irish College becoming more separatistic. In 1967, David Kingdon, principal of the Irish College, warned of potential separation at a BRF conference, and this was to be realized among the Irish Baptist churches in the next decades. Under **Barrington R. White**'s principalship, Regent's Park College, Oxford, became more inclined toward the concerns of the BRF in the 1970s. The fellowship influenced the longer-term direction of the BU through younger pastors like David Coffey (who helped found Mainstream in 1978); Raymond Brown, principal at Spurgeon's College; Paul Beasley-Murray (pastor at Altrincham, Cheshire); and Douglas McBain (a leading charismatic and pastor at Lewin Road, Streatham). Coffey went on to become president of the BU in 1986, secretary for evangelism in 1988, and general secretary in 1991. McBain was elected London area superintendent in 1989. Significant publications associated with the BRF include *Liberty in the Lord* (1964), which was signed by 16 Baptist ministers, and *Baptists at the Crossroads* (1968), which contained the provocative paper delivered at the 1967 BRF Conference by David Kingdon.

In 1964, prominent ministers in Victoria, **Australia**, including Wilbur Cook at Kerang and Alec White from Mentone, responded to growing concerns over ecumenism in the Baptist Union of Victoria by calling for the establishment of a Baptist Revival Fellowship to promote spirituality and missions and oppose ecumenism and **liberal** theology. The Australian movement was modeled upon the existing British Baptist organization, but it failed to have a significant impact, in part because it appeared to a majority of leaders to be divisive. The 1964 meeting involved about 250 attendees.

BAPTIST UNION OF AMERICA. *See* FINNISH BAPTIST UNION OF AMERICA.

BAPTIST UNION OF GREAT BRITAIN AND IRELAND (BU). The main body of Baptists in Britain, comprising congregations in

England and others affiliated to it, which also maintain membership with the Baptist Union of **Wales** and the Baptist Union of **Scotland**. The BU, which dropped "and Ireland" from the name in 1989, traces its origins back to the early years of the 19th century when leaders like **John Rippon** and **Joseph Ivimey** sought to unite the Baptist cause throughout Great Britain. Churches in fellowship with the BU have been called "Union Baptists."

Through the *Baptist Annual Register*, begun in 1798, Rippon advocated a union that he thought should be international; Ivimey wrote an article for *The Baptist Magazine* in 1811 that stated "union was essential to prosperity." The outcome of these catalysts was a meeting at Carter Lane Church in June 1812 at which 60 ministers agreed that union was desirable. The articles drawn up advocated cooperation for better communication among the churches and support of **missions.** One year later, again in Rippon's vestry, the BU was given shape by 45 ministers who signed 12 articles. The doctrinal basis, shorter than the ancient confessions, was **Particular Baptist** in substance and reflected the congregations represented by the ministers. During the early period of the BU's fragile history, the term "denomination" came into popular usage among those associated with the body. A combination of overarching political events, the crisis among the missionaries at Serampore, and interest in other forms of domestic mission, however, engendered disinterest and doomed the BU after 1817.

In 1831, a new attempt was made to reshape the BU by involving more churches, largely in response to initiatives among the Congregationalists to form a union, and the vast changes wrought in English society by the introduction of the Reform Bill. Although small in scope, the 1831 reorganization is usually considered the birth of the modern union. Gradually, important related organizations— including the missionary societies, the **Hanserd Knollys** Society (historical), and others—began to meet and to function in closer cooperation, and national periodicals like *The Baptist Magazine* and *The Baptist Record* began to give space to the interests of the BU. Over the years, by mid-century, a long list of distinguished Particular Baptist leaders also came to be associated with offices in the BU, including **Francis A. Cox, John Howard Hinton, John Mockett Cramp, William Harris Murch, James Hoby,** and **Edward**

Steane. The focus of the BU included issues of public concern in education, political recognition of dissenters, and theological differences.

The latter half of the 19th century witnessed vast changes in the life of the BU. In 1865, the missionary efforts relating to Ireland were brought under the aegis of one society, and this led to the natural inclusion of Ulster congregations in the lists of what became the Baptist Union of Great Britain and Ireland. In 1866, a separate Welsh Baptist Union was formed with a similar body taking shape in Scotland in 1869. These bodies became affiliates of the BU in 1872. While the BU remained essentially a body politic of churches, other groups—theological colleges, associations, and recognized societies—began to send representatives to the sessions as well. From 1863, a merger of **General Baptists** of the New Connexion and the BU was discussed, and this was achieved in 1891. In 1887, a major theological controversy, which caused great strife in the BU, surfaced in the ministry of **Charles Haddon Spurgeon**, who opposed both theologically **liberal** trends and the closer affiliation with General Baptists, constituting as Spurgeon called it a "downgrading of the Union's purposes." In 1887, Spurgeon withdrew from the BU. *See also* DOWNGRADE CONTROVERSY; WALES.

In 1898, **John Howard Shakespeare** became secretary of the BU and moved the cause beyond the "downgrade troubles." A Twentieth Century Fund added to the resources of the BU, and through Shakespeare the BU became a charter member of the National Free Church Council. In 1891, the BU began publishing *The Baptist Times*, a weekly newspaper, which in 1910 was amalgamated with *The Baptist*. A new hymnbook appeared in 1900, a Young People's Union in 1904, a Baptist Insurance Company in 1905, and the Baptist Women's League and the Baptist Colonial Society in 1910 (actually the second usage of Colonial Society). In 1905, the BU became a charter member of the **Baptist World Alliance** and hosted its first World Congress meeting at London. Symbolic of the maturity of the BU, an imposing edifice on Southampton Row in London opened in 1903, known as Baptist Church House.

In the 20th century, the BU has facilitated participation by British Churches in all of the major events of the international family, including the **European Baptist Federation** and the World Council of

Churches, of which it became a founding member. In addition, important advances at home have also been the result of closer cooperation within the BU: Regent's Park College was moved to Oxford in 1938; a plan for a Northern Baptist College at Manchester, first proposed in 1903, was realized in 1964; Carey Press and Kingsgate Press were united in 1949; and after many years of debate, the BU's strategic new location at Didcot in Oxfordshire was achieved when the London headquarters building was sold in 1989. Important leaders such as **Ernest Payne**, a historian; **David S. Russell**, a renowned biblical scholar; and Bernard Green and David Coffey, both pastors, have served as general secretaries of the BU in the post–World War II era.

Theological debates that had their origins in the mid-19th century played an important role in the BU in the 20th century. The Evangelical Alliance, with which many BU congregations have been identified, and Charles Spurgeon were galvanizing agents toward a conservative evangelical orientation. The numerical decline of BU membership drove the articulation of this position through the **Baptist Revival Fellowship**. Partly in response, but more in affirmation of Christian cooperation and a desire for Baptists to participate fully in the emerging **ecumenical** communities in Europe and the world, the **Baptist Renewal Group** came forth in 1968. Evangelicals were increasingly unhappy with the 19th-century Declaration of Principles of the BU, particularly the statement on the divinity of Christ. They wanted a confession like the Evangelical Alliance or a return to the Second London Confession (1678). Beginning in the 1960s, yet another force emerged to be reckoned with, the charismatic movement's influence upon Baptist churches that emphasized the gifts of the Spirit and radical changes in worship patterns. Baptist ministers were active in the formation of Mainstream, founded in 1978, to work for renewal within the BU and Manna Ministries, a charismatic renewal effort that promoted the gifts of the Spirit among the churches. A noticeable shift in training patterns for Baptist ministry and laity was seen among the historic colleges of the BU, Regent's Park, Northern, Cardiff, Bristol, and Spurgeon's, as well as London Bible College and, later, its London School of Theology. Among the more ecumenical and theologically progressive voices, many urged church unity conversations among Protestants and Catholics through the Churches' Unity Commission (1974) and the Churches' Council for Covenanting (1979), which looked toward adopting the Ten Propositions, a major national ecumenical statement. Baptists did not join the Churches' Council, but sent observers to a process that ultimately failed on the matter of episciopal ordination in apostolic succession. Some Baptists remained firm in their ecumenical resolve, carrying forth as the "1980 Group" and a reorganized British Council of Churches, Churches Together in England (1990), in which Baptists were later much involved.

Structurally, the Baptist Union of Great Britain consists of local churches, associations of churches, colleges, and a variety of related organizations such as the Baptist Historical Society, Baptist Men's Movement, Baptist Ministers' Fellowship, the Federation of Lay Ministries, the National Council of Baptist Women, and the Alliance of Baptist Youth. A consultation in 1996 led to the restructuring of the BU to include 12 **associations** in England and one in Wales, with local congregations involved in clusters (often including other than Baptists) and teams of superintendents accountable to the associations. There are seven affiliated theological colleges and the **Baptist Missionary Society** is the recognized overseas agency of the churches. The headquarters of the BU is located at Baptist House at Didcot in Oxfordshire (which it shares with the Baptist Missionary Society).

As of 2006, there were 2,007 churches and 138,305 members affiliated with the BU. *See also* GENERAL BAPTISTS; PARTICULAR BAPTISTS; SCOTLAND.

BAPTIST WORLD ALLIANCE (BWA). The international body of Baptists to which most Baptist unions and conventions worldwide belong. Founded in 1905, the BWA was the idea of **John H. Shakespeare**, **William H. Whitsett**, and **James H. Rushbrooke**, as well as being in some ways the successor to the **Baptist Congress**. The first international congress of the BWA was held in London, England, where 3,250 delegates attended. The BWA has grown steadily over the years to a global membership of unions/conventions and members from every continent. A **voluntary** association of the unions, the BWA provides a forum for fellowship, witness, and study, and addresses in particular the issue of **religious liberty**. Its major divisions include **Evangelism** and Education, Study and Research, Promotion and Development, and Baptist World Aid. There are three auxiliaries: the Women's Division, the Men's Department, and the Youth Division. Recently, forums and affinity groups have been established. Internationally, the BWA constituency is divided into regions: the **European Baptist Federation**, the **All-Africa Baptist Fellowship**, the **Asian Baptist Fellowship**, the **Latin American Baptist Fellowship**, and the **North American Baptist Fellowship**.

The General Council of the BWA meets at the Annual Gathering to debate resolutions, hear reports from each division, and reflect and represent the members in a particular region where the meetings are held. Every five years, or quinquennium, the BWA World Congress is held where 5,000 to 10,000 Baptists assemble to hear reports, derive inspiration, and pass resolutions, including election of officers and adoption of a budget and a five-year theme. Upon action of the congress, the BWA may engage in dialogue (called theological conversations) with other Christian groups; the BWA has concluded conversations with Roman Catholics, Lutherans, the World Council of Reformed Churches, and the Mennonite World Conference, and has begun discussions with the Orthodox Ecumenical Patriarchate. While the BWA is not a constituent member of the World Council of Churches (WCC), officers of the BWA attend WCC committee meetings and administrative and educational events from time to time.

The BWA has no authority over any church or union and consists primarily of denominational heads and elected denominational representatives. The BWA is funded by contributions of its member bodies, much of its budget being made up from North American and European bodies and individuals. Until 2004, the U.S. **Southern Baptist Convention** (SBC) provided the largest single amount. That same year, the SBC withdrew from the BWA. Also in 2004, state Baptist conventions in Texas, Virginia, and Missouri officially joined the BWA as member unions and brought along significant support. In 2005, the BWA celebrated its centenary in Birmingham, England. In recent years, the BWA established two awards in the area of human rights: (1) in 1991, former BWA secretary Carl Tiller and his wife, Olive, established with a $10,000 gift the quinqennial award that has been given to Jimmy Carter (1995), Pastor Simeon of Myanmar (2000), and Loren Bethell (2005); (2) the annual Denton and Janice

Lotz Award for Human Rights, created in 2006 with gifts of $125,000, has been awarded to Gustavo Parajon of El Salvador (2006) and Joao and Nora Matwawana of Nova Scotia/Angola (2007).

The BWA has produced several periodicals, notably the *Baptist World* (1905–) and the *Proceedings of the Baptist World Congress* (1905–) and has administrative offices at McLean, Virginia, a suburb of Washington, D.C. Presidents of the BWA have included **John Clifford**, James H. Rushbrooke, and F. Townley Lord (1893–1962) (U.K.); Robert S. MacArthur (1841–1923), **Edgar Y. Mullins**, George W. Truett (1867–1944), C. Oscar Johnson (1886–1965), V. Carney Hargroves (1900–1986), Theodore F. Adams (1898–1980), and Duke K. McCall (1914–) (U.S.); **William Tolbert** (Liberia); **G. Noel Vose** (Australia); Knud Wumpelmann (1922–) (Denmark); Joao F. Soren (1908–) and Nilson Fanini (1932–) (Brazil); John MacNeill (1855–1933) (Canada). General secretaries of the BWA (with years of service) have been James H. Rushbrooke (1928–1939); Walter O. Lewis (1939–1948); Arnold T. Ohrn (1948–1960); Josef Nordenhaug (1960–1969); Robert S. Denny (1969–1980); Gerhard Claas (1980–1988); Denton Lotz (1988–2007); and Neville Callam (2007–). Callam is the first general secretary from the Two-thirds World.

As of 2005, the BWA included 215 Baptist unions and conventions comprising a membership of almost 38 million persons and over 157,000 churches. *See also* ECUMENISM, BAPTIST INVOLVEMENT; HUMAN RIGHTS.

BAPTIST WORLD MISSION (BWM). Mission agency formed in 1961, originally called the World Conservative Baptist Mission. In the 1950s, two theological traditions emerged within the **Conservative Baptist** movement in the United States. One known as the "soft policy" group maintained relations with neo-evangelicals, while the other, called the "hard core," was composed of more militant **fundamentalists**. Eventually, in 1961, the "hard core," continuing as the Conservative Baptist Fellowship and led by Bryce Augsburger (1922–1988), Ernest Pickering (1928–), and **Richard Clearwaters** organized the World Conservative Baptist Mission, after 1966 known as Baptist World Mission. Its emphases were fundamentalistic and separatist, and to ensure doctrinal purity, a self-perpetuating board was provided for in 1967. In 1997, the Grace Independent Baptist Mission of Sellersville, Pennsylvania (founded c. 1965), merged with Baptist World Mission, enlarging its outreach. BWM specializes in **evangelism**, church planting, and Christian education. Work is conducted in over 25 countries on every continent, and over 4,000 **independent Baptist** churches support the organization. The home base is in Decatur, Alabama, and a newsletter, *World Witness*, is published.

BARBADOS. Island where **Southern Baptist** work commenced in 1972, originally known as the Windward Islands Mission. The Barbados Baptist Convention was founded in 1974, with headquarters at St. Michaels. In 1978, Barbados Baptist Theological College was started, later named the Baptist Theological College for the Caribbean.

As of 2006, there were 421 members in four churches affiliated with the Barbados Baptist Convention.

BARBUDA. *See* ANTIGUA.

BARNES, WILLIAM WRIGHT (1883–1960). Southern Baptist educator and church historian, born at Elm City, North Carolina. Barnes was educated at Wake Forest College and Southern Baptist Theological Seminary, where he earned the Th.D. degree in church history. He began his career as a teacher in Cuba under the Southern Baptist Home Mission Board (1904–1905) and served as principal of El Colegio Cubano-Americano in Havana (1909–1912). In 1913, following **Albert H. Newman**, Barnes was elected to the position in church history at Southwestern Baptist Theological Seminary in Ft. Worth, Texas, which he held until 1953. Barnes was a widely published historian of the **Southern Baptist Convention** (SBC), sometimes to the irritation of SBC leaders. His *Southern Baptist Convention 1845–1953* (1954) was highly edited to obscure problematic interpretive comments he had made, and his *Southern Baptist Convention: A Study in Ecclesiology* (1923) became a classic treatise in American church historiography.

BARNETTE, HENLEE HULIX (1911–2004). Southern Baptist educator and ethicist, born at Taylorsville, North Carolina. He was educated at Wake Forest College and Southern Baptist Theological Seminary, where he earned his Th.M. and Ph.D. degrees. Barnette taught at Howard College (1946–1947), Stetson University (1947–1951), and Southern Seminary (1951–1977). He is credited with bringing the study of Christian ethics into serious focus at Southern Seminary and mentoring scores of students. During the civil rights movement of the 1950s and 1960s, Barnette took controversial and courageous stands, including hosting Martin Luther King Jr. at the seminary in 1961. He was often criticized for his stands, resulting in loss of gift funds to Southern Seminary. Denied a senior professorial status at Southern Seminary, in 1977 he moved to the University of Louisville Medical School where he taught until 1992. Barnette was considered a racial pioneer among Southern Baptists and authored several books, including *Introducing Christian Ethics* (1961).

BARROW, DAVID (1753–1819). American Baptist minister, born in Brunswick County, Virginia. Barrow was ordained in 1774 and served a circuit of churches at Black Creek, Virginia. He itinerated in Virginia and North Carolina and served in the War for Independence. In 1778, Barrow was molested and nearly drowned by a crowd of mockers. Following the war, he moved to Kentucky and served the church at Mount Sterling. There he became a zealous abolitionist and his congregation divided over the issue of **slavery**. In 1807, he helped to form an **association** of emancipators, and the following year, he published the earliest defense of abolition among the Baptists of the United States, *Involuntary, Unmerited, Perpetual, Absolute, Hereditary Slavery Examined, on the Principles of Nature, Reason, Justice, Policy and Scripture* (1808).

BEASLEY-MURRAY, GEORGE RAYMOND (1916–2000). English Baptist biblical scholar and theologian, born in London, England. He was educated at Spurgeon's College and Kings College, University of London (M.Th.), and Cambridge University (Ph.D). Beasley-Murray served Ashurst Drive Baptist Church in East London (1945–1948) and, later, Zion Baptist in Cambridge before moving in 1950 to become Tutor in New Testament and also church history at Spurgeon's College. From 1956 to 1958, he taught New Testament at the International Baptist Seminary at Rueschlikon, Switzerland, where he interacted with Oscar Cullmann, Karl Barth, Eduard Schweizer, and Emil Brunner. From 1968 to 1973, Beasley-Murray returned to Spurgeon's as principal, turning aside an invitation to become the John Rylands Professor of Biblical Criticism and Exegesis at Manchester University in 1959. In 1973, Beasley-Murray was invited to accept the James Buchanan Harrison Chair in New Testament Interpretation at Southern Baptist Theological Seminary in Louisville, Kentucky, where he taught until his retirement in 1980. While principal at Spurgeon's College (1958–1973), he moved the college from a narrow **evangelical** position to an engaged evangelical openness and the position of being the leading ministerial training school of British Baptists. At his instigation, Spurgeon's became a degree-granting institution.

Beasley-Murray was active in the **ecumenical** movement in Britain and beyond, for instance, serving on the 1967 Ipswich Christian Unity Meeting, the World Council of Churches, and the National Union of Protestants. Beasley-Murray was involved in two controversial moments in British Baptist life. His 1952 Cambridge doctoral study that focused on Mark 13 asserted that Jesus had a limited understanding of eschatological events as an explanation for Jesus' statements about an imminent Parousia (Second Coming). This caused a firestorm among evangelicals in the **Baptist Union**, and Beasley-Murray later changed his mind on the meaning of the passage. The second incident concerned his response to **Michael Taylor**'s theological lecture at the Baptist Union Assembly in 1971. Ultimately, Beasley-Murray resigned as chairman of the Baptist Union Council in protest of Taylor's Christology. Among his published works are *Baptism in the New Testament* (1962) and *Jesus and the Kingdom of God* (1986).

BEDDOME, BENJAMIN (1717–1795). English Baptist minister and theologian, born in Henley-in-Arden, United Kingdom. He was educated at Bristol Baptist College and the Independent College at Mill End, London. Beddome served the congregation at Bourton-on-Water for over 50 years and exhibited the high caliber of Calvinistic Baptists of the 18th century. He was the first to produce a Baptist catechism in a series of questions and answers (1752), and he composed numerous hymns for worship, including the oft-used "Father of Mercies, Bow Thine Ear." He also published in 1820–1822 an eight-volume guide to worship. The College of Rhode Island awarded Beddome the honorary M.A. degree.

BEISSEL, JOHANN CONRAD (1690–1768). American German **Seventh Day Baptist** minister, born at Eberbach, Germany. He was apprenticed as a baker, but due to his extraordinary religious beliefs, he was banished from the Palatinate in 1720. Beissel emigrated to the colony of Pennsylvania, where he was influenced by Peter Becker (1687–1758), the founder of the Church of the Brethren. In 1721, Beissel formed his own colony at Mill Creek, Pennsylvania, the members of which referred to themselves as **Solitary Brethren**. In 1725, he was baptized by Becker and created yet another colony at Ephrata near Lancaster, Pennsylvania. He composed over 1,000 hymns and a unique musical genre, Paradaisical Wonder Music.

BELARUS. When the Baptist movement reached what became Belarus, the churches were part of the Russian Empire and thus included in the historical development of Russian Baptists. For instance, L. D. Priimachenko went to Tiflis (Tblisi) in **Georgia** to investigate the Baptist position and was baptized in 1884 at Vladikavkaz. He returned to Belarus to start the first Baptist church in the region.

Growth in the Baptist community occurred after the turn of the century with churches at Kha'ch in 1907 and Gomel in 1908. The Grodzensky region was fertile soil for early Baptists. With more freedom under the early Communist regimes, Baptists in Belarus organized a Belorussian Union at Minsk in 1927, which was closed under Stalin after 1929. Congregations in Belarus then related to the Russian Union and, later, the All-Union Council of Evangelical Christians-Baptists when it was organized from 1991 to 1993. At that time, a separate union for Belarus was again organized, the Sayuz Yevangel'skikh Khrystsiyan Baptystav Belarusy (Union of Evangelical Christians-Baptists of Belarus).

As of 2006, there were 315 churches and 14,000 affiliated with Sayuz Yevangel'skikh Khrystsiyan Baptystav Belarusy.

BELCHER, JOSEPH (1794–1859). English, Canadian, and, later, American Baptist minister, born in Birmingham, England. He was ordained to the **ministry** at Somersham, Huntingdonshire, where he served as **pastor**, 1819–1825. He then was minister at Folkstone (1825–1831); Paradise Chapel, Chelsea (1831–1834); and Greenwich (1834–1842). During his tenure as a Baptist minister in Britain, Belcher was a leader in denominational affairs. He was active in the **Baptist Home Mission Society** and the Baptist board charged him in 1832–1833 to collect statistics and a membership roster for Baptist ministers in the newly formed **Baptist Union**, of which he served as first secretary (1832–1840). In 1843, Belcher emigrated to North America, serving Granville Street (1845) and Salem Chapel (1846), both in Halifax, Nova Scotia; Mount Tabor, Philadelphia (1847); and East Thomaston, Maine (1849–1851?). In the United States, Belcher was a prolific author, writing biographies of George Whitefield (1714–1770), Robert Raikes (1735–1811), **William Carey**, and **Robert Haldane**, as well as editing the works of **Andrew Fuller**. Belcher's ministry in Halifax, Nova Scotia, was cut short by a highly publicized schism in the church there, largely instigated by Belcher's personality and his overly British perspective on matters of **polity** and the question of open communion.

BELGIUM. An outgrowth of Baptist missions in France, Baptist work began in 1895 when French Baptists started the church at Ougrée and, later, at Mont-sur-Marchienne. Missionary work has been sponsored by U.S. Southern and American Baptists, as well as Canadian Baptists and the **Baptist Bible Fellowship** since 1962. More recently, the **Conservative Baptist** Foreign Mission Society opened a mission in Belgium at Brussels. In 1922, the Unie van baptisten in Belgie (Union of Baptists in Belgium) was formed, and as of 2006, the Unie included 30 churches and 1,100 members.

BELIEVER'S BAPTISM. *See* BAPTISM.

BELIEVER'S CHURCH TRADITION. Baptists in England, North America, and beyond have been classified as believer's churches. The first Baptistic confession of faith described the congregation as a "true church of true believers." By this is meant that individuals exercise faith in Jesus Christ as personal Savior and accept the Lordship of **Christ** in their lives. Congregations are composed of believers; they are not defined as a parish or by assumption through a **sacramental** process like paedo-baptism followed by confirmation.

Believer's churches have been identifiable since New Testament times: Jesus said "where two or three are gathered together, there I am" (Matt. 18:20). Throughout the historical record of the church, believer's churches have existed as in the examples of the Cathari and the Lollards. Beginning in the 15th century, related groups of reformed congregations banded together in the Radical Reformation to constitute what historians now refer to as believer's churches as a stream or type of Protestant Christianity. A working definition according to Donald Durnbaugh, a historian of the movement, is "a covenanted and disciplined community of those walking in the way of Jesus Christ." This includes an earnest desire to be a Christian, regular meetings together, good works, **discipline**, mutual aid, **baptism**, attention to **Scripture**, and submission to Jesus Christ. From the 16th century, those in the close circle of the believer's churches include the Mennonites, Brethren, Baptists, Amish, and Hutterites, to name the major subcategories. In more modern development, particularly in North America, many sects and smaller churches, such as the Pentecostals, may consider themselves believer's churches by this definition.

Beginning in 1967, leaders of several believer's churches began to meet periodically together to reflect theologically on their growing similarities. This was in part a response to the **ecumenical** movement, and in part a sui generis coming together. Conferences have dealt with the ordinances, the nature of the church, **missions, voluntarism**, dissent, and renewal. The Believer's Church Conferences now represent a wide variety of groups and scholars as well as leaders of the churches. Primary to the Baptist participation are the **Southern Baptists**, American Baptists, and Canadian convention Baptists.

BELIZE. Central American country formerly called British Honduras. Baptist missionary effort was undertaken in 1822 by the **Baptist Missionary Society**. A church was constituted in 1825 and the work grew slowly. In 1977, **Southern Baptists** began missionary work in

British Honduras, eventually creating what became the Baptist Association of Belize. In 1979, the **Baptist Bible Fellowship** began its work.

As of 2006, there were 48 churches with 1,965 members affiliated with the Baptist Association of Belize.

BELLAMY, FRANCIS (1855–1931). American Baptist minister, born at Mount Morris, New York. Bellamy was educated at the University of Rochester and Rochester Theological Seminary; he was ordained at Little Falls, New York Baptist Church, which he served 1879–1884. Subsequently, Bellamy was pastor at Dearborn (1884–1890) and Bethany (1890–1891) Baptist churches in Boston, Massachusetts. Increasingly liberal in his views, he felt uncomfortable in the Baptist movement and left the ministry for a career in journalism. First, he served as an editor for *The Youth's Companion*; later he was the editor of the *Illustrated American Magazine*. At the conclusion of his career, Bellamy worked in advertising and for the Silver Burdette Publishing Company. With the support of his publisher, Daniel Ford, and his editor, James B. Upham, Bellamy submitted a model pledge of allegiance to the American flag to the *Youth's Companion*. The pledge was published anonymously on September 8, 1892, and, owing to the wide distribution of American flags by Mr. Ford, it became a national institution. U.S. presidents Grover Cleveland (1837–1908) and Benjamin Harrison (1833–1901) both lent support to the pledge being widely adopted.

BENEDICT, DAVID (1779–1874). American Baptist minister and historian, born at Norwalk, Connecticut. He graduated from Brown University and was ordained to serve the church at Pawtucket, Rhode Island. Benedict had a great interest in Baptist history and particularly the expansion of the denomination. In 1813, he published the first of his Baptist histories, followed by a definitive edition in 1848. His work was considered a reliable source of congregational and associational data in the mid-19th century. Benedict's subsequent autobiography, *Fifty Years among the Baptists*, is useful for its pre–Civil War reflections on the maturing denomination. His half-brother, Stephen (1801–1868), was a prosperous cotton manufacturer and Baptist deacon in his brother's church and left a considerable legacy to the **American Baptist Home Mission Society**. Benedict College in South Carolina was named for Stephen.

BENIN. Country in western Africa earlier known as Dahomey. Baptist development dates back to 1851 when T. J. Bowen (1814–1875), a missionary to Nigeria, visited what is now Benin. In 1969, the Southern Baptist **Foreign Mission Board** appointed its first missionary, who helped to begin a church at Abomey in 1974 and another at Porto Novo in 1976. Two **associations** have been formed; no convention as yet exists.

As of 2006, there were 210 churches and 8,000 members in the Union of Protestant Baptist Churches in Benin.

BENNETT, CEPHAS (1804–1885). American Baptist missionary, born at Homer, New York. Bennett was a printer, following that trade all his career. He developed an interest in religious publishing and produced a **Bible** dictionary in 1827 while he printed the *New York Baptist Register*. In the early years of New York Baptist life, he published numerous Baptist tracts and minutes under the name "Bennett and Bright." In 1827, he indicated an interest in publishing the Bible that **Adoniram Judson** was producing, and the **Baptist Board of Foreign Missions** appointed him to **Burma** for the project. In 1829, Bennett became the first American missionary printer, settling first at Moulmein and, later, at Rangoon. He began the American Baptist Missionary Press, and in 1862, he organized the Burma Bible and Tract Society. A longtime resident of Rangoon, Bennett published major historical works relating to Burmese life.

BERMUDA. Chain of islands in the north Atlantic Ocean where the Baptist movement is traced to **Southern Baptist** missionary work, which began in 1956 among American military personnel. The **Foreign Mission Board** has sponsored several initiatives over the years which have resulted in successful church planting. Also, the **National Baptist Convention, U.S.A.**, sponsored a congregation in Hamilton.

As of 2006, there were three churches and 330 members affiliated with the Bermuda Baptist Fellowship.

BIBLE. Book that serves as the Baptists' guide for faith and practice and instructs local churches and individual believers on faith, conduct, and **polity**. Baptists have held from their beginning that they are "people of the Book." The version of the Bible that Baptists first used was the Geneva edition of 1560. Baptists also widely used Alford's *New Testament* and Young's *Literal Translation* (1862).

Only in response to the large number of copies available in the early 19th century through the Bible Society movement did Baptists in the United States adopt the Authorized, or King James, Version (1611) as their standard. Some even declined in this context, preferring to prepare an edition that recognized the proper translation of *baptizo* as "immerse"; this "Baptist Bible," which appeared in 1850, was short-lived. **Scripture** memorization, doctrinal formulation, and devotional aids all popularized the King James Version (KJV) through the mid-20th century.

When the Revised Standard Version (RSV) was issued by the National Council of Churches of the United States in 1946, many Baptists declined to use or authorize the new version because of its translation of Isaiah 7:14: "Behold a young woman shall conceive . . ." This led to a proliferation of Scripture translations from **conservative evangelical** sources, which found widespread use in Baptist churches in North America. These have included the Berkeley Edition (1958), the Amplified Bible (1965), and the New International Version (1973). Many Baptists use a modernized edition of the KJV, known as the New King James Version (1982). Popular across the denomination in the United States are various editions of Scripture with notations, including the Scofield Reference Bible (1909, 1967), the Thompson Chain Reference Bible (1908, 1978), and the Ryrie Study Bible (1976). Also widely used are paraphrase editions like the Charles Williams Translation (1937), the New Testament in Modern English by J. B. Phillips (1961), and the Good News Bible (1976). In recent years, in Great Britain, Baptist churches have gravitated to the New English Bible (1970), the New International Version (1979), or the Revised English Bible (1989). More recently in North America, many congregations have adopted either the New International Version, the New King James Version, or the New Revised Standard Version (1989), and in study use the Jerusalem Bible (1966). The major concerns for new translations include nuances suggested by archaeology and linguistics and the use of inclusive English language. *See also* SCRIPTURE, AUTHORITY OF.

BIBLE COLLEGES, BAPTIST. Colleges that stress the priority of **Scripture** studies in preparation for **ministry**. Perhaps the oldest example of such a Bible college among Baptists is the **Freewill Baptist** Biblical School founded at Parsonfield, Maine, in 1840. Its curriculum and approach to the **Bible** was progressive for the era. Next in order was the Gordon Missionary Training School, opened in 1881 in Boston, Massachusetts.

In the 20th century, the Bible college movement has been associated with emerging Baptist groups and other groups that are antagonistic to higher education as found in church-related or "Christian" liberal arts colleges, universities, and graduate theological seminaries. The differentiating characteristics found in these Baptist Bible colleges are (1) a more practical ministry and missionary curriculum; (2) a confessional statement that mandates the entire curriculum is based upon and derived from the Bible; and (3) practical **missionary** work is required of all students. Examples of the use of Bible colleges among emerging Baptist groups are the schools of Eastern Europe, such as at Odessa, **Ukraine**, and Bucharest, **Romania**. Institutions that have an inherent bias against "higher" education are found among the **General Association of Regular Baptists**, the **Baptist Missionary Association**, the **Baptist Bible Fellowship**, the **Liberty Baptist Fellowship**, and other **independent Baptists** in the United States. Bible colleges, not necessarily of a **fundamentalist** theological persuasion, are also found among **black Baptists**, notably the American Baptist Theological Seminary (1924) and the National Baptist Missionary Training School (1936) in Nashville, Tennessee, related to the **Southern Baptist Convention** and the **National Baptist Convention, U.S.A**. In Great Britain, a number of Baptists have been trained at London Bible College, founded in 1943. *See also* THEOLOGICAL EDUCATION.

BIBLE DEFENSE LEAGUE. Group formed in May 1925 at Milton, Wisconsin, by and for **Seventh Day Baptists** who desired "to throw off the incubus of rationalism" which threatened evangelical Christianity. Akin to the **Baptist Bible Union** among First Day Baptists, the Bible Defense League was part of the **fundamentalist-modernist** division among 20th-century Baptists. Seventh Day Baptists involved in the Bible Defense League were less divisive than others in Baptist fundamentalism and essentially carried forth an editorial campaign in a bimonthly magazine called the *Exponent*. For three years there were also meetings of the league between sessions of the General Conference (1925–1927), after which the Committee of Six on Denominational Harmony recommended that freedom of private judgment should be exercised and both sides of the debate should be presented in the columns of the *Sabbath Recorder*. From 1928 to 1931, a "modernist" page appeared and from 1929 to 1931, the "Fundamentalist" page was regularly issued. Seventh Day Baptists ultimately settled down to a moderate evangelical position, concluding for the most part that modernism had reached its peak and did not reflect the majority of Seventh Day congregations.

BICKEL, LUKE WASHINGTON (1866–1917). American Baptist missionary, born at Cincinnati, Ohio. In his youth, Bickel was an apprenticed seaman and rose to the rank of captain in the merchant marine. After studies at Spurgeon's College in London and a missionary appointment with the British Baptist Publication Society, Bickel applied to the **American Baptist Missionary Union** for appointment. A gift from a Glasgow merchant for a gospel ship made possible Bickel's appointment in the Far East. In 1898, he began a mariner's mission in the Inland Sea of Japan aboard the *Fukuin Maru*. At many of the islands, he created **Sunday Schools** and preaching stations; in 1916, he reported work on 60 islands in cooperation with other denominational groups.

BILL, INGRAHAM EBENEZER (1805–1891). Canadian Baptist minister, editor, and historian, born at Cornwallis, Nova Scotia. He was baptized by **Edward Manning** in 1824 and served the church at Nictaux for 23 years. Bill also served churches in Fredericton and St. John, New Brunswick, and was one of the popular preachers and **revivalists** of his era. An ardent advocate of education, though lacking a formal education himself, Bill traveled to the United States and Great Britain in support of Acadia College, raising in the United States over $3,000 in 1844. In 1852, he became editor of the *Chris-*

tian Visitor, which he edited for 20 years. Bill was a farsighted **pastor** and leader, advocating female education and progressive worship forms. He introduced the use of pipe organs to his church at Nictaux. In 1880, he published *Fifty Years with the Baptist Ministers and Churches of the Maritime Provinces of Canada*, a major primary source for the region.

BISHOP, NATHAN (1808–1880). Educator and denominational leader, born at Vernon, New York. Bishop graduated from Brown University and became school superintendent in Providence, Rhode Island, and Boston. Bishop moved to New York City in the 1880s and became involved in denominational work. He served from 1874 to 1876 as corresponding secretary of the **American Baptist Home Mission Society** (ABHMS), and at his retirement he paid its debt of $30,000. Bishop was particularly interested in **black Baptist** education, and in his honor, the ABHMS named its college in Marshall, Texas, after Bishop.

BITTING, CHARLES CARROLL (1830–1898). Baptist minister and denominational leader, born at Philadelphia, Pennsylvania. Following collegiate studies at Lewisburg and Madison Universities, Bitting served churches in Virginia. While **pastor** at Alexandria, Virginia, during the Civil War, he refused to take the Oath of Allegiance to the United States and was forced to ride as a hostage on the front of a railroad locomotive against southern raiders for the day's trip from Alexandria to Orange County Courthouse. After the Civil War, Bitting became secretary of the Southern Baptist **Sunday School Board** and, in 1872, regional secretary for the **American Baptist Publication Society**. Later Bitting again served congregations in Virginia and Maryland. He was one of a select group of post–Civil War leaders to serve in both the major conventions, thus reversing the trend toward regionalism in Baptist life.

BLACK BAPTISTS. The black Baptist tradition is culturally diverse and involves congregations in North America and the Caribbean Islands. Essentially, the black experience reflects an admixture of African American and/or Caribbean cultures with Regular Baptist polity.

The initial black Baptist expressions were found among the slave communities in the British colonies in North America. White preachers preached among the slaves and underground congregations emerged, notably on William Byrd III's (1728–1777) plantation in Virginia in 1742. Freedom of interpretation and spontaneity in worship attracted large numbers of blacks to the Baptist tradition even before emancipation.

The first formally organized black Baptist church began in 1778 at Silver Bluff, South Carolina, under the direction of **George Leile** and **Andrew Bryan**. Later, in 1787, the Springfield Baptist Church was founded at Augusta, Georgia, and the First African Baptist Church in Savannah, Georgia (1788).

In the Canadian context, black Baptist churches date from 1782 when **David George** started a congregation at Shelburne, Nova Scotia. From this group eventually stemmed the African Baptist Association in 1854.

Black Baptist institutional life includes **associations**, national **conventions**, and educational institutions. While early congregations were related to Regular associations in northern cities, by the 1850s black leaders sought control of their own relationships and structures and joined forces with abolitionists and sympathetic Republican Party members. This led to the **American Baptist Free Mission Society**, which was established in 1843 in part to affirm Afro-American social equality. The **American Baptist Home Mission Society** (ABHMS) also assisted in the formation of many churches, cooperative bodies, and schools in the black communities. Their work began directly in 1862 in the District of Columbia and, later, in South Carolina. The major effort of the ABHMS was in training leaders for work among the freedmen, thus much money was raised to assist a group of academies, colleges, and universities across the South to train black leaders. The yearning for black organizations, however, led predictably to the formation of the **American Baptist Missionary Convention** in 1840 and the Western Colored Baptist Convention in 1853. This led eventually to the uniting of the Consolidated American Baptist Missionary Convention in 1866—and, later, to the **National Baptist Convention of the United States of America** (NBCUSA) in 1896—starting a heritage of black-led organizations (discussed below) that won the support and cooperation of the white societies.

Early Associations. The first associations emerged in the Ohio Valley in the antebellum era: Providence (1834, Meigs County, Ohio), Union (1836, Cincinnati, Ohio), Wood River (1839, St. Clair County, Illinois). In Upper **Canada** (now Ontario), the Amherstburg Association was formed along the northern shore of Lake Erie in 1841. There were approximately nine black Baptist associational bodies active in the United States before the Civil War and two in what is now Canada.

Black Baptist Education. Among the major black Baptist educational institutions (with date established) were Roger Williams University (Nashville, Tennessee, 1864), Shaw University (Raleigh, North Carolina, 1865), Wayland Seminary (Washington, D.C., 1865), Storer College (Harper's Ferry, West Virginia, 1866), Richmond Theological Seminary (Richmond, Virgina, 1867), Atlanta Baptist College (Atlanta, Georgia, 1867), Mather School (Beaufort, South Carolina, 1869), Benedict College (Columbia, South Carolina, 1870), Florida Institute (Live Oak, Florida, 1873), Bishop College (Marshall, Texas, 1881), Jackson College (Jackson, Mississippi, 1877), Leland College (New Orleans, Louisana, 1870), Alabama Colored Baptist University (Selma, Alabama, 1878), Spelman College (Atlanta, Georgia, 1881), Simmons University (Louisville, Kentucky, 1873), Hartshorn Memorial College (Richmond, Virginia, 1884), Walker Institute (Augusta, Georgia, 1885), Arkansas Baptist College (Little Rock, Arkansas, 1887), Bible and Normal Institute (Memphis, Tennessee, 1887), Coleman Academy (Gibbsland, Louisana, 1887), Spiller Academy (Hampton, Virginia, 1891), Waters Normal Institute (Winton, North Carolina, 1887?), Houston Academy (Houston, Texas, 1893), Jeruel Academy (Athens, Georgia, 1893), and Hearne Academy (Hearne, Texas, 1896). Southern Baptists cooperated with the NBCUSA in 1924 to establish the American Baptist Theological Seminary, a Bible college and missionary training institute in Nashville, Tennessee. The National Theological Institute was formed in 1864 to sponsor schools in Washington, D.C.; Virginia; South Carolina; and Georgia. In many cases, either the ABHMS or the **Freewill Baptists** early assisted the majority of the schools.

In addition, another group of colleges emerged on a more independent basis: Guadaloupe College (1884) and Houston College (1885), both in Texas; Virginia College and Theological Seminary (1888); Western College, Missouri (1890); Friendship Baptist College, South Carolina (1891); Meridian Baptist Seminary, Mississippi (1897); Central City College, Georgia (1899); Central Texas College (1903); Morris College, South Carolina (1905); Lee and Hayes University, Maryland (1914); Williams and Jones University, Maryland (1928); Central Baptist Seminary, Kansas (1921); and Northern Baptist University, New Jersey (1921). Several of these schools enjoyed the patronage of black Baptist State conventions.

Formation of State Conventions. As associations grew in number and benevolent concerns proliferated, black Baptists organized numerous state conventions—the General Association of Colored Baptists in Kentucky (1865), Florida Bethlehem Baptist State Convention (1874), Colored Baptist Convention of Maryland (1898), and Baptist Missionary and Educational Convention of Tennessee (1872), to cite several examples. Most were linked directly from their beginnings with the NBCUSA or one of its predecessors.

Formation of Black Baptist National Conventions. Responding to the need for black-led national missionary organizations, the Consolidated American Baptist Missionary Convention was formed at Nashville, Tennessee, in August 1867. This organization sponsored **Sunday School** agents and missionaries throughout the southern states, until its demise in 1879. The next national organization was the Baptist Foreign Mission Convention of the United States, organized in Montgomery, Alabama, in 1880. In the West, the American National Baptist Convention was formed at St. Louis in 1886. In 1895, these two regional bodies merged their interests to form the NBCUSA. In order to have a black-led foreign mission enterprise, the **Lott Carey Baptist Home and Foreign Mission Convention** was founded in 1897. In 1907, black Primitive Baptists in the South formed a national body, the National Primitive Baptist Convention of the U.S.A., mostly as a racially defined outgrowth of the white Primitive Baptists. A disagreement over management of the publication house of the NBCUSA led **Richard H. Boyd** in 1915 to form the National Baptist Convention of America (unincorporated) (NBCA). In 1961, under the influence of **Martin Luther King Jr.** and Gardner

C. Taylor (1918–), the **Progressive National Baptist Convention** was formed. A schism in the NBCA in 1988 led to the establishment of the **National Baptist Missionary Convention of America** (NBMCA). *See also* PRIMITIVE BAPTISTS.

Recent Trends. In the past decade, there are signs of increased communication and cooperation among the American national organizations of black Baptists. Facilitating this are the **Baptist World Alliance**, the Baptist Joint Committee on Religious Liberty, and the Hampton Conference. In January 2005, a major gathering of black Baptists in the United States was held in Nashville, Tennessee, when over 10,000 delegates met in a convention. Representing over 13 million black Baptists from the NBCUSA, the NBCA, the PNBC, and the NBMCA, the leaders were Gardner Taylor, Jesse Jackson, and William J. Shaw. Greater cooperation is also seen in support for educational institutions such as Interdenominational Theological Center in Atlanta and American Baptist College in Nashville. The major black Baptist groups also cooperated in the New Covenant Baptist meetings held in Atlanta in January 2008. *See also* AFRICAN UNITED BAPTIST ASSOCIATION.

BLACK ROCK CONVENTION. *See* PRIMITIVE BAPTISTS.

BOARDMAN, GEORGE DANA, JR. (1828–1903). American Baptist minister and educator, born at Tavoy, Burma. The son of **George Dana Boardman Sr.** and **Sarah Hall** (later **Judson**), George was the first surviving child of the missionary children born overseas to an American Baptist missionary. At the death of his father, he was sent to the United States to be raised and became the stepson of **Adoniram Judson** when his mother married Mr. Judson in 1834. George was educated at Brown University and Newton Theological Institution, after which he entered the pastoral ministry. He served Barnwell, South Carolina, Baptist Church (1855–1856); then Second Baptist, Rochester, New York (1856–1864); and finally First Baptist Church, Philadelphia, Pennsylvania (1864–1894). Boardman was a widely regarded orator in Philadelphia and taught at Temple University and the University of Pennsylvania. Brown University awarded him an honorary doctorate in 1866, as did the University of

Pennsylvania in 1889. His lectures on **Bible** exposition were well attended in Philadelphia and published widely during his lifetime.

BOARDMAN, GEORGE DANA, SR. (1801–1831). American Baptist missionary, born at Livermore, Maine. Boardman was in the first graduating class of Waterville College and remained briefly as a tutor on its faculty in 1822. In 1823, he sought an appointment of the **Baptist Board of Foreign Missions** and was accepted. He moved to Andover, Massachusetts, where he planned to enter seminary, but was diverted to serve as missionary to African people in that town. He was ordained at North Yarmouth, Maine, and entered the mission service in 1825. He and his wife, **Sarah Hall Boardman Judson**, embarked for **Burma**, but were detained at Calcutta where they lived with the English Baptist missionaries for two years. Eventually the Boardmans settled at Moulmein, Burma. After some years, he served at Tavoy where he became the pioneer missionary to the Karens. Boardman traveled extensively in the backcountry and gathered the first church at Tavoy. His health failed from respiratory illness and he died at Tavoy after an arduous journey. Boardman's wife, Sarah, later married **Adoniram Judson**.

BOGARD, BENJAMIN MARCUS (1868–1951). Southern Baptist and, later, Missionary Baptist minister, born at Elizabethtown, Kentucky. He was educated at Georgetown College and Bethel College in Kentucky and ordained at Woodland Church in 1888. Bogard served a series of country churches in Kentucky (1888–1892), as well as congregations at Princeton (1892–1894) and Fenton (1894), both in Kentucky; Charleston, Missouri (1894–1899); and Searcy, Arkansas (1899–1903). Bogard, a leading **Landmarkist**, became a well-known debater among Southern Baptists, taking exception to what he called "conventionism." His major public debates occurred in Texas, Indiana, Kentucky, and Arkansas, over Campbellism, Darwinian evolution, and Christian union among non-Baptists. Bogard joined forces with other Landmarkists in Arkansas and challenged the basis of representation in the **Southern Baptist Convention** (SBC) and the basis of support for missionary work that Bogard and others thought included too much administration. Bogard's following left the SBC and became organized in 1902 as the General Association in

Arkansas and, later, the **Baptist Missionary Association**. He was a staunch defender of Baptist successionism, the view that an unbroken line of Baptist churches existed from the year A.D. 31. His lasting institutional legacy was the Missionary Baptist Seminary in Little Rock, Arkansas.

BOHEMIAN BAPTISTS. *See* CZECHOSLOVAK BAPTIST CONVENTION OF THE UNITED STATES AND CANADA.

BOLIVIA. Baptist life in Bolivia is dated from the establishment at Oruro in 1898 of the first congregation by **Archibald Reekie**, a Canadian Baptist. In 1941, a biblical institute was founded at Cochabamba (later to become a theological seminary), and the Unión Bautista Boliviana was organized in 1936. Following the construction of a railroad from **Brazil** to **Peru**, the Brazilian Baptists began an aggressive missionary outreach in Bolivia in 1952 and formed the Convención Bautista Boliviana. In 1961, the Brazilian Baptists organized a theological school at Santa Cruz, the Seminario Teológico Bautista Del Oriente Bolivia. The Southern Baptist **Foreign Mission Board** entered Bolivia in 1977 at the invitation of the Brazilian work and the Maranatha Baptists, the International Baptist Missions entered the field in the 1960s, and the **Baptist Bible Fellowship** began a mission in 1978.

As of 2006, there were 276 churches and 27,361 members affiliated with the Unión Bautista Boliviana, and 49 churches and 7,000 members affiliated with the Convención Bautista Boliviana. The periodical, *El Centinela Boliviano* (*The Bolivian Sentinel*) (1945–), is associated with the Unión Bautista.

BOOTH, ABRAHAM (1734–1806). English Baptist pastor, born at Alfreton. He was converted during a revival in the Midlands and became superintendent of a congregation at Kirkby Woodhouse in 1760. Although this church was related to the **General Baptists**, Booth became a Calvinist and published significant theological treatises, including *Glad Tidings to Perishing Sinners* (1796). He was called to Little Prescot Street Church, Goodman's Fields, where he was ordained, and from this church, he became a leading figure among London Baptists. He was a prime mover in founding the theological college at Stepney as well as the Itinerant Society; he was also the first London minister to lend support to the **Baptist Missionary Society**. It was Booth who introduced **William Carey** to Dr. **John Thomas** in the service of the British East India Company, who in turn quickened Carey's interest in that region. Booth was remembered as an unostentatious man who gave large sums of money to benevolent causes, among which was the **antislavery** movement. Booth was one of the most widely read Baptists of the 18th century; among his many works were *The Reign of Grace: From Its Rise to Its Consummation* (1768) and *Paedobaptism Examined* (1784).

BOSNIA and HERZEGOVINA. Baptist experience began in Bosnia during the period of the Austro-Hungarian Empire. In 1862, Franz and Maria Tabory were baptized in Bucharest, Romania, and they moved shortly afterward to Sarajevo with Franz becoming a Bible **colporteur**. The next year, August Liebig, a German missionary in Romania, also moved to Lukovac and conducted **baptisms**. A third stream of Baptist life in Bosnia began with the ministry of Adolf Hempt, a Serbian. Hempt was baptized in Budapest and conducted missionary work in Sarajevo, actually creating the first congregation about 1877. Following World War I, the Baptist churches in Bosnia joined the Baptist Union in Yugoslavia. In 1992, with the dissolution of Yugoslavia and the ravages of civil war, Bosnian Baptists are rebuilding.

As of 2006, there were 15 churches in the area, including Tuzla, Zivinice, Sarajevo, Zenica, and Novi Tranik, with about 300 members in Bosnia and Herzegovina.

BOTSWANA. The South African Baptist Missionary Society was first to enter the territory now called Botswana in 1966. This work was transferred to the Southern Baptist **Foreign Mission Board** in 1968. The first congregation was formed at Francistown in 1970, and the churches organized a **convention** in 1978.

As of 2006, there were 17 churches and 657 members affiliated with the Baptist Convention of Botswana.

BOYCE, JAMES PETIGRU (1827–1888). Southern Baptist minister and educator, born at Charleston, South Carolina. Boyce was educated at the College of Charleston, Brown University, and Princeton Theological Seminary. His mentors were **Francis Wayland** at Brown and A. A. Hodge (1823–1886) and Charles Hodge (1797–1878) at Princeton. From 1848 to 1849, he edited the *Southern Baptist* and then served First Baptist Church, Columbia, South Carolina (1849–1851). In 1855, Boyce became a professor of theology at Furman College and in 1859 a founder of Southern Baptist Theological Seminary. At Southern, he was the first chair of the faculty and taught in New Testament, theology, homiletics, and church history. It was he who induced **Basil Manly Jr.** and **John A. Broaddus** with others to join the original Southern Seminary faculty. When the Civil War forced the closure of the school, Boyce raised funds for its reopening and eventual removal to Louisville, Kentucky. He was president of the **Southern Baptist Convention** from 1872 to 1879 and again in 1888. A double predestinarian Calvinist, Boyce also defended **Richard Fuller**'s views on **slavery**. In 1882, he published *Abstract of Systematic Theology*, reprinted for many years by the Southern Baptist **Sunday School Board**. A connoisseur of fine wines, he died in France while seeking a cure for gout. Boyce's writings have enjoyed renewed recognition from the 1980s in the **Founders Ministries** among Southern Baptists

BOYD, RICHARD HENRY (1843–1922). Black Baptist minister and publisher, born at Noxubee, Mississippi. Raised a slave in Mississippi and Texas, upon emancipation Boyd was converted and soon ordained to the Baptist ministry. In 1872, he rallied black congregations to form the first black Baptist **association** in Texas, and he rose to important positions in the **General Baptist** Convention of Texas. In 1896, he was elected the manager of the National Baptist Home Mission Board. An entrepreneur, Boyd negotiated a publishing arrangement with the Southern Baptist **Sunday School Board** to offset the influence of the **American Baptist Publication Society**, and he later formed the publishing board for the **National Baptist Convention** (NBCUSA) in 1897. He was financially very successful in this endeavor but differed greatly with the leadership of the NBCUSA about matters of ownership and control. Between 1905 and 1915, Boyd engaged in an acrimonious debate with the NBUSA, and he finally withdrew and helped to form a new group of black

Baptists, the **National Baptist Convention of America** (NBCA). Boyd was the author or editor of numerous practical works for the churches, including the *National Baptist Pastor's Guide* (1900), the *National Baptist Hymnal* (1903), and *A Story of the National Baptist Publishing Board* (1915).

BRAZIL. As early as 1859 Southern Baptists in the United States planned to begin **missions** work in Brazil. Thomas J. Bowen (1814–1878) preached in Rio de Janeiro in 1859–1860. A church of American emigrants was formed in 1871 at Santa Barbara. The first missionaries were dispatched from the Southern Baptist **Foreign Mission Board** in 1881. At Bahia, the first Brazilian congregation was constituted in 1882, largely the work of William Bagby (1855–1939). In 1907, the Convención Bautista Brasilena was formed, and the next year a college and seminary were opened at Rio de Janeiro. In 1953, as British missionaries left China, the **Baptist Missionary Society** began a new work in Ponta Grossa in coopera-tion with **Southern Baptists**. British influence upon the formation of the Parana Baptist Convention was significant thereafter.

In addition to the missionary efforts mentioned above, other inde-pendent Baptist groups contributed to mission work in Brazil: in 1922, Eric Nelson (1862–1939) gained support of the Amazon Valley Faith Baptist Mission and started a work in the Amazon Valley; in 1935, **Baptist Mid-Missions** (BMM) from the United States estab-lished an extensive mission in Brazil at Juazerio and, later, at Man-aus and Boa Vista; the **Association of Baptists for World Evange-lism** started a mission in 1942; Conservative Baptists began a church planting mission in 1946 and sponsored seminaries in Brasilia, São Luis, and Teresina; the Baptist General Conference opened a mission in 1955 in cooperation with the Brazilian Baptist Convention; the **Baptist Bible Fellowship** (BBF) started its mission in 1952; and in 1963, the Japan Baptist Convention also appointed missionaries to Brazil. In 1913, the first **Seventh Day Baptist** congregation was started in Brazil.

Brazilian Baptists themselves developed an aggressive overseas missionary program after World War II, opening fields in **Portugal**, Macao, and **Angola**. Extension also occurred into **Bolivia**. The Brazilian Baptist Convention has been publishing *O Jornal Batista*

(*Baptist Journal*) since 1901. In 1942, the Baptist Publishing House was founded in Rio. The Brazilian Baptist Convention encompasses an **evangelism** board, a Christian ethics commission, and a woman's missionary union. Theological schools exist at Recife (1902), Rio (1908), São Paulo (1901), and Belém (1955). Brazilian Baptist life was greatly advanced by the Tenth Baptist World Congress in Rio in 1970, which drew approximately 170,000 people.

As of 2006, there were 6,766 churches and 1,045,500 members affiliated with the Brazilian Baptist Convention, and 2,687 churches with 290,827 members affiliated with the National Baptist Convention of Brazil. Brazil has the most theological schools of any single Baptist national group. Thirty-six institutions or programs are dispersed throughout the country, several in key cities: Bauru, Teresina, São Paulo, Santo Andre, Pôrto Alegre, Rio de Janeiro, Itaperuna, Natal, São Goncalo, Ijui, Goiânia, Osasco, Brasília, Curitiba, Fortaleza, Juazeiro do Norte, Campinas, Campo Grande, Niterói, Feira de Santana, Vitória, Belo Horizonte, Dourados, Recife, Manaus, Salvador, Campos Goitacazes, Araguaina, Cuiabá, São Luis, and Belém.

BRINE, JOHN (1703–1765). English Baptist minister, born at Kettering. He was self-taught, and converted to Baptist beliefs under **John Gill**. In 1726, Brine was called to serve Jordan's Well, Coventry, Church, and in 1729, he was elected **pastor** at Curriers' Hall, St. Paul's Alley, Cripplegate, which he served until his death. Closely allied with John Gill, Brine was among the most theologically Calvinistic of the **Particular Baptists**. The author of over two dozen sermons and pamphlets published in seven volumes, he declined to address the condition of the unconverted, and this caused his ministry to wither by mid-century, an obvious product of extreme Calvinism. Among his most famous works were *Certain Efficacy of the Death of Christ* (1743) and *A Vindication of Divine Justice* (1754).

BRISBANE, WILLIAM HENRY (1906–1878). Baptist physician and editor, born at Black Swamp, South Carolina. Brisbane was educated at Charleston Medical School and became a plantation farmer and editor, in addition to his medical practice. **Francis Wayland**'s book *Elements of Moral Science* (1835) influenced Brisbane against **slavery**, and he freed his slaves and began a career as an abolitionist. Opposition to his views caused him to move to Ohio and, later, Wisconsin, where he wrote on **antislavery** topics. During the Civil War, Brisbane served as a chaplain in the Wisconsin Cavalry and, later, as tax commissioner in South Carolina during Reconstruction. He helped to organize the Port Royal Experiment, which assisted in the training of former slaves. Brisbane published a famous antislavery work, *Slaveholding Examined in the Light of the Holy Bible*, in 1847.

BRITISH HONDURAS. *See* BELIZE.

BRITISH VIRGIN ISLANDS. The **Baptist Missionary Association of America** (BMA) started a Baptist **mission** in the islands in 1956. As of 2007, there were two congregations affiliated with the BMA, with 500 members, and one congregation affiliated with the **Southern Baptist Convention**, with about 250 persons.

BROADDUS, ANDREW (1770–1848). American Baptist minister, born in Caroline County, Virginia. He was self-educated in a frontier cabin, converted, and then baptized about 1789. He entered the Baptist pastoral ministry and served churches in central Virginia: Upper King and Queen, Salem, Bethel, and Fredericksburg. Repeatedly offered prestigious congregations in urban areas in the South and North, Broaddus declined and favored the small, rural church. He was a well-known preacher and scholar, writing for the *Religious Herald* on various philosophic subjects, notably a response to the writings of Thomas Paine (1737–1809). Also an accomplished hymn writer, Broaddus published three volumes, among which were *Sacred Ballads* (1790) and the *Dover Selection of Spiritual Songs* (1828). His son, Andrew Broaddus Jr. (1818–1900), succeeded him as pastor at Salem Church in Caroline County, and his grandson, Andrew Broaddus III (1853–1926), followed in that pastoral ministry and leadership among Virginia Baptists.

BROADDUS, WILLIAM F[POSSIBLY FERGUSON] (1801–1876). American and, later, Southern Baptist minister, born at Woodville, Virginia. Privately educated, Broaddus was first a schoolteacher. He was ordained in 1824 at the "F.T." Church in Rappahannock County, Virginia, after which he served the Shiloh and Mt. Salem churches.

In his early career, Broaddus was an opponent of **revivalistic** techniques, but this changed dramatically in 1831 at Upperville where he observed the benefits of protracted meetings and other new measures, and he became a promoter of these strategies. This won for him the criticism of hyper-Calvinists in Virginia, yet he persisted in holding meetings and organizing new congregations and **associations** along these lines. Because of his stand, Broaddus was denied a seat in the Ketocton Association in northern Virginia. In 1833–1836, he served the churches at Bethel and Long Branch, and then he moved to Kentucky for a decade. From 1840 to 1850, he served pastorates in Lexington, Shelbyville, and Versailles, Kentucky. Returning to Virginia in 1853, Broaddus served Fredericksburg Baptist until captured in the Civil War. He was arrested by Union troops in 1862 and taken to prison in Washington, D.C., where he was retained for a political prisoner exchange with the Confederate government. Following his release, Broaddus was minister at Charlottesville, Virginia (1863–1865), and again served the congregation at Fredericksburg until his death (1865–1876). He was one of the most effective promoters of education and **mission** among Virginia Baptists, a charter trustee of Richmond College (for which he raised $20,000) and of the Virginia Baptist Education Society. Broaddus was also known for his stance against strong drink, being an author of a plea to the Shiloh Association for total abstinence in 1840. Broaddus published several important tracts on **baptism**, 1835–1858.

BROADUS, JOHN ALBERT (1827–1895). Southern Baptist theological educator, born at Culpeper County, Virginia. Educated in a private school, he taught school from 1844 to 1846 and then studied at the University of Virginia, where he graduated with an M.A. in 1850. That year, Broadus became pastor of the Baptist church in Charlottesville, Virginia, and tutor in classical languages at the University of Virginia. In 1858, he became one of the founding faculty members of Southern Baptist Theological Seminary in Greenville, South Carolina. During the Civil War, he was a chaplain in Robert E. Lee's (1807–1870) army, after which he returned to the seminary and facilitated its rebuilding and move to Louisville, Kentucky. While he taught New Testament and homiletics, his primary publications were in preaching: *On the Preparation and Delivery of Sermons* (1870),

Lectures on the History of Preaching (1876). His *Harmony of the Gospels* (1893) was a standard text for many years. In 1889, Broadus delivered the Lyman Beecher Lectures in Preaching at Yale University, one of two Southern Baptists selected for that honor.

BRONSON, MILES (1812–1883). American Baptist missionary, born at Norway, New York. He was educated at Hamilton Literary and Theological Institution (later Colgate University) and upon graduation was appointed a missionary to Assam for the **Baptist Board of Foreign Missions**. Arriving in northeastern **India** in 1837, Bronson set up work among the hill tribes, and he pioneered work among the Garo people in 1863. In 1841, he began a school at Nowgong and he commenced his literary work creating the first Assamese-English dictionary, which he finished in 1867. Bronson theorized that the Assamese language was the key to reaching the remote tribes, and this proved to be correct; learning that language resulted in thousands of Christian converts in northeast India. During his only furlough, Bronson served as pastor of the Springfield, New York, Baptist Church. The leading American Baptist missionary of his era to India, Bronson published 19 works in Naga, Garo, and Assamese, including the *Naga Catechism* (1839) and *A Dictionary in Assamese and English* (1867).

BROTHERHOOD OF THE KINGDOM. Group founded on July 9, 1892, in the New York City apartment of **Walter Rauschenbusch**, a young German Baptist minister. The group of six founding clergy, including Rauschenbusch (1861–1918), Samuel Zane Batten (1859–1925), Spencer B. Meeser (1859–1939), **Nathaniel Schmidt**, **William Newton Clarke**, and Leighton Williams (1855–1935), was an outgrowth of the **Baptist Congress** and focused on the reassertion of the doctrine of the Kingdom of God and its practical application in human society. The organization was kept to a minimum and the members engaged in **Bible** study, theological revision, social reform, and advocacy of Christian unity. Over the next 30 years, the brotherhood became an international fellowship and helped to influence church organizations to accept the **social gospel** agenda. Notable among its converts were the leaders of the Northern Baptist Convention, formed in 1907, which in 1910 formed a social service department of the denomination.

BROWN, JOHN NEWTON (1803–1868). American Baptist minister and denominational publisher, born at New London, Connecticut. He was educated at Hamilton Literary and Theological Institution (later Colgate University) and served pastorates in Exeter, New Hampshire (1829–1839), and Lexington, Virginia (1845–1849). For six years (1839–1845), he taught theology and pastoral relations at New Hampton Institute. In 1849, Brown was appointed educational secretary of the **American Baptist Publication Society**, where he remained for a key decade, building the printed resources of the society in response to the growth of frontier and overseas missions. Brown will ever be associated with the preparation of the New Hampshire Confession of Faith (1830–1833), which he principally authored with two other ministers, for use among the Baptist churches in New Hampshire. The **Confession** became widely used, as well as his church **covenant**, because he included both in his *Baptist Church Manual* (1853) of church **discipline**, distributed to virtually every missionary Baptist congregation in the United States.

BROWN, NATHAN (1807–1886). American Baptist missionary, born in Ipswich, New Hampshire. He was educated at Williams College and studied at Newton Theological Institution before serving a church at Rutland, Vermont; teaching school; and editing the *Vermont Telegraph*, a weekly religious paper. In 1832, the **Baptist Board of Foreign Missions** appointed Brown and his wife to join the **Adoniram Judsons** in **Burma**. Judson convinced Brown to open a new field in Assam, and he settled at Sadiva. Brown translated several tracts and hymns into Assamese and organized an **association** of churches in Assam. While on furlough in the United States in 1855, Brown resigned from the board and joined the **American Baptist Free Mission Society** (ABFrMS), editing their periodical, the *American Baptist*, and the *Journal and Messenger*. His strongly held abolitionist views were widely known. After the Civil War and the merger of the ABFrMS and the **American Baptist Missionary Union**, Brown returned to Japan to translate the New Testament into

Japanese, a project he finished in 1879. A highly regarded linguist, Brown helped to organize the American Philological Society. Brown published over 35 works, including *Catechisms in Thai and Assamese* (1837), the *First Assamese Hymnbook* (1845), and a *History of Assam, by a Native Pundit* (1844).

BROWN, NICHOLAS (1729–1741). Baptist entrepreneur and philanthropist, born at Providence, Rhode Island. He was a merchant in the spermacetti candle business, the first American businessman to create formally a monopoly, which he did among candlemakers in New England. During the French and Indian War, Brown was a privateer, and during the American Revolution, he secretly obtained clothing for the Continental troops. In the constitutional debates in the 1780s, Brown was a Federalist and helped to secure Rhode Island's support. In 1767, his contribution to the Baptist college of Rhode Island secured its relocation to Providence, and his firm built the first building, University Hall, on Brown family property. He was also a principal benefactor to the Charitable Baptist Society, the corporation of First Baptist Church in Providence.

His son, Nicholas (1769–1841), was educated in University Hall and developed a lifelong affection for the College of Rhode Island, serving as a trustee and its treasurer. In 1804, he gave $5,000 for the endowment of a professorship in belles lettres, and the name of the university was changed to honor the family's generosity. In 1823, the younger Brown gave funds to erect Hope College, named for his sister, and he built Manning Hall.

BRYAN, ANDREW (1737–1812). American black Baptist minister, born in Goose Creek, South Carolina. Named for his master, Jonathan Bryan (fl. 1780–1800), who was converted under **George Leile**, Bryan rose to leadership in the Savannah community of **black Baptists**, following the pastorate of Leile. At length, Bryan was ordained by his uncle, **Andrew Marshall**, and in 1788, he organized the first African Baptist Church of Savannah at Yamacraw, near Savannah. He purchased his freedom and bought a lot for his church of 700 members. The growth of the congregation was such that twice it divided into two more congregations. Collectively, these African congregations were known as "**Ethiopian**" churches.

In a celebrated incident in the 1780s, Andrew and his brother, Sampson, held night meetings of his congregation, and suspected of inciting insurrection, they were publicly whipped for the incidents. In 1790, Bryan and his church were admitted to the Georgia Baptist Association, bringing important recognition to his congregation and ministry.

BULGARIA. Baptist congregations in Bulgaria are the result of **missionary** work, immigration, spontaneous **Bible** study groups, and Bulgarians who traveled abroad. The first church was founded at Kazanlik in 1876 by **Ivan Kargel** (1849–1937), a German from St. Petersburg. The second congregation at Ruse (1888) led to the formation of a Romanian-Bulgarian Association (Evangelski Baptistki Alliance) in the 1890s. A congregation at the capital, Sofia, was started in 1899. Under the leadership of Peter Doycheff (1859–1913), the Soius na Evangelski Baptistki Zurkvi v Bulgaria (Bulgarian Baptist Union) was formed in 1908. Especially as a result of the **London Conference of 1920**, the **North American Baptist Conference** (German) in the United States assumed sponsorship of missions in Bulgaria from 1924. For a time in the 1920s, the Danish Baptists also supported a mission to Plovdiv. In 1995, the **Baptist Bible Fellowship** opened a mission in Bulgaria.

As of 2006, there were 75 churches and 4,500 members affiliated with the Soius na Evangelski Baptistki Zurkvi v Bulgaria. The periodical is the *Evangelist* (1920–1938), afterward renamed *Khristiyanski priyatel* (*Christian Friend*) (1939–).

BUNYAN, JOHN (1628–1688). English Independent and Baptist minister and writer, born at Elstow, Bedfordshire. At first Bunyan was a tinker by trade. He was converted in the mid-1650s and baptized in 1655 by John Gifford, the Baptist minister in Elstow. Bunyan became **pastor** of the church in Elstow which was related to the **Particular Baptists** and the Independents. In 1660, he was arrested for preaching and imprisoned for 12 years. During this time, he left prison frequently to preach outdoors and also composed *The Pilgrim's Progress*, an allegory considered to be one of the finest pieces of English literature in print. Upon his release in 1672, Bunyan became England's most celebrated preacher. He produced a tract in 1673 in which he declared that **baptism** should not be an obstacle to admission to the Lord's Table. In his posthumous autobiography, *Grace Abounding to the Chief of Sinners* (1679), Bunyan revealed that his conversion had been influenced by his reading of a passage from the Apocrypha, Ecclesiasticus 2:6; having such a revelation from the Apocrypha was an extraordinary circumstance among the Particular Baptist community, which limited its understanding of the biblical canon to 66 books. Bunyan is recalled by a memorial window in Westminster Abbey in London, the only Baptist so honored.

BURKINA FASO. Formerly called Upper Volta, Baptist **missionary** work in this nation was an outgrowth of work in **Ghana**. In 1971, the **Southern Baptists** commissioned a missionary to Burkina Faso. Centers of Baptist work include Ouagadougou and Koudougou. The **National Baptist Convention of Burkina Faso** was formed in 1977. In 1994, the **Baptist Bible Fellowship** also opened a mission in Burkina Faso.

As of 2006, there were 60 churches with 3,000 members affiliated with the Union of Evangelical Baptist Churches in Burkina Faso. There is a school, the Rural Baptist Training Center, located at Kondougou.

BURMA. County also known as Myanmar, where Baptists established an early mission. In 1814, **Adoniram** and **Ann Judson** established the American Baptist mission in Burma in the city of Ava. After them, the mission expanded from the urban areas to the hill tribes and eventually to **Siam** and **China**. American Baptists invested heavily in Burma, especially with remote tribes: Elisha Abbott and Henry Van Meter began formal work among the Karens in Bassein in 1852; Josiah **Cushing** prepared a Shan translation of **Scripture**, beginning his work in 1867; **Francis Mason** commenced a **mission** among the Kachins in 1873. Institutional development by Baptists was extensive throughout the 19th century. At Insein, the Karen Theological Seminary was established in 1845, and a widespread system of Baptist girl's and boy's schools added much to the denomination's rapid growth. In 1871, the **American Baptist Missionary Union** established Rangoon Baptist College, which eventually became Burma Baptist College. At the end of the 19th century, there were 15 associations of Baptist churches, united by the Burma Baptist Missionary

Convention, founded in 1865. At the high point of Baptist missionary activity in Burma (about 1880), there were the following missions: Rangoon (1813), Moulmein (1827), Tavoy (1828), Karen (1831), Bassein (1840), Henthada (1853), Swaygyeen (1853), Toungoo (1853), Prome (1854), Thongzai (1855), Zeegong (1876), and Bhamo (1877). An important asset to the Burmese Baptists was the establishment in 1830 by **Cephas Bennett** of the American Baptist Mission Press at Moulmein.

In 1966, all Baptist missionaries were withdrawn at the request of the Burmese government. As of 2006, there were 4,522 churches with 1,142,655 members affiliated with the Myanmar Baptist Convention; the Self-Supporting Kayoin Baptist Mission Society included 69 churches with 11,543 members; and the Myanmar **Seventh Day Baptist** Conference, established in 1964, encompassed 15 churches and 2,560 members. Over the years, the following periodicals have been associated with Baptist life in Burma (Myanmar): *Myitta Taman*, *Burma News*, and the *Burman Messenger*. There are presently 10 Baptist-related theological schools in Myanmar: Bassein, Chi State, Insein (3), Kutakai, Moulmein, Myitkyina, Rangoon, and Taunggyi.

BURROUGHS, NANNIE HELEN (1883–1961). American black Baptist denominational leader, born at Orange, Virginia. The child of skilled slaves, Burroughs received an education in Washington, D.C., and sought a teaching position in the Washington schools. Turned aside on the basis of color, she became a clerk and bookkeeper for the newly formed **National Baptist Convention of the United States of America** (NBCUSA) in 1895 and settled at Louisville, Kentucky. She was elected the first president of the Women's Auxiliary of the NBCUSA and became the corresponding secretary in 1900. She used her position to organize black women, establishing a voluntary organization, the Association of Colored Women, and in 1909, the National Training School for Women and Girls both in Washington, D.C. Burroughs followed **Booker T. Washington**'s program of self-help for blacks, calling her version "the bible, the bath, and the broom." Her work eventually extended across denominations and she was recognized as a pioneer in the National Association for the Advancement of Colored People.

BURTON, ERNEST DEWITT (1856–1925). American Baptist minister and educator, born in Granville, Ohio. He was educated at Griswold College and Denison University, from which he graduated. At first, Burton taught in public schools in Xenia and Cincinnati, Ohio, later entering Rochester Theological Seminary, from which he graduated in 1882. In 1883, he was ordained to the Baptist ministry and became professor of New Testament Greek at Newton Theological Institution until 1892 when he was elected to the chair of the Department of New Testament and Early Christian Literature at the University of Chicago. In that position, Burton worked in tandem with President **William Rainey Harper** in the area of Old Testament and Oriental Studies. In 1922, he became acting president of the university and a year later, president. In his short two years in that role, Burton increased the endowments to over $54 million and greatly expanded the medical school. Burton was a widely renowned scholar, editing *The Biblical World* and *The American Journal of Theology*. He published a *Harmony of the Gospels* (1894) and was chair of the China Education Commission, which influenced theological education in the Orient.

BURUNDI. Baptist witness in what was formerly Ruanda-Urundi dates from 1928 when Danish Baptist missionaries Johann and Niels Peter Andersen went there and established a church in 1931. A Union of the Baptist Churches of Ruanda-Urundi was constituted in 1960, but it divided in 1962 when the two countries were politically divided. In 1980, the (U.S.) Southern Baptist **Foreign Mission Board** opened a mission in Burundi, strengthening ties with the wider Baptist world.

As of 2006, there were 87 churches and 25,505 members affiliated with the Union of Baptist Churches in Burundi.

BUSHER, LEONARD (fl. 1615–1620). Baptist writer, about whom little is known. He was probably of Dutch descent, but part of his life was spent as a citizen of London, perhaps in exile. Busher's vocation, at least in London, was that of laborer. About 1614, he petitioned Parliament with a plea for freedom of conscience, entitled *Religion's Peace*. In this famous treatise, Busher argued that coercion by fire and sword was dangerous to king and state, a means of increasing the kingdom of antichrist. His book appears to have been written in Amsterdam and carried to England to support the Baptist case for **religious liberty**. Significantly, Busher also advocated adult **baptism** by immersion, becoming one of the first Baptists to do so. In his older years, he appeared again at Delft.

BUTLER, JOHN JAY (1814–1891). American **Freewill Baptist** minister, theologian, and educator, born at Berwick, Maine. Butler was educated at Berwick Academy, Parsonfield Seminary, Bowdoin College, and Andover Theological Seminary. Holding several teaching appointments before seminary graduation, Butler was one of the first faculty members at the Free Baptist Biblical School in Whitestown, New York, in 1844. In 1854, he moved to the chair of systematic theology at New Hampton Institution in Vermont. In 1870, Butler relocated with that institution to Cobb Divinity School of Bates College in Maine. From 1873 to 1883 he taught sacred literature at Hillsdale College in Michigan. Butler published a one-volume systematic theology, *Natural and Revealed Theology* (1861) and a *Commentary on the New Testament* (1870–1871). He was considered the principal theologian of the Freewill Baptist movement in the 19th century, a virtual authority on matters of doctrine. Butler is credited with keeping the mainstream of the theologically **Arminian** Free(will) Baptist movement from joining the **holiness** movement by maintaining a progressive stance on the doctrine of "entire sanctification."

BUZZELL, JOHN (1766–1863). American **Freewill Baptist** minister and editor, born at Barrington, New Hampshire. He became a school teacher and was influenced by the preaching of **Benjamin Randal**. He was baptized by Randal in 1791 and began preaching in the Freewill Baptist Connection. In 1798, Buzzell moved to Parsonfield, Maine, where he served for 65 years. He became Randal's successor as the leading minister in the Connection and started many congregations across northern New England. Buzzell edited *A Religious Magazine* (1811–1813) and was a founding editor of the *Morning Star*, the official newspaper of the denomination. During his pastoral years in Parsonfield, Buzzell was also principal of Parsonfield Seminary, the first educational institution of the Freewill Baptists. His published *Life of Benjamin Randall* (1827) was the first history of the movement, and he also compiled *Psalms, Hymns and Spiritual Songs* (1823), the first hymnal of the Freewill Baptists.

– C –

CALL TO MINISTRY, BAPTIST CONCEPT OF. Baptists have joined other Christians, primarily in the Reformation traditions, in affirming the nature and necessity of a call to **ministry**. John Calvin (1509–1564) in particular noted the importance of a calling to ministry in his Ecclesiastical Ordinances of 1541. Likewise, English Congregationalists distinguished between an "immediate" call from God and a "mediate" call through the church. Baptists speak consistently of an internal or "secret" call upon an individual from God to ministry. This is not to be for material reasons, but one based on a true and pure sense of service to God and edification of the Body of Christ. In the interview process with potential candidates for ministry, Baptists typically will expect to hear of the experience of the internal call and how it appears to derive from God alone. There is also the importance of the external call of a congregation. Church leaders will recognize the validity of the inner calling and respond with support for use of one's gifts to ratify a call. This may be accompanied by a license to ministry or license to preach. During the licentiate period, the effectiveness of one's gifts comes to ratify one's verbal articulation of an internal call. Ultimately, the external call is an invitation from a congregation to practice specified ministry in a particular place. **Ordination** may follow among most Baptist groups. Typically, Baptists maintain that an internal call is for life, while an external call may be related to the particular set of circumstances. During the 18th and 19th centuries, Baptists joined others in being concerned about "hireling ministers" and an "unconverted ministry." This has led to high expectations of personal commitment and a genuine sense of call to ministry.

CALLENDAR, ELISHA (1680–1738). American Baptist minister, born at Boston, Massachusetts. Callendar graduated from Harvard College in 1710, the first native-born American Baptist minister to obtain a higher education. His education and **ordination** recognition indirectly were made possible by the influence of **Thomas Hollis**, an English Baptist philanthropist. Cotton Mather (1663–1728) attended Callendar's ordination, representing the regional Congregationalist Standing Order. Callendar served the First Baptist Church in Boston for 20 years (1718–1738) and helped to extend its influence as the center of New England Baptist life.

CALLENDAR, JOHN (1706–1748). American Baptist minister and historian, born at Boston, Massachusetts. Callendar was educated at Harvard College, receiving support from the **Hollis** foundation in England. In 1731, he succeeded **John Comer** as co-pastor in Newport, Rhode Island, where he served until his death. He collected early Baptist historical materials, which **Isaac Backus** used in his history. He also authored *An Historical Discourse on the Civil and Religious Affairs of the Colony of Rhode-Island and Providence Plantations in New England in America* (1739), a pioneering work in American religious history.

CAMBODIA. Baptist work in Cambodia is relatively recent, owing to earlier Roman Catholic and Buddhist traditions and military conflicts of the mid-20th century. Several U.S. Baptist groups have attempted missionary work indirectly and more directly of late. The **Association of Baptists for World Evangelism** opened its mission in 1996; the **Baptist Bible Fellowship** opened in 1997. In 1980, the Association Baptiste du Cambodge was founded.

As of 2006, there were 180 churches with 6,730 members affiliated with the Association Baptiste du Cambodge. **Southern Baptists** have a mission comprised of 45 churches with about 3,000 members.

CAMEROON. Baptists were the first Protestant group to evangelize Cameroon. In 1845, the **Baptist Missionary Society** (BMS) began work there, led by **Alfred Saker**, and in 1886, BMS transferred the work to the Basel Mission, sponsored by the Reformed Church in Switzerland. Within three years, a "Berlin committee" was organized of German Baptists, and this group gradually evolved into the support base for a permanent Cameroon mission. In 1890, August Steffens (1861–1893), an American German Baptist, opened a mission in Cameroon, which signalled a new era of **missionary** work as well as support from the American churches. Eventually, the center of Baptist work became Soppo. A German-based organization, the Neuruppin Mission Society, handled all of the appointments. Gradually, the American German churches assumed the leadership for Cameroon, and in 1931–1935, the **North American Baptist Conference** adopted the country as a major mission priority, creating the Cameroon Baptist Mission. In 1951, the Cameroon Baptist Convention was founded, as well as a Bible training center, which later became the Cameroon Baptist Theological College. Significant medical missionary work followed, beginning at Mbingo in 1948. The European Baptist Mission Society, following the earlier German Baptist involvement, joined in support in 1954.

As of 2006, there were 900 churches with 900,000 members affiliated with the Cameroon Baptist Convention; 376 churches and 48,050 members affiliated with the Union of Baptist Churches; and 66 churches with 5,000 members affiliated with the Eglise Baptiste Camerouaise of the Cameroon.

CAMPBELL, ALEXANDER (1788–1866). Presbyterian and, for a time, American Baptist minister, born at Ballymena, Ireland. In 1807 Alexander joined his father, Thomas (1763–1854), emigrating to western Pennsylvania after he finished his studies at the University of Glasgow. Alexander had come under the influence of the **Haldanes**, and with his father he tried to create a fellowship that was **evangelistic** and non-creedal. At length, the Presbyterian Synod in western Pennsylvania rejected the admission of the Campbells' "Christian Association," and the group organized itself as a separate church at Brush Run, Pennsylvania. Alexander was ordained in 1812 and began a dialogue with local Baptists. His family was baptized by immersion, and after a sustained doctrinal dispute in which Alexander rejected the **Philadelphia Baptist Association**, the church was admitted to the Redstone Baptist Association in 1813.

Over the next several years, Campbell's views on **baptism,** the **Lord's Supper**, Christian organizations, and **ordination** (to mention a few of the areas in which his opinion differed) separated him from the mainstream of Baptists, and he withdrew in 1829 to create the "Reformer" movement, later to become the Disciples of Christ. From 1823 to 1830, he edited and published *The Christian Baptist*. Between 1825 and 1830, numerous Baptist congregations were swayed to the Campbellite position; eventually, a western apologetic grew up among Baptist **associations**, producing new periodicals, numerous public debates, and at least two camps of Baptists, those supportive of missionary societies and the anti-mission Baptists. After his Baptist career concluded, Alexander Campbell enjoyed a long-term leadership of the Christian Church/Disciples of Christ tradition. Among Baptists, Campbell is best known for his publication *Christian Baptism with Its Antecedents and Consequents* (1851) and his published accounts of debates over baptism and church **polity** in which he participated from 1820 to 1850.

CAMPBELL, ROBERT CHARLES (1924–). American Baptist minister and educator, born in Phoenix, Arizona. He was educated at the Eastern Baptist Theological Seminary, first graduating from the college division and then from the theological school. Under the tutelage of New Testament scholar Carl H. Morgan, Campbell completed his doctorate in theology, also at Eastern. While a graduate student, Campbell served in youth and pastoral ministries in Philadelphia at the Baptist Temple and the 34th Street Baptist Church. In 1949, he became assistant professor, first in biblical languages and, later, in Christianity, at Eastern Baptist College, where he taught for two years. In 1953, he was named associate professor of New Testament at California Baptist Theological Seminary, where he became academic dean the next year. Serving at California Seminary, Campbell achieved national attention as a Bible lecturer for NBC radio and television broadcasts "Frontiers of Faith" and "The Art of Living." In the late 1950s, he also served as an adjunct professor in New Testament at the University of the Redlands and Claremont Graduate School of Theology. In 1973, Campbell became the general secretary of the newly reorganized **American Baptist Churches in the U.S.A.** He was considered the candidate of the evangelical community, which had criticized the directions of the denomination under previous leadership. As chief executive of American Baptists, Campbell was a key bridge between the **ecumenical** and **evangelical** communities, serving on the boards of the World Council of Churches and the general council of the **Baptist World Alliance**. In 1987, Campbell became president of the Eastern Baptist Theological Seminary where he served until retirement in 1989. Among his published works are *The Gospel of Paul* (1973) and *Jesus Still Has Something to Say.* (1987).

CAMPOLO, ANTHONY, JR. (1935–). American Baptist minister and educator, born at Philadelphia, Pennsylvania. Campolo graduated from Eastern Baptist College and the Eastern Baptist Theological Seminary, taking the doctoral degree in sociology from Temple University. His entire academic career was spent teaching sociology at Eastern Baptist College (later Eastern University) in St. Davids, Pennsylvania. In addition to his teaching, Campolo started an international youth ministries organization, and he organized several voluntary **associations** for relief in Haiti, **evangelical** renewal, and the Evangelical Association for the Promotion of Education. Campolo has spent many years as a popular religious lecturer and speaker on every continent; he has also advised political figures, including President **Bill Clinton** during his moral crisis over Monica Lewinsky. Often a center of controversy, Campolo claimed in his 1983 book, *A Reasonable Faith*, that **Christ** is present in every believer, and this caused Campus Crusade for Christ to cancel one of his speaking events. A subsequent investigation in the American evangelical community, led by J. I. Packer at Regent College, ensued and found Campolo theologically naïve and injudicious, but not heretical. In the 1990s, Campolo hit on another controversial topic—his position on homosexuality, advocating committed relationships, has offended many traditional evangelicals. In Campolo's honor, Eastern University named its graduate division Campolo College of Graduate and Professional Studies. He is the author of 28 books, including *A Denomination Looks at Itself* (1971) and *Let Me Tell You a Story: Lessons from Unexpected Places and Unlikely People* (2000). *See also* PRESIDENTS OF THE U.S., BAPTIST.

CANADA. The first Baptist congregations in Canada emerged from the New Light movement in Nova Scotia. About 1765, **Ebenezer Moulton**, a Baptist from Massachusetts, formed preaching stations along Nova Scotia's Annapolis Valley, including a permanent one at Horton (now Wolfville). The congregation languished before the American Revolution and was reconstituted in 1778. In the same period, another early congregation of the Six Principle type was started at Sackville, New Brunswick, but it ceased within a decade. By 1800, there were nine congregations represented at the first meeting of the Nova Scotia Baptist Association. An academy was started to train Christian leaders in 1828 at Horton, which later evolved into Acadia University.

Maritime Baptist life also grew with the settlements of New England planters (and after the Revolution, United Empire Loyalists) in New Brunswick. In Nova Scotia, the influence of **Henry Alline** was important in charting the early history of Baptist church development. A separate **association** was formed in that province in 1821. Sensing the need for ministerial training there, New Brunswick Baptists started the New Brunswick Seminary in 1836, which survived until 1872.

The **Freewill Baptists** of the New England region of the United States entered the Maritime Provinces via itinerant preachers in the early 1800s and started several churches. In 1836, the quarterly meetings in Canada became the first Free Christian Baptist movement, which evolved into the Free Baptist General Conference (1866, 1898), distinct from the U.S. branch. With a close theological affinity to the Allinite tradition, the Freewill Baptists spread through the provinces and even created a few congregations in Quebec and Upper Canada (later Ontario), before merging with the regional associations and **conventions** of Regular Baptists after 1890. In the 1880s, the **holiness** movement affected the Free(will) Baptists in Canada, and after a schism, the **Reformed Baptist Alliance** of holiness congregations was formed.

In the central Canadian provinces, the earliest Regular Baptist congregations were found at Caldwell's Manor (1794), Hallowell (1796), Thurlow (1796), Bastard (1803), Clinton or Beamsville (1807), and Charlotteville (1810). North and east of Lake Ontario, it was Baptist ministers from upstate New York and Vermont who first planted churches. Likewise, the churches of the Niagara peninsula were largely the result of Baptist missionaries from New England and central New York State. Later, in the Ottawa Valley, **John Gilmour** and John Edwards (1780–1842) led a group of Scottish Baptists, who had experienced the **Haldanite** revivals in Scotland, to form several churches. The earliest congregations in the Montreal region were from time to time sponsored by British Baptists, who through the Baptist Colonial Missionary Society, and, later, the **Baptist Missionary Society**, supported missionaries from 1838 to 1850. The first association in Upper Canada met in 1802 at Thurlow.

Gradually, four epicenters of Baptist life in central Canada grew up in the mid-19th century: Montreal, Woodstock, Brantford, and Toronto. The struggle to establish a theological school illustrated the competition between these communities. At Montreal in 1838, Canada Baptist College was begun; in Woodstock in 1860, the Canadian Literary Institute opened; in Toronto in 1881, the Toronto Baptist College began its institutional pilgrimage to what became McMaster University in 1888; at Brantford in 1959, the Baptist Training Institute held its first classes.

In the western provinces, it was missionary labor from Ontario and Quebec—and to a lesser degree, the Maritime Baptists—that led to the formation of churches. **Alexander "Pioneer" McDonald** assisted in the constitution of the first church at Winnipeg in 1873. Immigrant families were a focus for American Baptist domestic missions as well as Canadian efforts; this work included Russians, Galicians, Ukrainians, Germans, and Swedes. Eventually, four separate conventions formed the Baptist Union of Western Canada in 1909. Educational institutions (with year of establishment) include Brandon University, Manitoba (1899); Baptist Leadership Training School, Calgary, Alberta (1948); and Carey Hall Theological College in Vancouver, British Columbia (1979).

Mention should also be made of the Francophone Baptist community in Quebec province, which also had its origin in the Haldanite movement. **Louis Roussy**, an evangelist for the Commission of the Churches of Switzerland Associated for Evangelization (supported by the Haldanes), joined **Henriette Feller** in 1835, and the two of them pioneered the development of an institute that trained children at the secondary level. In 1966, the Union des Eglises Baptistes Françaises au Canada was formed from the former Grand Ligne Mission by the eight surviving congregations. Centered in Montreal with the union is the Faculté de Théologie Evangélique, a **Bible college** level training school opened in 1982.

Canadian convention Baptist organization has historically been focused on the regional level. Four major conventions/unions were constituted to provide interchurch relations, **missions**, and educational resources: the United Baptist Convention of the Maritime Provinces (1905) (later the Atlantic Provinces 1963), the Baptist Convention of Ontario and Quebec, the Union des Eglises Baptistes Françaises, and the Baptist Union of Western Canada. Congregations also cooperated in the Baptist Federation of Canada from 1944 to 1994, at which time it was merged with the Canadian Baptist International Ministries to form Canadian Baptist Ministries, headquartered in Mississauga, Ontario. Built largely on the pattern of the U.S. **Baptist Joint Committee on Public Affairs**, the federation created in 1983 a Canadian Baptist Public Affairs Committee, which focused upon church-state issues and was staffed by volunteers in Ottawa. It was superceded in 1983 by a reorganized Committee on Public Affairs, a more internal group based in Mississauga, Ontario. The oldest of the national organizations is the foreign mission enterprise, variously called the Foreign Mission Board of the Baptist Convention of Ontario and Quebec, the Canadian Baptist Foreign Mission Society, the Canadian Baptist Overseas Mission Board, Canadian Baptist International Ministries, and, most recently, Canadian Baptist Ministries; it was founded in 1866 as an auxiliary to the **American Baptist Missionary Union**.

Outside the main streams of the three "conventions" of Canadian Baptists are the **Fellowship of Evangelical Baptist Churches in Canada**, the **North American Baptist Conference** (NABC), the **Baptist General Conference** (BGC), and missionary work by U.S. **Southern Baptists**. The NABC churches are an outgrowth of the mission among German-speaking Baptists in the United States, as the BGC in Canada is the result of missions among Swedish churches in the United States. The General Conference Baptists in 1955 assumed control of the Vancouver Bible College and operated the school until 1978. In 1953, Southern Baptists began support for Canadian work, beginning at Vancouver, British Columbia, from which other missions have spread across Canada. As of 1995, there were 28 congregations related to the **Baptist Bible Fellowship**, a **fundamentalist** Baptist group working in Canada since 1971. In the area of **theological education**, Baptists in Canada of varying kinds operate eight schools from Vancouver to Nova Scotia.

In **polity** and style, Canadian Baptists are a blend of English, Scottish, and American traditions. Emphasis is upon the local congregation, which calls its **pastors** and is usually formally constituted. Organization beyond the local church is centered on regional conventions. Mission and benevolent work as well as education is conducted through cooperative agencies, the "convention" Baptists controlling the executive boards of denominational bodies, while others cooperate with interdenominational evangelical groups or parent organizations in the United States. Convention Baptists, Southern Baptists, and the NABC are affiliated with the **Baptist World Alliance**. Only the Baptist Convention of Ontario and Quebec is affiliated with the **Canadian Council of Churches**.

Mainstream Baptists have published *Baptist Missionary Magazine* (1827), the *Christian Messenger* (1837–1884), *The Messenger and Visitor* (1885–1905), *The Maritime (Atlantic) Baptist* (1905–), and the *Canadian Baptist* (1854 –1998), while Fellowship Baptists publish the *Evangelical Baptist* (1952–). The Canadian Baptist Historical Society, founded in 1865, has been reconstituted at McMaster Divinity College and carries forth programs of heritage education and conferences.

As of 2006, there were 1,136 churches with 173,100 members affiliated with the conventions/unions in Canadian Baptist Ministries. *See also* AFRICAN UNITED BAPTIST ASSOCIATION; BLACK BAPTISTS; CONVENTIONS; FELLOWSHIP OF EVANGELICAL BAPTIST CHURCHES IN CANADA.

CAREY, LOTT (1780–1829). Black Baptist pastor and missionary, born near Charles City, Virginia. Carey was born on a plantation and went to work as a hired laborer in a tobacco warehouse in Richmond, Virginia. He purchased his freedom and attended classes at William Crane's School. Carey attended services at First Baptist Church, where he was **pastor** and began preaching among the black population. He became interested in foreign **missions**, and in 1815, he helped to found the Richmond African Missionary Society, which became an auxiliary to the **General Missionary Convention**. In 1821, Carey was appointed a missionary to western Africa by the **Baptist Board of Foreign Missions**, in conjunction with the American Colonization Society and his Richmond Society. At first, Carey worked in **Sierra Leone** but was forced to go to Cape Montserrado (later **Liberia**). There he set up a school and a medical service in the new colony. Carey also organized and served Providence Baptist Church at Monrovia. In 1828–1829, he served as vice governor, and then acting governor, of the colony of Liberia. Carey was killed in an accident while defending the capital against insurgents.

CAREY, WILLIAM (1761–1834). English Baptist pastor and missionary, born at Paulerspury. He was educated through the efforts of his schoolteacher father and read widely, especially in the subject areas of natural science and geography. Carey was apprenticed to a shoemaker and associated with people who held Dissenter views and strong Christian convictions. In 1782, he met **Andrew Fuller** and was baptized by **John Ryland** in the River Nene. Carey served a church at Moulton and continued to study politics and geography. At a meeting of the Northampton Baptist Association in 1786, he presented a plan for evangelizing the heathen and was largely dismissed by **John Collett Ryland** and others. Later, in 1792, Carey published a book, *A Solemn Enquiry*, which asserted the obligation of Christians to evangelize the heathen peoples of the world. This book became the most quoted tract in the history of modern missions.

Carey and 12 others organized in 1792 the Particular Baptist Society for Propagating the Gospel among the Heathen, in short the **Baptist Missionary Society**, of which he became the first appointee to **India**. Arriving in India in 1793, Carey set up a mission at Serampore and turned to large translation projects. He organized a press and built a church, the Lall Bazaar Chapel. His translation work produced results in six languages, and his numerous publications include *Dictionary of the Bengalee Language* (1815–1839) and *Memoir Relative to the Progress of the Translations of Sacred Scriptures, in the Year 1815* (1816). Considered the most learned man of his era in India, Carey was appointed a professor of Sanskrit at Fort William College. Thanks to scores of biographies, Carey became a model as a premier international citizen and missionary builder.

CARIBBEAN BAPTIST FELLOWSHIP (CaBF). As part of the regional organization of the **Baptist World Alliance** (BWA), the CaBF was organized at Lake Yale, Florida, in 1970. Thirteen member bodies comprised the original fellowship from the islands of the Greater and Lesser Antilles. The CaBF was a direct result of the combined efforts of the Crusade of the Americas, which began in 1965. The CaBF describes itself as a **voluntary association** that advances education; **mission**; communication; relief; **evangelism**; Baptist **polity**, practice, and justice; and **religious liberty**. The CaBF is one of the six regional fellowships of the BWA and publishes *The Caribbean Baptist*.

CARIBBEAN DIASPORA BAPTIST CLERGY ASSOCIATION. An **association** of Baptist ministers and congregations in the United States that brings together Caribbean immigrant pastors, and their interests, who are living in communities dispersed from their homelands in the West Indies. It was first suggested in 1993 by Roy Henry, president of the **Jamaica** Baptist Union, at a meeting at Bronx Baptist Church in New York City. In the 1990s, the idea earned the support of the Jamaica Baptist Union Mission Agency, and it now relates to the **Caribbean Baptist Fellowship** of the **Baptist World Alliance**. The association draws from congregations in Connecticut, Massachusetts, Pennsylvania, New York, and Maryland. It was formally constituted 30 March 2008 and includes 12 congregations and 3,000–5,000 members.

CARNELL, EDWARD JOHN (1919–1967). American Baptist educator and theologian, born at Antigo, Wisconsin. A graduate of Wheaton College and Westminster Theological Seminary, Carnell undertook two doctorates simultaneously at Boston University and Harvard. His respective dissertations resulted in major works on Reinhold Niebuhr and Soren Kierkegaard. A product of a **conservative** evangelical Baptist background, Carnell pursued a Reformed theological agenda under the tutelage of Gordon Clark at Wheaton College, Cornelius Van Til at Westminster Theological Seminary, and Edgar Brightman at Boston University. He was considered one of the outstanding young theologians of his era as he began his teaching career at Gordon College in 1945. Four years later, Carnell was selected as the inaugural president of Fuller Theological Seminary in 1949. Carnell was the author of nine books, the most important of which were *An Introduction to Christian Apologetics* (1948) and *The Case for Or-*

thodox Theology (1959). Usually included with **Carl F. H. Henry**, Harold J. Ockenga, and **Bernard Ramm**, Carnell was one of the original "neo-evangelical" theologians. His death occurred under suspicious circumstances, with some friends believing that it was a suicide from a narcotic overdose.

CARPENTER, CHAPIN HOWARD (1835–1887). American Baptist missionary, born in Milford, New Hampshire. Educated at Harvard College and Newton Theological Institution, Carpenter was appointed by the **American Baptist Missionary Union** (ABMU) to go to **Burma** in 1863. Commencing in 1864, he taught in the Karen Theological Seminary and superintended the Bassein Mission of 70 congregations. For two years, 1874–1875, Carpenter was president of the Rangoon Theological Seminary, after which he returned to Bassein. Working for 11 years among the Karens, he developed a policy of self-support and urged the ABMU to adopt this plan for all of their missionary work. The board declined the plan, and Carpenter resigned from the ABMU in 1886. Later, he and his wife, Harriet, began an independent Baptist mission among the Ainos of **Japan**, on a self-support principle. Carpenter's publications include *The Anglo-Karen Handbook and Reader* (1875) and *Self-Support, Illustrated in the History of the Bassein Karen Mission from 1840 to 1880* (1883).

CARROLL, BENAJAH HERVEY (1843–1914). Southern Baptist minister and educator, born in Carroll County, Mississippi. He was educated at Baylor College and invested much of his professional career there. Following military service in the Civil War as a Texas Ranger (he was among the last Confederates to surrender), Carroll held pastoral ministries in Texas, from 1870 to 1899. He became professor of theology and **Bible** at Baylor in 1872 and retired in 1905. Carroll built the Bible Department into a distinguished faculty, out of which emerged Southwestern Baptist Theological Seminary. He was the first president of the seminary from 1908 to 1914. He advocated the reestablishment of the Southern Baptist **Sunday School Board**, and he defended the Home Mission Board against incursions of the **Gospel Mission** movement. Carroll wrote a 13-volume commentary on the Bible, *An Interpretation of the English Bible* (1916–1917), intended for the use of preachers, and in his era, he was one of the most popular preachers in the **Southern Baptist Convention**.

CARROLL, JAMES MILTON (1852–1931). Southern Baptist minister and educator, born at Montecello, Arkansas; the brother of **Benajah Hervey Carroll**, who baptized him. He was educated at Baylor University, graduating with a B.A. in 1877. Following **ordination** in 1874, Carroll served numerous small churches in central Texas: Dog Town, Anderson, Oakland, Macedonia, Washington, Good Hope, and finally Corpus Christi (1880–1882) and Lampasas (1882–1887). He became active in promoting **Sunday Schools** and church planting and was appointed a missionary for the Texas Baptist State Convention (1889–1892) and General Superintendent of Missions (1892–1894); he also served as an agent for the Texas Baptist Education Commission (1898–1899). Carroll edited the *Missionary Messenger* and *Texas Baptist Statistics* (1895). He became president of Howard Payne College in 1911, concluding his career as pastor at Riverside Park, San Antonio, in 1912. Among his outstanding achievements were a *History of Texas Baptists* (1923) and his famous lecture "The Trail of Blood" (1931), which he delivered thousands of times in defense of historic Baptist sacrifice and an unbroken line of Baptists throughout history, later referred to as **successionism**.

CARSON, ALEXANDER (1776–1846). Scotch-Irish Presbyterian and, later, Baptist minister, born at Stewartstown, County Tyrone, Northern Ireland. Carson was educated at the University of Glasgow, and his first pastorate was the Presbyterian church in Tubbermore, Ireland (1798–1805). Under the influence of Haldanite itinerants, Carson was converted to Baptist principles about 1805. He preached in rented halls and open fields after leaving his Presbyterian pastorate. In 1814, he built a new meetinghouse at Tubbermore and was highly regarded in the region. Carson was a gifted intellectual, first demonstrating his linguistic abilities when he refuted a translation by Professor Lee, a specialist in Oriental languages at Cambridge, and, later, with his treatises, *Baptism: Its Mode and Subjects* (1831) and *History of Divine Providence* (1833). He also provided the linguistic basis for **Robert Haldane**'s *Commentary on the Romans* (1842). Following his preaching the annual sermon for the **Baptist Missionary**

Society in 1846, Carson's ministry was cut short by a fall from a pier in Liverpool from which he died a few days later.

CARTER, JAMES EARL, JR. (1924–). Southern Baptist layman and United States president, born in Plains, Georgia. He attended Georgia Western College and Georgia Institute of Technology, later graduating from the United States Naval Academy. Carter served as a midshipman, one of the pioneering officers of the U.S. nuclear submarine fleet. From this service, he frequently styled himself a "nuclear physicist." Upon leaving the Navy, Carter took over his father's peanut farm at Plains and grew the business considerably. He entered politics, and in 1971, "Jimmy" Carter was elected governor of Georgia. In 1976, he was elected the 39th president of the United States, defeating the incumbent Gerald R. Ford on a populist Democratic Party platform. Carter in turn was defeated by Ronald Reagan in 1980. He returned to private life and became engaged in various humanitarian projects, including his own Carter Center initiatives and Habitat for Humanity. In recognition of his many efforts over a long period, Carter was awarded the Nobel Prize for Peace in 2002.

Carter has been a lifelong Baptist, active in various parts of Baptist life. In 1935, Royall Callaway, **pastor** at Plains, baptized Carter. Callaway was a premillennialist and had conections to Bob Jones University, a noted **fundamentalist** institution. In 1962, Carter was ordained a Baptist deacon under the pastorate of Robert Hanna, who held progressive views in the area of race relations. Upon taking up the Georgia governorship, Jimmy and his family joined Northside Baptist Church in Atlanta, but frequently attended Roswell Street Baptist Church in Marietta, where his friend the Reverend Nelson Price was minister. In 1977, while he was president, Carter and his family joined the First Baptist Church in Washington, D.C., where the Reverend Charles Trentham was minister. Carter taught a **Sunday School** class at First Baptist while he was president. Returning to live in Plains in 1981, the Carters reconnected with Plains Church, which had undergone a split. The Carters became active at Maranatha Baptist Church, where the former president continues to teach a Bible class. Shunned by Southern Baptist conservatives, Carter helped to unite the theologically moderate **Southern Baptist Convention** factions and in 2008 was the leading voice in convening the New Covenant Baptist meetings in Atlanta.

CARVER, WILLIAM OWEN (1868–1954). Southern Baptist minister and educator, born in Wilson County, Tennessee. Carver was educated at the University of Richmond and Southern Baptist Theological Seminary where he earned the Th.D. degree. He served churches at Concord (1889–1891) and Deatsville (1896–1907), Kentucky, and Hermitage, Tennessee (1891–1893). Carver began his teaching career at Boscobel College (1893–1896) and then moved to Southern Seminary from 1896 to 1953. He first taught New Testament, then comparative religions, finally moving to **missions**, where he formed the first missiology department in Southern Baptist life in 1899. Carver was one of the most widely traveled and highly respected Southern Baptists of his era. He toured the mission fields of the **Foreign Mission Board** in 1900, 1907–1908, and 1922–1923. He was active in the Faith and Order movement and the World Council of Churches. His great legacy was the formation of the Women's Missionary Training School at Louisville, later named the Carver School of Missions and Social Work. Among his 20 published books are *Missions in the Plan of the Ages* (1909) and *Christian Mission in Today's World* (1942).

CASE, ISAAC (1761–1852). New England Baptist missionary, born at Rehoboth, Massachusetts. With no formal education, Case was ordained in 1783 as an evangelist. He was influenced by **Isaac Backus** and Job Macomber (d. 1820), a Baptist church planter in Maine, and itinerated in Massachusetts and Vermont. He started a congregation at Thomaston, Maine, in 1784, the first of several churches that owe their origins to him: Bowdoinham, East Brunswick, and Readfield. In 1800, Case began his work as a **missionary**, first for the Bowdoinham (Maine) Association, then in 1802 for the Massachusetts Baptist Missionary Society (MBMS). He was the first appointed American missionary to **Canada** and helped to organize the Maritime Baptist associations. In 1804, Case formed the Maine Baptist Missionary Society on the MBMS plan. Case's missionary endeavors did much to launch American Baptist influence into the Maritime Provinces of Canada.

CASE, SHIRLEY JACKSON (1872–1947). Canadian and American Baptist historian and educator, born at Hatfield Point, New Brunswick. Raised in a **Freewill Baptist** family and educated at Acadia University, Case taught at Horton Academy (1896) and New Hampton Institute (1897–1901), where he taught Greek. He then continued his studies at Yale (B.D., Ph.D.), where he majored in biblical studies and early Christianity. He served as pastor at two Congregational churches in Connecticut, Bethlehem (1902–1903) and Beaver Falls (1903–1906). Case took a teaching post in history at Bates College in 1906 and in 1908 moved to the University of Chicago Divinity School, where he first taught New Testament and, later, was chair of the Church History Department. In 1925, because of Case's international influence, he was designated "professor of the history of Christianity," a trend-setting title. As dean of the Divinity School (1933–1938), he developed the **Chicago School** of interpretation, creating a prestigious graduate program in religious studies and recruiting faculty such as William Warren Sweet (1881–1959). In retirement, Case taught at Bexley Hall (1938–1939) and the Florida School of Religion in Lakeland (1940–1947). An advocate of the sociohistorical method, he revitalized the American Society of Church History as its president and edited the influential *Journal of Religion*. Among Case's book-length publications are *The Evolution of Early Christianity* (1914), *Jesus through the Centuries* (1932), and *The Origins of Christian Supernaturalism* (1946).

CASTLE, JOHN HARVARD (1830–1890). American and Canadian Baptist minister and educator, born at Philadelphia, Pennsylvania. Castle was educated at the Baptist University at Lewisburg and Rochester Theological Seminary. He served pastorates at Newburgh, New York, and West Philadelphia, Pennsylvania; in 1872, he accepted the call of Bond Street Church in Toronto, Upper Canada. Castle developed a close friendship with Senator **William McMaster** and became the choice as the first principal of the Toronto Baptist College, over which the senator exerted great influence. Castle designed the curriculum and taught theology at the college, which at McMaster's death in 1887 became McMaster University. Near the end of his life, Castle penned the semiautobiographical words to

"Jesus, Wondrous Savior," a popular Baptist hymn in Canada and the official hymn of McMaster University.

CASWELL, ALEXIS (1799–1877). American Baptist minister and educator, born at Taunton, Massachusetts. Upon his graduation from Brown University, he became one of the original faculty members at Columbian College in Washington, D.C., where he taught ancient languages. Caswell also studied theology under **William Staughton** and Hebrew under **Irah Chase** while at Columbian. He left the college in 1827 to start the first Baptist church in Halifax, Nova Scotia, where he was ordained. In 1828, after only a year, he returned to Brown to the chair in mathematics and natural philosophy under President **Francis Wayland**. Caswell introduced new scientific techniques to Brown and was one of the most highly respected scientists of his era. In 1868, at an advanced age, Caswell became president of Brown University and enhanced its reputation greatly. In 1867–1868, he served as president of the **American Baptist Missionary Union**, the highest-ranking elective position among Baptists in the northern United States.

CATHCART, WILLIAM (1826–1908). English and American Baptist minister, born at Londonderry, Northern Ireland. Cathcart was educated at the University of Glasgow and Rawdon Academy. He served the Baptist church at Barnsley in Sheffield (1850–1853) and then emigrated to the United States on account of antiestablishment principles. In 1853, he went to the church at Groton, Connecticut, and four years later to Second Baptist, Philadelphia, Pennsylvania (1857–1884), which he served for 27 years until his health failed. Cathcart served as president of the American Baptist Historical Society (1876–1884), greatly increasing its collections, and he wrote on the papal system and Baptists in the American Revolution. His monumental work was a two-volume *Baptist Encyclopedia* (1881), which made him a household name in church libraries, while his lesser-known work, *The Papal System: From Its Origin to the Present Time* (1872) marked an important emphasis. Bucknell University conferred on him the doctor of divinity degree in 1873.

CENSURE. *See* DISCIPLINE, CHURCH.

CENTRAL AFRICAN REPUBLIC. In 1921, **William Haas** of **Baptist Mid–Missions** in the United States established a mission in the area of French Equatorial Africa that would later become the Central African Republic; important stations were at Sibut and Bangui and, later, at Kaga Bandoro. Two years later, in the extreme southwestern part of the country, the Swiss Baptist Mission was established in 1923. A third effort was established in 1928 by the **World Baptist Fellowship**, an American **fundamentalist** group.

As of 2006, there were 152 churches and 45,600 members affiliated with the Fraternal Union of Baptist Churches of the Central African Republic; 60 churches with 14,113 members affiliated with the Baptist Churches Union; and 224 churches with 60,000 members affiliated with the Association of Baptist Churches of the Central African Republic.

CEYLON. *See* SRI LANKA.

CHAD. Although Baptist presence in Chad is not numerically great, Baptists were the initial Protestant witness in the country. In 1925, **William Haas** of **Baptist Mid-Missions** opened a work at Balimba, and there was later work at Koumra, which included a hospital and **Bible** institute in the 1930s. In 1963, an association of Baptist congregations in Chad was separated from the main work in **Central African Republic**, but the mission was closed in 1974, in response to government demands. Many Baptists were persecuted.

Beginning in 1993, U.S. **Southern Baptists** began a mission in Chad, with the work centered at N'djamena.

CHAMBERLEN, PETER (1601–1683). English Seventh Day Baptist physician and prominent layman, of Huguenot stock. Chamberlen graduated from Emmanuel College, Cambridge; studied at the universities of Heidelberg and Padua; and was admitted to the Royal College of Physicians of London in 1628. As royal physician to three monarchs of England, he had access that was denied to many others. A progressive doctor, he urged the organization of midwives into a sisterhood, and he pioneered new techniques of medical practice. Chamberlen belonged to the Baptist church at Lothbury and was given to **Fifth Monarchy** ideas. In 1659, at his urging, the congregation adopted Sabbatarian views and migrated to Mill Yard as one of the earliest **Seventh Day Baptist** congregations. He favored greater cooperation among the sects and brought much prominence to his despised group by his medical reputation. Chamberlen was a powerful advocate of the Baptist persuasion, as illustrated in his *Master Bakewell's Sea of Absurdities Concerning Sprinkling Calmly Driven Back* (1650).

CHAMPION, LEONARD GEORGE (1907–1997). English Baptist minister, educator, and historian, born at Bristol. He was educated at Bristol Baptist College and studied New Testament under Martin Dibelius (1883–1947) at the University of Heidelberg, where he received a Th.D. Following graduate studies, he served as **pastor** at Minehead (1934–1938) and Rugby (1938–1951) before returning to Bristol Baptist College as tutor and, later, as principal until his retirement in 1972. In his groundbreaking study of **Andrew Gifford**, *Farthing Rushlight* (1961), Champion challenged the prevailing historiography of **W. T. Whitley** and **A. C. Underwood** (who stressed the London Baptist community) with the importance of Bristol Baptists and the West Country. Champion also contributed key essays on evangelical Calvinism as well as the Baptist ministry. His publications include *The Church in the New Testament* (1951).

CHAPEL CAR EVANGELISM. A program initiated by the **American Baptist Publication Society** (ABPS) and the **American Baptist Home Mission Society** that focused upon new church development and **evangelism** in the western and southern United States, 1891–1946. The idea of applying railroad technology to evangelism was first proposed by Wayland Hoyt (1838–1910), **pastor** of First Baptist Church, Minneapolis, Minnesota, in 1890. With Boston W. Smith (1851–1908) of the ABPS, he formed a Chapel Car Syndicate on New York's Wall Street to finance the idea; the syndicate was composed of business leaders such as Charles L. Colby, John R. Trevor, James B. Colgate, Eugene J. Barney, and others. The first car, Evangel, was dedicated in May 1891, to be followed by Emmanuel (1893), Glad Tidings (1894), Good Will (1895), Messenger of Peace (1898), Herald of Hope (1900), and Grace (1914). The chapel cars were modified Pullman train cars that included a miniature chapel with a pump organ provided by the Estey Company, and a fully furnished apartment for the missionary family. The cars were originally towed free of charge by major railroads onto sidings of new towns where worship services were held and **Sunday Schools** organized. Once the church was under way and plans were laid for a more permanent structure, the car and missionary were moved to another location. Among the states/territories where the cars were employed were West Virginia, the Pacific Northwest, Montana, the Dakotas, Minnesota, Nevada, Colorado, California, Arizona, Arkansas, and Idaho. The chapel car program ended in 1946 when the railroads no longer moved the vehicles without charge and the cars themselves needed costly repairs. Several of the chapel cars were transformed into permanent structures or museum exhibits; one of the wooden cars is on display at Prairie Village, South Dakota, and one of the metal cars is at the American Baptist Assembly at Green Lake, Wisconsin. *See also* COLPORTEURS.

CHASE, IRAH (1793–1864). American Baptist minister and educator, born at Stratton, Vermont. Chase was educated at Middlebury College and Andover Theological Seminary. Ordained an evangelist, he itinerated in western Virginia and in 1818 joined **William Staughton** as a theological teacher in Philadelphia and, later, as a member of the first faculty at Columbian College in Washington, D.C., for seven years. In 1825, New England friends lured Chase from Washington to accept the first professorship at the new Newton Theological Institution in Massachusetts. In addition to teaching biblical theology for 20 years at Newton, Chase designed the curriculum on the Andover model for the first postcollegiate theological school of the Baptists in the United States. Chase published several devotional and doctrinal works, the most significant of which was *The Design of Baptism, Viewed in Its Relation to the Christian Life* (1851).

CHATER, JAMES (1802–1829). English Baptist missionary, born at Bourton-on-Water. A graduate of Bristol Baptist College, he was appointed by the **Baptist Missionary Society** (BMS) in 1806. He arrived in Serampore later that year but was informed that the governor-general of **India** had ordered an end to itinerant preaching and decreed that Chater should leave the colony. Chater first explored the possibility of a mission to **Burma**, and traveled between Serampore and Rangoon until 1812, involved in translation work. When the BMS abandoned its Burma plans in 1812, Chater moved to Colombo, Ceylon, where he opened the Society's Sinhalese work. His outstanding accomplishment there was the translation of the entire Bible into the Sinhalese language. Chater died at sea en route to Britain. His published works introduced the Sinhalese mission to Baptists: *Dialogue between a Buddhist and a Christian* (1825) and *A Grammar of the Cingalese Language* (1815).

CHICAGO SCHOOL. A particular intellectual tradition at the University of Chicago in the first three decades of the 20th century. Beginning with the reorganized university of the 1890s under **William Rainey Harper**, theologians, biblical scholars, and historians began to apply the social sciences to the study of religious subjects. This led to an elaborate system of investigation of the contextual issues surrounding theological formulations. Basic to the Chicago School was the presupposition that ideas and institutions evolved and, therefore, that historical study was absolutely essential to proper interpretation of text and tradition. Advocates like **Shirley Jackson Case** held that there must be a concern for the total environment in which historical events occurred, and Case and his colleagues utilized other methodologies such as literary analysis and archaeological evidence to support historical hypotheses. The evolutionary pattern underlying the Chicago School implied not only that history emerged from one epoch to another but also that ideas and institutions evolved from lower to more sophisticated forms, which many termed a "genetic approach."

The chief proponents of the Chicago School were William R. Harper in Old Testament, **Ernest Dewitt Burton** in New Testament, Shirley Jackson Case in church history, and **George W. Northrup** and **George Burman Foster** in theology and philosophy of religion. The impact of these thinkers was enormous, considering the number of people who studied at Chicago and served on faculties elsewhere, and the development of curriculum studies and publications that affected the Association of Theological Schools in the United States and **Canada** and educational developments outside North America. Among Baptists, most faculties in Northern Baptist circles included at least one Chicago-trained member, if not large dependencies: Crozer, Rochester, Central, McMaster, Newton, and the liberal arts colleges like Bucknell, Bates, Colby, Rochester, and Colgate. Likewise, in the **Southern Baptist** tradition, both Southern Baptist Theological Seminary and Southwestern Baptist Theological Seminary had faculty members trained in the Chicago School.

CHILE. The Baptist movement entered Chile in the 1890s under the leadership of Daniel T. MacDonald (1852–1939). At Cajon in 1908, the Unión Evangélica Bautista de Chile was formed; with the entry of U.S. Southern Baptists in 1917, the term "**convention**" in 1936 replaced the term "union." Under the auspices of the **Foreign Mission Board**, many churches were started in the 1930s and 1940s; an antimission schism occurred in 1940, which led to the creation of the Iglesia Bautista Nacional. At Temuco, since 1936, there is a Baptist College, with a second institution later established there, and a theological seminary operates at Santiago. In 1953, the **Association of Baptists for World Evangelism** began church planting in Chile; in 1954, **Baptist Bible Fellowship** missionaries arrived in Chile.

As of 2006, there were 326 churches and 27,781 members affiliated with the Convención Evangélica Bautista de Chile, and 41 churches with 2,206 members affiliated with the Iglesia Bautista Nacional.

CHINA. The first Baptist missionary to the Chinese people was **William Dean**, appointed by the **Baptist Board of Foreign Missions** in 1834. Dean worked in the Chinese community in Bangkok, **Siam**, and, later, transferred his work to **Hong Kong**. At the conclusion of the First Opium War in 1842, Baptist **missionary** work began in earnest in the coastal cities and South China. American Baptists concentrated in Hong Kong and Swatow, while **Southern Baptists** focused upon Canton. British Baptists first commenced a China mission at Ningbo through the General Baptist Missionary Society in 1845, but discontinued it in 1854. British interest shifted north in 1860, first at Shanghai, then at Yantai; this effort was renewed considerably after 1870 under the leadership of **Timothy Richard**.

An American Baptist, **William Ashmore**, opened a theological school at Swatow in 1871, and in 1899, a China Baptist Publication

Society was started, as Swedish Baptists also opened their mission in Shantung. In East China, American Baptists began work in Shanghai and Nanjing; in 1906, the two groups, U.S. Northern and Southern Baptists, jointly opened a seminary at Shanghai. In Szechuan Province, work also began in West China in 1889, and in 1893, missions were conducted in Central China in cities like Hankow, Hanyang, and Wuchang. Indigenous Chinese Baptist associational life emerged in the late 19th and early 20th century as a product of the missionary conferences and as a response to antiforeign uprisings: the Chekiang Baptist Association (1873) evolved into the Chekiang-Shanghai Baptist Convention in 1918, the Hakka and Ling Tong Conventions in 1925, and the China Baptist Council in 1922 as a national coordinating body.

Other Baptist groups organized mission efforts to China in the new century, including the U.S. **Baptist General Conference,** which assumed support for a mission to Manchuria, begun in 1909 and which later included Russian refugees in that province. The **Baptist Bible Fellowship** began a mission in China in 1933 as its oldest field. In the aftermath of World War II, **Baptist Mid-Missions** from the United States established a mission at Shanghai in 1947, which was closed three years later.

After the Chinese field was closed in general to foreign missionaries in 1949–1953, Chinese Baptists suffered greatly and in many cases participated in the Three Self Movement, emerging in 1986 in a postdenominational society. Some also joined the underground movement of churches. External missions involving Western support have recently been conducted through the Amity Foundation and indirectly through the China Christian Council. It is not possible to calculate the numbers of Christians in China who might consider themselves Baptists, especially since government policy dictates a "postdenominational era" of Christian presence in the country.

CHIPMAN, THOMAS HANDLEY (1756–1830). Canadian Baptist minister, born in Newport, Rhode Island. His family emigrated to Nova Scotia when he was a child. Chipman was converted under the preaching of evangelist **Henry Alline** and baptized at Horton, the oldest congregation. In his first churches, Chipman took an open communion stance, later converting to closed communion, Baptistic principles. The pastor at Bridgetown, Nova Scotia, he was a founder of the first **association** in that province in 1800. In 1809, he went to Nictaux where he served for 20 years. With **Edward Manning** and **Harris Harding**, Chipman is considered one of the patriarchs of the Baptist movement in the Canadian Maritimes.

CHRIST, DOCTRINE OF. Doctrine that is of fundamental importance among Baptists. The earliest English **confessions of faith** expressed in detailed terms the nature and importance of Jesus Christ. The divine nature and special lineage of Jesus is affirmed as well as Mary's virginal conception. With the historic creeds of the church, Christ is affirmed to have lived as a human being, to have been crucified and buried, and to have risen from the dead as Savior and Lord. As mediator of a new covenant, Jesus becomes perfectly and fully Prophet, Priest, and King of the church of God, and these roles cannot be transferred to any other. Other names given to Christ are "Doctor," "Apostle of our profession," and "Angel of the Covenant." Christ is said to govern his church, and his church expects his second coming to reign among the saints. Christ is the chief expression of the Godhead that empowers and defines the church. In contrast to the Roman Catholic doctrine that Christ gave special authorities to St. Peter, Baptist doctrine holds that Christ gave power to every congregation to receive and cast out and to excommunicate members. Twenty-one of the articles of the First London Confession dealt with Christology, and the doctrine is the subject of one major article devoted to Christ's role as mediator in the Second London Confession. The Orthodox Creed gave six articles to Christ and is similar to the First London Confession.

The Lordship of Christ is also an important concept to Baptist Christians. Early English Baptists spoke of the doctrine in terms of the "Crown Rights of the Redeemer." In other words, since Jesus redeemed his people, they in turn owe him their allegiance in every phase of their lives. Just as subjects of an earthly monarch owe that person loyalty, so also do God's people owe it to Christ to abide by his teachings. As **William Kiffin** said in 1639, "Christ's kingly power in His Church was committed not to a Hierarchy, neither to a National Presbytery, but to a Company of Saints in a Congregational Way." This idea was modified in the democratic context of the United

States and elsewhere to become the Lordship of Christ or, in the **social gospel**, the "righteous rule of God in all human affairs."

From time to time among Baptists, varying interpretations of the nature of Christ have created sharp differences of opinion. Among the **Strict Baptists** in England, for instance, a debate arose in the 1860s over whether Christ's human nature preexisted the Incarnation. This "**Sonship**" question produced at least three divisions among the Strict Baptists. In contrast, Baptists in New England found **Asa Messer**'s Arian understanding of Christ unacceptable: he held that Jesus was preeminently the Son of God, but derived of himself, not from God. Messer was forced to resign as president of Brown University in 1836.

No major modification in mainstream Baptist understanding of the doctrine of Christ occurred until the later 19th century. Under the influence of the social gospel and higher critical views of **Scripture**, the humanity of Jesus became more relevant than the question of divinity for some. Jesus was seen as an example of total submission to God and an ethical teacher who personified his ideals. Ultimately, the authority of Christ emerged when he sacrificed his life for the ideals he taught. **Liberal** Baptist theologians such as **William Newton Clarke**, **Douglas Clyde MacIntosh**, **Gerald Birney Smith**, and later process theologians held this view; related to this position was that of Michael Taylor, former principal of Northern Baptist College in Manchester, England, who in a speech to the 1971 Assembly of the Baptist Union emphasized that Jesus was fully and completely man. This had very serious repercussions in the British Baptist community and spawned a new interest in orthodox Christology. Most Baptists, however, have continued to hold orthodox views of the person and work of Jesus Christ.

CHRISTIAN, JOHN TYLER (1854–1925). Southern Baptist educator and historian, born at Lexington, Kentucky. He was educated at Bethel College and served pastorates at First Baptist, Chattanooga, Tennessee (1883–1886); East Baptist, Louisville, Kentucky (1893–1900); Second Baptist, Little Rock, Arkansas (1904–1911); and First Baptist, Hattiesburg, Mississippi (1913–1919). Christian was a prime mover in the establishment of a theological school at New Orleans, Louisiana, in 1917 and served as professor of church history at Baptist Bible Institute (1919–1925). He was a consummate collector of books and built a substantial collection at what became New Orleans Baptist Theological Seminary. His publications include *Close Communion* (1892), *Baptism in Sculpture and Art* (1907), and *History of the Baptists* (1923).

CHURCH, BAPTIST DOCTRINE OF. The Baptist understanding of the church is fundamental to Baptist theology and practice. It is based upon characteristics inherited from the Puritans and Separatists as well as some unique elements. Key passages of **Scripture** inform Baptist understanding: 1 Corinthians 1:1–17; Ephesians 4:1–8; Colossians 1:17–18; Hebrews 6:1–2; Revelation 2–3. **John Smyth**, pioneer of the English Baptist movement, characterized the church as a "true church of true believers." By this he meant to emphasize the basis of Christian experience and faith commitment of an authentic Christian fellowship. Other examples of the church, such as the Church of England, Smyth held to be "antichrist."

In the confessions of both the **General** and **Particular Baptists**, the church is primarily a local congregation, but there is recognition of the catholicity of Christ's body, namely, by the church universal.

Across the 17th and 18th centuries, a debate arose among English Baptists over the primary purpose of the church. Particular Baptists such as **John Gill** stressed the elect nature of the church and held that the primary purposes of the church were worship, nurture, and fellowship of the saints. Later in the 18th century, however, others such as **Andrew Fuller** argued that a primary purpose of the church and the Christian **ministry** was to preach the gospel, to offer salvation to nonbelievers. This position has been widely regarded as "evangelical Calvinism" and opened the Baptist movement to placing a high value upon **missions** and **evangelism**.

Important to the Baptist concept of the church are **confessions of faith** and **covenants**. From the Puritan and Separatist traditions, Baptists followed the practice of writing confessional documents that described their theological beliefs. The purpose of confessions was to hold out the precise details of belief for new members and **discipline** of errant members, and to assert the identity of a congregation among other churches in the community. A covenant, on the other hand, served as a commitment between members and before

God concerning membership responsibilities and ethics. The purpose of the covenant was to bind together voluntarily the members of a congregation to each other.

As early as the 17th century, Baptist theological writers have recognized the mixture of persons in the church body. Some are given to pure doctrine and others to error; no church is perfect. But Baptists have equally believed that each church is called of God to be faithful and contains under the Lordship of **Christ** all that is needful to be the church.

From the doctrine of the church flows the Baptist understanding of the **sacraments/ordinances** and mission. *See also* DISCIPLINE, CHURCH; POLITY, BAPTIST.

CHURCH, PHARCELLUS (1801–1886). American Baptist minister, born at Geneva, New York. Church graduated from the Hamilton Literary and Theological Institution and served the church at Poultney, Vermont, for three years, from 1825 to 1828. In 1836, he became pastor at First Baptist, Rochester, New York, where he spearheaded a relocation movement for the Baptist college in Hamilton, New York. When this failed, Church helped to organize the Baptist-related University of Rochester and Rochester Theological Seminary. For a brief time, he was pastor at First Baptist, Montreal, Lower **Canada** (1852–1853). Church was a close friend of **William Colgate**, a New York manufacturer, who invited him to experiment with what was probably the first set of rubber pantaloons for baptismal services. Church wrote on a wide variety of topics, including *The Philosophy of Benevolence* (1836), *Permanency of the Pastoral Relation* (1845), and *Danger and Death of Missionaries* (1847).

CHURCHING. *See* DISCIPLINE, CHURCH.

CLARENDON CODE. A series of English parliamentary statutes passed between 1661 and 1665 to nullify religious dissent, named for Edward Hyde (1609–1674), the first Earl of Clarendon and lord chancellor of England, though his actual influence on this legislation was indirect at best. The first statute, The Corporation Act (1661), required members of municipal bodies to take the oaths of supremacy and allegiance and stated that future applicants were to have taken the sacrament in the Church of England in the 12 months prior to their appointment. This measure made it impossible for Baptists and other dissenters to have employment or commissions in government. A second law, the Act of Uniformity (1662), required that all Anglican clergy fully consent to every prescription in the *Book of Common Prayer*. This included all university professors, schoolmasters, and private tutors. Imprisonment and severe fines were levied for non-compliance. Baptists and other dissenters were thus effectively barred from university and educational posts. The Conventicle Act (1664) disciplined all persons over 16 years old who attended a **Nonconformist** service at which more than four people joined the family in attendance. Repeated offenders could be transported out of England for seven years. Under this statute, many Baptists had to resort to clandestine meetings as their meetinghouses were seized. A fourth statute, the Five Mile Act (1665), targeted clergy and lecturers who might try to return to a town in which they had previously served in the **ministry**, unless they took an oath not to alter the government of the church or state. Those ministers who had left the Church of England to pursue Nonconformist ministries could thus not legally serve in the same communities.

The result of this total legislation was to exact much difficulty and privation upon numerous dissenters and in particular the Baptists. In 1667, Clarendon was dismissed as lord chancellor and limited relief ensued for Nonconformists in the intriguing policies of King James II, who attempted to restore Catholicism under the guise of being more tolerant toward Anglican Nonconformity. The enforcers of the Clarendon Code were a combination of Royal troops and Anglican clergy.

CLARKE, JOHN (1609–1676). English and, later, American Baptist minister and physician, born in Suffolk. He attended a university, most likely on the continent, and became a physician in London in the 1630s. Clarke was a pious man, much involved in local church life. In Puritan Massachusetts and New Hampshire in the 1630s, he leaned toward some of the teachings of Ann Hutchinson and the Antinomians, drawing the suspicion of the authorities. He joined a company of settlers who ultimately purchased land from the Indians and established in 1638 a colony on Aquidneck near Rhode Island, which they named Newport. There Clarke established himself as a leading citizen. He was active in the town church, and when it experienced internal conflicts in 1643–1644, he helped to reshape it as a Baptist congregation (becoming the second oldest in the United States). In 1652, he wrote *Ill Newes from New England*, which made the case against religious persecution as he had witnessed it in the instance of **Obadiah Holmes**. Clarke returned to England for 12 years, among other duties to enable the colony of Rhode Island to obtain a charter. He was the principal author of the Rhode Island charter, which guaranteed religious rights and liberties, though he also personally cherished the vision of a Christian commonwealth. In 1669, following five years in the Rhode Island Assembly, he was designated deputy colonial governor. Theologically, Clarke was a consistent Calvinist, and he was a gifted student of biblical languages. More than anyone else, Clarke deserved the title "Father of American Baptists."

CLARKE, WILLIAM NEWTON (1841–1911). American and Canadian Baptist minister and theologian, born at North Brookfield, Massachusetts. He was educated at Hamilton College and the Theological Department of Madison University. In 1863, he entered the pastoral ministry at Keene, New Hampshire, followed by the First Baptist Church, Newton Centre, Massachusetts. In 1880, Clarke moved to Montreal to be **pastor** at Olivet Baptist Church, which he served for 11 prosperous years. In 1883, he became the first New Testament professor at Toronto Baptist College, remaining there through 1887. That year, he returned to the American scene as pastor of First Baptist Church in Hamilton, New York. Upon the sudden death of Madison University president and theologian **Ebenezer Dodge**, Clarke stepped in and became the professor of theology at what became Colgate Theological Seminary. In several important works, including *An Outline of Christian Theology* (1909), Clarke pioneered the theological position of **evangelical liberalism**. At his death, he was one of the most highly respected and quoted theologians in North America. Clarke's autobiography, *Sixty Years with the Bible* (1909), is considered a classic in defining the transition to the New Theology.

CLEARWATERS, RICHARD VOLLEY (1900–1996). American Baptist and, later, **independent Baptist** minister and educator, born at Wilmot, Kansas. He was educated at Moody Bible Institute, Kalamazoo College (B.A.), Northern Baptist Theological Seminary (Th.B.), and the University of Chicago (M.A.). He served student pastorates at Wilton Center, Illinois, and at Lawton and Kalamazoo, Michigan (1929–1935). In 1935, Clearwaters became pastor at Calvary Baptist Church, Cedar Rapids, Iowa. In 1940, he accepted the call to serve Fourth Baptist Church, Minneapolis, Minnesota, which he served until 1982. Clearwaters worked with **William B. Riley** to lead the Minnesota Baptist Convention away from the control of the Northern Baptist Convention (NBC), which Riley thought was dominated by modernists. Clearwaters taught and served as an administrator in Riley's Northwestern Schools, 1942–1957.

With the passing of Riley, Clearwaters aligned himself with the Conservative Baptist Fellowship in the NBC and was one of the founders of the **Conservative Baptist Association**, of which he served as president in 1951–1953. In 1956, he founded in his church Central Baptist Seminary, intended to be a major institution of the Conservative Baptist movement; he was president of the school from 1956 to 1987. A schism occurred in the denomination, however, leaving Clearwaters alienated from the Conservative Baptist movement and the school became an independent seminary. In the early 1950s, Clearwaters led in the reorganization of Pillsbury Academy, formerly affiliated with the Minnesota Baptist Convention, and he helped to found the Pillsbury Baptist Bible College at Owatonna, Minnesota. In 1942, he was awarded the honorary doctorate by Northern Baptist Theological Seminary.

CLEMENTS, KEITH WINSTON (1943–). British Baptist minister, theologian, and **ecumenical** leader, born at Guilin, China, the son of Baptist missionaries. He was educated at Oxford and Cambridge Universities, earning the M.A. in theology at each and a B.D. at Oxford and, later in life, the Ph.D. at the University of Bristol for his accumulated work. Clements served Downend Baptist Church in Bristol 1971–1977 and then joined the faculty of Bristol Baptist College as tutor in theology (1977–1990). A leading theologian among British Baptists, he was editor of the Baptist Historical Society and active in doctrine and ecumenical affairs for the **Baptist World Alliance**. In 1990, he became secretary for the Council of Churches of Britain and

Ireland, and from 1997 to 2005 he was general secretary of the Conference of European Churches in Geneva. Clements was much involved in the World Council of Churches, serving on its Faith and Order Commission. He became an authority on the work of German theologians Frederich Schleiermacher and Dietrich Bonhoeffer and published critical biographies of each. He has been a scholar in residence or lecturer at Whitley College in Melbourne, Australia, and at several institutions in the United States. In 1993, Clements was Selected Preacher at Cambridge University. Among his published works are *A Patriotism for Today:* (1986) and *Faith on the Frontier: A Biography of J.H. Oldham* (1999).

CLIFFORD, JOHN (1836–1923). English Baptist minister and denominational leader, born at Sawley, England. Clifford was educated at Midland Baptist College and the University of London. A **General Baptist**, he served the Praed Street Baptist Church in Paddington and was a prime mover in uniting the old General and **Particular Baptist** factions in the **Baptist Union of Great Britain and Ireland** (BU). Clifford applied the principles of the **social gospel** in his ministry, and as president of the BU, he advocated progressive thought, in keeping with the intellectual and moral trends of a progressive era. He was considered the chief adversary of **Charles H. Spurgeon** in the theological strife of the BU in the 1880s, though the two men were openly cordial to each other. Clifford was elected the first president of the **Baptist World Alliance**, 1905–1911. Clifford was a prodigious author, completing over 70 works, the most enduring of which are *The Attitude of Men of Science to Christianity* (1874), *Is Life Worth Living?* (1880), *The Free Churches of London: Their Faith and Future* (1895), *Socialism and the Teaching of Christ* (1898*), and *Clericalism in State Education* (1912). In recognition of Clifford's contribution as a Progressive English Baptist, **Australian** Baptists named their publication arm "Clifford Press" in 1947.

CLINTON, WILLIAM JEFFERSON (1946–). Baptist layman and 42nd president of the United States, born in Hope, Arkansas. Originally named William Jefferson Blythe III, Clinton was educated at Georgetown University, Yale University Law School, and as a Rhodes Scholar, at Oxford University. He taught at the University of

Arkansas Law School in the 1970s. Clinton was elected attorney general (1976) and governor of Arkansas (1978), and in 1992 he was elected president of the United States on the Democratic ticket, with fellow Baptist Albert Gore of Tennessee as vice president. Clinton served two terms in the White House, after which he has been a popular platform speaker, a humanitarian projects fund-raiser, and advisor to the presidential ambitions of his wife, Hillary Rodham Clinton.

As a Baptist, Clinton began attending Park Avenue Baptist Church in Hot Springs, Arkansas, and at 10 years old, publicly professed his faith and was baptized in that church. Later during his time as governor, Clinton joined Emmanuel Baptist Church in Little Rock and sang in the choir. As president, many assumed he would join First Baptist Church in Washington, D.C., where **Harry Truman** had attended; however, he followed his wife to Foundry United Methodist Church where they were active. Because of his personal difficulties and Congressional impeachment, Clinton was considered somewhat of a pariah by **Southern Baptists**, although he was close friends with American Baptist confidants like **Anthony Campolo** and Robert Seiple, the latter whom he named as an ambassador at large for **human rights**. Former president Clinton took an active role with former president **James (Jimmy) Carter** in organizing the New Covenant Baptists in Atlanta in January 2008.

CLOSED COMMUNION. *See* LORD'S SUPPER.

CLOUGH, JOHN EVERETT (1836–1910). American Baptist missionary, born at Frewsburg, New York. Clough was educated at Burlington College and Upper Iowa University, after which he was a schoolteacher. He became interested in foreign **mission** service after hearing **William Dean** tell of his China experiences, and he was accepted by the **American Baptist Missionary Union** for **India**. The Cloughs arrived in Nellore in 1865, and a year later moved to Ongole to work with the Telugus. His work prospered greatly, and the extra demands of his mission almost broke Clough's health. In 1876, a famine occurred that affected 60 million people; Clough devised a plan to employ hundreds of workers in the construction of the Buckingham Canal and in food distribution. Hundreds of converts were made from among the Telugus, and in one day, July 3, 1878, Clough supervised the **baptism** of 2,222 persons in the Gundlacumma River at Velumpilly. Twenty-four native ministers were ordained on April 16, 1880, to meet the needs of the Ongole field. In 1894, he married Emma Rauschenbusch (1859–1940), sister of Walter, and during a second major famine in India in 1896–1897, Clough again set up a work camp to organize relief and employment. During this period, he experimented with some of **Walter Rauchenbusch**'s ideas concerning the **social gospel**. At the conclusion of his active career, Clough was highly regarded in missionary annals and enjoyed heroic status in India. He was the principal literary exponent of the great revival in *From Darkness to Light: A Story of the Telugu Awakening* (1882), and his own story was told by his wife in *Social Christianity in the Orient: The Story of a Man, a Mission and a Movement* (1914).

COATS, THOMAS (1809–1883). Scottish Baptist industrialist and philanthropist, born at Paisley. He joined the family textile firm of J. and P. Coats and greatly expanded its enterprise in thread making, employing 10,000 persons in his mills. He was particularly interested in the engineering side of the business that he ran with his brother, Peter, for a number of years. As an outgrowth of his industrial success, Thomas Coats developed a philanthropic interest in education and his religious faith. In 1873, he was elected chairman of the Paisley School Board, and he enabled a number of Scottish Baptist projects. At the time of his death, Coats bequeathed 1.3 million pounds to Christian endeavor. In 1894, the Storie Street Baptist Church in Paisley built a new edifice and named it in honor of the benefactor, Thomas Coats Memorial Church. The church is a striking example of Gothic architecture and a formal liturgical tradition.

COFFEEHOUSE MEETINGS. Beginning in the late 17th century, **Nonconformist** ministerial gatherings began to associate in coffeehouses, which for social purposes rivaled the public houses and provided an alternative to alcoholic consumption. Baptists in London began meeting this way, and the result was the formation of permanent **associations** and funds. In 1714, **Benjamin Stinton** established a group at the Hanover Coffeehouse in London, composed of both **General** and **Particular Baptists**. This soon divided in 1724, and the Particular Baptists opened their own ministerium at the Gloucestershire Coffeehouse. The Hanover Coffeehouse club accomplished several worthwhile objectives, including assisting French refugees after the revocation of the Edict of Nantes (October 1685), improvement of the overall Baptist reputation by discouraging public disputes with radical groups like the Quakers, the repair of the Horsleydown **Baptistery** for use of the London congregations, and the formation of a united Baptist **ministry**, which eventually would join other Nonconformists in the **Three Dissenting Denominations**. The Baptist Board met at the Jamaica Coffeehouse, Coles Coffeehouse, and Blackwell Coffeehouse between 1767 and 1820. The General Baptist Fund and the Particular Baptist Fund were direct results of the respective coffeehouse meetings, and the establishment of the Sunday School Society was at the King's Head, Swithin's Alley. At times, the Crown and the Church of England held the coffeehouse gatherings in contempt, such as the one kept by James Jones in Southwark in the 17th century, as seditious associations.

COLBY, GARDNER (1810–1879). American Baptist philanthropist, born at Bowdoinham, Maine. Colby opened a dry goods store in Boston in 1830, eventually becoming involved in the **China** trade and real estate speculation in Boston. During the Civil War, he amassed a fortune in producing woolen clothing for the Union Army, and thereafter he became president of the Wisconsin Central Railroad, which he helped to build in the northern plains states. Colby used his money to support several educational institutions, including Newton Theological Institution and Waterville College, the latter of which changed its name in his honor after receiving a gift of $50,000. Colby was also a trustee of Brown University and was involved in the work of the **American Baptist Missionary Union**.

COLGATE, WILLIAM (1783–1857). American industrialist and Baptist lay leader, born at Hollingbourne, England. In his early years, Colgate was apprenticed to John Slidell of New York in soap making; within three years, he started his own company and perfected processes for scenting soaps and manufacturing various soap and petroleum products. His interest in the church was manifested in his generous support of scores of Baptist **voluntary** causes, from home **missions** to education and **Bible** translation. He was a member of most of the societies in the Northern Baptist community, and he helped to sustain several projects, including a translation of **Scripture** by the American Bible Union in 1850. Colgate was one of the leading philanthropists in the Baptist tradition, and his work was carried on through his two sons, James (1818–1904) and Samuel (1822–1897). The legacy of the Colgate family in higher education was honored in 1888 when Madison University in Hamilton, New York, was renamed Colgate University.

COLLIER, THOMAS (fl. 1650–1690). English Baptist minister, born in Wessex. Little is known about Collier's early life. His opponents referred to him as a "base, mechanical fellow, a husbandman," which suggests he was a farmer and lay preacher. At one time, Collier was expelled from Guernsey and, later, imprisoned at Portsmouth. He was ordained at Bridgwater in 1654. He evangelized widely and formed an **association** of churches in the West. In 46 years, Collier published as many tracts, engaged in significant debates at Axbridge and Wiveliscombe, and championed the rights of Jews. In 1655, he was appointed a general **messenger** to the associated churches of Wessex, and in 1656 and 1678, he issued **confessions of faith**. His emphases kept the churches of the West from fanatical directions, particularly the **Fifth Monarchy** ideas of **Henry Jessey**. In the 1660s, he was involved in planting new churches, in 1672 taking out a license for North Bradley. Collier issued a systematic theology of sorts, called *Body of Divinity*, which contained anti-Calvinistic thinking and which caused his enemies to refer to him as an Arian and Socinian. Five prominent London **Particular Baptists**, including **William Kiffin** and Nehemiah Cox (fl. 1670), visited Collier about 1676 to moderate his theological views, apparently without success. Shortly thereafter in 1677, the Particular Baptists issued the Second London Confession of Faith to affirm the theology of the Westminster Confession. Collier convened a similar meeting of the association in the West and issued yet another confession in 1691. Despite his often brash behavior, Collier was the most significant figure among Baptists in the West before 1689, and he survived to see the effects of toleration. Among his several published works are *A Brief Discovery of the Corruption of the Ministry of the Church of England* (1647) and *A Looking-Glass for the Quakers* (1657).

COLOMBIA. Initial Baptist missions in Colombia began in 1941 when Southern Baptists J. L. Hart (1877–1966) and Henry Schweinsberg (1910–1996) investigated the possibilities of church development in Colombia. Schweinsberg began the first congregation in 1942 at Barranquilla. An initial coalition of churches formed in 1949, the Convención Colombo-Venezolana, and, later, a separate Convención Bautista Colombiana formed in 1952. The Convención Bautista Colombiana publishes *Heraldo Bautista* (Baptist Herald) (1942–) and has supported a theological school at Cali since 1952. In 1929, the **Association of Baptists for World Evangelism** established churches resulting in the Iglesia Bautista Independiente. In 1971, the **Baptist Bible Fellowship** entered Colombia, and the **American Baptist Association** has a mission in the country.

As of 2006, there were 152 churches and 32,000 members affiliated with the Convención Bautista Columbiana. A theological school, Seminario Teológico Bautista Internacional, is located at Cali.

COLPORTEURS. Beginning in the 19th century and first associated with the **Bible** society movement in Britain and the United States, **Scripture** distribution agents were sent forth to conduct **evangelical** missions in Europe, Africa, Asia, and Latin America. A significant number of them were Baptists and remained in the field to start churches, notably **J. G. Oncken** in Germany and James Thompson in Latin America. The **American Baptist Publication Society** employed numerous colporteurs from the 1830s to conduct horseback missions in conjunction with the **American Baptist Home Mission Society** in the western and southern states. The first of the horse-drawn colportage wagons was placed in service in Jackson, Michigan, in 1897, with about 80 others put in service over the following two decades. The wagons contained storage room for bedding, clothes, food, and a tent and cook stove. In 1891, the first railroad **chapel cars** were placed in service by the **mission** agencies. In 1906, a chapel cruiser boat, the *Mamie Beal*, was commissioned in Coos Bay, Oregon, with five others which plied the western coastal routes in California, Oregon, and Washington through 1921. Chapel car automobiles were used in the United States beginning in 1923. Outside the United States, other Baptists used the methods of the colporteurs, including **Luke Bickel** in **Japan**, who commanded the boat *Fukuin*

Maru, and the **Evangelical Baptist Mission** in Mali, which in 1960 employed the *Niger Gospel Boat* on the Niger River. *See also* CHAPEL CAR EVANGELISM.

COLUMBIA BASIN MISSION. An independent **fundamentalist** Baptist domestic mission founded in 1940. The work was started to evangelize small towns in the Pacific Northwestern United States, specifically the region created by the Columbia Basin Irrigation Project of the U.S. government. **Mission** works were established in Washington State in 1940 and in Idaho in 1941. With the formation of the **Fellowship of Baptists for Home Missions** in 1950, the Columbia Basin Mission merged its efforts with that larger work.

COMER, JOHN (1704–1734). American Baptist minister, born at Boston, Massachusetts. Originally apprenticed in the glover's trade, Comer sought an education and was assisted by Increase Mather at Harvard; he also attended Yale College as its first Baptist student. Comer was ordained by his uncle, **Elisha Callendar**, and served the church in Newport, Rhode Island, 1726–1729. Comer advocated the "sixth principle" of the **laying on of hands**, which proved to be unpopular. He moved to Swansea to a congregation that accepted this view. His death at 30 deprived the early New England Baptists of an educated leader who showed promise among the urban churches. Comer's diary, published in 1893, is an important source for New England Baptist history in the first half of the 18th century.

COMMUNION, HOLY. *See* LORD'S SUPPER.

COMPERE, LEE (1789–1871). English Baptist and, later, Southern Baptist minister and missionary, born in Harborough, England. Compere studied theology with **John Sutclif** and embarked upon a mission to **Jamaica** in 1815. Attempting to work at Old Harbor and Kingston, he succumbed to the tropical climate and went to the United States in 1817. With the assistance of **Richard Furman**, he made further studies and moved about the South conducting **missions** with the Indians and starting churches. Remarkably, he was present at the formation of most of the early Baptist state **conventions** in the South, including South Carolina, Georgia, Alabama, and

Mississippi. While serving as superintendent of the **General Missionary Convention**'s Creek Mission in Alabama in the 1820s, he prepared a complete vocabulary and translated portions of **Scripture** into the Creek language.

CONE, SPENCER HOUGHTON (1785–1855). American Baptist minister, born at Princeton, New Jersey. Cone studied at Princeton College and took up a career in the theater. He served as a journalist in the War of 1812 and wrote in support of the James Madison presidential administration. Eventually, he entered the Baptist **ministry**, preaching at a small church in the Washington, D.C., Navy Yard. His success led to his appointment as chaplain to the U.S. House of Representatives, 1815–1816. Cone became **pastor** of the Baptist church in Alexandria, Virginia (1816–1823), moving in 1837 to the Oliver Street Church in New York City, which he served for 18 years (1823–1841), and finally served First Baptist, New York (1841–1855). With Deacon **William Colgate**, Cone assisted the formation of many benevolent enterprises, housing the **American Baptist Home Mission Society**'s office in his church, and was president of the General Missionary (Triennial) Convention from 1838–1841. Cone's most important literary achievement is *The Terms of Communion at the Lord's Table* (1824).

CONFESSIONS OF FAITH. Historically, Baptists have understood themselves as "noncreedal." By this is meant that the historic creeds of the churches are nonbinding on the conscience and thus may not be used for **discipline**, worship, or definitional purposes. Rather, Baptists affirm **liberty of conscience** and prefer to interpret the **Bible** as guided by the Holy Spirit and the church. Confessions of faith, however, are a popular means of expressing doctrinal definition and the theological traditions of congregations, **associations,** and institutions. The idea of a confession of faith derives from a **voluntary** statement of specific beliefs. Based on Matthew 28:19–20, Baptists believe that Christians have a responsibility to witness to their faith and to agree on matters of common understanding.

The first confessional statements were issued by individuals, notably **John Smyth**, the se-Baptist. Smyth wrote a series of 20 doctrinal assertions in 1610 (and probably another in 1611) to define his beliefs for possible dialogue with the Dutch Mennonite community. This became a pattern among early English **General** and **Particular Baptists**, as they sought to differentiate themselves from heterodoxy on the one hand and also from each other.

The primary examples of English Baptist confessions of faith of the 17th century were the First and Second London Confessions. The First London Confession was issued by seven congregations in the greater London area to define Baptist beliefs against critics who slandered Baptists as Münsterites. It contained 52 articles on topics such as Jesus Christ, the church, the **ordinances**, and the magistracy. In 1677, the Second London Confession was written to demonstrate Baptist theological affinity with Presbyterians and Congregationalists as all sects faced persecution under the **Clarendon Code**. The Second London Confession was based upon the Westminster Confession of Faith and was decidedly more Calvinistic than the First London Confession of 1644. It contained 32 articles. Other important 17th-century confessional statements included the Midland Confession (1655), the Somerset Confession (1656), and the Orthodox Creed (1679).

In the American colonies, the Second London Confession evolved as the Philadelphia Baptist Confession, first issued by Benjamin Franklin (1706–1790) in 1742. A number of congregations put forward confessions of faith, notably the First Baptist Church of Boston (1665) and the First Baptist Church of Charleston, South Carolina.

In order to provide a uniform format, if not a theological tradition, publishers issued many editions of the Philadelphia Confession along with standard covenants and rules of order. In 1833, the New Hampshire Baptist Convention authorized the preparation of a new confession, and this became a popular doctrinal statement for many local churches, notably in the southern states. The New Hampshire Confession affirmed concepts of biblical inerrancy and spoke only of the local congregation when defining the church.

As the debate over the authority of **Scripture** broke out in the early 20th century, various groups created confessional statements that asserted high views of Scripture and the autonomy of local congregations. **Strict Baptists** in Britain, **Fundamental** and **Conservative Baptists** in the United States, and **Fellowship** Baptists in **Canada**, to name the major groups, still adhere to confessional statements, usually based upon the 1689 London Confession or the 1832 New Hampshire Confession or some derived statement. American Baptists rejected any confession save the New Testament, and **Southern Baptists** adopted the "**Baptist Faith and Message**," which has metamorphosed through three editions: 1925, 1963, and 2000. Likewise, institutions also wrote doctrinal statements into their identities to serve as protocols for governance. Examples of the use of theological statements in the institutional setting were Spurgeon's College in Great Britain (1856) and Southern Baptist Theological Seminary (1859), Northern Baptist Theological Seminary (1913), and The Eastern Baptist Theological Seminary (1925) in the United States. Most fundamentalist schools and Baptist Bible colleges followed this pattern as well. While the confession of faith has not usually been binding upon church membership, it has been used to define faculty orthodoxy and assess missionary appointments. The Southern Baptist Convention has made the "Baptist Faith and Message" (2000) binding upon all convention agencies and related organizations.

CONGO, DEMOCRATIC REPUBLIC OF. Formerly known as Zaire, and prior to that, the Belgian Congo, Baptist missionaries from the **Baptist Missionary Society** began work along the Congo River in 1878. At São Salvador, Lukolela, Bolobo, Yakusu, Leopoldville, and Kimpese in the east, British Baptists focused upon church planting and education and created a system of schools. In 1884, the Livingstone Inland Mission offered its Congo field to the **American Baptist Missionary Union** (ABMU), and the ABMU accepted the seven stations and nine missionaries. The primary outreach of the American Baptist mission was at Banza Manteke, Palabala, and, later, at Vanga and Sona Bata. A significant revival broke out at Banza Manteke in 1886 under the ministry of **Henry Richards**; a thousand converts were won in a few weeks in what came to be known as the "Pentecost on the Congo." In 1929, American Baptists opened a station at Kikongo, which led to hundreds of converts. Baptist missionaries from Sweden conducted a successful mission in the Bandulu region, and, later, the **Conservative Baptist** Foreign Mission Society (CBFMS) in Goma and **Baptist Mid-Missions** (BMM) to the east and north of Kikwit, where they have established a **Bible** school and medical work.

Baptist missions in the Congo grew organizationally by the turn of the century. In 1903, the General Conference of Missionaries of the Protestant Societies Working in Congo Land was organized and included Baptists, a native council was created in 1936, and, later, the American and British Baptist work joined in the collective efforts of the Protestant Council of the Congo. Education became a primary investment of Baptists in the Congo, including the Lower Congo Training School, which was merged in 1908 with the Congo Evangelical Training Institution at Kimpese. In 1933, the school became the Ecole de Pasteurs et d'Instituteurs (Pastors' and Teachers' School), offering a theological course, a Bible college curriculum, and a teacher training course.

Following the Congo's independence from Belgium in 1960, and subsequent Protestant ecumenical reorganization of the Eglise du Christ au Zaire, missionary and indigenous work has been divided according to "communities," with three Baptist communities originally emerging: Communauté Baptiste du Bas-Fleuve (CBBF), Communauté Baptiste du Moyen-Fleuve (CBMF), and Communauté Baptiste du Haut-Congo (CBHC). After further negotiations, the Communauté Baptiste du Fleuve Zaire (CBFZ) was formed, which related to the British Baptist Missionary Society; the Communauté Baptiste du Zaire Ouest (CBZO), which related to the **American Baptist Foreign Mission Society**; and the Communauté Baptiste au Bandundu, which related to the Swedish Baptists. **Independent Baptist** congregations, sponsored by BMM and other agencies, have existed since 1921 at several locations in the country, including Sibut, Crampel, and Ouango. The CBFMS began a mission in 1946, centered in Kivu and Shaba provinces. The **Baptist Bible Fellowship** began a mission in Congo in 1957.

As of 2006 there were 30 churches and 24,371 members affiliated with the Communauté Baptiste au Bandundu; 274 churches and 93,800 members affiliated with the Communauté Baptiste au Kivu; 600 churches and 252,000 members affiliated with the Communauté Baptiste du Zaire Ouest; 221 churches with 274,092 members affiliated with the Communauté Baptiste du Fleuve Zaire; and 15 churches with 15,488 churches affiliated with the Communauté des Eglises Baptistes Autonomes. There are seven Baptist-related institutions in the Congo located at Bendela, Bolobo, Kimpese, Kinshasa, and Kisangani.

CONGO, REPUBLIC OF. Baptists are not numerically strong in this nation, which was formerly the French Congo. In the early colonial history of the Congo, the U.S. **American Baptist Missionary Union** organized churches, which became part of the Evangelical Church of the Congo. The Örebo Mission of Baptists in Sweden established itself in the north of the Congo, and significant growth was seen in the 20th century, including a **Bible college** established in 1954. **Baptist Mid-Missions** likewise assumed responsibility for a mission in Congo in 1953, which had previously belonged to the Unevangelized Fields Mission and the Congo Gospel Mission.

With a change of governments in 1978, mission work ceased and Baptists were outlawed. What churches survived became part of the Evangelical Church of the Congo, which numbers over 50 churches and 2,000 members.

CONGREGATION OF THE DEAD. *See* STRICT BAPTISTS.

CONNER, WALTER THOMAS (1877–1952). Southern Baptist theologian and educator, born in Cleveland County, Arkansas. He was educated at Hardin Simmons and Baylor Universities and Southwestern Baptist Theological Seminary. Conner also studied at Rochester Theological Seminary and the University of Chicago; he earned the Ph.D. from Southern Baptist Theological Seminary. He was professor of theology at Southwestern Seminary from 1910 to 1949 and gave shape to its theological position. The author of 15 books, Conner was the link between Southwestern Seminary founders **Benajah H. Carroll** and **Lee R. Scarborough**, and the more modern Southern Baptist conservative evangelical stance. His position included an understanding of the inspiration of **Scripture** without espousing a theory such as inerrancy, and a balanced view of the divine and human elements in the **Bible**. His publications were far ranging, covering doctrinal issues, the Holy Spirit, and the cults, especially the Jehovah's Witnesses and Mary Baker Eddy (1821–1910). Conner was one of the most respected theologians of

his era in the **Southern Baptist Convention** (SBC); among his protégés were James Leo Garrett and **James William McClendon**. Conner authored *Christian Doctrine* (1924) and *The Work of the Holy
Spirit* (1949).

**CONSERVATIVE BAPTIST ASSOCIATION OF AMERICA
(CBA).** A fellowship of autonomous congregations that originally
withdrew from the Northern Baptist Convention (NBC) in the
United States in 1947. For two decades previous to the schism, numerous **pastors** expressed opposition to the trend of Northern Baptists toward more **liberal** interpretations of **Scripture** and historic
Baptistic theology. Of major concern in the 1930s and 1940s was the
"inclusive policy" of the **American Baptist Foreign Mission Society**, which allowed for missionaries of widely differing theological
positions to be commissioned for international service. This led to
the first stage of the Conservative Baptist movement, a Fundamental Baptist Fellowship among NBC churches, and subsequently, a
foreign mission organization. For many years, Conservative Baptist
congregations were forbidden to have fellowship with the American
(Northern) Baptist Convention. The Fundamental Baptist Fellowship became in the 1940s the Conservative Baptist Fellowship, and
for many years maintained ties with the Conservative Baptist Foreign Mission Society and what became the Conservative Baptist Association. In 1961, a schism occurred and the "hard core" Conservative Baptist Fellowship broke its ties with the Conservative Baptist
movement.

Comprising what has been known as the Conservative Baptist
movement are the CBA, the Conservative Baptist Foreign Mission
Society (1943; after 1994, CB International, and since 2005, World
Venture), and the Conservative Baptist Home Mission Society (1950;
now restructured as Delta Ministries, Mission to the Americas, and
Titus Ministries-church renewal); none of which are controlled by the
CBA. There are 20 state and area **associations**, representing 29 states
and organized into nine regions. Within North America, Conservative
Baptists define themselves as "a covenantal fellowship of regional
church associations." Foreign mission work is conducted in 46 coun-
tries. Also related to the movement are three seminaries: Western
Conservative Baptist Seminary in Portland, Oregon; Denver Semi-

nary in Colorado; and, with the **Baptist General Conference**, the Conservative Baptist Seminary of the East in Dresher, Pennsylvania. Undergraduate schools include Judson Baptist College in Portland, Oregon; Southwestern Baptist Bible College in Phoenix, Arizona; New England Bible College in Portland, Maine; and International College in Honolulu, Hawaii. Headquarters for the major Conservative Baptist organizations are in Denver and Littleton, Colorado. The CBA Association publishes the *Conservative Baptist* (1971–) and, as of 2006, includes 1,200 churches and about 200,000 members. *See also* BAPTIST WORLD MISSION.

CONSERVATIVE TRADITION. Conservative, or conservative evangelical, tradition can be identified in North American Baptist thought at about the turn of the 20th century. As schools and writers questioned time-honored values such as the authority of **Scripture**, others responded by "conserving" the great truths of the faith. After the publication of the *Fundamentals* in 1915–1919 and the formation of the World's Christian Fundamentals Association in 1919, many Conservatives took the name "**fundamentalist**" because it identified them with a particular set of doctrinal formulae. In the 1920s, fundamentalism evolved as a shrill and schismatic critique of **liberalism** and modernism. For many this was too strong a position, and they sought a moderating stance, which became "conservative," and, later, under the influence of Baptist theologians like **Carl F. H. Henry**, "conservative evangelical." Specifically this means a doctrinal stance that is orthodox, **evangelical**, and not dogmatic in nonessential areas such as the inerrancy of **Scripture** and the second advent of Christ. In the area of social ethics, Conservatives tend to support right to life, traditional marriages, heterosexuality, Christlike speech, and abstention from the use of tobacco, alcoholic beverages, and the illegal use of drugs. Manifestations of a conservative stance among Baptists are found in the moderate **Southern Baptist** movement, the American Baptist evangelical tradition, the Conservative Baptist Association, and several **black Baptist** groups in the United States. *See also* FUNDAMENTALISM, BAPTIST; LIBERAL TRADITION.

CONTINENTAL BAPTISTS. Related to the **Reformed Baptist** movement, a group of Calvinistic Baptists located in the southern

United States began to hold conferences in 1981 to revive Calvinistic theology and the thought of **Charles H. Spurgeon** in particular. One of the leading **pastors** in the movement, Ronald McKinney, began a periodical in 1978 titled *Sword and the Trowel*, which emulated Spurgeon's paper by the same name. McKinney also sponsored conferences on Baptist theology. McKinney's group for a time was close to the Reformed Baptist position, but preferred the First London Confession of Faith (1646) to the 1689 Confession. Further distinguishing McKinney's group was an affirmation of preaching and a broader doctrine of the church. Referred to as the "Sword and Trowel Baptists," they adopted the name "Continental Baptists" in 1983 and followed an associational **polity**. Many of the approximately 40 congregations also share an affinity with the **General Association of Regular Baptist Churches**.

CONVENTIONS. Use of the terminology "convention" among Baptists arose in the United States in the first decades of the 19th century. Probably derived from the political use of the term to designate a gathering of persons according to a certain perspective or with a common agenda, exemplified in the Constitutional Convention of 1787 and the Hartford Convention of 1814, "convention" gained use among Baptists as a means of organizing themselves at the national and then state levels. In 1813, **Luther Rice** recalled that he had originated the idea of a national convention to which state conventions or auxiliaries would relate. The result was the **General Missionary Convention of the Baptist Denomination in the United States of America for Foreign Missions**, also known as the Baptist General Convention or the General Missionary Convention; it became a model for further organizations in the United States and, globally, where American missionary work has been conducted. The first state convention was the South Carolina Baptist Convention (1821), of which **Richard Furman** was a leading proponent.

In **Canada** the convention terminology was borrowed from U.S. experience, and the first provincial use of the term was the Baptist Convention of Nova Scotia, New Brunswick, and Prince Edward Island in 1846. Subsequent provincial conventions were formed in the central provinces as follows: the Regular Baptist Missionary Convention (1854) and the Canada Baptist Missionary Convention East

(1858); these two were united in 1888 as the Baptist Convention of Ontario and Quebec. In the western provinces, the first convention formed was the Baptist Convention of Manitoba (1880), which was reorganized in 1884 as the Baptist Convention of Manitoba and the Northwest, followed by the British Columbia Baptist Convention in 1897. The Baptist Convention of Western Canada was formed in 1907 to unite the mission programs of the scattered churches; it became in 1909 the Baptist Union of Western Canada. Subsequent to the formation of the Baptist Union, separate conventions were organized as units of the Union in Alberta (1910), British Columbia (1910), Manitoba (1910), and Saskatchewan (1910). An attempt in 1908–1909 to create a national Baptist Union of Canada was aborted in Ontario and Quebec. *See also* POLITY, BAPTIST.

CONWELL, RUSSELL HERMAN (1843–1925). American Baptist minister and educator, born at South Washington, Massachusetts. He graduated from Yale College and entered the U.S. Army during the Civil War. Afterward, he became a lawyer in Minnesota, ultimately becoming an immigration agent for that state. In 1879, following the death of his wife, Conwell turned to religion and was converted. Soon afterward, he assumed the pastorate of a small church in Lexington, Massachusetts, and revived the church. In 1881, he moved to Grace Baptist Church in North Philadelphia, a struggling, debt-ridden congregation. Within 10 years, he was **pastor** of a church of over a thousand and easily one of Philadelphia's outstanding orators. The Baptist Temple became, under his pastorate, a leading example of an institutional church, providing education and community services to a wide variety of people. In 1884, Conwell founded Temple University and, later, the Good Samaritan Hospital, the beginnings of the medical school. He is best remembered for his oft-preached sermon "Acres of Diamonds" (1888), which was based on his startling Civil War encounter with personal valor in a young soldier named Johnny Ring. Conwell was a popular author on a variety of subjects, including *Why the Chinese Emigrate* (1871), *History of the Great Fire in Boston* (1873), *The Story of the Presidents from Grant to Arthur* (1878), *The Life of Charles Haddon Spurgeon* (1892), and *Why Lincoln Laughed* (1922).

COOK, HENRY (1886–1970). English Baptist minister, born near Tillicoultry, Scotland. His family emigrated to Canada, but he remained in Britain where he was educated at the Baptist College in Glasgow, becoming a prize student. Cook served pastorates at Govan, Leamington Road, Blackburn (1910–1921); Blenham, Leeds (1921–1925); and Ferme Park, London (1925–1939). He entered denominational service on various committees of the **Baptist Union** (BU), served as president of the **Baptist Missionary Society** in 1940, and became general superintendent of the London area for the BU (1941–1955). He was elected president of the BU in 1955. From 1955 to 1959, Cook was associate general secretary of the **Baptist World Alliance**. His books, *The Why of Our Faith* (1924) and *What Baptists Stand For* (1947), were considered definitive of Baptist beliefs in the era. William Jewell College in Missouri awarded Cook an honorary doctorate in 1955.

COOK, THOMAS (1808–1892). English Baptist philanthropist and evangelist, born at Melbourne, Derbyshire. Early in life, he was apprenticed to his uncle in the trade of wood turning. He was converted in the **General Baptist** Church at Leicester and was influenced by Joseph Winks, a publisher in that town. From 1828 to 1832, Cook served as a General Baptist associational Bible reader and evangelist in Rutland County, traveling over 2,500 miles in one year. Later, while a wood turner at Market Harborough, Cook was converted to the **temperance** movement by a Roman Catholic priest, and he also became an advocate of antitobacco smoking. To assist a local temperance association, Cook organized an excursion trip by train from Leicester to Loughborough in 1841, the first of its kind. This was so successful that he took up organizing excursions in Britain and abroad and became wealthy as a result. His travel agency at Leicester published schedules and handbooks, and Cook himself organized the first round-the-world tour in 1872–1873. He traveled throughout the world, touring the **mission** stations of both General and **Particular Baptists**, making his reports in prominent periodicals. His work in the travel industry especially aided teetotalers, who often travelled together as a cultural experience. In 1840, Cook founded the *Children's Temperance Magazine*, four years later the *National Temperance Magazine* and the *Youth's Temperance Magazine*. Cook's own books included numerous tourist guides and a *Memoir of Samuel Deacon* (1889).

COOPERATIVE BAPTIST FELLOWSHIP (CBF). A coalition of mostly former U.S. **Southern Baptists** who felt the need to respond to the changes in the life of the Southern Baptist Convention (SBC), which was perceived to be moving in theologically and administratively unacceptable directions. In 1990, the last attempt of a moderate faction in the SBC to elect a president, Daniel Vestal, failed. Vestal immediately began rallying moderates and with the assistance of Cecil Sherman, Walter Shurden, and John Hewitt, the Consultation of Concerned Baptists was held in Atlanta, Georgia, in August 1990. Within a year, the Cooperative Baptist Fellowship evolved, holding its first general assembly in Atlanta on May 6, 1991, with 6,000 delegates in attendance. The ideals of the new CBF included upholding biblical teachings; advocating education over indoctrination; supporting the inclusion of ministries of mercy and justice, in addition to preaching and teaching, in **missions**; stressing the servant role of **pastors** and affirming the giftedness of women for ministry; and putting forth the hope of a fellowship that would be ecumenical and inclusive. Cecil Sherman was chosen as the first coordinator, an equivalent of executive director or general secretary. In 1993, Keith Parks, former executive of the SBC **Foreign Mission Board**, was chosen global missions coordinator, signaling a priority on global missions. Regionally, CBF state bodies were formed, imitating the Southern Baptist state conventions: Florida (1991), Kentucky (1991), Missouri (1991), South Carolina (1991), Alabama (1992), Georgia (1992), Mississippi (1992), North Central Region (1992), Oklahoma (1992), Tennessee (1992), Louisiana (1993), Virginia (1993), Northeast Region (1996), North Carolina (1994), Arkansas (1994), Texas (1996), and the Mid-Atlantic Region (1998).

The CBF has established "partnerships" with Baptist and other Christian groups, notably the **American Baptist Churches**, **Baptist Joint Committee for Religious Liberty**, **Baptist World Alliance**, Arab American Friendship Center in Michigan, Habitat for Humanity, and Wycliffe Bible Translators. In their many overseas mission projects, team ministries and cooperation with other groups are practiced. As of 2006, there were 165 missionaries under appointment among 20 people groups, particularly in Europe, Asia, and North Africa.

CBF is administered by a coordinating council of 83 members, who are elected at the general assembly. The executive offices of the CBF are located in Atlanta, Georgia, with 1,854 churches and 700,000 members supporting the program, as of 2006. General assemblies have been held across the South, in Texas, Georgia, Alabama, Virginia, Florida, and North Carolina, profiling CBF as essentially a southern group. The annual budget exceeds $17 million. The CBF participates in the retirement and benefits program of the American Baptist Churches in the U.S.A.; in 2007, the two groups shared a joint session among their concurrent annual (biennial) meetings held in Washington, D.C.

COSTA RICA. A significant number of early Baptists in Costa Rica were blacks, the result of efforts by the Baptist Missionary Society of **Jamaica.** In 1888, a church was established in Puerto Limón. In 1941, **Landmarkist** Southern Baptists opened a church in the country, and **Southern Baptist** mission work commenced in 1947. Six congregations organized the Convención Bautista de Costa Rica in 1947, and in 1951, a Baptist seminary, Instituto Teologico Bautista, opened at San José. Other Baptist groups in Costa Rica include La Iglesia Bautista Nacional (1945); the Asociación Bautista Costarricense (1955), an ultrafundamentalist group; and the **Baptist Bible Fellowship** (since 1970). The **American Baptist Association** also sponsors work in Costa Rica.

As of 2006, there were 22 churches with 2,006 members affiliated with the Convención Bautista de Costa Rica, and 22 churches with 1,450 members affiliated with the La Iglesia Bautista Nacional de Costa Rica.

COSTAS, ORLANDO ENRIQUE (1942–1987). Puerto Rican and American Baptist minister, missiologist, and theological educator, born at Ponce, Puerto Rico. His parents were Methodist, but Costas attended a Baptist school in Puerto Rico. He was educated at Bob Jones Academy in South Carolina and Nyack Missionary College in New York. Later, he studied at Trinity Evangelical Divinity School, Wheaton College Graduate School, and Northwestern University, ultimately earning his M.Div. degree at Garrett Theological Seminary. In 1965, Costas became a pastor at Yauco, Puerto Rico, and was ordained in the **American Baptist Churches** of Puerto Rico. In 1966–1969, he was **pastor** of Iglesia Evangelical Bautista in Milwaukee, Wisconsin, where he was active in social ministries and civil rights. He was named to the Wisconsin State Committee on Human Rights. From 1970 to 1976 he was under appointment of the Latin American Mission in San José, Costa Rica, where he taught at the Seminario Biblica Latinoamericana and concurrently served as Secretary for Research and Communication of the Institute for In Depth Evangelism as well as Secretary for Theological Studies.

During this period, Costas authored eight books on various subjects in homiletics, history, and evangelism. In 1976, he completed his Th.D. at the Free University of Amsterdam under Johannes Verkuyl. For the next four years, Costas served as a missionary under the Board of World Mission of the United Church of Christ (U.S.) and worked as an editor of the major project on the history of Christianity in Latin America. In 1980, he accepted the position of Thornley B. Wood Professor of Missiology and Director of Hispanic Ministries at Eastern Baptist Theological Seminary in Philadelphia. There he created the Eastern School of Christian Missions to serve the special needs of the Hispanic and black churches. From 1984 to 1987, Costas was dean at Andover Newton Theological School, during which time he lectured at Mansfield College in Oxford and was a Visiting Scholar of the Ecumenical Institute of Advanced Theology in Jerusalem. Among his many published works were *The Integrity of Mission* (1979); *Christ Outside the Gate: Mission beyond Christendom* (1982); and *Liberating News: A Theology of Contextual Evangelization* (1989).

CÔTE D'IVOIRE. *See* IVORY COAST.

COTTON GROVE RESOLUTIONS. Between 1846 and 1850, **James R. Graves** and John L. Waller (1809–1854) carried on a literary debate on Baptist identity in their respective Tennessee and Kentucky Baptist newspapers. Waller, editor of the *Baptist Banner* and, later, the *Western Recorder*, stressed the faith of persons baptized, while Graves emphasized the proper form, later to be known as a "**landmark**." Often ridiculing Waller, Graves challenged him to a public confrontation. A mass meeting of concerned Baptists (Waller was not present) met at Cotton Grove in Hardeman County, Tennessee, on June 24, 1851. They considered a presentation by Graves, who presented five propositions that stemmed from the question of whether recognition should be given to paedo-baptists. He questioned whether Baptists could recognize churches with a different government, different standards of membership, and different doctrines, practices, and **ordinances**. He held that ministers of such churches should not be recognized and that Baptists should not call such practitioners "brethren." Following a broad discussion, the meeting agreed to endorse the position or "resolutions," and Graves achieved much publicity from the event, holding that it was as definitive as Martin Luther's Ninety-five Theses. The Cotton Grove Resolutions are generally held to be the first definition of the Landmark Baptist movement. *See also* LANDMARKISM; LOCAL CHURCH PROTECTIONISM.

COUNCIL OF BAPTIST CHURCHES IN NORTHEAST INDIA (**CBCNEI**). An umbrella organization of Baptists in **India**. As a result of the missionary work primarily of American Baptists in northeast India, the Assam Baptist Convention was founded in 1914. While an important step, this organization lacked administrative accountability and the support of the various churches. American Baptists in the 1940s looked to greater autonomy of the Indian churches and assisted in the formation of an improved body the Council of Churches in Assam in 1950. In 1954, this evolved to become the Council of Churches in Assam and Manipur and in 1959, the Council of Baptist Churches in Northeast India. Within this body, over 30 language groups exist, for which American Baptists produced translations of **Scripture** for 19 tribes during the pioneer missionary period of the 19th century.

As of 2007, there were six conventions and 90 associations affiliated with CBCNEI, with a total of 924,554 members in an affiliated 6,024 churches. The headquarters of CBCNEI is located in Guwahati, Assam.

COUNCIL OF CHURCHES OF THE EVANGELICAL CHRISTIANS AND BAPTISTS (CCECB). *See* RUSSIA.

COVENANTED BAPTISTS OF THE UNITED STATES AND CANADA. *See* PRIMITIVE BAPTISTS.

COVENANTS. Since their earliest development, Baptists have understood the value of covenants as **voluntary** promissory statements. Borrowing heavily from Puritan and Separatist theology and practice, the first Baptists under **John Smyth**'s leadership covenanted together in 1607–1608 "as the Lord's free people . . . to walk in all his wayes made known, or to be made known to them, according to their best endeavors whatsoever it should cost them, the Lord assisting them," closely resembling the words of the covenant of the ancient church in 1591. Puritans had written covenants to remind themselves of God's provisions for the saints and their obligations toward God and the visible church. The use of covenants has a much broader history among Baptists in the United States than elsewhere. This is perhaps due to the widespread use of covenants in the New England Congregationalist community.

Unlike their predecessors in **Nonconformity**, Baptists usually stress the horizontal relational nature of covenants, that is, the relationships and obligations between church members. Typically, a covenant is a statement of relationships and expectations of members that is signed at least originally by all of the membership. When a covenant has been written and signed, a church is said to be constituted; as such, it reflects the consensus of the membership and is entirely voluntary. Among the more famous church covenants are the **William Screven** Covenant of 1682, Samuel Jones's (1735–1814) covenant printed in his 1798 *Treatise of Church Discipline*, and the covenant published in 1836 as an appendage to the New Hampshire Confession of Faith (1833), likely the work of **J. Newton Brown**. The Brown covenant is widely accepted in varying versions as "*the* church covenant."

On regular occasions, many congregations recite the covenant together, such as at celebrations of the **Lord's Supper** or in the reception of new members. In the latter 19th century, some American churches had a Saturday set aside for a covenant service, prior to the Lord's Supper on Sunday. Covenants can also be used to define the boundaries of church membership in order to **discipline** an errant member who appears to be in violation of a provision of membership.

Similarly, new converts may be instructed in the faith and life of a congregation by use of the covenant. Most covenants are not more than a few paragraphs in length. The provisions of a church covenant usually include a definition of membership, obligations concerning the **sacraments/ordinances**, care for each other, financial support for the church and attendance at its meetings. Some covenants also list ethical expectations of members such as abstinence from antisocial behavior, alcoholic beverages, and criticism of the church. Theologically, it is assumed that the grace of God allows (if not enables) the performance of covenanted obligations.

In recent years, covenants have lost relevance in North America, while elsewhere the **confession of faith** may have more meaning. An interesting use of the concept of the covenant is found among the **American Baptist Churches in the U.S.A.**, where beginning in 1973, each of the regional organizations agreed to a "covenant of relationships" with the national societies and the local churches. The covenant thus provides the uniting force in a voluntary polity of complex church corporations. In 2007–2008, an emergent movement in the United States, Baptists Covenanting Together, also called the New Baptist Covenant, brought together several major Baptist bodies for cooperation and witness January 30–February 2, 2008 in Atlanta, Georgia. The proposed "covenant" was based upon Luke 4:18–19 and involved creating an authentic and prophetic Baptist voice for complex times, an emphasis upon traditional Baptist values, and the promotion of peace with justice, care for the marginalized, promotion of **religious liberty**, and a respect for religious diversity.

COX, FRANCIS AUGUSTUS (1793–1853). English Baptist minister, born at Leighton Buzzard. He studied at Bristol College under **John Ryland** and then graduated from the University of Edinburgh. He served the church at Clipstone and for 42 years at Hackney in London. Cox was a promoter of foreign **missions**, the Baptist Irish Society, and relations with Baptists in the United States. He and **James Hoby** visited the United States in 1836 and wrote extensively of their findings. Cox served as secretary to the body of ministers of the **Three Dissenting Denominations** and was a founder of the Liberation Society. A devoted voluntarist, he was a member of the Evangelical Voluntary Church Association and the British Anti-State

Church Association, and led the anti-Maynooth drive and the Anti-Corn Law League. Fond of educational projects, Cox played a prominent role in the founding of University College and London University in 1827. At the jubilee of the **Baptist Missionary Society** in 1842, Cox was its official historian and he was president of the **Baptist Union** in 1834, 1845, and 1852. Cox was widely published and his works include *Female Scripture Biography* (1817), *The Baptists in America* (1836), *History of the Baptist Missionary Society* (1844), and *On Christian Union* (1845).

CRAMP, JOHN MOCKETT (1796–1881). English Baptist and, later, Canadian Baptist minister and educator, born at St. Peter's, Isle of Thanet, England. He was educated at Canterbury and Stepney Theological College in preparation for his **ordination** to the Baptist ministry. In England, Cramp edited the *Baptist Magazine* (1825–1828), was a publisher, and was active in various denominational boards and societies. In 1844, he accepted under **missionary** appointment the presidency of Canada Baptist College in Montreal, operated by the Canada Baptist Missionary Society and the Baptist Colonial Missionary Society in England. The school collapsed in 1849, and Cramp moved to Acadia College in Nova Scotia in 1851 as the second president of that school. He revived the college's sagging finances, was active in the **temperance** movement, and served the Horton (Wolfville) Baptist Church. In 1853, he became the first principal of Acadia's theological institute, serving again as president from 1860 to 1869. Cramp was an active writer, completing *An Essay on the Obligation of Christians to Observe the Lord's Supper Every Lord's Day* (1827), *History of the Baptists* (1871), *A Memoir of Madame Feller* (1876), several anti-Catholic works, and a series of newspaper articles chronicling the history of Maritime Baptists (1860–1863).

CRANDALL, JOSEPH (1761–1858). Canadian Baptist minister, born at Tiverton, Rhode Island. Crandall was converted under the evangelistic ministry of **Henry Alline** in the Chester, Nova Scotia, area. He was further awakened under the influence of **Harris Harding** and **Joseph Dimock** in 1795. Following a vivid vision of a call to preach and baptize, Crandall began his ministry in Liverpool, where he was a founding **pastor** until 1799, when he went to New Brunswick. He became the first regularly ordained Baptist pastor in New Brunswick, being set apart by **Edward Manning** and Joseph Dimock in Sackville. Crandall served at Salisbury until his death. He was a founder of the Nova Scotia Association in 1800 and the separate New Brunswick Association in 1822. Crandall was elected to the New Brunswick Assembly in 1818, campaigning broadly for civil and **religious liberty**, and became president of the New Brunswick Baptist Education Society in 1836. He died at 97 having preached his last sermon six weeks before.

CRAWFORD, ISABEL ALICE HARTLEY (1865–1961). American Baptist missionary, born at Cheltenham, Ontario. The daughter of a Canadian Baptist educator, Isabel was educated at the Baptist Missionary Training School in Chicago. In 1893, she was appointed a missionary to the Kiowa Indians of Oklahoma by the Woman's American Baptist Home Mission Society. During her tenure at Elk Creek, Crawford advocated Indian rights in the face of encroachment upon lands dedicated to the tribe. At Saddle Mountain in 1901, she superintended the construction of a church building. In 1905, while serving at Saddle Mountain, she assisted in the celebration of the **Lord's Supper**, perhaps the first Baptist woman to do so. She was heavily criticized for this action by the **American Baptist Home Mission Society** and the Indian Baptist Association; she was ultimately forced to resign her commission. In later years, Crawford lectured widely on Indian rights and in 1918 interceded in a dispute between the Presbyterians and Baptists on the Allegany Reservation in western New York. She was the first white woman missionary to be buried in the Indian Cemetery at Saddle Mountain, Oklahoma, a tribute to her affection for Indian peoples. The story of her early work is found in her book *Kiowa: The History of a Blanket Mission* (1915).

CRAWFORD, TARLETON PERRY (1821–1902). Southern Baptist and, later, **Independent Baptist** missionary, born in Warren County, Kentucky. He graduated from Union University in Murfreesboro, Tennessee, and was appointed a missionary to **China** in 1851 by the Southern Baptist **Foreign Mission Board** (FMB). Crawford and his wife served at Shanghai (1852–1863) in an educational mission and, later, in North China at Tengchow (1863–1893). During the American Civil War, Crawford invested in Chinese real estate and became independently wealthy; this prompted a connection with his **Landmarkist** upbringing, and he began to argue that missionaries ought to be self-supporting. After an unsuccessful attempt to persuade the FMB to accept his position, which he called "gospel missionism," he left the service of the board and became an Independent. Crawford's ideas were popularized in his *Evolution in My Mission Views* (1903). Crawford's views have been widely adopted by Independent Baptists in the United States, though not citing his name.

CRAWLEY, EDMUND ALBERN (1799–1888). Canadian and American Baptist minister and educator, born at Ipswich, England. Crawley emigrated as a child to Cape Breton Island and graduated from King's College, Windsor, Nova Scotia. His first career was that of a Halifax lawyer, but in 1828 he entered the **ministry**, having been converted by area **evangelicals** and drawn into the Baptist movement. He took courses at Brown University and Andover Theological Seminary, under the influence of **Alexis Caswell**. Ordained in Providence, Rhode Island, Crawley returned to be the **pastor** at Granville Street Baptist Church in Halifax, his home congregation. Crawley spearheaded the drive for a Baptist university in the Maritimes, which became Acadia University. A founder of the Nova Scotia Baptist Education Society on the New England plan, he was associated with Acadia at various times as professor of theology, president, and fund-raiser from 1838 until his death. Between 1856 and 1865, Crawley went to the United States and was involved in a disastrous financial scheme involving a mining company; he also founded Mt. Auburn Female Seminary in Cincinnati, Ohio, and was president of Limestone Springs Female Academy in Spartanburg, South Carolina, from 1856 to 1860. During the Civil War, he taught at a private school in Shelby, North Carolina. Returning to Acadia, he became the first principal of Acadia's theological school. Crawley was awarded a doctor of divinity degree by Brown University in 1844. His most notable publication is *A Treatise on Baptism* (1835).

CROATIA. Heinrich Meyer, the Baptist apostle to Hungary, indirectly originated the work in what is now Croatia. Meyer baptized Nicola Zrincak of Zagreb, who in 1883 began a mission in Zagreb.

Other early missions were commenced by Julius Peter, a German missionary who traveled throughout Yugoslavia, and Adolf Hempt, a convert of Germans who focused his efforts in Novi Sad. Under the leadership of Vinko Vacek, the Croatian Conference was organized in 1921, followed by the Serbo-Croatian Union, organized in 1922. This second body became the Savez Baptistickih Crkava (Baptist Union of Croatia) in 1924, which survived until World War II. During the period when Croatia was included in Yugoslavia, 1945–1991, Baptists in Croatia cooperated as part of the Baptist Union of Yugoslavia; with the independence of Croatia in 1991, the Savez Baptistickih Crkava u Republici Hrvatskoj was reconstituted. *Glas Evandjelia* (1923–1941; 1959 to present as *Glasnik*) was begun as the official newspaper of the Union, published first at Daruvar.

As of 2006, there were 50 churches and 2,000 members affiliated with the Savez Baptistickih Crkava u Republici Hrvatskpo. In 1997, the **Baptist Bible Fellowship** also entered Croatia.

CROSBY, THOMAS (1683–1751). English Baptist educator and historian, born at London. Early in his life he went to sea and trained at the Royal Mathematical School. He was supported by the Church of England but adopted Baptist views and was baptized. He joined the strategic Horsley-down Church under **Elias Keach** and married the daughter of the next **pastor, Benjamin Stinton**. Stinton introduced Crosby to many **associations** and the larger **Nonconformist** community in London. When Stinton died in 1719, Crosby advocated **John Gill** and, under some adversity, managed to have the pastoral selection prevail. Crosby was accused of fraudulent accounting practices and was expelled from the church. He joined a congregation at Unicorn Yard and was expelled from there in 1742 on account of questionable business practices and a bad temper. Over several decades, Crosby compiled the first published *History of the Baptists* (4 volumes, 1738–1740), based on the work of Benjamin Stinton and partly as a reaction to inadequate treatments in existing religious histories.

CROWN RIGHTS OF THE REDEEMER. *See* CHRIST, DOCTRINE OF.

CROZER, JOHN PRICE (1793–1866). American Baptist industrialist and philanthropist, born at Springfield, Pennsylvania. His career started as a laborer in a lumber mill, where he developed clever mechanical adaptations to water power. He opened his own cotton milling center at Upland, Pennsylvania, and successfully marketed his goods in nearby Philadelphia. Crozer was baptized by **William Staughton** and was greatly influenced by his **pastor**'s interest in **voluntary associations**. He was elected to prominent positions in the **American Baptist Home Mission Society** and in the **American Baptist Publication Society**, which his son-in-law, Benjamin Griffith (1821–1893), managed. He took a special interest in book distribution and **Sunday Schools**. During the Civil War, Crozer's profits soared, and he became one of the leading philanthropists in the Baptist community. He gave an endowed chair to the Baptist University at Lewisburg, Pennsylvania (later Bucknell University), and established an orphanage. After Crozer's death, his family used his estate to endow a theological school in Upland, Pennsylvania, named Crozer Theological Seminary.

CUBA. Baptist work relating to Cuba dates from 1886 when Southern Baptists first worked among Cubans in Florida. Foreign **mission** effort commenced at the conclusion of the Spanish-American War in 1898. Following consultation between the **American Baptist Missionary Union** (ABMU) and the **Southern Baptist Convention**, it was agreed that Southern Baptists would take missionary responsibility for the four western provinces, while the **American Baptist Home Mission Society** took the same responsibility for the two eastern provinces and **Puerto Rico**. The first church was started at Santiago in 1899 by Hartwell R. Mosely (1863–1926), an appointee of the ABMU. By 1903, the Convención Bautista de Cuba Oriental (Convention of the Eastern Provinces) was formed, and in 1920, a Cuban Baptist Home Mission Society was founded. In 1905, a Cuban-American College was started at Havana, out of which emerged El Cristo Colegios Internacionales. The first attempts in theological education came in 1947, when a seminary was started at Matanzas in cooperation with the Southern Baptist mission, Presbyterians, and Methodists; however, this soon proved inadequate.

Therefore, in 1949, the Cuban Baptist Convention of the East established at Santiago its own theological school with the support of American Baptists. Owing to a significant number of Haitian refugees in eastern Cuba, missionary work was conducted, and in 1940, in the Province of Camagüey, a Haitian Baptist Convention was organized, eventually with over 30 congregations. The first Southern Baptist congregation was started at Havana in 1905. American **Freewill Baptists** began missionary work on the island in 1941, with whom the Convención Bautista Libre de Cuba has been affiliated. La Convención Bautista Occidental published *La Voz Bautista* (The Baptist Voice) (1908–1965) prior to the Revolution of Fidel Castro. In 1955, the **Baptist Bible Fellowship** commenced a mission in Cuba in the **fundamentalist** tradition.

As of 2006, there were 319 churches with 25,000 members affiliated with the Convención Bautista de Cuba Oriental; 209 churches with 16,687 members affiliated with the Convención Bautista de Cuba Occidental; 31 churches and 3,040 members affiliated with the Fraternidad de Iglesias Bautista de Cuba; and 36 churches with 2,000 members associated with the Convención Bautista Libre de Cuba (Free Baptist Convention of Cuba). Presently, there are two schools in Cuba: Eastern Cuba Baptist Theological Seminary at Santiago de Cuba and Seminario Teologico Bautista de Cuba Occidental at La Havana.

CUSHING, ELLEN HOWARD WINDSOR (1840–1915). American Baptist missionary and educator, born at Kingston, Massachusetts. Converted at a Charles G. Finney crusade in Boston in 1857, Cushing was first a Congregationalist then a Baptist. At 21, she volunteered for service with the Port Royal Experiment, where she assisted freed slaves in entering postwar society. Later (1840–1905), Ellen and her husband, Josiah N. Cushing, went to **Burma**, where they collaborated on an English-Shan dictionary. In 1892, on furlough, she accepted a position with the Woman's American Baptist Foreign Mission Society of the East; realizing the need of a school to train single women missionaries, she started the Baptist Training Institute in Philadelphia (later Ellen Cushing College in Bryn Mawr, Pennsylvania). Back in the mission field in 1905, when Josiah died, Cushing completed his massive dictionary project. With her husband, she published *A Grammar of the Shan Language* (1871) and *A Shan and English Dictionary* (1881).

CZECHOSLOVAK BAPTIST CONVENTION OF THE UNITED STATES AND CANADA. An organization of Czech-speaking Baptist congregations in North America established by leaders in the German Baptist community in Chicago in 1909 to serve the needs of the immigrant Slovaks and Czechs in that area. Between 1909 and 1913, Polish work was also supported, but a decision was made to separate the conventions. Originally, there were two Bohemian Baptist churches, as they were called in the United States. A publishing ministry began among the Slavic churches, as well as a **missionary** outreach to Czechoslovakia. During the Marxist era, emphasis shifted to missionary work in **Haiti**, until 1993, when support was redirected to the unions of **Slovakia** and the **Czech Republic**. A general board of 51 members directs the work of the convention, which holds an annual assembly at Phillippi, West Virginia, the headquarters. The convention publishes *Slavna nadeje* (Glorious Hope). As of 2006, there were five churches in the United States and **Canada** with about 1,500 members affiliated with the convention.

CZECH REPUBLIC. Czech Baptists identify with early Hussite and Czech Brethren traditions, although modern Baptist witness is traced to the mid-19th century. **Colporteurs** of the British and Foreign Bible Society baptized believers in the 1860s in the region of Bohemia. **Henry Novotny** formed a church at Hledsebe near Prague in 1885, and a Baptist union was founded in 1919. Mission assistance was provided by the British and American Baptists plus the Scottish Bohemian Mission. With the downfall of Marxist government in Czechoslovakia in 1992, the Czech Republic and the **Slovak Republic** emerged as separate nations, thus necessitating separate Baptist organizations in 1993. In 1994, the Baptist Theological Seminary in Rüschlikon, Switzerland, relocated to Prague, the Czech Republic, where it related to the Protestant Faculty of Charles University; degree programs at the institution were closed temporarily in 1998. The union publishes *Rozsievac* (The Sower) (1930–). The **Baptist Bible Fellowship** opened a mission in 1992, and the following year, the

Conservative Baptist Foreign Mission Society began a mission in Prague.

As of 2006, there were 36 churches and 2,351 members belonging to the Bratrska Jednota Baptistu (Baptist Union of the Czech Republic).

– D –

DAGG, JOHN LEADLEY (1794–1884). Southern Baptist minister and educator, born at Middleburg, Virginia. Early career positions included schoolteacher and physician's apprentice. He also served in the military in the War of 1812. Dagg became an itinerant preacher in 1817 and won an invitation to succeed **William Staughton** at Fifth Baptist Church, Philadelphia, in 1825. In 1834, he turned to education, first as president of a manual labor school in Pennsylvania and ultimately as professor of theology and president of Mercer University in Macon, Georgia. Dagg was the first published theologian of the **Southern Baptist Convention**, producing its first systematic theology in 1859. He set the tone of later Southern Baptist theologians by laying down the rule of a biblical basis for all doctrine. Throughout his career, he suffered from a crippled body and partial blindness. Among Dagg's significant works are *Essay in Defense of Strict Communion* (1845), *A Treatise on Church Order* (1858), *Elements of Moral Science* (1859), and *A Manual of Theology* (1871).

DAHOMEY. *See* BENIN.

DANA, HARVEY EUGENE (1888–1945). Southern Baptist educator, born at Vicksburg, Mississippi. Dana was educated at Mississippi College and Southwestern Baptist Theological Seminary where he earned the Th.D. in New Testament. From 1920 to 1928, he served as professor of New Testament and Greek at Southwestern and then took further studies at the University of Chicago and Dubuque Theological Seminary. Dana went to Central Baptist Theological Seminary in Kansas City, Kansas, where he assumed the chair in New Testament and was president from 1938 to 1945. Central was jointly sponsored by the Southern and Northern Baptist Conventions, and

Dana had an unusual opportunity to influence students north and south. His scholarly work included New Testament criticism, the application of form criticism to the fourth gospel, and an exhaustive study of the New Testament term "ecclesia." Dana collaborated with Julius R. Mantey (1890–1981) at Northern Baptist Theological Seminary in the authorship of a textbook in introductory Greek, which was a classic textbook for many generations. His published works include *A Manual for the Study of the Greek New Testament* (1923), *The New Testament World* (1928), and *A Manual of Ecclesiology* (1941).

DANISH AND NORWEGIAN CONFERENCE(S). As Norwegian emigrants moved into the American Midwest, the **American Baptist Home Mission Society** (ABHMS) took the opportunity to conduct **missions** among them. An immigrant, Hans Valder (1813–1899), was the first Norwegian appointee of the ABHMS, and he organized the first American Norwegian congregation at Indian Creek, Illinois, in 1848. The first Danish congregation was established at Raymond Township, Wisconsin, in 1856. Because the Danish and Norwegians shared a common European heritage and often settled in close proximity, the two congregational groups easily blended into an associative life. In the 1850s, churches were started in Wisconsin, Minnesota, Michigan, and Iowa, most from former Lutheran relationships. Five congregations—four Danish and one Norwegian—comprised the first meeting of the Danish-Norwegian Baptist Conference of the Northwestern States in 1864 at Raymond, Wisconsin.

One of the chief obstacles to the expansion of the conference was the lack of a trained ministry. At first, the Danish and Norwegian candidates joined the Swedish educational program at Morgan Park in Chicago. When the Swedes decided upon a separate seminary in St. Paul, the Scandinavian Department of the reorganized University of Chicago Divinity School, as it came to be called, came under the influence of the Danish-Norwegians. This program attracted a number of students from **Denmark** and **Norway**, who later returned to Europe. In 1910, the Norwegian educational interest was moved from the university to an affiliation with the Northern Baptist Theological Seminary, where it continued for a number of years.

Attempts were made over the years (from 1890 to 1910) to organize a general conference encompassing Danes and Norwegians, similar to the national conferences for the Germans and Swedes. A consensus was not reached between the two groups, and in 1910, separate conferences were incorporated. The Norwegian Conference created a mission board, which sent workers to the Dakotas, the eastern states, the far West, and **Canada**. The churches in Canada became the joint responsibility of the Baptist Union of the Western Provinces. Close relations in the United States with the Northern Baptist Convention (NBC) were strengthened in 1939 with associate membership for the Norwegian Conference in the NBC; eventually in 1957 the Norwegian Baptist Conference was merged with the American Baptist Convention (ABC).

Among the Danes, several state conferences were organized in the late 19th century, notably in Minnesota, Wisconsin, Illinois, and Iowa. In 1910, the Danish Baptist General Conference held its organizing session at Harlan, Iowa, with 48 congregations represented. By 1915, a pension fund and women's and youth work had been organized under the conference. Canada was adopted as a mission field in 1928, with the first church established at Calgary in 1929. From 1912 to 1925, the Conference supported a seminary program at Des Moines University in Iowa, after which the program affiliated with the Northern Baptist Theological Seminary in Chicago. Like the Norwegian Conference, the Danish Baptist General Conference also accepted associate membership in the NBC and merged with the ABC in 1958.

In addition to producing a hymnal, the Danish and Norwegian churches cooperated in publishing *Oliebladet* (Olive Leaf) (1877–1887) and *Vaeteren* (Awakener) (1887–1910). From the separation of the two conferences, the Norwegians produced *Missionaeren* (The Missionary) (1910–1956), while the Danes published *Vaeteren* until 1958.

DAVIES, BENJAMIN (1814–1876). Welsh and Canadian Baptist minister and educator, born at Werne, Carmarthenshire. He was educated for the ministry in **Wales**, at Bristol Baptist College, and the University of Glasgow; he received a Ph.D. degree in Oriental studies at the University of Leipzig. Davies emigrated to **Canada**

in 1838, on the recommendation of **John Gilmour**, to head up the new faculty of Canada Baptist College in Montreal. As such, he became the first theological educator in Canada to have an earned doctorate. The college failed from an overly scholastic program and lack of local support; Davies returned to England to become principal at Stepney College, 1843–1846. His tenure was short due to lack of administrative ability, and in 1847, he went back to Canada for 10 years as professor and chairman of classical literature at McGill University in Montreal. In 1857, Davies returned to England as tutor in Old Testament and classical languages under **Joseph Angus** at Stepney and, later, Regent's Park, distinguishing himself as a teacher and scholar. He was one of the principal revisers of the English **Bible** and brought the fruits of German higher criticism to English **Nonconformity**. Davies was the translator of Gesenius's *Hebrew Grammar* and *Lexicon*, and he compiled and translated *The Paragraph Bible*.

DAVIS, NOAH (1802–1830). American Baptist minister and publisher, born at Salisbury, Maryland. Early in life he worked as a clerk in the Philadelphia firm of Fassitt and Langstroth. In 1819, he was baptized at Sansom Street Baptist Church by **William Staughton**. Licensed to the **ministry** by his home church in Salisbury, he returned to Philadelphia to study in Staughton's theological school and moved with the school to Washington, D.C., when it became Columbian College. Frustrated in his attempts to become a foreign missionary because of frail health, Davis moved to a pastoral ministry at Drummondtown, Virginia (on the Eastern Shore), and then to a church in Norfolk, Virginia. While in Norfolk, he preached to the soldiers at Old Point Comfort and started a Seaman's Friend Society. In 1824, he wrote to a friend in Washington (likely **Luther Rice**) urging the establishment of a denominational tract society on the model of the American Tract Society. Thus, the Baptist General Tract Society (BGTS) was organized in 1824 with Davis as its manager. He moved the BGTS to Philadelphia in 1826, and it prospered under his leadership. Never of strong stamina, Davis died after a brief illness—in the same month, according to his epitaph, in which he was born, baptized, ordained, and married—in the month of July.

DEACON. The office of deacon in Baptist **polity** and practice is derived from the biblical tradition in acts of lay **ministry**. Based upon the Greek term *diakonos*, meaning "servant," a deacon was originally a person who waited upon tables, and this evolved to apply to those laypersons in each congregation who took care of the needs of the congregation, both financial and pertaining to the **sacraments/ordinances**. Early Baptists recognized the need for a regular lay ministry and elected deacons from among the church membership, according to the qualifications in I Timothy 3:8–13. Generally, deacons serve for a stated term of three to five years; some congregations limit their reelection, while others do not. In practice, Baptist deacons observe watchcare over the congregation, offer advice and insight, prepare and distribute the elements of the **Lord's Supper**, and assist with the details and preparation of candidates for **baptism**. In the absence of a **pastor**, a deacon may officiate at the Lord's Supper. With the pastor and elders, where appropriate, deacons may form a team of spiritual ministry for congregations, teaching, preaching, and counseling where needed.

In the United States, deacons can be the governing board in a congregation. They may administratively supervise the compensated ministry, provide care for the membership themselves, and adjudicate matters of church **discipline.** Typically, deacons arrange for supply of preaching in the absence of a pastor and may form a pulpit search committee for new pastoral leadership. Among U.S. Southern Baptists, deacons may be ordained by the **laying on of hands** and may be elected for life.

DEACONESSES. Term applied to female deacons in some Baptist contexts and also to a professional women's service movement. In the 19th and early 20th centuries, women who served in local church roles were often designated deaconesses to distinguish the use of **deacon** for males. In some instances, the wife of a deacon was designated a deaconess. Following a pattern in German Lutheran circles from the 1830s, where women served in missions of health and welfare roles in hospitals, homes, schools, and orphanages, Baptists in Great Britain began commissioning women deaconesses in the London area in 1890 with the dedication of the Deaconness Home and Mission. The prominent **pastor, F. B. Meyer**, was a leading supporter. Training for this work was provided by institutes and colleges at London (West Ham Mission), Camden Town, Putney, and finally, Carey Hall, Birmingham, in conjunction with the United Missionary College. After World War I, the **Baptist Union** (BU) assumed administration of this work and for a time the women's movement filled the void created by males serving in the military. In the 1950s, interest in professional deaconess work declined, and the deaconesses seemed to be a second track to women serving in pastoral ministries. Sensing an injustice, the BU moved in 1975 to close out the deaconess tradition by listing all of the remaining women deaconesses on the accredited roster of ordained ministers. A parallel movement in the Northern Baptist family in the United States developed with the support of **Walter Rauschenbusch** and Leighton Williams in New York, who founded a Baptist Deaconess Home in New York City in 1894. A second project was started in Chicago in 1914 under the auspices of the German Baptist Conference. By the 1950s, these institutions had been transferred to other auspices and the deaconess movement faded. In Australia, deaconesses were appointed to have oversight of women in local churches, beginning in 1869. More broadly in the 1890s a band of "Sisters of Mercy" appeared in various states to assist the sick, poor, strangers, and those who appeared to be fallen and depraved. The order of deaconesses faded by the 1960s, with greater recognition of women as candidates for ordination. Among British Baptists, deaconesses were marked by uniforms and bonnets and the title of "Sister," but elsewhere Baptist deaconesses were not marked by any form of unique dress.

DEAN, WILLIAM (1807–1895). American Baptist missionary, born at Eaton, New York. He was educated at Hamilton Literary and Theological Institution (later Colgate University) and was appointed by the **Baptist Board of Foreign Missions** to **Siam** to work among the Chinese. When **Hong Kong** was transferred to British sovereignty in 1842, Dean moved there and organized the first Protestant church among the Chinese. Later, he returned to Bangkok where as a missionary of the **American Baptist Missionary Union** (ABMU), he became a close confidante of the Siamese king, Chulalongkorn (1868–1910). Among Dean's literary achievements were translations of **Scripture** into Chinese, a catechism, and a hymnal. Dean has the distinction of being the first American missionary to work among the Chinese, and he helped train most of the first generation of Baptist missionaries to the Chinese people. His published works include *Chinese Scriptures* (1849) and *The China Mission; Embracing a History of the Various Missions of all Denominations among the Chinese* (1859).

DENMARK. The Baptist movement in Denmark, though small, claims the oldest congregation in Scandinavia. It was founded in 1839 at Copenhagen, the result of mission efforts by **J. G. Oncken** and his close associate, **Julius Köbner**. The church at Copenhagen suffered much persecution and its early **pastors**, the Monster brothers, were several times imprisoned. Köbner returned to the Copenhagen church as pastor in 1865 and a period of growth and extension ensued. From 1849 to 1952, the Baptists were a nonrecognized **dissenter** group, receiving assistance from time to time from the **American Baptist Missionary Union**. For a time, Danish Baptists were part of the German Baptist Union, and many of their pastors were trained at the Danish-Norwegian Seminary in Chicago, Illinois.

As of 2006, the Danske Baptistsamfund, formed in 1865, had 50 churches and 5,054 members. A Folkehojskole was opened at Gistrup in 1899 and expanded to seminary status in 1918. Later, the theological seminary was moved to Tollose near Copenhagen. A periodical, *Baptisternes Ugeblad* (*Baptist Weekly*), is published (1853–). In addition to the indigenous work, the **Baptist Bible Fellowship** has a mission in Denmark, begun in 1980.

DENNE, HENRY (fl. 1640–1660). Anglican and, later, English Baptist minister and controversialist, born at Well, Ickham. He was educated at Cambridge and in 1630 was ordained at St. David's. He became curate at Pirton and remained there for a decade. About 1642, Denne became convinced of the wrongfulness of infant **baptism**, and he converted to Baptist principles. He was baptized in 1643 and became a member of the church in Bell Alley, where he also preached. In 1644, authorities apprehended him for preaching, and he was jailed at Cambridge and London. One of his fellow prisoners in London was Daniel Featley (1582–1645), author of *The Dippers Dipt*, whom Denne challenged to a debate in 1645. Denne's printed version became the classic treatise *The Foundation of Children's Baptism Discovered and Rased* (1645). He preached in the outdoors and baptized candidates in rivers, drawing persecution upon himself. In 1646, Denne joined Cromwell's army, where he served with distinction. In 1658, he held a two-day disputation at St. Clement Dane's Church, which brought him much attention. Denne published six works, including treatises on the Quakers and Levellers. Among his other significant works are *The Doctrine and Conversation of John Baptist* (1642) and *Antichrist Unmasked in Two Treatises* (1646).

DIEFENBACKER, JOHN GEORGE (1895–1979). Baptist layman and prime minister of Canada, born at Neustadt, Ontario. Following service in World War I, he was educated at the University of Saskatchewan (B.A., 1915), earning an M.A. in political science and economics and, later, his law degree there. Diefenbacker practiced criminal law in the province and in British Columbia, becoming one of the more dramatic courtroom figures of his era. In 1940, he was elected from the Lake Centre, Saskatchewan riding, and in 1956, he became leader of his party, the Progressive Conservatives. As Canada's 13th prime minister (1957–1963), Diefenbacker led in passage of the Canadian Bill of Rights of 1960, the empowerment of aboriginal peoples, and the Royal Commission on Health Services, and he appointed the first woman to a cabinet post in Canadian history. Defeated in 1967 by Robert Stanfield of Nova Scotia, he remained a Member of Parliament until 1979. From 1969 to 1979, he was also chancellor of the University of Saskatchewan. Diefenbaker was the son of deeply committed Baptists in the Hanover, Ontario, church where his mother played the organ. While in Ottawa, he attended First Baptist Church, and his funeral in Saskatoon involved Baptist clergy, William R. Wood and Fred Bullen.

DIGGERS. One of the several dissenter sects that emerged in England in the mid-17th century around greater freedom to interpret **Scripture** and find new ethical applications. Diggerism was a radical outgrowth of the **Leveller** movement, which blended egalitarian politics with theology. Gerard Winstanley (fl. 1648–1652) was likely the original Digger; he preached a reorganization of land cultivation in England, so as to benefit the poor and attach all classes more directly to agrarian means. He used Scripture to justify communal cultivation of town commons, paraphrasing Scripture, "True religion and undefiled is to let every one quietly have earth to manure." Calling themselves "True Levellers," the Diggers were so called because in some places, notably St. George's Hill in 1649, they dug up and planted public lands. A number of colonies were started across southern England from 1647 to 1650.

Digger thinking always placed a high value on education and particularly on women's education. As Winstanley's own theology became more radical and the seizure of public lands drew negative reaction from the Commonwealth, Diggerism faded into other religious pursuits. The Digger movement for a time included Levellers, **Ranters**, and Baptists, notably **Henry Denne**. Like other groups, the Diggers reflected the fluidity of 17th-century English dissenter identity. *See also* LEVELLERS; NONCONFORMITY; RANTERS; SEEKERS.

DIMOCK, JOSEPH (1768–1846). Canadian Baptist minister, born in Newport, Nova Scotia. Self-educated, he was swept into the **New Light** revival of **Henry Alline** and immersed in 1787. He preached as a New Light for a time and became gradually more orthodox in his views, being ordained at Chester, Nova Scotia, in 1793. Dimock was a leading player in the transition of many New Light congregations into the Baptist tradition. In 1800, he was elected moderator of the Nova Scotia Baptist Association at its first meeting. He also advocated education and **missionary** organizations and was considered one of the Maritime Baptist fathers.

DISCIPLINE, CHURCH. Discipline of members and congregations has taken a variety of forms in the Baptist tradition. As early as the 1660s, Baptist congregations in Great Britain and North America responded to breaches of the **covenant** or **confession of faith**, or aberrant behavior, with degrees of punitive or corrective action. First was admonition, which involved a meeting with **deacons** and the **pastor** who presented the allegations and sought conformity with membership expectations. If this did not produce desired results, censure was next. Censure involved public announcement of the infraction, aiming for changed behavior through embarrassment and peer pressure.

Failing these two measures, excommunication was the last disciplinary action and this amounted to being removed from the membership by vote of the members, as well as being deprived of all benefits
of the church. Such excommunicated persons could be restored by
vote of the members.

In the United States during the 19th century, many Baptist congregations instituted prudential committees, which handled matters of
church discipline and freed the deacons from what was essentially a
negative task. Formal acts of church discipline have become rare
among many Baptist groups, as the pastor and deacons prefer counseling to discipline, and in general, congregations have become more
lenient or timid about such matters. In Appalachia and certain areas
in the South, particularly Texas, "churching" was practiced against
persons who were found to be guilty of moral infractions, breaking
civil or criminal laws, doctrinal deviation, or divorce and drunkenness. Persons who have been "churched" are typically excluded from
the membership roster and denied access to the ordinances. It is now
a fairly rare practice.

Church discipline could also take place among congregations
within an **association**. If a church breached the rules of the association, perhaps by allowing an unorthodox practice or doctrinal position, the congregation could be admonished and, if uncorrected, disfellowshipped or excluded. This has remained a practice in many
associations in the United States, where, for instance, a congregation
that expressed support for **women** in ministry by calling a woman to
be its senior pastor was disfellowshipped by its association in 1987,
and others have been disfellowshipped in Ohio and California for
openness to the practice of homosexuality.

DISFELLOWSHIPPING. *See* DISCIPLINE, CHURCH.

DISPENSATIONALISM. A theological tradition that divides world
history, biblical history, and teleology into a series of periods or dispensations of God's relationships with humanity. Often associated
with chiliasm, or the belief in a literal 1,000-year reign of **Christ** at
the future end of human history, evidence of a kind of dispensationalism is found in the early church fathers, notably Ignatius
(c. 35–107), Justin Martyr (c. 100–165), and Tertullian (c. 160–220).

Later, the Waldensians and Paulicians evinced this tendency in doctrine. In the 17th century, some members of the Baptist community adopted dispensationalist views as part of the **Fifth Monarchy Movement**.

Dispensationalists hold that God relates differently to humans in different periods of human history. In the "Age of Law," for instance, God called upon the faithful to observe the Mosaic law and this was accounted to them for righteousness. In contrast, during the "Age of the Church," God required people to accept Christ as Savior and become members of the church universal. Following the Great Tribulation is the Millennial Kingdom, or "Kingdom Age," when all will acknowledge the Lordship of Jesus Christ. The last dispensation is the "Age of New Heavens and Earth," wherein the saints of God will dwell eternally. A feature of many dispensational calculations is pretribulationism, whereby the church will be "raptured" from the world prior to the beginning of seven years of worldwide calamity, culminating in the Battle of Armageddon. Such raptured saints, plus the "dead in Christ," will return with Christ at his Second Coming to reign with him on earth. Other dispensationalists opt for a "midtribulation," "partial rapture," or "posttribulation" rapture theory concerning the translation and gathering of the saints. Dispensationalists base their theological system upon literalistic interpretations of prophetic utterances, such as Ezekiel 38–39, Daniel 9–12, Matthew 24–25, and the entire book of Revelation, to identify the major biblical passages.

Modern dispensationalism owes its origins to the teachings of John Nelson Darby (1800–1882), an English **Bible** teacher and founder of the Plymouth Brethren movement. Darby held a pessimistic view of human history and taught that through a series of prophetic events, Jesus would secretly rapture the true church and return triumphantly to establish his literal kingdom. Darby organized his understanding of God's relations with mankind into seven dispensations covering all of **Scripture**. Darby's influence was felt in the United States and **Canada** through his personal visits, via Dwight L. Moody, and through the Bible conference movement. Baptist teachers such as **Henry G. Weston**, **William Bell Riley**, **Elmore G. Harris** of Toronto, and Arno C. Gaebelein (1861–1945) of New York were early leaders of the dispensationalist revival of the 20th century. The Scofield Reference Bible, edited by Cyrus I. Scofield (1843–1921) and first published in 1909, was popular among Baptists as the first annotated version of the Scriptures popularly produced for laypersons. In the period 1915–1930, dispensationalist theology became permanently wedded to **fundamentalism** when **conservative evangelical** ministers accused **liberal** teachers of denying supernaturalism, including the literal Second Coming of Christ. Dallas (Texas) Theological Seminary, under the leadership of Lewis Sperry Chafer (1871–1952) and John F. Walvoord (1910–2002), prepared numerous Baptist ministers and teachers in the dispensationalist position, although nondenominational itself. Among the categories of Baptists in which dispensationalism is popular are the **General Association of Regular Baptist Churches**, **Landmark** Baptists, the **Baptist Bible Fellowship**, and most independent fundamentalist Baptists. Among Baptists in **Germany**, dispensationalism has been a significant influence, especially with the closer cooperation of various Brethren churches with the union of Baptist churches from the early 20th century.

DISSENTERS. *See* NONCONFORMITY.

DIXON, AMZI CLARENCE (1854–1925). American Baptist minister, born at Shelby, North Carolina. He was educated at Wake Forest College and briefly at Southern Baptist Theological Seminary, and he served pastorates at Immanuel Baptist, Baltimore, Maryland (1882–1890); Hanson Place, Brooklyn, New York (1890–1900); Ruggles Street, Roxbury, Massachusetts (1901–1906); and the independent Chicago Avenue Church, Chicago, Illinois (1906–1922). Just after the turn of the century, Dixon became a devotee of Dwight L. Moody (1837–1899) and followed his revivalistic methods. Dixon opposed theological modernism, evolutionary teaching, and the **social gospel**. In 1909, he began editing a series of tracts called *The Fundamentals*, thus creating a major watershed in American religion. His own contribution to the series defended the infallibility of **Scripture**. When other Baptist **pastors**, notably **T. T. Shields** and **William B. Riley** created the **Baptist Bible Union** (BBU) in the 1920s, Dixon joined their efforts until he noticed that the movement was too stridently critical of mainstream church relationships. One of the authors of the BBU **confession of faith** in 1923, Dixon resigned from the board in

1925. He was characterized as a moderate **fundamentalist** and was the author of numerous **evangelical** works, including *Evangelism: Old and New* (1905).

DOANE, WILLIAM HOWARD (1832–1915). Baptist industrialist and composer, born at Preston, Connecticut. A graduate of Woodstock Academy, he became a bookkeeper in his family's firm. He developed several tools and machines for woodworking and amassed a fortune in his own firm, the J. A. Fay Co. In 1862, following a severe illness, Doane became interested in music and spent the remainder of his life writing and publishing Christian music. He collaborated with **Robert Lowry** and Fanny J. Crosby (1820–1915). Lowry edited the *Baptist Hymnal* in 1888, the most widely used hymnal in the denomination. Doane's compositions include "Take the Name of Jesus with You," "To God Be the Glory," and "Jesus, Keep Me Near the Cross."

DODGE, EBENEZER (1819–1890). American Baptist minister and theological educator, born at Salem, Massachusetts. He was educated at Brown University under the tutelage of **Francis Wayland** and, later, at Newton Theological Institution. In addition, he studied theology in Berlin under the noted teachers F. A. G. Tholuck (1799–1877) and August J. Dorner (1846–1920). He taught at the Western Baptist Theological Institute in Covington, Kentucky, in the 1840s, and then served as **pastor** at New Hampton and New London, New Hampshire. In 1853, Dodge was elected professor of biblical criticism and interpretation at Hamilton Theological Seminary and to a chair in evidences of revealed religion at Madison University. In 1861, this latter role evolved into a professional chair in doctrinal theology, which he renamed Christian Theology. In 1868, Dodge was elected president of Madison University, having turned down professorships at Rochester and Newton seminaries. He led the university into one of its prominent periods, following the "Removal Controversy," which sought to relocate the school to Rochester, New York, and resulted in a damaging split among faculty and the churches. In addition to his administrative duties, Dodge also acquired the status of senior theological faculty member in the institution. **William Newton Clarke** and **Nathaniel Schmidt** greatly admired Dodge as their mentor. Among his published works were *The Evidence of Christianity* (1869) and *Lectures in Christian Theology*, made available to his students at Madison.

DOMESTIC MISSIONS. *See* AMERICAN BAPTIST HOME MISSION SOCIETY; BAPTIST HOME MISSION SOCIETY.

DOMINICAN REPUBLIC. The first Baptists in the Dominican Republic were **Baptist Mid-Missions** from the United States, who established a mission in the republic in 1947. Next were the **Southern Baptists**, who arrived in 1962 to begin work at Santo Domingo and, later, Santiago; more recently, the **Baptist Bible Fellowship** started a mission in 1996. The Convención Bautista Dominicana was organized in 1968. An important chapter in Baptist history was written in 1971 when Paul and Nancy Potter, Southern Baptist missionaries, were killed at Santiago.

As of 2006, there were 22 churches and 1,299 members affiliated with the Convención Bautista Dominicana. *See also* MARTYROLOGY, BAPTIST.

DOUGLAS, THOMAS CLEMENT (1904–1986). Canadian Baptist minister and politician, born at Falkirk, **Scotland**. First trained as a printer, he studied for the ministry at Brandon College and served the Baptist church at Weyburn, Saskatchewan, in 1931–1933. A product of the **social gospel** movement, "Tommy" Douglas developed an interest in programs to relieve poverty and unemployment during the Great Depression. In 1935, he was elected from the Weyburn District to the Federal House of Commons on the Canadian Commonwealth Federation (CCF) ticket. In 1944, Douglas switched to the provincial CCF ticket for Saskatchewan and won a landslide victory. For the next 17 years, Douglas was premier of that province and head of the first socialist government in North America. In 1961, he resigned to become head of the national New Democratic Party. When he was premier in Saskatchewan, he fostered legislation in support of collective bargaining, minimum wages, social welfare, free medical care, and rural electrification. Douglas's ideas on socialized medical care became the basis for Canadian national policy in the 1960s.

DOWNGRADE CONTROVERSY. A theological and ecclesiastical disagreement among English Baptists in the last two decades of the 19th century. By the 1880s, **Charles H. Spurgeon** and a following of Baptist ministers were increasingly concerned over trends in the Baptist and **Nonconformist** communities toward a departure from traditional Calvinistic doctrines such as eternal punishment, the substitutionary atonement of Christ, and, at the root, the authority of **Scripture**. From Spurgeon's perspective as one of London's leading **pastors** and Christian voluntarists, the antidote was to develop and affirm a doctrinal statement such as that of the Evangelical Alliance. In the spring of 1888, Robert Shindler (1823–1903), a Baptist minister at Addlestone and friend of Spurgeon's, published two unsigned articles in Spurgeon's paper the *Sword and Trowel*, which under the title "Downgrade," attacked the **General Baptists** for their **Arminian** doctrines, which Schindler thought would lead to Arianism and Socinianism. Presumably the articles had Spurgeon's approval. Spurgeon himself became openly critical of other Baptists whom he suspected of unhealthy tendencies: John G. Greenhough (1843–1911?), James Thew (1846–1922), W. E. Blomfield (1862–1934), Richard Glover (1837–1919), and **Samuel G. Green**. Spurgeon considered **John Clifford** leader of the General Baptists in the union, his main adversary, and sometimes described him as the "arch-heretic."

In October 1887, Spurgeon withdrew from membership in the **Baptist Union** (BU), and this sent a shockwave through an unsuspecting Baptist community. While some of Spurgeon's associates withdrew with him, most, even those members of his Pastor's College, remained to seek a way of reconciliation. **Joseph Angus** drafted a "declaration" in which the history of the BU and its basic theological tenets were clearly stated, and he presented it to Spurgeon's representatives. Spurgeon declined to accept it, and in January 1887, a delegation consisting of James Culross (1824–1899), John Clifford, and Samuel H. Booth (1824–1902) met with Spurgeon to try to convince him to reverse his opinions. Spurgeon refused and accused the BU of being a "confederacy in evil," not naming anyone in particular. The rift opened wider, fueled by further phrases of condemnation from Spurgeon, and patience among the leadership of the BU declined. In January 1888, Spurgeon's resignation was accepted; in February, Angus's Declaratory Statement was adopted; and John

Clifford's leadership in the BU was solidified. The BU went on to receive the full integration of the General Baptists, a six-point doctrinal statement was adopted, and perhaps the largest and most prestigious of its churches, the Metropolitan Tabernacle, was permanently dissociated from both the BU and the London Baptist Association.

Within the greater British Baptist family, the issues profoundly affected relations with Irish Baptists, where Hugh D. Brown (1858–1917), a close follower of Spurgeon, led the churches away from affiliation with the BU. The Downgrade Controversy had far reaching effects upon the Baptist community on both sides of the Atlantic, legitimating the practice of schism over doctrinal differences, and laying a sure foundation for the type of doctrinal purity witnessed in the **fundamentalist** crusade in the next century.

DUNKERS. *See* GERMAN BAPTIST BRETHREN.

DUNSTER, HENRY (1612–1659). English and, later, American paedo-baptist minister and educator, born at Bury, England. He graduated from Magdalen College, Cambridge University, and entered the Anglican ministry. Disliking King Charles I and Presbyterians alike, Dunster moved to New England in 1639. Almost immediately due to his rare educational attainments among Dissenters, he was selected to be president of the fledgling Harvard College, and he thrived in that role for almost a decade. About 1652, however, he changed his mind about **baptism,** and he refused the **sacrament** for his third child. He was admonished and put on trial 1653–1655, ultimately resigning from his presidency and losing his residence. Dunster assumed a Baptistic position on the matter of believer's baptism and moved to Plymouth Colony in Massachusetts where he joined an Independent church.

DUTTON, ANN WILLIAMS COLES (1692–1765). English Baptist writer, born at Northampton. Not formally educated, she became a member of John Hunt's Baptist congregation at Castle Hill in Cambridgeshire. Dutton moved to London about 1720, marrying and being widowed twice. She married a third time to Benjamin Dutton, a clothier, and they moved to Great Gransden, where he became a **Nonconformist** minister. Ann was a prolific writer of about 50 pamphlets and tracts, covering topics as diverse as the Christian life, the Holy Spirit, and biblical themes. Her theological perspective was Calvinistic, and she was marked as a woman of great poetical gifts. Among Dutton's many works are *A Narration of the Wonders of Grace* (1734), *Brief Hints Concerning Baptism* (1746), and *A Letter on Perseverence Against Mr. Wesley* (1747?).

– E –

EARTHEN VESSEL **BAPTISTS.** *See* STRICT BAPTISTS.

EATON, ISAAC (1724–1772). American Baptist minister and educator, born at Montgomery, Pennsylvania. Self-educated in theology, he also studied medicine. Eaton became **pastor** of the Hopewell, New Jersey, Baptist Church in 1746, which he served until his death. In 1756, the **Philadelphia Baptist Association** voted to support the establishment of a Latin grammar school under Eaton's care at Hopewell, which he operated concurrently with his pastoral work. The prime purpose of this school was to train ministers for the Association, and since it was a preparatory institution, it was expected that graduates would enter collegiate studies at Princeton or Philadelphia. Among Eaton's students were **Samuel Jones**, **Hezekiah Smith**, and Isaac Skillman (1740–1799), in addition to several graduates who became lawyers and physicians. Eaton is credited with establishing the first educational institution among Baptists in America. A sample of Eaton's thinking about ministerial formation is found in "The Qualifications, Characters and Duties of a Good Minister of Jesus Christ" (1755), a sermon he preached at the ordination of **John Gano**. *See also* EDUCATION, BAPTIST VIEWS ON.

ECUADOR. Two missionaries of the Southern Baptist **Foreign Mission Board**, Bill M. Haverfield (1917–1991) and E. Gordon Crocker (1922–), began work at Quito in 1950 and several associations formed in the mid-1960s. In 1972, the Convención Bautista del Ecuador was constituted. A theological seminary at Guayaquil opened in 1961, later relocated to Quito. In 1975, the **Baptist Bible Fellowship** opened a mission in Ecuador.

As of 2006, there were 196 churches with 20,000 members affiliated with the Convención Bautista de Ecuador.

ECUMENISM, BAPTIST INVOLVEMENT IN. From their beginnings Baptists on every continent have been involved in dialogue and sometimes cooperation with other Christian groups. In the first three decades of the **General Baptist** movement in England, Baptists were closely allied with the Dutch Mennonite community. This led to the first Baptist congregation under **John Smyth** seeking refuge with the Dutch Mennonite congregation at Singelkerk in Amsterdam. Ultimately, some Baptists withdrew under **Thomas Helwys** and returned to England, where correspondence between Baptists and Mennonites carried forth until about 1630. The Mennonites declined serious relations with the General Baptists due to the schismatic nature of the latter movement. In the 1670s, the **Particular Baptists** in England drew close to the Presbyterians and tried to demonstrate their doctrinal affinities (except for **baptism**) with the Westminster Confession of Faith. Toward the end of the 17th century, several English General Baptists were friendly with the Unitarian movement and numerous congregations adopted that theological position.

The advance of **William Carey** in 1792 in calling for cooperation in world missionary outreach signaled a major interest among British Baptists toward cooperation with other Christians at the end of the 18th century. Similarly, Baptists were at the forefront in England and **Wales** in forming **voluntary** societies, often in conjunction with other Christians. Among the outstanding examples were the **Sunday School** Society (1785) and the British and Foreign Bible Society (1804).

In the United States, Baptists often evolved along fairly sectarian lines. Doctrinal differences over the mode of baptism caused wide differentiation between Baptists and other Protestant groups, and open criticism of Roman Catholics by prominent authors like **William Cathcart** separated Baptists from Catholics. But, with other evangelical Protestants, many Baptists also supported the American Bible Society (1816) and the Sunday School Union (1817), exhibiting an early cooperative spirit. Toward the middle of the 19th century, many Northern Baptists participated in the Evangelical Alliance and came to understand themselves as mainstream **evangelicals. Freewill**

Baptists cooperated with Free Communion Baptists and frequently joined causes with Regular or Calvinistic Baptists. There were serious differences expressed in several published debates between Baptists and Campellites (Disciples of Christ/Christian Church).

Serious engagement of organized ecumenism began in the American Baptist community with the merger of the Northern Baptist Convention (NBC) and the Free Baptist General Conference in 1911. In 1913, the NBC joined the Federal Council of Churches of Christ as a charter member. This alienated many and encouraged others, causing Northern Baptists, for instance, to decline discussions in 1918 with the Presbyterians toward organic union. In the wake of this sentiment, however, numbers of Northern Baptists joined in local and regional ecumenical relations, such as holiday observances, councils of churches, relief projects, and the Home Mission Council. In 1948, the NBC joined the World Council of Churches (WCC), the first North American Baptist body to do so. Among the several ecumenical organizations in which American Baptists have participated are the International Council of Religious Education, the Foreign Missions Conference of North America, the Missionary Education Movement, the Home Missions Council, the National Protestant Council on Higher Education, the United Stewardship Council, the United Council of Church Women, and Americans United for the Separation of Church and State. Subsequent to the American Baptists joining the WCC, the **Seventh Day Baptist** General Conference also joined. Membership in the National Council of Churches and other educational organizations has allowed some Baptists to be aware of church school curriculum writing, social action projects, and theological education among other major Protestant groups. Perhaps the most extensive amount of ecumenical relationships is enjoyed in the Association of Theological Schools in the United States and **Canada**, where Baptists of almost all persuasions who have accredited seminaries interact and attend policy-making meetings on at least a biennial basis. This has led to countless projects in cooperative education across confessional lines.

Southern Baptists have rather staunchly resisted most formal ecumenical involvement. Influenced by the **Landmarkist** movement, they have not joined, for theological reasons, most regional or national cooperative bodies. The high-water mark of irenic feeling was reached in 1914 when Southern Baptists expressed a desire to partic-ipate in the Faith and Order movement, but soon the tide turned to supporting only convention-related efforts. In the case of the **North American Baptist Fellowship**, the **Baptist World Alliance** (BWA), and the **Baptist Joint Committee on Public Affairs**, the Southern Baptist Convention (SBC) participated through 2004, later determin-ing to chart its own course of external relationships. During the 1960s and 1970s, Southern Baptists supported observer status in WCC dis-cussions of Faith and Order and meetings of the National Council of Churches, but this drew sharp criticism from conservatives and the discussions were curtailed in the 1980s. In the far-reaching mission-ary context of the SBC, noncooperation with ecumenical missions and local councils is required by Southern Baptists for aid to those churches, and this greatly impedes Southern Baptist involvement worldwide. Against this prevailing disinclination toward ecumenism, many Baptists in the South took pride in the establishment of the Ec-umenical Institute at Wake Forest University in 1968, which has sponsored dialogues with several Protestant groups and Roman Catholics. The **Cooperative Baptist Fellowship**, an outgrowth of the SBC in the 1990s, has placed a high priority on cooperation with other Baptist bodies. From the 1990s, representatives of the Southern Baptists convened conversations with the Churches of Christ; after 2000, this dialogue was carried forth by Texas Baptists and lodged in Abilene Christian University and Hardin-Simmons University, both located in Abilene Texas.

The **black Baptist** movement in the United States has a long record of involvement in ecumenical concerns and organizations. To-gether with white Baptist groups, black Baptists have been related to other groups in significant ways, for instance the **National Baptist Convention, U.S.A.**, related to the American Baptist movement, and the **National Baptist Convention of America**, related to the SBC. Beyond Baptist organizations, both major black conventions sup-ported cooperation with the National Association for the Advance-ment of Colored People (NAACP) and the National Equal Rights League as early as 1916. In 1918, a campaign for membership in the NAACP was launched among National Baptists. With the advent of the **Progressive National Baptist Convention** in 1961, fully com-mitted to ecumenism, black Baptists cooperated with the Congress on

Racial Equality, the Southern Christian Leadership Conference, and the National Council of Churches of Christ in the U.S.A. A number of prominent Baptist black Americans were leaders in the ecumenical task, including **Adam Clayton Powell Jr.**, **Martin Luther King Jr.**, **Howard Thurman**, **Benjamin E. Mays**, and **Jesse Jai MacNeill**.

In Great Britain, Baptists pioneered international ecumenism, and it was the founding of the Evangelical Alliance in 1846 that brought Baptists into recognition of cooperative Christianity. **Baptist W. Noel**, **Charles H. Spurgeon**, and others favored cooperation with other evangelical voluntarisms in both the Evangelical Alliance and the Exeter Hall meetings. Later, the establishment of the Free Church Council drew Union Baptists into a new form of ecumenism with Presbyterians, Congregationalists, and Methodists. Over the years, the close ecumenical relations have been maintained by British Baptists with the Congregationalists.

John Clifford, a leader among the Baptists, joined Hugh Price Hughes (1847–1902) in 1892 in convening in Manchester the first congress of **Nonconformists**. This Free Church Council became an annual gathering that organized free churches in the face of Anglican influence in Parliament and the Conservative Party. **John H. Shakespeare**, the secretary of the **Baptist Union** (BU), called for the establishment in 1919 of the Federal Council of Evangelical Free Churches, in which Baptists were heavily involved. In 1939, the Federal Council and the Free Church Council merged (with the support of the BU) into the Free Church Federal Council. When the British Council of Churches was formed in 1942, Baptists were among its members, as Baptists were represented in each phase of the International Missionary Council, Life and Work, and Faith and Order movements leading up to full membership with the establishment of the WCC in 1948. In more recent years, **Ernest A. Payne** led the BU into playing important roles in the World Council of Churches; Morris West, principal at Bristol Baptist College, helped shape the *Baptism, Eucharist and Ministry* document at Lima in 1982; and **Michael H. Taylor** was a prominent member of the WCC Commission on Theological Education 1971–1992. British Baptists were also active in local ecumenical projects throughout the country, with Keith Jones, an area minister in the North and, later, associate general secretary of the BU; Douglas Sparks, a staff person with the BU; and Neville Clarke of South Wales Baptist College as prominent members of organizations like regional ecumenical councils and the BU's Advisory Committee on Church Relations. John Nicholson, later BU superintendent for the North, served as the ecumenical officer of the British Council of Churches and field officer of the Churches Unity Commission 1975–1979, a key post in the era.

Elsewhere in the international family of Baptists there is considerable support for involvement in ecumenical affairs. In Western Europe, it is common for Baptist unions to participate in national ecumenical bodies; in Eastern Europe, it became important to unite a Christian witness under Marxist regimes. Thus, in the Baltic States, **Hungary**, and **Poland**, to name a few places, cooperation in the face of anti-Christian governments was necessary and proved productive from the 1940s through the downfall of Marxist regimes. In Canada, Baptists in one convention are members of the Canadian Council of Churches, and in two other conventions Baptists are members of the Evangelical Fellowship of Canada. Officially, in various parts of the world, Baptists have related to Methodists, Presbyterians, and other Reformed bodies; Lutherans and Catholics have in the last few decades also opened discussions with Baptists.

In **India**, major cooperation and even integration has occurred as large numbers of congregations in West Bengal, Orison, and Bihar voted to enter the Church of North India after it was constituted in 1970. British and U.S. Northern Baptist work in China, long cooperative with other Protestants, has been drawn into a postdenominational movement since the Cultural Revolution, and those who held Baptist sentiments have been found in projects like the China Christian Council and the Amity Foundation. In the Southern Hemisphere, in 1905 the BU of **New Zealand** was engaged in union discussions with the Churches of Christ, reflecting a genuine openness toward other Christians and the BU later joined the WCC as a full member. In Australia, **Silas Mead** in South Australia led his considerable following of churches in the 1870s and 1880s in discussions with Presbyterians and Congregationalists on the subject of open membership and baptism and was a cofounder and teacher in a theological school that involved the three traditions. Later, though initially involved in the Faith and Order movement through the 1940s and discussions that led to a national Australian Council of Churches, Australian Baptists steadfastly opposed involvement in the WCC and in 1962 resolved in the BU of **Australia** not to seek affiliation with the WCC. Two important 20th-century influences against Baptist participation in the WCC were U.S. Southern Baptist presence in New South Wales and the 1950 campaigns of American **fundamentalists** like Carl McIntire and **T. T. Shields**. Australian Baptists over the last half century have cooperated in interdenominational projects in mission and social service.

The BWA has been a major catalyst toward introducing a reluctant Baptist family to Christian cooperation. From its inception, the BWA has maintained cordial relations with other world communions, and with the advent of the WCC, the BWA has supported observer status at most major meetings and activities of the WCC. In the 1980s, Gunter Wagner and **Thorwald Lorenzen,** both faculty members at the International Baptist Seminary in Switzerland, served as official representatives in Geneva, as did **Keith Clements** from his position in the European Conference of Churches. Significantly, the BWA has engaged in theological dialogues with Roman Catholics, the Lutheran World Federation, the World Alliance of Reformed Churches, and the World Mennonite Conference. Negotiations have also been held with the Ecumenical Patriarchate of the Eastern Orthodox Churches. Related to the Roman Catholic conversations, there has been a recent resurgence of interest among conservative evangelical Baptists who affirm many of the pronouncements and attitudes toward non-Catholics expressed by Pope John Paul II. A recent publication, *The Legacy of John Paul II: An Evangelical Assessment* (2007), contains essays by Clark Pinnock and Timothy George. *See also* BAPTIST WORLD ALLIANCE.

EDUCATION, BAPTIST VIEWS ON. Baptist views on, and involvement in, education have varied across time and cultures. In their early development as **General Baptists**, **Particular Baptists**, and **Seventh Day Baptists**, leadership in these traditions came from a fairly high level of educational attainment, including academies, universities, and professional training. Among some early Baptists, there was a distinct disinclination toward formal **theological education** as competitive with spiritual preparation and fitness for **ministry**. Nevertheless, Baptists attended Dissenter academies and after Toleration in 1689 opened their own schools, frequently associated with a church; for example, the Broadmead Baptist Church, Bristol, England in the 1680s. In the 18th century, American Baptists pioneered educational efforts with **Isaac Eaton**'s Grammar School (1756) in Hopewell, New Jersey, and the College of Rhode Island in Providence (1764). More and more Baptist ministers by the 19th century studied at least partially in a college or seminary, except those in the **Primitive** and Old School Baptist groups. As the missionary expansion took place both at home and abroad, the opening of academies, schools, colleges, and seminaries became essential steps in establishing Baptist institutional life. Many of these schools, unfortunately, lacked sufficient funding and interest from Baptists and either closed or devolved into public or private institutions. Rare historically has been the Baptist collegiate institution whose student population is primarily Baptist. It is of interest that even modern **fundamentalist** Baptist groups, who often strenuously oppose "higher education," have created a significant number of educational institutions, holding to the importance of reinforcing their beliefs in a context of Christian education. *See also* HIGHER EDUCATION.

EDWARDS, MORGAN (1722–1795). British Baptist and, later, American Baptist minister and historian, born at Trevithin, **Wales**. Edwards was educated at Trosnant Academy under John Mathews and, later, at Bristol Baptist College under Bernard Foskett; initially, he was ordained to serve a church in Cork, Ireland, where he remained for nine years. In 1761, Edwards took the advice of Dr. **John Gill** and accepted the pastoral call of the First Baptist Church of Philadelphia, Pennsylvania. He served that church until 1771, when a dispute about his drinking habits caused his severance. Edwards also itinerated in the colonies as one of the first commissioned evangelists of the **Philadelphia Baptist Association**. After 1771, Edwards traveled and lectured from his base at Pencader, Delaware. He compiled the first history of Baptists in the United States, entitled *Materials toward a History of the Baptists* (7 vols, 1770–1772) and based on a model suggested by the work of Welsh Baptist historian Joshua Thomas (1719–1797). In the 1760s, Edwards was a prime mover in the Philadelphia Baptist Association for the establishment of the College of Rhode Island, and he suggested a union of Baptists in the United States. During the American Revolution, Edwards was a Loyalist, which caused him great difficulty in the Baptist community.

EGYPT. Baptist witness in Egypt commenced in 1931 with the establishment of a congregation by **Southern Baptists**. The **Baptist Bible Fellowship** opened a mission in Egypt in 1963. The organization of Baptists, formed in 1955, is known as the General Baptist Evangelical Convention of Egypt, as it is registered with the government.

As of 2006, there were 13 churches with 1,300 members affiliated with the General Baptist Evangelical Convention of Egypt, and 10 churches with 320 members affiliated with the Baptist International Mission in Egypt, a U.S.-based **fundamentalist** group.

ELDER. Term used among Baptists for a variety of purposes to designate both lay and clergy persons. Beginning in the 17th century, following the usage of the New Testament the **pastors** of local Baptist congregations were called elders. This term in the United States, especially in New England, became the title of pastors rather than "reverend," which was associated with the Episcopal or Presbyterian churches. Later, most likely under the influence of Brethren or Presbyterian usage, senior lay leaders in the congregation were called "elder," usually understood to be superior to **deacons** in their election to their office.

Among some Baptist groups, like the **Freewill Baptists** in the Northeast, there was a distinction between the "teaching elder," who administered the **ordinances/sacraments** and preached the Word, and the "ruling elder," who led the congregation when the teaching elder itinerated. The ruling elder cared for the welfare and **discipline** of the congregation in addition to supervising the officers, such as deacons. In the mid-20th century, **Reformed Baptists** in the United States, some American and **Southern Baptists**, and some congregations in **Canada** have adopted a multiple eldership, by which is meant a group of spiritual leaders who as a body provide for the various ministries of the congregation. In this case, there is not necessarily a single pastor; rather the pastoral office is divided among those of various personal gifts: teaching, pastoral care, administration, and so forth. Generally speaking, the deaconship is the more common terminology among Baptists to designate lay spiritual oversight within a local congregation. *See also* POLITY, BAPTIST.

ELLA THING MEMORIAL MISSION. In 1895, amidst the expansion of missionary endeavor from North America, an independent Baptist mission was launched at Clarendon Street Baptist Church in Boston, Massachusetts. With Pastor **Adoniram J. Gordon**'s encouragement, S. B. Thing, a deacon in the Clarendon Street Church, set up a memorial fund in 1895 to honor his only daughter, Ella. The first candidates were drawn from the Gordon Missionary Training School and went to **Korea**. The concentration of the mission was in the Korean hinterland, specifically at Kongju and Kanggyung. In 1905, the mission withdrew from Korea and moved to **Japan**, perhaps because of Korean aversions to bathing and the impact of this thinking upon baptismal practices. The work in Korea was assumed by **Malcolm Fenwick** and the Church of Christ in Korea. *See also* FENWICK, MALCOLM; KOREA.

EL SALVADOR. William Keech (fl. 1890–1915), a missionary of the **American Baptist Home Mission Society**, entered San Salvador in 1911, placing emphasis upon development of schools. The centers of American Baptist work were San Salvador and Santa Ana. The first organization of churches, the Baptist Convention of El Salvador, was organized in 1934. A second organization, the Associación Bautista de El Salvador, was formed among the churches in 1967. The **National Baptist Convention, U.S.A.**, began a work there in 1937. Through connections with U.S. **Southern Baptists** in Guatemala, an agreement for cooperation was struck and the Associación took on support from the Southern Baptist **Foreign Mission Board**. In 1976, the **Baptist Bible Fellowship** opened a mission in El Salvador in the **fundamentalist** tradition.

As of 2006, there were 57 churches with 4,427 members affiliated with the Associación Bautista de El Salvador, and 27 churches with 753 members affiliated with the Federacion Bautista de El Salvador. A publication, *Boletin de Fraternidad Bautista (Bulletin of the Baptist Fraternity)*, is published by the associación. The Baptist-related theological seminary for El Salvador is located in Santa Ana.

ENGLAND. *See* BAPTIST UNION OF GREAT BRITAIN AND IRE-
LAND; GENERAL BAPTISTS; LEG OF MUTTON BAPTISTS;
PARTICULAR BAPTISTS; SEVENTH DAY BAPTISTS.

EPHRATA COMMUNITY. *See* BEISSEL, CONRAD; SOLITARY
BRETHREN.

ESTEP, WILLIAM ROSCOE (1919–2000). Southern Baptist educator and historian, born at Williamsburg, Kentucky. He was educated at Berea College, with a theological degree from Southern Baptist Theological Seminary and a Th.D from Southwestern Baptist
Seminary. Estep furthered his education at Union Seminary; the Universities of Oxford, Zurich, and Basel; and in San Jose, Costa Rica.
He served pastorates in Kentucky, Oklahoma, and Texas but primarily taught church history at Los Angeles Baptist Seminary
(1946–1947) and Southwestern Baptist Seminary (1954–1990),
where he eventually became a Senior Professor. Estep specialized in
questions of Baptist identity and the **Anabaptist** contribution to the
early Baptist movement. He steadfastly defended the **Anabaptist
Kinship Theory** and stood at counterpoint to other notable Baptist
historians. Bilingual in English and Spanish, Estep taught at several
Latin American Baptist schools and was published in Spanish.
Among his notable works are *The Anabaptist Story* (1963, 1975) and
Baptists and Christian Unity (1967).

ESTONIA. In the 19th century, several attempts were made to establish evangelical churches in Estonia, which were always met
with intense persecution from Lutherans and Orthodox. Beginning
in the late 1870s, German Baptists were influential in teaching believer's **baptism**, and a baptism was held at Hapsal in 1884. This
action, which was held in frozen waters, impressed the public and
many converts were added. In 1922, a revival occurred with about
a thousand converts, and the same year a seminary was opened at
Kegel, the result of the **London Conference of 1920**; it was later
removed to Tartu.

As of 2006, there were 83 churches and 5,952 members in the
Eesti Evangeeliumi Kristlaste ja Baptistide Koguduste Liit.

ETHIOPIA. Baptist missionary work in Ethiopia commenced in 1950 with missionary appointments by the **Baptist General Conference of America**. Their first congregation was organized at Ambo, with later works at Bekoji and Gendeberet. In 1965, **Southern Baptists** entered the country and set up a station in the Menz-Gishe District. Through 1977, Southern Baptist missionaries worked closely with the Orthodox churches, since Baptists were forbidden to work independently in Ethiopia. A Baptist organization, the Ethiopian Evangelical New Covenant Baptist Church, has, since 1978, assisted several groups in coordinating a Christian witness. The **Baptist Bible Fellowship** has had a mission in Ethiopia since 1960.

As of 2006, there were 51 churches and 8,009 members affiliated with the Baptist Evangelical Association in Ethiopia, and 66 churches with 13,000 members affiliated with the Ethiopian Addis Kidan Baptist Church.

ETHIOPIAN BAPTIST CHURCHES. Name applied to black Baptist churches in the American South. In the 1780s, the congregations of the Savannah, Georgia, region started by **George Leile**, **Andrew Bryan**, and **Andrew Marshall** were referred to by white Baptists as "Ethiopian," doubtless as a generic term for Africa, indirectly inspired by scriptural usage. It was also used to signify black churches for **black Baptists**.

EUROPEAN BAPTIST CONVENTION (EBC). Following World War II, mission work sponsored by the **Southern Baptist Convention** in the United States created churches of English-speaking people across Europe. Congregations were largely associated with U.S. military installations in the NATO command network and had a common Southern Baptist perspective. In 1958, the Association of Baptists in Continental Europe was formed, and in 1964, an association of almost 50 churches became the European Baptist Convention. As of 1995, there are 30 churches and 2,379 members in the EBC. The EBC produces a periodical called *Highlights* (1963–).

EUROPEAN BAPTIST FEDERATION (EBF). The root of a continental organization of Baptists in Europe can be traced to the

London Conference of 1920, where comity agreements and relief projects following World War I were agreed upon under the aegis of the **Baptist World Alliance** (BWA). Turmoil again ensued with the instability in Europe in the 1930s followed by World War II. As the various unions of Baptists in Europe matured after the war, a federation of national Baptist unions was formed in 1949 under the sponsorship of the BWA. BWA associate general secretary Walter O. Lewis convened a meeting of the Committee of Seven that included Henry Cook (Great Britain), Jacob Meister (Germany), Manfredi Ronchi (Italy), Henri Vincent (France), Emil Pfister (Switzerland), A. A. Hardenburg (Holland), and Bredahl Petersen (Denmark). This group drew up a constitution; sought the assistance of the U.S. Northern and Southern Baptists, who had existing missions in Europe; and named W. O. Lewis as the first staff person from the London base of the BWA.

Since 1949, various programs and divisions have been formed for the EBF. The EBF holds congresses every five years and promotes mission and education projects. Its divisions include Theology and Education, Mission and **Evangelism**, Communications, and External Relations. The EBF has made education a major emphasis, helping to establish with the BWA the Theological Assistance Group (1980s), the European Baptist Theological Teacher's Conference (1954), the Summer Institute in Theological Education (1978), EUROLIT (1980, which provides pastor's libraries), the Lay Conference Committee (1971), and the International Baptist Lay Academy in Budapest (1987). After 1992, the EBF also gained oversight of the International Baptist Theological Seminary, which was established at Rüschlikon, Switzerland, in 1949 and removed to Prague, the **Czech Republic,** in 1995. Among other organizations associated with EBF are the European Baptist Mission, the European Baptist Press Service, the European Baptist Women's Union, and several institutes relating to Baptist and Anabaptist studies, training and education, and mission and evangelism. The EBF's offices are located at Bad-Hamburg, Germany, and it is one of the six regional fellowships of the BWA. A distinguished roster of presidents have served the EBF, including Hans Luckey (Germany), Eric Ruden (Sweden), Jacob Broertjes (Netherlands), Michael Zhidkov (Soviet Union), Andrew MacRae (Scotland),

Knud Wumpelmann (Denmark), David Russell (U.K.), Stanislav Svec (Czech Republic), Vasile Talpos (Romania), Piero Bensi (Italy), Theodor Angelov (Bulgaria), and Birgit Karlsson (Sweden). General secretaries have included Karl Heinz Walter (1989–1999), Theo Angelov (1999–), and Tony Peck (2003–).

As of 2006, there were 49 **conventions**/unions in 46 countries belonging to the EBF.

EVANGELICAL BAPTIST MISSIONS (EBM). In September 1928, a missionary from Africa; a **pastor**, Edward Drew; and six members of the Madison Avenue Baptist Church in Paterson, New Jersey, met to form a new mission sending agency, the Africa Christian Missions. The first missionary was Joseph McCaba (1899–1973), who had served as an independent missionary in **Nigeria** from 1925 to 1927; McCaba returned to the Niger Colony of French West Africa, later called the Republic of **Niger**, and served until 1948 when he became the field director of the EBM. The EBM was adopted by the **General Association of Regular Baptists** in 1938 and changed its name twice: Christian Missions, Inc. (1946), and Evangelical Baptist Missions (1957). Since its founding, the EBM has supported work in Africa, **Canada**, **Martinique**, and **Algeria**, primarily in francophone areas. Its doctrinal stance is premillennial and **fundamentalistic**.

EVANGELICALISM, BAPTISTS AND. The term "evangelical" has an evolved meaning in the history of Christianity. In the early church, "evangelical" pertained to the "good news," or gospel, of Jesus Christ, derived from the Greek term *euangellos*. During the Reformation of the 16th century, the German form of the word, *evangelische*, denoted the Protestant churches, such as the Lutheran and Reformed. The watermarks of such churches were the authority of **Scripture**, the Lordship of Christ, and a practicing Christian discipleship referred to as the **priesthood of all believers**. In the 18th century in North America, the **Great Awakening**—a period of **revivals** associated with John Wesley (1703–1791) and Jonathan Edwards (1703–1758), among others—produced a following known as "evangelicals," who were considered proponents of renewal or revival in the churches. There was an increasing emphasis upon religious experience and overt manifestations of religious enthusiasm.

In the 19th century, as revivalism became more widespread and, under leaders like Charles G. Finney (1792–1875), more doctrinaire and formulaic, the term "evangelical" became less an adjective and more a noun to define a growing number of people who wanted to be classed as supportive of certain emphases. These included the authority of the **Bible** and the need for conversion, a new life in Christ, and a passion for **evangelism** and **missionary** outreach. As mainstream denominational life grew more complex and defined, those with evangelical sentiments seized upon the **voluntary association** form of organization and produced scores of new Christian endeavors using an essentially entrepreneurial form of Christianity that became synonymous with evangelicalism. In 1846, organized evangelicalism took a great leap forward in the formation of the Evangelical Alliance, which gave widespread respect to the term amidst the traditional and established churches.

In the 20th century, the term "evangelical" was adopted by those wanting to defend or recover the fundamentals of the faith, until several **liberal** theologians, notably **William N. Clarke**, spoke of their position as "evangelical liberals," because they did not want to lose the warmth of religious experience in their own theological systems. This led to the more definitive use of the word "fundamentalist," and the temporary abandonment of the term "evangelical." Those who wanted a more generic term were caught in the theological middle and were accused of compromising their faith principles by being too open. In the 1950s, a movement, somewhat derisively called "neo-evangelicalism," grew up among open fundamentalists who wanted dialogue with more liberal and orthodox mainstream thinkers. Also to be accounted for were the younger scholars and leaders of an evangelical disposition who came to pastorates and teaching positions in the denominational circles. **Carl F. H. Henry** was a primary Baptist leader of this movement.

Gradually, evangelicalism emerged again among smaller groups and individuals as a viable term in the 1960s. The revitalized National Association of Evangelicals in the United States, the Evangelical Fellowship of **Canada**, the World Evangelical Fellowship, and the Lausanne Covenant tradition gave new life to organized evangelicalism, which now included charismatics and those who argued for a social conscience in tandem with evangelism. Baptist evangelist

Billy Graham has been a leading proponent of bridging the traditional denominations and the more highly doctrinally defined evangelical community.

Baptists have always inculcated the historic emphases of evangelicalism, such as authority of Scripture, necessity of conversion, the Lordship of Christ, a missionary imperative and discipleship. In this sense, adjectivally, Baptists are evangelical. In addition, Baptists have for the most part been supportive of revival traditions, themselves becoming in the United States one of the chief beneficiaries of the revivals. Baptists in Great Britain likewise joined in significant individual numbers the Evangelical Alliance, marking Baptists among the evangelical coalitions. In the 20th century, Baptists can be found among all of the shades of the evangelical tradition: **fundamentalism**, neo-evangelicalism, the World Evangelical Fellowship, the National Association of Evangelicals, and others. However, many Baptists in the mainstream convention and union organizations have declined to be entirely classed as evangelicals, in part because they hold that Baptists predated the formal organization of evangelicals, Baptists having pioneered the same emphases. Also, some Baptists believe that evangelicalism's demand for doctrinal statements and confessions is contrary to the historic Baptist emphasis of noncreedalism. Many Baptists feel that in cooperating with other non-Baptist groups, their doctrine of the church and **ordinances** is diluted, and thus Baptist identity is compromised.

Outside the United States, many Baptist groups have been collectively referred to as "evangelical churches," where there is a particular establishment church in existence, in contrast particularly to Roman Catholic and Orthodox Christians. This is the case in Eastern Europe, where—under Marxist governments and, later, under Orthodox establishment—Baptists, Mennonites, Adventists, and Methodists are called evangelicals. In Latin America, non-Protestants are referred to as evangelicals and this includes the Baptists of varying sorts. Even in **Canada**, Baptists are historically known as part of the evangelical denominations, along with Methodists, Presbyterians, and the Free Church of Scotland.

Baptists, then, typically defend their right to the use of the adjective "evangelical"—and it may even be imposed upon them—while separating themselves necessarily from the organizational side of the evangelical movement. There are numerous outstanding Baptists who also adopt the term's use as a noun, being individual evangelicals in order to maintain fellowship with other believers across confessional lines.

EVANGELISM, BAPTIST VIEWS ON. From their earliest development, Baptists have understood evangelism as both a command of Jesus **Christ** and a process of sharing the gospel, or Good News. In the written gospel narratives (Matt. 28:19, 20; Mark 16:7–9; Luke 24:48; John 20:21) and the Acts of the Apostles (1:8), Jesus clearly commissioned his disciples to move throughout the world to share the Good News that "God so loved the world that He gave His only Son that whosoever believes in Him might have eternal life" (John 3:16). Baptists have taken this commission specially (though not exclusively) to themselves, and evangelism has thus become an important characteristic of Baptist faith and life. Theologically, Baptists assume that salvation is entirely of God, not of works (Eph. 2:8ff), but that God graciously ordains that other humans should be part of the announcement of the Good News as well as exemplifying its effects in their lives. Most Baptists hold that evangelism should be followed by a commitment to become a member of a local congregation, which implies believer's **baptism** by immersion and other acts of personal discipleship and faithfulness (Acts 8:26–39; 16:30–34).

In their early development, some Baptists in Britain and North America debated whether evangelism was to be conducted for all persons or for an "elect" of God. Some held that evangelism was an awakening by the Holy Spirit of the elect, while others believed it was the church's responsibility to preach the gospel so that people led of God's Spirit could respond at will. These differences have survived in the **Strict**, **Primitive**, or Calvinistic Baptist groups on the one hand, and the more open, or **Arminian**, groups on the other.

Evangelism has been a high priority in local church activity. Most Baptists believe it is the responsibility of every believer to share the gospel. Some groups, such as the **Southern Baptists** and others in the **fundamentalist** groups, pray for evangelism, witness to others, and hold special services or opportunities where evangelists can call forth public decisions in response to a sermon. **Billy Graham**, following earlier evangelists like Billy Sunday (1862–1935), has come to symbolize "crusade" evangelism. Still other Baptists in North America and Europe can be seen preaching in public places or conducting house-to-house visits, two other long-used Baptist strategies of evangelism. In the 1960s and 1970s, Baptists in the American Baptist Convention affiliation stressed "corporate evangelism," in which they emphasized a Christian witness to social and economic structures in addition to a call for personal acceptance of Christ, generated from the **social gospel** thinking of **Walter Rauschenbusch** and others. Symbolically, evangelism occupies a prominent place among many Baptist groups. Many Baptist newspapers and journals are titled "messenger" or "herald" or "sower." "Proclamation" is also a common term that emphasizes sharing the gospel through preaching and teaching. *See also* PRIMITIVE BAPTISTS; STRICT BAPTISTS.

EVANS, BENJAMIN (1803–1872). English Baptist minister, educator, and historian, born at Bilston. Early in life, he was employed as an artist, later studying theology with **William Steadman** at Horton. He was pastor at Scarborough (1825–1862), the largest and most influential congregation in the northeast of Yorkshire. Evans was active in many of the **voluntary associations** of his day, including the Society for Liberating Religion from State Patronage and Control, the Archaeological Society, and the Bethel Mission to Seamen. He is said to have traveled thousands of miles in an open gig in support of denominational causes. At 64 years old, Evans founded the Theological College at Bury and assumed the chair in ecclesiastical history there. He established and edited the *Baptist Record*, largely for the benefit of **Strict Baptists**. His historical work was considerable: he wrote a two-volume history, *The Early English Baptists* (1862–1864), in which he undertook pioneering research in the British Museum and the archives in Amsterdam, and he completed the histories of Rawdon College and Horton Academy (1854). He corresponded officially with Baptists in the United States and contributed to the library of the American Baptist Historical Society. The University of Rochester in New York awarded Evans an honorary D.D. in 1857.

EVANS, CHRISTMAS (1766–1838). Welsh Baptist minister and evangelist, born at Llandyssul. He was first a farmer; from a study of the

Bible, Evans began to preach informally. Baptized as an adult by Timothy Thomas in 1788, he was ordained two years later by the Welsh Baptists as an itinerating **missionary**. Early in life Evans suffered several mishaps, including being waylaid and beaten, the result of which was the permanent loss of one eye and facial disfiguration. This made him somewhat of a curiosity, and coupled with his great preaching abilities, Evans drew vast crowds. While he spent much of his focused **ministry** in Anglesey, he held open air campaigns across **Wales** and in parts of England. Not only did his preaching renew the Baptist movement in the first decades of the 19th century but also his work helped to revive the Welsh language. He was well-known for his narrative sermon on the Gadarene Demoniac, whom he portrayed. Evans was Calvinistic, much appreciative of **John Gill**. He supported mission societies and a compensated ministry. Christmas Evans's published sermons were reprinted regularly in Welsh and English well into the 19th century.

EXECUTIVE MINISTER. Terminology that is applied among American Baptist churches and certain Canadian Baptists to describe the senior executive officer of a state **convention**, city society, or regional convention. The title succeeds that of agent, corresponding secretary, executive secretary, or general secretary found in early 19th-century Baptist polity at the provincial, state, or city level of administration in North America.

Before the American development of Baptist polity and terminology, "general superintendent" and "**messenger**" were used in the English tradition, and the compensated corresponding secretary (at least for expenses!) of a missionary society was typical, as in the **Baptist Missionary Society** from 1792 and the **Baptist Union** from 1832. In the United States, this pattern was seen in Massachusetts from 1802. British Baptists have continued the use of "superintendency" vocabulary into the present.

The executive staff of the early American societies were also voluntary. The first state-convention-paid employee appears to have been John Peck (1780–1849), general agent of the Baptist Missionary Convention of the State of New York, beginning in 1825. As the statewide Baptist communities organized and became involved in missionary activity, a definite need for supervision arose and each one in turn appointed such persons to administrative and traveling tasks. When the

American Baptist Home Mission Society (ABHMS) was organized in 1832, it developed patterns of cooperation with the various state **associations** and conventions, and this often led to funding of the general secretary role as a missionary superintendent. The ABHMS followed this pattern in the development of western U.S. state conventions, appointing its senior missionary as an administrator, for instance, in Minnesota, the Dakotas, California, and Washington State.

In 1919, the **New World Movement** called for the state secretaries to become collecting agents for the Northern Baptist Convention and its auxiliaries, and this led to a national role for the secretaries and the formation of the Organization of State Convention Secretaries in the 1920s. The use of the term "corresponding" or "executive secretary" continued to be popular through the 1950s.

Reorganization of state and national bodies took place in the 1960s, with fundamental changes occurring in 1972–1973. The first instance of the new title "executive minister" in the United States occurred in 1977 among regional secretaries of the **American Baptist Churches**. This title, provided for in the Report of the Study Commission on Relationships of December 9, 1976, became the title of all state and city secretaries, originally 37 in number. It conveyed both a regional and national accountability. Among Canadian Baptists, the term "executive minister" appears to have been adopted in the later 1970s, first in the Baptist Union of Western Canada in response to the Janssen Report, issued by an ABHMS consultant to the Baptist Convention of Ontario and Quebec, Lawrence H. Janssen (1921–1995).

The executive minister is usually accountable to a board or council of a convention and has oversight of the staff and program of the organization. The office has influence only in the life of member congregations and has limited ceremonial importance at assemblies where the elected voluntary officers preside over sessions. In certain circumstances, the executive minister may be the supervisor of the area or of regional ministers. Sociologically, the executive minister assumes many of the functions associated with the episcopacy in other denominations, including registrar of the ministerial roster, conflict resolution, and pastoral ministry to local church **pastors**. *See also* AMERICAN BAPTIST HOME MISSION SOCIETY; AREA MINISTER; POLITY, BAPTIST.

– F –

FALWELL, JERRY (1933–2007). U.S. independent, fundamentalist Baptist minister, educator, and political activist, born at Lynchburg, Virginia. Falwell studied at Lynchburg College, but withdrew to complete his education at Bible Baptist Seminary in Arlington, Texas. He started a congregation in the lower-middle-class west end of Lynchburg, first meeting in the Donald Duck Bottling Company warehouse. The congregation grew dramatically at Thomas Road Baptist Church, spurred on by an extensive bus ministry to its Sunday School and evangelistic preaching by Falwell that was broadcast first on radio, then national and international television as "The Old Time Gospel Hour." (Falwell took the name from his own religious conversion while listening to evangelist Charles Fuller's radio program, the "Old Time Revival Hour.") In 1971, he started Lynchburg Baptist College that evolved to Liberty University, Lynchburg Baptist Theological Seminary, and Thomas Road Bible Institute. Falwell's finances were often in jeopardy, with several investigations by the U.S. government, and in the early years, this led to a precarious existence for the schools.

Falwell's creation of the Moral Majority in 1979 led to a national political coalition that brought about the election of Ronald Reagan to the U.S. presidency, gave Falwell media credibility, and attracted wide interest to his university and church. He purchased a mountainside near Lynchburg, Virginia, and built a campus of 20,000 students that included a law school, a theological school, and a nationally ranked athletics program. In 2006, the Thomas Road Baptist Church moved to the university site to shared facilities that accommodate 10,000 resident students. In 2006, his two sons, Jerry Falwell Jr. (1962–) and Jonathan Falwell (1966–), took over the operations of the university and the church, respectively, under a family-controlled board of trustees. Among Baptists, Falwell founded the Liberty Baptist Fellowship; was affiliated with the Baptist Bible Fellowship, International; and contributed to the **Southern Baptist Convention** through its regional state affiliate in Virginia. Falwell's considerable legacy in publishing and outreach is continued through Jerry Falwell Ministries, Inc.

FAMILISTS. Name applied to a 17th-century English religious sect related to the early Baptist movement. The "Family," or "House of Love," was established about 1540 in Emden, Westphalia, by Hendrik Nicklaes (1502–1580?). Although the Elizabethan Act of Uniformity attempted to eliminate groups like the Familists, they continued underground in conventicles. The Family was organized as a perfectionist brotherhood, with hopes for the establishment of a thousand-year reign of **Christ** and his saints, which would be ushered in by an outpouring of the Holy Spirit. Familist organization drew upon **Anabaptist** patterns, with three classes of priests and no apostolic succession. Members were subject to the **discipline** of the brotherhood. Ethically, the Family was pacifistic and refused to take oaths. Seventeenth-century writers, notably the Presbyterian Thomas Edwards (1599–1647), considered the Familists as the root of radical ideas and behavior, influencing Quakers, Baptists, and **Fifth Monarchists**. A significant number of Familists evolved into Quakers, some surviving into the 1680s in Ely, England. In 1636, Governor John Winthrop of Massachusetts criticized Hanserd Knollys for "familistical" tendencies. *See also* DIGGERS; LEVELLERS; RANTERS; SEEKERS.

FAUNCE, WILLIAM HERBERT PERRY (1859–1930). American Baptist minister and educator, born at Worcester, Massachusetts. He was educated at Brown University and Newton Theological Institution, later spending a year in advanced studies at the University of Jena in **Germany**. Faunce served the pastorate of State Street Baptist Church in Springfield, Massachusetts, and from 1889 to 1899, Fifth Avenue Baptist in New York City. An able orator and thinker, he served as lecturer at the University of Chicago and as campus preacher at Harvard University. Faunce was elected president of Brown University in 1899 and expanded the program of the university in buildings and curriculum. Among his accomplishments, Faunce had the charter changed to allow for a non-Baptist president, in defense of religious freedom of the institution. This caused a great uproar in the Northern Baptist Convention and led ultimately to the separation of Brown as a church-related institution. A second tumultuous incident occurred in Faunce's career when McMaster University in **Canada** conferred upon him an honorary degree and drew the wrath of **conservative evangelicals** in the Baptist Convention of Ontario and Quebec.

Faunce was a leading **liberal** thinker of his era, interested in the historical-critical study of **Scripture** and the ethical issues inherent in the Christian faith. He defended the United States' entry into World War I and later championed the League of Nations. His Lyman Beecher Lectures at Yale in 1908 were published as *The Educational Ideal in Ministry*. In retirement, Faunce toured the mission fields of the Baptists, taking particular interest in **China**, and he was president of the World Peace Foundation. Faunce's published works include *The Social Aspects of Foreign Missions* (1914), *Religion and War* (1918), and *What Are the Fundamentals?* (1923).

FELLER, HENRIETTE ODIN (1800–1868). Canadian Baptist educator, born at Montmagny, **France**. About 1833, Henriette Feller met Henri Olivier (fl. 1800–1840), who introduced her to the Swiss Evangelical Movement, and she joined his church at Lausanne. At length, Olivier and his wife moved to Lower **Canada** (now Quebec) in 1834 to conduct missionary work. They induced Henriette and another young person, **Louis Roussy**, to come to Canada, and Henriette arrived in 1835. In 1836, she moved to a rural location at Grand Ligne, where she and Roussy started a school and did **evangelistic** work as the Mission de la Grande Ligne en Canada. Frequently, they suffered persecution and fled to upstate New York, for instance, in 1837. Support for Feller's work was broadened, and a permanent mission house was erected in 1840. Over the next 20 years, Baptist congregations increased in the region, leading to the eventual formation of the Union des Eglises Baptistes Françaises (French-Speaking Union of Canadian Baptists).

FELLOWSHIP OF BAPTISTS FOR HOME MISSIONS (FBHM). An independent American domestic missionary agency that conducts **evangelism** and church planting in the United States. Formed in July 1941 of missionaries and laymen at the First Baptist Church, Elyria, Ohio, the FBHM grew out of **fundamentalist** discontent with the Northern Baptist Convention and was adopted by the **General Association of Regular Baptist Churches** as its home mission agency. The FBHM's stated objectives were evangelization of the unsaved and establishment of New Testament churches. Several organizational mergers have taken place: the Montana Baptist Fellowship (1941) joined in 1948, and in 1950, the Western Baptist Missions (including the **Columbia Basin Mission**) and the West Virginia Fundamental Baptist Mission united with the FBHM. A national council and an advisory council guide the work of the mission, whose headquarters are located in Elyria, Ohio. The FBHM published the *Home Fellowship News*.

FELLOWSHIP OF BRITISH BAPTISTS (FBB). Formed in 1994, the FBB owes its origin to the suggestion in 1991 of **Baptist Union of Great Britain** general secretary Bernard Green (1925–) that those with common interests should consult and plan together. The FBB is composed of representatives of the Baptist Unions of **Scotland**, **Wales**, Great Britain, and the **Baptist Missionary Society**; it meets at least annually for fellowship, consultation, and mission planning. The FBB represents all of the mainstream Baptists in Britain and Northern Ireland in a less formal mode than in the historic national/regional structures.

FELLOWSHIP OF EVANGELICAL BAPTIST CHURCHES IN CANADA (FEBC). In the mid-1920s, against the background of the **fundamentalist**-modernist controversy in the United States, a schism broke out in the Baptist Convention of Ontario and Quebec. Led by **Thomas Todhunter Shields**, an investigation was launched in 1923–1925 into modernist tendencies at McMaster University, specifically concerning the appointment of **L. H. Marshall** as professor of pastoral theology. The 1926 convention adopted a resolution of censure against Shields, and the following year the convention voted to **disfellowship** 13 churches. Immediately, a new group was formed behind the leadership of Shields, the Union of Regular Baptist Churches of Ontario and Quebec. A further split occurred in 1931–1933, which spawned a loosely knit group in 1933, the Fellowship of Independent Baptist Churches of Canada. The doctrinal basis of this fellowship affirmed **voluntary association** and premillennialism. Related to this movement were the Fundamentalist Baptist Young People's Association (1927) and the Muskoka Baptist Conference (1931).

In the late 1920s, several Baptist churches in Alberta and British Columbia also coalesced around fundamentalistic principles and formed the British Columbia Regular Baptists (1927) and the Regular Baptist Missionary Fellowship in Alberta (1930). For a time, these western movements sought a relationship with the U.S. **Southern Baptists** who had started mission churches in the region. Ultimately, the Southern Baptist connection broke down, and Southern Baptists organized their own separate work in Canada. Between 1950 and 1953, merger discussions took place between the major groups of fundamentalist Baptists, and the result was the establishment of the Fellowship of Evangelical Baptist Churches in Canada in Toronto in October 1953. Over the years, FEBC Baptists have supported mission work through **Baptist Mid-Missions** and the **Association of Baptists for World Evangelism**, two U.S.-based organizations, as well as their own work, the **Japan** Regular Baptist Mission at Takaoka (1952), and missions at Ellichpur, **India** (1963), and in **Indonesia** (1967).

In 1938, the FEBC formally began a francophone mission in northern Quebec, which encompassed 76 churches and 4,700 members as of 1995. There is also a theological school, Seminaire Baptiste Evangélique du Québec, in Montreal, founded in 1974.

For educational purposes, in the central region, the FEBC related to the London (Ontario) Baptist Bible College and Central Baptist Seminary in Toronto, which were merged in 1993 to become Heritage Baptist College and Seminary in Hespeler, Ontario. In the western provinces, a separate educational heritage evolved: in 1934, the Regular Baptist Churches of the Prairies founded the Western Baptist Bible College, which closed in 1940. In 1945, the Regular Baptists of British Columbia and the Prairies opened the Northwest Baptist Bible College at Port Coquitlam, British Columbia, which in due course became the Northwest Baptist Theological College, now a member of the Associated Canadian Theological Schools in Langley, British Columbia. Numerous ministerial students in the FEBC family have been trained at the Ontario Theological Seminary (later Tyndale University College and Theological Seminary) in Toronto and also at various conservative evangelical schools in the United States.

The FEBC includes three national agencies: FEBInternational, Chaplaincy Services, and French Ministries. A national council that executes the decisions of the FEBC consists of 12 members who represent national officers, regional and agency members. The group publishes the *Evangelical Baptist* (1953–) and claims 493 congregations and 71,073 members across Canada (2006).

FELLOWSHIP OF EVANGELICAL BAPTIST CHURCHES IN EUROPE. An organization of conservative **evangelical** Baptists, who, in 1967, banded together for fellowship and mission to greater Europe and beyond. Included in the coalition are the **Strict Baptists** of England, Evangelical Baptists of **France**, and the Irish Baptists. The fellowship is characterized by a doctrinal statement and opposition to ecumenical organizations such as the **Baptist World Alliance**.

FENWICK, MALCOLM (1863–1935). Canadian **evangelical** and later Korean Baptist **missionary** and minister, born at Markham, Ontario. He worked on a model farm in Ontario and then went to Manitoba. Fenwick was called to foreign mission service while attending the Niagara Bible Conference. He married Fanny Hinds, who had taught for the Methodists in **Korea** and studied under **Adoniram J. Gordon**. About 1893, Fenwick met Gordon and was influenced by his teaching. In 1894, with Joseph Douglas of Toronto, Fenwick started the Corean Itinerant Mission, which supported him later in Korea. His ministry in Korea was based in Sorai and Wonsan, where he conducted a school. In 1901, Fenwick merged his work with the **Ella Thing Memorial Mission** to form the Church of Christ in Korea. Fenwick served from 1909 to 1914 as the "kammok," or superintendent-**pastor**, of this body and earned a reputation as an authority figure in the church. Over the years of his missionary work, Fenwick gradually evolved into a Baptistic thinker, with definite leanings toward the **conservative evangelical** tradition. *See also* KOREA.

FIFTH MONARCHY MOVEMENT. A 17th-century movement among Baptists and others in England that exhibited biblical literalism applied to the political context. Among the **General** and **Particular Baptists** and other Nonconformists in the 1640s were those who understood the **Scriptures** literally and took a special interest in the apocalyptic passages in the biblical books of Daniel and Revelation.

A few hundred people during the last years of the reign of King Charles I, led by Col. Thomas Harrison (1606–1660), concluded that **Christ** was due to return to earth as a king and establish the fifth monarchy of Daniel 7:1–8. The new kingdom was thought to be composed of saints, without priest or **sacrament**, law or oath, king or government. They expressed an interest in putting Charles I to death in order to hasten the coming of Christ's kingdom.

When Oliver Cromwell (1599–1658) accepted power over the Commonwealth in December 1653, Fifth Monarchists opposed Cromwell, proclaiming him an apostate and the little horn of Daniel's prophecy. Cromwell's takeover brought calculations of the biblical 1,260 days until the end of the great tribulation and plans for an insurrection to overthrow the "beast." Fearing an insurrection, Cromwell had many Fifth Monarchists, including Harrison, thrown into prison. In 1660, Harrison was hanged, drawn, and quartered; this incited Thomas Venner (d. 1661), a cooper, to rise up against the government, resulting in a violent defeat of the Fifth Monarchists at Cripplegate. Such political events, plus errors of calculation, proved the falsity of the Fifth Monarchy idea, and most of the chiliastic sentiment died.

Many of those who held a literalistic biblical hermeneutic, however, found in the recovery of the sabbath a new cause, and they shifted to the **Seventh Day** movement, which included some Baptists and others. The major Baptist activists and writers in the Fifth Monarchy Movement were **Henry Jessey**, **Hanserd Knollys**, John Pendarves (1622–1656), Henry Danvers, **Peter Chamberlen**, and **Vavasor Powell**. In order to clear the name of Baptists from charges of extremism, both General and Particular Baptists published a document, *The Humble Apology of Some Commonly Called Anabaptist* (1660), the first joint effort of all Baptists. The contributions of Fifth Monarchist Baptists include the application of new hymns to old tunes. See also DIGGERS; DISPENSATIONALISM; LEVELLERS; RANTERS; SEEKERS.

FIJI. The first Baptist work in Fiji dates from 1969 and numbers around 1,100 members as an independent association of 2 churches. As of 2006, there were 14 churches and about 1,000 members associated with the Fiji Baptist Convention, related to the **Southern Baptist Convention.**

FINLAND. Baptist development in Finland evolved as an outgrowth of Swedish Baptist missionary endeavor and from crosscurrents of relationships. As early as 1854, Carl J. M. Mollersvard (1832–1901) preached on Foglö Island, and a chapel was erected at Jakobstad in 1871. In 1870, Esaias Lundberg, baptized by a Swedish sailor, founded the first Finnish-speaking congregation; later, John Hymander (1803–1877) went to Stockholm to be baptized and returned to form a congregation at Parikkala. A district union of the Swedish-speaking churches was established in 1883 and renamed in 1893, "Conference of the Baptist Denomination in Finland." Some strife occurred between the Swedish-speaking churches and what became the Suomen Baptistiyhdyskunta (Finnish Union), formed in 1903; the Swedish-speaking congregations separated from the Finnish-speaking churches in 1922, essentially creating a second organization, Svenska Baptisternas i Finland. A newspaper, *Kodin ystava* (Friend of Homes), began publication in 1896 and a **Bible** institute opened in 1949. The Swedish churches publish *Missions Standaret* (1914–), and the Finnish churches publish *Tootuuden kaiku* (Echo of the Truth). Theological education is conducted at a Bible school in Tampere. In addition to the indigenous work, **Baptist Mid-Missions** from the United States established a mission in 1980.

As of 2006, there were 11 churches and 692 members in the Suomen Baptistiyhdyskunta, and 19 churches and 1,271 members in the Svenska Baptisternas i Finland.

FINNISH BAPTIST UNION OF AMERICA. At the beginning of the 20th century, significant numbers of Finnish emigrants went to the United States and intermingled, particularly with the Swedish communities in the Great Lakes region. At length, missions were conducted and two congregations emerged in 1900: Worcester, Massachusetts, and Felch, Michigan. The preaching of pioneer **evangelist** Matts Esselstrom (1868–1949) and Albert M. Wickstrom (1872–1951), a physician and **Bible** teacher, were important catalysts in church development.

A conference, the Finnish Baptist Mission Union of America (also known as the Baptist Union of America and, after 1947, the Baptist Mission Union of America), was formed in 1901 at Austin, near Chicago, Illinois. It served primarily to send out evangelists to Finns and Swedes in the United States and **Canada**, focusing mainly on Michigan, Minnesota, Wisconsin, and Illinois. The Union published for a time *Finnoka Missions Posten* (Mission Post) (1906–). In the 1940s, the union included about 19 churches and 1,000 members. After 1948, the congregations were invited to affiliate with the **Baptist General Conference** (Swedish) and most were absorbed into its work. For a period in the 1940s, the Union was also affiliated with the Northern Baptist Convention.

FIVE PRINCIPLE CALVINISTIC BAPTISTS. In the U.S. colonial New England context, a coalition of churches emerged between 1639 and 1740 in Massachusetts, Rhode Island, and Connecticut known as Five Principle Calvinistic Baptists. The name signified their affirmation of historic Calvinistic doctrines as stated in the Westminster **Confession of Faith** (1646): total depravity, unmerited favor, limited atonement, irresistible grace, and the perseverance of the saints. The Five Principle Calvinistic Baptists were divided into two camps: those who worshipped on the first day and those who worshipped on the **seventh day**. The Sabbatarians had two congregations before 1740, Westerly and Newport, Rhode Island. The first-day churches included those at Boston, Swansea, Tiverton, Rehoboth, Sutton, Bellingham, Leicester, South Brimfield, and West Springfield in Massachusetts, and at Wallingford in Connecticut. Generally, the Five Principle Calvinistic Baptists in New England closely imitated the **Particular Baptists** in England and **Wales** in the 17th century. *See also* GENERAL BAPTISTS.

FLEISCHMANN, KONRAD ANTON (1812–1867). American German Baptist minister, born in Nuremberg, Germany. In his youth, Fleischmann traveled in **Switzerland** and **Germany**, ultimately being converted under the Swiss Separatists. He studied for the ministry under Karl von Rodt, experienced persecution from the Reformed Church in Switzerland, and emigrated to America in 1839. He came under American Baptist influence and was commissioned by the

American Baptist Home Mission Society as a missionary to the Germans in eastern Pennsylvania. In the winter of 1841, Fleischmann was part of a great revival in central Pennsylvania. The next year he moved to Philadelphia where he baptized five candidates and gathered the first German Baptist Church in the United States. In 1851, he organized the first German Baptist Conference, and in 1853, he began publication of *Der Senbote des Evangeliums* (The Gospel Messenger). Fleischmann is considered the founding father of the German Baptist movement in the United States. *See also* NORTH AMERICAN BAPTIST CONFERENCE.

FOOT WASHING. A recognized **ordinance** among several Baptist groups, including some **Primitive Baptists**, **black Baptists**, **Glasites**, and the **Scotch Baptists** of the 19th century. The washing of feet in the ancient Near East was done for practical purposes of cleanliness and comfort, where people traveled by foot and wore open sandals. Usually a servant in the family or household washed the feet of newly arrived travelers (Gen. 18:4; Judg. 19:21; II Sam. 11:8; Canticles 5:3).

Three passages in the New Testament indicate that the washing of feet was relevant to the early Christian community. In John 13:14–15, Jesus washed the feet of his disciples and asserted that they ought to wash the feet of each other. This passage has meant for some in the Brethren tradition (and some Baptists) that it should become a gospel ordinance practiced by believers in the church. In the early 19th century, a debate arose among New England Baptists to that end. Among the objections raised were whether foot washing was meant to be universal, that it had never being recorded as part of New Testament liturgy, that it would take excessive time, that it would be difficult for men and women to wash each other's feet, and that the task seemingly implied by I Timothy 5:9–10 in which a woman appears to have the task of washing people's feet as part of her household service would be deemed too exclusive. These objections prevented foot washing from becoming a widely accepted gospel ordinance among Baptists.

In the instances where foot washing is practiced, the ceremony, called the pedalavium, is simple. At a service, which begins with self-examination, the text is commonly John 13. The congregation is divided according to sex, with men serving men and women serving women. Among **German Baptist Brethren**, the oldest sibling first washes the feet of the first sibling on the right and that person in turn washes the feet of the one on his or her right, until the entire company has participated. The leader uses a small basin of tepid water to dip a towel, then with dried hands from another towel, may shake the hand of the one served and perhaps use the kiss of peace or offer a prayer. The first male and female initially gird themselves with the drying towel, in the form of a servant.

Most Baptists have taken foot washing as a symbolic gesture to teach humility and servanthood, actually practicing it rarely, such as only during Lent or Passion Week.

FOREIGN MISSION BOARD, SOUTHERN BAPTIST CONVENTION (FMB). The Southern Baptist Foreign Mission Board in the United States is the largest missionary organization belonging to the Baptist family. In 1845, with the organization of the **Southern Baptist Convention** (SBC), one of the first tasks was to promote foreign missions, and the Board of Foreign Missions was set up in Richmond, Virginia. The original governing body included officers of the SBC, plus several elected by the SBC, and a board of managers local to the Richmond area. **James B. Taylor** was chosen corresponding secretary and served until 1871. The first mission fields were **China** and Africa and, after the American Civil War, **Italy**. Negotiations were held with the **Baptist Board of Foreign Missions** (BBFM), with which Baptist churches in the South had previously cooperated; one missionary under appointment to the BBFM, **J. Lewis Shuck**, transferred to the southern FMB. During the American Civil War, operations of the FMB virtually closed down for four years. Afterward, under the leadership of **Henry A. Tupper**, expansion into China, **Nigeria**, Italy, **Mexico**, and **Japan** took place. Tupper also resurrected the appointment of female missionaries, with Lulu Whilden and the **Moon** sisters in 1873, and shepherded the establishment of the auxiliary Woman's Missionary Union in 1888. Important steps were taken in 1851, with the first female appointment, Harriet Baker (fl. 1850), and the FMB's first commissioning service that year, and in 1875, with the appointment of black missionaries W. J. David (1850–1919) and W. W. Colley (1847–1879) to Yoruba Land.

During the early years of its evolution, the FMB experimented with several scenarios of appointment and work, as in **Sierra Leone** where in 1855 the board assumed the support of personnel from other sources. In its expanding witness after the turn of the century, however, the FMB confronted the issue of cooperation in world mission with other Baptist and Christian organizations. In 1916, the board approved a policy of complete autonomy at home and abroad, rejecting arbitrary territorial boundaries and any form of cooperation that was not accountable to the SBC and under its control. This autonomy has often meant that Southern Baptist missionaries work in fields already occupied by other Baptists. Much of the initiative of the FMB, however, has been in previously unevangelized fields. Since 1845, Southern Baptists have worked in 155 countries; as of 2006, they were operating in 117 nations/people groups with over 5,000 missionaries. The FMB has received 50 percent of the annual Cooperative Program receipts since 1925, and the remaining funds for overseas work have come from the annual Lottie Moon Christmas Offering. The annual budget for the FMB is $288.9 million (2006).

In 1997, with the reorganization of the SBC, the FMB became the International Mission Board (IMB) of the SBC. The FMB's official publication has been *The Commission* (1849–1850; 1938–). The IMB claims to relate to 135,252 churches with 8.8 million members overseas (2006).

FORTRESS MONROE CONFERENCE. Following the era of Civil War and Reconstruction in the United States (1861–1877), the Baptist communities of the North and South competed in missionary efforts, particularly among the black population. Representatives of the **Southern Baptist Convention** (SBC) requested a meeting with the **American Baptist Home Mission Society** (ABHMS), which had long operated schools, colleges, church planting programs, and **chapel car evangelism** in the southern states. Ostensibly, the SBC wanted the ABHMS to cease its work in the region. On September 12–14, 1894, the representatives met at Fortress Monroe, Virginia, the site of a federal prison during the Civil War where the president of the Confederacy, Jefferson Davis, had been incarcerated. A series of agreements were reached, which provided for assumption of greater influence in the schools for **black Baptists**, cooperation in mission work among blacks, and a principle of comity, whereby the two Baptist groups would not compete in the same region and would instead focus their energies upon fields not already occupied by either. The Fortress Monroe Conference established a principle of mutual recognition of the two major U.S. Baptist groups, until the SBC voted in the mid-1940s to establish churches in the northern states because of migration of southerners to the North.

FOSDICK, HARRY EMERSON (1878–1969). American Baptist minister, born at Buffalo, New York. Fosdick was educated at Colgate University and Union Theological Seminary and later took a master's degree at Columbia University. His early mentor was **William Newton Clarke** at Colgate. He served three pastorates: First Baptist, Montclair, New Jersey (1904–1915); First Presbyterian Church, New York (1918–1925); and Park Avenue Baptist Church, New York City. Under Fosdick's leadership, Park Avenue evolved into Riverside Church in the Morningside Heights area of New York's Upper West Side. During World War I, he served with the American Expeditionary Forces in Europe and developed a pacifist position. As a pulpiteer, Fosdick had few equals, and he quickly became one of the most highly quoted clergymen of his era. In his Park Avenue congregation were **John D. Rockefeller** and James **Colgate**; Rockefeller built a new edifice on Fosdick's irenic theology, Riverside Church, dedicated in 1931.

At the outbreak of the **fundamentalist** crusade, Fosdick preached a sermon, "Shall the Fundamentalists Win?" which became a battle cry for both the **liberal** camp and fundamentalists. His pastoral approach to the **Bible** and popular dependence upon the documentary hypothesis of the origins of the Pentateuch (*The Modern Use of the Bible*, 1924) brought popularity as well as scorn, and his stance on civil rights and against war likewise galvanized people. Fosdick also devoted his communications gifts to Union Seminary, teaching practical theology there from 1908 to 1946. He was the weekly preacher on the "National Vespers Hour," an influential **ecumenical** radio broadcast. Fosdick was awarded an honorary doctorate from the University of Glasgow. Fosdick's hymn, "God of Grace and God of Glory," is popular among all Protestants and has been an unofficial theme hymn of American (formerly Northern) Baptists. Memorable

Fosdick publications include *What Shall We Do with Jesus?* (1922), *Science and Religion* (1924), and *The Unknown Soldier* (1934).

FOSTER, GEORGE BURMAN (1857–1918). American Baptist minister and theologian, born at Alderson, West Virginia. He graduated from West Virginia University and studied theology in German universities at Berlin and Göttingen. In the 1880s, Foster served congregations at Morgantown, West Virginia, and Saratoga Springs, New York, preferring a career in academic life. In 1892, he took a teaching position in philosophy at McMaster University in Toronto, Ontario, later moving to the University of Chicago Divinity School in 1896 at the invitation of **William Rainey Harper**. A controversial systematic theologian, Foster developed his theology on the basis of human experience and moved in the then fashionable streams of pragmatism in American intellectual thought. A member of the famous "**Chicago School**," Foster was described as one of the most intellectual theologians ever to develop in the Baptist tradition, and he influenced many **liberal** thinkers, including **Douglas Clyde MacIntosh**. Due to his vague statements of orthodox Christian doctrines, Foster was expelled by the Baptist Ministers Conference of Chicago in 1906–1907. He was transferred from the Divinity School to the Department of Philosophy of Religion in the Graduate School in order to alleviate the criticism from the constituency. Foster's major works include *The Finality of the Christian Religion* (1906) and *The Function of Religion in Man's Struggle for Existence* (1909).

FOUNDERS MINISTRIES. A theologically confessional coalition of congregations and individuals in the greater **Southern Baptist** (SBC) family that adhere to classic formulations of Baptist doctrine. Beginning in 1982 at Southern Baptist Theological Seminary in Louisville, Kentucky, leaders gathered for annual conferences stressing Calvinistic Baptist doctrines as articulated in the Second London Confession and the Southern Seminary Abstract of Principles. Initially, the gatherings were known as the Southern Baptist Founders Conferences, meeting at Rhodes College in Memphis, Samford University in Birmingham, and Southern Seminary (SBTS) in Louisville. The Founders assert themselves to be a ministry of teaching and encouragement promoting the doctrines of **grace** and experiential application to local churches. They call upon members to declare their fidelity to some combination of the First London (1644), Second London, (1678), Southern Seminary (1859) (non-negotiable), and/or the New Hampshire Confession of Faith (1833). A stated goal of Founders is to reform the SBC so as to restore its theological integrity. The influence of Southern Seminary president Albert Mohler and SBTS professor of theology Tom Nettles is evident, as is the historic writing of **James Pettigrew Boyce,** one of the founders of the seminary. In recent years, the Founders movement has held national and regional theological conferences, an online Study Center, a *Founders Journal* (online), and a list of churches, members, and orthodox speakers for commendation to congregations. While almost exclusively SBC, the Founders have numbers of independent Calvinistic churches and ministers who want to be included in the listings. Prominent among those associated with the Founders are John Piper, a Baptist General Conference minister; J. I. Packer of Regent College; and Timothy George, dean at Samford University Divinity School. In 1998, owing to the growth of members, the name was changed to Founders Ministries, and Tom Ascol, pastor of Grace Baptist Church, Cape Coral, Florida, was named the executive director of Founders Ministries. As of 2007, there were 807 subscribing congregations in the United States, and congregations or members in 35 countries outside the United States. The largest numbers of U.S. congregations are found in Texas, Florida, and Georgia. Founders Ministries are linked to other evangelical causes, including the Alliance of Confessing Evangelicals and *Reformation Today*. *See also* CONFESSIONS OF FAITH.

FOX, WILLIAM (1736–1826). Baptist businessman and humanitarian, born at Clapton, England. Fox was apprenticed a draper and mercer and operated his own successful business at an early age. He was a member of **Benjamin Beddome**'s congregation at Bourton-on-Water but later moved to London. He became a **deacon** at Prescott Street Church in London under the **ministry** of **Abraham Booth** and engaged in numerous humanitarian efforts, including feeding and clothing the hungry. In May 1785, at the King's Head Tavern in the Poultry, London, he introduced a plan for universal education that reached the attention of a number of important thinkers, including Robert Raikes (1735–1811). In collaboration with Raikes, Fox began in 1785 the Society for the Establishment and Support of **Sunday Schools** throughout the Kingdom of Great Britain, which aimed to teach children to read the **Bible** and fulfilled Fox's dream of universal education. He was treasurer of the **Baptist Home Mission Society** and a friend of political leaders Granville Sharp (1735–1813) and William Wilberforce (1759–1833).

FRANCE. Early France was the scene of several significant **baptisteries**, and during the Middle Ages, the Albigensians and Waldensians found refuge in the country's eastern mountains. Modern Baptist life in France reaches back to 1810 in French Flanders, when, through a home **Bible** study at Nomain, persons were first baptized and a church was organized after 1815 by Henri Pyt (b. 1797?), a disciple of **Robert Haldane**. Some of Pyt's followers became active **colporteurs** for various societies in France. Later, with assistance from the **American Baptist Missionary Union**, another mission began with **Casimir Rostan** and Isaac Willmarth (1804–1891). The first church was constituted in 1835 at Douai, while Rostan and Willmarth concentrated their efforts at Paris. A "school of the prophets" to train Christian workers was formed at Douai about 1839 and later moved to Paris. The Fédération des Eglises Evangéliques Baptistes de France (French Baptist Federation) was formed in 1919, uniting the Fédération des Eglises Baptistes du Nord de la France with the Association des Eglises Baptistes Franco-Suisses. In 1920, Arthur Blocher led a secession over theological issues, and in 1921, R. Dubarry and M. G. Guyot, with six churches, formed the Association Evangelique d'Eglises Baptistes de Langue Française, with congregations in France, **Belgium**, and **Switzerland**, plus missions in Madagascar and **Martinique**.

There were also British Baptist missions in Brittany, and the Welsh Baptists sponsored missions among the Bretons, centered in Morlaix. Since 1962, the **Conservative Baptist** Foreign Mission Society has conducted a mission in conjunction with the Baptist Evangelical Alliance of East and North Paris. **Baptist Mid-Missions** from the United States have a French center, located at Bordeaux with a Bible institute, and the **Baptist Bible Fellowship** began a mission in 1970.

In 1984, the **Association of Baptists for World Evangelism** opened a mission in France.

As of 2006, there were 111 churches and 6,284 members in the Fédération des Eglises Evangéliques Baptistes de France. The French Baptist periodical is *Croire et Servir* (*Believe and Serve*) (1924–). There is a Baptist-related theological school in Paris.

FREE BAPTISTS. *See* FREE(WILL) BAPTISTS.

FREE CHRISTIAN BAPTIST CONFERENCE. *See* FREE(WILL) BAPTISTS.

FREE COMMUNION BAPTISTS. *See* FREEWILL BAPTISTS.

FREE GRACE GENERAL BAPTISTS. *See* GENERAL BAPTISTS.

FREEDOM OF CONSCIENCE. Terminology common among Baptist writers on **religious liberty**. On the basis of Acts 5:29 and Galatians 5:1, humans possess in the image of God a conscience, or moral decision-making capability, which is free to choose good or evil. Conscience can be coerced by other individuals, the church, or the state. Baptists oppose any form of coercion of the conscience. This generally includes freedom to decide whether to worship or not, to join with a congregation, to change ecclesiastical affiliations, to nurture children and new adherents to the faith, to choose religious instruction, to express and propagate one's faith, to travel in the interests of religion, to associate for religious purposes, to contribute to religious causes, to make judgments on issues for religious reasons, and to have free access to religious information. The key element in freedom of conscience is the **voluntary** nature of one's choice. *See also* RELIGIOUS LIBERTY; VOLUNTARISM.

FREEWILL BAPTISTS (FWB). A North American phenomenon that began in the **ministry** of several preachers in the colony of New Hampshire in the 1770s. Theologically, Freewill Baptists are akin to, but not connected with, the **General Baptist** movement. **Benjamin Randal** was foremost among the early itinerants in advancing the Freewill Baptist "connexion." Like other 18th-century awakeners, he traveled to preaching stations in Vermont, New Hampshire, and Maine in the United States across a period of three decades, emphasizing free grace, free will, and free communion. Many of Randal's preaching stations eventually became permanent monthly meetings. Elder **John Buzzell**, successor to Randal, is credited with shaping the denominational structure.

As the "connexion" multiplied, the monthly meetings combined to form "quarterly meetings," roughly equivalent to Regular Baptist associations. By the 1820s, several quarterly meetings had united to form a "Yearly Meeting," the equivalent of a state convention. Finally, in 1827 the first Freewill Baptist General Conference met at Tunbridge, Vermont, uniting the entire movement nationally with a single purpose, reporting procedure, and statistical directory. Later, other **voluntary associations** followed: the Freewill Baptist Book Concern (1831), the Freewill Baptist Foreign Mission Society (1832), the Freewill Baptist Home Mission Society (1834), and the Freewill Baptist Education Society (1840). The unusual terminology "meetings," employed by the Freewill Baptists to identify their **polity**, was derived from Randal the founder, who appears to have syncretized elements of Quaker, Methodist, and Congregationalist polities into his own experience.

In 1841, the Freewill Baptists merged with the Free Communion Baptists, a group of churches mostly located in New York State. Free Communion Baptists affirmed open communion, experiential religion, trinitarianism, and high ethical standards. The group was supportive of voluntary organizations for benevolent purposes and liberally gave to Freewill Baptist enterprises. The resulting denomination was referred to as the "Free Baptists." The Freewill Baptist congregations in the Canadian Maritime provinces in 1836 organized themselves as the Free Christian Baptist Conference and cooperated fully with the U.S. Free Baptist General Conference. *The Morning Star* (1826–1911), a Freewill Baptist newspaper, was merged into *The Watchman*.

The Free(will) Baptists maintained correspondence with several theologically **Arminian** groups, including the New Connexion of General Baptists in England. This led to the visit of a delegation of New Connexion Baptists, **Jabez Burns** and **Joseph Goadby**, to the United States in 1848 and a reciprocal visit by Noyes to Britain the same year. On an earlier visit by British General Baptist missionary **Amos Sutton**, the Freewill Baptists formed their own foreign mission society and adopted him as their first missionary.

The Free Baptists in the northern states were the sole major theologically Arminian group in the 19th century in the United States and **Canada** not to adopt perfectionistic theology. As much as any influence, this was due to the writing and teaching of **John J. Butler** at Cobb Divinity School in Maine. A group of churches in the Canadian Maritime Provinces, however, left the main movement in 1888 and formed the **Reformed Baptist Alliance**, emphasizing holiness themes.

Merger conversations with the Regular (Calvinistic) Baptists of the North began in 1904. Alfred Williams Anthony brought the union discussions to fruition in 1911. A publicity campaign took place between 1904 and 1911 to convince local congregations to accept the union. Yearly conferences were integrated into the respective regular state conventions, and several of the institutions were adopted by the American Baptist Board of Education. Many of the isolated congregations, notably the mother congregation at New Durham, New Hampshire, identified with a rural **evangelicalism** and declined the merger; some later joined one of the **conservative** Baptist denominations. Of the roughly 1,100 congregations at the time of the merger, about one half joined the convention. For several years the Free Baptists also considered merger with the Christian Church and the Congregationalists, declining both.

At the time of union, the following educational institutions existed: Bates College (Maine, 1855), Hillsdale College (Michigan, 1855), Rio Grande College (Ohio, 1876), Keuka College (New York, 1888), and Storer College, (West Virginia, 1867). Earlier institutions, which had closed before union, include Parsonfield Academy (Maine, 1832), Stratford Academy (New Hampshire, 1834), Smithville Seminary (Rhode Island, 1839), the Biblical School (Dracut, Massachusetts, 1842), Geauga Seminary (Ohio, 1844), Whitestown Seminary (New York, 1844), New Hampton Institute (New Hampshire, 1853), Cheshire Academy (Ohio, 1858), Pike Seminary (New York, 1859), Wilton Collegiate Institute (Iowa, 1860), Green Mountain Seminary (Vermont, 1862), Lyndon Literary and Biblical Institute (Vermont, 1869), and Cobb Divinity School at Bates College (Maine, 1870).

Later, in a related group, the Holiness Bible Institute in Woodstock, New Brunswick (1936), evolved into the Bethany Bible College in Sussex, New Brunswick, related to the **Reformed Baptist Alliance**, a holiness offshoot of the Freewill Baptist movement in Canada.

Southern or Original Free Will Baptists. This terminology is applied to a U.S. southern group of Arminian Baptists who emerged in North Carolina in the first decade of the 19th century. There is no evidence for a connection with the General Baptists of the coastal region, who were defunct by the late 18th century, but some modern Free Will Baptist historians find their origins in the collection of diverse Arminian Baptists in the wake of that former movement in the 1790s. Perhaps as early as 1812, but more likely about 1829, an annual conference commenced meeting in eastern North Carolina, centered at New Bern and led by two elders, James Roach and Jesse Heath. These **pastors** corresponded with *The Morning Star* and styled themselves "Original Baptists" and later "Original Free Will Baptists," also adopting an English General Baptist confession of faith of 1660.

The Bethel Conference, as it came to be called, continued to be the epicenter of the movement in North and South Carolina, beset by theological struggles in the 1840s caused in large measure by the influence of the Disciples of Christ, with which many of the churches affiliated in 1845. Those remaining 38 congregations constituted the North Carolina General Conference of Original Free Will Baptists the same year. By 1904, 14 conferences or **associations** from six states constituted the North Carolina General Conference. In 1916, under the influence of the **holiness movement** and growing opposition to the union of Free Will Baptists with Calvinistic Baptists in the northern states, a renewed body was born, the Co-operative General Association of Free Will Baptists. In 1921, the southern churches coalesced with the Midwestern churches to form the General Conference of Original Free Will Baptists in the United States. Over the years, the denomination has constituted mission departments, lady's aid societies, orphanages, and **Sunday School** work. A denominational paper, the *Free Will Baptist Advocate* (1873–) was published beginning at Elm City, North Carolina.

From 1898 to 1925, the Free Will Baptists operated the Free Will Baptist Theological Seminary at Ayden, North Carolina; designed as a training school for ministers, it evolved as a church-related high school program. Its successor, Eureka College, operated from 1926 to 1929 and was closed due to financial insolvency. Thereafter, churches in the Free Will Baptist movement operated **Bible** colleges such as Zion Bible School at Blakely, Georgia (1930); the Bible School at Smithfield, North Carolina (1933); and the Carolina Bible Institute at Pine Level, North Carolina (1975). The Free Will Baptist Bible College, Nashville, Tennessee, opened in 1938, just as the denomination became a "national" entity—the National Association of Free Will Baptists (1935). This educational tradition, under the influence of graduates of Bob Jones University, provided a **fundamentalist** alternative to Mount Olive College, Mount Olive, North Carolina, the mainstream school founded in 1945.

As of 2005, the National Association of Free Will Baptists operated a denominational press; foreign and home mission agencies; an assembly ground at Cragmont, North Carolina; and a national headquarters at Antioch, Tennessee. That year, there were 2,399 churches and 187,183 members in connection with the association.

Pentecostal Free Will Baptist Church. The holiness movement influenced the Free Will Baptist movement in the southern states and eventually created a new form of the denomination. In 1912, a holiness minister, G. B. Cashwell, introduced the emphases of the Azusa Street Revival into the churches of the Cape Fear (North Carolina) Conference of the Free Will Baptist movement, and soon thereafter, "Free Will Baptist Holiness," which referred to the second blessing or "entire sanctification," became a dominant motif in this regional conference. Three other conferences were organized along these lines, and in 1959, the body incorporated as the Pentecostal Free Will Baptist Church. The headquarters of the organization of churches is at Dunn, North Carolina, as is the official school, Heritage Bible College. The publication is the *Messenger* (1912?–).

Connections with Other Freewill and General Baptists. Attempts have been made by some modern historians of the movement in the American South to connect it to either the General Baptists organized by **Paul Palmer** in North Carolina or the English General Baptists. These connections involve only similarity of ideas rather than actual historical connections. More appropriately, the southern Free Will-

Baptists have considered relationships with groups like the Disciples of Christ, the General Association of General Baptists, and the Churches of God, General Conference (Winebrennarians).

FRENCH-SPEAKING BAPTIST CONFERENCE OF NEW ENGLAND. In the late 19th century, significant numbers of franco phone emigrants moved from Quebec to New England for seasonal employment and jobs in factories. In conjunction with the Grande Ligne Mission in Canada, efforts were made at **evangelization** and church planting. In 1895, a Conference was organized to coordinate missionary outreach in the region. In the 1940s, the Conference was affiliated with the Northern (American) Baptist Convention, and the Conference shared the publication *L'Aurore* with the Grande Ligne Mission.

FULLER, ANDREW (1754–1815). English Baptist minister and denominational leader, born at Wicken. Raised on a farm and lacking much formal education, Fuller read widely, much interested in the writings of **John Bunyan**. He was converted at 16, and five years later, he became the **pastor** at the Baptist Church in Soham. In 1782, he moved to the church at Kettering, which he served until his death. Fuller was the principal advocate of a renewal movement among **Particular Baptists**, called "**evangelical** Calvinism." He held that God has a grand redemptive design in which the church has an important role to hold up the free grace of God. It was Fuller's theological stance, as articulated in his famous treatise *The Gospel Worthy of All Acceptation* (1781), that catalyzed the formation of the **Baptist Missionary Society** (BMS) in 1792. Fuller was a close confidant to and exerted considerable influence on **William Carey**, with whom he labored in establishing the denomination in overseas missions. He served as the secretary of the BMS from 1792 to 1815. The movement of renewal that followed his teaching, called "Fullerism," broke the rigid determinism of "Gillism," which had prevailed among Particular Baptists since the ministry of **John Gill**. Fuller's other notable published works include *Life of the Rev. Samuel Pearce* (1799), *Thoughts on Open Communion* (1800), and *Strictures on Sandemanianism* (1812).

FULLER, RICHARD (1804–1876). Southern Baptist minister, born at Beaufort, South Carolina. He was educated at Harvard College and first entered a career in law. In 1832, Fuller was converted under the **revival** ministry of Daniel Baker and became convinced of a call to **ministry**. Fuller left his career and became **pastor** of the Beaufort Baptist Church in 1832, where his ministry extended to the slaves of the plantation community. In 1846, he moved to the pastorate of Seventh Baptist, Baltimore, and later formed a new congregation, Eutaw Place Baptist, Baltimore. He engaged in a series of published debates with President **Francis Wayland** of Brown University in which Fuller advocated a pro-slavery position. He was a principal advocate of the formation of the **Southern Baptist Convention** and preached its first annual sermon. Fuller supported the rebuilding of Southern Baptist Seminary after the Civil War, and he did much to attempt to heal the rift between Northern and Southern Baptists. Fuller was considered one of the great oratorical preachers of the 19th century and had numerous sermons published. Among Fuller's published works are *The Psalmist: A New Collection of Hymns for the Use of the Baptist Churches* (1843), *Domestic Slavery Considered as a Scriptural Institution* (1845), and *Baptism and Terms of Communion* (1850).

FUNDAMENTAL BAPTIST CONGRESS OF NORTH AMERICA. *See* FUNDAMENTALISM, BAPTISTS.

FUNDAMENTAL BAPTIST FELLOWSHIP. *See* BAPTIST WORLD MISSION; CONSERVATIVE BAPTIST ASSOCIATION OF AMERICA.

FUNDAMENTAL BAPTIST WORLD WIDE MISSION. A local church-administered, fundamentalistic mission sending agency founded in 1985 by Ernest Campbell and Teddy Heale, **pastor** of East Side Baptist Church in Memphis, Tennessee. Members of the **mission** board include **fundamental** Baptist pastors from the near region. As of 2007, the mission supported about 35 missionaries on five continents, the largest number of which were deployed in church planting ministries in **Mexico** and the United States.

FUNDAMENTALISM, BAPTIST. The fundamentalist agitation among Baptists in the United States and beyond began in 1906 over the teaching of perceived **liberal** ideas in denominational schools, especially the theological seminaries. Concerns emerged in Chicago over teachers and approaches at the University of Chicago, in Philadelphia at Crozer Seminary, in Toronto at McMaster University, and in Boston at Newton Theological Institution. The Baptist community followed the lead of the World's Christian Fundamental Association, an interdenominational body, and pockets of concern began to meet regularly, notably in the Northeast and Great Lakes regions. In New York City, **Cortland Myers**, pastor at Calvary Baptist Church, first raised the issues as a national concern, followed by articles in the widely read newspaper the *Watchman Examiner*; articles by S. M. Lindsay and **William B. Riley** were widely quoted. Subsequently, in 1919, 25 Baptist pastors from metropolitan New York called for a meeting for prayer and consultation. The next year, 3,000 "delegates" assembled in Buffalo, New York to, organize. A "Group of Seven" was appointed to continue as an executive committee on "Conferences on Baptist Fundamentals," the name given to the ongoing body. *See also* CHICAGO SCHOOL.

At least two groups were evident among the Baptist fundamentalists: the militant leaders—including W. B. Riley of Minnesota, **John Roach Straton** of New York City, **Thomas T. Shields** of Toronto, and **J. Frank Norris** of Fort Worth, Texas—and the moderates, who included **Curtis L. Laws** of Philadelphia, Frank M. Goodchild (1860–1928), **Amzi C. Dixon**, and **Jasper C. Massee**. The militants, whose spokesman was often Riley, made sharp demands, while the moderates, led by Massee, preferred to work for change through convention structures. Various views were exhibited including, for example, on the doctrine of the Second Coming of Christ.

Moderate fundamentalists came to define what would evolve into Baptist evangelical thought. J. C. Massee at first held to five fundamentals: the inspiration of **Scripture**, the deity of Christ, the spiritual nature of the church, a divine call to the **ministry**, and an emphasis upon **evangelism**. He was also a premillennial Calvinist, but not of the familiar Princetonian variety associated with Benjamin B. Warfield (1851–1921) and J. Gresham Machen (1881–1937), two defining Presbyterian theologians of the era. Frank M. Goodchild, similarly, was not opposed to critical study of the **Bible**, a high educational standard, **religious liberty**, and social service. The moderate faction eventually gravitated to three epicenters: Philadelphia, Chicago, and Boston. In Chicago, Northern Baptist Theological Seminary became the graduate school of fundamentalists; in Philadelphia, the Eastern Baptist Theological Seminary developed an **evangelical** doctrinal stance; and in Boston, Gordon Missionary Training School became an alternative to Newton Theological Institution. Each of these schools devised a doctrinal statement that reflected identifiable constituencies affirming the infallibility of Scripture and the classic evangelical positions on the virgin birth of Christ, the atonement, the depravity of man, and the return of Christ, without a necessarily premillennial interpretation.

Militant fundamentalism, on the other hand, focused on the inerrancy of Scripture; literal damnation of unsaved people after death; the absolute substitutionary atonement of Christ; Christ's return according to a pretribulational, premillennial scheme; restrictive lifestyle (antialcohol and antismoking); and an insular public and foreign policy, which emphasized the forward march of Western capitalism. The more militant factions focused their efforts on the formation of doctrinally restrictive training schools, devoid of ideas like evolution, social science theory, **ecumenical** relationships, and the value of comparative religions. T. T. Shields and W. B. Riley took over the operation of Des Moines University in Iowa for a time. When that failed, Shields opened Toronto Baptist Seminary in Ontario and Riley began the Northwestern Schools in St. Paul, Minnesota. J. Frank Norris started a **Bible college** in his church at Fort Worth, eventually called the Bible Baptist Seminary.

Organized fundamentalism in the first generation took several forms among Baptists in North America. Among the first were the **General Association of Regular Baptist Churches in the United States** (1932) and the **Fellowship of Independent Baptist Churches of Canada** (1933), the latter of which became the **Fellowship of Evangelical Baptist Churches in Canada**. Under the leadership of J. Frank Norris, a third stream evolved, first called the Premillennial Baptist Missionary Fellowship, later the **World Baptist Fellowship** (1931), and then the **Bible Baptist Fellowship**, out of which grew the Baptist Bible Fellowship (1950). Also included in this category was the **Liberty Baptist Fellowship**, formed in 1977 by **Jerry Falwell** of Lynchburg, Virginia. Various smaller movements of Baptist fundamentalists can also be found among independent groups, notably the Independent Fundamental Churches of America and those in harmony with Bob Jones University in Greenville, South Carolina. Because of their doctrinal stances, other small bodies could be considered fundamentalistic, including the **Landmarkist** groups in the southern states, the **General Association of General Baptists**, and the Original **Freewill Baptists**. **Baptist Mid-Missions** and the **Association of Baptists for World Evangelism** coordinate the overseas efforts of many of the fundamentalist Baptist churches in the United States. Among **Seventh Day Baptists**, fundamentalism was manifested in the **Bible Defense League**.

A second generation of Baptist fundamentalists can be identified during the era of World War II. Disaffection with the appointment policy of the Northern Baptist Convention in its overseas work, plus continued concern for educational philosophies of the older theological schools, led to the formation of the Fundamental Baptist Fellowship, and later, another schism that produced a second generation of Baptist fundamentalists. In 1943, the Conservative Baptist Foreign Fellowship was formed to reflect the need for change in the Northern Convention. This led ultimately to the **Conservative Baptist Association** with its loose federation of schools and programs. This generation had little impact upon the **Southern Baptist Convention** (SBC), which was beginning to move aggressively north and west in its home mission programs.

Noteworthy in the second generation of fundamentalists was the evolution of both the moderate and militant positions from that of the first generation. Replacing Massee, Laws, and Goodchild in the northern states were **Carl F. H. Henry**, Cuthbert G. Rutenber (1909–2003), James D. Mosteller (1915–1977), and even later theological writers like Clark Pinnock (1937–), **Dale Moody**, and Millard Erickson (1932–). These "neo-evangelical" writers favored cooperation and dialogue and thus often made a greater contribution to a broader alliance of evangelicals than to the ongoing denominational battles of the 1950s and 1960s. Characteristic of these theologians was the desire to work within the existing conventions, as seen in Henry, Rutenber, Mosteller in the American Baptist Convention,

Erickson in the **Baptist General Conference**, and Clark Pinnock in the SBC and later the Baptist Convention of Ontario and Quebec. But the militant fundamentalists also gained strength through men like **John R. Rice**, **Robert T. Ketcham**, **Richard Clearwaters**, and Lee Roberson (1909–2007) in both the North and South. Rice and Roberson helped form the **Southwide Baptist Fellowship**, Ketcham was a founder of the General Association of Regular Baptist Churches, and Richard Clearwaters found fellowship first among the Conservative Baptists, but later became an Independent Baptist.

A third generation of fundamentalists among Baptists evolved within the two major conventions in the United States in the 1970s. Among Southern Baptists, widespread disaffection arose over unacceptable (to some) interpretations expressed in official Bible commentaries in 1962 and 1970. **Pastors** of leading Southern Baptist congregations—such as W. Amos Criswell (1909–2002) of First Baptist, Dallas; **Adrian Rodgers** of Bellevue Baptist Church, Memphis, Tennessee; and Charles Stanley (1932–) of First Baptist, Atlanta, Georgia—used their growing constituencies to launch a platform of change from the theological moderation of the SBC. Criticism of the six theological seminary faculties across the SBC widened and a hardened doctrinal position was evident at annual meetings of the national convention. Under the careful planning of **Paul Pressler III**, a judge from Houston, Texas, who vowed to restore the biblical basis of the SBC, officers were elected to transform the convention structures to be in perceived harmony with its roots and their agenda. By 1995, each of the seminaries had been reorganized with new faculty leaders and trustees, and the SBC's boards were reorganized and staffed by sympathetic leadership. Spokesmen external to the SBC, such as Jerry Falwell of Lynchburg, Virginia, and Pat Robertson (1930–) of Virginia Beach, Virginia (himself a former Southern Baptist), were influential in creating a rarified national media atmosphere for change. Representing a significant subgroup of fundamentalist Southern Baptists are those associated with **Founders Ministries**, a Calvinistic, confessional group of churches and individuals.

In the **American Baptist Churches in the U.S.A.**, a gradual decline in membership statistics and a seemingly perpetual need to reorganize led to concern for a more well-defined evangelical direction. Although a series of quiet ecumenical evangelicals were elected to prominent positions from the 1970s, the social activism and broad inclusivity positions of the national agencies led to the establishment of **American Baptist Evangelicals**, an aggressive group calling for a return to a biblically defined position and rejecting alternative lifestyles and politically correct policies.

Baptist fundamentalism has coalesced at regional, national, and international levels as well as within existing conventions or unions. For instance in Europe, the Fellowship of Evangelical Baptists in Europe has met periodically since an initial conference in 1967 at Northwood in the United Kingdom. Similarly, the Fundamental Baptist Congress of North America has met in conferences, 1963–1978. The International Baptist Fellowship, which sponsored the first congress of fundamental Baptists, has held meetings in 1962, 1965, 1973, 1976, 1979, and 1992 in various locations.

Baptist fundamentalism reached Britain in the decade of the 1920s, though it did not have the impact it did in North America. Conservative attacks upon higher criticism seemed to emerge from the Keswick Conferences in the 1870s, as well as from Spurgeon and the **Downgrade Controversy**. Early English Baptists were broader in their outlook on biblical criticism than their American counterparts; the widespread appreciation of biblical scholars like **H. Wheeler Robinson** at Rawdon and T. H. Robinson at Cardiff was not to be assuaged. Yet in 1919, J. W. Thirtle and James Mountain set up an organization parallel to the North American pattern, the Baptist Bible Union. Several transatlantic Baptist connections were noticed: A. C. Dixon and T. T. Shields both had stints of service in England; Dixon served the Metropolitan Tabernacle in London from 1911 to 1919 and was followed in that pulpit by H. T. Chilvers and J. C. Carlile, both of whom nurtured the interest of transatlantic fundamentalism in the 1920s. British Baptist fundamentalism was never as militant as its North American cousin.

Because Baptists revere Scripture and tend toward a transparent, or literal, understanding of the Bible, the temperament of fundamentalism continues to be evident in the various branches of the denomination. What could be identified as fundamentalist doctrines, such as revealed truth in Scripture, the virgin birth of Jesus, and a literal second advent of Christ, may be found in most parts of the Baptist community, adhered to more or less militantly. *See also* CONSERVATIVE

TRADITION; EVANGELICALISM, BAPTISTS AND; LIBERAL TRADITION.

FURMAN, RICHARD (1755–1825). American Baptist minister, born at Esopus, New York. The Furman family moved in the 1750s to the colony of South Carolina, where Richard received an informal education. At 19, he became the Baptist **pastor** at High Hills, South Carolina Church, and he became a regionally known orator. During the American Revolution, he was a prominent patriot and was sought by British general Lord Cornwallis. For a time, Furman fled the state for Virginia, where he came in contact with tidewater politicians like Patrick Henry (1736–1799). Following a continued pastorate with High Hills, in 1787, Furman became pastor of First Baptist, Charleston, and the oldest and most prestigious congregation in the state. He followed the lead of Baptist organizers in the North and helped to form **missionary** societies and educational ventures. In 1814, he was a principal mover in the founding of the **General Missionary Convention** of Baptists in the United States and served as its first president. He responded quickly to the call of the **Judson** Mission in **Burma** and was **Luther Rice**'s closest confidant in the South. In 1821, he shaped the South Carolina Baptist State Convention, which he saw as an auxiliary to the national convention. Furman promoted higher education for the southern churches as a part of the work of the Triennial Convention in 1817 and was a founder of Columbian College in Washington, D.C. Furman University in Greenville, South Carolina (1850), was named in his honor. Furman's famous sermon on the death of George Washington was entitled "Humble Submission to Divine Sovereignty the Duty of a Bereaved Nation" (1799) and represents one of the best examples of a public eulogy offered by a Baptist in the United States.

FYFE, ROBERT ALEXANDER (1816–1878). Canadian and American Baptist minister and educator, born in St. Philippe, Quebec. He spent a year at Hamilton Literary and Theological Institution (later Colgate University) and graduated from Newton Theological Institution. Fyfe served churches at March Street, Toronto (1844–1848), and Perth, Ontario (1848–1849), and was on the faculty of Canada Baptist College in Montreal (1843–1844). During the 1840s, debate over the distribution of the Clergy Reserves (a land preserve for the benefit of the churches), Fyfe led a courageous crusade against church establishment in Upper Canada and became the chief advocate of religious **voluntarism** in the province. He also favored a national body of Baptists, and he worked hard for the short-lived Canada Baptist Union in 1844 and following. In 1849, Fyfe took the pastorate in Warren, Rhode Island, which he served until 1853, when he moved to the Baptist church in Milwaukee, Wisconsin (1853–1854). He returned once again to a Toronto pastorate at Bond Street (formerly March Street) until, in 1857, he helped to organize the Canadian Literary Institute at Woodstock. The founding principal of the Institute, Fyfe gave many of the lectures, particularly specializing in theology. He engineered a curriculum of Christian education, which became a model for Toronto Baptist College and McMaster University. Among his protégés were John McLaurin (1839–1912) and **Alexander McDonald**, two pioneer Canadian missionaries. Fyfe was able to persuade his good friend, Senator **William McMaster** of Toronto, to support the idea of a Christian university, but Fyfe died before the dream was realized.

– G –

GADSBY, WILLIAM (1773–1844). English Baptist minister, born at Attleborough, Warwickshire. Gadsby had no formal education and as a youth was apprenticed to the craft of ribbon-weaving. He was converted and turned to preaching part time. He served **Particular Baptist** congregations at Hinckley and Desford from 1798 to 1800, settling at Hinckley until 1805. From 1805 to 1844, he was minister at Back Lane Chapel, Manchester. Gadsby was a masterful preacher and built a considerable following among the working classes, forming 40 congregations in the Lancashire, Yorkshire, Cheshire, and Derbyshire regions. Frequently, Gadsby traveled to London to preach at Red Cross Street, Gower Street, and Zoar chapels to raise money for his ministries in the north of England. He is said to have traveled over 60,000 miles and preached nearly 120,000 sermons in his career. Gadsby was a firm opponent of Fullerism, advocating instead a high Calvinism; he also opposed the formation of the **Baptist Union of**

Great Britain and Ireland, with which he had no fellowship. He and his followers, called "Gadsbyites," are considered the origin of what would become a major branch of the **Strict Baptist** position. Gadsby's thought is well articulated in his published works, including *Doctrinal Antinominianism Refuted* (1850?) and *An Everlasting Task for Arminians* (1828).

GALUSHA, ELON (1791–1856). American Baptist minister and social reformer, born at Shaftsbury, Vermont. In 1816, he became a member of the Whitesboro, New York, Baptist Church, which he appears to have served as **pastor** until 1830. From 1830 to 1833 Galusha was pastor of Second (Broad Street) Baptist in Utica, New York. While a pastor, he served as a **missionary** to Michigan Territory and founded the first Baptist Church at Pontiac. He was elected president of the Baptist Missionary Convention of New York in 1823, and in 1824 he founded the *Baptist Register*, a prestigious denominational paper. Active in the establishment of a firm financial basis for Hamilton Literary and Theological Institution (later Colgate University), he moved to Rochester, New York, in 1834 and formed the Second Baptist Church, an institution that was later instrumental in forming Rochester Theological Seminary. While in western New York, he was an **antimasonic** enthusiast in the late 1820s, and he helped form a local **antislavery** society in Rochester. In 1842, he moved to Lockport and the next year announced his adoption of Millerite views. Galusha alienated himself temporarily from the Baptist mainstream and was forced in 1844 to withdraw to the Baptist Church at Perry, New York, where he worked hard for the **Adventist** cause. Even when **William Miller**'s predictions of the end of the world did not materialize, Galusha held the movement in western New York together and did much to ensure the evolution of the Adventist denomination. Highly regarded by Joshua Himes (1805–1895) and William Miller, Galusha was restored to the Baptist movement in 1856; however, he did not withdraw his Millerite views.

GAMBIA. In 1978, the **Association of Baptists for World Evangelism** opened a mission in the country. Later, **Southern Baptist** missionaries arrived in Gambia in 1982. As of 2006, there were five churches with 479 members in the Baptist Union in the Gambia.

GAMBRELL, JAMES BRUTON (1841–1921). Southern Baptist educator and editor, born in Anderson County, South Carolina. He fought in the American Civil War, earning a reputation as a sharpshooter and a scout for General Robert E. Lee (1807–1870). At the conclusion of the war, he became pastor of the Oxford, Mississippi, Baptist Church (1865–1877) and was educated at the nearby University of Mississippi. In 1877, Gambrell became editor of the *Baptist Record* for 16 years. For a term, 1893–1896, he was president of Mercer University in Macon, Georgia. In 1896, Gambrell moved to Texas and became a home **missionary** for the state convention until 1910, when he became editor of the *Baptist Standard*, where he served for four years. In 1912, Gambrell was a founder of Southwestern Baptist Theological Seminary, continuing to serve the Consolidated Board of Missions of Texas, and he was president of the **Southern Baptist Convention** for four terms, from 1917 to 1921. Gambrell's published work includes *Baptist, Why and Why Not* (1900) and *Lectures on Ecclesiology* (1919).

GANO, JOHN (1727–1804). American Baptist pastor and military chaplain, born at Hopewell, New Jersey. Originally a farmer and self-educated in a Presbyterian home, Gano early converted to Baptist principles, uniting with the Hopewell, New Jersey, congregation. Following a tour of the southern colonies in which he met George Whitefield (1714–1770), Gano was ordained in 1754 and became **pastor** of the Scotch Plains, New Jersey, church. In 1756, he moved to the South but returned in 1760 to become the founding pastor of the First Baptist Church in New York City, where he remained for 26 years. In 1777, Gano joined Governor George Clinton's (1739–1812) New York Brigade in the Revolution and served with distinction, often under fire. There was a popular belief that he baptized George Washington (1732–1799), but no evidence exists for this event; General Washington did commend Gano's military exploits. After the war, Gano traveled to the West and started a church at Duck Creek (now Cincinnati, Ohio), and served a congregation at Town Fork, Kentucky. The brother-in-law of **James Manning**, Gano was a promoter of Rhode Island College and the missionary expansion of the Baptists. Although disabled by a stroke, he was carried to camp meetings in Kentucky, where he preached with power.

GATES, FREDERICK TAYLOR (1853–1929). American Baptist educator and businessman, born at Maine, New York. He was educated at the University of Rochester and Rochester Theological Seminary; he served the Central Baptist Church in Minneapolis, Minnesota, 1880–1888. As part of his service to the Minnesota Baptist Convention, Gates was asked by **George A. Pillsbury** to head up a campaign to raise $50,000 to endow Pillsbury Academy at Owatonna, Minnesota. Gates's success with this project led to his being named executive secretary of the newly formed **American Baptist Education Society** in 1889. That year, **John D. Rockefeller** asked Gates to raise $1 million toward the newly constituted University of Chicago, which Rockefeller planned to match. In time, this friendship grew and Gates came to manage Rockefeller's iron ore projects in Minnesota, coordinating resources, finance, and transportation interests. By 1893, Gates devoted himself entirely to Mr. Rockefeller's philanthropic work, distributing millions of charitable dollars to Rockefeller's interests. Gates was president or chair of 13 different companies and the Northern Baptist Convention's General Education Board, 1907–1917. During the years he worked with John D. Rockefeller, Gates managed over $600 million in charities and helped set up the Rockefeller Foundation, with estimated assets of over $125,000,000.

GAUNT, ELIZABETH. *See* MARTYROLOGY, BAPTIST.

GENERAL ASSOCIATION OF GENERAL BAPTISTS (GAGB). *See* GENERAL BAPTISTS.

GENERAL ASSOCIATION OF REGULAR BAPTIST CHURCHES (GARBC). An outgrowth along theological lines of the Northern (American) Baptist Convention (NBC) in the United States. In 1932, 22 congregations withdrew from the NBC to form the GARBC. Their concerns included modernist teachings, inequality of representation in the NBC, control of missionary work, and the principle of conventionism. The member churches are considered part of Baptist **fundamentalism**, along with, for instance, the **Conservative Baptist Association**, the **Baptist Bible Fellowship**, and the **Baptist Missionary Association**. The term **"association"** is preferred, in contrast to "convention." "Regular" Baptist refers to their understanding that they are the true heirs of consistent Baptist teachings, rather than the two great conventions. Association churches are Calvinistic and subscribe to the New Hampshire Baptist **Confession of Faith** (1833), with a premillennial interpretation.

The GARBC is governed by a Council of Eighteen; it maintains the Regular Baptist Press and is related to the **Association of Baptists for World Evangelism**, **Evangelical Baptist Missions**, Baptist Church Planters, **Baptist Mid-Missions**, Baptist Missionary Builders, and other domestic missionary organizations. The GARBC has approved four **Bible colleges**—Baptist Bible College of Pennsylvania, Clark's Summit, Pennsylvania; Faith Baptist Bible College, Ankeny, Iowa; Spurgeon Baptist Bible College, Mulberry, Florida; Pillsbury Baptist Bible College, Iwatonna, Minnesota (Pillsbury and Spurgeon dissolved in 2008) and three undergraduate schools: Cedarville College, Cedarville, Ohio; Cornerstone Baptist College, Grand Rapids, Michigan; and Western Baptist College, Salem, Oregon. There are four approved theological seminaries: Baptist Bible Seminary, Clark's Summit, Pennsylvania; Faith Baptist Bible Theological Seminary, Ankeny, Iowa; Grand Rapids Baptist Seminary, Grand Rapids, Michigan; and Northwest Baptist Seminary, Tacoma, Washington. The periodical is the *Baptist Bulletin*, (1935–). As of 2005, there were 1,415 churches and 129,407 members in the GARBC.

GENERAL BAPTISTS. The term "general" has usually been applied to groups of Baptists who hold to an unlimited view of Christ's atonement, that is, they believe that **Christ** died for all persons. In some contexts, the terminology "General Baptist" is used synonymously with the **Arminian** theological tradition, but this is not always accurate.

English General Baptists. The first General Baptists emerged in England following the teachings of the earliest Baptists, including **Thomas Helwys** and others. Helwys clearly advocated a general view of the atonement of Christ. About 1626, churches of this persuasion were in correspondence with Waterlander Mennonites in Holland. The first **confession of faith** that was undeniably General Baptist was published in 1660 and reputedly had the sanction of over

20,000 persons. Two other General Baptist confessions were issued in 1679 and another by the General Baptists in Somersetshire in 1691. English General Baptists had a threefold order of **ministry**: **messengers**, **elders**, and **deacons**. The office of messenger was based upon 2 Corinthians 8:23 and was widely successful in holding together the disparate congregations. **Thomas Grantham** wrote of the role of the messenger and was the earliest systematic **theologian** of the General Baptist sort. The local churches were organized into **associations** and then into a national General Assembly, which first met in 1660. The assembly became a court of appeals for the entire connection and may have led to its demise for that reason. Another popular distinction of the General Baptists in England was the "sixth principle" based on Hebrews 6:1–2, in which it is held that the **laying on of hands** should be done to all newly baptized believers. English General Baptists also practiced **foot washing** and anointing the sick with oil (James 5:14, 15), and some refused to eat blood, on the basis of Acts 15:20. A much-debated issue in the assembly after the Revolution was psalm singing, the decline of which retarded their distinctive music.

As the 17th century waned, so also did the English General Baptists. Their churches were not well distributed in the towns, many congregations met in homes, their doctrine was rigid, ministerial education was frowned upon, and, significantly, many followed a leading and long-lived messenger, Matthew Caffyn (1628–1715), into Hoffmanite Christology and Socinian views. Throughout the 18th century several congregations retained their General Baptist nomenclature while evolving into Unitarian meetings or cooperating with **Particular** or **Seventh Day Baptists**. The remaining Old General Baptist congregations and associations for the most part joined fellowship with the reorganized **Baptist Union** in 1831.

New Connexion of General Baptists. This movement originated in the ministry of **Dan Taylor**, a Midlands preacher. On 6 June 1770, the Assembly of Free Grace General Baptists, soon to be called the "New Connexion," was founded to distinguish the **evangelical** zeal of Taylor and Gilbert Boyce from the rigidity and doctrinal laxity of the older General Baptists. Taylor wrote a doctrinal statement that was unabashedly Arminian and had a high Christology. By 1820, the Connexion had over 7,000 members in slightly less than 100 churches. Taylor and his following exhibited a mild form of **holiness** ethics particularly attractive among the working classes. Beginning in the 1850s, movement toward cooperation and later amalgamation with the Baptist Union began; under the leadership of **John Clifford**, the consummation of merger took place in 1891. The General Baptists operated a theological academy/college from 1797 to 1914. Periodicals include the *General Baptist Magazine* (1798–1800), succeeded by the *General Baptist Repository*, published at London from 1802 to 1821. *See also* THEOLOGICAL EDUCATION.

Colonial General Baptists in North America. Early in American Baptist history, General Baptists appeared in both New England and the South. As early as the 1680s, General Baptists were situated in South Carolina, and in North Carolina **Paul Palmer** apparently led in the formation of several General Baptist churches, according to **Morgan Edwards**. In New England, many of the first congregations were known as General Six Principle Baptists.

General Six Principle Baptists. Among the early Baptists in New England, this group took their doctrinal basis from Hebrews 6:1–2 and included the laying on of hands in their practices. Although mildly Calvinistic at first, most churches became Arminian. At one time in the late 17th century, the Six Principle Baptists claimed many of the prominent congregations, including First Baptist Church in Providence. Rhode Island was the center of their influence (12 congregations in Massachusetts and Rhode Island, and 3 in Connecticut) and they probably can claim the oldest associational meeting among Baptists in America, held in 1670. In most respects, the General Six Principle Baptists resembled their English General Baptist counterparts. In the 20th century, only a handful of congregations remain.

Freewill Baptists. The **Freewill Baptists** of New England and the Canadian Maritimes are also included in most discussions of the General Baptists, owing to their position on the atonement of Christ. The Free Communion Baptists, merged with the Freewill group in 1841, also held a general atonement position. *See also* FREEWILL BAPTISTS.

General Association of General Baptists. In 1823, a movement in the Old Northwest began with the preaching of **Benoni Stinson**, who articulated Arminian views. In 1870, an association was formed, the General Association of General Baptists (GAGB). With congregations in 15 states, the GAGB supports Oakland College and theological school in Indiana and publishes the *General Baptist Messenger* (1885–). As of 2006, there were 842 churches and 78,863 members in the GAGB. The historians of this movement argue for a connection with the original General Baptists of England; however, this is not historically established.

GENERAL MISSIONARY CONVENTION OF THE BAPTIST DENOMINATION IN THE UNITED STATES OF AMERICA FOR FOREIGN MISSIONS (GMC). Name given to the first national organization of Baptists in the United States. The GMC was formed at Philadelphia on May 18, 1814, and chartered in the state of Pennsylvania. The idea of a national body originated with **Luther Rice** while he traveled from Richmond, Virginia, in a stage coach. Doubtless the term "**convention**" was borrowed from political discourse of the era (e.g. "constitutional convention") and involved delegates from the state and local **associations** and individual contributing members, the latter category reflective of the single purpose **voluntary** society particularly popular in New England. Elements of the plan of the American Board of Commissioners for Foreign Missions (Congregationalist) were also seen in 1814, as the central purpose was originally to support overseas missionaries.

In 1817, the GMC's work was enlarged to include domestic missions and education for ministers, and in 1820 the actual purpose statement was expanded to include "other important objects relating to the Redeemer's kingdom." Another fundamental change occurred in 1826 when the GMC was reduced essentially to a single purpose missionary society, reflecting the financial woes suffered from the overextension into education and western U.S. **missionary** activity. A final modification was made in 1846 when the board structure was changed to reflect the departure of newly organized **Southern Baptist Convention** elements and the General Missionary Convention became the **American Baptist Missionary Union**.

The convention was popularly known as the General Missionary Convention, the Baptist General Convention, and the Triennial Convention, the latter because its principal manifestation involved a meeting of all the delegates every three years from 1814 to 1844, in an assembly. During the three interim years in each triennium, the

Convention's work was carried out by the **Baptist Board of Foreign Missions** or the Acting Board. *See also* AMERICAN BAPTIST CHURCHES IN THE U.S.A.; AMERICAN BAPTIST FOREIGN MISSION SOCIETY.

GEORGE, DAVID (1743–1810). American and Canadian black Baptist minister, born in Essex County, Virginia, the son of slaves. Suffering cruel treatment, he ran away as a young man to the colony of Georgia, where he lived and worked with the Creek Indians. Later, he was converted under the preaching of **George Leile** and Wait Palmer (c. 1740–1780). About 1775, he became the first regular **pastor** of the Silver Bluff Baptist Church, Georgia, the oldest **black Baptist** congregation in North America. In 1782, he was granted freedom and he joined the exodus of British Loyalists from Charleston, South Carolina, to Halifax and later Shelburne, Nova Scotia. There he gathered a congregation and preached broadly in Nova Scotia and what later became New Brunswick. In 1792, in response to limited political and social opportunities, George joined 1,200 other black settlers and emigrated to **Sierra Leone**, West Africa. Following a visit to England by George, the **Baptist Missionary Society** agreed to support missions in Sierra Leone, and George carried on extensive correspondence with **Samuel Pearce** and John Newton (1725–1807). George himself served a church at Freetown, supplementing his income by keeping an alehouse. George's principal publication was his autobiographical "Account of the Life of Mr. David George, from Sierra Leone in West Africa" printed in **John Rippon's** *Annual Register* in 1793.

GEORGIA. The oldest Baptist church in the Asian Republic of Georgia dates from 1919 at Tbilisi. An Armenian congregation was founded in the region in 1926. Over the years of Georgia's socialist government, the Baptists there were included in the All Union Council of Evangelical-Christians Baptists; in 1991, this changed and the churches in Georgia later formed Siouz Evangelskikh Christian-Baptistov Gruzii. Additionally, the **Baptist Bible Fellowship** (U.S.) opened a **fundamentalist** mission to the Republic of Georgia in 1995.

As of 2006, there were 72 churches and 5,085 members affiliated with the Soiuz Evangelskikh Christian-Baptistov Gruzii.

GERMAN BAPTIST BRETHREN. Name applied to the congregations of German **Anabaptists** who emigrated to the colony of Pennsylvania in the 1720s, also known as Dunkers, Taufers, or Tunkers, the latter being a term of derision. The movement dated back to 1521 and the Zwickau Prophets, who first preached and practiced adult **baptism** in Saxony. In 1708, a congregation was gathered at Alexander Mack's (1679–1735) home in Schwarzenau, where there was a baptism and commitment made to move to Pennsylvania. The small group settled in the Wissahickon Valley near Philadelphia. On Christmas Day 1723, a church was constituted near Roxborough, Pennsylvania, after which the group spread to Chester County and Conestoga country. The congregations practiced an eclectic group of experiences, unrelated to other Baptists, including the **Love Feast**, Kiss of Peace, and **foot washing**. The term "Brethren" was derived from Matthew 23:8, "you have only one master and you are all brethren."

As the movement grew, divisions occurred and two primary bodies emerged, the Brethren and the Ephrata community, or Beisselianer. Surrounded by English-speaking Baptists, the German Baptist Brethren came to look more like Anabaptists than Baptists. In more recent times, a fraternal ralationship between American Baptists and the Church of the Brethren emerged, which recognizes a common theological heritage and shared delegates to national **conventions**. *See also* FOOT WASHING; LOVE FEAST; SOLITARY BRETHREN; ZIONITIC BROTHERHOOD.

GERMAN BAPTIST CONFERENCE. *See* NORTH AMERICAN BAPTIST CONFERENCE.

GERMAN SEVENTH DAY BAPTIST BRETHREN. *See* SOLITARY BRETHREN.

GERMANY. Baptist life in Germany is almost inseparable from the ministry of **J. G. Oncken**. His work for various religious societies and eventually the **American Baptist Publication Society** and the **American Baptist Missionary Union** was critical in the development of both churches and institutions. In 1834, Oncken opened the first congregation at Hamburg; although authorities tried numerous times to close its worship and work, this became the center for Baptist witness. **Julius W.**

Köbner and **Gottfried W. Lehmann** joined Oncken as a triumvirate of missionaries and German Baptist leadership. In 1849, a Bund der vereinigten Gemeinden getaufter Christen in Deutschland und Dänemark (Union of United Baptist Churches in Germany and Denmark) was founded with Oncken as chairman; this union included churches in **Switzerland**, the **Netherlands**, and Eastern Europe as well. Lehmann led in the formation of the Predigerseminar (Preacher's Seminary) in 1880 at Hamburg, which served most of the churches in Europe. The publishing house, Oncken Verlag, was founded in 1878. The union also worked in both domestic and foreign missions.

Under pressure from the government, the Union of Free Church Christians (Bruedergemeinden plus Elimgemeinden) merged with the "Open" Brethren (Bruedergemeinden) to form in 1937 the Union of Free Christians (Bund freikirchlicher Christen); in 1941, this church body merged with the German Baptist Union (Bund Deutscher Baptisten), to form the Union of Evangelical Free Churches (Bund Evangelisch-Freikirklicher Gemeinden-K.d.oe.R.). Following World War II, Germany was divided and the Baptists of the German Democratic Republic (East Germany) had to create their own theological school, Theologisches Seminar, at Buckow in 1959, and in 1970, their own union, the Bund Evangelisch-Freikirchlicher Gemeinden in der DDR. **Baptist Mid-Missions** from the United States established a German mission at Munich in 1951, the **Baptist Bible Fellowship** began a mission in 1970, the **Association of Baptists for World Evangelism** in 1989, and the **American Baptist Association** also has a mission in the country.

In 1991, the two historic German Baptist unions were reunited, reflecting the political reunification of Germany. As of 2006, there were 850 churches with 85,194 members in the Bund Evangelisch-Freikirchlicher Gemeinden in der DDR, and 67 churches with 5,246 members affiliated with the English-speaking International Baptist Convention. The Bund comprises 13 associations or regional organizations, each with salaried program staff, notably in the area of youth ministries. Also, the Bund has official legal status as an Organization of Public Right and thus conforms to structural and pension expectations through the national government. The Bund publishes *Wort und Werk* (*Word and Work*) (1880–). There is a theological school and Baptist center at Elstal, which is heir to the one founded by J. G. Oncken in Hamburg.

Faculty members of the seminary are integrally related to the Bund. In addition to the mainstream Bund, since 1961, a separate group of ethnic German Baptists have emigrated from Russia and the former Soviet republics. These congregations have formed separate bunds or associations and began a bible seminary at Bonn in the 1990s. In 2008, the U.S. Southern Baptists opened a cooperative agreement with the seminary and several of the associations. These congregations are characterized by an emphasis upon leadership in the local church and a conservative-to-fundamentalist theological position.

GHANA. In 1914, **William Haas** of the **Baptist Mid-Missions** commenced a work at Bambili in what became Ghana. From 1957, this effort included church planting in Gold Coast, Ashanti, and British Togoland. The main Baptist work in this West African nation was the initiative of the Nigerian Baptists, beginning in 1947 with congregations at Tamale and Sekondi. **Southern Baptist** missionaries began work in Ghana in 1949. The Ghana Baptist Convention was formed in 1954 and separated from the Nigerian Convention in 1964. The **Baptist Bible Fellowship** began a mission in Ghana in 1987, as did the **Association of Baptists for World Evangelism** in 1993.

As of 2006, there were 1,000 churches with 75,000 members affiliated with the Ghana Baptist Convention. A Baptist Training Center is located at Tamale and a seminary at Kumasi.

GIFFORD, ANDREW (1700–1784). English Baptist minister, born in Bristol. One of the most eminent **pastors** of his era, Gifford was educated at Tewksbury Academy and Gresham College. He was called to the church at Wild Street in London in 1729. A long-forgotten moral lapse from his youth, involving allegations of homosexuality, became known and the congregation split. Gifford withdrew and formed the Eagle Street Church and served there until his death. Although ostracized by his fellow Baptist ministers in London, he was befriended by influential members of Parliament and was a well-known collector of coins. He was a close friend of the revivalist George Whitefield. Through Marischal College, Edinburgh University conferred on Gifford the doctor of divinity, and he worked for a time at the British Museum as a librarian. Gifford bequeathed his books, which included a copy of the Tyndale New Testament (sold in

1994 to the British Library) to the Bristol Baptist College, where they became the special collection known as the "Andrew Gifford Remains." *See also* SEXUALITY.

GILL, JOHN (1697–1771). English Baptist minister and theologian, born in Kettering. Gifted in the classics, Gill was educated at a local academy. He was called to be pastor of the Horsley-down, Southwark, Church in London in 1720; he died in that role 51 years later. Gill was an avid student of biblical literature and the Hebrew language, and in 1748, the University of Aberdeen awarded him the doctor of divinity degree for this scholarship. Gill became known for his extreme Calvinism, "unable to offer **Christ** to sinners because it did not respect the sovereignty of God." His **ministry** concentrated on the edification of an elect church. He published a major commentary on the books of the **Bible** (1728–1767) and a comprehensive systematic **theology** called *A Complete Body of Doctrinal and Practical Divinity* (1769). His influence upon churches in Great Britain and North America was termed "Gillism" and stood in contrast with "Fullerism" (also known as evangelical Calvinism), as the position of **Andrew Fuller** came to be called. Beyond his local congregation, Gill was a member of the Baptist Board and the **Three Dissenting Denominations**, one of the most influential Baptist leaders of his era. John Gill continues to be the preferred theologian of many theologically Calvinistic Baptists, including especially many **Strict Baptists** in Britain and **Primitive**, or Old School, Baptists in North America.

GILL, WILLIAM ATHOL (1937–1992). Australian Baptist minister and educator, born at Wauchope, New South Wales, **Australia**. He was educated at the Baptist College in Sydney, then Spurgeon's College in London; the International Baptist Seminary in Rüschlikon, Switzerland; and the University of Zurich, where he earned the doctorate in New Testament under Eduard Schweizer. Gill began his teaching carer at Queensland College 1971–1972, but was not reappointed for theological reasons. From 1972 to 1974, he taught at the Methodist Training College. He then won an appointment in 1974 as dean at Whitley College in Melbourne. In 1979, Gill took the chair in New Testament at Whitley, which he occupied until his death. However, in 1984, his reappointment at Whitley was challenged by theological **conservatives**, but he steadfastly defended his positions. Early in his teaching career, Gill was confronted by his Queensland students to look at alternative forms of ministry, and this led him to establish in succession three centers of radical discipleship and social justice: the House of Freedom, the House of the New World, and the House of the Gentle Bunyip, the latter name inspired by a children's story. The House of Freedom, in 1974, sent Gill as a delegate to the International Congress on Evangelism at Lausanne, and there he developed a friendship and working relation with world **evangelicals** like Samuel Escobar, Rene Padilla, John Howard Yoder, and Ronald Sider. He lectured widely on topics of social justice and transformation and authored *Life on the Road: The Gospel Basis for a Messianic Lifestyle* (1989) and *The Fringes of Freedom: Following Jesus, Living Hope, Working for Justice* (1990).

GILMOUR, JOHN (1792–1869). Canadian Baptist missionary, born at Ayr, Scotland. An apprenticed seaman, he was captured in 1809 and imprisoned in France for five years. In 1814, he was baptized, studied for the ministry, and began itinerant preaching. Gilmour was influenced by William Fraser (1800–1883) and John Edwards (1780–1842) to emigrate to **Canada**, and he settled at Montreal in 1830. He formed the St. Helen Street Church (later First Baptist) and served there for five years. At length, he traveled in the Ottawa Valley and founded churches across Upper Canada (now Ontario), his base being at Peterborough. His itinerant parish ran from Montreal in Lower Canada to Dundas in Upper Canada and he wielded a considerable influence of the **Scottish Haldanite** tradition. Gilmour helped to form the Ottawa Association, the Canada Baptist Missionary Society, and the *Canada Baptist Missionary Magazine*. In 1838, he was the prime mover in the establishment of Canada Baptist College at Montreal, the first Baptist institution of higher learning in central Canada. He traveled to Britain in 1836 to appeal for funds to begin a college and support missionaries, a trip which resulted in the **Baptist Missionary Society**'s appointment of educational and church planting missionaries in Canada and the formation of the Baptist Canadian Missionary Society.

GLASITES. Term used to designate the followers of John Glas (1695–1773), a minister of the Church of Scotland who, in 1728, founded a sect that aimed to restore the primitive church. Glasite congregations developed in the vicinity of Dundee, with a principal one at Perth. The practices of Glasites included **love feasts**, **foot washing**, the holy kiss, and abstinence from eating blooded meats; unanimity in congregational decision making was practiced and a strict **separation of church and state** adhered to. Because of their advocacy of the kiss of peace, Glasites were also derisively called "Kissites." Numerous dissenters from the Church of Scotland vacillated between Glasite convictions and Baptist practices; the principal flow of Glasite ideas came through Robert Sandeman, **Archibald McLean**, and **Alexander Campbell**. Glas himself became known as a "father of **voluntarism**." *See also* SANDAMANIANS; VOLUNTARISM.

GLOVER, TERROT REAVELY (1869–1943). English educator and Baptist leader, born in Bristol. The son of Baptist minister Richard Glover (1837–1919), Terrot graduated from Cambridge University and for most of his career was a fellow and lecturer in classics at St. John's College, Cambridge, where in later years he was University Lecturer in Ancient History. In 1896, he emigrated to Canada where he was professor of Latin at Queens University until 1901, when he returned to Cambridge where he held the prestigious office of Public Orator at the University. Glover was a popular lecturer (speaking on many occasions in Latin) and well-known for his scholarship. His book *Conflict of Religion in the Early Roman Empire* (1909) was regarded as a piece of first-rate scholarship on both sides of the Atlantic, and his later work *The Jesus of History* (1917) was widely circulated. His scholarship was confirmed in 1918–1921 when Oxford University appointed him Wilde Lecturer in Natural and Comparative Religion. Glover served as president of the **Baptist Union of Great Britain and Ireland** in 1924. Among Baptists, he was identified with the **liberal** tradition and often took severe criticism for his views. Followers of **Charles H. Spurgeon** attacked him in British circles, and **T. T. Shields** branded him the "English Pippin of Three Rotten Apples," along with **L. H. Marshall** and **Shailer Mathews**, in **Canada** in 1928. He was awarded the LL.D. degree by Queens University and McMaster University in Ontario and by the University of St. Andrews in Scotland.

GOADBY, JOSEPH (1801–1859). English Baptist minister, born at Ashby-de-la-Zouch in Leicestershire. Educated by his father, who was a **General Baptist** preacher, Joseph was apprenticed as a watchmaker.

He studied at the General Baptist Academy at Wisbech and served the churches at Manchester (1825–1826) and Dover Street, Leicester (1826–1848). In 1847, Goadby and Jabez Burns (1805–1876) were deputed by the General Baptist Assembly to visit the **Freewill Baptist** Triennial Convention in the United States, which resulted in close relations between the two **Arminian** groups. Goadby was recognized as one of the outstanding General Baptists of his era, serving as secretary to the General Baptist College, publisher of the *General Baptist Magazine*, and the chief advocate of the General Baptist Orissa Mission in **India**. He concluded his ministerial career as **pastor** at Wood-Gate, Loughborough (1848–1859).

GOBLE, JONATHAN (1827–1896). American Baptist missionary, born at Wayne, Steuben County, New York. Raised on a farm, he was convicted of arson and sentenced to jail in 1844. In a second altercation in 1846, Goble threatened the life of a Syracuse grocer and was sentenced to prison at Auburn, New York, for two years. While in prison, he became a Christian and was baptized three years later. He resolved to become a **missionary** and joined the U.S. Marine Corps to embark on the expedition of Commodore Matthew C. Perry (1794–1858) to **Japan** in 1851. Among the influences on Goble was Bernard John Bettelheim (1811–1850), a medical missionary to Okinawa who served as a translator for the Perry expedition. In 1854, following his return to the United States, Goble studied at Madison University. Preferring to act rather than study, he was commissioned in 1859 by the **American Baptist Free Mission Society** (ABFrMS) to serve as the first Baptist missionary to Japan. He arrived in Japan in 1860 and set up at Kanagawa. In 1868, he moved to Yokohama where he conducted an **evangelical** and translation **ministry**. At the end of 1864, he had completed the first Japanese translation of the Gospels. With the merger of the ABFrMS and the Regular Baptist movement, Goble was appointed by the **American Baptist Missionary Union** (ABMU) as a missionary in 1872. The next year, Goble was involved in a violent act in Yokohama, and he withdrew from the ABMU. He became engaged in a war of words with senior Baptist missionary **Nathan Brown** and this destroyed his reputation at home.

Among Goble's claims to fame was his patent in 1870 for the jinrikisha (rickshaw), a popular and convenient personal conveyance for cities; it originated as a cart for his disabled wife. In the later 1870s, Goble served as a **Bible colporteur** for the American Bible Society in distant areas of Kyushu. His health worn out, he returned a widower to the United States in 1884 and settled in Germantown, Pennsylvania. At length, his conduct was again unbecoming, and he was expelled from the Baptist-sponsored George Nugent Home for the Aged. He died after a diagnosis of dementia at St. Louis, Missouri. To his death, he continued to be a vocal critic of the ABMU. Goble clandestinely kept a diary during his voyage with Commodore Perry, and this book has survived to become a document of singular importance to historians.

GOBLE, JOSEPH HUNTER (1863–1932). Australian Baptist minister born at Rosebrook, Victoria State. The son of impoverished parents, he was apprenticed as a compositor and remained an active member of that union. Goble planted a congregation in Footscray, a suburb of Melbourne in 1895, which he served for 37 years. Goble became the leading Baptist minister of **Australia** from his church at Footscray, a kind of unofficial bishop among the Baptists. He served as president of the Baptist Union of Victoria, in 1905, and the first president of the Baptist Union of Australia, in 1926. He was an evangelical advocate of the social concerns, always a friend of working people, opposing practices that increased unemployment, the arms race, and military conscription. His church was for many years the largest congregation in Victoria and the largest **Sunday School**. A statue of Goble was erected on Geelong Road outside Melbourne by his following.

GOEN, CLARENCE CHARLES (1924–1990). Southern and, later, American Baptist minister and historian, born at San Marcos, Texas. He was educated at the University of Texas, Hardin Simmons University, and Southwestern Baptist Theological Seminary, completing a Th.D. in church history. For a time, Goen was **pastor** of congregations in Texas and Oklahoma and was ordained a **Southern Baptist** in 1948. Encouraged by **Robert A. Baker**, the senior historian at Southwestern, Goen completed his Ph.D. at Yale under Sidney Ahlstrom (1919–1984) and Roland Bainton (1894–1984). While Goen was at Yale, a promised post at Southwestern closed, and he instead took a teaching position at the newly formed Methodist-related Wesley Theological Seminary in Washington, D.C., and remained there from 1960 to his retirement. His principal contribution was *Revivalism and Separatism in New England, 1740–1800*, which focused on the development of the **Separate Baptists** of New England. He also examined the factors leading to separation of northern and southern Baptists before the Civil War. Goen served as president of the American Society of Church History (1982) and the American Baptist Historical Society (1974–1976), as well as holding positions among American Baptist churches in the Washington, D.C. area.

GOING, JONATHAN (1786–1844). American Baptist minister and educator, born at Reading, Vermont. He was educated at Brown University and remained after graduation to study theology with Asa Messer (1769–1836). Going served two pastorates: Cavendish, Vermont (1811–1815), and Worcester, Massachusetts (1815–1831). At Worcester, he was a statewide leader in educational issues, promoting a public school system, and within the New England region, he was the creation of Newton Theological Institution in 1825. In 1831, Going made a recuperative trip to the Old Northwest, where he encountered **John Mason Peck** in Illinois. Peck convinced him of the urgent missionary needs of the West, and Going became a devoted advocate of a separate domestic mission agency for the Baptists. At an adjourned meeting of the Seventh Triennial Convention in New York City in 1832, he helped to organize the **American Baptist Home Mission Society**, and he became its first corresponding secretary. In 1838, he resigned to become president of Granville Literary and Theological Institution (later Denison University) in Ohio. As president at Granville, Going established the faculty and institutional reputation and was highly regarded for his pastoral care of students.

GOLD COAST. *See* GHANA.

GOOD SHEPHERD MINISTRIES. An **independent** Baptist missionary organization founded in 1974 to conduct church planting, literacy work, and relief aid. With its home base in Rockledge, Florida, the organization focuses upon work in **Haiti**. Its periodical is *Good Shepherd Newsletter*.

GOODSPEED, THOMAS WAKEFIELD (1842–1927). American Baptist minister and educator, born near Glens Falls, New York. He studied at the old University of Chicago, finishing his degree at the University of Rochester with theological studies at the Rochester Theological Seminary. Goodspeed served the Baptist church at Quincy, Illinois (1866–1871), then as associate **pastor** to his brother Edgar at Second Baptist Church, Chicago (1871–1875). In 1875, he was named agent for the Baptist Union Theological Seminary and raised funds for the struggling institution while also serving as pastor at Morgan Park Baptist Church. Goodspeed's reputation as a fundraiser was considerable (he raised over $500,000 in 13 years), and he came to know closely **John D. Rockefeller** and **Frederick Gates**, the corresponding secretary of the American Baptist Education Society. Goodspeed helped Rockefeller to formulate a plan for a modern university in Chicago, and he brought both Rockefeller and Gates into the project. As well, he enlisted the leadership of **William Rainey Harper** as president of the institution in 1890. Beginning in 1890, Goodspeed was for 23 years the secretary of the board of trustees of the University of Chicago, writing its first history as well as biographies of **Ernest D. Burton** (1926) and **William R. Harper** (1928).

GORDON, ADONIRAM JUDSON (1836–1895). American Baptist minister, born at New Hampton, New Hampshire. He was educated at Brown University and Newton Theological Institution, choosing a lifelong pastoral **ministry**. For 26 years, he served Clarendon Street Baptist Church in Boston (1869–1895), making it a center of **evangelism** and **missions**. Gordon relied heavily upon evangelistic strategies of the era, especially those of Dwight L. Moody (1837–1899). His theological bent became increasingly **dispensationalist**, thus making him a popular speaker at **Bible** conferences. Within denominational circles, his church became a major contributor to the work of the **American Baptist Missionary Union**, earning for him the presidency of the organization. He eschewed rationalism and modern theological trends, and single-handedly revived the denomination's missionary program, adding, for instance, the African **Congo** field to the American Baptists. Gordon's educational legacy became the Boston Missionary Training School that he founded in his church in 1881 (later Gordon College, Gordon Divinity School, and Gordon Conwell Theological Seminary). Gordon published a number of popular works, including *The Holy Spirit in Missions* (1893), *How Christ Came to Church* (1895), and *Is Christianity True?* (1897).

GOSPEL FURTHERING FELLOWSHIP. An **independent** Baptist **missionary** organization founded in 1935 by George Rhodes, a missionary in Africa. The agency is based in Lebanon, Pennsylvania, and focuses on **evangelism**, church planting, and theological education in **Canada**, **Spain**, and Africa. The Mission publishes *News and Views of GFF*.

GOSPEL HERALD **BAPTISTS.** *See* STRICT BAPTISTS.

GOSPEL MISSION OF SOUTH AMERICA. An **independent** Baptist missionary organization founded in 1923 to foster **evangelism**, church planting, **theological education**, and broadcasting. Its home base is in Ft. Lauderdale, Florida.

GOSPEL MISSIONARY UNION. An **independent** Baptist **missionary** agency founded in 1892. It focuses its effort on church planting, broadcasting, **theological education**, and missionary orientation. With a home base in Kansas City, Missouri, the Union operates in 19 countries. It publishes the *Gospel Message*.

GOSPEL MISSIONISM. A movement among Baptists in North America that stresses the role local churches should play over the interests of societies in conducting **missionary** activity. A form of **local church protectionism** and related to **Landmarkism**, Gospel Missionism was advanced primarily by **Tarleton P. Crawford** and, to a lesser extent, **James R. Graves**. Gospel Missionists believed that the sole purpose of missions is **evangelism** and that local churches could choose their missionaries and support them directly. Further, missionaries should eventually be self-supporting. The Gospel Mission movement reached the apex of its influence in 1892 when several missionaries resigned from the service of the Southern Baptist **Foreign Mission Board** and followed T. P. Crawford.

GOSPEL STANDARD **BAPTISTS.** *See* STRICT BAPTISTS.

GOTCH, FREDERICK WILLIAM (1808–1890). English Baptist minister and educator, born at Kettering, England. He was educated at Bristol Baptist College and graduated from Trinity College, the University of Dublin. For a time, Gotch served the Baptist church at Boxmoor, Hertfordshire, and his first teaching position was in philosophical studies at Stepney College. He took a permanent teaching position at Bristol Baptist College (1845–1883), serving as president from 1868 to 1883. In 1868, he was chair of the **Baptist Union of Great Britain**. Among other theological concerns, Gotch rejected theories of inspiration for a system of interpretation he called "noncreedal Christocentrism." His scholarship was well respected. He contributed to the *Encyclopedia Britannica* and was author of the "Genesis to Deuteronomy" section of the Revised English Bible in 1881. Gotch was awarded an honorary doctorate by the University of Dublin in 1859.

GRACE, DOCTRINE OF. Generally speaking, Baptists follow the Reformed pattern of understanding of the grace of God. To quote the eminent 18th-century Baptist theologian, **John Gill**, "[grace] is no other than love unmerited and undeserved, exercising and communicating itself to them in a free and generous manner, which they are altogether unworthy of" (Gill, *A Complete Body of Doctrinal and Practical Divinity*, p. 82). Historically, grace is taken to be completely God's initiative and is in stark contrast to any human effort in salvation or discipleship. The New Testament teaching in Ephesians 2:4–10 is authoritative in this regard. The early Baptist divines spoke of "doctrines of grace," which included foreknowledge, predestination, election, regeneration, and perseverance. Preaching the doctrines of grace was synonymous with holding orthodox doctrine. The term "irresistible grace" is found in many early Calvinistic Baptist theological writings. Comprehensively, English **Particular Baptists** were influenced by the Westminster Confession of Faith (1646) and wrote of the "Covenant of Grace," which included effectual call (special grace), justification (saving grace), repentance (evangelical grace), sanctification (graces of the Spirit), and preservation (also called perseverance). In classic usage, the exercise of faith is considered to be an act of God's grace, and grace as a commodity provided by God, offsets the penalty of human sin.

By the 18th century, however, Baptists like **Andrew Fuller** and **Dan Taylor** in England and **Benjamin Randal** in the United States emphasized human response to the grace of God and various sorts of **Arminian**, or **FreeWill**, **Baptists** in England and North America followed this direction. More modern Baptists often speak of a more general understanding of grace, as it pertains to God's goodness to all of creation and to all peoples. In his 1899 *Outline of Christian Theology*, **William Newton Clarke** attempted to shift the Baptist focus from sovereign grace to stressing the motive of the freedom of grace in the character of God and defining grace primarily as love. God's love extends to all of creation and to human beings especially. The effect of this shift can even be noticed in contemporary Baptist thinkers like Millard Erickson, who identifies grace as part of the manifold of God's love and distinct from God's benevolent nature. For Erickson, grace is God's undeserved favors. **James McClendon**, another contemporary North American Baptist theologian, has no section of his systematic theology specifically devoted to grace, but altogether asserts the connection of grace with Jesus Christ, who is the center of the Christian faith. This lessening of classic Calvinistic tones has also been noticeable in the fewer number of doctrinal statements among mainstream American and British Baptists, though a reaction to this has occurred among those who wish to reemphasize "sovereign grace." The latter advocates include the **Strict** (or Evangelical) Baptists in Britain; in the United States, **fundamentalist** groups like the **General Association of Regular Baptists**, **Conservative Baptists**, **Independent Baptists**, **Sovereign Grace Baptists**, **Reformed Baptists,** the **Founders Movement**, and many **Southern Baptists** in the United States.

Other uses of the term "grace" pertain to the **sacraments**, though Baptists generally do not understand the sacraments/**ordinances** to convey grace and the "graces," by which is meant the gifts of the Spirit, that is, faith, repentance, love, joy, and hope (cf. chap. XVII, *Second London Confession*). In the Orthodox Creed (1679), "justifying grace" is said to be a "habit," wrought in the soul by the Holy

Ghost. Also, following the teaching of Hebrews 4:16, God is described as being seated on a "Throne of Grace" and as dispensing, through Jesus **Christ** as High Priest, "grace" to meet human needs. *See also* BAPTISM; LORD'S SUPPER.

GRACE BAPTISTS. *See* STRICT BAPTISTS.

GRAHAM, WILLIAM FRANKLIN (1918–). Southern Baptist minister and evangelist, born at Charlotte, North Carolina. He was educated at Bob Jones University and Florida Bible Institute, graduating from Wheaton College in Illinois. Raised a Presbyterian, he met **Mordecai F. Ham** (1877–1961), an evangelist, who greatly influenced Graham's conversion and call to full-time **evangelism**. During World War II, "Billy," as he became popularly known, preached on the radio and toured American military installations, conducting crusades. In 1947, **William Bell Riley** persuaded Graham to become president of Riley's **fundamentalist** school, the Northwest Bible Training Institute in Minneapolis, Minnesota, and Graham remained president for five years.

In 1949, Graham held his first major crusade in the Rose Bowl stadium in Pasadena, California, and a year later, he organized the Billy Graham Evangelistic Association with a team of evangelists, musicians, and the well-known soloist George Beverly Shea (1909–). Graham's relation to the Baptist community includes membership in a local Baptist church and delivering addresses at national denominational meetings and the **Baptist World Alliance**. During his crusades outside North America, he has enjoyed support from many groups, and he has advocated for Baptist communities, notably **Poland** and the former Soviet Union. Graham has been an unofficial chaplain to presidents and other public figures, delivering the prayer at several U.S. presidential inaugurations and prayer breakfasts.

GRANTHAM, THOMAS (1634–1692). English Baptist minister and theologian, born at Halton-Holegate, Lincolnshire. Originally a tailor, then a farmer, Grantham was baptized in 1653, and three years later became a **General Baptist** pastor at Halton-Holegate, where he assisted in forming several congregations. In 1666, he was ordained a **"messenger"** and for the next several years started churches at Norwich, Yarmouth, and Lynn. Several terms in jail allowed him the time to study and write, and he composed the first comprehensive, systematic General Baptist **theology** in 1678, *Christianismus Primitivus*. He was ecumenically minded and was buried in St. Stephen's Church, Norwich, owing to his friendship with the Anglican vicar. Grantham's theological works, more than any other General Baptist writer, were formative in establishing the theological position of the General Baptists. He was the first systematic theologian of any breadth in the Baptist movement.

GRAVES, JAMES ROBINSON (1820–1893). Southern Baptist minister and editor, born at Chester, Vermont. Self-taught, Graves took positions as a schoolteacher in Ohio and Kentucky. Moving to Nashville, Tennessee, in 1845, he studied for the **ministry** and was ordained. The next year, he became editor of *The Tennessee Baptist* and exerted a wide influence across the South and beyond. He wrote on issues of Baptist **polity** and **theology**, emphasizing "landmarks" of the faith. He debated leaders of other denominations, notably the Methodists and Disciples of Christ. In a dispute with the Southern Baptist Publication Society, he formed the Southwestern Publishing House, which produced many controversial works. A great preacher and enthusiast, Graves raised an endowment for Union University in Jackson, Tennessee, and established Mary Sharpe College in Winchester, Tennessee. He is generally accorded the leadership of the **Landmarker** Baptist movement, in which strict views of the authority of a local church and the requirement of **baptism** by immersion are propounded. *See also* COTTON GROVE RESOLUTIONS; LANDMARKISM; LOCAL CHURCH PROTECTIONISM.

GREAT AWAKENING. The revival movement in the American colonies in the mid-18th century. Less directly, the term "Great Awakening" applies to some influences of the Wesleyan Revival in Great Britain during the same era. Renewal occurred beginning in the 1720s in New Jersey among the Dutch Reformed congregations. Later, Presbyterians experienced revival in New Jersey and Pennsylvania. In the 1740s and 1750s, the Awakening was carried forth by several exponents, including Jonathan Edwards (1703–1758), George Whitefield (1714–1770), and James Davenport (1710–1757).

Of the three, Whitefield probably had the greatest direct impact upon the Baptists.

A significant number of "separate" congregations grew up around the emphases of the **revival**, perhaps as many as 300 in 10 colonies. Originally, the churches were primarily part of varying shades of the Congregationalist movement, but by the 1740s and 1750s, many adopted Baptistic principles and as congregations made the transition to Separate Baptists. Leaders of that movement include **Isaac Backus** and **Ebenezer Moulton**.

Benjamin Randal, a sailmaker of Portsmouth, New Hampshire, heard Whitefield preach, was eventually converted, and formed an itinerant **ministry** called the **Freewill Baptist Connexion**, which spread the revival fires through northern New England. Two other products of the Awakening were **John Gano** and **Oliver Hart**, who were both influenced by Whitefield.

In the Canadian provinces, the Awakening reached the Maritimes via Ebenezer Moulton and **Henry Alline**. In the 1760s, Moulton itinerated in the Annapolis Valley and formed at least two churches of the **New Light** persuasion. Alline itinerated throughout Nova Scotia and New England, focusing his efforts especially in the Annapolis Valley where several of his preaching stops survived as congregations. Alline established a peculiar revivalist, experiential understanding of the faith, which characterized the Baptist communities in Nova Scotia long after his death.

In 1754, a **pastor** in Toland, Connecticut, **Shubael Stearns** joined the revival movement, and with **Daniel Marshall**, moved south to Virginia, where, at Mill Creek, their evangelism produced extraordinary results. At length, Stearns and Marshall removed to Sandy Creek, North Carolina, where the Separate Baptist movement in the South took shape. Overall, the Baptists seem to have experienced the greatest surge of numerical growth in all regions, among all the denominations in the 18th century.

GREAT BRITAIN. *See* ENGLAND; SCOTLAND; WALES.

GREECE. In 1836, American Baptists, through the **Baptist Board of Foreign Missions**, commenced evangelistic work in Greece but withdrew due to opposition and shortage of funds. Two later attempts were made by the **American Baptist Missionary Union**, in 1851 and 1871, withdrawing in 1886. In more recent history, Baptists entered Greece, the first modern church being planted by Marcus Bousios at Athens in 1969. The Baptist movement is assisted by the Southern Baptist **Foreign Mission Board** and is officially designated the Evangelical Baptist Church of Greece. In 1993, the **Baptist Bible Fellowship** began a mission to Greece.

As of 2005, there were three churches and approximately 300 Baptists in Greece.

GREEN, SAMUEL GOSNELL (1822–1905). English Baptist minister and educator, born at Falmouth, England. He was educated at Stepney College and graduated from the University of London. He served two churches, High Wycombe (1845–1847) and Taunton (1847–1851), before taking a position at the Yorkshire Baptist College (Rawdon) as tutor in classics (1851–1863). In 1863, Green became principal at the college, serving until 1876. In 1876, he became the secretary of the Religious Tract Society through 1891. Among the most widely circulated popular writers on various biblical subjects, Green was the author of 18 books, including *A Handbook to Grammar of the Greek New Testament* (1870). His leadership at Rawdon College was considered progressive by some and latitudinarian by others; he was a catalyst in the establishment in 1866 by closed communion Baptists of the Bury Baptist College, later Manchester Baptist College.

GRENADA. Baptists came late to the islands, evangelizing from South American conventions. **Southern Baptist** missions in Grenada date from 1975, involving a transfer of missionaries from Guyana. Church development has been slow, and the community has remained a missionary enterprise.

As of 2005, there were four churches and about 400 members in the Baptist community of Grenada.

GRENFELL, GEORGE (1849–1906). English Baptist missionary, born at Sancreed, England. Active as a young person in the Birmingham Young Men's Missionary Society, Grenfell was educated at Bristol Baptist College. There he met **Alfred Saker**, who influenced his decision for missionary work in Africa. Convinced that **mission** stations should be established in the interior, he began his work for the **Baptist Missionary Society** in 1875 in present-day **Cameroon**. Eventually, his river explorations took him to the upper Congo, in the steps of Henry M. Stanley (1841–1904), where he helped to found the mission at Saõ Salvador. In order to advance the work, Grenfell supervised the construction of a steamboat, financed by Robert Arthington, an evangelical philanthropist of Leeds, England, which was disassembled and reassembled up river in 1884. Grenfell established stations at Lukolela, Yakusu, and Bolobo, where he built his home. For his work in exploring the interior of the Congo, Grenfell was presented with the "Chevalier of the Order of Leopold" by Belgian King Leopold II. Grenfell's published work includes *The Upper Congo as a Waterway* (1902), a significant geographical account.

GUADALOUPE. Baptist presence in the French West Indies, including Guadaloupe, has been small. **Southern Baptists** began missionary work on the islands in 1964, stressing medical ministries and **Sunday School** outreach.

As of 2005, there were seven churches and 750 members in the Convention Baptiste du Guadaloupe.

GUAM. Baptist presence on Guam began in 1922 with a **General Baptist** mission. Then followed U.S. military occupation, with a Baptist fellowship in 1959–1961, which related to the **Southern Baptists** (SBC). Southern Baptists also have mission work among the numerous Vietnamese refugees living in Guam. **Conservative Baptists** have had a mission since the early 1960s, and the **Baptist Bible Fellowship** also opened a mission on Guam in 1975.

As of 2001, there were three churches with about 1,190 members affiliated with the Guam Baptist Convention (SBC), and two churches with approximately 667 members related to the General Baptist Mission.

GUATEMALA. Paul C. Bell, Sr. (1928–) and William J. Webb (1912–1973), U.S. **Southern Baptists** from **Costa Rica** and **Panama**, visited Guatemala in 1946, which resulted in the **baptism** of 300 people and the formation of five new Baptist congregations that year. Later in the year, La Convención Bautista de Guatemala was formed. In

1947, a library, **colporteur** program, and Instituto de Pastores were begun. Southern Baptist support of **missions** in Guatemala commenced in 1947, when the president of the Baptist Seminary in Mexico transferred to Guatemala City and became the primary missionary there. In 1975, **Baptist Bible Fellowship** began its mission in Guatemala.

As of 2006 there were 273 churches with 36,107 members affiliated with the Convención Bautista de Guatemala. The Convención Bautista publishes *Nueva Era Bautista* (*New Era Baptist*). The Pablo Bell Baptist Bible Institute is located at Solala and a theological seminary is in Guatemala City.

GUYANA. The first **Southern Baptist** missionaries arrived at Georgetown, Guyana, in 1962. Brazilian Baptists were next to begin a **mission** in Guyana, with the assistance of the **Baptist Missionary Society** in 1991. In 1993, the **Baptist Bible Fellowship** opened a mission to Guyana. The Baptist Cooperative Convention was organized in 1973, relating to Southern Baptist work.

As of 2006, there were 33 churches and 1,823 members associated with the Cooperative Convention of Guyana. A Baptist-related theological institute is located in Georgetown.

– H –

HAAS, WILLIAM CLARENCE (1873–1924). American Baptist minister, and later **Independent Baptist** missionary, born at Mendon, Michigan. He was educated to be a schoolteacher and taught from 1889 to 1894. Haas became a **pastor** at Union City, Michigan (1894–1902); Manchester Baptist Church, Caldwell, Ohio (1902–1906); and Memorial Baptist Church, Columbus, Ohio (1906–1908). In 1908, he resigned to become a missionary to Africa. Frustrated in his attempts to gain appointment through the **American Baptist Missionary Union**, Haas accepted a call from the Africa Inland Mission in 1911 and served for a time at Mombasa, East Africa. His interest lay in French Equatorial Africa, however, which he entered in 1914, first at Bambili and later at Rafai. Following returns to the United States in 1916 and 1920, Haas was a principal organizer of **Baptist Mid-Missions** (BMM), soon to become the most extensive **fundamentalist** Baptist mission work in the United States. Just prior to his death, Haas had firmly established the BMM's work in Sibut and earned a reputation as a respected pioneer of African missionary work.

HAITI. Baptist mission labors in Haiti date from 1823, when the Massachusetts Baptist Missionary Society commissioned **Thomas Paul** of Boston to do work there on a short-term basis. Paul opened a church at Cap Haitien but returned to New England in 1824. During the 1840s, William Jones of Philadelphia went to Haiti under the auspices of the **American Baptist Free Mission Society** to train Christian workers for Africa. A century after Thomas Paul, American Baptists commenced work in Haiti in 1923 through the **American Baptist Home Mission Society**. The first church became the reopened facility at Cap Haitien. In 1848, a second stream of Baptist missions was started, this time by the **Baptist Missionary Society** at Jacmel on the southern coast. In 1885, the English mission was transferred to the Jamaican Baptist Missionary Society, and later, this mission was supported by the **Lott Carey Baptist Foreign Mission Convention** (LCBFMC). The LCBFMC concentrated its efforts particularly on the island of La Gonave. **Baptist Mid-Missions** from the United States established a station at Marigot in 1934, and in 1982, the **Baptist Bible Fellowship** opened a mission.

As of 2006, there were 93 churches with 70,000 members affiliated with the Convention Baptiste d'Haiti (organized 1923), and 354 churches with 17,440 members affiliated with the Baptist Haiti Mission. The Baptist theological seminary of Haiti is located at Cap Haitien.

HALDANE, JAMES ALEXANDER (1768–1851). Scottish Baptist minister and mariner, born at Dundee, **Scotland**. Following studies at the University of Edinburgh, Haldane served in the Merchant Marine and returned to Scotland about 1795. He began to preach at various rural locations and came under the influence of John Campbell, an iron worker and itinerant Congregationalist preacher. In 1797, James made his first preaching tour of the North of Scotland, based on the methods of Campbell. The next year with the assistance of his brother, **Robert Haldane**, he started a **voluntary** organization, the

Society for Propagating the Gospel at Home, and he recruited numerous young protégés. In 1799, Haldane began a **ministry** at what was called the Tabernacle or Circus Church in Edinburgh, which in 1801 was moved to Leith Walk to occupy a building that his brother helped to finance. In 1808, under the influence of writings of Archibald MacLean, a **Scotch Baptist**, and Lachlan Macintosh, Haldane was baptized. He was **pastor** at the Tabernacle for half a century and with his brother, Robert, exerted much influence on the development of **evangelical** and Baptist ministries through a theological school and the sending forth of missionary-pastors. Haldane's published works include *The Voluntary Question Political Not Religious* (1839) and *Man's Responsibility* (1842).

HALDANE, ROBERT (1764–1842). Scottish Baptist theologian and philanthropist, born at London. Haldane began studies at the University of Edinburgh but quit to join the Royal Navy. Completing his term at sea, he settled at the family estate at Airthney, near Stirling, and with his brother, **James Alexander Haldane**, he devoted himself to various forms of Christian endeavor. Robert's initial plan was to sell Airthney and set up at Benares in India a Christian colony of 30 persons to conduct **evangelism** and publish literature; the East India Company, however, declined his proposal. In 1808, he was baptized and moved about the circles of **Scotch Baptists** with increasing influence. He had an interest in the Serampore Mission, but this was channeled into mission work in **Scotland**. Haldane supported tract societies, **Sunday Schools**, and the resettlement of former **slaves** in **Sierra Leone**, West Africa. He went to Geneva and **France** in 1816–1819 to study and write; a number of students gathered about him, and a **revival** occurred among Protestant churches in the French-speaking communities. Among his students at Montauban, France, were Louis Gaussen (1790–1863) and J. H. Merle d'Aubigne (1794–1872). Haldane published a major study of the nature of the inspiration of **Scripture** and aided in establishing the Continental Society. His generosity extended to aid for many houses of worship in Scotland, including the Tabernacle in Edinburgh in which his brother served. Robert's most significant theological work was *The Evidence and Authority of Divine Revelation* (1816).

HALDANITE TRADITION. Terminology applied to the emphases and personalities involved in the outreach of **James** and **Robert Haldane** of **Scotland**. Many writers characterize the work of **revivalism** wrought through the brothers as nothing short of a Wesleyan revival. Against the infidelism generated by the French Revolution and troubles within the Church of Scotland, the Haldanes brought renewal through **voluntary associations** of outreach, publications, educational efforts, and **evangelical** preaching. Their philanthropy led to the establishment of institutions that transformed churches at home and abroad. The formation of the Free Church of Scotland in 1843 was influenced greatly by the Haldanes. Their seminary produced student **pastor**-missionaries who fanned out over Scotland, England, and **Wales**, as well as the Canadian provinces and indirectly in the United States. In **Canada**, for instance, John Edwards (1780–1842), William Fraser (1801–1883), and **John Gilmour**, three primary church planters, were of the Haldanite tradition. Although the work of the Haldanes came to an end in 1851 when James Haldane died, the tradition could be found wherever their disciples took up **ministry**.

HALL, ROBERT, JR. (1764–1831). English Baptist minister and theological controversialist, born at Arnesby, England. The son of **Robert Hall Sr.**, Hall was educated at Bristol Baptist College and King's College, University of Aberdeen. He took an assistant pastoral position under Caleb Evans (1737–1791) at Broadmead, but owing to rivalry with Evans, he moved to Cambridge to succeed **Robert Robinson**. At Cambridge, Hall developed a reputation as the city's finest preacher; he later served at Leicester and at Bristol a second time. He wrote widely on subjects such as freedom of the press, infidelity, and terms of communion. He was opposed to hyper-Calvinism and energetically supported open communion. A critic of **John Gill**, Hall referred to Gill's theology as "a continent of mud."

HALL, ROBERT, SR. (1728–1791). English Baptist minister and theologian, born in Northumbria. Hall was credited with having changed the course of the theological tradition of Old Calvinism when in 1770 he preached a sermon encouraging **evangelism**. His book, *Help to Zion's Travellers* (1781), was a major catalyst in the thinking of

William Carey. Hall settled at Arnesby in Leicestershire in a poor parish, and to support his family, he kept a small farm, all the while writing materials that defended the new directions of **evangelical** Calvinism among Baptists. His sermons were widely published after his death.

HAM, MORDECAI (1877–1961). Southern Baptist minister and **evangelist**, born in Allen County, Kentucky. He began his **ministry** in Bowling Green, Kentucky, and served First Baptist Church, Oklahoma City (1927–1929). As an evangelist, he itinerated widely; among his converts were **William F. "Billy" Graham** and Grady Wilson (1919–1987). Ham was a popular radio preacher who spoke of conversions numbering over 1 million during his ministry.

"HARD CORE" BAPTISTS. *See* BAPTIST WORLD MISSION.

HARDING, HARRIS (1761–1854). Canadian Baptist minister, born at Horton, Nova Scotia. Harding was converted under the ministry of John Payzant (1749–1834), a **New Light** Congregationalist preacher, and he united with the mixed communion congregation at Cornwallis. He went to Yarmouth as an evangelist in 1790 and settled there in 1797, serving the church for 60 years. Although Harding became a Baptist in 1799, his church did not join the Association until 1806, preferring a mixed communion stance. Harding suffered from personal defeats in his professional development, notably from a romantic affair in 1796, which led to a forced marriage, and accusations in 1798 of "new **dispensationalism**," which referred to his denial of structures and rules. In both instances, Harding presented a contrite response and rebuilt his **ministry** with solid **evangelism**. In 1806 and again in 1812–1813, he was involved in major awakenings in his community, the former resulting in 150 new converts. Exemplifying the **Second Great Awakening** in the Canadian Maritimes, Harding was considered one of the "fathers" of the Baptist movement in that region.

HARDING, THEODORE SETH (1773–1855). Canadian Baptist minister, born at Barrington, Nova Scotia. He was converted under the influence of **Harris Harding**, **Joseph Dimock**, and the

Methodist preacher Freeborn Garrettson. Harding was further converted to Baptist principles in 1795 and was called to the Horton (later Wolfville, Nova Scotia) Church in 1796. He served that congregation for 60 years. Harding was an active promoter of establishing Horton Academy and the Nova Scotia Baptist Education Society. He traveled extensively among the Baptist communities in the United States and gave spiritual insight to the founding of Acadia College. He was considered one of the "fathers" of the Maritime Baptist community. Between 1814 and 1820, Harding served as a home missionary in New Brunswick. He started this service opposed to closed communion; he returned an advocate of it. Two great **revivals** occurred during his ministry, 1841 and 1848–1849; both the church and the college were involved in the protracted meetings. Between 1832 and 1841, Harding baptized over 350 persons at Horton.

HARDING, WARREN GAMALIEL (1865–1923). Baptist layman and 29th president of the United States, born at Corsica, Ohio. He studied at Ohio Central College and became a newspaperman and eventually the publisher of the *Marion Star*. Harding rose to leadership in the Marion community, being elected to the Ohio legislature (1888), the lt. governorship (1903), and the U.S. Senate in 1914. A rising Republican during World War I, Harding was the successful presidential candidate in the election of 1920 against Democrat James M. Cox, in a campaign Harding conducted almost exclusively from the front porch of his home in Marion. As a Baptist, Harding was likely **baptized** in Blooming Grove, Ohio. He was later associated with Trinity Baptist Church in Marion, Ohio, before his presidency and at his second funeral. While in Washington, D.C., he attended Calvary Baptist Church and developed a friendship with the senior **pastor**, William S. Abernethy. Harding was a member of the Vaughn **Sunday School** class at Calvary Church, where he enjoyed fellowship with other prominent Washingtonians. President Harding's state funeral was conducted at the U.S. capitol by J. Freeman Anderson, assistant pastor of Calvary Baptist Church, in the absence of Dr. Abernethy.

HARPER, WILLIAM RAINEY (1856–1906). American Baptist educator, born at New Concord, Ohio. He graduated from Muskingum

College, Baptist Union Theological Seminary, Chicago, and Yale University (Ph.D.). Harper had a gift for the study of languages and completed his doctorate at age 19. For a time, he lectured at Denison University Academy and at his theological alma mater. Yale created a chair for him in linguistics, and he taught there with great success in 1886–1890. Harper became **Thomas Goodspeed**'s and **John D. Rockefeller**'s choice to build a great university at Chicago, and Harper designed the institution's curriculum. Among his achievements were a school that in five years counted over 2,000 students, a university press and extension school, and a scholarly publication, *Biblical World*. With **Ernest DeWitt Burton** and **Shailer Mathews**, Harper was a leader in the first generation of what became known as the **Chicago School** of religious scholarship.

HARRIS, ELMORE (1854–1911). Canadian Baptist minister, born at Beamsville, Ontario. He was heir to the family of Massey-Harris Industries, a major producer of farm machinery. Educated at the University of Toronto, Harris turned immediately to pastoral **ministry**. He served at Centre Street, St. Thomas (1876–1882); Yorkville, which became Bloor Street, Toronto (1882–1889); and Walmer Road in Toronto (1889–1895). Under his leadership, congregations expanded greatly and required new facilities. His pastoral ministry at Bloor Street included many of the faculty at Toronto Baptist College (later McMaster University); in 1908–1909, Harris led an investigation of perceived modernist teachings by Professor Isaac G. Matthews (1871–1959) at McMaster. For several years, Harris himself lectured at McMaster in **Bible**. Following his retirement from active pastoral leadership, Harris remained as a senior spiritual counsellor in the Walmer Road congregation, which he had founded and the property of which was donated by his family. He moved into the field of religious education in 1894, when he founded the Toronto Bible Training Institute (later Toronto Bible College). Serving as the first president of the school, Harris used the opportunity to showcase the institution to a wide variety of conservative **evangelical** leaders of the era, including Arno C. Gaebelein (1861–1945), C. I. Scofield (1843–1921), and W. H. Griffiths Thomas (1861–1924). These associations brought Harris a reputation as a leading Bible teacher and inclusion as a member of the editorial board of the first edition of the

Scofield Reference Bible (1909). He died of smallpox while on a **missions** exploratory trip in Delhi, **India**.

HART, OLIVER (1723–1795). American Baptist minister, born at Hopewell, New Jersey. Early influenced by **Great Awakening** preachers George Whitefield (1714–1770) and Gilbert Tennent (1703–1764), Hart adopted an **evangelistic** style and embarked on an itinerant ministry in the southern colonies. During the Revolution, he was an ardent patriot, serving as a member of the South Carolina Committee of Safety. He fled Charleston with a British bounty on his head, settling in Hopewell, New Jersey, as **pastor** from 1780 to 1795. Hart was firmly convinced of the associational principle and built up cooperation among churches wherever he served. In Charleston, shortly after his arrival in 1751, the first **association** in the South was formed. In Philadelphia, he greatly strengthened the oldest association in the United States. Hart was one of the most esteemed clergy of the 18th century, and two memorial sermons were preached at his funeral, one by **Richard Furman** in South Carolina, the other by **William Rogers** in Philadelphia. Hart wrote a few works that were published, including *Dancing Exploded* (1778) and *A Gospel Church Portrayed* (1791).

HARTSHORNE-FROYD REPORT. Following a reorganization of the **American Baptist Publication Society** in 1944, the Northern Baptist Convention (NBC) undertook a study of theological training for its churches. Hugh Hartshorne (1885–1967) and Milton C. Froyd (1908–1985) canvassed colleges, universities, theological seminaries, and ministers to make their report to the Board of Education and Publication in 1945. They found that 31.9 percent of the ministers serving in the NBC had no formal college training of any kind, and 19.1 percent had no theological training. Of the 68.1 percent who had at least one year of college, 19.8 percent received it in Baptist colleges, while 36.1 percent received it in other than denominational schools and 12.3 percent received their education in theological schools founded after 1900. Fifty-three percent of all Northern Baptist ministers had no training in Baptist schools, an alarming result of the survey. The report, published in 1945 as *Theological Education in the Northern Baptist Convention*, prompted the denomination to take steps to enhance leadership development, one of which was the calling of a Conference on Professional and Lay Leadership at Green Lake, Wisconsin, in August 1950. Scholarship funds were also increased for use in denominational schools. The Hartshorne-Froyd Report proved groundbreaking among Baptists in that it defined in sociological and organizational terms the profile of **ministry** and marked the participation of a Baptist group in social scientific research. *See also* THEOLOGICAL EDUCATION.

HARVEY, HEZEKIAH (1821–1893). American Baptist minister and theological educator, born at Hulven, Suffolk, England. As a child, he emigrated to the United States and was converted under the **ministry** of **Jacob Knapp**. Harvey was educated at Madison University and Hamilton Theological Seminary, and owing to his prowess with languages, remained in Hamilton as a tutor for two years. He served as **pastor** at Homer, New York (1849–1857), and Hamilton, New York (1857–1858). Due to poor health, he left the pastorate for a teaching career at the seminary, lecturing in church history and pastoral **theology**. In 1861, his teaching fields expanded to biblical criticism. For one year, he returned to the pastorate, in Dayton, Ohio, but soon health failure forced him back to Hamilton, New York. In 1869, Harvey resumed his teaching career at Hamilton and remained in biblical studies and pastoral theology for the rest of his career. He was one of the first seminary professors among Baptists to conduct a study tour of the Holy Land (1874), about which he was widely published. Harvey's works on Baptist **polity** were definitive for many generations. They include *The Church: Its Polity and Ordinances* (1879) and *The Pastor* (1879).

HASSELTINE, ANN (1789–1826). American Baptist missionary, born at Bradford, Massachusetts. She was educated at Bradford Academy and read widely in religious classics. In February 1812, she married **Adoniram Judson** of Malden, and in 1813, the couple became America's first foreign missionaries to **India**. Although sent out under the sponsorship of the Congregationalist American Board of Commissioners for Foreign Missions, Ann and her husband adopted Baptist sentiments upon landing in India. Ann was baptized by **William Carey** at Serampore. Difficulties with the colonial government forced the Judsons to relocate to **Burma**, where Adoniram became the pioneer Baptist missionary. She became involved in children's work and maintained an extensive correspondence. Owing to health problems, she returned to the United States in 1821 and worked to modify the policies of the newly formed **Baptist Board of Foreign Missions**. Returning to Burma in 1822, Ann encountered trying circumstances. Her husband was imprisoned in the Burmese civil war, and she continuously pled for his release. She died of a liver ailment and became an instant heroine of missions. Her inspiring story was told by **Emily Judson**, Adoniram's third wife.

HAZZARD, DOROTHY (fl. 1640). English Separatist and, later, Baptist leader. She was the spouse of Anthony Kelly and then Matthew Hazzard (both of Bristol), the latter an Anglican priest who held Parliamentary sympathies in the English Civil War. About 1640, Hazzard refused to conform and began a meeting of **Nonconformists** at a private home in Bristol. Described as a "Mother in Israel," Hazzard was among the first Separatists in Bristol. She fell under the influence of a Baptist preacher named Cann and followed his gospel order in organizing what became the Broadmead Church in the City of Bristol. *See also* WOMEN, IN BAPTIST LIFE.

HELWYS, THOMAS (c. 1570–1616). English Baptist pioneer, born at Bilbrough, England. Details of Helwys's early life are sketchy. He appears to have attended Gray's Inn where he prepared for the practice of law. His home at Broxtowe Hall, Nottinghamshire, was the venue for a conventicle formed by **John Smyth** about 1605. Helwys likely funded the removal of this group of Separatists to Amsterdam in 1608. The next year, the group adopted Baptist practices and became the first Baptist congregation. In Holland, Smyth and Helwys differed on doctrinal and social issues, Helwys determining to return to England. Back in England in 1612, Helwys published the first exposition of complete **religious liberty** in the English language, *The Mistery of Iniquity*, and addressed his case to King James I. He also helped to form that year the first Baptist congregation in England at Spitalfields, outside London. Because of Helwys's understanding of the unlimited nature of Christ's atonement, the church was considered the progenitor of the **General Baptist** tradition. Helwys likely died in Newgate Prison before 1616. Among his other published works is *A Short and Plaine Proofe by the Word and Workes of God That God's Decree Is Not the Cause of Any Man's Sinne or Condemnation and That All Men Are Redeemed By Christ* (1610?).

HENRY, CARL FERDINAND HOWARD (1913–2003). American Baptist theologian, born at New York City. He was educated at Wheaton College, Northern Baptist Theological Seminary, and Boston University, where he received his doctorate. Early in his life, Henry was a journalist, and this writing capability served him well throughout the remainder of his productive career. He taught at Northern Baptist Seminary, and in 1947, he became one of the founding faculty members of Fuller Theological Seminary in Pasadena, California. A confidant of **Billy Graham** (whose 1949 Rose Bowl Crusade Henry helped organize), the Fuller Family, and the oil magnate J. Howard Pew, Henry rose quickly in the ranks of American **evangelicalism**. His postwar book, *The Uneasy Conscience of Modern Fundamentalism* (1947), struck a new course for **conservative** evangelicals, emphasizing dialogue, a better educated leadership, and social awareness. With **Edward J. Carnell**, **Bernard Ramm**, Harold Ockenga, and **Harold Lindsell**, Henry took on the sobriquet of "neo-evangelical," by which he meant to recover a biblical word and provide a response to Barthianism. In 1956, he was the unanimous choice as founding editor of *Christianity Today*, and he was also editorially associated with World Vision. After his Fuller years, Henry taught at Trinity Evangelical Divinity School and The Eastern Baptist Theological Seminary. His great theological treatise, which he reckoned a successor to the work of **Augustus H. Strong**, was *God, Revelation, and Authority* (1976–1983). In it, Henry argued persuasively for the verbal plenary inspiration of the scriptures and the basis of theology to be the divine self-revelation. Henry was married to Helga Bender, a linguist and former missionary in the North American (German) Baptist Conference.

HIAWATHA LAND INDEPENDENT BAPTIST MISSIONS. An **independent fundamentalist** Baptist domestic mission founded in May 1942, at Escanaba, Michigan. The prime mover was Arthur A. Glen (d. 1952), a **colporteur** for the **American Baptist Home Mis-**

sion **Society** (1926–1933), who became disenchanted with the **liberalism** of the Northern Baptist Convention and resigned. A **pastor** in upstate Michigan for four years, Glen gathered several sympathetic **pastors** and formed the Hiawatha Land Independent Baptist Mission, whose objectives were **evangelism**, church planting, and assistance for ministers in the northern central states. In 1943, the mission was recognized by the **General Association of Regular Baptist Churches**.

HIGHER EDUCATION. The interest of Baptists in Christian higher education goes back to the origins of the denomination in England in the 17th century. Among the earliest **General** and **Particular Baptists** in England were several university-trained ministers of the Anglican or Puritan persuasion. Such names as **John Smyth**, **Thomas Helwys**, **Hanserd Knollys**, **Roger Williams**, and **Henry Denne** give ample evidence of the learning of the leadership.

In the years of the Puritan Commonwealth and the Restoration, Baptists and other **Nonconformists** were denied the opportunity to study in the universities at Oxford and Cambridge, as well as the schools and academies where the Established Church offspring received their primary educations. This led to clandestine academies and later recognized secondary institutions where Independents, Presbyterians, and Baptists were educated. In 1679, Edward Terrill (fl. 1680) of Bristol took the significant step of setting up a trust whereby ministers could be trained in the apprenticeship style by the **pastors** of his church, Broadmead Baptist in Bristol. This evolved in the 18th century into Bristol Baptist College. Several other theological schools were founded by the English Baptists in the 18th and 19th centuries, meeting the needs of the professional clergy. Others who aspired to be physicians, lawyers, or teachers found their way into the system and excelled at both Oxford and Cambridge, plus the "red brick" universities founded in the 19th century. The founding of the University of London upon nonsectarian principles, but with heavy Dissenter influences (and related colleges and lectures), was an exception to the English trend to send students through the ancient universities to receive a higher education. *See also* THEOLOGICAL EDUCATION.

In the United States, however, different circumstances ensued. Christian colleges emerged from the mid-17th century as bastions of the religious confessions that gave them life. Indeed, it has been shown by historians of higher education that the foundation of the American collegiate system was the church-related college. Baptists were privileged to make their mark in the pre-Revolutionary era with the establishment of the College of Rhode Island at Providence in 1764. This was the first of scores of institutions.

Throughout the 19th century, the Baptist system of state conventions, established before 1850, gave rise to state Baptist institutions, like Colby College (Maine, 1817), Colgate University (New York, 1819), Columbian College (Washington, D.C., 1821), Mississippi College (Mississippi, 1826), Furman University (South Carolina, 1827), Georgetown College (Kentucky, 1829), Denison University (Ohio, 1831), Richmond College (Virginia, 1832), Shurtleff College (Illinois, 1832), Kalamazoo College (Michigan, 1833), Mercer University (Georgia, 1833), Franklin College (Indiana, 1834), Union University (Tennessee, 1834), Wake Forest University (North Carolina, 1834), Howard College (Alabama, 1842), Baylor University (Texas, 1846), Bucknell University (Pennsylvania, 1846), Linfield College (Oregon, 1849), William Jewell College (Missouri, 1849), and Stephens College (Missouri, 1856).

Later collegiate-level institutions that enjoyed wide patronage in their respective states were Des Moines University (Iowa, 1865), Ottawa University (Kansas, 1865), Alderson, Broaddus (West Virginia, 1871), Pillsbury College (Minnesota, 1877), Sioux Falls University (South Dakota, 1883), Colorado Women's College (Colorado, 1888), Grand Island College (Nebraska, 1892), Oklahoma Baptist University (Oklahoma, 1914), and Ouachita University (Oklahoma, 1886). Several of these institutions did not survive financial crises caused in large part by insufficient interest and support from their Baptist constituencies. Others left the church relationship in favor of nonsectarian higher education: Brown University, University of Rochester, Bucknell University, Colby College, Colgate University, and the University of Chicago.

In **Canada**, the American style of school was seen in the development of Acadia University (1838), Canadian Literary Institute (1860) (later McMaster University), Prairie College (1879), Brandon College (1899), Okanagan College (1906), Atlantic Baptist University (1949), and Carey Theological College (1960). Similar to the secularization process in the United States, Canadian Baptists lost control over their three most prestigious universities in the 20th century: McMaster, Acadia, and Brandon. Baptist influence continues at McMaster and Acadia in the form of divinity colleges related to private, nonsectarian universities.

In other parts of the world where Baptist missions have been established, schools, universities, and special colleges have resulted from concerted efforts to offer egalitarian education. Notable are the Serampore College founded by **William Carey** in **India** and the Reekie School (1898) in Oruro, **Bolivia**. *See also* EDUCATION.

HINDUSTAN BIBLE INSTITUTE. An **independent** mission agency of Baptistic doctrine, founded in 1952 by Paul Gupta, a converted Hindu in Madras, **India**. The U.S.-based organization raises funds for educational and **evangelistic** efforts in India and sponsors short-term teams to India. The office is in Union Mills, North Carolina.

HINTON, JOHN HOWARD (1791–1873). English Baptist minister, **theologian**, and denominational leader, born at Oxford. He was educated in surgery at Oxford University, but under the influence of **Andrew Fuller** and **John Sutcliff**, Hinton transferred to Bristol Baptist College, where he completed two years. In 1811, he graduated from the University of Edinburgh. From 1816 to 1820, he served at Haverfordwest and, later, the Hosier St. Chapel in Reading (1820–1837); and Devonshire Square in London (1837–1863). In 1837, he was elected secretary of the **Baptist Union of Great Britain** and in the ensuing quarter of a century his leadership saved the feeble union. Hinton strongly favored **voluntarism** and the authority of local congregations and lamented the priority of overseas over domestic **missions**. A moderate Calvinist, he repeatedly stressed human responsibility in conversion and was severely criticized by the *Gospel Standard* and **Strict Baptist** movements. At the end of his **ministry**, Hinton rejected the moralising tendencies of **Nonconformist** theologians, favoring a more **evangelistic** approach and opposing the growing cooperation with the Congregationalist Union. A **pastor** again in Reading from 1863 to 1868, Hinton compiled seven volumes of his theological writings, as well as a history of the United States.

HISPANIC BAPTISTS. Since the establishment of American and Southern Baptist missions in the Caribbean and Mexico in the 19th century, Spanish-speaking Baptists have constituted a growing minority in the denominational family. There is a Baptist Convention in **Spain** (1928) and conventions in every Spanish-speaking republic in Latin America. Significant Hispanic communities in North America are located in Florida, New York, Pennsylvania, Texas, and Southern California. In 1928, a Spanish American Baptist Convention was founded in California. It sponsored the Spanish American Baptist Seminary in Los Angeles and a periodical, *El Paladin* (*The Champion*). The convention, which included about 10 congregations in 1940, was associated with the Northern Baptist Convention.

In **Puerto Rico**, the Baptist community is related primarily to the **American Baptist Churches** and within the United States there is the American Baptist National Hispanic Caucus, formed in 1970 at Green Lake, Wisconsin. The Hispanic community related to the American Baptist family is derived primarily from Puerto Rico, **Cuba**, **Mexico**, and **Nicaragua**. Likewise, **Southern Baptist** Hispanic churches tend to be derived from Mexico, and Central and South America. One of the most recent developments in North America is the emergence of a Hispanic Baptist community in **Canada**, where there is a seminary, founded in 1997 at Montreal, Quebec. The Hispanic community in Canada has been formed largely from emigrants from the Central American republics and is concentrated in Quebec, Ontario, and British Columbia. The Spanish Baptist Publishing House in El Paso, Texas, founded in 1906, is a major producer of Hispanic language educational materials.

HISTORICAL COLLECTIONS. Early in their history, Baptists began to collect historical materials for use in writing an official history. Probably the first to do so was **Benjamin Stinton**, brother-in-law of **Thomas Crosby**. Evidently **Joseph Ivimey** also used a wide variety of primary sources.

Morgan Edwards took an interest in uniting the many clusters of Baptists from New York to the southern colonies and prepared notes for further publication in a full-blown history. Several sets of his manuscripts were discovered after his death, only some of which were published. Edwards's notes became the important beginnings of

Baptist materials in North Carolina, Virginia, South Carolina, and Pennsylvania. Similarly, **Isaac Backus**, in compiling his history of Baptists in New England, brought together a substantial amount of letters and firsthand accounts of the various streams of Baptists from his section of the country.

In the first decade of the 19th century, **David Benedict** and **Luther Rice** collected a wide variety of materials for differing purposes. Benedict collected not only minutes of associations but he also requested regional leaders to write essays on the development of Baptist church life in their midst. Luther Rice, peripatetic missionary promoter among the Baptists in the United States, amassed a large amount of **associational** literature, which later found its way into the American Baptist Historical Society (ABHS).

The ABHS was the first systematic attempt in the United States to preserve materials relating to the Baptist enterprise. **Howard Malcolm**, a missionary promoter and writer; **John Mason Peck**; and William R. Williams (1804–1885) were among the originators of the society, which was created in Philadelphia in 1861. In 1896, a tragic fire destroyed much of the ABHS's collections. A parallel collection was started by **Samuel Colgate** of Orange, New Jersey, in 1888 and presented to Colgate University. This collection featured published reports and a rare book library of early English Baptist publications. In 1955, the ABHS merged its reconstituted holdings housed at Crozer Theological Seminary in Chester, Pennsylvania, with the Colgate Collection to form the largest body of Baptist historical literature and records in the world. The merged libraries were given a new home at Colgate Rochester Divinity School in Rochester, New York. In 1983, the ABHS opened an American Baptist Archives Center at Valley Forge, Pennsylvania, to administer the American Baptist denominational records at the headquarters site, in addition to the Colgate Library in Rochester. Also in 1983, a small museum with changing exhibits was started at the American Baptist Assembly at Green Lake, Wisconsin. In 2008, the ABHS relocated all of its collections to the Atlanta, Georgia, campus of Mercer University.

In most of the state regions in both the Southern and American Baptist families, there are important regional collections; among the oldest and largest are Virginia, North Carolina, Georgia, Texas, Illinois, Oregon, South Dakota, and Berkeley, California. Additionally, the **Baptist General Conference**, the **North American Baptist Conference**, and **Seventh Day Baptists** have archives related to their organizations. In 1949, the **Southern Baptist Convention** (SBC) created the Historical Commission, which in 1985 took over the Dargan-Carver Library of the **Sunday School Board**. This library and archives was for a time the repository for the national Southern Baptist agencies. However, due to reorganization of the commission structure of the SBC in 1995, the Southern Baptist Historical Society and many program facets of the Historical Commission broke away from the Nashville center in 1996 to be recreated at Oklahoma Baptist University.

Canadian Baptist efforts in historical preservation are also extensive. **John Mockett Cramp** collected many details for his serialized essays in Maritime Baptist history in the *Christian Messenger*. **Edward Manning**, pastor in Nova Scotia, left a large body of letters and associational items. In 1845, the Maritime Baptists organized a collection later to become the Baptist Archives at Acadia University. In the central provinces, historical preservation efforts began with the formation of the Canadian Baptist Historical Society in 1865, associated with **Robert A. Fyfe** at Canadian Literary Institute and later McMaster University in Toronto and Hamilton, Ontario. This collection also includes materials for the French Union, the national organizations, and the Baptist Union of Western Canada.

In Great Britain, the most significant collection of materials is the Angus Library, associated with Regent's Park College at Oxford. The provenance of this collection was Joseph Angus's personal library. Its strengths are original publications of 17th- and 18th-century Baptist literature and records of associations and societies, notably the **Baptist Missionary Society**. The **Strict Baptists** maintain their historical collection at Dunstable in Bedfordshire. Less extensive collections are to be found at Bristol Baptist College, Dr. Williams' Library in London, and the John Rylands Library at the University of Manchester. A small but significant collection of Welsh Baptist materials is kept at the union offices of the Welsh Baptist Union in Swansea, and a Scottish collection is kept at union offices in Glasgow.

In Europe, many unions have made efforts to preserve their historical materials. In Hamburg (since 1996 at Elstal) at the Baptist seminary are many items relating to **German** Baptists, notably papers associated with August and **Walter Rauschenbusch**. At Betelseminariat in Stockholm, the **Swedish Baptists** have an extensive collection, emphasizing education and missions as well as a museum exhibit. Likewise the theological seminaries in Tolose, **Denmark**, Stabekk, **Norway**, and Budapest, **Hungary**, maintain historical materials. The Southern Baptist-originated seminary at Rüschlikon, **Switzerland** (recently removed to Prague, **Czech Republic**) has a Baptist/ **Anabaptist** collection of mostly secondary materials.

Elsewhere in the Baptist family, many colleges maintain historical collections. Among these are the Baptist Historical Society of New South Wales, **Australia** (1974); Serampore College in **India**; **Hong Kong** Baptist College; and Central **Philippines** University.

Baptist historical serial publications include the *Chronicle* (1938–1957), *Foundations* (1958–1982), and *American Baptist Quarterly* (1982–), by American Baptists; *Baptist History and Heritage* (1965–), by Southern Baptists; and *Transactions of the Baptist Historical Society* (1908–1921) and its successor, the *Baptist Quarterly* (1922–), by British Baptists.

HOBART, ALVAH SABIN (1847–1930). American Baptist minister and theological educator, born in Whitby, Ontario, **Canada**. Upon the death of his mother, Hobart was raised in Vermont by his grandfather, the distinguished American Baptist minister Alvah Sabin (1793–1885). He was educated at Madison (later Colgate) University and Hamilton Theological Seminary. Ordained at Morris, New York, he served that church from 1874 to 1879 and then Mt. Auburn, Cincinnati, Ohio (1879–1885); First Baptist Toledo, Ohio (1885–1889); and Warburton Avenue, Yonkers, New York (1889–1900). Crozer Theological Seminary appointed Hobart professor of English New Testament in 1900, a post he held for 20 years. In the classroom, he became a master of biblical hermeneutics. From 1920 to 1923, he returned to the pulpit of Warburton Avenue and then retired. As a denominational statesman, he was in much demand, for instance, as a member of the investigation committee at Colgate in the **Nathaniel Schmidt** incident, and also as one of the committee on the union of Free Baptists and Northern Baptists, a merger that Hobart was the first to suggest. Among theological educators, he was an advocate of English **Bible** instruction. At Crozer, he dropped the Greek and

Hebrew language requirements and modernized the entire curriculum. Hobart also pioneered the extension course of education at Crozer, which assisted scores of pastors in remote locations. His published works include *Key to the New Testament* (1910) and *Religion for Men* (1912).

HOBBS, HERSCHEL HAROLD (1907–1995). Southern Baptist minister and denominational leader, born at Talladega Springs, Arkansas. He was educated at Howard College (later Samford University) and Southern Baptist Theological Seminary, where he was awarded the Ph.D. in New Testament. A **pastor** for most of his career, Hobbs served Vinesville (1929) and Berney Points, near Birmingham, Alabama (1929–1932); Crestwood, Kentucky (1937–1938); Calvary Baptist, Birmingham (1938–1939); Clayton Street, Montgomery, Alabama (1939–1941); Emmanuel Baptist, Alexandria, Louisiana (1941–1945); Dauphin Way, Mobile, Alabama (1945–1949); and First Baptist, Oklahoma City (1949–1972). Hobbs was one of the most widely respected leaders of the **Southern Baptist Convention** of his era, serving as president from 1962 to 1963 and chair of the Peace Commission in 1985, and preaching the annual sermon in 1957. Hobbs wrote hundreds of lessons for the Baptist **Sunday School Board** and preached over 700 sermons on the *Southern Baptist Hour*, a popular radio broadcast. In 1962–1963, Hobbs chaired the prestigious committee to revise the "**Baptist Faith and Message**" and this earned him a place as a prominent moderate theological voice among Southern Baptists, notably the **Mainstream Network**.

HOBY, JAMES (1788–1871). English Baptist minister, born in London. He was educated at Bristol Baptist College and served as assistant pastor at Maze Pond Baptist Chapel (1812–1823) and then as **pastor** at Birmingham, Weymouth, and Twickenham. In 1836, on behalf of the **Baptist Union**, Hoby joined **Francis A. Cox** and made an extensive tour of the Baptists in the United States and **Canada**. The report was published in 1836 as *Baptists in America: A Report of the Deputation*, and became a major resource in Britain for understanding the development and splintering of Baptist life in North America.

HOLINESS MOVEMENT, BAPTISTS AND. A collection of themes derived from the Methodist and revival traditions in the United States and Great Britain. From the time of John Wesley (1703–1791), some Methodists emphasized Christian perfection and wrote much about the doctrine of entire sanctification. With the **Second Great Awakenings**, particularly the stream fostered by Charles G. Finney (1792–1875), a Presbyterian **evangelist** in upstate New York, the notion of the perfectibility of individual Christian experience received new attention. In the **revivals** of 1858, led particularly by Walter C. (1804–1883) and Phoebe (1807–1874) Palmer and A. B. Earle (d. 1892), a holiness **theology** took definite shape. Advocates of the holiness position held that sanctification was instantaneous, not progressive, and this led to a recognition of a second work of grace after salvation. Theologically and ethically, the doctrine teaches that the roots of sin are removed by sanctification, but that the possibility of a lapse remains. Typically, persons could experience this work of grace in revival meetings or the regional camp meetings being held throughout the United States and Britain in the 1860s and 1870s.

Baptists in the northeastern United States in limited numbers responded to holiness preaching, and a few professed to have had an experience of entire sanctification. Likewise, during revival services in New Brunswick and Nova Scotia, **Canada**, in 1882–1883, prominent Free Christian Baptists had experiences. The result was a prolonged debate among the **Freewill Baptists** whose **Arminian** theology provided a context for emphasizing Christian experience. In 1888, a schism took place in which the mainstream Freewill Baptists rejected holiness theology on the grounds that it was unbiblical and that it was contrary to the teachings of their systematic theologian, **John J. Butler**. Those who favored an instantaneous experience in turn formed the **Reformed Baptist Alliance**, which in 1968 merged with Wesleyan Methodists in the United States. A similar set of circumstances occurred among Freewill Baptists in the southern United States when G. B. Cashwell in North Carolina had an experience of grace and led in the formation of the Cape Fear Conference of Freewill Baptists, later the Pentecostal Freewill Baptist Church.

The holiness movement also had a pronounced impact upon Baptists in **Russia**. Princess Natalie Lieven who maintained a grand home in St. Petersburg in the 1880s was the magnet for various evangelicals to attend preaching and Bible study. She had been moved to an experience of entire sanctification under the preaching of Col. Vasilii Pashkov. **Ivan Kargel** fell under this influence at the Lieven Palace and became a holiness advocate. His influence was felt among the group that coalesced as the Evangelical Christians. *See also* FREEWILL BAPTISTS; KARGEL, IVAN; REFORMED BAPTIST ALLIANCE.

HOLLIS, THOMAS (1659–1731). English Baptist philanthropist, born at Rotherham. Hollis was an active supporter of the Pinner's Hall open membership church in London. Hollis paid for the elaborate **baptisterion** at the church in Barbican for Baptists in London to use. He helped to found the **Particular Baptist** Fund in 1717. In response to the plight of Baptists in New England, he established at Harvard College the Hollis professorships, in exchange for recognition of Baptist ministers by the Congregationalist Standing Order. His gift gave preference to Baptists and thus established Baptists on a sound footing among New England sects. *See also* ARCHITECTURE, BAPTIST.

HOLMES, ELKANAH (1744–1832). American and Canadian Baptist missionary, born at Canterbury, New Hampshire. He served in the British military during the French and Indian War and later in the American Revolution as a chaplain. A frontiersman at heart, Holmes left his pastorate at Staten Island, New York, to volunteer for **missionary** service among the Iroquois of western New York. He first worked for the New York Missionary Society from 1796 to 1807, but his insistence on believer's **baptism** led to a rift, and the New York Baptist Missionary Society was formed, for which he also worked. He evangelized the British settlements on the Niagara Peninsula, starting several congregations, and lived in Upper **Canada** (now Ontario) during the War of 1812. In 1797, Holmes published an important manual of **polity**, which was widely used on both sides of the border.

HOLMES, OBADIAH (1607–1682). American Baptist minister, born at Manchester, England. Holmes emigrated to Massachusetts as part of the Puritan migration under Archbishop William Laud

(1573–1645). He settled first at Salem, then at Rehoboth, Massachusetts. In 1650, he adopted Baptist views and moved to Newport, Rhode Island, to enjoy greater religious freedom. In 1651, Holmes, **John Clarke**, and John Crandall traveled to Lynn, Massachusetts, to witness to a friend, and were imprisoned and fined. His whipping became the subject of works on persecution by John Clarke and **Roger Williams**. Holmes served as **pastor** of the Newport Baptist congregation from 1651 to 1663, in the absence of John Clarke. He maintained correspondence with London **Particular Baptists** and withstood a schism in the congregation, which eventually became Second Baptist Church. Holmes's steadfast opposition to Seventh Day views led to the establishment in Newport of a separate **Seventh Day Baptist** church in 1668. His theological confession, composed for the benefit of his brother Robert in England, was printed in the 1871 edition of **Isaac Backus**'s *History of the Baptists.*

HOLY COMMUNION. *See* LORD'S SUPPER.

HOLY SPIRIT, BAPTIST UNDERSTANDING OF. A universal Baptist "doctrine" of the Holy Spirit cannot be easily identified or summarized in a single, convenient statement. There is a long tradition of Baptist recognition of the work of the Spirit, with increasing attention to the gifts of the Spirit and the Spirit-filled life in the later 20th century.

None of the early Baptist confessions of faith have a separate section devoted to the Holy Spirit, as is the case, for instance, with the doctrines of **Christ** and the church. Instead, discussion of the Holy Spirit occurs in the context of the Trinity, the gathering of the church, witness to the person of Christ, and teacher of truth. As Quakers, **Seekers**, and **Ranters** spoke openly of "being in the Spirit" or "being led by the Spirit" in the 17th century, Baptists clearly wanted to differentiate themselves from these more radical, enthusiastic sects. Most early Baptists, therefore, adopted a generally Reformed view of the Holy Spirit as Paraclete and guide, preferring instead to emphasize the preeminence of Christ.

Beginning in the 18th century, and probably under the influence of the Wesleyans in Britain and the revivalist movement in the United States, Baptists began to awaken to manifestations of the Spirit in individual and collective spiritualities. **New Lights** emphasized the work of the Spirit in regeneration and sanctification, while Old Lights stressed education, nurture, and confessionalism. Camp meetings, **revivals**, outdoor **evangelism** and **missionary** endeavor of many kinds, all necessitated a strong belief in an immanent and personal manifestation of God, namely, the Holy Spirit. The influence of the **holiness** tradition upon particularly the **Freewill Baptists** led to correctives by theologians such as **John J. Butler**, who urged a traditional progressive understanding of sanctification, rather than instantaneous manifestations purportedly wrought by the Spirit.

With the growing attention in the 20th century to the Pentecostal traditions and the charismatic renewal movements, Baptists were forced to respond to the stimuli of media evangelists, small group development, and massive literature output about the Spirit upon church members. Not atypically, many Baptists in the United Kingdom were involved in the Spring Harvest movement and Manna Ministries, and in North America the Vineyard movement, both of which emphasized the extraordinary work of the Holy Spirit. In a few cases, ongoing **associations** of "Spirit-filled Baptists" exist in denominational families, such as the American Baptist Charismatic Fellowship, more recently called the Holy Spirit Renewal Fellowship.

In terms of doctrinal statements, Baptists generally have stressed the personhood of the Holy Spirit and referred to the Spirit in the third person ("he"). Additionally, the Spirit is understood to have been active in Creation, the inspiration of **Scripture**, the exaltation of Christ, the calling of believers, the cultivation of Christian character through presence in every believer, and the empowerment of believers for worship, evangelism, and service.

HOMOSEXUALITY. *See* SEXUALITY.

HONDURAS. Baptist life in Honduras was an outgrowth of missions in **Guatemala** and **El Salvador**. In 1946, the first congregation was organized at Choluteca and U.S. **Southern Baptist** William J. Webb (1912–1973) conducted preaching tours and established the work. In 1958, the Asociación de Iglesias Bautistas de Honduras was founded with five churches; a theological institute was opened a short time later at Tegucigalpa. In 1951, the **Conservative Baptists** from the

United States began a substantial work with a radio station; in 1955, **Baptist Mid-Missions** opened a mission at Utila on the Day Islands; in 1974, the **Baptist Bible Fellowship** opened a mission; and the **American Baptist Association** also has mission work in Honduras from the 1960s.

As of 2006, there were 444 churches and 25,000 members with the Convención Nacional Bautista de Honduras.

HONG KONG. The presence of Baptists in the city and province of Hong Kong may be dated from 1842 when **William Dean** and **J. Lewis Shuck,** missionaries of the American **Baptist Board of Foreign Missions**, embarked upon a church planting mission with the support of the **British Baptist Missionary Society**. Eventually, American Baptists left Hong Kong to indigenous leaders in favor of other ports in South **China**. Shuck became a **missionary** of the **Southern Baptist Convention** and for a time carried on the work under their auspices. In the 20th century, as the fields in mainland China closed, Hong Kong once again became a major focus of American and Southern Baptist missionary work in its own right, often connected with missions in **Macao**. Hong Kong Baptist College was established in 1956. In addition to regular Baptist work, **Baptist Mid-Missions** from the United States established a mission in Hong Kong in 1951, as an outgrowth of its closed China work, as did the U.S. **Association of Baptists for World Evangelism** (ABWE) in 1945; the U.S. **Conservative Baptist** Foreign Mission Society began a mission in 1963 in Kowloon and the New Territories, and the U.S. **Baptist Bible Fellowship** established a mission in 1969.

As of 2006, 152 churches with 65,721 members were affiliated with the Baptist Convention of Hong Kong; 7 churches with 1,800 members affliated with the Hong Kong Conservative Baptist Association; and 19 churches with 5,000 members in the ABWE in Hong Kong. There are two Baptist-related schools in Kowloon and one in Sha Tin. *See also* MACAU.

HOOTEN, ELIZABETH (c. 1600–1672). English **Nonconformist** preacher, born in Nottinghamshire. From scant evidence, some recent historians hold that Elizabeth Hooten may have been one of the earliest Baptist "she-preachers." In Thomas Edwards's (1599–1647) book *Gangrena*, a **woman** preacher who was believed to conduct **baptisms** ministered in the vicinity of Skegby, near Mansfield. She may well have been one of the "**shattered Baptists**" whom George Fox (1624–1691) encountered in 1648. Hooten was said to be Fox's first convert; later, she went on a mission for the Society of Friends and died in **Jamaica**.

HOVEY, ALVAH (1820–1903). American Baptist minister and theological educator, born at Greene, New York. A graduate of Dartmouth College and Newton Theological Institution, Hovey began his career as a schoolteacher. He returned to Newton in 1849 to teach Hebrew and church history. Later, he became professor of **theology** and Christian ethics. From 1868 to 1898, Hovey was president of the seminary, one of the longest and most distinguished tenures of a Baptist seminary administrator. His published writings include a biography of **Isaac Backus** and a systematic theology. During the Civil War era, he forcefully opposed **slavery** and he chaired the trustee committee at Brown University, which admitted women students. Hovey was also one of the organizers of the **Baptist Congress**.

HOWARD, JOHN (1726–1790). English Baptist philanthropist and reformer, born at Hackney. Early in life, he was apprenticed as a grocer but declined to continue in that trade. In 1756, Howard took a sea voyage and was captured and imprisoned in France. During his incarceration, he cared for sailors and took note of the deplorable conditions in the prison system. Returning to England, Howard was made a Fellow of the Royal Society in 1756, and he settled at Cardington, Bedfordshire. On his property, he constructed a model village and conducted education for **Nonconformist** children. From 1773 to his death, he traveled widely in England and Europe, at his own expense, conducting a tour and assessment of prisons, hospitals, lazarettos, and military encampments. In 1773, Howard was elected High Sheriff of Bedfordshire, and from this position he brought about reform of prison conditions in the counties. In 1777, he published a widely acclaimed study, the *State of the Prisons in England and Wales*, which initiated much reform of the system. A teetotaler and vegetarian, Howard was also an active Baptist layman, involved in **Samuel Stennett**'s church at Little Wild Street, London. He held

Stennett in high esteem and wrote affectionately of his worship services. Howard died at Khersom in southern **Russia**, while inspecting military outposts.

HOWELL, ROBERT BOYTE CRAWFORD (1801–1868). Southern Baptist minister and denominational leader, born in Wayne County, North Carolina. A graduate of Columbian College, his **ministry** began in Norfolk, Virginia, after which he moved to the pastorate of First Baptist, Nashville, Tennessee, from 1834 to 1850. Next he served Second Baptist, Richmond, Virginia, from 1850 to 1857. In each of these pastorates, he served with distinction, building large congregations. Howell served as president of the **Southern Baptist Convention** from 1851 to 1853 and again in 1855 and 1857, resigning under pressure from **James R. Graves** and the **Landmarkist** movement. One of the most prolific writers of the Baptist family in the United States, he wrote major works entitled *The Deaconship* (1846) and *The Terms of Communion* (1854). He debated with Campbellites and within his own denomination, with James R. Graves. Howell favored a strong denomination that was missionary minded in contrast to other more exclusivist views of the church.

HUBMAIER, BALTHASAR (c. 1480–1528). German religious reformer, born at Friedberg. He was educated at the University of Freiberg, where he earned an M.A. under the tutelage of Johann Eck (1486–1543), and in 1512, he was awarded the Th.D. degree at the University of Ingolstadt, again largely under Eck. Hubmaier earned a wide reputation as a pulpit orator from his service as a chaplain at the Church of the Virgin. In 1516, he moved to Regensburg as a preacher, where he became embroiled in an anti-Jewish movement. At length, he went to Waldshut in Württenberg as a zealous Catholic. Influenced by Swiss reformers and Erasmus (1469–1536), in 1522 Hubmaier began to rethink his theological position. In 1524, much affected by **Huldrych Zwingli** in Zurich, Hubmaier announced to his congregation at Waldshut a list of 18 theses, which included the principle of *sola fide* and an end to the Mass. He was married the same year. In 1525, Hubmaier moved beyond Zwingli to a position in support of believer's **baptism**, and he was baptized by William Roublin of Wytiken. Hubmaier's tract, *The Christian Baptism of Believers*

(1525), summarized his new beliefs. In 1526, he moved to Nikols-burg in Moravia where he mingled with chiliastic **Anabaptists**. By edict of Ferdinand of Austria, he and his wife were imprisoned at Greisenstein near Vienna. Under pressure, Hubmaier made several concessions to Catholicism and his having conspired against the state. His continuing Anabaptist views, however, led to his martyr-dom on March 10, 1528, at Vienna, while his wife was drowned in the Danube. Recovered historically in the 19th century, Hubmaier be-came a heroic figure among advocates of believer's baptism, and his defense of the position is considered the earliest and best theological presentation of the sacrament/ordinance.

HUDSON, WINTHROP STILL (1911–2001). American Baptist min-ister, historian, and educator, born at Schoolcraft, Michigan. His fa-ther was a U.S. Congressman from Michigan. Hudson was educated at Kalamazoo College, Colgate Rochester Divinity School, and the University of Chicago, where he completed the Ph.D. under Sidney Mead and William Warren Sweet. Hudson began his teaching career at the University of Chicago and in 1948 was successor to Conrad H. Moehlman at Colgate Rochester. He continued in this position as the James B. Colgate Professor of the History of Christianity until his re-tirement in 1979. During the final years of Hudson's work, he was also appointed in the Department of History at the University of Rochester. Hudson brought to the Rochester seminary **theological** identity a mild version of the **Chicago School**, and he mentored many theological students toward graduate studies at Chicago, Yale, and Rochester Universities. He was active in numerous roles in the American Baptist Convention at crucial perods, including president of the American Baptist Historical Society when the two great Bap-tist historical libraries were merged in to the Samuel Colgate Baptist Historical Collection in Rochester. He was a major contributor to the Green Lake theological conferences sponsored by the American Bap-tist Board of Education and Publication, and this led to classic essays like "Stumbling Into Disorder" and "The Associational Principle Among Baptists." Hudson became the leading reference point for Baptist identity among American Baptists for three decades. With **Norman H. Maring** at Eastern Baptist Seminary, Hudson coau-thored a **polity** and practice manual that served the denomination for generations. Beyond his work as a Baptist, Hudson earned the title Dean of American Religious Historians during the 1980s for his publication of *The Great Tradition of the American Churches* (1953) and *Religion in America* (1965). Thoroughly **ecumenical**, Hudson was a proponent of the **Puritan-Separatist Hypothesis** of Baptist origins and the overall Reformed theological orientation of his denomination and school.

HUMAN RIGHTS, BAPTISTS AND. Many Baptists have difficulties with the terminology "human rights" because of their Calvinistic heritage of the doctrine of the sovereignty of God. However, this has not diminished overall Baptist interest in and support for human rights concerns: physical, political, and spiritual.

The primary human rights issue for Baptists has been **religious liberty**, almost to the exclusion of other needs. From the time of **Thomas Helwys,** religious liberty has included the rights to freedom of conscience, education of children, propagation of the faith, and freedom to organize churches and religious associations.

In the early 19th century, human rights for many was equated with the abolition of slavery. Progressive Baptists in the American South, such as **David Barrow** and **William H. Brisbane**, advocated emancipation of slaves as an act of Christian responsibility. In the 1830s, **Freewill Baptists** and Regular Baptists in the northern states advocated abolition of slavery on the grounds of moral law and human rights. In the British context, **William Knibb** reminded readers of his observations of life in Jamaica in decrying the evils of slavery, and he advocated the emancipation of slaves to numerous members of Parliament in the 1832 session. Slavery was the overriding violation of human rights and it consumed Baptist moral energies well into the 1850s.

Later, Baptist **associations** in the northern United States organized various **voluntary** societies to alleviate poor housing conditions, exploitation of women and children, and the plight of black and immigrant communities. The Long Island Baptist Fresh Air Society (actually a camping ministry) and the Friendship House movement in northern Baptist cities illustrated these responses.

The Baptist community spoke out dramatically in the 1930s as totalitarian governments seized control in several European countries.

Of particular concern were Nazi **Germany** and Stalinist **Russia**. In 1939, the three major U.S. Baptist groups, Northern, **Southern**, and **National**, jointly issued the **American Baptist Bill of Rights**, which upheld basic human rights to personal spirituality, unconstrained religious expression, a free church in a free state, and complete religious freedom for all peoples, regardless of faith commitment. It was said that the governments of the United States and Great Britain were influenced by the position of their Baptist constituencies.

When the United Nations was formed in 1945, Baptists were granted Non-Governmental Organization status through the **Baptist World Alliance** (BWA), and this has facilitated a constant flow of human rights data as well as a forum for Baptists to express their concerns to representatives of various world governments. Under the leadership of **Thorwald Lorenzen**, a variety of human rights violations have come to the attention of the BWA and been addressed by resolutions and/or site visits. Of particular concern has been the use of torture by militants and unjust imprisonment by governments.

From the 1960s through the 1980s, many Baptists focused their energies on the civil rights struggle in the United States as well as on the apartheid conditions in South Africa. Support was forthcoming from the American Baptist Convention and several historically **black Baptist** groups for the work of **Martin Luther King Jr.** Likewise, it was a stated position of the General Board of the **American Baptist Churches** in the 1980s to support the **Sullivan Principles**, which increased pressure on U.S. corporations to withdraw investments from South Africa.

Currently, Baptist concerns for human rights focus on the abuse of governments with respect to the treatment of children, refugees, prisoners (political and military), genocide, minority groups, and military action as a tool to resolve conflict. Hunger; famine; natural disasters; sustainable development; violence against believers, churches, and ministers; vandalism borne of racial or ethnic strife; and uncontrolled disease epidemics are also of particular interest to several Baptist groups. Some would even argue that religious harassment within some Baptist groups over political control or doctrinal differences is a violation of human rights in a free society.

Advocacy for human rights is seen in the Human Rights Study Commission of the BWA (which has been under pressure since the

1980s to create a higher level of divisional status), the American Baptist Churches, the Southern Baptist Convention, the **Baptist Union of Great Britain**, the regional fellowships of the BWA, and the **Baptist Peace Fellowship of North America**. In 1998, the BWA developed a format to receive complaints and reports of the violation of human rights, which are reported to the general secretary for appropriate action. Increasingly, the language of human rights as intoned in the United Nations is being used in BWA circles, such as the widespread advocacy of "life, liberty, and security" as stated in the Universal Declaration of Human Rights. In 1991, the BWA created a quinquennial Human Rights Award in memory of Carl and Olive Tiller, and in 2006, the Denton and Janice Lotz Annual Award in Human Rights was established. Locations of particular concern to Baptists in the last 25 years have included Zaire (**Congo**), **Burma** (Myanmar), **China**, the Soviet Union, **Uganda**, **Rwanda**, **Liberia**, **South Africa**, **Ireland**, **Nicaragua**, **Mexico**, **Bolivia**, **Colombia**, **Peru**, **Argentina**, Australian Aborigines, **Kenya**, **Angola**, **Mozambique**, Afghanistan, **Iran**, Palestine, and Tibet. A smaller effort toward a Baptist witness for human rights is the Baptist Peace Fellowship of North America.

HUNGARIAN BAPTIST UNION OF AMERICA. Part of the **American Baptist Home Mission Society**'s witness to Slavic immigrants to the United States in the late 19th and early 20th centuries was the formation of Hungarian Baptist congregations. Many of these churches were clustered in northeastern Pennsylvania and the Great Lakes region. In 1908, at Homestead, Pennsylvania, the Hungarian Baptist Union was formed, which at once began publication of a newspaper, the *Gospel Messenger* (1908–). In 1913, a Hungarian Baptist Seminary was started at Scranton, Pennsylvania, later to be merged with the International Baptist Seminary in East Orange, New Jersey. Over the years, the union came to include about 30 churches in Pennsylvania, Ohio, and New Jersey. In 1940–1941, the union became an "Associated Organization" with the Northern Baptist Convention.

HUNGARY. In the interests of the Free Church tradition, Hungarian Baptists maintain an ideological historical connection with Swiss **Anabaptists** from the 16th century. Officially, Baptist work in Hungary is traced to the ministry of **Heinrich Meyer**, who arrived in Budapest in 1873 as an agent of the British and Foreign Bible Society. Also working for **J. G. Oncken**, Meyer baptized several candidates and a church was formed by 1874. Eventually two distinct groups emerged, a German-speaking and a Hungarian-speaking association. In 1892, a **mission** board was organized, and the Hungarian Baptist Union was formed in 1900, with a **confession of faith** adopted in 1902. In 1920, the separate factions were united in the Magyarorszagi Baptista Egyhaz. A theological school was founded at Budapest in 1921 as a result of the **London Conference of 1920**. In 1990, the International Baptist Lay Academy was established under the auspices of the **European Baptist Federation**. The **Association of Baptists for World Evangelism** started a mission in 1988, and in 1990, the **Baptist Bible Fellowship** opened a mission in Hungary, as did the **Conservative Baptist** Foreign Mission Society the same year.

As of 2006, there were 343 churches with 11,533 members in the Magyarorszagi Baptista Egyhaz. A newspaper, *Bekehirnok* (*Messenger of Peace*) (1894–), is published by the Hungarian Baptist Union.

– I –

ICELAND. Baptist **mission** work in Iceland has followed the presence of U.S. military personnel. **Southern Baptists** began a mission in Iceland in 1963, but four years later closed down the effort. The **Baptist Bible Fellowship** opened a mission in Iceland in 1982. One congregation located at Njardvik is independent of any outside group and had over 100 members as of 2001.

INDEPENDENT BAPTISTS. The term "independent" has been applied to Baptist congregations and some associative bodies who are distinguished for their opposition to mainstream Baptist organizations. The term is usually employed in the American context, though it is found among Baptists in **Trinidad** from 1890.

In the 18th-century United States, for instance, **Isaac Backus** stood outside the regular association for several years and was "independent," as was **Elias Smith** of Haverhill, Massachusetts, when he became critical of the leaders of the Warren Association. Deep antagonisms emerged in the 19th century among the anti-mission Baptists and later the "gospel mission movement." Many in the **Landmarker** movement were independent of "conventionism." As the **fundamentalist** movement emerged in the first decades of the 20th century, leaders like **J. Frank Norris, John R. Rice, T. T. Shields,** and others first tried to reform the conventions to which they related, then they organized various **associations** independent of any existing Baptist body.

A new wave of "independent" Baptists came forth after World War II, mostly in the United States, but expanding in the missionary context, which are not related strongly to any extra-congregational body. These congregations cherish their **autonomy** and exhibit strong individual pastoral leadership. The terminology "independent" must be understood in a context of selective associationalism, however, as most congregations that employ the label "independent" cooperate with some organization, for instance, the **Baptist Bible Fellowship,** the **World Baptist Fellowship,** the **Southwide Baptist Fellowship,** or the **Liberty Baptist Fellowship.** Independent Baptist missionary agencies have allowed the independent church movement to carry forth the same outreach programs that "convention-related Baptists" enjoy. Among the prominent independent Baptist mission agencies are the **Association of Baptists for World Evangelism, Maranatha Baptists, Baptist Mid-Missions,** and **Evangelical Baptist Mission.** There are also several colleges, **Bible schools,** and seminaries that meet the needs of independent Baptists, for instance, Bob Jones University (South Carolina), Tennessee Temple Schools (Tennessee), Baptist Bible College (Missouri), Dallas Theological Seminary (Texas), Liberty University (Virginia), Moody Bible Institute (Illinois), Baptist Bible College and Seminary (Pennsylvania), Toronto Baptist Seminary (Ontario), and the Northwestern Schools in Minnesota.

It should also be noted that the terminology of the capitalized "Independent Baptists" has recently seen a new usage among theologically moderate to **liberal** Baptist congregations in very different circumstances. For instance, there is an Independent Baptist Church in Lower Sackville, Nova Scotia, where the title means simply "non-Convention affiliated." In Waco, Texas, Seventh and James Baptist Church refers to itself as an independent Baptist church in the moderate to liberal tradition theologically (stressing that its governance lies within the congregation), since it voted to dissociate itself from the Southern Baptist Convention in 2003. The Waco congregation remains actively related to the Waco Baptist Association, the Baptist General Convention of Texas, and the Baptist World Alliance. *See also* WORLD BAPTIST FELLOWSHIP.

INDEPENDENT GOSPEL MISSIONS. An American **independent** Baptistic missionary organization founded in 1968 by David Bovard and Henry Campbell. It focuses its effort on **evangelism** and church planting, with about 150 missionaries in Africa, **India**, South America, the Caribbean, the **Philippines**, and **Korea**. Its home base is in Sharon, Pennsylvania.

INDIA. The first Baptist missions in India were commenced in the early 1790s through the work of **John Thomas**. He informed **William Carey** of the opportunity he had observed in two previous visits, and the two became the first Baptist missionaries to Bengal in 1792; they were sent by the newly organized **Particular Baptist** Society for Propagating the Gospel among the Heathen (later the **Baptist Missionary Society**). The first Baptist congregation in India was organized by Carey and his cohorts in November 1795 at **Serampore**, with the first **baptism** of a Hindu convert, Krishna Pal, in 1800. With the translation and evangelization work supervised by Carey, the growth of Baptists in India through an extension of mission stations was slow and dependent upon the missionary society for many years. The first **association** on the British model was formed in Bengal in 1842, and a loose association has existed in Barisal District from about 1880. American Baptist missionaries passed through India to other fields and eventually claimed their own Indian territory in Assam in the northeast in 1836. **Amos Sutton**, originally a British **General Baptist** missionary who arrived in 1824, came under the sponsorship of the American **Freewill Baptists** and began church planting in Orissa in 1836. Canadian Baptists began their Telugu work at Vizagapatam in 1836.

The development of indigenous Baptist organizations in India was much influenced by **ecumenism** and the strength of the work in certain regions. For American Baptists, these developments took shape

in Assam, a region of northeast India. In Assam, a Baptist association on the U.S. model was organized in 1851, followed by the All
Assam Baptist Christian Convention, organized in 1914. In the related region of Garo, the churches, which began as an indigenous
movement centered at Rajasimla, organized their separate Baptist
association in 1875 and a convention in 1867. Another field in the
Northeast under the auspices of the American Baptists was in Bihar
among the tea workers. In 1871, four workers walked 70 miles to be
baptized at Sibsagar, which became a center of the mission in that
area. A fourth region in which great results for Indian Baptist missions were realized was among the Naga peoples. An Assamese
evangelist, Godhula Babu, converted 24 young Naga men who were
baptized in 1872. Starting at Molung Kimong village in the Ao Naga
area, the movement spread to other Naga-inhabited areas as well.
The Nagaland Baptist Church Council, a contemporary umbrella organization, has 454,349 members in 1,347 churches and 20 associations (2007). Another fruitful field of work was begun in Manipur
State in 1896; there, a convention was organized in the early 20th
century. In 1950, all of the churches connected to the American Baptist Assam Missions were organized into an indigenous body at first
called the Council of Baptist Churches in Assam, and later renamed
the **Council of Baptist Churches of Northeast India**. More than
400 schools and five hospitals were part of this legacy. Other recent
Baptist convention-level organizations in the American Baptist tradition include the Arunachal Pradesh Baptist Convention (1995) and
the Banjara Baptist Sanghevur Malawo (1996), in the Andra Predesh
region.

   In Bengal Orissa, a field originally opened by the Freewill Baptists
but transferred to American Baptists in 1911, the Yearly Meeting was
nationalized in 1918 and the Home Mission Board was formed in
1935. The following year, with the support of American Baptists, the
Bengal-Orissa Mission joined the All India Baptist Union (see below), a body of mission coordination for the country. In the South India Baptist Mission, also an outgrowth of American Baptist efforts,
the American Baptist Telugu Mission became the Telugu Baptist
Convention in 1918 (in recent years, the Baptist Convention of Telugu Churches/Telugu Baptist Fellowship), which has as many as
1,484 preaching places in addition to over 700 churches (2007).

Aside from the numerous local and regional schisms, cooperation has more often characterized Baptist work in India, and this has been due to the impetus of missionary support organizations, plus the political independence and maturity of the nation. In 1939, the Baptist Union of India (formerly All India Baptist Union) was re-formed to promote fellowship and the sharing of ideas among the several Baptist missionary societies and churches working in Northeast, North, East, and South India. It included six missions from the United States, **Canada, Australia, New Zealand**, and Great Britain, plus seven language groups from India itself. In 1998, more than 700 Baptist churches from several conventions and unions joined together in forming the All India Baptist Federation.

The oldest educational institution among Baptists in India is Serampore College, begun in 1818. American Baptists started a theological seminary in 1872 under the tutelage of **A. V. Timpany** at Ramapatnam; the school was originally known as Brownson Theological Seminary, and in 1920, with the merger of the Canadian Baptist school, it became Union Theological Seminary. A significant educational center was developed at Jorhat, beginning in 1906 and inclusive of four kinds of education; in 1950, this became the location of Eastern Theological College. Perhaps no other national context has witnessed so widespread growth of Baptist schools, hospitals, clinics, social service centers, and other institutions as in India. The vast majority of these institutions were indigenized after 1948 when India won its independence from Great Britain and thereafter placed restrictions upon foreign mission influences. Presently, there are 20 theological schools related to various Baptist bodies in India, several in key centers: Andhra Pradesh, Assam, Meghalaya, Manipur, Mizoram, Nagaland, West Bengal, and Tripura. The great majority of theological schools (excluding Roman Catholics) in India are affiliated to the Senate of Serampore College. British Baptists have supported the Council of Baptist Churches in northern India in one form or another since 1901, and Canadian Baptists established missions among the Cicars in 1874, the Soaras in 1900, and the Oriyas in 1910.

In addition to the 19th-century Baptist work in India, U.S. **Southern Baptists** entered the country by appointing Dr. Jasper McPhail (1930–), a thoracic surgeon, to the Vellore Christian Medical College. McPhail urged the establishment of a hospital at Bangalore in 1962, with a medical mission under the direction of Ralph Bethea (1919–). The U.S. **Baptist General Conference** assumed in 1944 responsibility for mission work begun in 1912–1917 in Assam on the north bank of the Brahmaputra River at Manipur. Also, **Baptist Mid-Missions** from the United States established in 1935 a mission in Assam; the **Conservative Baptist** Foreign Mission Society established a mission in 1945 at Calcutta, Madras, and in Maharashtra and Madhya Pradesh states (where they work with Serampore College and Calcutta Bible College); and the **Baptist Bible Fellowship** established a mission in 1952. The **American Baptist Association** also has a mission in India. In 1900, a **Seventh Day Baptist** mission commenced, with a permanent congregation in 1925 in Calcutta and another established among the Telugus in 1950. Other works include the mission of the India Gospel League in 1906; the Separate Baptists in Christ in 1917; the India Association of General Baptist Churches, a mission of the U.S. General Association of General Baptist Churches; the Freewill Baptist Conference of India in 1935 (U.S. based); the Tripura Baptist Christian Union, a work established by the New Zealand Baptist Foreign Mission Society in 1938; the Rabha Baptist Church Union (1959); the Baptist Bible Believers Assembly (1968); the Association of Regular Baptist Churches of India established in 1935 by the U.S.-based Baptist Mid-Missions; and Baptist International Missions (1978), a fundamentalist U.S. mission.

As of 2007, there were over 40 Baptist conventions/major associations in India, including Apatani Christian Fellowship (120 churches, 40,000 members); Arunachal Pradesh Baptist Convention (412 churches, 41,725 members); Assam Baptist Convention (319 churches, 37,200 members); Association of Regular Baptist Churches of India (70 churches, 6,000 members); Banjara Baptist Sanhevur Malawo (126 churches, 2,881 members); Baptist Bible Believers Assembly (6 churches, 800 members); Baptist Church of Mizoram (410 churches, 60,172 members); Baptist Christian Association, affiliated with Conservative Baptists (145 churches, 2,762 members); Baptist International Missions (26 churches, 10,000 members); Baptist Union of North India (173 churches, 16,280 members); Bengal Baptist Union (173 churches, 16,280 members); Bengal-Orissa-Bihar Baptist Convention (85 churches, 16,500 members); Convention of Baptist Churches of the Northern Cicars (255 churches, 165,400 members); Convention of Krishna-Godvari Baptist Churches (60 churches, 50,000 members); Council of Baptist Churches in North India (470 churches, 60,000 members); Evangelical Baptist Convention of India (141 churches, 31,266 members); the Freewill Baptist Conference of India (47 churches, 23,000 members); Garo Baptist Convention (2,376 churches, 207,524 members); India Association of General Baptists (80 churches, 5,900 members); India Baptist Convention (60 churches, 5,900 members); India Gospel League (50 churches, 3,000 members); Karbi Anglong Baptist Convention (290 churches, 17,166 members); Karnataka Baptist Convention (1,403 churches, 24,493 members); Kuki Christian Church (350 churches, 80,000 members); Lairam Jesus Christ Baptist Church (87 churches, 13,779 members); Lower Assam Baptist Union (261 churches 20,700 members); Convention of Baptist Churches of Maharastra (54 churches, 8,125 members); Maharashtra Baptist Society (176 churches, 6,101 members); Manipur Baptist Convention (1,292 churches, 160,000 members); Nagaland Baptist Church Council (1,352 churches, 429, 479 members); North Bank Baptist Christian Association (894 churches, 85,818 members); Orissa Baptist Evangelical Crusade (3,240 churches, 430,000 members); Association of Oriya Baptist Churches (550 churches, 45,000 members); Samavesam of Telugu Baptist Churches (893 churches, 475,639 members); Separate Baptist in Christ (3 churches, 3,000 members); Seventh Day Baptist Churches (320 churches, 27,000 members); Tamil Baptist Churches (100 churches 4,000 members); Telugu Baptist Churches/Telugu Baptist Fellowship (764 churches, 979,700 members); the Tripura Baptist Christian Union of India (500 churches, 80,000 members); and the Zeme Baptist Christian Council (24 churches, 35,000 members). The total number of Baptists in India as of 2007 was about 32,000 churches and over 2.7 million members.

INDONESIA. Baptist work in Indonesia commenced in 1952 when a **Baptist Mid-Missions** missionary, Ernest Loong, left **China** to minister to Chinese in Indonesia. He started the initial Baptist congregation in Djakarta. Also in 1952, **Southern Baptist** missionaries entered Indonesia and organized their first church in 1953 at Bandung. In 1954, the Baptist Theological Seminary of Indonesia was opened at Semarang. By 1961, work began on Sumatra at Palambang; a station opened on Madura and one on Bali in 1970. The growth of Baptist missions led to the organization in 1973 of the Union of Indonesian Baptist Churches. Conservative Baptists have had an extensive **mission** in Indonesia since 1961 at locations like Java, Jakarta, and Sumatra; they established the Gospel Baptist Association of Indonesia. The **Baptist Bible Fellowship** opened a mission in Indonesia in 1972.

As of 2006, there were 123 churches with 9,600 members affiliated with the Convention of Indonesian Baptist Churches; 206 churches and 74,581 members affiliated with the Fellowship of Baptist Churches in Irian Jaya; 120 churches and 4,294 members affiliated with the Gospel Baptist Association of Indonesia; and 210 churches and 45,984 members affiliated with the Union of Indonesian Baptist Churches. There are four recognized Baptist theological schools in Indonesia: Pontianak, Manado, Semarang, and Tobelo.

INERRANCY OF THE BIBLE. *See* SCRIPTURE, AUTHORITY OF.

INGALLS, MARILLA BAKER (1828–1902). American Baptist missionary, born at Greenville, New York. Educated in local schools, she met in 1850 Lovell Ingalls (1808–1856), a furloughed American Baptist missionary to **Burma** who had served under **Adoniram Judson**. She returned to Burma with her husband in 1851 to continue his **mission** at Arracan. When Lovell died in 1856, Marilla traveled to the United States and arranged an appointment from the **American Baptist Missionary Union** for independent work in Burma. She returned to Lower Burma and settled at Thonze, a village located on the verge of the jungle. She endured persecution and health difficulties at Thonze, but remained as the railroad construction reached the village; her ministry consisted of tract distribution, libraries, and reading rooms. The nearby Buddhist monastery was a special object of her witness, and it was said that she led over 100 Buddhist priests to faith in Christ. On her return trip in 1866 through England, she secured a copy of the **Bible** signed by Queen Victoria, which she presented to the Queen of Burma at Mandalay in 1872, obtaining recognition of the Bible Women's Movement of Burma.

INITSIATIVNIKI. *See* RUSSIA.

INSTITUTIONAL CHURCHES. Terminology applied to urban congregations in the later 19th-century United States, which adapted their roles and outreach to an all-encompassing program. Beginning as inner city congregations that grew to substantial size and accompanying edifices, the churches were confronted with several social classes, variegated educational needs, and many opportunities for **evangelism** and outreach. An institutional church came to be defined as an organized body of Christian believers who found themselves in an uncongenial social environment and supplemented the ordinary methods of **ministry** with a system of "organized kindness" that reached all in its shadow. New programs included language training, vocational classes, soup kitchens, recreation, shelters, and summer camping outside the urban areas for school-age children. Such congregations sought to combine in the church the work of welfare agencies, social clubs, and settlement houses, on the premise that the church alone contains the potential cure for all social ills. The institutional churches were in many ways the embodiments of the ideals of the **social gospel movement**. **Edward Judson**, pastor of the Memorial Church on Washington Square in New York City, wrote the defining pastoral theology for institutional churches, and others like **Russell Conwell** in Philadelphia and **A. J. Gordon** of Boston also followed the pattern. In the latter two cases, major educational institutions were rooted in the local congregations. In more modern usage, the First Institutional Baptist Church of Phoenix, Arizona, a **black Baptist** congregation, uses the term in a corporate sense, to identify their legal status.

INTERNATIONAL BAPTIST FELLOWSHIP. *See* FUNDAMENTALISM, BAPTIST.

INTERNATIONAL BOARD OF JEWISH MISSIONS. An **independent** Baptistic missionary organization founded in 1949. It focuses its effort on **evangelism**, church planting, and broadcasting ministries among Jewish communities in Asia, **Brazil**, **France**, and **Spain**. Its home base is in Chattanooga, Tennessee.

INTERNATIONAL CRUSADES, INC. An **independent** Baptistic missionary organization founded in 1971. Support is given to **evangelistic** crusades, particularly in the **Philippines**. Its home base is in Dallas, Texas.

INTERNATIONAL MINISTRIES TO ISRAEL. An **independent** Baptistic missionary agency founded in 1944. Its focus is on Jewish missions in **Israel** and **Mexico**. It publishes the *Covenant Newsletter*.

INTERNATIONAL MISSION BOARD. *See* FOREIGN MISSION BOARD.

INTERNATIONAL PARTNERSHIP MINISTRIES. An **independent** Baptistic missionary organization founded by Chester Joines, **pastor** of Calvary Bible Church in Hanover, Pennsylvania, as American Technical Outreach Ministries in 1982. The agency focuses on theological education and leadership development in Africa, Asia, South America, and the Caribbean. Its publication is *Partnership News*, and the home base is Hanover, Pennsylvania.

INTERNATIONAL URBAN ASSOCIATES. A Baptistic missionary organization founded in 1989 by Northern Baptist Theological Seminary urban missiologist Raymond Bakke (1938–). It focuses on leadership development, research and training, and management consulting for the **mission** context. With a home base in Chicago, Illinois, it publishes the *International Urban Associates Newsletter*.

IRAN. U.S. **Southern Baptist** missionaries began work among Muslim students at the University of Teheran in 1968. A congregation was established in Teheran in 1972, with others created in Shiraz, Ahwaz, and Isfahan. The U.S. **Baptist Bible Fellowship** opened a work in 1966. In 1978, with the Islamic Revolution, Baptist missionaries were withdrawn.

IRELAND. Baptist work in Ireland began in earnest during the Cromwell Protectorate: between 1652 and 1654, 11 churches were established, and the English governor-general was a member of the movement. The congregation at Dublin later became the center for Irish Baptist life; it became the Baptist Society for Propagating the Faith in Ireland and related to the Baptist Irish Society, which was founded in England in 1813 by **Joseph Ivimey** and others. Another root of Baptist faith was in the work of **Alexander Carson**, who brought the Scottish **Haldanite** movement to Ireland and formed a congregation at Tobermore where, he spent 30 years. English Baptists organized the Irish Baptist Home Mission, and in 1888, this was transferred to the Irish Baptist Association in a move toward "home rule." In response, in 1895 the Association upgraded itself to become the Baptist Union of Ireland, partly in response to the **Downgrade Controversy**. Within this new union, two **associations** were formed in 1897, the Northern and Southern. In the 1920s, a separate relationship was recognized for the churches in Northern Ireland that belonged to the **Baptist Union of Great Britain and Ireland**.

In cooperation with the Baptist Union of Ireland are several voluntary organizations: Irish Baptist Home Mission (1888), Annuity Fund (1902), Total Abstinence Society (1904), Prayer Union (1908), Sunday School Union (1913), Orphan Society (1917), Irish Baptist Foreign Mission (1924), Women's Auxiliary (1928), Baptist Youth Fellowship (1943), and Irish Baptist Historical Society (1968). Irish Baptists carry forth missionary work in **France**, **Belgium**, **Peru**, and **Spain** and support a theological college at Belfast, which was founded by Hugh D. Brown as the Irish Baptist Training Institute in 1892 at Dublin. Generally separatistic, Irish Baptists declined to join the **Baptist World Alliance** and maintain fellowship with **evangelical** and **Strict Baptists** in Europe and Britain through the **Fellowship of Evangelical Baptist Churches in Europe**. In 1999, the Baptist Union of Ireland changed its name to the Association of Baptist Churches in Ireland. The *Irish Baptist* (1876–) is published by the Association. In 1977, **Baptist Bible Fellowship** opened a mission in Ireland, and in 1993, the **Conservative Baptist** Foreign Mission Society opened a mission in conjunction with the Baptist Union of Ireland.

As of 2007, there were 113 churches with 8,600 members affiliated with the Association of Baptist Churches in Ireland; in the Republic of Ireland itself, there were 19 churches with 680 members. The vast majority of Baptists are in the Northern Ireland region. Across the country there are a few **independent Baptist** churches with two to three dozen estimated members.

IRELAND, JAMES (1748–1806). American Baptist minister and evangelist, born in Edinburgh, **Scotland**. As a child, Ireland emigrated with his family to Virginia and by 1766 was a schoolteacher in the Shenandoah Valley. In 1769, he was baptized at Sandy Creek, North Carolina, and allied himself with the **Separate Baptists**, who in due course ordained him. He was a popular preacher in the region and was imprisoned in 1769–1770 at Culpepper, Virginia, for his public preaching. Accounts of his imprisonment indicate that local interests tried several means to kill Ireland, including suffocation with gunpowder smoke. He was ultimately released under the provisions of the Toleration Act, his incarceration becoming one of the most celebrated cases of Baptist persecution in the American colonies. Ireland served as **pastor** at Buck Marsh (Berryville) and Water Lick churches in Virginia. In the year 1802, Ireland received 52 members in one day into his church.

ISRAEL. Baptist missionary work in Israel began in 1921, when a Syrian, Shukri Mosa, established a church at Nazareth. Following the **London Conference of 1920**, Israel has evolved as part of the Southern Baptist **Foreign Mission Board**'s Europe and Middle East section. Before World War II, there were four congregations: Nazareth, Jerusalem, Tel Aviv, and Haifa. With additional missionary support, schools have been opened, and the Association of Baptist Churches in Israel (officially the Baptist Convention in Israel) was organized in 1964(?). The **American Baptist Association** also has a mission in Israel. From 1954 to 1956, Conservative Baptists also had a mission in Jerusalem and Haifa.

As of 2006, there were 19 churches with 800 members affiliated with the Association of Baptist Churches in Israel.

ITALIAN BAPTIST ASSOCIATION OF AMERICA. Missionary work among the Italian community in the United States began at Mt. Pleasant Baptist Church in Newark, New Jersey, in 1887. The first congregation was constituted in 1894 in Buffalo, New York. In the 1890s, the Italian Department was formed at Colgate Theological

Seminary to train ministers for these churches, and in 1898, the Italian Baptist Association of America was formed, and the number of congregations by 1940 grew to over 40. Largely an eastern states **association**, the churches publish *L'Aurora* (*Dawn*), and most of the congregations are also affiliated with the **American Baptist Churches in the U.S.A.**

ITALY. Baptist life in Italy began in 1863 with the work of English missionaries, James Calne in Bologna and Edward Clark in La Spezia. Following the dissolution of Roman Catholic establishment in 1871, the **Baptist Missionary Society** and the Southern Baptist **Foreign Mission Board** began support for missionaries and the **Southern Baptists** commissioned George Boardman Taylor, who began his work in 1873. Churches were started in Rome (1871), Turin, and other urban centers. In 1923, as an outgrowth of the **London Conference of 1920**, Baptist work was united, with the Baptist Federation founded in 1939. An Italian Baptist Union, separate from the **mission** work, was formed in 1956, and this assisted in the gaining of **religious liberty** in the country. Baptists cooperate with Methodists and the Waldensians in educational work; there is an educational program, Centro Filadelfia, at Rivoli and the periodicals are called *Il Testimonio* (*The Testimony*) (1883–), *Il Seminatore* (*The Sower*) (1876–), and *Bilychnis (Light)* (1912–). Literature distribution to various constituencies is a major thrust of Baptist mission in the country. Other groups include the **Conservative Baptist** Foreign Mission Society, since 1947; **Baptist Mid-Missions** from the United States, which established works at Naples (1951) and Salerno (1956); the **Baptist Bible Fellowship**, which has had a mission in Italy since 1978; and the **Association of Baptists for World Evangelism**, which opened its work in 1989.

As of 2006, there were 111 churches and 4,849 members in the Unione Cristiana Evangelica Battista D'Italia.

IVIMEY, JOSEPH (1773–1834). English Baptist minister and historian, born in Hampshire. Originally a tailor, Ivimey was a **pastor** at Wallingford and then Eagle Street, London. As a pastor he added 800 new members to the church and 20 candidates to the **ministry**. Ivimey was a strict communionist and Calvinist. A consummate **vol-**

untarist, he advocated abolition of **slavery**, education for the poor, and public almshouses. He was a devotee of the **Baptist Missionary Society**, the Baptist Irish Society, and the **Home Missionary Society**. In 1811, he proposed a **Baptist Union,** which was finally realized in 1831. Ivimey opposed the open communionism of **Robert Hall** and he staunchly supported "Fullerism," or **evangelical** Calvinism. He wrote a five-volume *History of the Baptists*, published in 1811.

IVORY COAST. The first Baptists in Ivory Coast came from **Nigeria** to work with Yoruba people. Beginning in 1947, **Conservative Baptists** began their mission, as did **Freewill Baptists** and later **Southern Baptists**; these three groups worked together in various types of **mission**. Freewill Baptists concentrated their efforts in Bible translation for the tribespeople. After 1966, Southern Baptists worked with the indigenous French, rather than the Yorubas. Abidjan became the center of Southern Baptist francophone missions in Africa. By 1979, the French-speaking churches near Abidjan organized an association, and by 1984, this group became the Association Baptiste Evangélique de Côte d'Ivoire and eventually the Eglises Evangéliques Baptistes Méridionales en Côte d'Ivoire. In addition to the older work, the **Baptist Bible Fellowship** opened a mission in Ivory Coast in 1988.

As of 2006, there were 100 churches and 10,000 members affiliated with the Eglises Evangéliques Baptistes Méridionales de Côte d'Ivoire.

– J –

JACKSON, JOSEPH HARRISON (1900–1990). American **black Baptist** minister and denominational leader, born at Jamestown, Mississippi. He was educated at Jackson College, Colgate Rochester Divinity School, and Creighton University and served pastorates in rural Mississippi; Omaha, Nebraska; and Philadelphia, Pennsylvania. In 1934, he became the corresponding secretary of the **National Baptist Convention** (NBCUSA) Foreign Mission Board, the leading position in the largest black Baptist denomination. In 1941, he assumed the pastorate of Olivet Baptist in Chicago (which he served for over 40 years), which positioned him to become the president of the denomination in 1953. He served in that capacity through 1982, the longest term in the denomination's history. During his presidency, Jackson courted government relationships, and the NBCUSA expanded into several relief projects. He opposed the militancy of the civil rights crusade and stood against the attempts of Gardner C. Taylor (1918–) and **Martin Luther King Jr.** to take control of the NBCUSA. His leadership style led to the schism in 1961, which created the **Progressive National Baptist Convention**. Among Jackson's publications are *Many But One: The Ecumenics of Charity* (1964) and *A Story of Christian Activism: The History of the National Baptist Convention, USA, Inc.* (1980).

JACOB, HENRY (1563–1624). English Separatist and Independent minister, born at Cheriton, Kent. He was educated at St. Mary Hall, Oxford, but did not enter the Church of England's ministry, holding that church to be in need of reformation. In 1590, he joined the Brownist sect and fled to Holland, where he conferred with other Marian exiles. Over the next 15 years, Jacob moved between England and Holland in the communities of Separatists. In 1616, he formed at Southwark a congregation on the plan of John Robinson (1576–1625); this became the first Independent, or congregational, church in England. Later, as it evolved in the 1630s, the church became the first **Particular Baptist** congregation. Jacob wrote on the subject of **religious liberty** and eventually moved to the colony of Virginia where he formed a settlement named after him, "Jacobopolis." He died in London.

JAMAICA. George Leile, a slave from Virginia, arrived in Kingston in 1782 and began preaching on the local race course. He gathered a congregation, and in 1791, built the first Baptist church in Kingston. In 1814, John Rowe was appointed by the **Baptist Missionary Society** to Jamaica; he settled at Falmouth and opened a school for the children of slaves. Other British missionaries followed, including **Lee Compere**, J. M. Phillippo (1798–1879), and Thomas Burchell (1799–1846). Among the most outstanding missionaries was **William Knibb**, who led the drive for emancipation of the slaves.

With a church in every parish on the island by 1841, Baptists made extensive contributions to Jamaica's history.

The Jamaica Baptist Union was organized in 1849, which in recent development includes departments for youth work, women's federation, and **evangelism**. In 1842, the Jamaica Baptist Missionary Society was founded to support missions in Africa and Central America. Efforts in **Cuba**, **Costa Rica**, **Haiti**, Cayman Islands, and West Africa have resulted. In 1843, Calabar Theological College was opened; in 1964, the college was federated with 10 other denominations in the United Theological College of the West Indies at Kingston, a major theological school for the region. The Jamaica Baptist Union published the *Jamaica Baptist Reporter* (1966–), a quarterly newsletter. In addition to the regular Baptist work, **Baptist Mid-Missions** from the United States established a Jamaican mission in 1929, with the assistance of Canadians; the Fairview Baptist Bible College, founded in 1963 at Savanna-la-Mar, resulted from this effort. The **Baptist Bible Fellowship** established a mission in Jamaica in 1972.

As of 2006, there were 311 churches and 40,000 members affiliated with the Jamaica Baptist Union.

JAPAN. Baptist witness in Japan dates from **Jonathan Goble**, a sailor on Commodore Matthew Perry's ship in Tokyo Bay in 1853. Goble returned to Japan in 1860 under the auspices of the **American Baptist Free Mission Society** and worked for 10 years. Later, the **American Baptist Missionary Union** (ABMU) commissioned **Nathan Brown** to Japan in 1873, also assuming the mission of Goble. Brown formed the first church in Yokohama about 1873, and in 1884, a theological school was founded also at Yokohama. The first Baptist church in Tokyo was founded in 1876. A number of the outer islands of Japan were reached by Capt. **Luke Bickel** for the ABMU; he operated a **colporteur** boat to more than 400 outposts from 1898 to the opening of World War I. In 1890, the Yearly Japan Baptist Conference of Missionaries was formed, and the Japanese Baptists organized the Japan Baptist Union at the same time. For a brief time, the Australian Baptist Missionary Society supported a mission at Hiroshima (1874–1877), begun by Wilton Hack (1843–1923). American **Southern Baptists** began work in Japan in 1889; it was seriously interrupted by World War II, after which the work was reorganized in 1947 as the Japan Baptist Convention.

The postwar mission of the **North American Baptist Conference** opened in Japan in 1951. Among the other American missions, the **Baptist Bible Fellowship** opened a mission in 1948 and **Baptist Mid-Missions** established a work at Tokyo in 1950, one of its earliest fields; the **Association of Baptists for World Evangelism** started a Japan mission in 1953; the **Conservative Baptist** Foreign Mission Society started a mission in Japan in 1947 and has over 70 churches together with the Sendai Baptist Seminary affiliated with the Conservative Baptist Association of Churches, begun by missionaries. The **American Baptist Association** also has a mission in the country, and since 1952, the **Fellowship of Evangelical Baptists of Canada** has a mission at Takaoka.

As of 2006, there were 329 churches with 34,033 members affiliated with the Japan Baptist Convention; 74 churches with 4,437 members affiliated with the Japan Baptist Union; 39 churches with 3,165 members affiliated with the Okinawa Baptist Convention; and 11 churches with 476 members affiliated with the Japan Baptist Conference. The Japan Conservative Baptist Association of Christians has 67 congregations with 2,603 members affiliated. There are six recognized Baptist-related colleges or theological schools in Japan: Fukuoka (two), Sendai, Yokohama, Kyogo-ken, and Kitakyushu.

JASPER, JOHN (1812–1901). American black Baptist minister, born in Fluvanna County, Virginia. Raised a slave, he worked on various plantations in Virginia. He became a Christian in 1839 and was baptized in the Richmond African Baptist Church. He began preaching and attracted throngs of listeners, owing to his rhetoric. During the American Civil War, Jasper was employed to preach among the sick and wounded in the Confederate hospitals. He received his freedom in 1864 and organized several black congregations, including Brown's Island, Third Baptist, Petersburg, Virginia, and Weldon, North Carolina. In accord with the Zetetic School of philosophy, Jasper advocated a curious theory of the rotation of the sun which in his sermons brought him both ridicule and applause because of its affinity with Joshua 10:14. His sermon "The Sun Do Move" was one of the classic sermons of the **black Baptist** tradition. He served as

pastor of the Sixth Mount Zion Baptist Church in Richmond, which included over 1,000 members in 1885.

JESSEY, HENRY (1601–1663). English Anglican and Baptist minister, born at West Rounton, England. Jessey graduated a top scholar from St. John's College, Cambridge, his favorite subjects being Hebrew and rabbinical literature. He became a personal chaplain to Brampton Gurdon (fl. 1650) and a wealthy Puritan, and he took up the study of medicine. In 1627, he was episcopally **ordained**, but was without a charge until he took Aughton in Yorkshire in 1633. Jessey was soon discharged for removing a crucifix and neglecting the use of parts of the liturgy; subsequently he became chaplain to Matthew Boynton of Barnston (d. 1651). With Boynton, he went to London in 1635 and later to Uxbridge. In midsummer 1637, Jessey became **pastor** of the Separatist Independent congregation founded by **Henry Jacob** and **John Lathrop** in Southwark. This congregation had suffered a schism in 1633 over **baptism**, and a second occurred when Jessey became pastor. Jessey examined the question, was baptized as a believer by **Hanserd Knollys**, and held immersion to be imperative.

Jessey's congregation suffered persecution and actually split in 1640 to avoid discovery. During the time he served the Baptist congregation, Jessey also preached at St. George's, Southwark, until he was ejected in 1660. He was one of the first missionaries to **Wales** in 1639, planting a congregation at Llanvaches. In 1646, he was reported to have participated in a healing service for a blind woman at Aldgate. During the Commonwealth, he served as a Trier and Expurgator for Cromwell (1654), and his minute knowledge of the **Bible** led to his appointment in 1652 to a committee to approve any new English translation of the **Scriptures**. In addition to serving as a teaching minister at Swan Alley, Coleman Street, Jessey also travelled extensively among the Baptist churches in the West and the eastern counties. He advocated citizenship for Jews and contributed generously to the charitable maintenance of 30 families. Suspected of **Fifth Monarchy** views, he was arrested in 1660 and later imprisoned until 1663. Following a trip to Holland to defend the rights of some of his parishioners, Jessey died at London.

JETER, JEREMIAH BELL (1802–1880). Southern **Baptist** minister and denominational leader, born in Bedford County, Virginia. Jeter was self-educated, and early in his career he served as an itinerant minister in the valley of Virginia and a small church at Morattico. In 1836, he became **pastor** at First Baptist, Richmond, moving to Second Baptist, St. Louis, Missouri in 1849–1852. His final pastorate was at Grace Street Baptist, again in Richmond. Jeter used his Richmond base to broaden his denominational influence considerably. For 15 years, he edited the *Religious Herald*, one of the outstanding state Baptist papers of the South. He was the first president of the Southern Baptist **Foreign Mission Board** (FMB) and set the denominational tone for overseas work. He was convinced of the need to improve relations between blacks and whites in his congregation, and against the advice of the city fathers, he provided a building for separate services for blacks, which became the First African Baptist Church in Richmond. He used **revivalistic** techniques in his church and city and was himself a popular preacher in Northern Baptist pulpits. Conciliatory toward his fellow Baptists of the North following the Civil War, Jessey was an ardent opponent of **Alexander Campbell**'s teachings.

JOHNSON, FRANCIS (1562–1618). English Separatist educator and **pastor**, born at Richmond, Yorkshire. He was educated at Cambridge University and in 1584 became a Fellow of Christ's College, Cambridge. As a Fellow, Johnson was responsible for the education of several undergraduate students, including the se-Baptist **John Smyth**. In January 1588 or 1589, Johnson preached a controversial sermon at Great St. Mary's in which he questioned basic foundations of the Episcopal form of church government. He advocated instead a Presbyterial system of governing the true church of **Christ**. After a year of trials and disputes, he was deprived of his fellowship and ejected from the university. Johnson then took up a career as a Separatist pastor in London and then in Middleburg, the Netherlands, where he served the church of the Merchant-Adventurers. In the ensuing decades, Johnson interacted with notable Separatists and proto-Baptists, including John Robinson, Robert Browne, John Greenwood, Henry Barrow, John Smyth, Thomas Cartwright, Henry Ainsworth, and **Henry Jacob**. As pastor of the famed Ancient

Church, Johnson wrote a **confession of faith** and was an influential disputant. Ultimately, though a certain mentor in John Smyth's early career, Johnson came to oppose Smyth's ideas of **baptism**, church government, and other similarities to **Anabaptist** thought.

JOHNSON, WILLIAM BULLEIN (1782–1862). Southern Baptist minister and denominational leader, born at John's Island, South Carolina. He first studied law, and then under the influence of Baptist luminaries like **Richard Furman** and **Oliver Hart**, he entered the **ministry** and served churches at Euhaw and Columbia, South Carolina, and then Savannah, Georgia. Also an educator and champion of **women**'s education, Johnson supported the establishment of the **General Missionary Convention** (GMC) in 1813 and Columbian College in 1821. President of the GMC from 1841 to 1844, he offered the **Baltimore Compromise** and later feared the predisposition of the national body to **antislavery** supporters. In 1845, Johnson was a prime mover in the organization of the **Southern Baptist Convention** (SBC) and served as the first president of that body. It was his influence that caused the SBC to adopt many of the characteristics of the GMC.

JOHNSONIANS. Name applied to followers of John Johnson (1706–1791) of Liverpool, an English **Particular Baptist** minister who advocated high Calvinism. Johnson, originally a **General Baptist**, developed a unique theological system, which destabilized many churches in the Lancashire and Yorkshire **associations** well into the 19th century. Because faith is a grace, Johnson taught, lack of it is no sin. He held to a modalist understanding of the Trinity and a millennarian interpretation of prophecy, and he was vehemently **local church protectionist** and opposed to cooperation, even with other Baptists. Johnsonian churches practiced the **laying on of hands** and one **ordinance**, water **baptism**. In the 18th century, **John Brine** and Samuel Fisher (1742–1803) opposed Johnson's teachings, and later, John Fawcett and **Andrew Fuller** were among his critics. Churches sympathetic to Johnson's teachings numbered 13 and were found in Liverpool, Halifax, Towchester, Chesterfield, London, Newark, Todmorden, Norwich, and Wisbech. The last of the Johnsonian congregations had disappeared by 1850.

JONES, SAMUEL (1735–1814). American Baptist minister born at Cefn y Gelli, Glamorganshire, **Wales**. His father was a wealthy emigrant to America in 1737, and Samuel was accorded an education in the College of Philadelphia, graduating with an M.A. in 1762. He was ordained by First Baptist Church of Philadelphia in 1763 and became **pastor** at the Baptist churches of Southampton and Pennypack, a united parish. In 1770, Jones resigned the church at Southampton and served the congregation at Pennypack (Lower Dublin) for 51 years. He became one of the leaders of the **Philadelphia Baptist Association** (PBA), and, by extension, the denomination at large. The PBA appointed him to compile a system of **discipline** (1798) and a *Book of Hymns*, published in 1790. He also drew up a map of the churches, probably the first of its kind in the United States, and served numerous years as either the moderator or composer of the circular letter of the PBA. Jones's booklet on the **laying on of hands** was a longtime authority in the American Baptist community. He was frequently called upon to constitute new churches in Pennsylvania and New Jersey and in 1763 helped to write the draft of a charter for the College of Rhode Island. The College of Rhode Island conferred the M.A. on him in 1769, and the College of Philadelphia conferred the D.D. in 1788.

JORDAN. Baptist presence in Jordan can probably be traced to American and British military personnel presence and Holy Land tourists early in the 20th century. In 1952, **Southern Baptists** took responsibility for a hospital at Ajloun, which also became an educational center. The Jordan Baptist Convention was organized in 1955. The **Baptist Bible Fellowship** opened its Palestine Mission in 1955, and the following year, the U.S. **Conservative Baptist** Foreign Mission Society began its work in Amman and Aqaba and helped to form the Free Evangelical Church. The **Baptist World Alliance** (BWA) maintains a special presence in Jordan: in 2008, the government of Jordan invited the BWA to be involved in constructing a proposed Baptism Center to commemorate the likely location of the baptism of Jesus at Bethany beyond Jordan; completion is set for 2009.

As of 2006, there were 20 churches and 1,200 members affiliated with the Jordan Baptist Convention. The Free Evangelical Church, an

Independent Baptist group, included about nine churches with 458 members as of 2001.

JORDAN, LEWIS GARNETT (1854–1939). American black Baptist minister and denominational leader, born at Meridian, Mississippi. Educated at Roger Williams University in Nashville, Tennessee, he initially served churches in Yazoo City, Mississippi (1876–1883) and successively at Second Baptist, San Antonio, New Hope, Waco, and St. Emmanuel in Hearne, Texas (1883–1990?). He served the pastorate of Union Baptist Church in Philadelphia, Pennsylvania (c. 1890–1896), after which he became a canvasser for the National Prohibition Party, which ultimately nominated Jordan for congressman-at-large in Pennsylvania. In 1896, he was elected corresponding secretary of the Foreign Mission Board of the **National Baptist Convention, U.S.A.** (NBCUSA), where he gave substance to the structure and program of overseas missions in the 25 years of his service to the Board. Among his accomplishments were the establishment of the headquarters in Louisville, Kentucky, central to the **black Baptist** community; the beginning of the Providence Industrial Mission in Nyasaland in 1900 and the Suehn Mission in **Liberia** in 1912; and the recognition of the pioneering work of **George Liele**. As part of his administrative successes, Jordan urged the creation of the Women's Auxiliary in 1900, and in 1896, he began the *Afro-American Mission Herald*, the first national black Baptist foreign mission periodical in the United States. In 1915–1916, when **Richard H. Boyd** led a schism of the National Baptist Convention, Jordan was a vocal opponent, and his leadership helped to avoid a larger defection of cooperating congregations. Jordan's historical work, *Up the Ladder in Foreign Missions* (1901), is considered a pioneering work in black Baptist studies. Jordan was a well-traveled denominational statesman, making four trips to Africa, two trips to Latin America, and four trips to the West Indies.

JUDSON, ADONIRAM (1788–1850). American Congregationalist and, later, Baptist missionary, born at Malden, Massachusetts. He was educated at Brown University and Andover Theological Seminary, graduating in the seminary's first class. In 1812, Judson became a catalyst in the formation of the American Board of Commissioners for Foreign Missions and was the leading candidate of that body for commissioned service in **India** in 1812. He and his wife, **Ann Hasseltine**, became America's first foreign missionaries to the East; upon arrival in Serampore after much study on the subject of **baptism**, he turned to Baptist principles and was baptized by **William Carey**. Judson was not allowed to remain in India and went to **Burma**, where he opened a new field for the newly formed **Baptist Board of Foreign Missions**. He concentrated on language study and produced a Burmese dictionary and a translation of the **Scriptures** into Burmese. His work was interrupted by imprisonment and great deprivation during the civil war in 1824. He remained in Burma, except for a furlough in 1845–1846, and married three times—to Ann Hasseltine, **Sarah Hall Boardman**, and **Emily Chubbock**, each of whom made literary and **mission** contributions in their own right. *See also* HASSELTINE, ANN.

JUDSON, EDWARD (1844–1914). American Baptist minister, born at Moulmein, Burma, the son of **Adoniram** and **Emily Judson**. He was educated at Brown University, earning the A.B. and M.A. degrees. For several years, 1867–1874, Judson taught languages at Madison (later Colgate) University, after which he was a **pastor** at Orange, New Jersey (1875–1881), and Judson Memorial Church in New York City. The Judson Memorial Church was designed to be a model institutional church in the Progressive Era, organizing projects and **ministrie**s to assist persons in special need. Judson also intended the downtown church to be a memorial to his father, and he prevailed upon his friendship with the **Rockefeller** and **Colgate** families to contribute to its construction and programs. Frequently, Judson traveled with John D. Rockefeller and **Frederick Gates**. In addition to his pastoral responsibilities, he taught pastoral theology at Colgate, 1897–1900 and 1905–1914, and homiletics at the University of Chicago, 1904–1905. One of his last projects was the completion of the Judson Centennial celebrations in 1914.

JUDSON, EMILY CHUBBOCK (1817–1854). American Baptist writer and missionary, born at Eaton, New York. As a child she lived a life of drudgery, collecting firewood and working in a woolen mill. Self-educated, Judson taught school in various central New York towns from 1832 to 1840, after which she took classes and taught English at Utica Female Seminary. She published several articles in national magazines and became a widely known fiction writer under the pseudonym Fanny Forester. In 1845, she met **Adoniram Judson**, and though he disapproved of her writings, they were married. She took on the project of producing the memoirs of **Sarah B. Judson**. The couple returned to **Burma** in 1846, and Emily assisted in her husband's translation work. Ill for the years 1848–1850, she left Burma after Adoniram died and devoted herself to an official edition of his memoirs. Among her published works were *Tripping in Author Land* (1846) and *The Memoirs of Sarah B. Judson* (1848).

JUDSON, SARAH HALL BOARDMAN (1803–1845). American Baptist missionary, born at Alstead, New Hampshire. She was educated in Danvers, Massachusetts, and married **George Dana Boardman**, a student at Waterville College in Maine. In 1825, the Boardmans were appointed as missionaries to **Burma** by the American **Baptist Board of Foreign Missions**, and they arrived at Moulmein that same year. Following early work at Tavoy among the Karens, George Boardman died in 1831, and Sarah was encouraged by **Adoniram Judson** to continue the work. She traveled widely in the jungles of Burma, evangelizing, translating, conducting **women's missions**, and organizing schools. By 1832, she was superintending five day schools with about 170 students. Her work was part of the Bengali school system, and she received a regular stipend from the government. Sarah married Adoniram Judson in 1834 and assisted him in several translation projects. A gifted writer and poet, Sarah died in 1845 of complications from the birth of her 10th child.

– K –

KARGEL, IVAN VENIAMINOVITSH (1849–1937). German, Russian, and Bulgarian Baptist minister and denominational leader, likely born in southern **Russia**. He was educated at **J. G. Oncken**'s Baptist seminary in Hamburg, at mission institutes held in 1869 and 1874–1875. Baptized by Nikita Voronin, the first Russian Baptist, Kargel was **pastor** of a **German** Baptist congregation at Tiflis in the

1870s. For a time, he worked in the Mennonite community in southern Russia in the Molotschna region (1873–1874). After his second period of study in Hamburg, he was pastor of the German Baptist Church in Soroczin, Volhynia (later on the Polish border.) In 1875, Kargel moved to St. Petersburg, Russia, where he worked with **evangelical** cell groups and was supported by the **American Baptist Missionary Union**. Owing to poor health, he left Russia in 1880 to plant Baptist churches in **Bulgaria**. After four years in Bulgaria, Kargel returned to St. Petersburg, where he imbibed holiness theology in the company of Victorian evangelicals associated with Princess Natalie Lieven. Again a leader among house-church groups, he encountered **Ivan Prokhanov**, who out-organized Kargel in one of the principal congregations. While Kargel and Prokhanov split over **polity** issues, eventually they again joined forces to unite the evangelical and Baptist movements in Russia. Kargel's statement of faith, which he drafted in 1913, became the doctrinal standard for the All-Union Council of Evangelical Christians-Baptists in 1944, thus crediting Kargel with being the leading Baptist **theologian** of the early Russian Baptists.

KAZAKHSTAN. As part of the sociopolitical results of the collapse of the Union of Soviet Socialist Republics in 1991, Baptist history in Kazakhstan has been separated as a distinct movement of its own. In 1917, eight families, primarily from Ukraine, moved to Alma Ata and established the first congregation of Baptists. Over the years, as scattered churches were formed, most related to the All Union Council of Evangelical-Baptists. In 1992, the Soyuz Tserkvey Evangel'skikh Khristian Baptistov Kazakhstana (Union of Evangelicals-Christians Baptists of Kazakhstan) was formed. The **Conservative Baptist** Foreign Mission Society began missionary work in Central Asia in 1994.

As of 2006, there were a total of 290 churches with about 11,000 members affiliated with the Soyuz Tserkvey Evangel'skikh Khristian-Baptistov Kazakhstana, the Korean Baptists in Kazakhstan, and the unregistered Baptist churches in Kazakhstan. In 2006, the Baptist Union (Soyuz) voted to quit membership in the **European Baptist Federation** and the **Baptist World Alliance** over issues of **women** ordained to ministry, charismatic influences, and perceived erosion of biblical authority.

KEACH, BENJAMIN (1640–1704). English Baptist minister and writer, born in Buckinghamshire. Keach was a tailor by trade who became a **General Baptist** pastor at Winslow. For his catechetical work *Child's Instructor* (1664), he was jailed and his book was burned. Keach rewrote the book from memory, and it was sold widely. In 1668, he went to serve the Southwark church in London and was the first **Nonconformist** ordained since the Restoration. In moving to London, Keach also moved to the **Particular Baptist** persuasion, probably under the influence of **Hanserd Knollys** and **William Kiffin**. He established the Horsley-down Church and introduced hymn singing, perhaps the first in all of England to do so. He operated a bookshop to supplement his income and to sell his over 40 works, defended the **laying on of hands** at **baptism** among the Particular Baptists, and managed to write a full-scale allegory before **John Bunyan** published *Pilgrim's Progress*. Keach was one of the most celebrated and quoted Baptist ministers of his era on both sides of the Atlantic. Among his many published works are *The Breach Repaired in God's Worship* (1691), *Spiritual Melody* (1700), and *Gospel Mysteries Unveiled* (1701).

KEACH, ELIAS (1667–1701). English Baptist and, later, American Baptist minister, born at Winslow, England. The son of the celebrated **Benjamin Keach**, he emigrated to Philadelphia at 19 and supported himself by masquerading as a minister. In a moment of self-disclosure, he recognized the error of his ways and sought the counsel of a local Baptist minister, Thomas Dongan (fl. 1680), of Cold Spring, Pennsylvania. Keach was subsequently **baptized** and ordained and served the congregation at Lower Dublin (Pennepack) faithfully from 1688 to 1692. He returned to London and organized a congregation at Pinner's Hall, where he preached to hundreds. Among his published works is *The Glory and Ornament of a True Gospel-Constituted Church* (1697).

KEITHIAN BAPTISTS. In the late 17th century, a division among Quakers occurred in Pennsylvania, which led to a small, short-lived company of Quaker-Baptists. Following the leadership of George Keith (1638–1716), which coalesced around differences over the doctrine of **Christ** and human ability in salvation, several meetings split from the main Quaker movement in 1691 and formed their own organization centered in Burlington, New Jersey. Some of the meetings—notably at Philadelphia, Southampton, and Lower Dublin, Pennsylvania—pursued New Testament practices like the **Love Feast**, Kiss of Charity, anointing of the sick, and believer's **baptism**. Probably the practice of baptism was introduced in 1797 by Abel Noble (fl. 1690–1700), a **Seventh Day Baptist**. But in 1700, a division arose among the new group over keeping of the Sabbath, and the Keithian Baptists gradually dissolved into other Christian fellowships. The last of the congregations was reorganized at Brandywine, Pennsylvania, as a Regular Baptist Church in 1715. The Keithian Baptists were characterized by plain speech and dress, pacifism, and a **confession of faith** composed in 1697 and based upon the Apostles' Creed.

KENYA. Baptist history in Kenya is quite recent. In 1956, a Southern Baptist missionary, Davis Saunders (1925–) arrived in Nairobi and the following year James Hampton (1929–) settled in Mombasa. With mission stations established among the tribespeople, the work grew rapidly. In 1971, the National Baptist Convention of Kenya was organized, and the same year the **Baptist Bible Fellowship** opened its mission. **Conservative Baptists** began their **mission** in 1972 and created the Conservative Baptist Fellowship of Kenya. In 1983, the **Association of Baptists for World Evangelism** started a Kenya mission.

As of 2006, there were 2,960 churches and 600,000 members affiliated with the Baptist Convention of Kenya; about four churches with about 150 members affiliated with the Conservative Baptist Fellowship of Kenya; and numerous Baptists involved in other Baptist groups: the African Christian Church and Schools, a group associated with Canadian Baptist Missions (74 churches, 6,200 members); the Good News Church of Africa, founded in 1958 (130 churches, 40,000 members); the Gospel Tabernacle Church, founded in 1943 (16 churches, 10,000 members); and the Independent Baptist Churches of East Africa, formed in 1964 as a mission of U.S. Independent Baptist Missions (30 churches, 30,000 members).

KETCHAM, ROBERT THOMAS (1889–1978). American and, later, Independent Baptist minister and denominational leader, born in Nelson, Pennsylvania. Educated by correspondence, he entered the pastoral **ministry** in 1912 and served at Brookville (1915–1919) and Butler (1919–1923), Pennsylvania; Niles (1923–1926) and Elyria (1926–1932), Ohio; Gary, Indiana (1932–1939); and Waterloo, Iowa (1939–1948). Almost from the outset of his ministry, Ketcham was identified with the Baptist **fundamentalist** movement. In 1919, he opposed the **New World Movement**, joined the fundamentalists in Buffalo in 1920, and addressed the **Baptist Bible Union** in 1923. Ketcham was among the first to announce separation from the Northern Baptist Convention (NBC) in 1928, and he organized the Ohio Association of Independent Baptist Churches in Columbus that year. When the **General Association of Regular Baptist Churches** (GARBC) met to organize a national movement in 1932–1934, Ketcham was a principal founder and was elected president in which he served, 1934–1938.

As editor of the paper *Baptist Bulletin* and GARBC National Representative from 1948 to 1966, Ketcham exercised a wide influence on Baptist churches in the northern United States. Frequently, he interfered in the affairs of a congregation to influence withdrawal from the NBC, as in the case of Smethport, Pennsylvania. Ketcham was considered persona non grata with the NBC, and he also had a bitter disagreement with other fundamentalist Baptists, notably **J. Frank Norris** in the 1930s. Elected president of the interdenominational, fundamentalist American Council of Christian Churches, he was awarded an honorary doctorate by Bob Jones University in 1961. Among his published works were *Communism in Baptist Ranks* (1935) and *Let Rome Speak for Herself* (1956).

KIFFIN, WILLIAM (1616–1701). English Baptist minister and theologian, born in London. Kiffin lost both his parents to the plague and was an apprentice to a glover. He attended Independent churches beginning about 1638, and by 1642 became a Baptist under the influence of **John Spilsbury**. About 1643, he helped to form what became the Devonshire Square Church in London, which he served as **pastor**/leader for 60 years. After an illness, Kiffin traded in Holland

and became a highly successful woollen merchant, as well as becoming an esteemed member of the Leathersellers Guild of London. During the Protectorate, he served Cromwell and was a member of Parliament for Middlesex in 1656. During the Restoration, Kiffin loaned King Charles II £10,000 and frequently secured the release of Baptist friends, imprisoned under the terms of the Conventicle Act. Two of Kiffin's grandsons were executed in the cause of **religious liberty**. King James II named him to be an alderman for the city of London, a task Kiffin found onerous. Kiffin lived to see the results of the "Glorious" Revolution of 1688 and helped to compose both the First and Second London Baptist **Confessions of Faith**. He was critical of **John Bunyan**'s stance on open communion and was an exponent of the **Particular Baptist** persuasion. Kiffin was the first Baptist known to have written an autobiographical sketch and his portrait, which hangs in Regent's Park College, Oxford University, is one of the oldest known depictions of an early English Baptist. Kiffin's life was detailed in *Remarkable Passages in the Life of William Kiffin, Written by Himself* (1823).

KINCAID, EUGENIO (1797–1883). American Baptist missionary, born at Wethersfield, Connecticut. He was educated at Hamilton Literary and Theological Institution (later Colgate University) and served pastorates in Galway, New York, and Milton, Pennsylvania, from 1822 to 1827. In 182?, he served as a domestic missionary for the Pennsylvania state **association**; in 1829, the **Baptist Board of Foreign Missions** (BBFM) appointed him a missionary to **Burma**. Following great difficulty with the government, Kincaid established himself among the Karens at Arracan. In 1837, he pioneered a mission to the Kachin peoples in the northern hills. In his later years in Burma, he became widely respected in the diplomatic community and in 1857 actually served as an official emissary of the United States to the Court of Ava. During his furlough in the United States in 1842–1849, Kincaid travelled on deputation for the BBFM and became a legendary hero in Alfred S. Patton's book *The Hero Missionary* (1858) for his stories of daring work in Burma.

KING, MARTIN LUTHER, JR. (1929–1968). American Baptist minister and civil rights activist, born in Atlanta, Georgia. He was educated at Morehouse College, Crozer Theological Seminary, and Boston University, earning the Ph.D degree at the latter, where he was mentored by E. J. Brightman (1884–1953). King served in the pastoral ministry at Dexter Avenue Baptist Church, Montgomery, Alabama (1954–1959), and finally as co-**pastor** with his father, Martin Luther King Sr. (1899–1984) at Ebenezer Baptist Church in Atlanta, Georgia (1959–1968). Later influenced by Mahatma Gandhi (1869–1948) and **Walter Rauschenbusch**, King developed a theology of nonviolent opposition to injustice, which he exhibited in several key demonstrations for civil rights of blacks. With **Ralph Abernathy**, he was an organizer of the Southern Christian Leadership Conference in 1957 and was active in the National Association for the Advancement of Colored People. He led major civil rights marches in Birmingham, Alabama (1962), Washington, D.C. (1963), and Selma, Alabama (1965). In 1964, King was awarded the Nobel Prize for Peace. As a Baptist leader, he helped to organize the **Progressive National Baptist Convention** in 1961, to affirm the values of the civil rights crusade and **ecumenism**. He was the first black minister to address the American Baptist Convention, meeting in Philadelphia in 1957. While speaking publicly in Memphis, Tennessee, in 1968, King was assassinated. Among his published work were *Strength to Love* (1963) and *Why We Can't Wait* (1964).

KINGHORN, JOSEPH (1766–1832). English Baptist minister, born at Gateshead-on-Tyne, Newcastle-upon-Tyne. He was educated at Bristol Baptist College and shortly thereafter was **pastor** at Fairford, Gloucestershire in 1788. In 1789, he embarked on a lifelong ministry at St. Mary's **Particular Baptist** Church in Norwich. Kinghorn, a bachelor, became a beloved member of the community, a self-professed **conservative**. When **Robert Hall**, for instance, advocated open communion, Kinghorn responded by defending a strict Baptist position and became widely known for his views on the matter. Kinghorn was an exceptional scholar and was offered a tutorship at Stepney Academy when it opened in 1810, which he declined in order to continue his pastorate. He traveled on behalf of the **Baptist Missionary Society**, challenging in particular the **Scottish** churches to greater support for **missions**. Among Kinghorn's numerous published works are *Scriptural Arguments for the Divinity of Christ* (1813) and *Baptism, a Term of Communion at the Lord's Supper* (1816).

KIRGHIZISTAN. Baptists have a history in Khirgizia since about 1950. In the wake of the political downfall of the Soviet Union in 1992, Baptists and other **evangelical** groups reordered themselves into unions in many of the former Soviet republics. In Kirghizistan, a union was formed in 1995, composed mainly of **Russian** and **German**-speaking peoples. As of 2006, there were 84 congregations with about 3,100 members affiliated with the union. A long-standing disagreement over **women** in ministry, the influence of the charismatic movement, and biblical authority, shared with Baptists in **Kazakhstan,** led the Khirghizi Baptists to sever ties with the **European Baptist Federation** and the **Baptist World Alliance** in 2006.

KIRKCONNELL, WATSON (1895–1977). Canadian Baptist educator and denominational leader, born at Port Hope, Ontario. He was educated at Queen's University where he obtained the bachelor's and master's degrees; later, at Oxford University, he earned the B.Litt in economics. Kirkconnell taught English at Wesley College, Winnipeg, and later at McMaster University, where in addition to his wide interest in humanities and linguistics, he launched a vigorous anti-Communist writing and speaking campaign during World War II. In 1944, he was one of the prime movers of the establishment of the Canadian Baptist Federation. From 1948 to 1964, he was president of Acadia University, the Baptist institution of the Canadian Maritime Provinces. Kirkonnell was well known for his linguistic skills, translating numerous works from Polish, Hungarian, and Slavic into English, as well as composing thousands of lines of poetry. Among his many published works are *Liberal Education in the Canadian Democracy* (1948), *Seven Pillars of Freedom* (1952), and *A Slice of Canada: Memoirs* (1967).

KISSITES. *See* GLASITES.

KNAPP, JACOB (1799–1874). American Baptist minister and evangelist, born in Otsego County, New York. He was educated at Hamilton Literary and Theological Institution, served as a schoolteacher, and was **pastor** for a time at Springfield and Watertown, New York. In 1833, Knapp entered a full-time **ministry** of itinerant **evangelism**. He adopted the "New Measures" of Charles G. Finney (1792–1875) and became the Baptist exponent of the **Second Great Awakenings**. He held major protracted **revival** meetings in Rochester, New York; New York City; Washington, D.C.; and Boston, Massachusetts. His style was often excessive, and he created deep divisions in the Baptist community. In upstate New York, Knapp was a leader in the "Removal Controversy," an unpopular campaign to move Baptist-related Madison University to Rochester. In Boston, he was accused of fraudulent practices and accepting gifts for his services. In 1837, he claimed that he had baptized 60 people in 28 minutes at Crooked Lake, New York. Knapp published a popular collection of revival hymns in 1845 and an autobiography in 1868.

KNIBB, WILLIAM (1803–1845). English Baptist missionary, born in Kettering, England. As an appointment of the **Baptist Missionary Society**, he went to Jamaica and served several churches and taught school at Kingston. Knibb was **pastor** at Port Royal, then at Savanna-la-Mar. In 1830, he was called to the church at Falmouth, on the north shore of the island. Gradually Knibb became openly critical of the slave code, becoming a popular hero with the black population but a pariah among the planter class. In 1832, he returned to Britain to travel widely on behalf of abolition; his was a major contribution to the bill of 1834, which abolished **slavery** in the British Empire. Again due in large part to Knibb's influence, slavery was abolished in Jamaica in 1838. Following his return to the island, he advocated education for the freed slaves and later died of yellow fever. Knibb's published work, *Colonial Slavery: A Defense of the Baptist Missionaries from the Charge of Indicting the Late Rebellion in Jamaica* (1832), was a catalyst in marshalling the forces of British **antislavery** sentiment. *See also* JAMAICA.

KNOLLYS, HANSERD (1598–1691). English and, for a time, American Baptist minister and writer, born at Cawkwell, Lincolnshire, England. Knollys graduated from Cambridge University and was ordained in the Church of England in 1629. In 1636, he resigned his membership in the church and was imprisoned for **Nonconformist**

preaching. Knollys escaped prison and fled to New England; he was turned away by the Congregationalists in Boston, and he served a church in Dover, New Hampshire (1639–1641). Afterward, he was a **pastor** for a short time on Long Island (1641), likely with Baptist sentiments. This congregation survived and relocated to Piscataway, New Jersey, naming the village for the town where Knollys had first gathered the congregation. He returned to England in 1643 and was co-pastor with **William Kiffin** and others in the early **Particular Baptist** community, often preaching to hundreds. A strong Calvinist, Knollys was jailed several times for preaching, and he wrote 11 works on historical, doctrinal, and linguistic topics. Among his works are *Christ Exalted* (1646) and *An Exposition of the Whole Book of the Revelation* (1689). Knollys was honored by the early naming of the British Baptist historical enterprise, the Hanserd Knollys Society.

KÖBNER, JULIUS (1806–1884). Danish Baptist minister, born at Odense, **Denmark**. The son of a Jewish rabbi, Köbner was trained as an engraver, settling in Schleswig-Holstein. In Hamburg, he encountered **J. G. Oncken** and was baptized in 1836. In 1839, Köbner visited Denmark and with Oncken organized the first Baptist church at Copenhagen. Years later, he served as **pastor** of the church, 1865–1879. A **revival** occurred during his **ministry** and the membership rose to 400. Köbner helped to organize the Baptist churches on the German plan and served as a resident theological professor for the other pastors. In 1848, he was the principal author of the "Manifesto of Free True Christianity for the German People," a landmark document in the development of a German Free Church. He composed the first Danish Baptist hymnbook, writing many of the poems himself. With Oncken and **G. W. Lehmann**, Köbner formed the "Kleeblat" (cloverleaf) or great triumvirate of European Baptist pioneers. Among Köbner's published works are *Die Glaubenstimme* (1849) and *Das Lied von Gott* (1873).

KOREA. Baptist history in Korea is dated from 1889 when **Malcolm Fenwick** (1863–1935), a Canadian **independent** missionary and later a Baptist, arrived to begin **evangelism**. Under the auspices of the Corean Itinerant Mission, which he helped to create, in 1896 Fenwick began a church at Sorai and later organized several congregations in the Tuman District. Another important stream of Baptist work commenced in 1895, when the first missionaries of the **Ella Thing Mission** arrived in Seoul. It was an outgrowth of Clarendon Street Baptist Church in Boston, Massachusetts, and it concentrated its effort in Kongju and Kanggyung. In 1901, the Corean Itinerant Mission merged with the Ella Thing Mission under the leadership of Fenwick, and the result was the formation in 1905 of Daihan Kitokkyohuay (Church of Christ in Korea).

The Baptist cause was fairly minimal until after the Korean War (1949–1953) when, following U.S. military presence, the **Southern Baptist** work in South Korea began in earnest. Daihan Kitokkyo Chimneyhuay, the Korea Baptist Convention, was formed in 1949. The first missionaries were John Abernathy and his wife (1896–?). A schism occurred in 1959 over relations between the Convention (which was under intense theological pressure from the International Council of Christian Churches) and the Southern Baptist Mission; the separate entities were reunited in 1968 as the Hankook Chimneyhuay Yunmaing (League of Korean Baptist Churches). In the 1980s, large churches have emerged in the vicinity of Seoul, the scene of the Baptist World Congress in 1990.

In addition to the regular Baptist work, **Baptist Mid-Missions** from the United States established in 1974 a work related to the Korea Baptist Convention, and in 1958 the **Baptist Bible Fellowship** opened its mission. Also, the **American Baptist Association** has a mission in Seoul, which includes a school.

As of 2006, there were 2,508 churches and 774,259 members affiliated with the Daihan Kitokkyo Chimneyhuay (formerly the Hankook). There are two recognized Baptist theological schools in Korea: Kyungkido and Tae Jun City.

KOREA GOSPEL MISSION. An **independent** Baptistic missionary agency founded in 1952. The **Mission** focuses on education and **evangelism** in South Korea. Its home base is in Seoul, South Korea, with recognition in the United States.

KYRGYZSTAN. Baptist beginnings in Kyrgyzstan are traced to 1882 when Mennonites from **Ukraine** entered the region. Mennonites and Baptists developed in tandem with each other, the Mennonites creating

German-speaking congregations. In 1907, R. G. Bershadsky and his wife, while traveling near Frunze, established a Baptist church at Pischpek (later Bischkek). Other churches were planted, and those associated with the All Union Council of Evangelical Christians-Baptists until 1991. With the reorganization of the Soviet Union, and the recognition of Kyrgyzstan as a separate state, 16 churches met in a congress in 1992 and formed the Union of Evangelical Christians-Baptists in Kyrgyzstan.

As of 2006, there were 64 churches and 24 groups with approximately 3,100 members affiliated with the Union. *See also* RUSSIA.

– L –

LAGERGRAN, CARL GUSTAF (1846–1941). Swedish and, later, American Baptist minister and educator, born at Ostersund, Jamtland, **Sweden**. He was educated at a local gymnasium and at the University of Uppsala, where he studied languages and philosophy. **Anders Wiberg** recommended Lagergran to serve the congregation at Uppsala, after which he was **pastor** at Sundsvall from 1883 to 1889. While in the pastorate, he helped organize a domestic missionary effort for Sweden and **Finland**, and he conducted a **Bible school**. In 1889, he was called to be dean of the Swedish Baptist Theological Seminary, then a part of the Baptist Theological Union in Morgan Park, Chicago, Illinois. He also served as professor of theology in that institution through 1922, writing a major systematic **theology** (1924), as well as his autobiography (1927). In 1912–1914, Lagergran supported the combination of Bethel Academy and the Swedish Baptist Seminary in Chicago, and the removal of both schools to St. Paul, Minnesota. For his distinguished service over many years, he was named a Knight of the Royal Order of the North Star by Swedish King Gustav V.

LAMBE, THOMAS (fl. 1635–1673). English General Baptist minister, whose birthplace is unknown. He first appears in records at Colchester, where he was imprisoned in 1639–1640 for preaching and baptizing. He is significant to Baptist history as a bridge figure between those who sprinkled and those who immersed and as one of the first to conduct itinerant preaching among the **General Baptists**. Likely a soap boiler by trade, he is not to be confused with the Thomas Lambe, pastor and merchant of London, of about the same era. He was a **Leveller** to the end of that party's progress and preached widely, presaging the General Baptist office of **messenger**. He served the church at Bell Alley, London, and was remembered by the Presbyterian Thomas Edwards (1599–1647) for his openness and revivalistic style. Sometime in the early 1640s, Lambe moved the congregation to Spitalfields and a split occurred over the **laying on of hands** at **baptism**, which he opposed. In his classic book *The Fountains of Free Grace Opened* (1645), he helped give General Baptists a theological reputation by openly advocating an **Arminian** position. He drew other preachers to his itinerating style, among who were **Henry Denne**, Samuel Oates (1610–1683), and Jeremiah Ives (fl. 1653–1674). Lambe was imprisoned in 1663 for attending a conventicle service, and according to **Thomas Crosby**, he died in 1673.

LANDMARKISM. A form of **local church protectionism** that emerged among Baptists in the United States in the 19th century. While Landmarkism is usually associated with Baptist life in the southern region, its origins are in New England.

Based upon scriptural references such as Proverbs 22:28, "Remove not the ancient landmarks which thy fathers have set," and Deuteronomy 19:14, "Thou shalt not remove thy neighbor's landmark, which they of old time have set in thine inheritance, which thou shalt inherit in the land that the Lord thy God giveth thee to possess it," the originators of the movement sought to observe strictly their definitions of Baptist identity, which was synonymous with unadulterated, historic Christian identity.

Within the frame of reference of New England Baptist congregational life in the early decades of the 19th century, rural Baptist churches and **associations** became alarmed with the buildup of extra-congregational organization. These new organizations included societies of various kinds and involved a push toward a national convention, thus creating a sense of Baptist denominationalism. The newer forms were advocated by leaders in the Middle States and South, and were particularly well supported by urban churches in the eastern cities. When the funding for many of the nationalists' agenda (including domestic and foreign **missions**, education, and publication) proved inadequate in the 1820s, New England Baptists moved to control the development of the new organizations and in their place instituted a style of limited purpose societies, which historians have later referred to as the "society model" of Baptist life. Well-educated thinkers such as **Francis Wayland** of Brown University advocated the society model, while others like **J. Newton Brown** and I. M. Person (fl. 1830) in New Hampshire provided a theological basis for local church protectionism. The movement also found adherents among the isolated churches of the Old Northwest and what became the **Primitive**, or Old School, Baptists.

James M. Graves held that the Landmark movement began in his own spiritual pilgrimage starting from confusion over different modes of **baptism** and the spiritual fitness of certain ministers and leading to a clear articulation of Baptist principles according to seven landmarks. He began to write about his positions in *The Tennessee Baptist* in 1846, and in 1851 called a major debate at Cotton Grove, Tennessee, where he claimed to have convinced a significant number of churches to accept his positions. In 1854, **James M. Pendleton** actually coined the term "Landmark" in a pamphlet that Graves published under the title *An Old Landmark Reset*. Graves argued that **William Kiffin**, the English **Particular Baptist John Clarke** of Rhode Island, and **Jesse Mercer** of Georgia were all Landmarkists because of the way each sharply defined Baptist identity before anyone actually used the term. For Graves and Pendleton, the issue was to carry out in their practice those principles that all true Baptists, in all ages, have professed to believe. *See also* COTTON GROVE RESOLUTIONS.

Modernity set in more rapidly in the East and North than in the South, and the churches in those two sections turned to missionary expansion at home and abroad, as well as to more sophisticated institutions of **higher education**. In the rural South, Landmarkism became a powerful force that some historians believe has been determinative in the making of **Southern Baptist** identity, especially with respect to **ecumenical** relations and denominationalism. Landmarkism may be identified as a critical factor in regions of the Southern Baptist Convention as diverse as the Southwest and upper Mississippi Valley. It was a contributing factor in the **Gospel Mission**

Movement of the 1880s and one of the negative factors that retarded the growth of a unified publishing program and educational system of Southern Baptists in the period 1860–1910.

Several schisms in Southern Baptist life have followed Landmark emphases. The anticonventionism of leaders like **Ben M. Bogard** and **J. Frank Norris**, plus the organizational rifts at the state level that led to the **Baptist Missionary Association** and the **American Baptist Association**, reveal strong Landmarkist tendencies. Landmarkism has become a tradition that includes a number of organizationally distinct bodies. Some Baptist bodies are both Landmarkist and **fundamentalist**. The more missionary-minded Landmarkists have carried the ideals far beyond North America to Asia, Africa, and Latin America in particular.

As fully elaborated, Landmark theology includes beliefs such as the following: Baptist churches are the purest, truest churches in the world; the church is essentially visible and local; the church is composed only of regenerate persons; repentence must precede baptism ("blood before water"); only a true church can perform the **ordinances** of the **Lord's Supper** and baptism; the Lord's Supper is not intended for fellowship with unbelievers; and a nonbeliever must not be admitted to a Baptist pulpit nor to the Lord's Supper. In more recent embellishments of Landmarkism, some advocates have equated the use of the term "kingdom" in **Scripture** with "church," and the historical position of "**Successionism**" is assumed by many writers. Among the important literature of the Landmark movement are works written by James M. Pendleton, *An Old Landmark Reset* (1854); James R. Graves, *Old Landmarkism: What Is It?* (1880); A. C. Dayton, *Theodosia Ernest: or the Heroine of Faith* (1856); Ben M. Bogard, *The Baptist Way-Book* (1927); and D. B. Ray, *Baptist Succession* (1949).

LATHROP, JOHN (d. 1653). English Independent minister. Almost nothing is known of his background except that he likely attended Cambridge University and accepted the curacy of Egerton. Lathrop resigned his position in 1622 and assumed the pastorate of **Henry Jacob**'s **Independent** Church in Southwark. In 1632, the bishop of London had the church raided during a meeting in the home of Humphrey Barnet, a brewer's clerk; Lathrop and 41 of the members were imprisoned at the Clink for 12 years. During Lathrop's incarceration, a schism took place, one group remaining true to Independency, the other following **John Spilsbury** and the practice of believer's **baptism**. Lathrop was given permission in 1634 to go into foreign exile. Before departing, he reorganized his congregation, which included **William Kiffin**. Lathrop fled to New England accompanied by 32 church members, and they settled at Scituate, and later Barnstable, Massachusetts. The Southwark portion of his congregation was apparently led for a time by **Samuel Eaton**, who was succeeded by **Henry Jessey**.

LATOURETTE, KENNETH SCOTT (1884–1968). American Baptist historian and educator, born at Oregon City, Oregon. He was educated at McMinnville (later Linfield) College and Yale University, receiving his Ph.D. at Yale in 1909. Latourette traveled for two years as a staff member and later missionary of the Student Volunteer Movement in China, teaching in the Yale in China program in Hunan Province in 1910. Being forced to return home due to illness, he taught at Reed College in Oregon (1914–1916) and Denison University in Ohio (1916–1921), before taking the D. Willis James Professorship of Missions at Yale Divinity School in 1921. Soon he began teaching courses in the university on the Far East, and his title was expanded in 1927 to include Oriental history. Latourette awakened scholarly and popular interest in the Far East, influencing many university departments around the world. In 1949, he was named Sterling Professor at Yale. His contribution to the discipline of church history was enormous, as witnessed in his major publications, *A History of the Expansion of Christianity* (7 volumes, 1937–1945) and his encyclopedic one-volume *History of Christianity* (1953). His peers elected him president of the American Society of Church History (1945), the American Historical Association (1948), and the Far Eastern Association (1954). In 1952, Latourette was elected president of the American Baptist Convention, in part recognizing his many years of service on the board of the **American Baptist Foreign Mission Society**.

LATVIA. The first baptism of believers in Latvia was observed in 1861 near Libau in the secrecy of night to avoid being detected by police.

Under much persecution, Baptist representatives presented a petition to Russian Czar Alexander II, who granted full **religious liberty** in 1879 to the Baptist community. Largely under the direction of the Memel Church in Lithuania, considered the mother congregation of the Letts, congregations were started at Windau, Sakkenhausen, and Riga. Beginning in 1875, Lettish Baptist Conferences were held. Under the leadership of Janis A. Frey (1863–1950), **pastor** at Dunamunde, the Latvian cause grew to include **Sunday Schools** and a publishing house. The Bund of Baltic Baptists was created in 1885, renamed in 1891 the Association of Latvian Baptists and again in 1908 the Union of Latvian Baptists. Missionary work among Lettish people was carried out in **Russia**, Siberia, **Brazil**, and later in **India** and **China**. With the coming of war, all Baptist meetings were banned and the leadership was exiled to Siberia in 1916. Frey returned to Riga in 1922 to start a theological school there as a result of the **London Conference of 1920**. In 1940, the Soviet government forbade the activities of the Union of Latvian Baptists, but the Germans restored the union in 1942. In 1945, the Baptist churches in Latvia were incorporated in the Soviet All-Union Council of Evangelical Christians-Baptists; this status ensued until 1991, when with Latvian independence, the union was reestablished as Latvijas Baptistu Draudzu Savieniba. The theological school at Riga was closed in 1940 but reopened in 1991.

As of 2006, there were 86 congregations and 6,680 members affiliated with Latvijas Baptistu Draudzu Savieniba.

LAWS, CURTIS LEE (1868–1946). American Baptist minister and editor, born at Aldie, Virginia. He was educated at the University of Richmond and Crozer Theological Seminary. Laws served pastorates in Baltimore, Maryland (1893–1908), and Brooklyn, New York (1908–1913). While in the charge of Greene Avenue Baptist in Brooklyn, Laws facilitated the merger of the *Watchman* (Boston) and the *Examiner* (New York). In 1911, he became editor for 27 years of the combined *Watchman-Examiner* weekly newspaper, the most widely circulated Baptist periodical in the United States. As a respected **evangelical** editorial opinion, Laws sought to recover historic Baptistic and biblical principles to the denomination, especially in the Northern Baptist Convention (NBC). He was an organizer in

1920 of the **fundamentalist** movement at the Buffalo meeting of the NBC, always a moderate and pro-NBC voice. Eschewing terms like "**conservative**," "premillennial," and "**Landmarker**," he coined the term "fundamentalist" in an editorial in the *Watchman-Examiner* in 1920. Believing fundamentalists were part of a "historic and holy succession," he held to the Philadelphia and New Hampshire Baptist **confessions of faith** as definitions of the theological traditions. Laws was associated in 1925 with the founding of the Eastern Baptist Theological Seminary in Philadelphia, whose chapel bears his name. Among Laws's book publications is *Baptist Fundamentals* (1920).

LAYING ON OF HANDS. Also known as "imposition" and considered by some to be an **ordinance**. The laying on of hands occurs at three occasions in Baptist practice: following believer's **baptism**, the **ordination** of **deacons**, and the ordination of **pastors**.

Following Believer's Baptism. In Acts 8:14–18, the order of reception into the Christian faith involved preaching, prayer, baptism, and the laying on of hands to impart the Holy Ghost. Early Baptists in England, particularly the **General Baptists**, coupled this teaching with the supposed confession of Hebrews 6:1–2, to require the laying on of hands on all believers following baptism. In the North American colonies, from the late 17th century through the late 18th century, both General **Six Principle** and Calvinistic Baptists ordained the laying on of hands for this purpose. The Philadelphia Confession of Faith (1742), a modification of the Second London Confession of Faith (1677), included an article on the laying on of hands but asserted that the purpose was not to receive extraordinary gifts of the Spirit, but to receive the promise and graces of the Spirit, such as comfort, strength, and confirmation of the presence of the Spirit in one's life. The practice was abandoned by the end of the century among most Regular Baptist congregations in the United States.

The Ordination of Pastors. In the tradition of Old Testament identification of leaders, as in I Samuel 16:12–13, the New Testament churches practiced "setting apart" candidates for **ministry**; "fasting, prayer, and the laying on of hands" were observed (Acts 13:2–3). I Timothy 4:14 suggests that the New Testament church believed that a gift was conveyed and that the presbytery (eldership or ordained ministry) had the responsibility for the act. Baptists with other Christians make the laying on of hands an important component of an ordination service. After appropriate remarks have been made, the candidate kneels in front of the congregation or **associational** gathering and ordained clergy are asked to come forward to place their hands on the head of the candidate, offer remarks quietly to the candidate, and/or say a personal prayer. An alternative form is to have several clergy place a hand on the candidate's head at the same time and one person offers a prayer of ordination. By placing the hands on the head of the candidate, Baptists believe that the spiritual power of ministry is symbolically passed to the candidate, the participating ministers affirm personally their support of the candidate, and the candidate signals his or her submission to the authority of the church. When the laying on of hands is concluded, the candidate rises and is recognized as a minister in full standing.

The Ordination of Deacons. Among some Baptists, deacons may also participate in a laying-on-of-hands ceremony. Deacons may be asked to represent the congregation as part of the ordination of a pastor. Deacons themselves may be ordained, and the laying on of hands is carried forth much as above, except that deacons join pastors in placing their hands on the head of the candidates. In the case of deacons, several may be ordained at once. Early Welsh Baptists and later **Southern Baptists** in the United States (among others) practiced the laying on of hands with deacons.

LEBANON. Baptist presence in Lebanon doubtless stems from British and American military personnel and tourists in the middle years of the 20th century. The first Baptist **mission** was established by **Southern Baptists** in 1948; the first congregation was located at Beirut, and subsequent church planting occurred throughout the Christian sectors. In 1955, the Lebanese Baptist Convention was organized, later the Arab Baptist Seminary was opened in 1960, and a major Arabic language press was begun, which became the center for Baptist witness among Arab peoples. In 1958, the **Baptist Bible Fellowship** opened a mission in Lebanon, broadening the Baptist presence in the country.

As of 2006, there were 27 churches and 2,000 members affiliated with the Lebanese Baptist Convention. There is a recognized Baptist theological school at Beirut.

LEE, ROBERT GREENE (1886–1978). Southern Baptist minister, born at Fort Mill, South Carolina. He was educated at Furman University and Chicago Law School. Lee highly esteemed the president of Furman, **Edwin Poteat,** and modeled his life on Poteat's oratorical abilities. "R. G." Lee turned aside careers in law and teaching at Furman University to be a **pastor.** He served churches at Saluda (1918), Edgefield (1918–1921), and Chester (1921–1922), South Carolina; First Baptist, New Orleans, Louisiana (1922–1925); Citadel Square, South Carolina (1925–1927); and Bellevue Baptist Church in Memphis, Tennessee (1927–1960). Lee became one of the most outstanding preachers of his day, speaking in the quintessential Southern Baptist style of the 20th century. He was well-known for his **evangelistic** sermon "Pay Day . . . Some Day," first preached at Edgefield, South Carolina, and 900 times thereafter. Lee developed a widespread reputation for large numbers of decisions for Christ and **baptisms** at his church in Memphis. He was elected a rare three times to the presidency of the **Southern Baptist Convention**, in 1949, 1950, and 1951.

LEG OF MUTTON BAPTISTS. Marius D'Assigny (1643–1717) in his survey of Baptists of 1709 found that at Lambert Street, Whitechapel, there was a congregation that practiced eating meat, particularly leg of mutton, at the **Lord's Supper.** Presumably this was recognition of the connection with the Passover Meal and earned the group the name Leg of Mutton Baptists.

LEHMANN, GOTTFRIED WILHELM (1799–1882). German Baptist minister and denominational leader, born in Hamburg, **Germany**. As a youth, he was in contact with Mennonites in Friesland and followed his father's occupation as an engraver. Lehmann came to know **J. G. Oncken** and followed his example in converting to Baptist principles. In 1837, immediately after his **baptism,** Lehmann became **pastor** at a new church in Berlin, where he remained for many years. With Oncken and **Julius Köbner**, Lehman constituted the "Kleeblat" (cloverleaf), a trio of German Baptist leaders.

LEILE, GEORGE (c. 1750–1800). American and, later, Jamaican black Baptist minister, born a **slave** in Virginia. About the beginning of the American Revolution, Leile was converted under the **ministry** of Matthew Moore of South Carolina, who also baptized him and received him into his church. Ultimately, Leile's master gave him his freedom in order to become a minister. Among the Savannah River plantations, Leile preached, was ordained, and gathered a congregation, which became the first African Baptist Church in the United States. Fleeing his former owners who attempted to reclaim him as a slave in the 1780s, Leile fled to **Jamaica** in 1782 and became the first **missionary** there. To support himself, he worked at the Customs House in Kingston and preached at the race course. In 1791, he reported to the English Baptist **John Rippon** that he had baptized 500 people, who became the nucleus of the Windward Road Church in Kingston. This led English Baptists to begin their support for missions in Jamaica. Leile wrote an early church covenant for Jamaica and quietly advocated **religious liberty** and **human rights**, as well as mentoring other ministers, notably Moses Baker, who served in St. James Parish.

LELAND, JOHN (1754–1841). American Baptist minister, born at Grafton, Massachusetts. Leland was not formally educated, and was quickened in his religious profession under the **ministry** of **Elhanan Winchester**. In 1773, he conducted a preaching tour of Virginia and returned there for 15 years of ministry. He was finally ordained in 1786, and two years later reported 300 **baptisms** on a preaching tour of the South and middle states. In 1791, he returned to Cheshire, Massachusetts. Leland resisted a settled pastorate and wrote widely on various subjects, notably **religious liberty**. He opposed governmentally established religious holidays and chaplains to governments paid by tax dollars. In 1804, in a celebrated incident, he delivered a large gift of Cheshire cheese to U.S. President Thomas Jefferson (1743–1826), for whom Leland had great affection. It is widely held that Leland had a significant impact at least indirectly upon James Madison (1750–1836) in his political understanding of the **separation of church and state**. Among Leland's most famous published works are *The Rights of Conscience Inalienable* (1791) and *The Government of Christ a Christocracy* (1804). The John Leland Center for Theological Studies, founded in 1997, carries forth the tradition of Leland in the greater Washington, D.C./Virginia region.

LEVELLERS. A mid-17th-century English **dissenter** movement that coincided and interacted with the rise of the Baptists. Inspired by religious, political, and economic motives that opposed monopolies, religious compulsion, property taxes, debt imprisonment, and capital punishment, the Levellers reached a peak of influence about 1645. The movement was diffuse, united by three leaders: John Lilburne (1614–1657), Richard Overton (fl. 1642–1663), and William Walwyn (fl. 1649). Leveller propaganda shared a common heritage with **Separatists** and Baptists, and it was not uncommon for Baptists to have Leveller sympathies. Overton, a printer, had been a follower of **John Smyth** in 1615, but by the 1640s, he developed a radical position denying the immortality of the human soul, and while a distant **General Baptist** associated with the church at Bell Alley, London, he was a leading Leveller. Other Baptists known to be part of the movement were **Thomas Lambe** (fl. 1635–1673), Samuel Highland (fl. 1645–1649), William Allen (1614–1677), and Edmund Chillenden (fl. 1645–1656). Levellers in fact helped to give a clear focus to Baptists and other dissenters as soldiers, artisans, skilled workers, and "mechanicks."

As the theological and political position of Leveller writers became increasingly radical, many Baptists broke ranks. In addition, Levellers were an increasing irritant to Oliver Cromwell (1599–1658), and the Leveller plan for a coming democratic kingdom conflicted with the eschatological aspirations of millennialists and a theocratic kingdom. Some Baptists, such as **William Kiffin**, openly opposed the Levellers before various tribunals. Ultimately, the defeat of the king's forces at Burford and the death of Charles I in 1649 brought the Leveller cause to a bitter conclusion, with its Baptist adherents having drifted back to their more conservative positions. As with other dissenter traditions, Baptist engagement with radical ideas illustrated the fluidity of 17th-century dissenter identity. *See also* DIGGERS; FIFTH MONARCHY MOVEMENT; RANTERS; SEEKERS.

LIBERAL TRADITION. Among Baptists, the term "liberal" has both negative and positive connotations, depending upon the context. In the positive sense, liberal usually refers to thinkers and positions that affirm progressive social thought and religious ideals, **human rights**, and social reform. From the later 19th century, particularly in North America, liberalism was a flowering of at least two elements inherent in the Baptist character. As several theological analysts have shown, the liberal spirit owed much to the pietism and experiential bases of religion on the one hand, and the heritage of **religious liberty** on the other. Among Baptists, religious fervor, such as that felt in the **revival** tradition, replaced orthodox creedalism and confessionalism. This, coupled with an impulse of free thought, can be seen in many of the avant garde liberal **theologians** from about 1880 to 1930, a substantial number of whom were Baptists. Liberal thought among Baptists, however, also has a much older history.

In the 17th century, at least from an "establishment" point of view, Baptists (especially **General Baptists**) were considered a liberal sect. Ideas like religious liberty, **separation of church and state**, believer's **baptism**, and belief in free will, plus some Baptists' identification with **Seekers**, **Levellers**, and **Ranters**, reinforced the liberal reputation of the movement. Baptist liberal thinking was also applied to openness on key theological issues, such as admission to the **Lord's Supper** and the nature of the atonement. But other concerns were also evident, including singing in the church, the role of **women**, involvement in contemporary political and social movements, and relations with other churches and theological traditions.

Eighteenth-century liberal Baptist thinkers were associated with opposition to **revivalism** and enthusiastic expression, like Harvard alumnus Jeremiah Condy (1709–1768) of First Baptist, Boston. Others were advocates of education, ordination, soul freedom, and separation of church and state, like **John Leland**. Some liberal thinkers, such as **Elhanan Winchester**, held Unitarian or **Universalist** views. In the early 19th century, those who supported missionary activity, the formation of **associations** and **conventions**, **higher education**, and social reforms were often labeled liberals. **Freewill** and Free Communion Baptists were among those groups considered liberal among Regular Calvinistic Baptists in the United States, largely because of their openness to inclusion of persons regardless of social status. In Britain, in the early 19th century, **Robert Aspland**, formerly a **Particular Baptist** minister who studied at Bristol and Aberdeen and then joined the General Baptist movement, became successively a Unitarian and then a Presbyterian, editing the *Universal*

Theological Magazine, a publication associated with contemporary liberal thought. Later, advocates of the **Baptist Union of Great Britain and Ireland** and those who favored a lessening of the distinctions of Calvinism were among those considered liberal, among who were **Robert Hall**, **Andrew Fuller**, and **Joseph Ivimey**. More recently, **Michael H. Taylor**, principal at Northern Baptist College in Manchester from 1970 to 1985, espoused a liberal position on the doctrine of **Christ** in his 1971 address before the Baptist Union Assembly, which caused quite a stir among the Union churches.

Liberal Baptist thinkers since the mid-19th century have utilized a critical historical or scientific approach to the interpretation of **Scripture**, rather than a simple proof text method and assumptions about the divine origins of the **Bible**. Among such writers and scholars in the British context were **Samuel G. Green**, S. A. Tipple (1828–1910), and **James Martin**, and in the United States, **Asa Messer**, **William Newton Clarke**, **Nathaniel Schmidt**, and **Crawford H. Toy**. Messer was forced to resign from the presidency at Brown over doctrinal matters early in the century. Schmidt and Toy were actually the defendants in educational heresy proceedings and dismissed from their respective institutions for their liberal positions. Toward the end of the 19th century in the United States, influenced by progressive thought, university education in the sciences, and a growing awareness of social problems, some Baptist thinkers became more interested in Christian social reform than in personal **evangelism** and church planting; among these were **Walter Rauschenbusch**, Leighton Williams (1855–1935), and **William H. P. Faunce**. The "**Chicago School**" came to be synonymous with liberal thought, emphasizing critical scientific investigation of the Scriptures, a comparative religions approach to the uniqueness of Christianity, interfaith dialogue, and the application of the social sciences to theological disciplines. Exponents of this tradition included **William Rainey Harper**, **Shirley Jackson Case**, **Ernest Dewitt Burton**, **George Burman Foster**, and **Douglas Clyde Macintosh**.

In the Canadian Baptist context, liberalism has been termed "modernism" and has been associated with McMaster University and to a lesser degree Brandon University in Manitoba and Acadia University in Nova Scotia. Each of these schools was influenced by the methods at the University of Chicago in the early decades of the 20th century.

In the mid-1920s, the theological faculty at McMaster was reorganized, and some of the churches in the Toronto region felt the trend pointed toward an unacceptable view of Scripture and teaching of scientific theories of the earth's origins. The arts faculty became predominant over the theological studies. For those who remained in the Baptist Convention of Ontario and Quebec, liberalism became synonymous with the university's right to explore knowledge; for those who left the affiliation of the convention, liberalism became a negative description of mainstream Baptist life.

As a pejorative label, "liberal" has been used by Baptist **evangelicals** and **fundamentalists** to categorize their theological and ethical adversaries. Among the typical liberal tendencies noted by these groups are not holding to an orthodox view of the authority of Scripture, denying in many cases the deity of Christ and the personhood of the Holy Spirit, the transcendence of God, miraculous events, the physical return of Christ, and a literal understanding of direct theistic creation. Traditional **conservative evangelicals** often associate certain ethical liberties and attitudes with liberalism, including the enjoyment of alcoholic beverages in the North American context, smoking tobacco products, use of drugs for other than medicinal purposes, dancing, rock music, premarital sex, permission of divorce, use of profanity, and human sexual orientations other than heterosexual. Also considered liberal in the realm of social and political thought are aggressive civil rights advocacy, support for abortion rights, pro-feminist thought, liberation theology, toleration of Marxist ideology and governments, membership in **ecumenical** organizations, and openness to socialist and pluralistic religious policy in government legislation. See also CONSERVATIVE TRADITION; EVANGELICALISM, BAPTISTS AND; FUNDAMENTALISM, BAPTIST.

LIBERIA. Baptist mission in Liberia dates from the arrival of **Lott Carey** in 1821. He established a church at Monrovia in 1822 under the auspices of the **Baptist Board of Foreign Missions**. Many early missionaries died of fevers in Liberia; Ezekiel Skinner was a notable medical missionary who served for four decades, arriving in 1834. The Liberia Baptist Association was formed at Monrovia in 1835. In 1856, the **American Baptist Missionary Union** transferred its

Liberian mission to the **Southern Baptists**, who were assisted by **black Baptists** in the United States. Southern Baptists terminated their work in 1875 (they returned in 1960), leaving the **mission** to a U.S. black body, the Consolidated American Baptist Foreign Mission Convention, and **Jamaican** Baptists. In 1880, various churches and **associations** combined to form the Liberia Baptist Missionary Convention at Marshall, later to be called the Liberian Baptist Missionary and Educational Convention. This body has worked closely with U.S. black Baptists. An outgrowth of this work was the establishment of Ricks Institute in 1887, which continues to the present. The school was named for Moses Ricks, a Liberian Baptist farmer who donated funds to purchase land for the campus.

In addition to the regular Baptist work, **Baptist Mid-Missions** from the United States established a mission in 1938 among the Kpelle people at Sua Koko. In 1954, this mission established the Baptist Bible Institute in Monrovia and two years later a Baptist press. The **General Association of Regular Baptists** established their mission in 1968. In 1976, a theological seminary was opened under Southern Baptist auspices.

As of 2006, there were 229 churches and 60,000 members affiliated with the Liberia Baptist Missionary and Educational Convention, Inc. The Liberia Baptist Theological Seminary is located at Paynesford City.

LIBERTY BAPTIST FELLOWSHIP (LBF). Group formed in 1977 to support and enlarge the emphases of **Jerry Falwell**, a fundamentalist **pastor**/evangelist, and the Thomas Road Baptist Church in Lynchburg, Virginia. From its beginning, the LBF was administered personally by Falwell (who served as executive chairman until his death) and influenced by graduates of Liberty University, a **fundamentalist** Baptist institution in Lynchburg. The purposes of the LBF include providing fellowship for pastors of like faith, mutual accountability, support for planting new churches in the United States, assistance for pastors of new congregations, and a certifying body for licensing and recognition of chaplains. The fellowship elects officers from a church constituency of several hundred pastors, and a periodical, the *Liberty Baptist Fellowship Newsletter*, has been issued since 1977.

As of 2007, there were 333 member churches and 28 chaplains affiliated with the LBF. Several of the pastors in the fellowship are also identified with the **Baptist Bible Fellowship** or the **Southwide Baptist Fellowship**. Also associated with the LBF is Liberty Baptist Mission, founded in 1978 at Thomas Road Baptist Church. The Mission has work in seven countries and focuses on **evangelism** and **theological education**.

LIBYA. With the production of oil in the 1960s, American presence in Libya was expanded and Baptist missionaries entered the country on a limited basis. In 1962, U.S. **Southern Baptist** missionaries created a church, consisting of Americans, at Tripoli. In 1970, the American presence left the country and mission work ceased.

LINDSELL, HAROLD (1913–1998). Baptist minister, editor, and theological educator, born in New York City. He was educated at Wheaton College (B.A.); the University of California, Berkeley (M.A.); and New York University (Ph.D). Raised a Presbyterian, Lindsell became a Baptist by conviction and was ordained at First Baptist Church, Columbia, South Carolina, in 1944. Lindsell's first teaching position was in church history and missions at Columbia Bible College in South Carolina (1942–1944). He then studied church history at Northern Baptist Theological Seminary, where he became a close colleague of **Carl F. H. Henry**. In 1949, he joined Henry, Everett Harrison, and Wilbur Smith as the inaugural faculty at Fuller Theological Seminary in California. He became dean and later vice president at Fuller. In 1964, Lindsell left Fuller to become associate editor of *Christianity Today*, an evangelical fortnightly magazine, for one year, also teaching Bible at Wheaton College (1967–1968). From 1968 to 1978, he was editor of *Christianity Today* and drew international attention to its contents and **evangelicalism** in general. Following his editorship, Lindsell taught apologetics at Simon Greenleaf School of Law in Anaheim, California, 1984–1989. Lindsell was a vocal advocate of biblical inerrancy and a close confidant of evangelist **Billy Graham**. He helped to organize Graham's International Conference on World Evangelism at Lausanne, Switzerland, in 1974. Lindsell was also president of the **Baptist Faith and Message** Fellowship, an influence group seeking to turn **Southern**

Baptists toward inerrancy. Of Lindsell's 20 books, his most prominent published works are *The Battle for the Bible* (1976) and *The Bible in Balance* (1979).

LITERATURE OF BAPTISTS. From their beginnings in the 17th century, Baptists have made a substantial literary contribution. Within the first generations, the primary achievements were theological treatises like **John Smyth**'s *Differences in the Churches of the Seperation* (1608–1609) and **Thomas Helwys**'s *Mistery of Iniquity* (1612). In addition, Baptist identity was forged by the publication of **confessions of faith,** essentially pamphlet-sized 50-to-60-page (maximum) discourses on doctrinal categories with **Scripture** references. Printed in London, these pamphlets were distributed through dissenter channels and booksellers across the kingdom and to North America. As English Baptists interacted with other dissenters and churchmen in debates, the literary work continued in broadsides and treatises on topics of ecclesiological and practical interests. Toward the end of the century, a new genre appeared, that of the allegory, made famous by **John Bunyan**'s *Pilgrim's Progress* and **Benjamin Keach**'s *The Glorious Lover* (1696).

The publishing work of the Baptist Union's Kingsgate Press and the **Baptist Missionary Society**'s Carey Press (after 1949 Carey Kingsgate Press) carried forth British Baptist literary accomplishments until the press was discontinued in 1969. More recently, Paternoster Press in Carlisle, Cumbria, has published a number of Baptist scholarly works.

The first Baptist title to be produced in North America was John Russell's *A Brief Narrative . . . Concerning the First Gathering and Further Progress of a Church of Christ in Gospel Order in Boston* (1680). By the mid-18th century, the confession of faith was popularized again in the printing of the Philadelphia Confession by Benjamin Franklin in 1742. This document went through several printings and was popularly found on the southern and western frontiers. Yet another type of literature appeared in 1770 with **Morgan Edwards**'s *Materials toward a History of the American Baptists*. Alongside came **Isaac Backus**'s *History of New England, with Particular Reference to the Denomination of Christians Called Baptists* (1777). As congregations, as well as their **pastors**, in Boston region and the

Delaware Valley became more prominent, funeral orations and dedication tracts were printed: noteworthy were those for **James Manning**, **Richard Furman**, and **Samuel Stillman**. A great literary leap forward occurred with the appearance of the periodicals the *Georgia Analytical Repository*, the *Massachusetts Baptist Missionary Magazine*, and the *Latter Day Luminary*. These works displayed a cohesiveness and hunger among the scattered churches for religious and secular intelligence, as well as giving opportunities for literary expression to pastors and laypersons.

As the 19th-century advancement of the denomination occurred, Baptist literature fell easily into categories: Bibles; newspapers and magazines; minutes of organizations; theological treatises; catalogs of institutions; educational manuals and books; works of fiction; historical works; and congregational programs. Newspapers became the weekly or monthly communications of prominent state organizations: noteworthy would be the *Biblical Recorder* (North Carolina) and the *Religious Herald* (Virginia) and, among urban centers, Boston's *Watchman* and New York's *Examiner.* In these papers, one finds not only specific data of churches and persona, but also theological and sociopolitical opinion and line drawings of churches. Every **association** printed annual minutes that contained not only statistics, but actions of the body and an annual sermon, usually on an assigned topic. Theological treatises came to include works on **baptism**, the **Lord's Supper**, the **deaconship**, and the first systematic theologies (**Francis Wayland**'s *Elements of Moral Science* and **John L. Dagg**'s *Manual of Theology*). The **American Baptist Publication Society** (ABPS), and later the **Sunday School Board** of the **Southern Baptist Covention** (SBC), produced educational materials for Bible study, children's instruction, and manuals of **polity** and practice. Each of the ethnic and racially defined groups had a publishing arm that produced a unique form or language literature. "Theodosia Ernest" represents the kind of literature intended to teach morality through fictional characters. David Benedict (1811–1848) and Thomas Armitage (1886) wrote major historical treatises that became the fare of early Baptist libraries and identity making. Finally, there is an abundance of locally produced literature from congregations that included membership rosters, worship programs, dedication brochures, and local church histories.

In the 20th century, Baptists became major producers of Christian literature. In the United States, through the ABPS and the Sunday School Board's quarterlies and magazines, churches were taught the faith from a Baptist orientation. This literary production also enabled the global missionary outreach of these organizations. Judson Press, the book-publishing arm of ABPS, and Broadman Press, similarly connected with the SBC Sunday School Board, printed significant amounts of books, studies, biographies, and Bible commentaries. Competition from nondenominational producers of church school literature, however, led to the demise of American Baptist literature in the 1980s, while theological rigidity among Southern Baptists led to the new channel of Smyth and Helwys Publishers in competition with Broadman Press and the Sunday School Board. Also noteworthy in the literature of Baptist scholarship from a theologically moderate perspective is Mercer University Press, founded in 1979.

Baptist writers have included thousands of pastors, **theologians**, and laypersons. Among those with recent notoriety are Howard Thurman, *The Inward Journey* (1973), John Grisham, *A Time to Kill* (1982) and *The Pelican Brief* (1992); Bill Moyers, *Moyers on America* (2004); and Albert Gore, *An Inconvenient Truth* (2006). Grisham, a former lawyer and politician, has sold over 235 million books.

LITHUANIA. In 1841, the German Baptists formed a Baptist congregation at Memel, which had great impact upon the Lettish peoples. Similarly, in 1879, a second German Baptist congregation was commenced at Kaunas, eventually to be independent in 1889. Following World War I, other Baptist works were started among Russian-speaking emigrants and a theological school was started as a result of the **London Conference of 1920**. In 1933, a Lithuanian Baptist Union was formed at Klaipeda, and reformed in 1989 in the same city. In 1991, the **Baptist Bible Fellowship** opened its mission in Lithuania and in 1997 the **Conservative Baptist** Foreign Mission Society began a work in Lithuania.

As of 2006, there were seven churches and 374 members associated with the Lietuvos Evangeliku Baznyciu Sajunga (Lithuanian Evangelical Baptist Union).

"LIVING FAMILY." *See* STRICT BAPTISTS.

LOCAL CHURCH PROTECTIONISM. A term applied to the tendency among Baptists in the United States to safeguard the rights and privileges of the local congregation. In the 1820s, the anti-missionary spirit resisted all interference and competition from societies, **conventions**, and **associations**. In 1833, the Baptist Convention of New Hampshire published a **confession of faith** in which the church was defined in purely local terms. Later, in the 1840s and 1850s, the **Landmarkist** movement in the upper South spawned a whole new round of local church protectionism, which influenced greatly the entire future of the **Southern Baptist Convention**. Doctrinally, the idea of local church protectionism is defended on the basis of New Testament evidence of the strength and power of the local church. In many Baptist circles, it has been called a Baptist distinctive usually referred to as the **autonomy of the local church**.

LONDON CONFERENCE OF 1920. A watershed event in modern Baptist history whereby agreements were reached on the postwar relief and development of Baptists in Europe. During World War I, much of the Baptist community established in the 19th century was scattered, if not destroyed. Representatives of the U.S. Southern Baptist **Foreign Mission Board**, the **American Baptist Foreign Mission Society** (Northern Baptist Convention), and the British **Baptist Missionary Society** (BMS) toured Europe in 1920 to ascertain appropriate rebuilding steps in the Baptist community.

At a meeting in London, England, on July 19–23, delegates from the mission agencies and representatives of most of the European bodies met to plan for the future. A three-year relief program under the aegis of the **Baptist World Alliance** (BWA) was undertaken, and certain mission territorial "mandates" were agreed upon, some jointly supported: **Spain**, **Italy**, **Yugoslavia**, Hungary, **Ukraine**, **Romania**, southern **Russia,** to be administered by the U.S. **Southern Baptist Convention**; **France**, **Belgium**, **Switzerland**, Czechoslovakia, **Poland**, **Norway**, **Denmark**, northern Russia, and the Baltic States, by the U.S. Northern Baptist Convention; France, Italy, Czechoslovakia, **Finland**, all three Baltic States, and the **Netherlands**, by the BMS; **Bulgaria**, Poland, and **Austria**, by the German Union and the German Conference in North America; and **Portugal**, by **Brazil**.

These relationships were to be completely voluntary, and native work was to be preferred over missionary appointments. **Religious liberty** was to be a top priority, and sound relations with civil authorities were a goal. The London Conference authorized the establishment of a "commissioner" to coordinate relief efforts and make presentations to respective European governments. The venerable **James H. Rushbrooke** of Great Britain was chosen as commissioner, and his report was published in 1923 as *The Baptist Movement in the Continent of Europe*, a classic source on European Baptists. New **theological schools** were started in Spain, Portugal, **Latvia**, **Lithuania**, **Estonia**, Czechoslovakia, Hungary, and Romania. Much of the complexity of relations between European Baptists and their North American counterparts may be traced to the London Conference of 1920.

LORD'S SUPPER. The **ordinance** of the Lord's Supper—also called the breaking of bread, the **sacrament** of Holy Communion, or the Eucharist—is considered of primary importance to Baptists. Baptist understanding of the Lord's Supper is derived from Matthew 26:26–29, Mark 14:22–25, Luke 22:17–20, and 1 Corinthians 11:23–34.

Early English Baptists followed the patterns their ministers had learned in the Anglican and Puritan traditions. The Supper was considered by many to be sacramental, though this terminology was often eschewed because of its connection with Roman and Anglican superstitions. More appropriate was the Calvinistic understanding of a sacrament, namely, a sign of the grace of God that nurtures and confirms true believers. The term "ordinance" was used to designate a teaching of Christ for the whole church, and this was more palatable to the nascent Baptist community. The Lord's Supper is referred to as an ordinance in most of the early confessions, excepting the Orthodox Creed (1679) where the term "sacrament" is also used.

The Lord's Supper was usually prepared for church members who had been baptized as believers, and this practice was called "closed," or "close," communion. In "open communion" congregations, such as that of **John Bunyan** at Bedford, the invitation was given to all professing believers, regardless of baptized status as an infant or adult. The term "mixed communion" was used in Britain and later in the American colonies to denote the practice of admitting baptized believers and paedo-baptized Christians to the Table.

In normative Baptist practice, a table is set in the midst of the congregation, around which gather the **deacons** and **pastor**, who will serve the elements. Two elements are used: bread and wine, later to be replaced by grape juice. Usually the bread is cut into one-inch cubes and the grape beverage is served in either a single chalice or individual communion cups. The deacons take the bread first, and then the wine (grape juice), to the congregation in their places. A deacon offers a prayer of thanksgiving over each element, and after the minister serves the deacons and a deacon serves the minister, all partake of the bread, then the cup in the same manner. After all have been served, a hymn is sung and the congregation is dismissed. Great care is taken to reenact the Last Supper of Jesus and his disciples, as recorded in the Gospels and 1 Corinthians 11. The Pauline passage is more common than the Gospels as a reference in the service for many Baptists, particularly because it lays stress upon the spiritual preparation of the believers.

Baptists have disagreed and written widely on various aspects of the Lord's Supper. In the beginning, the controversy centered on who should be admitted. In Britain, **Robert Hall** understood the Lord's Supper as a sign of the church's unity and thus practiced open communion. **Joseph Kinghorn**, on the other hand, held that communion belongs to the church and only those admitted to the church through the waters of **baptism** should be invited to the Lord's Table. In the United States, these positions were advocated by **Benjamin Randal** and the **Landmarkist** movement, respectively, the latter led by **James R. Graves** and others.

Some Baptists also debated over the terminology of "sacrament" and "ordinance." Then followed the question of wine or grape juice. In Britain, between 1820 and 1880, a transition from wine to unfermented grape juice took place. Francis Beardsall (1799–1842) in 1835, Jabez Burns (1806–1876) in 1841, and the **Strict Baptists** by 1850 all led in the transition, which reflected the teetotal movement and new theological/biblical rationales. In one congregation at Bolton in the 1870s, a "two-cup" solution emerged for a time, with both wine and grape juice served as alternatives in the same service. Similarly, with the processing of grape juice in the United States and the introduction of germ theories of disease transmission, grape juice served in small, individual glasses became the preferred administration of the cup in most Baptist churches by the 1880s. **Alvah Hovey** defended the use of wine on scriptural grounds, and Abraham Coles (1813–1891) propounded the use of unfermented grape juice.

In the 19th century, there was some interest in taking the ordinance to sick or invalid persons, but in England this was overruled by those who believed it was too close to the high church practice of a priest taking the reserved sacrament as an act of mercy. Moreover, it was held that ordained persons wherever possible should preside at the Table in order to maintain proper church order. This hearkened back to **John Gill** and later **Andrew Fuller** among the **Particular Baptists**. **Scotch Baptists**, who recognized a plurality of elders, were an exception to this practice in Britain and North America. In the United States, elders as pastors presiding at the Supper were the common practice; a question arose over women and unordained persons presiding when **Isabel Crawford** celebrated the Lord's Supper in 1905 at Saddle Mountain, Oklahoma, and had to resign from her **missionary** work for violating mission Board policy.

Typically, among the Baptists, the Lord's Supper is celebrated on the first Sunday of each month and on special occasions throughout the year, such as Holy Week and Advent. Among some groups, the Pedalavium (**foot washing**) Service and **Love Feast** may accompany the Supper. In the mid-19th century, there was an attempt by several English Baptists, notably **John M. Cramp, James Haldane**, and **Charles H. Spurgeon** to adopt a weekly celebration, but again this was viewed as too close to the establishment sacramentarian practice. Some English Baptists and many American Baptists have recovered the sacramental dimension in recent years, while most Baptists prefer the terminology of "ordinance." *See also* BAPTISM; FOOT WASHING; LOVE FEAST.

LORENZEN, THORWALD (1936–). German and Australian Baptist theologian and educator, born at Hamburg, **Germany**. He was apprenticed in the firm of Deutsche Phillips but emigrated to **Australia** in 1959. During his early working career there, he became a Christian believer. Lorenzen took his B.A. at Sydney University and studied for ordination as a Baptist minister at Morling College, New

South Wales. He served congregations at Lansdowne (1963–1964) and Avalon (1964–1966) in Australia. He then returned to Europe to study at the Baptist Theological Seminary at Rüschlikon, **Switzerland,** where he earned the B.D. and Th.M. He took his Ph.D. in New Testament under Eduard Schweizer at University of Zurich, publishing on the Gospel of John. Lorenzen served on the faculty at the International Baptist Seminary from 1969 to 1995, gaining the professorship in 1982. From 1983 to 1985 he was acting president of the school. He also taught from 1971 to 1974 at Southeastern Baptist Seminary and then at Eastern Baptist Theological Seminary in 1987. In 1995, Lorenzen returned to Australia to become **pastor** of Canberra Baptist Church until his retirement in 2005.

During most of his career, Lorenzen was active in the **European Baptist Federation**, the **Baptist World Alliance** (BWA), and the World Council of Churches, as well as various organizations in Australia. In the BWA, he was chair of the **Human Rights** Commission (1985–1990; 1995–2000), chair of the theological conversation with the Lutheran World Federation, and the official representative of the BWA to the World Council of Churches in Geneva (1985–1990; 1994–1995). A prolific author and speaker on topics in ecumenism and human rights, he has published numerous treatises, including *Torture: A Moral Outrage: A Summons to Christian Action* (1984) and *Resurrection and Discipleship* (1995). Since his retirement, Lorenzen has lectured at Whitley College and served as professor of theology and Principal Researcher at Charles Sturt University and St. Mark's Theological Centre.

LOTT CAREY BAPTIST FOREIGN MISSION CONVENTION (LCBFMC). One of the major national expressions of **black Baptist** organizations in the United States, named for **Lott Carey**, a pioneer Baptist missionary to Africa. As the new **National Baptist Convention of the United States of America** (NBCUSA) took shape under the leadership of **Elias C. Morris**, several pastors objected to the NBCUSA's attitude of black separatism toward white Baptists. This led to a schismatic movement in 1896–1897. A coalition met at Shiloh Baptist Church in Washington, D.C., in December 1897, led by several prominent clergy, including Joseph E. Jones (1850–1922), A. W. Pegues (1859–1929), Calvin S. Brown (1859–1936?), and

William T. Johnson (1866–1942), to form the Lott Carey Baptist Foreign Mission Society. Most of the **pastors** were from eastern states, were employed by the **American Baptist Home Mission Society** (ABHMS), and were educated at either Shaw University in Raleigh, North Carolina, or the Richmond Theological Institute in Virginia, both schools supported by the ABHMS. A distinct contribution to the development of black Baptist foreign missions, the LCFMC changed its name from a society to a convention in 1903. It is the only distinct Baptist foreign missionary convention in the United States, and as such, it administers 133 missionary efforts in **Guyana**, **India**, **Kenya**, **Liberia**, and **Nigeria**. Sixteen states and the District of Columbia have affiliate organizations. The purpose of the LCFMC includes **evangelism**, education, and healing ministries. In the national convention, there are four divisions: Parent Body, Women's Auxiliary, Layman's League, and the Auxiliaries. A number of churches that are affiliated with the LCFMC are dually aligned with one of the National Baptist Conventions or the **American Baptist Churches in the U.S.A.** The LCFMC publishes the *Lott Carey Herald* (1908–). As of 2006, there were 3,500 churches with 1,225,000 members affiliated with the LCFMC.

LOVE FEAST. The Love Feast, also called by some the Agape Meal, is a historic **ordinance** among **German Baptist Brethren** and some other Baptist groups. Celebrated in conjunction with the **Lord's Supper**, the Love Feast is a reenactment of the Last Supper, which Jesus celebrated at the Feast of the Passover. Following the Pedalavium, or **foot washing** service, participants face each other across large tables and prepare for a full meal. In some instances, a meal consists of many staples like lamb stew, while in other situations, the meal has symbolic elements like coffee or chocolate or wheat biscuits. Bread and apple butter are common in the German Baptist tradition. The meal is eaten in absolute silence and prayerfully. When this portion of the meal is concluded, members turn to the distribution of the unleavened bread and the wine which constitute the traditional Lord's Supper or Holy Communion. The purpose of the Love Feast is both to fulfill the scriptural drama of Matthew 26:17–25 and to allow a time for communal fellowship and reconciliation with other members of the congregation. *See also* FOOT WASHING; LORD'S SUPPER.

LOWRY, ROBERT (1826–1899). American Baptist minister and hymnist, born at Philadelphia, Pennsylvania. Lowry graduated from the University at Lewisburg (later Bucknell) in 1854 with valedictory honors. He was called the same year to First Baptist Church, West Chester, Pennsylvania. In 1858, he moved to Bloomingdale Baptist in New York City, and then to Hanson Place Baptist in Brooklyn, where under his leadership, 400 new members were added. In 1869, Lowry took the position of Crozer Professor of Rhetoric at the University of Lewisburg, concurrent with a call to the First Baptist Church of Lewisburg. He retired from teaching in 1875 and became chancellor of the university until 1882. With the reorganization of the university, Lowry moved to a church in Plainfield, New Jersey, which he served for nine years, until he lost his hearing. He was the author of scores of popular hymns and gospel songs, including "Shall We Gather at the River," "Nothing but the Blood," and "Low in the Grave."

LUND, ERIC (1852–1933). Swedish Baptist and, later, American Baptist missionary, born at Selja, Mora, **Sweden**. He was educated at Betelseminariat in Stockholm and Harley College, London. While studying at the H. G. Guiness Mission Institute, he became interested in **missionary** work and went to **Spain**, where he preached and distributed **Bibles**. For his **evangelistic** work, he was imprisoned. In 1882, Lund became a missionary of the **American Baptist Missionary Union** (ABMU), having established relationships with Filipino Baptist students. When the ABMU decided to enter the **Philippine** field after the Spanish-American War, Lund was one of the first missionaries appointed. In 1900, he founded the American Baptist mission among the Visayas at Jaro. At length he took charge of the **Bible school** at Jaro and taught preaching and Baptist doctrine from 1900 to 1912. His **theology** was dogmatic and anti-Catholic, as revealed in over 200 tracts, a Bible dictionary in Visayan (1931), and translations of the New Testament into Panayan, Cebuan, and Samaryan. He edited the journal *Revista Homiletica* (*Homiletic Review*) for many years and was awarded an honorary doctorate by Des Moines University in 1913.

– M –

MABIE, HENRY CLAY (1847–1918). American Baptist minister and educator, born in Belvidere, Illinois. Influenced by **Charles Hill Roe**, he was educated at the University of Chicago where he received the B.A. and B.D. He was ordained at Rockford, Illinois, in 1869 and served there as **pastor** (1869–1873), and later at Oak Park, Illinois (1873–1876). In 1876, Mabie moved to First Baptist, Brookline, Massachusetts (1876–1879), and from there he went to First Baptist, Indianapolis, Indiana (1879–1884); Belvidere, Illinois (1884–1885); First Baptist, St. Paul, Minnesota (1885–1888); and Central Baptist Church, Minneapolis (1885–1890). In 1890, Mabie was named corresponding secretary of the **American Baptist Missionary Union**, where he served until 1908. After leaving the mission board, he served as Davis Professor of Systematic Theology at Rochester Theological Seminary (1908–1909), and subsequently at the Seminary as lecturer on the theory and practice of **missions**. In his retirement, he lectured across the United States on various university and seminary campuses, including a number of distinguished lectureships, one of which was published as *Unshaken Kingdom* (1917). His "Personal Manifesto," delivered in 1917, included a full-blown declaration of **religious liberty** and the purposes of **voluntary** organizations as *ecclesiolae in ecclesia*. His best remembered work is *The Meaning and Message of the Cross* (1906).

MACAU. Baptist work in Macau dates from 1836, when **J. Lewis Shuck** went there for the **Baptist Board of Foreign Missions**. In 1910, a preexisting independent **mission** in Macau was assumed by the **Southern Baptists**, and their work began in earnest. With the flood of refugees from mainland **China** after 1949, missionary staffing was increased and included many of the missionaries formerly in China. In 1952, the **Hong Kong**–Macau Baptist Mission was organized, which evolved into the Hong Kong Baptist Association. As of 2006, there were six churches with 750 members in the Igreja Baptista de Macau and a congregation of about 150 members, the Igreja Baptista Bama, related to Burmese Baptists.

The U.S. **Conservative Baptist** Foreign Mission Society also established a mission in Macau in 1986. Still largely considered a mission field for Baptists, Macau has three congregations with about 80 church members associated with the Igreja Baptista Conservator. *See also* HONG KONG.

MACEDONIA. Baptist work in Macedonia can be dated from 1928, when the Methodist congregation at Radovis turned to the Baptists because the Methodists were not legally recognized. That same year, Vinko Vacek visited Skopje, the capital of Macedonia, baptized several persons, and established **missions** throughout the region. Later, beginning in 1936, Macedonian congregations were an outgrowth of missionary work of the Belgrade church and part of the Baptist Union of Yugoslavia. The ravages of civil war in the wake of the 1991 dissolution of Yugoslavia left the Baptist movement greatly reduced. In 1991, the Sojuz na Hristijanite-Baptisti vo Republika Makedonija (Union of the Baptist Christians in the Republic of Macedonia) was formed.

As of 1995, there were two congregations with less than 50 members, which are related to Sojuz na Hristijanite-Baptisti vo Republika Makedonija.

MACEDONIA WORLD BAPTIST MISSIONS. Founded in 1967, Macedonia World Missions has work in 16 countries with about 65 missionaries overseas. With headquarters in Lawrenceville, Georgia, the **mission** publishes *Focus on the Field*.

MACEDONIAN MISSIONARY SERVICE. Founded in 1973 by Harold Williams (1936–) and Leon Jasper (1936–), the Macedonian Missionary Service has work in 30 countries involving about 40 short-term missionaries. Major support is derived from churches affiliated with the **American Baptist Association**. The organization is headquartered in Lakeland, Florida, and publishes the *Macedonian Call*.

MACINTOSH, DOUGLAS CLYDE (1877–1948). Canadian and, later, American Baptist minister and theologian, born at Breadalbane, Ontario. Macintosh served **mission** congregations in the Baptist Convention of Ontario and Quebec, after which he was educated at McMaster University and the University of Chicago, where he earned the Ph.D. degree. Macintosh taught for two years at Brandon College in Manitoba, where he organized the Department of Theology, and then he took a position in **theology** at Yale Divinity School in the United States. Ordained at the Hyde Park Baptist Church in Chicago, he became the Timothy Dwight Professor at Yale. Macintosh evolved into one of the leading **liberal** thinkers of his era, espousing first a pragmatism, and later an empirical, approach to theology. In the 1930s, he was involved in a celebrated case with the U.S. government over his application for U.S. citizenship, which was denied because he refused to take an oath to bear arms in defense of the United States. His position was that he was loyal ultimately to God in such matters. Among his 18 published books are *The Reasonableness of Christianity* (1925) and *The Problem of Religious Knowledge* (1940).

MACKENZIE, ALEXANDER (1822–1892). Scottish and, later, Canadian Baptist political leader, born in Logierait, **Scotland**. Trained as a stonemason, in 1842, he emigrated to **Canada** settling at Port Sarnia in Upper Canada as a builder. He became editor in 1852 of the **liberal** *Lambden Shield*, and in 1851, he was elected to the provincial parliament. With the establishment of the Dominion of Canada in 1867, Mackenzie was elected to the House of Commons (under dual representation) and became a leader in the first Liberal government, 1867–1878. Among his outstanding achievements as the second prime minister of Canada (1872–1878) were the building of the Canadian Pacific Railroad, which he personally advocated, and the establishment of the Supreme Court of Canada. Known for his economic liberalism, social egalitarianism, and mistrust of institutional authority, he successfully achieved uniform elections and the secret ballot in Canada. A strict temperance advocate, his government pushed through the Canada Temperance Act in 1870, and the unpopularity of the legislation was a factor in the ultimate defeat of his government. Mackenzie, known as a religiously pious man, joined a Baptist congregation in Irvine, Scotland, which was influenced by the **Haldane** brothers. Later in Canada, he was an active member of the Bunyan Baptist Church near Sarnia, Ontario, where he led in worship services. While in Ottawa, Mackenzie attended First Baptist Church on Parliament Hill. When he moved to Toronto, he became a member of historic Jarvis Street Baptist Church. Mackenzie followed the pattern of leaders like **R. A. Fyfe** in advocating a **voluntary** religious system.

MACLAREN, ALEXANDER (1826–1910). English Baptist minister, born in Glasgow, **Scotland**. He was educated at Stepney College and first served the church at Portland Chapel, Southampton. In 1858, he went to Union Chapel, Manchester, where he remained until 1903. At Union Chapel, Maclaren became the premier expository preacher of his day and attracted throngs of hearers. He disdained pastoral work, keeping records, organization, and elaborate music. He was twice elected to the presidency of the **Baptist Union** and presided over the first congress of the **Baptist World Alliance** at London in 1905. Maclaren published 32 volumes of sermons, as well as works on mysticism, religious equality, and Free Church history. His literary popularity extended to North America, where his expository materials were used across Protestantism.

MACLAY, ARCHIBALD (1778–1860). American Baptist minister, born in Killearn, **Scotland**. Maclay came under the influence of **Robert Haldane**, who assisted him in preparing for the **ministry**. His first work was as a supply preacher in Fifeshire. As a Congregationalist, Maclay took an appointment as a missionary to **Jamaica**, but owing to government opposition, he went to New York instead. He started Congregational Church on Rose Street in that city, but after studying the **Scriptures** was led to Baptist sentiments. He and friends then began the Tabernacle Baptist Church (later Mulberry Street Church), and this congregation prospered for many years under Maclay's leadership (1809–1837). He was heavily involved in **voluntary associations**, notably the **Bible** society movement. He left his pastorate in 1837 to become a general agent for the American and Foreign Bible Society. Dissatisfied with translation policies in the society, Maclay assisted in establishing in 1850 the American Bible Union, a breakaway movement to protect Baptist emphases in translation. His literary efforts produced works about Bible translation, hymnology, and published sermons.

MACNEILL, JESSE JAI (1913–1965). American **black Baptist** minister and educator, born in North Little Rock, Arkansas. He was educated at Shurtleff College, Union Theological Seminary, and Columbia University. His first **ministry** was pastoral, serving Tabernacle Baptist Church, Alton, Illinois (1932–1939), after which he became editor of young people's literature with the **Sunday School** Publishing Board of the **National Baptist Convention, U.S.A.** (1943–1944). In 1944, MacNeill became dean of the School of Religion at Bishop College and also completed his seminary degree at Virginia Union School of Theology. He became involved in the World Council of Churches (WCC) in 1947; as a member of the WCC, he attended the Ecumenical Institute at Bossey. He gave international lectures at the **Baptist World Alliance** Youth Meeting in Stockholm, Sweden, in 1949, and was a consultant to W. A. Visser't Hooft (1900–1985) for the Second Assembly of the WCC in 1954. MacNeill served as **pastor** at Tabernacle Baptist Church in Detroit, Michigan (1947–1961), and pioneered **ecumenical** activity in that metropolitan area. At the American Baptist Seminary of the West (1961–1965), he was the first black faculty member appointed in any American Baptist theological school. Through travel seminars, personal advocacy, and membership in urban and statewide councils of churches, MacNeill became one of the foremost black Baptist ecumenists of the 20th century.

MADAGASCAR. As early as 1813, American Baptist pioneer missionaries **Adoniram Judson** and **Luther Rice** planned a Baptist **mission** in Madagascar. Independent Baptists from the United States began a mission in the country in 1932, which embodied a split from an earlier mission established by the London Missionary Society. The **Conservative Baptist** Foreign Mission Society likewise entered Madagascar in 1966, with work at Antananarivo, Fianarantsoa, and Mahajanga. Finally, the Southern Baptist **Foreign Mission Board** began its mission in 1987.

As of 2006 there were about 55 churches with 3,000 members associated with the Association of Bible Baptist Churches in Madagascar. The Malagasy Baptist Association is associated with the Conservative Baptists.

MAINSTREAM. A 20th-century **evangelical** renewal movement among the churches of the **Baptist Union of Great Britain and Ireland** (BU). In 1977–1978, in response to the perceived numerical and spiritual decline in the BU, and somewhat as a successor to the **Baptist Revival Fellowship**, a group of pastors and educators (many of whom were associated with Spurgeon's College) took to developing a fervent commitment to the gospel as articulated in the Declaration of Principle and the program and work of the Baptist denomination. Taking a centrist approach, the leaders avoided the extremes of the charismatic movement and Separatist tendencies. Mainstream became a series of meetings typically following the formal sessions of the annual BU assemblies, featuring exciting worship, drama, and evangelical speakers. Prominent leaders of Mainstream included Raymond Brown, principal at Spurgeon's College; Paul Beasley-Murray; David Coffey, who served as secretary; and Jack Ramsbottom of Kidlington. By the 1980s, Mainstream became a major force in the makeover of the BU, tracking through subscribers to its *Newsletter*. Gradually, the charismatic **pastors** in the BU made inroads into Mainstream, forging a diverse alliance with more traditional evangelicals. In the decades of the 1980s and 1990s, Mainstream embraced B. R. White at Regent's Park, Douglas McBain, John Briggs, and Steve Chalke. From 1980, the Swanick Conferences were to become major features of the Mainstream movement and concentration was placed upon influencing the structures of the BU.

MAINSTREAM BAPTIST NETWORK. An influence group of theologically moderate Baptists founded in 1997 in Oklahoma. Leaders like Bruce Prescott, Dan S. Hobbs, Pat Clement, and Bob Stephenson from leading Oklahoma congregations in Oklahoma City, Norman, and Shawnee, organized the Mainstream movement to oppose the **fundamentalist**-resurgent takeover of **Southern Baptist** agencies and institutions. They strongly oppose biblical inerrancy and changes to the "**Baptist Faith and Message**" (1963 edition, largely authored by Oklahoma Baptist minister, Herchel H. Hobbs); they affirm **women** in ministry and **ecumenical** Christianity. Based originally in Oklahoma, the movement has grown to include Baptists in Texas, Alabama, Georgia, Louisiana, and Missouri. Mainstream groups later formed in Virginia, North Carolina, South Carolina, Tennessee, Illinois, Florida, Mississippi, and Arkansas. At one time, Texas Baptist leaders like **Herbert Reynolds** and Richard Jackson proposed that the Mainstream group might become a new, moderate Baptist movement in the U.S. Other

Texas Baptists, like Phil Lineberger of Sugarlands, Texas, are influential in the developing coalition of organizations. Affiliated to the Mainstream Network are state Baptist papers in North Carolina, Texas, Kentucky, and Missouri, and nationally, the Associated Baptist Press. Organizational links exist with the Baptist History and Heritage Society, the Roger Williams Fellowship, and the Baptist Joint Committee on Religious Liberty. Bruce Prescott, a pastor from Texas, was elected executive director of Mainstream Network in 1998, and the network publishes a newsletter, the *Mainstream Messenger* (1998–). From time to time, the network sponsors regional events (Dallas, 2007) to raise awareness of its objectives. The Mainstream Network closely monitors Southern Baptist life, especially terminations of missionaries and institutional staff for perceived theological reasons.

MALAWI. In 1892, Australian Baptists formed a mission near Bantered, which was the first Baptist effort in the former British colony of Nyasaland. Shortly afterward, the **Seventh Day Baptists** entered the country (in 1899) and developed about 50 congregations; also, in 1900 from the United States came the **National Baptist Convention of the United States of America**, eventually helping to form the African Baptist Assembly in 1945. **Southern Baptists** entered Malawi in 1959, and an outgrowth of Southern Baptist work was the formation of the Baptist Convention of Malawi in 1970.

As of 2006, there were 787 churches and 72,810 members affiliated with the African Baptist Assembly, Malawi, Inc.; 1,375 churches with 175,000 members affiliated with the Baptist Convention of Malawi; and 300 churches with 19,000 members affiliated with the Evangelical Baptist Church of Malawi.

MALAYSIA. The first Baptists in Malaya, later Malaysia, came from Shadow, **China**, in 1905. Church development began in 1937 at Aloe Star and Peek. In 1952, the U.S. **Southern Baptists** organized a Malayan Mission with stations at Kuala Lumpur and Singapore. As the China mission field closed, both North American personnel and Chinese leadership immigrated to Malaya and strengthened the work there. The church in Kuala Lumpur, organized in 1952, became a point of church planting for all of Malaya. In the 1960s and 1970s,

Baptist missions were extended into Borneo, Sarawak, and Brunei. In 1953, the Malaya Baptist Theological Seminary opened at Penning. As of 2006, there were 324 churches and 22,853 members affiliated with the Malaysia Baptist Convention. The Convention publishes the *Malayan Baptist* (1920–).

MALI. Beginning in 1951, the Evangelical Baptist Missions of the United States began a work in what is now Mali in the city of Gao and another at Timbuktu in 1952. In 1964, **Conservative Baptists** from the United States opened a mission and **Southern Baptists** entered the country in 1983.

As of 2006, there was one congregation with 120 members in the Baptist community of Mali and one church with 53 members in the Eglise Baptiste du Septicemia Jour (**Seventh Day Baptist**).

MALTA. Malta has a small community of Baptists of recent origin. The **Baptist Bible Fellowship** opened a **mission** in 1983. As of 2001, there was one congregation affiliated with the Bible Baptist Fellowship with less than 50 members and one congregation with 80 members from the Evangelical Baptist Church (established in 1926).

MANLY FAMILY. A prominent family in U.S. Southern Baptist life in the 19th and early 20th centuries. The first of the family was **Basil Manly Sr.** (1798–1868), born in Pittsborough, North Carolina. He was educated at the College of Charleston, graduated with honors, and was ordained to serve the Edgefield, South Carolina, Church (1822–1826). He became **pastor** of prestigious First Baptist Charleston, which he served until 1837. Manly was the president of the University of Alabama for 18 years and enlarged its interests greatly. During this period, Manly was active in Alabama state Baptist work and prepared the resolution in 1844, which posed a hypothetical case to the **General Missionary Convention** to determine if they would appoint a slaveholder as a missionary. This was considered inflammatory, and the responses led to a hardened position of southern regionalism, which Manly advocated. When his term as president of the university ended, Manly returned to Charleston to serve the Wentworth Street Church in 1855, and after a short time he served as an **evangelist** in Alabama. He was active with his son,

Basil, in establishing the Southern Baptist Theological Seminary at Greenville, South Carolina, in 1859, and in promoting what became Furman University.

Basil Manly Jr. (1825–1892), the son of Basil Sr., was also a **Southern Baptist** minister and educator, born at Edgefield, South Carolina. He was educated at the University of Alabama and Newton Theological Institution, and graduated from Princeton Theological Seminary in 1847. He served in the pastoral ministry of small churches in Sumter County, Alabama (1848–1850), and later First Baptist Church, Richmond, Virginia (1850–1854). He founded the Richmond Female Institute in 1854 and was its president from 1854 to 1859. In 1859, **James Boyce** asked Manly to join the inaugural faculty of Southern Baptist Theological Seminary in Greenville, South Carolina, as professor of Old Testament. Manly drew up the seminary's doctrinal basis, the "Abstract of Principles." During the American Civil War, he served various churches and in 1871–1877 was president of Georgetown College in Kentucky. During this same era, he helped to establish the Southern Baptist **Sunday School Board** and was its first president. In 1877, he returned to Southern Seminary, now in Louisville, Kentucky, and during his final term (until 1892), he helped to build the outstanding reputation of its faculty. His book *The Biblical Doctrine of Inspiration* (1888) helped to countermand the difficulties raised by his colleague, **Crawford H. Toy**. Manly was a gifted and prolific writer of about 20 hymns, the most famous of which is "Soldiers of Christ in Truth Arrayed." His literary efforts produced catechetical aids for young people, historical treatises, published sermons, and collections of hymns.

Finally, the family included **Charles Manly** (1837–1924), second son of Basil Manly Sr. He was educated at the University of Alabama and Princeton Theological Seminary. Charles was ordained to serve the Tuscaloosa, Alabama Baptist Church from 1859 to 1871, after which he was pastor at Murfreesboro, Tennessee (1871–1873), and Staunton, Virginia (1873–1880). While in Alabama, he taught and was president at Alabama Female College, and in Tennessee, he was president of Union University. He was pastor of the Greenville, South Carolina, Church from 1880 to 1881, after which for 18 years he was president at Furman University (1881–1897). Having set the school on firm foundations, Manly returned to pastoral **ministry**, serving churches in Lexington, Missouri, and Lexington, Virginia from 1897 to 1914.

MANNING, EDWARD (1766–1851). Canadian Baptist minister, born in Ireland. He was converted under the **evangelistic ministry** of Congregationalist John Payzant (1749–1834) and ordained to serve the Congregational church at Cornwallis, Nova Scotia. He embraced Baptist sentiments and was baptized by **Thomas H. Chipman** in 1798. Soon thereafter, he brought his church into the Baptist association, and he served the congregation for over 50 years. Considered one of the "fathers" of the Maritime Baptists, Manning was one of the founders of Horton Academy and Acadia University and a historian of the Maritimes, supplying **David Benedict** with materials for his *History of the Baptists* (1848).

MANNING, JAMES (1738–1791). American Baptist minister and educator, born at Elizabethtown, New Jersey. Manning was educated at the Baptist academy at Hopewell, New Jersey, under **Isaac Eaton** and the College of New Jersey, earning the highest honors in his class. After a year of travel in the colonies, Manning accepted the invitation of the **Philadelphia Baptist Association** to start a grammar school in Warren, Rhode Island. This he did in 1764, and commenced a new Baptist congregation as well. Upon the securing of a charter in that year, Manning became the first president of the College of Rhode Island. In 1767, he assisted in the formation of the Warren (Rhode Island) Baptist Association. The decision was made to move the college to Providence in 1770, and Manning set about building the campus. In addition, he accepted the call of First Baptist Church in Providence and superintended the construction of their meetinghouse in 1774, one of the most impressive church edifices of the era. In 1786, Manning was chosen to represent Rhode Island in the Confederation Congress; he later shifted to support the new constitution in 1787 and used his considerable influence to carry the support of the state. His longtime friendship with the **Nicholas Brown** family made possible the firm establishment of the College of Rhode Island, and the family later honored Manning by building the chapel in his memory. *See also* ARCHITECTURE, BAPTIST CHURCH.

MARANATHA BAPTIST MISSION. Founded in 1961 by James W. Crumpton, Maranatha Baptist Mission is an **independent** Baptist overseas agency which relates to the Independent Fundamental Baptist Churches. As of 1995, the organization had missions in 24 countries, including **Australia**, Europe, Africa, South America, and the Far East, with 1,180 missionaries. Headquarters is located in Natchez, Mississippi, and the mission publishes *Maranatha Publications*.

MARING, NORMAN HILL (1914–1998). American Baptist minister and church historian, born at Crozer Theological Seminary in Upland, Pennsylvania. He was educated at Furman University and the Collegiate Division of the Eastern Baptist Seminary, after which he earned the M.A. and Ph.D. degrees at the University of Maryland under Richard Hofstadter and Wesley Gewehr. Following his theological degree from Eastern, he served churches in Berwyn and Cumberland, Maryland. In 1948, Maring became professor of church history at Eastern and served the school for 35 years. From 1972 to 1978, he was academic dean of the seminary. Maring was a valued resource for three generations of American Baptists, particularly in the areas of denominational **polity** and identity. He offered a "conservative, but progressive" theological position and was mentor to several senior American Baptist leaders. His outstanding publication, *A Baptist Manual of Polity and Practice* (1963, 1991), has been used broadly in the Baptist family, and his *Baptists in New Jersey: A Study in Transition* (1964) was hailed for its approach to regional church history. In retirement, Maring served on the American Baptist Denominational Identity Commission (1984–1986) and taught at Southern Baptist and Southeastern Baptist seminaries.

MARKS, DAVID (1805–1845). American Freewill Baptist minister and **evangelist**, born in Shandaken, New York. In 1818, he walked more than 300 miles and returned to enroll at Brown University, only to be disappointed with an inadequate offer of financial assistance. Marks was baptized in 1819 and embarked upon an itinerant **ministry** among **Freewill Baptist** churches in western New York and Canada at only 15 years old. Known as the "boy preacher," he finally settled in a pastorate at Portsmouth, New Hampshire (1834–1836), but moved to plant a congregation in Rochester, New York (1836–1837), and afterward at Varysburg, New York (1838–1842). Marks was the principal founder of the Freewill Baptist Book Concern for his denomination. In 1842, he moved to Oberlin, Ohio, to further his studies, establishing high schools at Strafford, New Hampshire, and Chester, Ohio. Ultimately, the strain of his efforts took its toll, and he died at 40 years old. A remarkable feat for his age, he wrote on religious experience, catechetical subjects, and hymnology.

MARNEY, CARLYLE (1916–1978). Southern Baptist minister, born at Harriman, Tennessee. He was educated at Carson Newman College and Southern Baptist Theological Seminary. In 1946, Marney received the Th.D. degree from Southern Seminary in church history, his dissertation entitled, "The Rise of Ecclesiological Externalism to 337 A.D." He served churches at Ft. Knox (1941–1944), and Immanuel, Paducah, (1946–1948) Kentucky; Austin, Texas (1948–1958); and Myers Park Baptist Church in Charlotte, North Carolina (1958–1967). During his Texas pastorate, Marney served as adjunct professor in Christian Ethics at Austin Theological Seminary and published an acclaimed book, *Faith in Conflict* (1957). In 1967, with assistance from foundations and the denomination, he opened at Lake Junaluska, North Carolina, the Interpreter's House, a **ministry** of renewal, instruction, and self-integration. Openly critical of denominational structures and alienated from the administration of the **Southern Baptist Convention**, Marney moved in an **ecumenical** direction and was increasingly critical of racism and **fundamentalism**. He became a nationally recognized lecturer and commentator on religious experience. His academic activities included serving as adjunct professor of preaching at Duke University Divinity School from 1972 to 1978 and as visiting professor of humanities at Virginia Military Institute in 1978. In 1976, he was awarded an honorary doctorate at the University of Glasgow, largely for his work in clergy professional rehabilitation. Marney was the author of over 20 books, including *The Recovery of the Person* (1963).

MARSHALL, ANDREW (c.1755–1856). American **black Baptist** minister, born in South Carolina, the son of an English soldier and a slave woman. He was raised on a plantation and owned by several masters. He purchased his freedom in 1785 and became a Christian about the same time. When President George Washington (1732–1799) toured the southern states in the 1790s, Marshall accompanied him as a servant and wrote of his experiences. Considered one of the outstanding preachers of his era, Marshall succeeded **Andrew Bryan** in 1806 as **pastor** of Second Baptist Church (later named the First African Baptist Church) in Savannah, Georgia, which he led to over 3,000 members. During the course of his **ministry**, he is said to have baptized 3,800 persons and seen over 4,000 converted. About 1820, Marshall was whipped publicly for advocating the plight of his slave brothers, and this increased his notoriety in Georgia. His theology was Calvinistic, based upon an appreciation of **John Gill**, the English Baptist writer. In order to raise money for a new building for his church, Marshall toured the northern states in 1856, preaching in many prominent Baptist pulpits. His funeral procession was one mile long with over 58 carriages in train, including persons of both races.

MARSHALL, DANIEL (1706–1784). American Baptist minister and **evangelist**, born in Windsor, Connecticut. He was converted in 1745 under the preaching of George Whitefield (1714–1770) and became a self-proclaimed **missionary** to the Mohawk Indians of upstate New York. In 1746, Marshall moved to Conecocheague, Pennsylvania, and then to Winchester, Virginia. In Winchester in 1754, he joined a frontier Baptist congregation related to the **Philadelphia Baptist Association**. About 1756, in response to French frontier hostilities, he moved to Hughwarry, North Carolina, and then to neighboring Abbot's Creek, where he was ordained **pastor**. Closely associated with **Shubael Stearns**, his brother-in-law, Marshall became an itinerant **Separate Baptist** pastor in the next few years, serving Beaver Creek, South Carolina, and then Horse Creek, Georgia, near Augusta. At length, he was ordered not to preach in the colonies of South Carolina and Georgia. But, against government decrees, he settled in 1771 at Kiokee, Georgia, and conducted a successful ministry, organizing the first Baptist congregation in the colony. Daniel's wife, Martha Stearns Marshall (fl. 1750), was said to be a church planter and evangelist herself, of no little reputation. In 1784, Marshall presided over the inaugural meeting of the Georgia Baptist Association.

MARSHALL, LAURENCE HENRY (1882–1953). English and, later, Canadian Baptist minister and educator, born at Louth, England. Initially educated at Rawdon College, he graduated in arts and divinity from the University of London, gaining both the Dr. Williams and **Baptist Union** scholarships. He spent two years studying in **Germany**, first under C. G. A. von Harnack (1851–1930) and G. A. Deissman (1866–1937) at Berlin, then under Adolf Julicher (1857–1938) and Wilhelm Heitmuller (1869–1926) in Marburg. After postgraduate work, he was **pastor** at Prince's Gate, Liverpool (1911–1919), and Queen's Road, Coventry (1920–1925). In 1925, Marshall was elected to the vacant chair in theology at McMaster University in Toronto, a move that caused much controversy in Ontario. **T. T. Shields** led an attack upon Marshall's reputation in the Baptist Convention of Ontario and Quebec, which prompted Marshall to deliver an able defense of **religious liberty**. Although the McMaster administration won the floor fight at the convention, Marshall returned to England in 1930 to become pastor at Victoria Road, Leicester. In 1936, he returned to Rawdon as tutor in New Testament and pastoral theology and became principal in 1948 on the death of **A. C. Underwood**. Marshall's book, *The Challenge of New Testament Ethics* (1946), was long considered a classic in the field. In **Canada**, his appointment at McMaster became a symbol of the **liberal** tradition adopted at the university.

MARSHMAN, HANNAH (1767–1847). English Baptist missionary, born at Bristol, England. Educated in local schools and orphaned at 12, she lived in London and was baptized at Westbury Leigh Church. In 1791, she married **Joshua Marshman** and they settled at Bristol, where Joshua studied at Bristol Baptist Academy. The couple offered themselves for **missionary** service and embarked for **India** in 1799, settling at Serampore with **William Carey**. Aside from her family responsibilities, Hannah helped to organize the school plan that her husband initiated. She returned to England in 1820 for two years, during which time she promoted the Indian schools and the Serampore Mission. Upon her return to India, she took over the administration of Serampore's female schools after **William Ward** died, and she assumed the care of several families in the Christian community. Hannah Marshman is credited among Christians and educators in

India with introducing and advocating **women**'s education. She is recalled throughout the century as a role model for aspiring missionary candidates.

MARSHMAN, JOSHUA (1768–1837). English Baptist missionary, born at Westbury Leigh, England. He was educated in primary school and read very widely. At Bristol in 1794, he took charge of a school and was baptized at Broadmead Baptist Church. He studied at Bristol Baptist College with an emphasis in Hebrew and Syriac. In 1799, Marshman and his wife, **Hannah Marshman**, offered themselves to the **Baptist Missionary Society** for service in **India**. He worked with **William Carey** in translation and the operation of boarding schools with his wife. With Carey and **William Ward**, Marshman was considered part of the "Serampore Trio." Following an extensive study of Chinese, Marshman produced a Chinese grammar in 1814 and the first Chinese **Bible** in 1821. His literary efforts were wide-ranging on topics relating to Christian witness in India, education, translation missions, and a memoir of the first Serampore missionaries (1827). Brown University in Rhode Island conferred the doctor of divinity degree on him in 1811.

MARTIN, JAMES (1821–1877). English Baptist minister and scholar, born at Hackney, England. He was educated at Madras House School and later at Stepney College under **Benjamin Davies** and **F. W. Gotch**. After his graduation from the University of London, he studied under Dr. Ward's Trust in **Germany** at the University of Bonn in 1847. Martin served pastorates at Lymington (1848–1855); Charlotte Chapel, Edinburgh (1856–1858); Derby Road, Nottingham (1858–1869); and then Collins Street, Melbourne, Australia (1869–1877). Martin was a catalyst for the publication of German theological scholarship into English, translating 20 works for the Edinburgh publisher, T and T Clark, notably his contemporaries Karl F. Keil (1807–1888), Franz Delitsch's (1813–1890) Old Testament commentaries, and E. W. Hengstenburg's (1802–1869) *Christology of the Old Testament* (1856).

MARTINIQUE. Martinique, formerly part of the French West Indies, has a small Baptist population. The first Baptists were likely associated with **Evangelical Baptist Missions**, beginning in 1945. This group numbers about four churches and 300 members. In 1977, **Southern Baptists** began missionary work on the island as part of their work in **Guadaloupe**; in 1978, the work in Martinique was separated from Guadaloupe to form a new mission **association**.

As of 2001, there were five churches with about 200 members associated with the Association des Eglises Evangelical Baptistes.

MARTYROLOGY, BAPTIST. From the earliest period of Baptist development there have been instances of persecution and loss of life for one's religious principles, or in the conduct of **ministry** and missionary service. One of the founders of the **General Baptist** persuasion in England, **Thomas Helwys**, likely died in prison for his religious convictions. Others in the 17th century who gave their lives include Benjamin and William Hewling, grandsons of **William Kiffin**. Benjamin (c. 1663–1685) and William (c. 1665–1685) took up arms against the Duke of York (later King James II) because of his perceived Catholic tendencies, were imprisoned at Newgate, and were executed at Lyme and Taunton, respectively, in September 1685. The last woman to be executed in England for her religious views was a Baptist, Elizabeth Gaunt (fl. 1660–1685). She was found guilty of harboring a man named Burton who was suspected of complicity in the Rye House Plot, and she was tried and burnt at the stake at Tyburn near London on 23 October 1685.

While there is ample evidence of persecution, loss of property and position, and corporal punishment in the early American scene, there is no known case of martyrdom among Baptists in the American colonies in the 17th or 18th centuries. A famous example of punishment of Baptists involved **Obadiah Holmes**, who joined Joseph Crandall and **John Clarke** in 1651 on a visit to Lynn, Massachusetts, to provide spiritual care for a blind friend, William Witter (fl. 1650). When the authorities found out the plan, they imprisoned Holmes, and after a trial in which he refused to pay his fine of 30 pounds, he was flogged 30 times. In the next century, **James Ireland** in Virginia was imprisoned for preaching in Culpeper, Virginia; while he was in prison, attempts were made upon his life to halt his witness.

It is in the missionary context that several Baptist ministers and laypersons lost their lives in the 19th century. **Lott Carey** was killed in an explosion in **Liberia**, apparently the victim of an insurrection in 1829. Many writers hold that **Ann Hasseltine Judson** and **Sarah Hall Boardman**, to mention just two missionary wives, essentially died for the cause of **missions** in **Burma**.

A famous story among the Baptist communities of Eastern Europe concerns a boy named "Frank" who in the 1870s attended the **Sunday School** started by Henry and Amalie **Novotny** in Prague. Warned not to return to the Baptist church, the boy was beaten and abused by a local Catholic priest who opposed Protestantism. Frank's love for the **Scriptures** and Sunday School were widely known, and after he died from his injuries, he became a folk hero among Sunday School students across Czechoslovakia.

During much of their history, Baptists in **Russia** have suffered greatly from government persecution. Pastors such as Andreas Erstratenko (1863–?), who was banished to Siberia in 1891 and remained to begin a church there, and Ivan Savelieff (1858–?), who was banished from Transcaucasia to Siberia from 1894 to 1904, illustrate the harsh treatment inflicted on Baptists by the government of Imperial Russia. Although many names are not available, it is certain that numerous Baptists lost their lives in prisons during the Stalinist purges and later. For instance, N. Odintsov (1871–1939) suffered a violent death for **evangelical** labors, as did Peter Vins, a missionary in Siberia who died in a prison in 1929, a victim of the "anti-God" law of that year.

Likewise, **China** was the scene of Baptist martyrdoms. During the period of the Boxer Rebellion (1900), in Shansi Province, 112 of the Chinese Christian community were killed for their connection with the English Baptist Mission. Choa Hsi Mao, with his wife and sister and mother, were beheaded in July 1900.

Two outstanding examples of martyrdom occurred in the **Philippines** and **Bolivia** in the 1940s. On the Island of Pansy in the Philippines, American Baptists maintained hospitals, which were placed in jeopardy by the advance of the Japanese army in April 1942. In accord with the "scorched earth" policy of the Allied forces, the hospital buildings were destroyed and the missionary personnel fled to a prearranged mountain retreat called "Hopedale." For several months, up to 22 people survived, until the Japanese located them and executed 11 missionaries and relatives on December 19, 1943. Those who gave their lives were a nurse, Jennie Clare Adams (1896–1943); a teacher, James Howard Lovell (1896–1943); Lovell's wife, Charm Moore Lovell (1895–1943); an educational administrator, Dorothy Antoinette Dowell (1889–1943); a teacher, Singe Amelia Erickson (1898–1943); a medical doctor, Frederick Waller Meyer (1892–1943); Meyer's wife, Ruth Schacht Meyer (1892–1943); a college administrator, Francis Howard Rose (1884–1943); Rose's wife, Gertrude Coombs Rose (1885–1943); an evangelist, Earle Frederick Rounds (1901–1943); Rounds's wife, Louise Cummings Rounds (1904–1943); and the Rounds's son, Earle Douglas Rounds (1934–1943).

A celebrated Baptist martyrdom occurred in Bolivia in 1949. While on a preaching tour of the interior altiplano, the Reverend Norman Dabbs (1912–1949), a Canadian Baptist missionary, and seven other Bolivian Baptist leaders were stoned and killed, while six others were left for dead on 8 August 1949 at Merk'Amaya. The murder of Dabbs became an instant international incident, and the Christian community responded with horror. Many new leaders in Bolivia were recruited for ministry as a result of the martyrdom.

Baptist leaders in **Korea** lost their lives in the military advance of the Communists following World War II. At a rate comparatively higher than other Korean Christian groups, Baptists were martyred in significant numbers: in 1950, 61 Baptists were killed by the Communists. A specially remembered incident involved the president of the Korean Baptist Convention, Jong-Duk Yi (1884–1950), who was shot to death in the marsh of the Kum on 28 September 1950.

More recently, **Southern Baptist** missionaries to the **Dominican Republic**, Paul E. (1932–1971) and Nancy (1935–1971) Potter, were killed at their home in Santiago on July 7, 1971. The Potters had been serving in the Dominican Republic since 1966, opening the mission station in Santiago. The deaths were apparent homicides and may have been related to robbery. While not directly associated with Christian witness, the Potters died in the course of their **ministry**.

Over the three and a half centuries of their development, Baptists have suffered persecution; estrangement of goods, property, and family; and death for their faith. In this regard, they fit the pattern of religious dissenters through the course of Christian history.

MASON, FRANCIS (1799–1874). American Baptist missionary, born at York, England. In his youth, Mason was an apprenticed shoemaker, self-taught in literature and mathematics. He emigrated to the United States in 1818 and studied theology at Newton Theological Institution. He was appointed a missionary to **Burma** in 1829 by the **Baptist Board of Foreign Missions**. Mason settled at Tavoy, replacing **George Dana Boardman**, serving 20 years as a translator, administrator, and seminary teacher. He is especially remembered for the growth of the **mission** at Toungoo: more than 6,000 converts were baptized and over 100 churches begun in a decade under his leadership. In the late 1850s, his wife, Ellen (1817–1894), assumed leadership in the mission and caused a stir by claiming a special revelation from God. From 1865 to 1871, the **American Baptist Missionary Union** withheld its support until Ellen's teachings were withdrawn, ultimately restoring his funding. Mason was a linguistic scholar with few peers, publishing over 30 **Scripture** translations in Pali, Burmese, and Sanskrit. He also published a scientific study on natural life in Burma, historical mission treatises, and mathematical subjects for which he was elected a member of the Royal Asiatic Society. His biography is told in *The Story of a Workingman's Life* (1870).

MASSEE, JASPER CORTENUS (1871–1965). American Baptist minister, born at Marshallville, Georgia. He graduated from Mercer University and attended Southern Baptist Theological Seminary for one year. He served congregations in Kissimmee, Florida (1893–1896); Orlando, Florida (1897–1898); Lancaster, Kentucky (1899–1901); Mansfield, Ohio (1901–1903); Raleigh, North Carolina (1903–1908); Chattanooga, Tennessee (1908–1913); Dayton, Ohio (1913–1919); Brooklyn, New York (1919–1922); and Boston, Massachusetts (1922–1929). Following pastoral ministry, Massee pursued a career as an evangelist and was professor of homiletics at the Eastern Baptist Theological Seminary from 1938 to 1941. Massee perfected an **evangelistic** style that included thematic nights in protracted meetings, pulpit responses to contemporary social phenomena, pledge cards for ethical commitments, and **Bible** exposition. During his pastoral **ministry** at Tremont Temple in Boston, 2,500 persons joined the church in seven years.

With **Curtis L. Laws** and **William B. Riley**, Massee joined the **fundamentalist** crusade in 1920 and became the presiding officer of the newly formed Fundamentals of the Faith Conference at Buffalo in 1920. As president of the Fundamentalist Federation (1920–1925), he led an investigation of Baptist schools to ferret out modernism. Massee, considered a moderate fundamentalist, became increasingly concerned over the bitter spirit of more radical colleagues in the movement, notably **John R. Straton** and **J. Frank Norris**. Opposing a split in the Northern Baptist Convention, Massee left the fundamentalist movement in 1925, blaming the **Baptist Bible Union** for divisiveness in the denomination. He held to five "fundamentals of the faith," and while openly centrist in the denominational struggles, he exhibited anti-intellectual characteristics and opposed the **social gospel**. Massee was a widely circulated author, publishing over 30 books on topics ranging from doctrine to ethical issues and sermons.

MASTER'S MISSION, THE. An independent, doctrinally Baptistic missionary organization, founded in 1979 by Paul Tisdale and Robert Van Campen. Tisdale was a former Africa Inland Missionary in **Kenya**. The Master's Mission currently supports about 40 projects or **missionaries** in Kenya and elsewhere in Africa, and **Mexico**. Its publication is *Mission News*, and the headquarters are located in Robbinsville, North Carolina.

MASTON, THOMAS BUFORD (1897–1988). Texas Baptist educator and ethicist, born in Jefferson County, Tennessee. He was educated at Carson-Newman College and Southwestern Baptist Seminary, where he earned a doctorate in religious education. Later, he earned a Ph.D. at Yale University under H. Richard Niebuhr and also studied with the southern sociologist, Howard Odum. From 1922 to 1963, he taught ethics at Southwestern Baptist Seminary, though he was never ordained to the ministry. Maston was the most influential **Southern Baptist** ethicist of his era, publishing over 25 books, including *Christianity and World Issues* (1957) and *Biblical Ethics* (1967). His work was institutionalized in the establishment of the Christian Life Commission of the Baptist General Convention of Texas in 1950. As a Baptist historian, he is remembered for his 1962 book on **Isaac Backus**, prepared largely from primary sources. The annual T. B.

Maston Lectures, sponsored by the Baptist General Convention of Texas, features outstanding thinkers on various ethical questions.

MATHEWS, SHAILER (1863–1941). American Baptist educator and denominational leader, born at Portland, Maine. He was educated at Colby College and Newton Theological Institution. He began his teaching career at Colby, where he first taught history and later New Testament Interpretation from 1889 to 1897. **Ernest D. Burton** induced him to accept a position at the new University of Chicago where his efforts flourished. Mathews introduced the scientific study of religion and guided the school to a distinctive approach utilizing the social sciences and called the "**Chicago School**." He argued for contextual studies and evolutionary patterns of history to understand Christian dogma. His book *The Faith of Modernism* (1924) was a cogent and positive response to the attacks of **fundamentalists**. Mathews was not ordained, but was one of the shapers of the Northern Baptist Convention and particularly its social action emphases. He was also one of the most popular teachers in the religious lecture circuit of his era. Mathews's published works number over 50 items, notably *The Life of Christ* (1901) and *Creative Christianity* (1935).

MAURITIUS. Originally known as the Isle of France, Baptist work began here with the arrival of **Adoniram Judson** and **Luther Rice** in 1814. For a short time, the American **missionaries** remained on Mauritius until Judson left for **Burma** and Rice returned to the United States. Not until 1978 did Baptists return, via the Southern Baptist **Foreign Mission Board**, among Chinese believers. As of 2001, there was a small association of one church, numbering about 200 members.

MAYS, BENJAMIN ELIJAH (1894–1984). American **black Baptist** minister and educator, born at Epworth, South Carolina. He was educated at South Carolina State College, Bates College, and the University of Chicago, where he received the Ph.D. degree. He taught mathematics at Morehouse College (1921–1924), while also serving as **pastor** at Shiloh Baptist Church in Atlanta, Georgia. From there, Mays moved to teach English at Orangeburg State College in South Carolina (1925–1926). He then served as executive secretary of the

Urban League in Tampa, Florida (1926–1928) and national student secretary of the Y.M.C.A. (1928–1930), and he conducted research on the black church in America for the Institute of Social and Religious Research (1930–1932). In 1934, Mays entered educational administration, his lifelong ministry. He served as dean of the School of Religion of Howard University (1934–1940) and president of Morehouse College (1940–1967). One of the eminent leaders in black higher education, Mays was a consultant to government and private organizations, including the Ford Foundation, the Peace Corps, and the United Nations. He served as president of the United Negro College Fund from 1958 to 1961, and he received over 50 honorary degrees, probably the most among the Baptist family worldwide in any era. Mays was an authority on the black church in America and the symbolic leader of the movement to establish a high standard for black education. He was the author of several published works, including *Seeking to Be Christian in Race Relations* (1957) and *Born to Rebel* (1971).

MCCALL, DUKE KIMBROUGH (1914–). Southern Baptist minister and theological educator, born at Meridian, Mississippi. He was educated at Furman University (B.A.) and Southern Baptist Theological Seminary (Th.M, Ph.D.). He was **pastor** at Broadway Baptist, Louisville, Kentucky (1940–1943), and then he was named president of Baptist Bible Institute (later New Orleans Baptist Theological Seminary). After World War II, McCall took the position of executive secretary of the Executive Committee of the **Southern Baptist Convention** (SBC), the highest-ranking administrator of Southern Baptists. He also served as treasurer of the SBC during that period. In 1951, he became president of Southern Baptist Theological Seminary and remained in that position for 31 years, until he was named chancellor of the seminary (1982–1990). McCall made a significant contribution to Southern Baptist education and convention life. He was the first person to serve as president of two theological seminaries, New Orleans and Southern. At New Orleans, he recommended the transition to a postgraduate identity. In Louisville, he stood against the challenge of several faculty to his appointment prerogative and terminated several faculty in 1958. As executive secretary of the convention, McCall created the senior administration and readied the

SBC for its years of great advance. In 1980, he was elected president of the **Baptist World Alliance**, and he traveled widely on behalf of its interests through 1990. McCall authored several works, including *Broadman Comments: What Is the Church?* (1958) and *A Story of Stewardship* (1990).

MCCLENDON, JAMES WILLIAM (1924–2000). Baptist theologian, born in Louisiana. Mcclendon was educated at the U.S. Naval Academy and took another B.A. at the University of Texas. Later his theological degrees were completed at Southwestern Baptist Seminary and Princeton Seminary, and his doctorate at Southwestern under **Walter T. Conner**. As one of the best prospects in the Southern Baptist family in the 1950s, McClendon was recruited by Golden Gate Baptist Seminary, where he taught until his advocacy of **Martin Luther King Jr.** and the civil rights movement cost him a tenured position. He moved to the Jesuit-related University of San Francisco, until he was fired a second time over his position on the Vietnam War. He then took several short teaching appointments at Stanford, Temple, and Notre Dame universities. From 1970 to 1989, he was professor of theology at the (Episcopal) Church Divinity School of the Pacific and the Graduate Theological Union. Following his formal retirement, he became a Distinguished Scholar in Residence at Fuller Theological Seminary. Always a theological outsider, McClendon was a pacifist who was labeled a "neo-**Anabaptist**" for his usage of the decapitalized term "baptist." He was much taken with narrative approaches to theology and led the critique of foundationalism in the 1980s. He married a second time to a graduate student, Nancey Murphy, also a prominent philosopher of science and an anti-foundationalist. He was the author of a three-volume systematic theology: *Ethics* (1986), *Doctrine* (1994), and *Witness* (2000).

MCCOY, ISAAC (1784–1846). American Baptist missionary, born in Fayette County, Pennsylvania. Lacking an adequate education, he was ordained to the Baptist **ministry** in 1810 at Maria Creek, Indiana, where he was **pastor** from 1810 to 1817. He was appointed by the **Baptist Board of Foreign Missions** (BBFM) to work with the Miami Indians in Illinois and Indiana. In 1822, he moved to Michigan and settled among the Potawatomi Indians and became a government teacher. In 1825, as the government moved the tribes west of the Mississippi, McCoy devised an enlightened plan for an Indian Territory, and he worked for the government during the removal. He operated a **mission** among the Delawares and Shawnees in Kansas in the 1830s. In 1842, McCoy created the American Indian Mission Association to unite all Indian missions. Ultimately, he moved his allegiance from the BBFM to the newly formed Domestic Board of the **Southern Baptist Convention** in 1846. Because of his dealings with the U.S. government, McCoy was often the target of criticism of the anti-missionary Baptists led by **Daniel Parker**.

MCCRACKEN, ROBERT JAMES (1904–1973). Scottish, **Canadian**, and, later, American Baptist minister, born at Motherwell, Scotland. He studied at the University of Glasgow (M.A., B.D.) and in **Scotland** served churches in Edinburgh (1928–1932) and Dennistown (1932–1938). He lectured in theology at the Scottish Baptist College and was a delegate to the Conference on Faith and Order in Edinburgh. In 1938, McCracken moved to McMaster University in Hamilton, Ontario, where he taught theology. In 1946, he succeeded **Harry Emerson Fosdick** as senior **pastor** at Riverside Church in New York City, the most prestigious pulpit among Northern Baptists. He served the church (among whose members was **John D. Rockefeller**) until his retirement in 1967, during which time he also taught homiletics at Union Theological Seminary in New York. McCracken was the author of a number of books, including *The Making of the Sermon* (1956), a popular homiletics textbook, and, following Dr. Fosdick's lead, *What Is Sin? What Is Virtue?* (1966).

MCDONALD, ALEXANDER (1837–1911). Canadian and American Baptist **missionary**, born at Osgoode, Ontario. He was educated at Canadian Literary Institute (later McMaster University) under the tutelage of **Robert A. Fyfe** and a close friend of Robert McLaurin (1839–1912) the first Canadian Baptist overseas missionary. In 1873, McDonald arrived in Ft. Garry (later Winnipeg), Manitoba Territory. Within two years, he established the first Baptist congregation there, which came to be the first in the Canadian West. He started a second church at Stonewall in 1879 and assisted in the constitution of the Red River Association in 1880. In 1882, McDonald transferred to

Grafton, North Dakota, where he served that congregation as a home missionary **pastor**. In 1893, he became the first pastor of the First Baptist Church in Edmonton, Alberta, where he served for two years before commencing a new congregation at Strathcona, near Edmonton. For his many church plantings, he was popularly known as "Pioneer McDonald" and is the parent of the Baptist movement in western **Canada**.

MCGLOTHLIN, WILLIAM JOSEPH (1867–1933). Southern Baptist educator and historian, born at Gallatin, Tennessee. He was educated at Bethel College, Southern Baptist Theological Seminary, and the University of Berlin, where he received his Ph.D. McGlothlin was professor of church history at Southern Baptist Seminary (1894–1919), after which he was president at Furman University (1919–1933). He greatly enlarged Furman and brought it accreditation. The first David T. Porter Professor of Church History at Southern Baptist Seminary (1904–1919), McGlothlin published *Baptist Confessions of Faith* (1910), *Infant Baptism in History* (1915), and *The Course of Christian History* (1917). He was instrumental in critically examining the original documentation exhibiting relationships between Baptists and Swiss **Anabaptists**.

MCKINNEY, BAYLUS BENJAMIN (1886–1952). Southern Baptist minister and hymnist, born in Heflin, Louisiana. McKinney was educated at Louisiana College and Southwestern Baptist Theological Seminary, and later at the Bush Conservatory of Music in Chicago. In 1919, he joined the faculty of music at Southwestern Seminary and taught there until 1931. McKinney developed a popular following as a music minister in **evangelistic** meetings and special events in the **Southern Baptist Convention**. In 1931, he became the director of music at Travis Avenue Baptist Church in Ft. Worth, Texas, the city's most prestigious congregation. The **Sunday School Board** of the Southern Baptist Convention called McKinney in 1935 to be its first music editor, and his greatest accomplishment in that role was the compilation of the *Broadman Hymnal* in 1940. He was the author or composer of 483 pieces of work, including gospel songs, hymns, and choruses. Among his better known hymns are "Send a Great Revival!", "Glorious Is Thy Name," and "Wherever He Leads I'll Go."

MCLEAN, ARCHIBALD (1733–1812). Scotch Baptist minister, born at East Kilbride, Lanarkshire. As a young man he heard George Whitefield (1703–1770) preach and was much impressed. He was apprenticed a printer in 1746 and followed that trade as a printer and bookseller in Glasgow from 1759 to 1766. After a year in London, McLean left the Presbyterian Church and became a follower of the **Glasites**. He continued in the printing business as a superintendent for the Donaldson Company, in Edinburgh, from 1767 to 1785. In 1763, he was involved in a dispute with the Glasgow Glasites over a point of church **discipline**, and left their fellowship with Robert Carmichael (d. 1774) to build a New Testament church. The two leaders sought the advice of **John Gill**, who baptized Carmichael, who in turn baptized McLean in 1765.

In 1768, McLean and Carmichael became co-elders of a congregation in Edinburgh, calling themselves and their new movement "**Scotch Baptists**." Following the principles of Robert Sandeman (1718–1771) plus a stricter ethic and believer's **baptism**, McLean interacted with leaders of the Baptist community, notably **Andrew Fuller**, with whom he frequently debated. After the death of Carmichael in 1774, McLean became the sole **pastor** of the church at Edinburgh. His influence was felt in northern England, in Yorkshire and Lancashire, basically characterized by a multiplicity of church elders and primitivist practices; McLean was popular in North Wales among the **Particular Baptist** churches. His followers were often referred to as "McLeanists" or "McLeanites." His works were published in six volumes, and he was awarded an honorary M.A. degree in 1793 by Brown University in Rhode Island.

MCLOUGHLIN, WILLIAM GERALD (1922–1992). Historian of Baptist life and thought, born at Maplewood, New Jersey. McLoughlin was educated at Princeton and Harvard Universities (A.M., Ph.D.), where he specialized in American civilization. He taught his entire career at Brown University, emphasizing in his scholarship from time to time Baptist experience and **religious liberty**; in 1981, he was named Annie McClelland and Willard Prescott Smith Professor of History and Religion at Brown. McLoughlin trained numerous Baptist students and was the author of 16 books. Among his most important works were *New England Dissent* (2 volumes, 1971), an updated, comprehensive history of Baptists in New England; the *Diary of Isaac Backus* (3 volumes, 1979); and *Modern Revivalism* (1958). His biography of **Billy Graham** (1958) was based upon careful observation of Graham at crusades, and so forth, and was expected to be the authoritative work on the life of the 20th-century **evangelist**. However McLoughlin made some assessments of the revivalist's techniques that the Graham organization felt were unfair and damaging, and the Graham organization protested McLoughlin's material. He continued to turn out major scholarly works about **evangelical** life and characters, **revivalism**, and Indian **missions**, while espousing numerous activist causes.

MCMASTER, WILLIAM (1811–1887). Canadian Baptist denominational leader, born in Tyrone County, Ireland. He was not formally educated and after emigrating to York, Upper Canada (now Ontario), took a minor position with a dry goods company and later took over the business, moving it to Toronto. To further his trading interests, McMaster founded his own financial house, the Bank of Commerce, becoming its first president in 1867. He served on the legislative council of the province of Upper **Canada** and was appointed to the first Senate of the Dominion of Canada in 1867. He was an active Baptist layman, a member of the Jarvis Street Church in Toronto and various societies and boards of the denomination in Ontario and Quebec. He took an interest in **Robert A. Fyfe**'s plan for a Christian university at Woodstock, Ontario, but later shifted his support to a Toronto-based institution called the Toronto Baptist College, which he largely founded in 1881, also writing its doctrinal basis. McMaster helped to secure a charter for the College, which was renamed McMaster University at his death in 1887. His estate, which amounted to just under $1 million, was the most substantial gift of its kind in all of Canada to be given at that time to a religious institution.

MEAD, SILAS (1834–1909). English and Australian Baptist minister, born at Curry Mallett, Somersetshire, England. He was educated at Stepney-Regent's Park College in London for the ministry and took the B.A. and M.A. degrees in Eastern languages at the University of London in pursuit of possible **missionary** service with the **Baptist Missionary Society**. He also completed the LL.B. degree at London.

Much influenced by **Joseph Angus**, he was recommended to a Baptist congregation in Adelaide in the colony of South **Australia**, and he arrived there in 1861. Mead built an influential congregation on Flinders Street, with a seating capacity of 1,000 and an impressive Gothic building. By 1885, he had baptized 1,000 persons. Considered by many to be the father of South Australian Baptists, Mead helped to establish much of the denomination's infrastructure in the country: chapters of the Australian Baptist Foreign Mission in each state, a strengthened associational life, the Baptist Bible Translation Society (1864), and a denominational newspaper, *Truth and Progress* (1868). He was also a founder of the Society of Christian Endeavour of South Australia and was tutor of exegesis at Union College in Adelaide for fourteen years; in both of these roles he was a keen advocate of open membership and church unity among Baptists, Presbyterians, and Congregationalists. He returned to England to become principal of Harley College, a missionary training institution founded by H. Grattan Guiness, where he served 1897–1901. Mead was the author of *Scripture Immersion* (1867), a popular work on **baptism**.

MERCER, JESSE (1769–1841). Southern Baptist minister, denominational leader, and historian, born in Halifax County, North Carolina. Lacking formal education, he plunged into pastoral **ministry** at several towns in Georgia and was remembered as an effective revivalist. Mercer opposed the "New Measures" of Charles G. Finney (1792–1875) and others, preferring long periods of prayer and exhortation. He served three congregations simultaneously while conducting a far-reaching career in education. He began an academy at Salem, Georgia, in 1796 and wrote an authoritative history based upon his own observations, *History of the Georgia Baptist Association* (1838). He believed strongly in the **associational** principle and **missions**, writing major treatises on these topics, as well as on Baptist **polity**. Mercer was president of the state Baptist convention for almost 20 years, and Mercer University in Macon, Georgia, was named in his honor. Brown University conferred an honorary doctorate on Mercer in 1835.

MESSENGER, BAPTIST UNDERSTANDING OF. The title of messenger first began to appear in Baptist usage among the English

General Baptists in the 1650s. It designated traveling ministers who visited the churches, celebrating the **Lord's Supper**, resolving questions of church **polity**, and sometimes doing **evangelical** work. **Particular Baptists** also employed the office of messenger in the 17th century. Messengers came to symbolize the larger connection and eventually served as superintendents of areas of England. The office of messenger was fully defined in the work of **Thomas Grantham** and seems to have had an effect upon American colonial General Baptist development in the Carolina Colony. As the General Baptists declined in the 18th century, so the office of messenger dropped out of usage. It was ultimately recovered in the **Baptist Union** development of area minister.

A second usage of the term "messenger" was developed among **Southern Baptists** and others in the United States. Under the influence of **Landmarkism**, Southern Baptists eschewed the northern churches' use of the term "representative" to associational meetings, holding that no one could "represent" a Baptist congregation. Those persons who attended **convention** and **association** meetings on behalf of local churches thus came to be called "messengers," because they carried messages between their congregations and other bodies.

MESSER, ASA (1769–1836). American Baptist minister and educator, born in Methuen, Massachusetts. He turned from farming to tutorial studies under **Hezekiah Smith**, who prepared him for Rhode Island College, where he graduated in 1790. Messer, a brilliant student, was appointed tutor at the college in 1791 and rose to professor of languages and natural philosophy by 1799. He was ordained to the Baptist **ministry** at First Baptist, Providence in 1801, although he never served a congregation. From 1802 to 1836, Messer was president of Rhode Island College, during which time he was an able administrator and developer of what emerged as Brown University. He secured the Brown family munificence, started a medical school, and extended the faculty. Messer cherished liberty of speech and conscience, and this led him into difficulty with Baptist authorities. Described as an Arian, he held an unorthodox position on the doctrine of **Christ**. At length, he was forced to resign as president and turned to local politics and farming in Rhode Island. The University of Vermont gave him an LL.D. in 1812, and Harvard Divinity School awarded him the doctor of divinity degree in 1820.

MEXICO. Protestant and Baptist works in Mexico are synonymous in the earliest period of development. In 1827, James Thompson (fl. 1825–1845), a **colporteur** for the British and Foreign Bible Society, conducted **evangelical** work; he was followed by James Hickey (1800–1866), a colporteur and Baptist minister from Texas who started the first Baptist church at Monterrey. Later, Thomas Westrup (1837–1909) commenced **missionary** efforts for the **American Baptist Home Mission Society** in 1870. Due to legal restrictions in Mexico, leaders were trained at the Spanish-American Baptist Seminary in Los Angeles, California, until 1947, when a theological school was opened at First Baptist Church in Mexico City. In 1880, the Southern Baptist **Foreign Mission Board** set up their first work at Saltillo, with the center of American Baptist missions in Mexico City. In 1894, a unifying step was taken with the organization of the Baptist Association of Central and Southern Mexico. Later, in 1903, the Convención Nacional Bautista was founded, and it cooperated with both major U.S. Baptist mission bodies, American and Southern Baptists. In 1946, the **fundamentalist Baptist Bible Fellowship** (BBF) opened one of its earliest fields in Mexico and for a time it drew congregations away from affiliation with the Convención. A Seventh Day Baptist work was established in Mexico in 1965.

As of 2006, there were 1,550 churches with 150,000 members affiliated with the Convención Nacional Bautista de Mexico. The Convención Nacional Bautista publishes *La Luz* (*The Light*). There are two Baptist-related seminaries in Mexico, one in Mexico City and the other at Edo de Mexico.

MEYER, FREDERICK BROTHERTON (1847–1929). English Baptist minister, born in London, England. Following an early career in business, he studied at Regent's Park College and the University of London, receiving his B.A. Meyer served as student pastorate at Richmond, then as assistant at Pembroke, Liverpool (1870–1872), and **pastor** at Priory Street, York (1872–1874); Victoria Road, Leicester (1874–1888); Regent's Park Chapel, London (1888–1892); Christ Church, Lambeth (1892–1907); a second pastoral **ministry** at

Regent's Park Church (1909–1915); and a second term at Christ Church, Lambeth (1915–1922). Meyer was a greatly influential pastor, serving as president of the **Baptist Union** in 1906 and taking world **mission** tours in 1889, 1901, and 1907. He made 12 preaching tours to North America, the last one in 1922. Beginning in 1878, his preaching filled Melbourne Hall, England. Dwight L. Moody (1837–1899) was a close friend of Meyer's, stemming from the 1873 tour Moody made to Britain, in which he preached in Meyer's church. Later in 1891, Meyer was Moody's guest at the Northfield, Massachusetts Bible Conferences Moody hosted. Meyer's published works totaled over 5 million copies of over 500 titles in his name, distributed worldwide. Meyer has been credited with being the guiding light behind the Baptist **deaconess** movement among British Baptists. His important works include *The Exalted Life* (1896), *My Daily Prayer* (1913), and *A Winter in South Africa* (1908). McMaster University in **Canada** conferred the doctor of divinity degree on Meyer in 1911.

MEYER, HEINRICH (1842–1919). German Baptist minister and missionary, born at Grossbussek, **Germany**. He became a **colporteur** and conducted missionary tours into Eastern Europe, choosing **Hungary** as his home in 1873. His work was supported by the British and Foreign Bible Society, and he ministered in the tradition of a Baptist throughout Hungary and **Serbia**. Twelve Baptist congregations in Hungary alone are said to be the result of Meyer's **ministry**. He created a connection among the churches he served, the so-called Free Baptist Convention, which crossed numerous national boundaries. Meyer is considered the father of the Hungarian Baptist movement.

MIDDLE ASIA. Following the political reorganization of the Soviet Union in 1991–1992, Baptists in the Soviet republics who had cooperated with the All-Union Council of Evangelical Christians-Baptists sought to reorganize on a state-by-state basis. Where there were insufficient Baptists to support a single union or convention in the Asiatic republics, several joined in 1992 to form Soyuz Evangel'skikh Khristian Baptistov Srednoy Azyi (the Union of Churches of Evangelical Christians-Baptists of Middle Asia). The population of the region is predominantly Muslim. This union includes churches in Tadzhikistan, Turkmenistan (3 churches, 200 members), and Uzbekistan (10 churches, 6,000 members). The union cooperates with the Evro-Asiatskaya Federatsia Evangel'skikh Khristian Baptistov (Euro-Asiatic Federation of Evangelical Christians-Baptists) and the **European Baptist Federation**.

As of 2006, there were 31 churches with 2,836 affiliated with the soyuz; in Uzbekistan, there were 15 Korean Baptist congregations with about 3,000 members.

MILLER, WILLIAM (1782–1849). American Baptist preacher and, later, **Adventist** leader, born in Pittsfield, Massachusetts. Self-taught, he became a farmer in Poultney, Vermont, in 1803, and later Low Hampton, New York, serving in local political offices and the U.S. Army in the War of 1812. Taunted by his friends for his deistical religious beliefs, he began a serious study of the **Bible** about 1816 and focused on the return of Christ's prophecies. Miller calculated that Jesus Christ would return in 1843 and announced this in a public lecture in 1831. In 1833, the Low Hampton Baptist Church granted him a license to preach and he circulated widely and spoke to large audiences on prophetic themes. His published lectures, *Evidence from the Scriptures and History of the Second Coming of Christ about the Year 1843* (1836), made him a sensation. Joshua Himes (1805–1895), a publicist, adopted Miller's views and campaigned in print for the Advent emphases. The two purchased a tent and toured the northeastern United States, holding 120 camp meetings in 1842–1844. When Miller's predictions did not materialize in 1843, many of his followers suffered great disappointment. In 1845, he helped to organize the Adventist Church and became its titular head. Baptists eventually rejected Miller's views and charged **associations** and congregations to avoid contacts with the Adventists. *See also* ADVENTISM.

MINISTRY, BAPTIST UNDERSTANDING OF. Baptists have understood ministry in terms of service, from the original language of the New Testament, "doulos." All members of the church, or Body of Christ, are servants and ministers, and are expected to be witnesses and provide care for one another. Clergy, or ordained ministers, are gifted for certain kinds of service and set apart accordingly. Ordained ministry concerns preaching, pastoral care, and the administration of the **sacraments/ordinances**, though the latter service is shared with **deacons**. Ministry is a gift from God, as well as an opportunity within the church empowered by the Holy Spirit. Baptists have typically understood the offices of ministry in the New Testament in a functional way, as opposed to a hierarchy as assumed by other denominations. Thus, the *episcopos* (bishop) is an overseer ministry of the pastor, and the *presbuteros* (**elder**) is likewise associated with the pastor of a local congregation. In this way, Baptists evolved with one of the most egalitarian ideas of ministry among Protestant sects.

Titles for Baptist ministers have varied through the centuries. In American colonial experience, the term "elder" was used up to the War of Independence. Perhaps as a concession to the egalitarian mood of the times or the maturation of the denomination in urban regions, many ministers adopted the use of the title "reverend," which had previously been reserved for the learned clergy of the established churches. Once the College of Rhode Island was functioning (1764), its graduates placed their degrees (A.B., M.A.) after their names, and to this list was added a long list of those awarded honorary doctorates in divinity. **Samuel Stillman**, **Isaac Backus**, **Hezekiah Smith**, **Thomas Baldwin**, and **James Manning** all enjoyed the use of educational and ecclesiastical credentials in their titles. *See also* DEACON; ELDER.

MISSIONARY BAPTISTS. Nomenclature applied to several groups of Baptists across the American South.

(1) A western branch is centered in Arkansas. At the 1901 meeting of the Arkansas State Baptist Convention in Hope, Arkansas, questions arose over the issues associated with **Landmarkism** and in particular the work of **W. H. Whitsett** and the organizationally centralizing tendencies of **Southern Baptist Convention** leaders. Behind the leadership of **Ben M. Bogard**, a collection of churches affirming the rights of local congregations and **associations** over **conventions**, met at Fort Smith to consider organizing a new association in which churches would control **missions** and benevolence. The result was the formation of the State Association of Missionary Baptist Churches of Arkansas, the first of the Missionary Baptist movement, which later spread throughout the Southwest as a reaction to the

Southern Baptist Convention. In the beginning, 150 churches comprised the Arkansas General Association, with later asssociations organized in Alabama, Missouri, Texas, Oklahoma, and Mississippi. In 1910, a publishing company was formed; in 1919, the Missionary Baptist College was founded at Sheridan, which lasted until its bankruptcy in 1933. An orphanage was operated at Texarkana from 1903. The Missionary Baptists are clearly Landmarkists, although they prefer not to use the terminology "Landmarkist" because of its sectarian tone. Rather, they stress the New Testament congregational principle, coupled with mostly local missionary outreach and **evangelism**.

(2) In the East, another group calling themselves Missionary Baptists, and located in the Carolinas, Tennessee, and Kentucky, have a more austere perspective: they oppose the sale of alcohol, the practice of abortion, and the teaching of sex education in public schools. These Appalachian Missionary Baptist churches are small and rural, with characteristics of behavior similar to **Primitive Baptists**. They uniformly use the King James Version of the Bible and are opposed to the use of indoor **baptisteries**, robed choirs, theological education for ministers, and **women** in ministry. There is little to no relationship between the two groups using the name "Missionary Baptist," except that both are disinclined, if not adversarial, to the Southern Baptist Convention. *See also* BAPTIST MISSIONARY ASSOCIATION.

MISSIONARY EVANGELISTIC FELLOWSHIP. Founded in 1940 by John Rhodes, a **missionary** to **China** and **Japan**, Missionary Evangelistic Fellowship is related to the **Independent** Baptist movement and sponsors work in six countries. It focuses on support for training national workers. Its headquarters are located in Buffalo Center, Iowa.

MISSIONARY FLIGHTS INTERNATIONAL. Founded in 1964, Missionary Flights International provides support for Baptist missionaries in aviation ministries. With headquarters located in West Palm Beach, Florida, it publishes *Flight Briefing*.

MISSIONS, BAPTIST. The missionary impulse among Baptists of most kinds stems from a literal and personalized interpretation of the Great Commission, Matthew 28:19–20. Most Baptists believe this was a challenge and command of **Christ** to go, teach, and baptize in His name. When coupled with Mark 16:15 and Acts 1:8, the commission becomes a fourfold task: in places familiar (Jerusalem), nearby and receptive (Judea), nearby and indifferent or antagonistic (Samaria), and virtually everywhere (to the "uttermost parts of the earth"). In the 17th century, Baptist missions concentrated on personal **evangelism**, and local churches expended efforts on expansion of their **ministries** in the urban areas of Great Britain. Later in the century, missions were conducted in North America, such as in the Carolinas and New England, mostly on an individual basis.

High Calvinistic theology propounded by great London preachers like **John Gill** and **John Brine** did little to promote an interest in missions from the late 17th century to the first decades of the next. The 18th century, beginning with Baptists in the west of England, witnessed a resurgence of interest in missionary activity, with Baptists in the forefront of all English-speaking Protestants. Beginning in mid-century, prayer meetings were held in Britain; leaders like **Andrew Fuller, John Sutclif**, and **William Carey** laid a theological basis for the Great Commission; and **voluntary** groups sprang up for various benevolent enterprises. Chief among them was the **Baptist Missionary Society**, formed at Kettering, England, to evangelize the heathen, a relatively new concept for churches. Soon the missionary impulse hit the churches of the American colonies; in Philadelphia and New England, **associations** sent forth commissioned evangelists or missionaries to take tours of regions in the summer months. This led to missionary endeavor in what became **Canada** and the continental interior. Indian missions were popular in the West and South. In the 1780s, work among the slave and free **black** communities in Georgia led to missionary work in **Jamaica** and other Caribbean islands.

The largest organizational outreach of missions occurred in the 19th century and followed denominational boundaries. In Britain, both **Particular** and **General Baptists** formed societies and concentrated upon different fields at home and in **Ireland**; high Calvinists formed the **Strict Baptist** Mission in 1861. From the United States, Baptist missionaries were commissioned from the **Baptist Board of Foreign Missions** (1814–1845) (later the **American Baptist Missionary Union**, 1846–1905, and afterward the **American Baptist**

Foreign Mission Society, 1905–); the **Freewill Baptist** Foreign Mission Society (1832); the **Foreign Mission Board** of the **Southern Baptist Convention** (1845–); the **Seventh Day Baptist** Mission Society (1842); and the **American Baptist Free Mission Society** (1843). In the European Baptist context, German Baptists in the later 19th century sent missionaries and trained indigenous leaders for much of eastern and southern Europe, and the Swedish Baptists cooperated with other Baptists in the **Congo**, **China**, and Eastern Europe.

The 20th century saw yet more organizations develop within the Baptist tradition and along theological lines, such as the Strict Baptist Mission (U.K.), Örebo Mission (**Sweden**), and in the United States: **Baptist Mid-Missions** (1920); Africa Christian Missions, later **Evangelical Baptist Missions** (1929); the **Association of Baptists for World Evangelism** (1928); **World Baptist Fellowship** (1928); the **Conservative Baptist** Foreign Mission Society (1943); and **Baptist International Missions** (1965).

Also, the growth of Baptist overseas sending agencies has been phenomenal. The Association of Baptists for World Evangelism employs 1,250 missionaries in 70 countries; Baptist Mid-Missions has over 1,000 missionaries in 50 countries; and the Baptist Bible Fellowship International has 836 missionaries in 170 countries. Among the older boards and agencies, the Baptist Missionary Society employs 150 full-time workers on four continents, and the American Baptist Foreign Mission Society, in conjunction with the Woman's American Baptist Foreign Missionary Society, as of 2007, had under appointment 107 missionaries in 29 countries. Canadian Baptist Ministries (formerly Canadian Baptist Overseas Mission Board) had 42 workers or couples in 20 countries. As of 2006, the largest outreach of all Baptist mission organizations was administered by the Southern Baptist International Mission Board, which employed 5,160 missionaries in over 110 countries. As of 2007, the total number of overseas Baptist missionaries from all sending agencies worldwide exceeded 10,000 persons under appointment.

Elsewhere in the international Baptist family, there are examples of the maturation of mission fields that in turn have assumed missionary responsibilities themselves. Included among these are the Canadian Baptist Foreign Mission Board (1873), the Brazilian

Baptist Foreign Mission Board (1907), the Baptist Union of **South Africa** (1892), and the Jamaican Baptists. The **Baptist World Alliance**, formed in 1905, itself encourages missions through its programs of evangelism and education.

MIXED COMMUNION. *See* LORD'S SUPPER.

MOLDOVA. The first Baptist congregations formed in Moldova were at Kishinev in 1908. Simyon V. Rakhmanov was among the early Baptist ministers in the region. Over the years of the 20th century, Moldovan churches became part of the All-Union Council of Evangelical Christians-Baptists in the Soviet Union. In 1992, however, as the Moldovan Republic declared its independence, the Baptist community organized its own body, the Uniunea Bisericilor Crestine Evanghelice-Baptiste Din Moldova (Union of Evangelical Christians-Baptists of Moldova), representing most Baptists in the Republic. The **Baptist Bible Fellowship** appointed missionaries to Moldova in 1992.

As of 2006, there were 400 churches with 21,400 members affiliated with the Uniunea Bisericilor Crestine Evanghelice-Baptiste Din Moldova (Union of Evangelical Christians-Baptists of Moldova). Offices of the union are located in Chisinau.

MONGOLIA. Baptist work in Mongolia is relatively recent, owing to government restrictions. **Southern Baptist** witness in Mongolia dates from 1992, when a small congregation was gathered in Ulaanbataar. In 1994, this congregation became the first formally recognized Baptist church in Mongolia. In 1995, the U.S. **Conservative Baptist** Foreign Mission Society established a work in Mongolia. As of 1995, there were an estimated 100 Baptist adherents in Mongolia.

MONTANA BAPTIST FELLOWSHIP. An independent fundamentalist Baptist domestic mission in the United States founded in 1941. The object of the organization formed in Indianapolis, Indiana, in September that year was to plant new congregations in Montana. Eventually, in May 1948, the Montana Baptist Fellowship was merged with the **Fellowship of Baptists for Home Missions**.

MONTGOMERY, HELEN BARRETT (1861–1934). American Baptist lay leader and **mission** promoter. Born at Kingsville, Ohio, she was educated at Wellesley College and became a schoolteacher. Helen married William A. Montgomery of Rochester, New York, who operated a successful component manufacturing business in the early automobile industry. His wealth gave Helen many social and civic opportunities, which she placed at the disposal of her church and denomination, the Northern Baptist Convention. She was a key figure in the unification of the western and eastern branches of the Woman's American Baptist Foreign Mission Societies in 1914, and she wrote and traveled widely on behalf of women in missions. Montgomery advocated establishing the World Day of Prayer, and she translated the Greek New Testament into a popular edition for the **American Baptist Publication Society** in 1924. Helen was elected president of the Northern Baptist Convention in 1920—the first woman president of any mainstream denomination in North America—and in this role she presided over the stormy debates with **fundamentalists**. She collaborated in several mission trips and publications with **Lucy Waterbury Peabody**. Among Helen's several published works are *Western Women in Eastern Lands* (1910), *From Jerusalem to Jerusalem* (1929), and *The Preaching Value of Missions* (1931).

MONTSERRAT. In 1975, **Southern Baptists** commenced a mission in Montserrat. As of 2005, a small Baptist community in one congregation of 300 members existed in Montserrat.

MOODY, DALE (1915–1992). Southern Baptist minister and theologian, born at Stamford, Texas. He was educated at Baylor University, Southern Baptist Theological Seminary and Oxford University, where he received the D.Phil. degree. In 1948, Moody assumed the Joseph Emerson Brown Chair at Southern Baptist Seminary in Christian Theology and taught there until 1983. He was a popular teacher and broadly involved in Baptist and **ecumenical** organizations. He was the only Baptist and second Protestant to teach at the Pontifical Gregorian University in Rome, Italy (1969–1970), and he was a visiting professor at the Ecumenical Institute for Advanced Studies in Jerusalem in 1973 and 1976. Moody, whose theological pilgrimage ran from **dispensationalism** to Southern Baptist biblicalism, admitted being influenced by **A. T. Robertson** and **W. O. Carver** as well as Paul Tillich (1886–1965) and Emil Brunner (1889–1966).

As the theological reorientation of the **Southern Baptist Convention** (SBC) took shape in the 1970s, Moody became an antagonist of the inerrancy movement and "unthinking conservatism." In 1982–1983, as a retired distinguished professor at Southern Seminary, he openly took exception with the seminary's doctrinal statement, "The Abstract of Principles," on the matter of the "perseverance of the saints," holding to the possibility of apostasy. This drew the ire of SBC **conservatives** (particularly in Arkansas), who demanded Moody's dismissal. His postretirement status became much celebrated, and the seminary trustees voted not to renew his annual contract after 1983. Moody continued to teach at other schools, notably American Baptist-related Eastern Baptist Theological Seminary in Philadelphia, Pennsylvania. He was a widely published author, his outstanding books including *The Hope of Glory* (1964) and *The Word of Truth* (1981).

MOODY, DEBORAH (fl. 1630–1640). American colonial Baptist thinker, likely born in England. In 1640, she settled in Salem, Massachusetts, and was admitted to the Congregational Church. In 1642, she concluded that infant **baptism** was not scriptural and persuaded others in the congregation of her position. The clergy sought to dissuade her but to no avail; subsequently, she was brought before the Court of Sessions in Salem and admonished. Under intense pressure, she left to settle among the Dutch on Long Island in 1643, where her wealth and education gave her much influence in the colony of New Netherland. Eventually, she became a Quaker.

MOON, CHARLOTTE (1840–1912). Southern Baptist missionary, born at Viewmont, Virginia. She was educated at Virginia Female Institute and in the women's department related to the University of Virginia, one of the best-educated women of her era. Following a brief career in school teaching, "Lottie" was appointed by the **Foreign Mission Board** (FMB) of the **Southern Baptist Convention** to **China**, where she joined her sister, Edmonia (1851–1908), in 1873. Ultimately, Edmonia returned to the United States, and Lottie embarked on a long career in Shantung Province, China. She started schools, conducted **evangelism**, and cared for the plight of **women**. Her influence on Baptists in the United States was great: in the 1880s, it was her idea to organize support, which eventually became the Woman's Missionary Union. She also advocated greater opportunities for women missionaries under the FMB. An annual offering among Southern Baptists is named in her honor.

MOORE, JOANNA PATTERSON (1832–1916). American Baptist missionary, born in Clarion County, Pennsylvania. She was educated at Rockford Seminary (Illinois) and became a schoolteacher. During the American Civil War, Moore experienced a call to **missions** that first focused on overseas work. She visited the freed **black** communities along the Mississippi River and decided to devote herself to domestic missions. She won a designation from the **American Baptist Home Mission Society** without remuneration to work on Island 10 in the Mississippi. There she taught reading, personal hygiene, and skills to freed women. At Helena, Arkansas, after the war, she earned a wide reputation for teaching soldiers to read. With the formation in 1871 of the Woman's American Baptist Home Mission Society, Moore was its first appointee. With a base in Louisiana, amidst stiff opposition from white Christians, Moore worked among women in domestic education groups she called "fireside schools." This program was made formal in 1892 and promoted daily **Bible** reading and the development of personal spirituality in the black community. Among the sick and poor, she established the Bible bands, and she edited *Hope* magazine. At length she established a base in Nashville, Tennessee, from which she trained workers for the entire Reconstruction South. At her death, Moore was buried in a black cemetery, honoring her work in that community. Her published works include *Fireside School Manual* (1895) and *In Christ's Stead* (1902).

MOREHOUSE, HENRY LYMAN (1834–1917). American Baptist minister and denominational leader, born at Bagnall, New York. He was one of the first graduates of Baptist-related University of Rochester and Rochester Theological Seminary, and first embarked on a political career in the Republican Party. His decision to enter the **ministry** took him on a tour of the Civil War southern states, and he noted the needs particularly of the free black population. A gifted administrator, Morehouse moved from pastorates in Saginaw, Michigan, and East Rochester, New York, to become, in 1879, corresponding secretary of the **American Baptist Home Mission Society** (ABHMS); he greatly expanded the ABHMS work among blacks, French Canadians, and American Indians. In 1891, he stepped down to become field secretary of that society, and observing antagonism with **Southern Baptists** over territorialism, Morehouse organized the **Fortress Monroe Conference** in 1894. In 1898, he recommended the unification of the northern Baptist societies, and he became the chief architect of the Northern Baptist Convention, organized in 1905. For 38 years the head of the ABHMS, Morehouse was a highly respected leader of what became **American Baptist Churches in the U.S.A.** Morehouse College, an undergraduate school in Atlanta, Georgia, founded for black men, was named in his honor. Morehouse was the author of several definitive books, including *Baptist Home Missions in North America* (1883) and *Relationships between the General Denominational Societies and State Conventions* (1913).

MOROCCO. Baptist witness in Morocco is late in origin and limited by government restrictions. In 1966, **Southern Baptist** missionaries began a work in Melilla with a Spanish congregation. Later, the work was transferred to Rabat. Outreach is also maintained in Tangiers and Fes, particularly among the U.S. military personnel. As of 2001, there were three congregations with 167 members associated with the Baptist Convention of Morocco, which is affiliated with the U.S. Southern Baptists.

MORRIS, ELIAS CAMP (1855–1922). American black Baptist missionary and denominational leader, born in Murray County, Georgia. He was born in slavery and after the Civil War, he took up shoemaking and secured an education. Settling in Arkansas, he worked closely with the **American Baptist Home Mission Society** in founding Arkansas Baptist College, a school for Freedmen. He was elected president of the Negro state convention and helped to form the **National Baptist Convention of the United States of America** (NBCUSA). In 1915, he was president of the NBCUSA when **Richard H. Boyd** sought control of the National Baptist Publishing Board. Morris stood firm, although he lost the publishing board to

Boyd. Morris frequently represented **black Baptists** across the United States and at the **Baptist World Alliance** and was widely respected among the Baptist family.

MOULTON, EBENEZER (1709–1783). American and, later, Canadian Baptist minister and controversialist. Born in Windham, Connecticut, Moulton was a leading **pastor** and itinerant in the **New Light** awakenings in New England and Nova Scotia in the 18th century.

Ordained in 1741 at Brimfield by regular Calvinistic Baptists from eastern Massachusetts, Moulton soon shifted to the New Light position and itinerated broadly. In 1748, he led a split in the Brimfield church, forming a new **Separate Baptist** congregation. With other Baptist pastors in Massachusetts concerned over oppressive taxation to support the "standing order," Moulton was a primary leader in successive petition campaigns to the Massachusetts General Court on behalf of a united Baptist community. In the 1750s, he is credited with helping to give New England Baptists a sense of identity and unity. For a time, in conjunction with his pastoral duties, he worked in mercantile pursuits, until he was bankrupted in 1763 and fled to Nova Scotia.

In Nova Scotia, Moulton became the pioneer planter of the Baptist faith. He itinerated broadly along the eastern coast of the Bay of Fundy and in the Annapolis Valley, baptizing converts upon request. His New Light principles and closed communion **polity** soon made enemies in the isolated settlements. At Horton (later Wolfville), he formed in 1765 what became the oldest surviving Baptist church in **Canada**, but was forced to withdraw from the village by Congregationalists of the open communion kind. In 1773, Moulton returned to Brimfield, Massachusetts, his former debts having been forgiven.

MOYERS, BILLY DON (1934–). Southern Baptist minister, government administrator, and television journalist, born at Hugo, Oklahoma. "Bill" Moyers was educated at the University of North Texas and the University of Texas, later earning his theological degree at Southwestern Baptist Theological Seminary. Ordained a Baptist minister, he had planned to pursue graduate studies at Edinburgh University, but instead went to work for Lyndon Baines Johnson. He worked for a television station owned by Mrs. Lady Bird Johnson and became associated with the family as the Kennedy/Johnson administration came to office in 1961. From 1961 to 1963, he was deputy director of the Peace Corps, and then he worked for President Johnson as a staff assistant 1963–1965 and then White House press secretary, 1965–1967.

Following his years in public service, Moyers entered the field of television journalism and was an early personality on the Public Broadcasting Network, developing in 1971 his own commentary show, *Bill Moyers' Journal*. The broadcasts featured prominent public personalities and earned Moyers international fame as an observer of U.S. military involvement, economic trends, and the culture wars issues of the 1990s. He is a staunch critic of the resurgent "takeover" of the **Southern Baptist Convention**, yet a strong advocate of Baptist ideals such as **freedom of conscience**, **religious liberty**, and **human rights**. He was given a Lifetime Emmy Award for his work as a television journalist in 2006. Among his many books are *Genesis: A Living Conversation* (1996) and *Moyers on America: A Journalist and His Times* (2004).

MOZAMBIQUE. The Swedish Baptists were the first to establish churches in Mozambique, beginning in 1892. Later, in 1949, Portuguese Baptists began a mission. A Baptist convention was formed in 1960. Swedish Baptists in 1918 started a mission, later to be developed as Missão Baptista Escandinava. This group has evolved as the Igreja União Baptista, the union of Swedish efforts and the **South Africa** General Mission.

As of 2006, there were 120 churches and 40,000 members affiliated with the Convenção Bautista de Mozambique, and 1,178 churches with about 400,000 members affiliated with the Igreja União Baptista. There is a Baptist-related theological school at Maputo.

MULLINS, EDGAR YOUNG (1860–1928). Southern Baptist theologian and educator, born in Franklin County, Mississippi. Early in life, he worked in several trades, becoming a telegrapher. Educated at Texas Agricultural and Mechanical College, and Southern Baptist Seminary, he became a **pastor** at Harrodsburg, Kentucky

(1885–1888); Lee Street, Baltimore, Maryland (1888–1895); and First Baptist, Newton Centre, Massachusetts (1896–1899), one of the few Baptist pastors of the post–Civil War era to serve in both the North and the South. In 1899, he began a 30-year teaching career at Southern Baptist Theological Seminary in the field of systematic theology. In that role, he became the principal **theologian** of Southern Baptists, publishing widely; his books on Baptist doctrines became standard texts. Mullins became president of the seminary in 1899 and led in the expansion and modernization of the school. As president of the **Southern Baptist Convention** from 1921 to 1924, Mullins raised the consciousness of Southern Baptists to social concerns, and as president of the **Baptist World Alliance** in 1928, he traveled extensively on behalf of **religious liberty**. Among the over 40 titles that Mullins published are *The Axioms of Religion* (1908) and *The Christian Religion in Its Doctrinal Expression* (1917).

MURCH, WILLIAM HARRIS (1784–1859). English Baptist minister and educator, born at Honiton, England. Baptized by **John Rippon** at Carter's Lane, he began preaching at 14 years old. His education consisted of training at Wymondley College. In 1806, he became assistant pastor at Sheppard's Barton, Frome, and three years later the sole **pastor** until 1827. That year he accepted the tutorship in **theology** at the Baptist Theological College at Stepney, where he remained until his health failed in 1844. From 1845 to 1851, Murch served the church at Rickmansworth, Hertfordshire, and in 1856, he started a new congregation at Kensington, Bath. At the denominational level, Murch was secretary of the **Baptist Union** from 1834 to 1846 and of the Baptist Board from 1837 to 1843. One of the most respected clergy of his era, Murch received an honorary degree from Brown University in Rhode Island in 1837. He was the editor of *A New Selection of Hymns* (1838), in wide use by the Baptist Union churches.

MUSIC, IN BAPTIST WORSHIP. Slow to become a regular aspect of Baptist worship, the purpose of music is to enhance the worship quality (in addition to readings, prayers, offerings, and reflection), provide a greater variety of spiritual experience, and guide persons engaged in worship along a particular theme. Music can be a dominant use of worship time, it can be definitive of the character of a congregation, and it can be used for increasing emotional and religious intensity. Some Baptist congregations are known for their great choirs (First Baptist, Dallas, Texas) or Christian rock singers (Chris Tomlin, Kirk Franklin); others are defined as either "formal," "informal," or "contemporary" by the music presented. Studies of the Baptist **revival** tradition have also demonstrated that music can be used to carefully set a tone ("Rock of Ages"), develop an attitude of contrition ("Just as I Am, Without One Plea") or exhilaration ("All Hail the Power of Jesus' Name"), or support the theological idea of a sermon ("Christ Receiveth Sinful Men").

Music among Baptists most likely occurs as congregational singing. Singing became a controversial issue for English Baptists in the 17th century. While there was little doubt that recitation of psalms was an acceptable form of worship, any type of chanting (as in the Anglican or Catholic traditions) was unacceptable, as was any musical form that was brought into the church from the external culture. Apparently, during the Puritan Commonwealth years, Baptist soldiers practiced singing psalms. **Seventh Day Baptists** used **Lord's Supper** hymns at Colchester as early as 1657. Solo singing was practiced in the 1660s, as Katherine Sutton's published collection reveals, and it is obvious that **John Bunyan**'s followers sang hymns. **Benjamin Keach** was among the first to advocate widespread use of singing, and he published in 1691 the first Baptist hymnbook intended for congregational use, *Spiritual Melody*. **Joseph Stennett** produced a collection of communion hymns in 1697 and hymns for **baptism** in 1712. The *Bristol Hymnbook* was produced in 1769 by Caleb Evans (1737–1791) and others for use in the West Country, which included material by other English writers. Among Scottish Baptists, John Glas produced a collection of hymns for **Glasite** congregations in 1749, and William Sinclair compiled a collection for his church at Keiss in 1750. Subsequent Scottish Baptist hymnals were published in 1786, 1818, 1900, 1933, and 1962, several patterned on English Baptist editions. *See also* STENNETT FAMILY.

The broad acceptability of Isaac Watts's (1674–1748) hymns pushed other Baptists to compose and publish hymns and psalm collections. From 1760 to 1800, Baptists enjoyed a "golden age of hymnody." In 1787, **John Rippon** published his *Selections* in which the tunes were identified for the first time. The **General Baptists** enjoyed wide use of *Barton Hymns* (1785), later preferring the *New Connexion Baptist Hymnal* (1879), which paralleled *Psalms and Hymns* among the **Particular Baptists** (1858). Reflecting the union of the two groups, the *Baptist Church Hymnal* of 1900 was published for a new century, to be succeeded by a revised edition in 1933 and a new *Baptist Church Hymnal* in 1954, which included the Baptist churches of **Australia**, **New Zealand**, and **South Africa**. The contemporary *Baptist Church Hymnary*, which reflects an **ecumenical** interest, was first produced in 1962. Welsh folk tunes from the Old Country became popular across the Baptist family and are found in many Baptist hymnals and songbooks, for instance, the popular tune "Cym Rhonda." Since the 18th century, Welsh singing festivals have occurred annually in Wales, Pennsylvania; in eastern coastal U.S. ports; and in certain parts of Australia.

Great variety of music composition took place in the United States. As the Baptist community matured there in the 19th century, the more urbane churches gravitated toward a group of popular composers and arrangers, such as Lowell Mason (1792–1872), Thomas Hastings (1784–1872), and William Bradbury (1816–1868). In the South, West, and rural areas, *The Sacred Harp* (1844) reflected Baptist folk culture. **William Howard Doane** edited the *Baptist Hymnal* (1883), which created a greater appreciation for liturgy and reflected the influence of the Oxford movement in Britain. Many Baptists joined with other **evangelicals** after the mid-19th century in using music first composed for **Sunday Schools** and camp meetings, in church worship experiences. By the mid-20th century, **Southern Baptists** led the denomination worldwide in producing new music and publishing songs and hymnbooks in various languages for local churches and in the **missionary** contexts. Gradually, music among almost all Baptist groups became a vivid expression of Christian experience, and the typical worship service came to be punctuated with both congregational and choral singing. As several writers have shown, the hymnals that Baptists compiled and used in public services and private devotions provided the worship resource found by Anglicans in the *Book of Common Prayer* and the Presbyterian *Book of Worship*. Like Methodists and other evangelical groups, many important themes and phrases indicative of popular Baptist theology (salvation, sanctification) are found in Baptist hymns and gospel songs.

The involvement of choral and instrumental music among Baptist churches followed patterns in other evangelical sects. In the urban churches, choirs were noticed in the early decades of the 19th century, doubtless imitating Congregationalists, some Lutherans and Brethren (who employed German forms), and Methodists. By the 1960s, it was a dominant feature of Sunday morning worship in Anglo-North American Baptist churches to have a fully robed choir that sat either behind the pulpit or in a rear balcony and performed a practiced anthem or hymn. Choir practices usually occurred as an add-on to midweek prayer services and provided a unique subculture in the congregation. At special times of the year, such as Christmas and Easter, choirs performed cantatas, some energetically taking on Handel's *Messiah* in parts, or similar works by Faure, Verdi, or Bach, or in recent, contemporary use, pieces by the English composer John Rutter. An ever popular choral selection at Easter is "The Holy City" (1892), by Frederick Weatherly and Michael Maybrick. The individual talent in choirs has produced solos and multiple singers (duets, trios, gospel quartets) who bring "special music" to a service. Urban black Baptists typically provide for large choirs and feature multiple soloists as prominent parts of their services, combining syncopated rhythm with music. Choirs are also prominent features of Baptist life in the Baltic countries, **Wales**, **China**, and Latin America. The **Billy Graham** crusades, which feature large choirs, are an important model for congregational imitation, especially as local choir members have participated in regional crusades over the years of Dr. Graham's ministry. Also in the context of Baptist choral expression are the various levels of children's choirs that appear typically at Christmas and Easter and are important opportunities for education and inculturation.

In the cultural shifts of the 1970s among white churches, however, choirs in many British and North American Baptist churches of a smaller size were gradually supplanted by worship teams and ministries that brought contemporary music and forms patterned after jazz, rock, and country singers to the services. Four factors may be identified in the application of these forms to Baptist tastes in music: the growing influence of the Pentecostal and black gospel traditions; the popularity of recorded gospel music; a trend toward more informal patterns of worship; and the perceived need to attract more adolescent age people to Baptist worship. Caught in "generation gaps," many churches have "blended" patterns for different age groups to include both choirs and worship teams. Concurrent with this change, however, has been a demise of music education in Baptist colleges and seminaries as well as full-salaried positions for organists and ministers of music. To a limited extent among **fundamentalist** Baptists, Baptist **Bible colleges** have stemmed this tide by continuing to stress music ministries.

Baptists have relied principally upon the harpsichord (18th century, along the East Coast of the U.S. and in the cities of Britain), the piano(forte), and the organ, for accompaniment of hymn singing and as background for pauses in the proper parts of the service (offerings, readings). Many Baptist churches allow for musical "preludes" and "postludes" but struggle to achieve the attention of worshippers during the performances. Occasionally, where talent exists or can be remunerated, Baptist services feature special instruments such as brass horns, woodwinds, stringed instruments, accordions, and harps. Among North American churches, where there is opportunity for more contemporary services, there is frequent use of guitars, base guitars, synthesizers, keyboards, and prerecorded music through amplifier systems. Recapturing other denominational and evangelical music traditions, Baptist congregations also employ orchestras and bell/chime choirs, both comprised of members of the congregation. Once anathema, but now quite widespread in use, are percussion instruments like drum kits, tambourines, and cymbals. In England, the Spring Harvest annual meetings have been promotive of new gospel songs ("Shine, Jesus, Shine!") and instruments.

From the 1830s through the 1990s, the purchase and contruction of an organ was a sign of musical sophistication for many Baptist churches in the British Isles, Germany, **Canada**, Australia, and the United States. For some, this meant a pipe organ that adorned the front or rear of a sanctuary. Noting a new era in worship, the first pipe organ in Scottish Baptist life was installed at Dublin Street Church in Edinburgh in 1864. In the United States, the instrument caught on even more quickly. Popular in frontier settings and revival meetings were the portable pump organs like those manufactured by the Estey Company of Brattleboro, Vermont (1846–1960). Estey also built small pipe organs for local congregations. For others after World War

II, it meant an electric or, later, an electronic organ, such as those manufactured by the Hammond Organ Company of Addison, Illinois (1934–1975). The most prominent organist/composer in a Baptist setting in the 19th century was **Robert Lowry** in Pennsylvania and in the 20th century, Virgil Fox at Riverside Church in New York City. More than any other instrument, pianos have been a mainstay of Baptists around the world, from hymn accompaniment to **Sunday School** services and religious music performed in the home. For many years, Baptist ministers in the Southern, black, and American Baptist traditions were encouraged to learn to play the piano or marry a person who could play the instrument in order to assure quality of accompaniment in worship.

It should be noted that certain smaller bodies of Baptists have rejected instrumental music, choirs, and even singing. These would include various Old School and Old Regular Baptists, Sovereign Grace Baptists, and some independent congregations. Here one sees the influence of the noninstrumental movement in the Campbell-Stone tradition. *See also* WORSHIP IN THE BAPTIST TRADITION.

MYANMAR. *See* BURMA.

MYERS, CORTLAND (1864–1941). American Baptist minister, born at Kingston, New York. He was educated at the University of Rochester and Rochester Theological Seminary. His pastorates included First Baptist, Syracuse, New York (1890–1893); First Baptist, Brooklyn, New York (1893–1909); and Tremont Temple, Boston, Massachusetts (1909–1921). Myers was a widely regarded pulpit orator, reflecting **conservative evangelical** views of his era. Among his published works are *Midnight in a Great City* (1896), *The Dangers of Crooked Thinking* (1924), and *How Do We Know?* (1927). His sermons at Tremont Temple were published in popular pamphlet form and circulated throughout the northeastern United States.

MYLES, JOHN (1621–1684). English and, later, American Baptist minister, born at Newton-Welsh, Hertfordshire. Myles matriculated at Brasenose College, Oxford, after which he began preaching in **Wales** about 1645, likely as an Independent. In 1649, he was in London as part of a Baptist Church at the Glasshouse, under Edward Draper. That same year he returned to Wales and formed the first Baptist church at Ilston on the Gower Peninsula. He became a Trier under the Cromwell government and did much to advance the Baptist cause in the 1650s. Myles and some of his Ilston congregation emigrated to Massachusetts in 1663, where they settled at Rehoboth and later in Swansea. At times, Myles was an irritant to the civil authorities; at other times, he served amicably as the sole town minister. At Swansea, a town named for the Welsh seaport where the Baptist congregation originated, he practiced mixed communion and conducted a school. He maintained cordial relations with his Congregationalist friends and was one of the most respected Baptists of the 17th century on both sides of the Atlantic. In 1656, Myles published *An Antidote against the Infection of the Times; or a Faithful Watchword from Mt. Sion to Prevent the Ruin of Souls.*

– N –

NAMIBIA. In 1961, the South African Baptist Missionary Society began missionary work in Namibia, while three years later **Southern Baptists** entered the country. Major church centers were established at Tsumeb, Oshakati, and in Kavango. The Baptist Convention of Namibia was formed in 1984, supported by the Baptist Union of **South Africa** and composed largely of white members.

As of 2006, there were 49 churches and 3,500 members affiliated with the Baptist Convention of Namibia and a group of three churches and 400 members associated with the Baptist Union of South Africa.

NATIONAL ASSOCIATION OF FREEWILL BAPTISTS. *See* FREEWILL BAPTISTS.

NATIONAL BAPTIST CONVENTION OF AMERICA (NBCA). Commonly referred to as the unincorporated convention of **black Baptists** in the United States, and also formerly known as the "Boyd Baptist Convention" because of its connection with **Richard H. Boyd**. The NBCA traces its origins to 1889–1890, with the founding of the Baptist Foreign Missionary Convention of the United States in Montgomery, Alabama.

The NBCA was incorporated in Louisiana in 1987, and one of the initial actions was to assert that the National Baptist Publishing Board was not the property of any **convention**. Further organizational evolution occurred in 1988 when a controversy over the control of the National Baptist Sunday Church School, the Baptist Training Union Congress, and the National Baptist Publishing Board again became an issue. Five hundred leaders met in Dallas, Texas, to form a new convention related to the Boyd family, the **National Missionary Baptist Convention of America**, while 700 leaders met in San Antonio to advocate central control of the NBCA. The NBCA has eight boards and 11 auxiliary bodies. The boards are autonomous: Foreign Missions, Home Missions, Benevolence, and Education to mention the major ones. Auxiliaries include Women, Brotherhood, Youth, Pastor's Conference, Ministers' Wives, and Matrons. There are 120 state/regional organizations related to the NBCA. The NBCA supports missionary work in **Ghana**, West Africa, **Cameroon**, **Jamaica**, Virgin Islands, and **Panama**. Schools that have the approbation of the NBCA are Union Baptist Seminary, Florida Memorial College, and Morris College. The denominational periodical is the *National Baptist Voice* (1915–).

As of 2006 there were 12,336 churches with an aggregate membership of 3,106,000 in the NBCA.

NATIONAL BAPTIST CONVENTION OF THE UNITED STATES OF AMERICA (NBCUSA). The oldest and largest of the **black Baptist** national denominations in the United States. The origins of the NBCUSA lie in the merger of the National Baptist Educational Convention, the **Baptist Foreign Mission Convention of the United States**, and the **American National Baptist Convention** to form the National Baptist Convention of the United States of America in May 1895. In 1900, the Baptist General Association of the Western States and Territories joined. As a result of a dispute over the ownership of the National Baptist Publishing Board in 1915, that led to a major schism, the constitution was amended and the organization became the National Baptist Convention, U.S.A., Inc.

Boards of the NBCUSA originally included Home Missions (1886), Education (1893), **Sunday School** Publishing (1896), Baptist **Temperance** (1899), and the Women's Convention (1900). In recent years, these have been reduced to three: Sunday School Publishing, Home Missions, and Foreign Missions. Auxiliary organizations include the National Baptist Layman's Movement, Women's Convention, and Congress of Christian Education. There are 171 state/regional affiliated organizations. Missionary work is conducted in **Sierra Leone, Malawi, Swaziland, South Africa, Nicaragua, Jamaica**, the **Bahamas**, and **Barbados**. The NBCUSA supports the following schools: Shaw University, Shaw Divinity School, Central Baptist Theological Seminary, National Baptist College, Selma University, American Baptist Theological Seminary, and Morehouse School of Religion. Missionary work is conducted in two regions of the world: Africa and the Caribbean. The NBCUSA publishes *The Mission Herald* (1897–).

As of 2006, there were 33,000 churches and 8.5 million members affiliated with the NBCUSA.

NATIONAL BAPTIST MISSIONARY CONVENTION OF AMERICA (NBMCA). A major black organization of U.S. Baptists, founded in 1988 after a dispute within the **National Baptist Convention of America** over control of the National Baptist Publishing Board. The purpose of the NBMCA is to serve its constituent congregations as an agency of Christian education, church extension, and missionary efforts, both domestic and overseas. As well, the NBMCA seeks to safeguard **religious liberty** and engage in social and **ecumenical** development. The NBMCA is seen as a "restoration" of the original purposes of the **National Baptist Convention of the United States of America** of the 19th century. Among the agencies of the NBMCA are the Home Mission, Foreign Mission, Education, and **Evangelical** boards. The auxiliaries include the Brotherhood and the Women's Missionary Union. An executive committee makes policy for the denomination. The headquarters of the NBMCA is at Greater Temple of God Missionary Baptist Church in Los Angeles, California. The NBMCA supports the publication, *National Baptist Union Review* (1896–).

As of 2007, there were about 300 churches and 400,000 members claimed to be associated with the NBMCA.

NELSON, REUBEN EMANUEL (1905–1960). American Baptist minister, educator, and ecclesiastical leader, born at Lake, Minnesota. He was educated at Des Moines University and Bethel Theological Seminary. He also studied at Andover Newton Theological School and Yale Divinity School. Nelson was the son of Swedish immigrants who responded to the witness of the **American Baptist Home Mission Society**. He was **pastor** of congregations in Iowa and Minnesota before teaching New Testament at Bethel Seminary. The first stage of his ministry was spent among the **Baptist General Conference**. In 1939, at the peak of the **fundamentalist** impact on the Northern Baptist Convention in the Upper Great Lakes region, Nelson became the state secretary of the Minnesota Baptist Convention 1939–1943. This placed him in controversies involving property and institutional rights and at cross purposes with fundamentalist and **conservative** Baptist leaders like **William Bell Riley** and **Richard Clearwaters.** Nelson next took a similar executive post in the Detroit, Michigan, Baptist City Mission Society (1943–1945). From 1945 to 1950, he was the secretary of the General Council on Missionary Cooperation of the Northern Baptist Convention. In 1950, as the Northern Baptist Convention was renamed and reorganized to become the American Baptist Convention, Nelson became the first general secretary of the denomination and remained in that position until 1959. He helped to define the role of general secretary as a spiritual leader of American Baptists, the executive administrator of denominational programs, and a "head of communion" with other international religious leaders.

NEPAL. In 1962, missionaries of the **Baptist Missionary Society**, in cooperation with the **Council of Baptist Churches of Northeast India**, began work in Nepal. The Baptist mission became part of the United Mission to Nepal, which focuses on development efforts rather than establishing a national church body. A separate **mission** thrust of Naga Baptists in India, some of whom were relocated Nepalese, led to the establishment of the Nepal Baptist Church Council in 1992, with seven churches.

As of 2006, there were 90 churches or 200 fellowships with about 12,000 members affiliated with the council.

NETHERLANDS. Baptist thought and practices in what is now the Netherlands is traceable to the early **Anabaptists** of the 16th century. However, modern Baptist development evolves from the 1840s. **Julius Köbner**, a Danish colleague of **J. G. Oncken**, met Johannes E. Feisser, a Dutchman who had been pondering **baptism** as a believer. In 1845, Köbner baptized Feisser and several others at Gasselternijveen. Two other congregations soon followed at Amsterdam, from a **Bible** study group, and at Zutphen, from Mennonite foundations. Amidst a **revival** among **mission** works in the 1880s, a union was founded in 1881 with seven charter members. During the 1880s, there was serious doctrinal controversy in which churches left the union. At length, the organization recovered its unity and the work was expanded to include young people's work and a **theological seminary** in 1958 known as De Vinkenhof at Utrecht. From its beginning, the Union has published *De Christen* (*The Christian*) (1883–). There are also other Baptists involved in the Netherlands, notably the U.S. **Baptist Bible Fellowship** (1979), **Baptist Mid-Missions**, the U.S. **Conservative Baptist** Foreign Mission Society, and Canadian Baptist Ministries, which works in conjunction with the union.

As of 2006 there were 85 churches and 11,500 members affiliated with the Unie van Baptisten Gemeenten in Nederland.

NEWCOMEN, THOMAS (1663–1729). English Baptist minister and inventor, born at Dartmouth. He was apprenticed as an ironmonger and later he opened a business of this kind at Exeter. Newcomen read widely and experimented with engines, inventing in 1705 a steam engine that operated with an atmospheric chamber, and an arrangement of a rocking beam and pump. Newcomen's engine was soon constructed at numerous prominent collieries across England. For about 20 years at the turn of the century, he was **pastor** of the Baptist congregation in Dartmouth.

NEW GUINEA. *See* PAPUA NEW GUINEA.

NEW LIGHT BAPTISTS. During the 18th century in the American colonial context, the **Great Awakening** produced a profound effect upon religious development. Some churches were favorable to the **revival**, and scores were actually brought into being by revival preaching and then turned to spiritual matters. These pro-Awakening churches were derisively dubbed "New Lights" because of their insistence upon a conscious conversion experience. The enthusiasm of Quakers and others for an "inner light" probably inspired the negative label. Originally, most of the New Light congregations in New England were Congregationalists, many of whom in the 1740s turned to Baptistic principles, particularly believer's **baptism** over infant baptism, which the New Lights felt had no basis in **Scripture**. Frequently, Congregationalist church record books read "gone to the Baptists" to denote a member who had converted to Baptist principles. Among the many leaders of the New Light Baptists were **Isaac Backus**, **John Leland**, **Hezekiah Smith**, **Ebenezer Moulton**, **Shubael Stearns**, and Wait Palmer (1711–1795). The New Light movement in Virginia, influenced by New Englanders, produced leaders such as **James Ireland**, Samuel Harris (1724–1799), and **John Waller**.

Those who were opposed to the Awakening were similarly called "Old Lights," particularly in New England. Among the Old Light Baptists were Jeremiah Condy (fl. 1750–1765), **John Callendar**, and **Edward Upham**. By the end of the 1700s, the distinctions between Old Lights and New Lights were often greatly diminished, most New England Baptists having formed **associations** of pro-revivalistic sentiments. In the South, the New Lights were known as **Separate Baptists**, and many in this group largely merged with the Regular Baptists by 1801. *See also* SEPARATE BAPTISTS.

NEWMAN, ALBERT HENRY (1852–1933). American, Canadian, and Southern Baptist educator and historian, born in Edgefield, South Carolina. He was educated at Mercer University and Rochester Theological Seminary, as well as being trained in Middle Eastern languages under **Crawford H. Toy** at Southern Baptist Theological Seminary. In 1880, Newman was elected Pettengill Professor of Church History at Rochester Seminary, replacing R. J. W. Buckland

(1829–1877), who died. Four years later, however, he accepted one of the inaugural professorships in Toronto Baptist College (later McMaster University), where he served with great distinction until 1901. At that time, he went to Baylor University, where he helped to create Southwestern Baptist Theological Seminary and taught there from 1907 to 1913. Newman taught church history at Baylor, Mercer, Chicago, and again at McMaster. Newman was the premier Baptist and Free Church historian of his era in North America. He pioneered the study of anti-paedo-baptism and wrote 16 textbooks on church history and the history of the Baptists, including *A History of the Baptist Churches in the United States* (1894), *A History of Antipaedobaptism* (1897), and *A Manual of Church History* (1903).

NEW WORLD MOVEMENT. Following World War I, Baptists in the Northern Baptist Convention (NBC) in the United States were influenced by the **ecumenical** movement and spurred forward by the needs of the postwar period. One manifestation was the New World Movement, the first major fund-raising drive of the new convention. Between 1919 and 1924, the NBC sought to raise a single budget of $100 million from among its churches. Reminiscent of the Liberty Loan drives, each congregation was solicited once, thus ending the separate solicitations of the **independent** American Baptist societies. By 1924, about 50 percent of the $100 million was subscribed by 86 percent of the churches. Although the financial results were disappointing, the unifying effect upon the NBC and its overseas affiliates was remarkable in that schools and **missions** were combined into a single stewardship effort. One negative result of the New World Movement was the crystallization of **fundamentalist** identity, which opposed many of the directions of centralization in the NBC. For them, the New World Movement symbolized modernism and unwanted **ecumenism**.

NEW ZEALAND. Baptist work in New Zealand was originally an extension of English Baptist life. Economic pressures in England, a gold rush in New Zealand, and successful colonial advertising all enabled the early pioneers. Henry Daniell of Nelson was likely the first Baptist in the colony: he had been a member of Broadmead Baptist Church in Bristol. Joshua Robinson and his family arrived in Auckland from

London the next year. The first Baptist congregation was started in 1851 at Nelson by Decimus Dolamore, also an English Baptist. The Baptist Union of New Zealand, encompassing both islands, was organized in 1882, largely at the instigation of Alfred North, minister at Dunedin. North was also the driving force behind the New Zealand Baptist Missionary Society, founded in 1885. North had recently emigrated from England, where he had served as secretary to the Midlands Baptist Association. A school, the Baptist College of New Zealand, commenced in 1924; Church Extension was started in 1934; and a national Baptist Women's Missionary Union in 1952. Gradually, Baptists joined leading citizens of New Zealand, with Thomas Dick of Dunedin elected to Parliament in 1858 and Gilbert Carson of Waganui elected to the House in the 1890s.

Theologically, Baptist development in New Zealand was much influenced by graduates of Spurgeon's Pastor's College, and to a lesser extent, Stepney (Regent's Park). Over the years, major **theological** concerns have included the authority of **Scripture**, closed versus open membership, and relations with other Christians. Countering Baptist **ecumenism** in the Baptist Union, the U.S. **Baptist Bible Fellowship** began a mission in 1971, and U.S. **Baptist Mid-Missions** established a church in New Zealand in 1974. In cooperation with the Australian Baptist Missionary Society, New Zealand Baptists sponsored missionary work in **India** and East Bengal, later **Bangladesh**, in the early 20th century. Other missionary work has been started in **Papua New Guinea**, and beginning in 1886, at home among the Maoris. The Baptist Union publishes the *New Zealand Baptist* (1885–).

As of 2006, there were 90 churches and 12,000 members affiliated with the Baptist Union of New Zealand and six churches with 135 members in the Australasian Conference of **Seventh Day Baptists**. Carey Baptist College is located in Auckland.

NICARAGUA. As early as 1852, a Baptist congregation was started on Corn Island, the result of work through Baptists in **Belize**. Later, in 1889, Baptists from **Jamaica** sponsored a **missionary** work. Both the Northern and **Southern Baptist** conventions in the United States looked at Nicaragua as a potential mission field early in the 20th century. As a result of agreements reached at the missionary conference at Edinburgh in 1910, the **American Baptist Home Mission Society** began evangelization in 1917 in Nicaragua. The first church, largely begun by Eleanor Blackmore (1873–1943), was located in Managua, which became the center of Baptist life. Institutional development evolved, including Colegio Bautista in 1917; a seminary was relocated from **El Salvador** to Masaya in 1941; and the Cranska Memorial Hospital was built in 1930. The Convención Nacional Bautista was formed in 1936. In 1951, the Baptist Seminary was relocated to Managua, where it has had a major impact on Baptist life in Central America. Beyond mainstream Baptist organization, the U.S. **Baptist Bible Fellowship** opened a mission in Nicaragua in 1969.

As of 2006, there were 173 churches with 28,000 members affiliated with the Convencion Bautista de Nicaragua. There is a Baptist-related theological School at Managua.

NIGER. Baptist work in this West African nation began in 1929, when Joseph McCabe started a mission for what became the **Evangelical Baptist Missions** from the United States; this mission resulted in the creation of the Union des Eglises Evangéliques Baptistes in 1927. Later, in 1973, the **Southern Baptists** entered Niger with an extension of their work among the Yoruba people.

As of 2001, there was one congregation, Eglise Baptiste, an outreach of Baptist International Missions (U.S.) with approximately 120 members; one Southern Baptist congregation with about 100 members; and one church, Baptiste Eglise Internationale (1966), associated with Baptist International Missions with about 50 members.

NIGERIA. One of the important early fields of **Southern Baptist** foreign missions was Yorubaland, which later became Nigeria. Work began in 1850 with the preaching mission of Thomas J. Bowen (1814–1875). By 1853, he had organized a church and mission outpost at Ijaye. In the 20th century, the **Lott Carey Baptist Foreign Mission Convention** and the **National Baptist Convention of the United States of America** began missionary works, now cooperating in the Pilgrim Baptist Mission of Nigeria. In 1987, the **Baptist Bible Fellowship** (BBF) began a mission in Nigeria.

As of 2006, there were 9,300 churches and 2,500,000 members in the Nigerian Baptist Convention; a smaller group, the Mambilla

Baptist Convention, had 205 churches and 20,132 members. The Nigerian Convention publishes the *Nigerian Baptist* (1923–). There are six theological schools in Nigeria: Eku, Gongola State, Kaduna, Ogbomosho Western State, Owerri, and Oyo.

NILSON, FREDRIK OLAUS (1809–1881). Swedish and American Baptist minister, born near Gothenburg, Sweden. Baptized by a Danish minister, Forster, he was ordained at Hamburg by **J. G. Oncken**. Nilson organized the first congregation near Gothenburg in 1848. Seized for departing from the doctrine of the State Church, Nilson was banished from **Sweden** in 1851 and became the **pastor** of the Baptist church in Copenhagen (1851–1853). At length his following in Sweden persuaded him to emigrate to the United States, where he was pastor at Rock Island, Illinois, from 1853 to 1860 of the first Swedish Baptist congregation in the United States. In 1860, his banishment from Sweden was lifted by King Charles XV, and Nilson triumphantly went to Gothenburg as a Baptist pastor. In 1868, he again returned to the United States, settling at Houston, Minnesota, as a pastor. He later withdrew from the Baptist ministry, joining the Swedish Free Religious Society, a local Unitarian group.

NOEL, BAPTIST WRIOTHESLEY (1798–1873). English Baptist minister, born at Leightmount, Scotland. He was the son of a baronet and educated at Trinity College, Cambridge University. At first, Noel was an Anglican priest and took the parish at St. John's Chapel, Bedford Row. His **evangelical** preaching was widely regarded, and he was appointed a chaplain to Queen Victoria. With other prominent leaders, Noel was a founder of the Evangelical Alliance in 1846. At length, his sermons caused much disturbance and he converted to Baptist principles in 1849, being publicly baptized that year. From 1850 to 1868, he was minister at John Street, Holborn, and he then embarked upon an evangelistic **ministry**, traveling in the interest of the Evangelical Alliance and the Exeter Hall meetings. An ardent **voluntarist**, Noel criticized **Charles H. Spurgeon** for causing division among evangelicals over baptismal regeneration, and he refused to support united political action against state religion. More than 70 titles are attributed to Noel, including *Essay on Christian Baptism* (1849), *A Revival of Religion* (1851), and *The Rebellion in America*

(1863). In 1859, Brown University (U.S.) conferred an honorary doctorate on Noel.

NONCONFORMITY. A term used in the Elizabethan English historical context to describe Christians who were in communion with the Church of England, but who refused to conform to specified practices in the *Book of Common Prayer*, 1559 edition. In 1662, when Parliament required Anglican clergy to give complete consent to the 1559 edition, many were left outside the Church and the term "Nonconformist" took a more exclusive definition. Eventually, Nonconformity evolved as a political term with respect to the state, and its adherents organized to represent a new religio-political force in English politics. The word "Dissenter" is close in meaning to Nonconformist, originally referring to those Protestants who worshiped outside the established church.

By the mid-17th century, Dissenters and Nonconformists were roughly the same and included not only Presbyterians and Independents but also the Baptists, and in some instances, a host of sects that included **Diggers, Familists, Levellers,** Quakers, **Ranters,** and **Seekers.** Baptists, Congregationalists or Independents, Presbyterians, and sometimes Quakers constituted what was called "old dissent," while Methodists (divided between Calvinists and **Arminians**), from the 18th century, were part of the newer dissent. Baptists originally were a sect, but by the Act of Toleration sought recognition as a legitimate element of Nonconformity. Generally, Nonconformists held common principles such as high priority placed on religious experience, individual expression of the faith, **voluntarism, separation of church and state,** and **religious liberty.**

NORRIS, HANNAH MARIA (1842–1919). Canadian Baptist missionary and denominational leader, born at Canso, Nova Scotia. Educated at the Normal School in Truro, she taught school in her area, often visiting Micmac Indian camps. About 1869, while teaching at the Female Seminary at Acadia University, she was called to **mission** service in **Burma.** Lacking sufficient funds from the Canadian Mission Board, Norris began a crusade to organize **women** for missionary support and started the first of several societies in 1870 at Canso. In all, she organized 33 societies in three months, essentially creating the woman's missionary movement of the Canadian Maritimes. Norris married William F. Armstrong (1849–1918) and served for 48 years in Burma among the Telugus. Her specialty became "redemptive theologies" in Sgau Karen and Telugu folklore; she also developed strategies for **Bible** study in schools, orphanages, and local churches. Hannah equipped a Bible school for the **American Baptist Missionary Union** at Rangoon and traveled widely in its financial interest.

NORRIS, JOHN FRANKLYN (1877–1952). Southern Baptist and, later, Independent Baptist minister, born at Dadeville, Alabama. Norris graduated from Baylor University and Southern Baptist Theological Seminary, but became vehemently critical of higher education. He served three pastorates in Texas: Mt. Calm (1899–1903); McKinney Avenue, Dallas (1905–1908); and First Baptist, Ft. Worth (1909–1951), the latter reportedly paying him the highest ministerial salary in the U.S. South. From 1908 to 1909, he was editor of the *Baptist Standard*, the official paper of Texas Baptists. In the early 1920s, Norris joined with the **fundamentalist** movement, and from his pastorate at Ft. Worth, he launched a lifelong crusade against the **Southern Baptist Convention** (SBC) and religious modernism, withdrawing from membership in the SBC in 1931. He also served Temple Baptist Church, Detroit, Michigan, simultaneously with the Ft. Worth congregation from 1935 to 1951.

Norris was a flamboyant fundamentalist preacher, often involved in controversial behavior such as a celebrated indictment in 1935 for murder, from which he was acquitted. He denounced the New Deal, the Congress of Industrial Organizations, Columbia University, and the Federal Council of Churches of Christ. His open criticism of Southern Baptist leadership caused his ousting from the Pastor's Conference in 1914, from the local association in 1922, and from the state convention in 1924. Norris, in turn, started a new Baptist movement, the Premillennial Fundamental Missionary Fellowship, later known as the **World Baptist Fellowship**, and a school, the Bible Baptist Seminary in Arlington, Texas. His authoritarian leadership in later years led to a split within his group from pastors like **G. Beauchamp Vick**, who began yet another movement, the **Baptist Bible Fellowship** in 1950. Norris published several titles, including

The Gospel of Dynamite (1933) and *New Dealism Exposed: Communism in Baptist Circles* (1935).

NORTH AMERICAN BAPTIST ASSOCIATION. *See* BAPTIST MISSIONARY ASSOCIATION OF AMERICA.

NORTH AMERICAN BAPTIST CONFERENCE (NABC). Body formed in November 1851 at the First German Baptist Church of Philadelphia, Pennsylvania, and formerly known as the German Baptist Conference. Four churches and several laymen and missionaries created the conference to encourage the development of German-speaking Baptist churches in North America. The total membership of the churches at the time of formation was over 600.

From the outset, the German Conference was integrally related to the work of the **American Baptist Home Mission Society** (ABHMS) and the **American Baptist Publication Society**. The churches were listed among the English-speaking congregations for statistical purposes, ministerial candidates were trained in a special department of the Rochester Theological Seminary, and many of the churches received financial grants from the ABHMS.

The growth of the conference depended upon German immigration patterns, and areas in New York, Illinois, Missouri, and the Dakotas and in Upper **Canada** (now Ontario) and the Canadian prairies were of special missionary concern. Early leaders of the conference included **Konrad Anton Fleischmann** (1812–1867), August Rauschenbusch (1816–1899), and Alexander von Puttkammer (1801–1893).

Gradually, the scope of the conference's work expanded with the establishment of a missionary society, a publication society, regional conferences, and **associations**. In 1902, a conference separate to Canada was organized, as was a national women's union. By the 1970s, the number of churches exceeded 350 with a foreign mission program in four countries: **Cameroon**, **Nigeria**, **Japan**, and **Brazil**. Many of the North American churches became bilingual, then mostly English speaking in the 20th century.

Between 1920 and 1940, the relationship between the German Baptist Conference and the Northern Baptist Convention (NBC) was reevaluated by both parties. The ABHMS had long desired the foreign language groups to be assimilated into the mainstream, while the

German Conference affirmed the continuation of the German culture and language. When, in 1938, the NBC extended an invitation for associate membership in that body, the German Conference declined. Among the reasons listed were the possible isolation of German-speaking churches, the loss of the organizational achievements of the Conference, and less specifically, a perception of growing theological **liberalism** in the NBC. In 1946, the general conference was incorporated as the North American Baptist Conference; in 1954, a similar incorporation took place in Canada for the several churches there.

The headquarters of the NABC are located at Oakbrook Terrace, Illinois. From 1853 to 1983, the conference has published a German language paper, *Der Sendbote* (*The Messenger*), and since 1926, an English magazine, the *Baptist Herald*. In the United States, the conference supports one theological school, North American Baptist Seminary, and several homes and orphanages; in Canada there is a single campus for Edmonton Baptist Seminary and the Edmonton Baptist College, after known as Taylor University College.

As of 2006, there were 398 churches with 62,973 members affiliated with the NABC.

NORTH AMERICAN BAPTIST FELLOWSHIP (NABF). One of the six regional fellowships of Baptist conventions/unions related to the **Baptist World Alliance**. The NABF was formed in 1964 as an outgrowth of the Baptist Jubilee Advance and now includes ten member bodies: **American Baptist Churches in the U.S.A.**, **General Association of General Baptists**, **Southern Baptist Convention**, the **National Baptist Convention of the United States of America**, **National Baptist Convention of America**, **Baptist General Conference**, **North American Baptist Conference**, **Progressive National Baptist Convention**, **Seventh Day Baptist** General Conference, and Canadian Baptist Ministries. The NABF meets periodically to facilitate cooperative effort among the members. From time to time, NABF "affinity groups" of staff and volunteers from the member bodies meet to consider ways and means of doing mission and ministry in North American context.

NORTHERN BAPTIST CONVENTION (NBC). *See* AMERICAN BAPTIST CHURCHES IN THE U.S.A.

NORTHRUP, GEORGE WASHINGTON (1825–1900). Baptist minister, theologian, and educator, born at Antwerp, New York. He was educated at Williams College under the celebrated Mark Hopkins and at Rochester Theological Seminary under **Ezekiel G. Robinson**. Considered the outstanding student at Rochester of his era, upon his graduation, Northrup was invited to teach church history and continued at the seminary (1857–1867). He also served as **pastor** of First Baptist, Rochester, one of the premier congregations in the state. In moving to Chicago, Northrup shifted to the discipline of theology and became one of the Baptist leaders in developing the "New Theology." As the inaugural professor at Morgan Park, he organized a distinguished faculty at the Baptist Union Theological Seminary, ultimately including **William R. Harper**. As the new University of Chicago emerged in 1892, Northrup was asked to head up the Divinity School faculty, actually an integration of the Baptist Union Theological Seminary. He taught theology at the University of Chicago until his death, heralding what would come to be known as the **Chicago School**. Clearly one of the brightest **theologians** of the Baptist family at the end of the 19th century, Northrup was similar to **Augustus H. Strong** in that he retained traditional views on the authority of **Scripture**, while holding traditional Reformed dogma and premillennialism in low esteem. He was the author of *Lectures in Systematic Theology* (1881) and an important essay, "The Fatherhood of God," published posthumously in the *American Journal of Theology* (1901).

NORWAY. Two sailor-missionaries—a Dane, Frederik Rymker (1819–1884), and a Norwegian, Gotfred Hübert (1835–1922)—and a Swedish blacksmith, Ola B. Hanssen (1842–1925), began the Baptist work in Norway. The first churches appeared at Porsgrunn and Larvik in 1860. An associational meeting was first held in 1872 at Skien, and the first all Norwegian Baptist Union meeting was in Bergen in 1877. The union was officially organized in 1879 at Trondheim. The Norwegian Baptists in 1910 opened the first Free Church theological school at Christiana; later, with the assistance of American Baptists, a seminary, Baptistenes Teologiske Seminar, was opened at Stabekk, near Oslo. Baptists in Norway enjoyed a close relationship beginning in the 19th century with the Norwegian Baptist

Conference in the United States, as well as leadership from the Scandinavian Department of the Divinity School at the University of Chicago. Norwegian Baptists produce the periodical *Unions-Banneret* (*Banner*) (1880–1892; *Banneret*, 1892–). In 1971, the **Baptist Bible Fellowship** began a mission in Norway, and in 1978, the **Association of Baptists for World Evangelism** started its work in Norway.

As of 2006, Det Norske Baptistsamfunn (Norse Baptist Union) included 71 churches and 4,926 members.

NORWEGIAN BAPTIST CONFERENCE. *See* DANISH-NORWEGIAN BAPTIST CONFERENCE.

NOVOTNY, HENRY (1846–1912). Czech Baptist minister and denominational leader, born near Nachod, Bohemia. Recruited by American Congregationalist missionaries, he was educated at the Theological Institute on St. Chriscona in Basel, **Switzerland**, and at the Free Church College, University of Edinburgh. Following his studies, he returned to Prague to begin pastoral work for the Congregationalists. Under the influence of a Russian Baptist from **Poland**, August Meereis (b. 1847), Novotny was persuaded to adopt Baptist sentiments. In 1885 at Hled'sebe near Prague, Novotny formed the first Czech Baptist congregation, the first services of which were held in his home under great persecution. Later, he was also influential in the creation of the first Baptist congregation in Slovakia at Vavrisovo. He was the publisher of the first Czech Baptist periodical, *Pravda*, and the prime mover in the establishment of the Baptist Union of Czechoslovakia. Novotny wrote the first history of Czech Baptists, *The Baptist Romance in the Heart of Europe* (1939).

NYASALAND. *See* MALAWI.

– O –

OATES, WAYNE EDWARD (1917–1999). Southern Baptist educator and psychologist, born at Greenville, South Carolina. He was educated at Wake Forest College and Southern Baptist Seminary, where he earned the Ph.D. in psychology of religion. He also did further study at Union Theological Seminary in New York and the University of Louisville Medical School. Oates became an internationally renowned professor and author in the field of pastoral care and psychology of religion, teaching most of his career at Southern Seminary 1947–1974. Later, he taught at the University of Louisville Medical School. Oates pioneered the method in counseling known as "trialogue," involving the counselor, the counselee, and the Holy Spirit. He is also credited with coining the term "workaholic." The Wayne Oates Institute was founded in 1993 in Louisville, Kentucky, to promote education and research into holistic health and healing and continue his work. Oates authored 57 books, the most outstanding of which include *The Christian Pastor* (1951) and *Confessions of a Workaholic* (1971).

OLD GENERAL ASSOCIATION OF BAPTISTS. A regional body of **Landmarkist** Baptists formed in November 1905 at Texarkana, Texas. Churches were represented by "**messengers**" from seven states and two foreign countries. The purpose of the association was to unite congregations for **missionary** work and to coordinate a national fellowship. The name adopted was General Association of Baptists in the United States of America, shortened in 1924 to the Missionary Baptist General Association. The effectiveness of the association was short-lived, however, because the Baptist Missionary Association of Texas, for example, was older and larger. Thus, in 1924, the Old General Association of Baptists merged with the Texas Association to become the **American Baptist Association**.

OLD LIGHT BAPTISTS. *See* NEW LIGHT BAPTISTS.

OLD REGULAR BAPTISTS. Name applied to a group of Baptists in the United States who date their founding in 1825 with the formation of the New Salem (Kentucky) Association. As Regular Baptists, they are Calvinistic in the **Philadelphia Baptist Association** tradition and were once part of the United Baptist movement, which brought together the Regular and **Separate** Baptists. Several of the churches, however, were unsatisfied with that union, on the one hand not accepting the **revivalism** of the Separates and also the modernizing tendencies of the Regulars. "Old Regularism" emerged as a means to preserve older patterns in worship and lifestyle. The name was first applied in 1892.

The movement is characterized by basic Baptist principles, plus lined singing in worship, noninstrumental music, support for **Sunday Schools**, reluctance to cooperate with other Baptists, unaltered codes of conduct, the **ordinance** of **foot washing**, frequent hand shaking, and much spontaneity. Theologically, the Old Regulars reject absolute predestination and position themselves deliberately between the hyper-Calvinistic **Primitive Baptists** and the **Arminian** groups like **Freewill Baptists**. The churches of Old Regular Baptists are simple white frame meetinghouses, mostly rural in location. Ministers include not only **elders** of one congregation, but also traveling elders who move about the constituency for special meetings and celebrations of the **Lord's Supper**. **Baptisms** tend to occur later in life than among other Baptists.

There are 13 associations of Old Regular Baptists, ranging from Michigan to Florida and the Mississippi Valley; the center of the movement is in Kentucky and Tennessee. Other than **associations**, there are few evidences of Old Regular institutional life; an exception was the Old Regular Baptist Orphanage in Letcher County, Kentucky, which existed from the late 1940s to 1959. More recent statistics (1990) indicate about 288 congregations with 15,000 members associated with the Old Regular movement.

OLD SCHOOL BAPTISTS. *See* PRIMITIVE BAPTISTS.

ONCKEN, JOHANN GERHARD (1800–1884). German Baptist **missionary** and **pastor**, born at Varel. Self-taught, Oncken was first a schoolteacher and then he became a missionary for the Edinburgh Bible Society, and later the British Continental Society. He met an American Baptist theological educator, **Barnas Sears**, when the latter was touring Europe; Sears baptized Oncken on 22 April 1834. This propelled Oncken on a course as a Baptist missionary and church planter throughout Europe. He established a church at Hamburg in 1834 and served as its pastor for much of his career. His work was recognized by American Baptists, and he became the senior missionary of the **Baptist Board of Foreign Missions** in Europe. He evangelized the Austro-Hungarian Empire, the Balkan states, **Russia**, and Scandinavia. In many cases, he assisted in the establishment with governments of favorable conditions to preach and start congregations. Sometimes this meant imprisonment. No one was more important to the spread of Baptist principles and **religious liberty** in Europe. In 1849, Oncken was the prime mover in the establishment of a union among the German churches and a publishing house, which was later named after him. His sermons were published under the title *Licht und Recht* (1901).

OPEN COMMUNION. *See* LORD'S SUPPER.

ORDINANCES. In Baptist usage, the primary generic term for the religious rites of the church. In contrast with the term "**sacrament**," which some early as well as contemporary Baptists use, an ordinance is taught by **Christ** and clearly evidenced in the New Testament. The purpose of ordinances is symbolic and educational in that by participating in the ordinance, believers are drawn closer to Christ, their fellowship and witness is strengthened, and they act in obedience to a direct command of Christ. There are for most Baptists two ordinances, **baptism** and the **Lord's Supper**, but some would also argue that the **laying on of hands**, singing, **foot washing**, and preaching are also ordinances, that is, these are taught by Christ. *See also* BAPTISM; FOOT WASHING; LORD'S SUPPER.

ORDINATION. A term used among Baptists to designate those who are set apart for special **ministry**, called by some the "professional church leadership" of the denomination. In keeping with the practices of the New Testament churches (Eph. 4:12–13; Acts 6:4; 2 Cor. 4:1), ministry belongs to all, while some are set apart for the ministry of preaching, teaching, **evangelism**, pastoral care, administration, and missionary service (Eph. 4:11; Acts 13:2, 3). The process of ordination involves the local church, the **association**, sometimes a regional or national body, and a candidate. Once the candidate announces to his or her local church that he or she has felt a call of God to ministry, the local church usually issues a license to preach in order that gifts for ministry may be observed. After a reasonable time of training, education, and evaluation, the formal steps toward ordination take place. This involves a committee of an association, which examines the candidate's sense of call, doctrinal beliefs, practical experience, and gifts. In recent years among U.S. **Southern Baptists**, because of intense theological differences within the associations, ordination examinations have been conducted at the local congregational level, with other ministers participating from the geographical area. If the candidate passes the examination, a service of ordination, culminating in the **laying on of hands**, will take place. Usually Baptist candidates are ordained with a clear place of ministry in view.

Among Canadian and Australian Baptists, ordination has evolved in a sophisticated ecclesiological usage. In several unions in **Australia**, a tradition has emerged where the union both ordains and accredits one for ministry. There is recognition of three calls: one for the individual, one from the church, and one from the denomination. This practice was in contrast to the position of **William T. Whitley** in Victoria in the 1880s, who followed the British custom of the church ordaining and the union recognizing ministers. Eventually in several Australian states, colleges and society-type organizations came to ordain persons for their respective services. Likewise in Maritime **Canada**, central Canada, and western Canada, the Baptist Unions also examine candidates for ministry and maintain accredited lists of ministers. Australian Baptists have stipulated from the 1970s that ordination involves four tasks: proclamation, fellowship and nurture, teaching, and service. Among Canadian provinces, the provincial governments also certify persons to perform weddings, upon recognition of the respective ecclesiastical organization. Educational preparation, as determined by the union, has become mandatory in both Canada and Australia.

Although ordination among early English Baptists was practiced each time a minister went to a new congregation, the rite has long been considered a lifetime status as long as the candidate maintains his or her commitments. Some Baptists, however, do withdraw recognition of ordination from those who are not actively engaged in ministry. An ordained minister may be in full-time or part-time ministry. A certificate of ordination issued to the candidate has been common since the 18th century, and in the 20th century, candidates are listed on a roster kept in the union, association, or **convention** official records. The status of ordination usually carries the privileges of officiating at marriages, funerals, **baptisms**, and other occasions, and may in some cases allow the minister to enjoy tax/rate benefits in housing and income reporting, due to historically lower remuneration in ministry than other fields. Ordination of **deacons** is also recognized among Baptists, notably U.S. Southern Baptists, and allows for public recognition of lay ministry. *See also* MINISTRY, BAPTIST UNDERSTANDING OF.

ORIGINAL AND ANCIENT BAPTISTS. Terminology applied by British writers to the New Testament churches, which (the writers assumed) practiced believer's **baptism** and held other Baptist principles; terminology also applied to later Baptistic adherents. Some **Strict Baptists** refer to the earliest Baptists of the Calvinistic tradition, before the creation of the **Baptist Union of Great Britain** in 1831, as Ancient Baptists, in contrast with the Union Baptists, who in Strict Baptist teachings had erred from the faith. *See also* STRICT BAPTISTS.

ORIGINAL FREEWILL BAPTISTS. *See* FREEWILL BAPTISTS.

ORTHODOX BAPTISTS. Name given to a movement of **fundamentalist** Baptists who emerged in Ardmore, Oklahoma, in 1931. W. Lee Rector (d. 1945), a former professor at Oklahoma Baptist University and **pastor** at First Missionary Baptist Church in Ardmore, resigned to form the First Orthodox Baptist Church, also in Ardmore. His guiding principles included reaction to perceived modernism in the **Southern Baptist Convention**, a clear premillennial stance, and the basic Baptist **polity** and thought of **James M. Pendleton**. Eventually, Rector founded a school, the Orthodox Bible Institute, in 1944 and published a periodical, the *Illuminator*, later the *Orthodox Baptist* (1931–). *See also* DISPENSATIONALISM.

– P –

PAKISTAN. Principally an Islamic republic, Pakistan has been a difficult field for Baptist missions. In 1954, the **Conservative Baptists** embarked upon a mission, joined by Canadian Fellowship Baptists and, in 1984, by **Southern Baptists,** to which the official Baptist Convention is related. The Baptist community of approximately 1,000 members is centered in Karachi. The **Baptist Bible Fellowship** also opened a mission in Pakistan in 1959, and the Conservative Baptist Foreign Mission relates to the Indus Christian fellowship in the Sindh province, begun in 1954. The Conservative Baptists work in partnership with the Fellowship Baptists of **Canada.**

As of 2001, there were about 6 churches with 3,100 members affiliated with the Indus Christian Fellowship (CB International), and 14 churches with 1,140 members affiliated with the Baptist Convention.

PALMER, PAUL (fl. 1720–1740). American colonial Baptist minister, whose origins are unsubstantiated; some historians believe he was born in the colony of Maryland, while others hold that he may have been born in England and emigrated to the colonies as a **General Baptist messenger**. The American thesis holds that Palmer was baptized at Welsh Tract Church in Delaware and ordained in Connecticut. In either case, in 1720 he started at Chestnut Ridge what became the first Baptist congregation in Maryland. Within seven years, he settled in the northern region of Carolina colony and started the first Baptist congregation there in 1727. Over the next decade, he started about eight other churches. **Morgan Edwards** visited Palmer in 1738 and proclaimed him the father of the General Baptists of the South. Palmer, who may have been formally elected a General Baptist messenger before he left England, corresponded with General Baptists in England to receive financial assistance, which the English General Baptist Assembly approved in 1702.

PALMQUIST, GUSTAF (1812–1867). American Swedish Baptist minister, born at Solberga, Småland, Sweden. Originally a schoolteacher, he was converted in 1844 to **evangelical** principles. He met **F. O. Nilsson** in Stockholm and was persuaded to emigrate to the United States to be **pastor** to persecuted **Swedish** emigrants. He was baptized and ordained at Galesburg, Illinois, and settled at Rock Island in 1852. Commissioned by the American Baptist congregation at Galesburg, he organized the first Swedish Baptist Church in the United States at Rock Island. In 1854–1855, he was a commissioned missionary of the **American Baptist Home Mission Society** in New

York City, but withdrew to Rock Island in 1855. He returned to **Sweden** in 1857 and spent the remainder of his life in ill health, contracted during a bitter winter experience in Illinois.

PANAMA. Baptist life in Panama has great variety, beginning with the **Jamaican** Baptist Mission Society in conjunction with the **Baptist Missionary Society** in 1866. With the establishment of the Canal Zone in 1903, English language missions were established through the **Southern Baptist Convention**. The work in Panama became a base for **mission** expansion into other Central American countries. In 1959, the Convención Bautista de Panama was established and a theological school opened at Arraijan. The **Conservative Baptist** Foreign Mission Society began in 1962, and the U.S. **Freewill Baptists** began a mission the same year. In 1976, the **Baptist Bible Fellowship** also opened a mission in Panama.

As of 2006, there were 106 churches with 7,573 members affiliated with the Convención Bautista de Panama. Presently, there are two theological schools in Panama: Arraijan and Panama City.

PAPUA NEW GUINEA. Baptist witness in this nation began in 1949, the result of **Australian** missionaries with assistance from **New Zealand** Baptists. Early church planting was conducted at Baiyer River, Kompiam, Lumusa, and Tekin. By 1956, public baptismal services were held at Baiyer River and Lumusa. In 1969, a Baptist **Bible college** was opened, and in 1973 the first portion of the **Bible** translated into Kyaka Enga was completed. The **Baptist Bible Fellowship** opened a mission in Papua New Guinea in 1961, and in 1967, the **Association of Baptists for World Evangelism** started its mission in the country.

As of 2006, there were 395 churches and 38,000 members affiliated with the Baptist Union of Papua New Guinea. Presently, there are two Baptist-related theological schools in Papua New Guinea: Sepik and Western Highland Province.

PARAGUAY. The first Baptist mission work in Paraguay was begun by Argentine missionaries in 1919. The first congregation was started at Asuncion in 1920, and churches were included in the Misión Bautista del Rio de la Plata after 1945. The Convención Evangelica Bautista del Paraguay was organized in 1956. The **Association of Baptists for World Evangelism** began its mission in Paraguay in 1976, and the **Baptist Bible Fellowship** opened a mission in Paraguay in 1980.

As of 2006, there were 135 churches and 10,700 members associated with the Convención Evangelica Bautista. The Convención Evangelica Bautista publishes *Centinela* (*Sentinel*) (1964–). There is a theological institute located in Asuncion.

PARKER, DANIEL (1781–1844). Baptist minister and publisher, born at Culpeper County, Virginia. He was little educated and took to living at various locations on the Old Northwest frontier. Licensed by the Nail's Creek Baptist Church in Dickson County, Tennessee, he was ordained at the Turnbull (Tennessee) Baptist Church in 1806. Thereafter he moved to southeastern Illinois along the Wabash River in 1816. In Illinois, he became an ardent critic of Baptist **missions**, favoring instead individual congregational **ministry**. Parker opposed **Sunday Schools**, education, and missionary societies. He moved among congregations, preaching his doctrine of the "Two Seeds," and organized a successful campaign against the efforts of men like **Luther Rice** and **Isaac McCoy**. He was the **pastor** of Pilgrim Predestinarian Church in Lamotte, Illinois, 1817–1836, and published a newspaper, the *Church Advocate*, in 1829–1831. In 1834, he was in Texas where he began a branch congregation of his Illinois church. For one term, he was elected to the Illinois State Senate (1826–1827). Parker was well-known for his publications, *A Public Address to the Baptist Society of the Baptist Board of Foreign Missions* (1820) and *Views on the Two Seeds: Taken from Genesis, 3rd Chapter and Part of the Fifteenth Verse* (1826). Parker's views were condemned in 1855 in a publication by Tennessee **Primitive Baptist** John M. Watson in his treatise, *The Old Baptist Test*.

PARTICULAR BAPTISTS. Major type among early English Baptists, along with **General Baptists**. Particular Baptists were so called because they held that Christ's atonement applied to the elect of God only, or a particular group of persons.

The first Particular Baptist congregation may be traced to a London Independent, or Congregational, Separatist group established in 1616. **Henry Jacob**, an Oxford graduate, founded the church and later emigrated to Virginia, where he died. **John Lathrop**, a Kentish preacher, assumed pastoral duties until he emigrated to the New World about 1634. Three years later, **Henry Jessey**, a Yorkshire man and Cambridge graduate, became **pastor** and served for the next few years. The question of **baptism** was debated among the congregation as early as 1630, with some members under **Samuel Eaton** accepting believer's baptism about 1633. In 1638, a group of Baptist sympathizers behind the leadership of **John Spilsbury** separated itself from the Jessey congregation as the first Particular Baptist congregation. Between 1638 and 1641, further enlightenment about baptism occurred as Richard Blunt (fl. 1640), a **deacon** in the Spilsbury congregation, traveled to the **Netherlands** and received baptism by immersion from the Hansberger Collegians, a practice that he brought back to England.

In 1644, seven London-area Particular Baptist churches issued a **confession of faith,** which sought to distinguish the Particular Baptist movement from the maligned **Anabaptists** of Ulsterite infamy. Among the signers were **William Coffin**, John Pillsbury, Thomas Patience (d. 1666), and Samuel Richardson (fl. 1643–1658).

Particular Baptists grew dramatically under Cromwell's Protectorate, with numbers of the sect in the New Model Army, which planted churches and **associational** life as the army moved about the countryside. In 1689, the first general "**convention**" (as **Whitley**, called it) of Particular Baptists was held for all of those who agreed to the Confession of 1677. At the turn of the 18th century, the Particular Baptists, strengthened in the urban areas, were the leading Baptist group in England.

During the 18th century, Particular Baptist life matured at both the local church level and beyond. Numerous congregations developed substantial resources, for example the Horsley-down, Southwark, church served by **John Gill** for 51 years. Baptist ministers met in meetings for regular advice (as in the Hanover **Coffeehouse**) and to address political concerns, as part of the **Three Dissenting Denominations**. Education funds and measures to care for widows were instituted in the first decades of the 18th century. In 1770, Particular Baptists of the West Country rallied behind Bristol Academy in the formation of the Bristol Baptist Education Society. In this new **voluntary** tradition, Particular Baptists in 1792 formed the first overseas missionary body in the denomination to reach heathen peoples. Particular Baptists in the North began itinerating **missions**, which eventually became part of the home missionary movement. In 1813, Particular Baptist leaders like **Joseph Ivimey** worked to unite all Baptists in what became the **Baptist Union of Great Britain and Ireland** (BU) (1833). Some Particular Baptist congregations chose to retain the name to demonstrate their continuing Calvinistic ethos, following a historical lineage to **Strict** and, later, Grace Baptists. At length, in 1891, with the diminution of Calvinism due to the Wesleyan Revival and other factors, most Particular Baptists dropped the label and were fused with the remaining General Baptists in the BU. English Particular Baptists published in London a periodical, the *New Baptist Miscellany and Particular Baptist Magazine* (1827–1832).

In recent years, some theologically **conservative** Baptists in the United States and Canada have resuscitated the identity of English Particular Baptists because of their consistent confessional heritage and the Reformed theological orientation that is held in common. Among the centers of renewed interest in Particular Baptist thought are Southern Baptist Theological Seminary (the **Founders Ministries**); the Particular Baptist Press in Springfield, Missouri; and Toronto Baptist Seminary in Ontario, **Canada**.

PASHKOVISM. A religious movement in Imperial **Russia** that emerged in the 1870s and culminated in part as a component of the mainstream Baptist tradition. Granville A. W. Waldegrave, Lord Radstock (1833–1913), a Plymouth Brethren missionary from England, began a **mission** at St. Petersburg in 1874. One of his most ardent converts was Vasilii A. Pashkov (d. 1901), who gave himself vigorously to propagating the Christian faith in the empire. Pashkov and his followers sought to renew the Russian Orthodox Church as a kind of pietistic movement and appealed to Russians on this basis. The Pashkovites, as they were called, were open communionists and rejected the strict **discipline** of the Baptists.

In 1882, they organized the Society for Encouragement of Religious and Moral Reading, a group that ultimately won the approval of the Holy Synod. This society led in the production of a Russian Bible. Numerous people, including many early Baptist leaders, were led to faith by the literature the Pashkovites produced, and Pashkov himself aided the Baptists very generously, at one point purchasing a plot of land for a Baptist colony. Close cooperation ensued between Pashkovites and Baptists until 1903, when the Pashkovites were formally accepted into the Russian Baptist Union, and the name was changed to the Soyuz Yevangel' skikh Khristian-baptistov (Union of Evangelical Christians-Baptists), the term **"evangelical"** being preferred by the Pashkovites. *See also* RUSSIA.

PASTOR, BAPTIST UNDERSTANDING OF. Among almost all Baptist groups since the beginning of the 17th century, the pastor has been the spiritual leader of a local congregation. Baptists typically hold that the terms in the New Testament—presbyter (**elder**), bishop (*episcopos*), and pastor—all designate the same office.

Qualities required of a pastor include moral uprightness, an ability to lead one's family, graciousness, sobriety, temperance, self-control, spiritual discipline, trustworthiness, and honesty (I Tim. 3:1–8; Titus 1:5–9). The duties of a pastor are derived from the apostolic churches and include preaching the gospel, administration of the **sacraments/ ordinances**, leadership at weddings and funerals, and supervision of the governance and oversight of the congregation. Pastors of local churches also constitute together the presbytery of the associated churches.

Since the days of both the English **General** and **Particular Baptists**, the pastoral ministry has been understood as the primary ordained form of **ministry**. All others, such as missionaries, chaplains, educators, administrators, **evangelists**, and special workers, must be understood and assessed first for their fitness as pastors. Pastors are elected by the congregation, usually on nomination of a pulpit or selection committee, or in some cases by a committee of deacons. There is usually no term of office for pastors, the early experience being one of **ordination** for life in a given congregation and reordination where a pastor moves to another congregation. A long pastorate might be several decades, as with **John Gill** who served in London for half a century, or typically for 10 to 15 years. In North American experience in the 20th century, 7 to 10 years is more standard, with British experience being a bit longer in one place.

Among the more **fundamentalist** Baptist congregations, "pastor" can be a title and noun of address. This may signal an unusually authoritarian role and perception of a Baptist pastor, rationalized upon the leadership of **Christ** as a singular great teacher and example. In contrast, British and North American Calvinistic Baptists may practice a multiplicity of elders, and thus elect several "pastors" with differing and changing functions in the life of a congregation. Various bodies of Baptists frequently list the pastors of churches affiliated with an organization (i.e., associations, fellowships, and **conventions**), along with their credentials, and this establishes a formal ministerial roster of the approved and credentialed pastoral ministry. *See also* ASSOCIATIONS; POLITY, BAPTIST.

PATTERSON, LEIGHTON PAIGE (1942–). Southern Baptist minister and educator, born at Ft. Worth, Texas. Patterson's father, T. A. Patterson, was the general secretary of the Baptist General Convention of Texas 1961–1973. Paige was educated at Hardin-Simmons University and New Orleans Baptist Seminary where he received a doctorate in theology. One of the most influential teachers in his early development was **Clark H. Pinnock**. After serving several churches in Abilene, Texas; Fayetteville, Arkansas; New Orleans; and Dallas (1963–1975), Patterson became associated with W. A. Criswell at First Baptist Dallas and eventually was selected in 1975 to be the founding president of Criswell Bible Institute, an institutional expression of Southern Baptist **conservative evangelical** resurgence in the 1980s. In 1992, Patterson became president at Southeastern Baptist Seminary in Wake Forest, North Carolina, to begin the transition of that school toward the agenda of conservative evangelicals in the **Southern Baptist Convention** (SBC). During his presidency, he advanced the academic programs, adding a research doctorate to the curricula, several physical plant improvements, and the beginnings of a full-fledged undergraduate program of studies. In 2003, he accepted the presidency of Southwestern Baptist Seminary in Ft. Worth, Texas, thus returning him to his native state. At Southwestern, he has reshaped the faculty profile and strengthened the Southern Baptist influence in Texas through the newly organized Southern Baptist Convention of Texas. With **Paul Pressler**, Patterson is credited with being a principal architect of the profound changes in the SBC. He was twice elected to the presidency of the SBC (1998, 1999) and in that capacity influenced passage of the revised "**Baptist Faith and Message**" (2000). At both Southeastern and Southwestern seminaries, he has held professorships in theology, most recently the L. R. Scarborough Chair in Evangelism. Among his published works are *A Pilgrim Priesthood* (1982) and *The Church in the 21st Century* (2001).

PAUL, THOMAS (1773–1831). American **black Baptist** minister and missionary, born at Exeter, New Hampshire. He was baptized in 1789 and ordained to the **ministry** at Nottingham, West, New Hampshire. He served the African Baptist Church in Boston from 1805 to 1831, also organizing the Abyssinian Baptist Church in New York City in 1809. In 1823, he secured a missionary appointment from the Massachusetts Baptist Missionary Society to serve in **Haiti**; this service lasted for six months during which time he became a pioneer preacher on the island. His lack of knowledge of the French language inhibited his **mission**, however, and he returned to Boston. Reports of his missionary labors were printed in the *Massachusetts Baptist Missionary Magazine*.

PAYNE, ERNEST ALEXANDER (1902–1980). English Baptist minister, educator, and denominational leader, born at Clapton, England. He was educated at King's College, University of London, Regent's Park College, and Mansfield College, Oxford University. Following his Oxford studies, he served from 1928 to 1932 as **pastor** at Bugbrooke. From 1932 to 1940, he served in several roles with the **Baptist Missionary Society** and the **Baptist Union** (BU), resigning to accept a position as tutor at Regent's Park College, Oxford. In his 10 years with Regent's College, Payne specialized in ecclesiastical history and mentored a number of future Baptist leaders. During this period, he wrote a history of the Free Churches and advocated the **Anabaptist origins** of the Baptist movement. In 1951, he became the secretary of the BU, and as such, one of the most influential voices in English **Nonconformity**. Under Payne's leadership, British Baptists participated fully in the World Council of Churches, Payne serving as one of its presidents and as a member of the Faith and Order Commission. Within the BU until 1967, and well into retirement, he was an advocate of **religious liberty** and international **human rights** causes. Among Ernest Payne's many literary contributions are *The Prayer Call of 1784* (1941), *The Free Church Tradition in the Life of*

England (1944), *The Baptist Union: A Short History* (1959), and *Christian Baptism* (1959).

PEABODY, LUCY WHITEHEAD MCGILL (1861–1949). Baptist denominational leader, born in Belmont, Kansas. She attended classes at the University of Rochester and married a Rochester Seminary student, Norman Waterbury. Lucy taught for a time at Rochester School for the Deaf; later, she and her husband were appointed missionaries to **India** by the **American Baptist Missionary Union**. After five years' work with the Telugus at Madras, Norman died and Lucy returned to the United States. In 1887, she accepted the position of corresponding secretary of the Woman's American Baptist Foreign Mission Society of the East and married a wealthy Salem merchant, Henry Peabody. Peabody died in 1908, leaving Lucy with a considerable estate, which she devoted to various mission causes. She made the acquaintance of **Helen Barrett Montgomery** and the two women campaigned widely on behalf of women's missionary work, particularly in 1910 during the International Jubilee of Women's Missions. During the theological debates among Northern Baptists in the 1920s, Lucy lent her support to the **conservative evangelical** camp. She helped to establish the **Association of Baptists for Evangelism** in the Orient in 1927. Resigning from all of her Northern Baptist Convention responsibilities, she became an outspoken promoter of conservative causes, including the Eastern Baptist Theological Seminary in Philadelphia. Ultimately, rebuffed as a woman in leadership, she reduced her outreach to writing on missionary subjects and managing her benevolent projects. Among her more enduring works are *Henry Wayland Peabody-Merchant* (1909) and *Just Like You: Stories of Children of Every Land* (1937).

PEACEMAKING, BAPTIST. Although not one of the "historic peace churches," numerous Baptists have advocated various forms of peacemaking, based on the scriptural injunction, "Seek peace and pursue it" (Psalm 34:14). **Voluntary associations** and later denominational agencies have also taken pro-peace (or nonviolence) stances among parts of the Baptist family. Many early English Baptists fought in the New Model Army and viewed military service as a part of their civic responsibility. However, linked with **religious liberty**, Baptists like **Leonard Busher** published works that reinterpreted the theme of peace, *Religion's Peace; or a Plea for Liberty of Conscience* (1614).

Likewise in the American colonies, Baptists took a nonresistance position, like the **Rogerenes**. In the early American Republic, Baptist ministers like Henry Holcombe (1762–1824) of Charleston, South Carolina, and Philadelphia, Pennsylvania, and **Francis Wayland** of Boston, Massachusetts, and Providence, Rhode Island, were peace advocates and joined voluntary societies dedicated to peace concerns; Howard Malcolm (1799–1879) and **George Dana Boardman Jr**. also joined the movement.

In Great Britain, with the formation of the Society for the Promotion of Permanent and Universal Peace in 1816, several Baptist ministers, including George Pilkington (1785–1858), James Hargreaves (1768–1845), and William Stokes (d. 1881) were prominent in its membership. Even greater interest among Baptists for the cause of peace emerged in the 20th century, with the formation in Britain in 1929 of the Baptist Peace Fellowship, gathered by a Baptist pastor, W. H. Haden (1875–1952) of West Bridgford. This followed clear advocacy by British leaders like **F. B. Meyer**, **James Rushbrooke**, and **John Clifford**. In the United States, those who wished to offer support to conscientious objectors in the era of World War II formed the Baptist Pacifist Fellowship in 1939, including **Harry Emerson Fosdick**, Edwin M. Poteat Jr., and Edwin Dahlberg (1892–1986). This presaged in 1984 American and **Southern Baptists** in the U.S. forming the **Baptist Peace Fellowship of North America** (BPFNA). A major conference of 200 Baptists from 30 countries was held in Sjovik, Sweden, in 1988, at which a manifesto was issued. One of the important catalysts toward recognition among Baptists of the importance of pursuing peace was the endowment in 1964 of an award in the American Baptist Convention by Victor and Eileen Gavel in honor of Edwin T. Dahlberg. Among the prominent Baptist leaders in the modern peace movement were **Martin Luther King Jr.**, Muriel Lester (1883–1968), and **Howard Thurman**. The BPFNA publishes *Baptist Peacemaker* (1981–). *See also* POTEAT FAMILY.

PEARCE, SAMUEL (1766–1799). English Baptist minister, born at Plymouth, England. Early in his life he had an **evangelical** experience, and he was educated for the ministry at Bristol Baptist College. His sole pastorate was at Cannon Street Baptist Church in Birmingham from 1789 to 1799. Pearce knew **William Carey** before his missionary career and became one of Carey's most devoted supporters. He offered himself for **missions**, but owing to his organizational powers and reputation in the north of England, he was encouraged to work for missions at home. This he did by organizing an auxiliary society and carrying forth a system of prayer for missions among the churches. He traveled widely, speaking in England and **Ireland** on behalf of the **Baptist Missionary Society**. In 1794, he wrote to **William Rogers** of First Baptist Church, Philadelphia, urging him to appeal to American Baptists to create an **American Baptist Foreign Mission Society**. Pearce died of consumption; it has been speculated this was the result of a wearing schedule, which entailed travel among the poorer classes and straightened living circumstances. Pearce produced one major treatise in his short career, *The Scripture Doctrine of Baptism, with Some Historical Remarks on the Subject* (1794).

PECK, JOHN MASON (1789–1858). American Baptist missionary and denominational leader, born at Litchfield, Connecticut. Peck was largely self-taught, although he received some lectures in William Staughton's Theological School in Philadelphia. Following a pastoral ministry in Amenia, New York, in 1813–1815, Peck accepted an appointment of the Massachusetts Baptist Missionary Society as a domestic missionary in the West. In 1817, along with **James E. Welch**, Peck became one of the first missionaries of the **Baptist Board of Foreign Missions** from 1817 to 1820. He positioned himself at St. Louis and turned his attention to the Indian tribes in the vicinity. After only three years, the board withdrew its support, but Peck stayed in the field. He moved to Rock Spring, Illinois, where he began a school based on a combination of a high school and a literary and theological model coupled with a manual labor institute program. To support himself, he wrote extensively on the western territories and he edited newspapers, notably *The Pioneer and Western Baptist* (1830–1843). With the support of **Jonathan Going**, Peck helped to organize the **American Baptist Home Mission Society** in 1832. In 1843, he became the corresponding secretary of the **American Baptist Publication Society** and reduced its debt and greatly extended its outreach. In 1853, he helped to found the American Baptist Historical Society in recognition of the need to address Baptist identity. As an editor, Peck was an **antislavery** thinker, but refused abolitionism as too extreme. Peck's journal, *Forty Years of Pioneer Life: Memoir of John Mason Peck* (1864), is considered an important resource for the study of the Mississippi Valley region.

PEDALAVIUM. *See* FOOT WASHING.

PENDLETON, JAMES MADISON (1811–1891). Southern and, later, American Baptist minister, born in Spotsylvania County, Virginia. Pendleton was tutored by **Andrew Broaddus** and became a merchant. He moved to Kentucky, and further studied at an academy in Hopkinsville, Kentucky, under James Rumsey. After a brief career in school teaching, he served churches at Hopkinsville (1833–1836), First Baptist, Bowling Green (1836–1849), and Russellville (1849–1857). About 1852, Pendleton met **James R. Graves** who promptly won Pendleton over to a closed communion position. Graves invited Pendleton to write for his paper, the *Tennessee Baptist*, and Pendleton's work was well received. Two important classics emerged from his pen, *Three Reasons Why I Am a Baptist* (1856) and *An Old Landmark Re-Set* (1857). Pendleton immediately became a leader in the emerging **Landmarker** movement, although he never advocated Baptist successionism and held to the doctrine of the universal church.

In 1857, Pendleton was named to an endowed chair in theology at Union University in Murfreesboro, set up by Graves. There he served also as president of the institution (1859–1860) until it was forced to close at the threat of war. He also served as an editor of the *Southern Baptist Review* and of the *Tennessee Baptist*. He was an ardent opponent of Campbellism, Roman Catholicism, and infant baptism. Pendleton's position against **slavery** (he was a gradualist) angered Graves, and he was fired as associate editor of the *Tennessee Baptist* in 1861. In 1862, Pendleton became **pastor** at First Baptist Hamilton, Ohio, where he served until moving to the Upland Baptist Church in

Pennsylvania in 1865. At Upland, he had a close relationship with **Henry G. Weston** and the **Crozer** family, taught at Crozer Theological Seminary, and published a *Church Manual* (1867) and *Christian Doctrines* (1878), as well as other doctrinal and exegetical works.

PENTECOSTAL FREEWILL BAPTIST CHURCH. *See* FREEWILL BAPTISTS.

PERKIN, JAMES RUSSELL CONWAY (1928–). English and later Canadian Baptist minister and educator, born at Bugbrooke, Northamptonshire. He was educated at St. Catherines, Oxford (M.A., D.Phil.). He served in the Royal Air Force at the conclusion of World War II, and was early encouraged to advanced studies by his former pastor, **Ernest Payne**. From 1956 to 1961, he served the Baptist church at Altrincham, having been ordained to the ministry at Bugbrooke. Perkin won a **Baptist Union** Open Scholarship and studied at Strasbourg, where he taught Greek to theological students in French. Following a time of teaching at New College, Edinburgh University (1962–1965), he accepted a position as associate professor of New Testament Interpretation at McMaster Divinity College and McMaster University in Ontario (1965–1969). At that time, Perkin transferred his ordination credentials to the Baptist Convention of Ontario and Quebec. In 1969, he moved to Acadia University as professor and head of religious studies. In succession, he took on increasing administrative responsibilities at Acadia: dean of arts (1977); vice president, academic (1980); and president (1981–1993). During his presidency, facilities expansion took place, and in the academic area, a significant number of Rhodes and Commonwealth scholars graduated from the undergraduate programs. Regionally, Perkin took an interest in **ecumenical** ministry, and this led to his work with a historic congregation, the Covenanter Church in Grand Pre, in conjunction with the local United Church clergy. From the 1960s, he was well-known for his interest in church music and liturgy, producing with G. Gerald Harrop, *With Mind and Heart: Worship Aids for Leaders and People* (1978). This interest paralleled his work with the committee to publish the new Canadian Baptist *Hymnal* (1973), in which he contributed a number of signed responses and prayers, thus influencing worship across the country. Following his university presidency,

Perkin continued to teach English and religious studies courses and presided over the regional health services board in Western Nova Scotia. His Oxford dissertation was titled "Baptism in Nonconformist Theology, 1820–Present, with Special Reference to the Baptists," and his publications include *Seedtime and Harvest* (1982), *Morning in His Heart: Life and Letters of Watson Kirkonnell* (1986), and *Ordinary Magic: A Biographical Sketch of Alex Colville* (1995).

PERRY, RUFUS (1834–1895). American **black Baptist** minister and denominational leader, born a slave in Tennessee. Perry educated himself secretly, using the good resources of his Baptist preacher-father until his father ran away to Canada. Rufus was sold to a Mississippi slaveholder in 1852 but fled to Windsor, Ontario, where he taught school. Eventually, he took theological classes at Kalamazoo College and was ordained in 1861 to serve the Second Baptist Church, Ann Arbor, Michigan. Later, Perry was also **pastor** at St. Catherines, Ontario, and at Buffalo and Brooklyn, New York. In Brooklyn, he organized Messiah Baptist Church. After the Civil War, Perry devoted himself to educational efforts and administration. He superintended schools for freedmen and edited newspapers, including the *American Baptist* and the *National Monitor*. He became a corresponding secretary for the **Consolidated American Baptist Missionary Convention**, as well as the American Educational Association and the **American Baptist Free Mission Society**. Perry was an outspoken devotee of black leadership in black affairs. Following an electrifying address entitled "Light" at State University in Louisville, Kentucky, in 1887, that school awarded him the Ph.D. degree, possibly the first to a black Baptist clergyman in the United States. Perry's booklet, *The Cushite or the Children of Ham* (1887), is considered a classic of African American literature.

PERU. The initial Baptist work in Peru was an outgrowth of Argentine Baptist work. Under the influence of the Southern Baptist **Foreign Mission Board**, Argentine missionaries began churches north from Lake Titicaca in 1933. Independent Baptists working for the Amazon Valley Baptist Faith Missions established a church in 1935 at Iquitos. In 1950, the Convención Evangelica Bautista de Peru was started; in the 1950s, congregations opened in most of the major cities. Other

Baptist developments included independent Baptists associated with Misión Evangelica Bautista Irlandesa (the Irish Baptist Foreign Mission; 1927), Associación Bautistas Maranathas (1964), and the Associación Bautistas para Evangelistas Mundial (**Association of Baptists for World Evangelism**) initiated a work in 1929 related to another effort of **Baptist Mid-Missions** in the United States, which began its mission in 1947 at Lima and Cuzco. The **Baptist Bible Fellowship** opened a mission in Peru in 1958. Recently, the Baptists of eastern Peru have been involved in cooperative ministries with the Bolivian Baptist Union.

As of 2006, there were 155 churches and 10,000 members affiliated with the Convención Evangelica Bautista del Peru. The Convención Evangelica Bautista publishes *Destellos Bautistas* (*Baptist Stars*). There is a Baptist-related theological school located at Trujillo.

PETO, SAMUEL MORTON (1809–1889). English Baptist philanthropist, born at Woking, Surrey. Peto was apprenticed in various building trades and became a draftsman. He developed the firm of Griswell and Peto, a construction company, which built the Nelson Monument, the Houses of Parliament, and the Lyceum Theatre. The original firm dissolved in 1840, with Peto directing his energies into railroad construction on several continents, as well as in Britain. In 1846, he began railway construction on the Norwich section of the Northeastern Railway, where he met William Brock, the minister of St. Mary's, Norwich. Two years later, Peto built with his own money Bloomsbury Chapel in London, to which he persuaded Brock to come as **pastor**. Peto served in Parliament for Finsbury, Norwich (1859–1865), and later for Bristol (1865–1868). He led in the passage of the Church Rates Bill and the Peto Act, which prescribed the procedures for appointing trustees for dissenting places of worship. At length, Peto went bankrupt but recovered by entering the field of railroad building. Later in life, he was again able to support numerous Baptist causes. Peto also served as treasurer of the **Baptist Missionary Society** from 1855 to 1866. He published *The Resources and Prospects of America Ascertained during a Visit to the States in the Autumn of 1865* (1866).

PHILADELPHIA BAPTIST ASSOCIATION (PBA). The oldest Baptist association in the United States in continuous existence, founded in 1707. Consultative intermittent meetings were held as early as 1688. Originally comprising five small congregations, Lower Dublin (Pennepack), Piscataqua (Piscataway), Middletown, Cohansey, and Welsh Tract, the association spanned the Delaware River in Pennsylvania and New Jersey. Based upon English and Welsh Baptist models, this prototype of all American Baptist **associations** and extra-parish bodies, the PBA pioneered many features of Baptist life. The association handled queries about matters of order and church **discipline**, examination for **ordination**, supply of pastors, constitution of new churches, and special projects. In 1746, Benjamin Griffiths provided a classic definition of an association in the annual minutes; the next decade, the first educational institution of Baptists in America was sponsored in Hopewell, New Jersey; and in 1764, the PBA sponsored the establishment of a college in Rhode Island.

During the 1770s, the PBA grew strong enough to commission traveling evangelists to the other colonies and the pattern of leadership was passed to the north (Warren Baptist Association) and south (Charleston Baptist Association). The PBA was the nucleus of sentiment several times for a national organization of Baptists, notably in the 1760s and 1790s and again in 1812. Its churches, which numbered 81 (21,000 members) by 1940, included several of the most prestigious congregations in the United States. The PBA debated most of the significant social concerns of the day and affirmed typical Protestant positions, such as **religious liberty**, **antislavery**, **temperance**, and the need to maintain a watchful eye on the developing Roman Catholic community in the region. Following the Civil War, the PBA became essentially dominated by its urban congregations, although many historic churches in the surrounding Pennsylvania countryside remained faithful. This led, in due course, to the founding of the Philadelphia Baptist City Mission Society in 1880, which placed the association at the forefront of American Baptist urban mission development.

With the formation of a statewide **convention** in Pennsylvania, the PBA churches often dually aligned themselves with both bodies, and this resulted in cooperation in many projects. In the reorganization of the American Baptist Convention in 1972, the PBA became one of 37 recognized regional, state, or city organizations in covenant with the national denomination. In its membership are churches of various ethnic and racial groups, including **black Baptists**, Hispanic, German, and Chinese. As of 1995, the PBA included 123 churches with over 54,000 members involving nine ethnic groups. *See also* AMERICAN BAPTIST CHURCHES IN THE U.S.A.; ASSOCIATIONS, BAPTIST; EDUCATION; HIGHER EDUCATION; POLITY, BAPTIST.

PHILIPPINES. The **American Baptist Missionary Union** was the first Baptist organization to send missionaries to the Philippines, beginning in 1900 after the Spanish-American War. Under a comity arrangement for **evangelization** of the islands by the Evangelical Union of the Philippines, Baptists were given Panay and Negros Islands, with primary emphasis upon the indigenous Visayan peoples. The centers of the effort were Jaro and Iloilo. From this mission came the Baptist Conference of the Philippines in 1904. Educational institutions, including Jaro Industrial School (1905), Filamer College (1906), and Central Philippine University (1923), were started by missionary support. In 1925, a Philippine Baptist Home Mission Society was organized. As a result of American Baptist divisions over missionary methods, the **Association of Baptists for World Evangelism** began work in the islands in 1929, founding the Doane Evangelistic Institute at Iloilo, Panay, in 1930, and the Luzon Baptist District Association with Manila at its center in 1935. This same effort produced the Baptist Bible Seminary in Manila in 1948.

In 1943, 11 American Baptist missionaries were executed on the Island of Panay by the Japanese army. U.S. **Southern Baptist** interest in the Philippines commenced as large numbers of American troops were incarcerated on the islands during World War II and with the closing of the **China** field in 1949–1953. In 1948, Southern Baptist missionaries began work that would become the Convention of Philippine Baptist Churches and the Mindanao Baptist Convention of Southern Baptist Churches. The Philippine Baptist Theological Seminary was opened in 1952 at Baguio. Another U.S. group, the **Baptist General Conference**, began a mission in 1946 with a Baptist Theological College at Cebu. The **Baptist Bible Fellowship** opened a mission in the Philippines in 1948, as did the **Conservative Baptist** Foreign Mission Society, with a theological school founded at Quezon City in 1968. In 1974, a **Seventh Day Baptist** mission was established in the Philippines.

As of 2006, there were six Baptist groups organized in the Philippines: the Baptist Conference of the Philippines, with 323 churches and 23,240 members; the Convention of Philippines Baptist Churches, with 800 churches and 110,000 members; the General Baptist Church of the Philippines, with 252 churches and 7,667 members; the Luzon Convention of Southern Baptist Churches with 540 churches and 41,895 members; the Mindanao Baptist Convention of Southern Baptist Churches, with 889 churches and 52,166 members; and the Conservative Baptist Association of the Philippines, with about 150 churches with 21,000 members. There are 10 schools in the Philippines: Bacolad City, Baguio City, Cebu City (2), Davan City (3), Dagupan City, Iloilo City, and Negros. *See also* MARTYROLOGY, BAPTIST.

PHILPOT, JOSEPH CHARLES (1802–1869). English Baptist minister and editor, born at Ripple. He was educated at Oxford University and elected a fellow of Worcester College in 1827. As an Anglican rector he served the parish at Stadhampton; he was a popular **evangelical** preacher and built a substantial congregation. Philpot was converted to the Baptist position and baptized in 1832 by John Warburton, a former weaver. He served **Strict** and **Particular** congregations the rest of his life, at Allington, Oakham, and Stamford. For over 20 years, he edited the *Gospel Standard*, assuming the mantle of **William Gadsby**. Philpot's sermons were translated into Dutch and German as exemplars of the theme of sovereign grace. One of Philpot's favorite themes was to stand against **Arminianism**, and he frequently denounced John Wesley (1703–1791) and the Methodists. Among Philpot's published works are *The Eternal Sonship of Christ* (1861) and *Strict Communion Vindicated* (1873).

PILLSBURY, GEORGE ALFRED (1816–1898). American Baptist denominational leader and philanthropist, born at Sutton, New Hampshire. After a secondary education, Pillsbury worked in the grocery business and sheet-iron manufacture. By 1848, he entered a partnership in dry goods and became a local politician. In Concord, New

Hampshire, Pillsbury served as purchasing agent for a railroad, was elected mayor of the city, and served one term in the New Hampshire State legislature (1871–1872). In 1878, he moved to Minneapolis, Minnesota, and entered a partnership in flour milling with his son and brother. This became the Pillsbury-Washburn Flour Mills Co., the largest in the world of its era. Again involved in politics, Pillsbury was elected mayor of Minneapolis in 1884 and was an influential Republican. In Concord, he was a highly regarded lay member of First Baptist Church, and in Minneapolis, he superintended the construction at First Baptist Church of the largest ecclesiastical edifice west of Chicago, as well as the creation of the largest pipe organ in the West. He virtually built the campus of an academy at Owatonna, later named Pillsbury Academy. He also served as president of the St. Paul/Minneapolis Baptist Union, the Minnesota Baptist Convention (1880–1887), and the **American Baptist Missionary Union** (1888).

PINNOCK, CLARK HAROLD (1937–). Canadian Baptist theologian, born in Toronto, Ontario. He was educated at the University of Toronto in Near Eastern Studies and took a doctorate in New Testament theology at the University of Manchester under the celebrated Church of the Brethren scholar, F. F. Bruce. Following graduate school, Pinnock lived at L'Abri, Switzerland, in the colony established there by the American Reformed theologian Francis Schaeffer. In 1965, he took an initial academic post at New Orleans Baptist Theological Seminary, which was under the leadership of H. Leo Eddleman, a **conservative evangelical** Southern Baptist. With another Canadian colleague, Samuel Mikolaski, Pinnock helped to redefine New Orleans as a conservative evangelical bastion in the Southern Baptist tradition. While in New Orleans, he taught **Paige Patterson** and met **Paul Pressler III**, the aspiring strategists of a resurgence movement in the **Southern Baptist Convention**. Pinnock left New Orleans in 1969 to teach at Trinity Evangelical Divinity School, and in 1974, he left Trinity to teach at Regent College in Vancouver, British Columbia. His evolving views on **Scripture** and also on Calvinist thought created difficulties at each institution.

In 1977, McMaster Divinity College, associated with McMaster University in Hamilton, Ontario, invited Pinnock to give a lecture in which he advocated blame for the downfall of conservative theology in the Baptist Convention of Ontario and Quebec to the rise of **liberal** thought at McMaster University. As a move to assert its openness to evangelical thought, McMaster appointed Pinnock to succeed Russell Aldwinckle in Theology. Pinnock's years at McMaster were also fraught with controversy. Defining himself as a "pilgrim theologian," he wrote in favor of scriptural infallibility but also affirmed the theology of Pope John Paul II and the charismatic experiences in the widely publicized "Toronto Blessing," a Holy Spirit **revival** led by a **Fellowship Baptist** pastor, John Arnott. Yet Pinnock was also a key element in the recovery of McMaster's evangelical heritage. By the time of Pinnock's retirement in 2002 from McMaster, his following had shifted from traditional conservative evangelicals to large numbers of Pentecostals. His position in support of open theist colleagues like John Sanders almost brought a vote of expulsion in 2003 from the Evangelical Theological Society. Among Pinnock's numerous published works are *Set Forth Your Case* (1968), *The Scripture Principle* (1984), *Flame of Love* (1996), and *Most Moved Mover: A Theology of God's Openness* (2001).

POLAND. Polish Baptist development stems from the German Pietist movement and the mission work of **J. G. Oncken**. In 1858, Gottfried A. Alf (1831–1898) formed the first congregation at Adamow near Warsaw. In contrast with the German-influenced churches, Slavic and other language congregations also emerged. Under great persecution, partly because of their German origins, Polish Baptists finally united in 1942 and secured recognition from the government in 1946. The partition of lands to the east and west made it difficult to unite the Polish churches until the Marxist era. In 1907, a seminary was formed at Lodz (recently transferred to Radosc near Warsaw), and a newspaper, *Slowo Prawdy* (*Word of Truth*) was started in 1925. Among the other groups represented in Poland, the **Conservative Baptist** Foreign Mission Society began work in 1988, assisting in the establishment of a Baptist-related seminary at Wroclaw. In 1933, a division among Seventh-day Adventists led to the establishment of a **Seventh Day Baptist** work.

As of 2006, there were 79 churches and 4,700 members in the Koscio Chrzescijan Baptystow.

POLISH BAPTIST CONFERENCE IN THE U.S.A. With increasing numbers of immigrants from Poland and improved economic opportunities in the United States and **Canada**, significant numbers of Poles emigrated to the eastern industrialized regions of the United States. American and German Baptists began Polish mission work in Buffalo, New York, in 1890; Jozef Antozewski (1853–1934) founded the Fillmore Avenue Baptist Church in 1894. In the Chicago area, Polish **mission** was conducted by several German Baptist churches. By 1912, the scattered congregations formed the Polish Baptist Association at Pound, Wisconsin; this later became the Polish Baptist Conference in the U.S.A. By 1939, there were 38 churches; in Canada, an additional seven were founded. The conference supported missions to Polish people and raised support for aid to Poland. The conference has published the following periodicals: *Naszc Zycic (Our Life)* (1910–1917); *Zrodlo Prawdy (Source of Truth)* (1917–1930); *Zwiastun Prawdy (Herald of Truth)* (1930–1939). The conference has been related to the **American Baptist Churches in the U.S.A.** and the Baptist Convention of Ontario and Quebec.

POLITY, BAPTIST. Term applied to the organizational principles and behavior of a religious group. In Baptist experience of all kinds, the centerpiece of polity is the local congregation. All authority under **Christ** is vested in the local church and no external authority is superior. Its officers, mandate, relationships, and ministries are determined by its membership. A **confession of faith,** derived from the membership, may indicate the local church's theological identity, and a **covenant** agreed upon by the membership may define obligations and conditions of membership and **ministry**. A constitution and/or bylaws will likely profile the structures, procedures, and purposes of each local church. In some cases, mostly in North America and Great Britain, local churches will also be incorporated in order to achieve protection and opportunities under local laws. Among many Baptist groups, Baptist polity ends with the local church.

From the early 17th century, English Baptists associated among congregations. This led inevitably to the formation of permanent **associations**, which serve as advisory bodies to the local churches and help to facilitate certain functions that local churches prefer to do collectively. These functions include **ordination** of ministers, resolution of conflict, doctrinal interpretation and advice, and various forms of mission activity. Associations grew rapidly in the 18th century in England, **Scotland**, and **Wales**, and the vehicle was transferred to North America as well. At the end of the 18th century, the identity of the Baptist denomination was seen primarily in the collection of associations. Associations are usually defined by rules of order and procedure and are entirely **voluntary** bodies.

Emerging from the British community was the voluntary association, which provided a variegated form of organization for Baptists. These societies were composed of individuals who focused upon a particular task and drew up their own rules and membership qualifications. Sometimes these societies existed within churches, while others developed alongside congregations, or involved a mixture of Christians from many denominations. The society model of polity influenced Baptists broadly in shaping future permanent organizations at the denominational level; the society had a great appeal to Baptists because it fostered individualism and freedom of choice. The Bristol Education Society and the **Baptist Missionary Society** were pioneers of this model in British Baptist experience.

In 1813 and 1814, respectively, British and American Baptists created a new level of polity by organizing the union or **convention**. In Britain, the union eventually became the national assemblage of Baptists from churches and associations, which coordinated **mission** programs, stewardship, and ethical/political concerns. In the United States, the convention became a gathering of representatives of churches and associations interested in cooperating in mission—first overseas, then domestic—and education. With the formation of the **Southern Baptist Convention** in 1845, the convention became a unifying symbol of Baptist identity in the United States and a model of cooperation and advice for smaller Baptist bodies. Inevitably, some Baptists objected to the organizational unity and preferred to stress the inviolable local church; these have variously been referred to as "**Landmarkers**," "anti-missionary," or "**Primitive**" Baptists.

Beginning with associational rules and **Thomas Grantham**'s *Christianismus Primitivus* (1678), manuals of polity and practice have been produced to instruct churches and extraparish bodies on rules of decorum and structure. Among the more widely accepted authors have been **Elkanah Holmes** (1797), Samuel Jones (1798),

Edward Hiscox (1859), **James M. Pendleton** (1867), **Hezekiah Harvey** (1879), **Ben M. Bogard** (1927), William R. McNutt (1935), **Henry Cook** (1947), and **Norman H. Maring** and **Winthrop S. Hudson** (1963, 1991). Many Baptist unions require candidates for **ordination** to complete courses in Baptist polity and practice. *See also* ELDER; LOCAL CHURCH PROTECTIONISM; PASTOR, BAPTIST UNDERSTANDING OF.

POPKES, WIARD UDO (1936–2007). German Baptist theologian and educator, born at Westoverledingen-Ihren in East Friesia. He was educated at the International Baptist Seminary in Rüschlikon, Switzerland, completed his doctorate in New Testament at the University of Zurich, and served a congregation in Vikariat from 1957–1969. His entire teaching career (1967–2002) was spent as instructor in New Testament at the Baptist Seminary in Hamburg (later Elstal), **Germany**, with short terms teaching at the International Seminary in Prague and as an adjunct professor at the University of Hamburg. Popkes was a leader in his generation of important changes in European and German Baptist development. As chair of the board of trustees of the International Baptist Seminary in **Switzerland**, in the 1990s, he led the plan to dissociate the school from the U.S. **Southern Baptist Convention** and move it to Prague, **Czech Republic**. This came after a preferred plan failed; Popkes and Karl-Heinz Walter of the European Baptist Federation had tried to unite the Switzerland school with Popkes's own seminary at Hamburg, Germany. Popkes was a prime mover in the establishment of the European Baptist Teachers Fellowship, regularly bringing together educators from several Baptist institutions and unions in Europe. In addition, Popkes was a key faculty member in the relocation and reestablishment of the historic German Baptist seminary at Hamburg to Elstal in former East Germany that involved a merger with the former Baptist seminary at Buckow in East Germany. Popkes' career marked the sweeping changes in European political geography and the Baptist denomination in Post-Marxist Europe. Among his published works are *Christus traditus* (1967), *Der brief des Jakobus* (2001), and *Ein Gott und ein Herr: Zum kontext des monotheismus im Neun Testament* (2004).

PORTUGAL. The first Portuguese Baptist was likely Ignatius Fernandez (1757–1830), a candlemaker in Dinajpur, **India**. He was brought under the influence of **Baptist Missionary Society** personnel in India in 1796. As for Portugal itself, an English Baptist layman and protégé of **Charles Haddon Spurgeon**, Joseph Jones (1769–1868), began **evangelistic** work and formed the first Baptist congregation in 1888 at Oporto. In 1910, Brazilian Baptists heard of the work and sent Zachary C. Taylor (1851–1919), a **Southern Baptist** missionary, to Portugal. New congregations at Wisen (1913), Tondela (1914), and Lisbon (1922) resulted. The Portuguese Baptist Convention was started in 1920. Another Baptist beginning was the result of **Conservative Baptist** missionaries from the United States, who used the services of a former Brazilian Baptist missionary, João de Oliviera (1883–1958), who was associated with no less than 10 mission organizations, beginning in 1945. In 1949, they started several congregations and a seminary at Leiria was established in 1948; the seminary has changed hands several times and continues operation at present with Southern Baptist support. A cooperative body, União Baptista de Portugal, was formed in 1946, securing assent of 11 churches. Portuguese Baptists publish *O semeador Baptista* (*The Baptist Sower*) (1925–). Separate from the other Baptist works, the Conservative Baptist Foreign Mission Society began a work in central Portugal in 1945, the **Baptist Bible Fellowship** opened a mission in 1987, as well as the **Association of Baptists for World Evangelism** in 1978.

As of 2006, there were 68 churches and 4,400 members affiliated with Convencão Baptista Portuguêsa, and 3 churches with 150 members affiliated with the Conservative Baptist Mission. There is a Baptist-related seminary at Queluz.

PORTUGUESE BAPTIST CONGRESS IN THE UNITED STATES. Portuguese mission work in the United States dates from the 1890s when Francisco C. B. Silva (1863–1926) accepted an appointment from the **American Baptist Home Mission Society** in Oakland, California. Later Silva attended Newton Theological Institution and worked among the Portuguese in Massachusetts, especially the Bethel Baptist Mission in Boston and vicinity. In 1894, a chapel was constructed in New Bedford, Massachusetts, becoming the first Portuguese Baptist Church in North America. The congress was formed in 1919 to provide fellowship among the churches, which in 1940 numbered about 14. The congress became a cooperating organization of the Northern Convention, later **American Baptist Churches**.

POTEAT FAMILY. A prominent Southern Baptist family of several generations. Among the leaders were William Louis Poteat (1856–1938), son of James and Julia Poteat and the president of Wake Forest College (1905–1927). William was educated at Wake Forest and then did graduate studies at the University of Berlin and the Marine Biology Laboratory at Woods Hole, Massachusetts. He taught at Wake Forest (1878–1905) and blended science and religion in his teachings. He was active in the North Carolina Baptist Convention, the Anti-Saloon League, the North Carolina Academy of Sciences, and the North Carolina Conference of Social Services.

William's younger brother was Edwin McNeill Poteat Sr. (1861–1937), president of Furman University (1903–1918). Edwin was educated at Wake Forest and Southern Baptist Theological Seminary, with further studies at Berlin, Yale, and Johns Hopkins universities. He served pastorates at Chapel Hill, North Carolina (1884–1886), and Memorial Baptist Church, Philadelphia (1898–1903). Poteat was active in the Layman's Missionary Movement and the Interchurch World Movement (1918–1919) and worked for the Northern Baptist Convention General Board of Promotion. Following his presidency at Furman, he was professor of philosophy and ethics at the University of Shanghai in **China** and at Mercer University (1931–1934).

Edwin McNeill Poteat Jr. (1892–1955), son of Edwin McNeill Poteat Sr., was a Southern Baptist minister and educator, born at New Haven, Connecticut. A graduate of Furman University and Southern Baptist Seminary, he joined the Student Volunteer Movement and became a **missionary** to China. For four years, he taught philosophy at the University of Shanghai and then returned to the United States to be **pastor** at Pullen Memorial Baptist Church in Raleigh, North Carolina, and Euclid Avenue Baptist in Cleveland, Ohio (1937–1944). For one term (1944–1948), he was president of Colgate Rochester

Divinity School in Rochester, New York. He was also a member of the Committee on Worship of the National Council of Churches (1941–1955) and president of Protestants and Other Americans United for the **Separation of Church and State**. As a pastor, he advocated scientific advances and wrote on a great many subjects, including history, poetry, and liturgy—18 books in all, including *Jesus and the Liberal Mind* (1934) and *Mandate to Humanity* (1953). In the **Southern Baptist Convention**, he became known as an advocate of the **social gospel**, and even charged that Baptists had participated in social evils. He called upon his fellow Baptists to confess their sins and pursue racial and economic justice and **religious liberty**. In 1940, he delivered the Beecher Lectures in Preaching at Yale University. The Poteat family represented the **liberal** tradition in Southern Baptist life, raising questions of modernity and **ecumenism** within their own denomination and the larger Christian church.

POWELL, ADAM CLAYTON, JR. (1908–1972). American black Baptist minister and political leader, born in New Haven, Connecticut. The son of a prominent **black Baptist** clergyman, **Adam Clayton Powell Sr.**, Powell was educated at Colgate University (B.A.) and Columbia University (M.A.). He became minister at Abyssinian Baptist Church in New York City in 1937 following his father, where Adam Jr. served until 1960. He entered city politics in the 1930s, being elected to the City Council of New York in 1941, and founding and editing a civil rights newspaper, the *People's Voice*, in 1942. Powell was elected to the U.S. Congress in 1945 and subsequently 10 more times through 1967. A flamboyant orator, he was irreverent, audacious, and prophetic in his advocacy of nondiscrimination. Powell's personal life overwhelmed his career, however. In 1966, following an eight-year legal battle in which he was found guilty of slander, he took up residence on the island of Bimini. The following year, amidst charges of the misuse of public funds, the U.S. House of Representatives voted to censure him and, ultimately, to remove him from his congressional seat. In 1969, he was stripped of his seniority, but later the Supreme Court reversed his removal order. To complicate matters further, at the time of his death, two women vied for the right to determine Powell's funeral arrangements. Powell received honorary degrees from Shaw University in Raleigh, North Carolina, and Virginia Union University in Richmond, Virginia. His outstanding literary achievement is *Keep the Faith, Baby!* (1967).

POWELL, ADAM CLAYTON, SR. (1865–1953). American **black Baptist** minister, born at Martin's Mill, Virginia, the son of a German planter and a Negro-Indian woman slave. He was poorly educated and fled accusations in a gunshot incident in 1884. He worked in coal mines in Ohio and was dramatically converted in 1885, turning to the **ministry**. For a time, he worked in a hotel in Washington, D.C., and studied at Wayland Seminary. In 1892–1893, he was **pastor** at churches in St. Paul, Minnesota, and Philadelphia, Pennsylvania. In 1893, he was called to Emmanuel Baptist Church in New Haven, Connecticut, where he became a nationally famous black preacher. Abyssinian Baptist Church in New York City, deeply in debt, called him as pastor in 1908, and he remained there until his retirement in 1937. In his years at Abyssinian, he cleared the debt, helped the congregation to move uptown to a new location, and became a major spokesman for black racial pride. A longtime Republican, Powell switched to the Democrats in 1932 to support Franklin D. Roosevelt, and Powell led in the creation of programs to combat poverty in the Great Depression. A **liberal** social thinker who shifted from the position of **Booker T. Washington** to that of W. E. B. Dubois (1868–1963), Powell was a founder of the Urban League and the National Association for the Advancement of Colored People. The community base which his ministry created became the political base of his son, **Adam Clayton Powell Jr**.

POWELL, VAVASOR (1617–1671). Welsh Baptist minister and evangelist, born in Radnorshire, **Wales**. He was a graduate of Jesus College, Oxford University, and entered the Anglican ministry. He was influenced by Puritan thought and converted to the Independent cause; he was baptized in 1655. Powell was considered the greatest **evangelist** of his era, preaching across Wales and at London to great crowds and starting new churches. At Dartmoor, he started a congregation but later returned to Wales. From 1650, Powell enjoyed opportunities under the Act for the Better Propagation and Preaching of the Gospel in Wales, which allied him with government interests. A significant number of Welsh congregations followed his teachings:

Calvinistic, mixed communion, open membership, and **revivalistic**. His extreme republican views, such as advocating the right of lower classes to rule, and **Fifth Monarchist** sympathies drew the ire of Oliver Cromwell (1599–1658), and Cromwell had Powell imprisoned. Powell was incarcerated eight years in 13 prisons; he died at Fleet Jail in London in the 11th year of his confinement. Powell managed to publish nine works, including one of the first biblical concordances (1671) produced by a Baptist. His biography, also published in 1671, was influential over many generations among Welsh Baptists. Powell was the author of several polemics, including *A Short View of the Praelaticall Church of England* (1641) and *Common Prayer-Book No Divine Service* (1660).

PRAYER MEETING. A customary devotional and worship experience among Baptists since the 17th century. While the precise origins of prayer meetings are not known, it is likely that they were an outgrowth of small groups that met as illegal conventicles when more public meetings were unlawful. This was typical of Puritans and Separatists from the 1580s. Early congregational records, notably at Broadmead Baptist Church in Bristol, England, in 1640, indicate that church members gathered in homes for prayer between Sunday worship services. Some churches connected such meetings with the **Lord's Supper** and met at least monthly. In the later 18th century, the New Connexion of **General Baptists** produced tickets for participants in weekly prayer meetings, which in turn admitted members to the Lord's Supper; this practice was derived from the Methodists. It is also evident in British Baptist practice that prayer meetings were an occasion for lay leadership, many times in the absence of ministers, as at Birchcliff in Yorkshire. The General Assembly of **General Baptists** in 1724 urged the organization of "cottage meetings" to increase spiritual gifts.

The occurrence of prayer meetings among Baptists in America originated in the 17th century. Association circular letters enjoined prayer among the congregations as early as the 1720s. It appears that the idea of a mid-week prayer service was popularized in the mid to late 19th century in the **revivalist** tradition as a means of spiritual discipline between Lord's Days. With **Sunday Schools**, prayer meetings caught on as a regular part of church life for the faithful. In the 20th century, prayer meetings were common until the 1970s, when family activities and schedules complicated the weekly routine.

A typical prayer service consists of **Scripture** reading, a brief homily or reflection (hence the name of the service is often "prayer meeting and **Bible** study"), followed by sharing of prayer needs and concerns and a "season of prayer" in which several persons pray extemporaneously. The entire experience lasts about one hour in North American practice and occurs typically on Wednesday evenings. When the service occurs in a home rather than in the church building, it is referred to as a cottage prayer meeting.

PREEXISTERIAN BAPTISTS. *See* STRICT BAPTISTS.

PRESIDENCY OF THE UNITED STATES, BAPTIST INVOLVEMENT IN. Prior to 1900, Baptists could not claim a president, but there were Baptist influences upon those who did serve. There is a widespread myth that George Washington was baptized by immersion by a Baptist chaplain at Valley Forge during the American Revolution. Both Thomas Jefferson and James Madison had close friends in the Baptist ministry in Virginia. In Andrew Jackson's cabinet, Baptists were prominent. Thomas Lincoln, father of Abraham Lincoln, was a leader in the Pigeon Creek, Indiana, Baptist Church, and Abraham Lincoln may have been a sexton there. George Washington Baines, the maternal grandfather of Lyndon Baines Johnson of Texas, was a prominent Texas Baptist editor and president of Baylor University.

Four Baptists have served as presidents of the United States and one vice president was Baptist. **Warren Gamaliel Harding** was elected president in 1920 and served until his death in 1923. He was a member of a congregation in Ohio that related to the Northern Baptist Convention. **Harry S. Truman** of Missouri was raised a Baptist and was a lifelong member at Grandview Baptist Church in Missouri. Truman was thought of as belonging to the Southern Baptist family, though that denomination did not own his leadership. **James Earl ("Jimmy") Carter** was an active Southern Baptist layman in his home congregation at Plains, Georgia, when he was elected president in 1976. After his presidency, Carter became associated with the Cooperative Baptist Fellowship and other theologically moderate Baptists. **William Jefferson ("Bill") Clinton**, elected president in 1992, was a member of congregations in Hope and Little Rock, Arkansas, through his college years. Albert Gore, vice president under Clinton (1993–2001), was a Baptist in his home church in Tennessee and in Washington, a member at Georgetown Baptist Church.

PRESSLER, PAUL III (1930–). Texas jurist and Baptist layman, born at Houston, Texas. He was educated at Princeton University, the University of Texas Law School, and later at the National College of State Trial Judges. Pressler worked for the law firm of Vinson and Elkins in Houston and served for a term in the Texas State House of Representatives (1957–1959). He was appointed District Judge for the 133rd District in Houston, Texas, in 1970. From 1978 to 1992, he was a judge on the 14th Texas Court of Appeals (Houston) and active in the Texas Republican Committee. In 1978, he met with **Paige Patterson** at the Café Dumond in New Orleans to begin a collaboration in changing the structure and leadership of the **Southern Baptist Convention** (SBC) through a renewal of **conservative evangelical** theology. Pressler considered himself a keen student of organizational structures, and Patterson the quintessential conservative evangelical theologian. His first major achievement was the election of **Adrian Rogers** as SBC president in 1979. Pressler stepped down from the bench in 1992, confident of the direction of the denomination, to return to the practice of law and to serve as director of various organizations, including the National Association of Religious Broadcasters, the Southern Baptist International Mission Board, and the Free Market Foundation. Since 2000, Pressler has been a senior partner with Woodfill and Pressler and involved in mediation law. Politically, Pressler has long been an active Republican in Texas politics and supported Ronald Reagan, George H. W. Bush, and George W. Bush in their presidential campaigns. President George Bush intended to nominate Pressler as director of the Office of Government Ethics in 1989, but pressure from Southern Baptist moderates against the nomination persuaded Pressler against accepting the nomination. His 1999 book, *A Hill on Which to Die*, is considered an autobiography of the Southern Baptist resurgence movement. In 2007, Louisiana College named its Law School in honor of Judge Paul Pressler.

PRIESTHOOD OF ALL BELIEVERS. A generally accepted characteristic of most Baptists, the priesthood of all believers is an inheritance of the Reformation. Martin Luther (1483–1546) especially emphasized this doctrine. For Baptists of the 17th century, the notion of a hierarchical priesthood such as in the Church of England or Roman Catholicism was unacceptable and tended toward clericalism. Rather, each believer has direct access to God through Jesus Christ, the High Priest (Heb. 7:17–28; 1 John 2:1). Based upon **Scripture** references, such as Exodus 19:5–6, Revelation 1:6, 1 Peter 2:9, and Ephesians 4:12, Baptists teach that priestly **ministry** is conducted by one believer for others. Included in the priestly ministry of believers are intercessory prayer and service in the name of **Christ** for one another. Some Baptist writers also stress that the priesthood of all believers allows any believer to administer the **sacraments** (**baptism**, the **Lord's Supper**) to each other. In contemporary literature, the priesthood of all believers has often been expressed as the "ministry of the whole people of God" or the "mutual ministry of believers."

PRIME MINISTERS OF CANADA. *See* DIEFENBACKER, JOHN GEORGE; MACKENZIE, ALEXANDER; TUPPER, SIR CHARLES.

PRIMITIVE BAPTISTS. Movement that originated in 1832 among rural Baptist communities in Maryland and Delaware. These first Primitive Baptists are also called the "Old School," anti-missionary, or "Hard Shell" Baptists. On 28 September 1832, a group of 22 ministers convened as the "Black Rock Convention" to oppose tract societies, **Sunday Schools**, missionary societies, the Bible Society, colleges and theological schools, and protracted meetings. They issued a series of resolutions and an account of their proceedings, and called upon others to subscribe to a new periodical, the *Signs of the Times*. Their reasoning was that societies and new measures were human inventions of a modern age and were not found in the New Testament; as such, these practices were contrary to the spirit and power of **Christ**. They refused to cooperate with others in the regular Baptist **associations** on the basis of "Can two walk together, except they be agreed?" (Amos 3:3). They styled themselves "Old School Baptists" because the title distinguished them as belonging to the "school of Christ"; in actuality, the terms "New School" and "Old School" had some currency among Presbyterians and Congregationalists on the matter of using "means" (human instrumentality) to advance the gospel (New School people used "means").

A second emergence of this U.S. Primitive Baptist tradition occurred in the Chemung (New York) Baptist Association in 1835. Leaders there called for disassociation from other Baptist associations that supported missionary societies and educational institutions. The same rationale was used, namely, that there was no New Testament basis for such organizations. The desire of these churches was to adhere to the order of the "primitive" church. Within a decade, there were 1,600 congregations and over 60,000 members in the movement.

In 1900, a key organizing meeting of Primitive Baptists in the United States was held at Fulton, Kentucky. Behind the leadership of Elder James Oliphant, those present agreed to reaffirm the 1689 London Confession, providing modifications for language clarity purposes only in what became called the "Fulton General Address." In 1981, the London Confession was again reprinted, with some dissent from several elders who felt the **Bible** should be the only standard and others making a distinction between "time salvation" and those biblical texts relating to eternity.

Primitive Baptists in the U.S. have provided various kinds of observers with opportunities to examine a microcosmic community of Baptists. The **German** social scientist Max Weber (1864–1920) visited the Primitive Baptist community at Mt. Airy, North Carolina, in 1904. He drew several useful conclusions about the application of Calvinism in religious communities and typified the Primitive Baptists as a sect. Other more recent studies by various sociologists and anthropologists of Appalachian religious culture continue to mark the importance of the group.

In 1910, among Georgia Primitive Baptists, a major split occurred over the use of musical instruments in worship, advocating **Sunday Schools**, holding "fleshly" revival meetings, and remunerating ministers. Two factions emerged: the Old Liners and the Progressives, the former being absolutely opposed to changes, and the latter being open to new ways.

As of 1995, there were approximately 1,700 churches and about 64,000 members associated with various segments of the U.S. Primitive

Baptist movement, including the Absoluters, the Old Liners, and the Progressives. Primitive Baptists of different persuasions publish several periodicals, including *Signs of the Times* (1833–), the *Primitive Baptist* (1885–), *Baptist Witness* (1952–), and *Banner Herald* (1918–) (formerly the *Pilgrim's Banner* [1893–1918], which merged with the *Primitive Herald* [1916–1918]). In 1958, the radio broadcast "Baptist Bible Hour" was adopted by many Primitive Baptists and has enjoyed the support of many churches, despite its being a use of the media.

A second category of Primitive Baptists is found among black Americans. Following the Civil War, black Primitive Baptists in the southern United States separated from the white churches and formed a movement of black Primitive Baptists. As of 2005, there were over 500 congregations and about 50,000 members associated with the group.

The third major group of Baptists to adopt the nomenclature "Primitive" was a cluster of several churches in New Brunswick, Canada. In 1875, a breakaway conference of Free Baptists under the leadership of Elder George Wightfield Orser (1813–1885) was organized at East Florenceville, New Brunswick. It was made up of seven churches, formerly a part of the General Conference of Free Christian Baptists. Within a decade, congregations from Maine and Massachusetts joined the new conference. However, when this conference sought a charter from the New Brunswick legislature, they were denied the use of the name "Free Baptists" under pressure from the preexistent Free Christian Baptists who were numerous in the province. In 1898, the new group obtained a charter under the name "Primitive Baptists." By the 1980s, the group had dwindled sharply in numbers, and in 1981 they voted to join the American Freewill Baptists, becoming the Atlantic Canada Association of the National Association of Freewill Baptists. Popularly known as "Orserites," they were never Calvinistic in theological outlook as were the U.S. Primitive Baptists.

PROGRESSIVE NATIONAL BAPTIST CONVENTION (PNBC). The most **ecumenical** of the major American **black Baptist** denominations. The roots of the organization are found in a 1961 dispute at the annual meeting of the National Baptist Convention in Kansas City over the election of the president of the **National Baptist Con-**

vention of the United States of America. **Joseph H. Jackson** sought his fourth two-year term as president against a movement among delegates to elect Gardner C. Taylor (1918–) of New York City. Jackson won, in part by manipulating the election. A related issue was the question of support for **Martin Luther King Jr.** and the civil rights movement, which the Taylorites wanted but the followers of Jackson opposed. When it appeared futile to bring about change in the "tenure" of the incumbent, 33 delegates from 14 states convened on 14–15 November 1961, at Cincinnati, Ohio, and founded the Progressive National Baptist Convention. Lavaughn Venchael Booth (1919–2002), **pastor** of Zion Baptist Church in Cincinnati, was considered the leading voice in the new movement. Timothy Moses Chambers (1899–1977) was elected president of the PNBC, while Taylor and King played a major role in shaping the principles of the organization.

Like the other national black Baptist organizations, the PNBC includes boards for Home Missions, Foreign Missions, Christian Education, and Pensions. The convention participates in most ecumenical bodies, including the National Association for the Advancement of Colored People, the Southern Christian Leadership Conference, and the Urban League. From its inception, the PNBC has maintained a cooperative agreement with the **American Baptist Churches in the U.S.A.** Its support for educational institutions is extended to Chicago Baptist Theological Seminary, Central Baptist Theological Seminary, Morehouse School of Religion, Virginia Union School of Theology, Shaw University, and Howard University School of Divinity. Missionary work is sponsored in **Haiti**, **Liberia**, **Nigeria**, and other parts of West Africa. The PNBC periodical is *Baptist Progress* (1912–), an older black Baptist news magazine.

As of 2006, there were 1,200 congregations and an estimated 2.5 million members related to the PNBC, many of which are dually aligned with other Baptist bodies.

PROKHANOV, IVAN STEPANOVICH (1869–1924). Russian Evangelical and Baptist minister, writer, and educator, born in the Caucasus. The son of Molokan parents, he was educated at Bristol Baptist College and the New Congregational College in Bristol. Later, he graduated from the theological faculty of the University of Berlin and did further studies at the University of Paris and Hamburg. In 1890,

Prokhanov returned to Russia to become a leader in the development of the Evangelical movement. A composer of hymns (he compiled a hymnal, *Gusli*) and editor of a journal, *Besseda* (*Dialogue*), he had a dream to unite Russian evangelicals, including Baptists, under a scheme similar to the Evangelical Alliance. He went to England for studies for several years, and then returned to Russia as an engineer and educator. During his time in England, Prokhanov continued to publish his journal, which he sent by mail back into Russia. About 1898, he joined **Ivan Kargel** in a Baptist congregation in St. Petersburg, but by 1905, Prokhanov had separately organized the young people into his own house church. A theological rift occurred between Prokhanov's following, which favored broader relationships with evangelicals, and the Kargel group, which held a position similar to closed communion. During the last years of Czarist Russia, Prokhanov petitioned the government for a charter to start a Russian Baptist university, and this was granted just as the Bolshevik Revolution erupted. He made a strong case for the libertarian ideals of Baptists and their strong patriotism. After the Soviet takeover and during an era of relative freedom in the early 1920s, Prokhanov attempted in 1926–1927 to blend New Testament teaching, Communist agricultural ideals, and **Anabaptist** community models into a commune he called the "City of the Sun," or "Evangelsk," to be located in Siberia. His greatest achievement was to be his work in organizing the All Russian Evangelical Conference in 1909 that would become a major component of the All-Union Council of Evangelicals-Baptists, uniting several believer's church factions. Prokhanov was elected vice president of the **Baptist World Alliance** in 1911.

PROKOFIEVITES. *See* RUSSIA.

PUERTO RICO. From 1898, Baptist work in Puerto Rico has primarily been related to the American Baptists. Just after the United States occupied Puerto Rico in 1899, Hugh McCormick (1860–1929), a missionary of the **American Baptist Home Mission Society**, arrived at Rio Piedras to begin church planting. The location at Rio Piedras insured that it would become a center for education, including the university and the Evangelical Seminary (founded originally in Coamo in 1907), in which Baptists participate with five other denominations. Other educational ventures include the Grace Conaway Institute (1914) and the Barranquitas Academy (1926). A convention of churches, Iglesias Bautistas de Puerto Rico, was formed in 1902 and is a recognized regional organization of the **American Baptist Churches in the U.S.A.** Following U.S. military presence on the island, **Southern Baptists** began mission work in Puerto Rico in 1964, having started a congregation in the early 1950s. In 1965, an association of Southern Baptists was formed.

As of 2001, there were 82 churches with 27,000 members affiliated with the Iglesias Bautistas de Puerto Rico.

PULSFORD, THOMAS (1793–1871). English Baptist minister and revivalist, born in West Ansty, Devonshire. Baptized at Tiverton, he served the church at Limpley Stoke, and from 1819 to 1839, he served as **pastor** at Torrington. In 1839, he was appointed evangelizing agent for the **Baptist Home Mission Society**. Pulsford focussed his efforts in northern England and produced a widespread **revival** experience among the churches in 1847. He used "means" much akin to those of American Presbyterian revivalist Charles G. Finney (1792–1875): protracted meetings twice per day and three times on Sundays, tracts, **prayer meetings**, inquiry meetings, and the anxious bench. In the years 1842–1843, it was estimated that Pulsford helped to convert as many as 500 persons at towns like Newark and elsewhere in the north. Following an assessment of Pulsford's work, it was agreed that he should not hold protracted meetings after 1844, and he took a settled pastorate in the Southwest. Pulsford was the author of *Helps for Revival Churches* (1846).

PURITAN-SEPARATIST HYPOTHESIS. A historical theory that seeks to explain the origins of the Baptist movement with reference to the English Puritan tradition. Since the later 19th century, British and American Baptist historians have debated whether Baptists were an outgrowth of the **Anabaptists** or a sect that emerged as part of the overall Puritan Reformation of 1560–1650. Following the clues laid forth in the studies of English **Separatism** and Congregationalism, where a congregational form of church government arose along with a strong commitment to biblical authority, proponents of the Puritan-Separatist hypothesis hold that the earliest Baptists came to be connected with **Francis Johnson** (1562–1618), a Cambridge theologian, and his protégés, John Robinson (1572–1625) and **John Smyth**. A distinct connection of doctrinal and ecclesiastical similarity, if not personal relationships, has been demonstrated to exist from Johnson to Smyth and the first **General Baptists**, and also from **Henry Jacob** and what became the **Particular Baptist** movement. Those who propound this thesis see no necessary connection between English Separatists and European Anabaptists and hold that the burden of proof lies upon those who would affirm such a connection. Rather, it was a particular view of church government and the widespread influence of the **Scriptures** in the vernacular that produced the first Baptists as an entirely distinct group. Among the historians who have advanced the Puritan-Separatist hypothesis are **Henry C. Vedder**; **William T. Whitley**, Barrington R. White of Oxford, **Winthrop S. Hudson** at Colgate Rochester in New York; **Norman H. Maring** at Eastern Baptist Seminary in Philadelphia, Pennsylvania; Ken R. Manley at Whitley College in Melbourne, Australia; and H. Leon McBeth at Southwestern Baptist Seminary in Ft. Worth, Texas. *See also* ANABAPTIST KINSHIP THEORY.

– R –

RACE, BAPTISTS AND. The issue of race has played a significant role in Baptist identity from the 16th century. At its beginning, the Baptist movement was essentially white and English speaking, but as Baptists emigrated to North America, Africa, and Australasia, issues of race began to emerge. Baptists interacted with indigenous groups by either attempting to evangelize them and/or assimilate them into Euro-American cultures. Baptists conducted missions to the Native Americans in New England and New York in the 18th century, establishing segregated congregations. In the 19th century, Baptists produced a flurry of missionary efforts in the Northwest and South among tribes, ultimately supporting both the removal of tribes from their native lands and the establishment of the reservation system. Congregations on the reservations were segregated. Likewise, in **India**, **Burma**, **China**, and Africa, missionary congregations established among indigenous peoples were almost exclusively non-white, and the missionaries typically lived in compounds with native workers assisting them. The assumption underlying the missionary effort was that it was the burden of the Europeans and North Americans to bring the rest of the heathen world to a Christian orientation and culture.

Racial identity was especially pronounced in regions where slavery existed, notably in the United States and the British Empire. Unlike some leading Quakers or Methodists who early developed **antislavery** postures and limited integration of blacks and whites, Baptists have a history of racially segregated congregations. In late 17th-century English Baptist life, there is evidence of Baptist complicity in the slave trade, as in the various enterprises of Edward Terrill of Bristol. This passed to the societies of Islanders in the West Indies and Africa. Various voices were heard within the Baptist community against slavery, notably **William Knibb**, who eventually influenced the abolition of slavery in Britain.

Hundreds of Baptists in the southern, northern, and western United States were slaveholders. Slave churches in the Baptist tradition in the United States were segregated from whites until later in the 18th century. In colonial Virginia, South Carolina, and Georgia, some black congregations met in white meetinghouses, some were part of extended white congregations, and still others were under the general oversight of white Baptist associations. Through the American Civil War, white congregations in the South seemed to follow the social and legal sanctions against blacks, though there is evidence of Baptist cooperation in the Underground Railroad operations in the South to assist slaves attempting to flee to the North and Canada. A notable leader in this movement was **William H. Brisbane**. *See also* BLACK BAPTISTS.

The earliest development of Baptists in Africa was along racial lines, first in **Sierra Leone**, where former American slaves who had first relocated to Nova Scotia settled finally in coastal Africa under the leadership of **David George**. In the 1820s, a colony of American former slaves was organized in **Liberia** under the Baptist missionary **Lott Carey**. In **Jamaica**, West Indies, **George Leile** in the 1780s pioneered a segregated church in Kingston.

As Baptists in the United States followed a segregated organizational history after the Civil War, their missionary outreach was likewise segregated. Generally, **black Baptists** supported missions in Africa and the West Indies, where the white **mission** organizations from the United States had little-to-no investment. This changed in the 1970s as racial attitudes among **Southern Baptists** evolved and the **Foreign Mission Board** stepped up its work in Africa and the Indies, where black Baptist numbers increased substantially in countries like **Kenya, Ghana, Ivory Coast**, and **Nigeria** in Africa, and **Haiti, Dominican Republic**, and **Barbados** in the Indies. The colorful complexion of Baptists worldwide was noticeably beginning to change in the **Baptist World Alliance** context, where leaders of black organizations in the United States and later Africa attended and were elected to positions of prominence from 1905 forward.

In discussing issues in which racial identity plays a role, racial slavery and abolitionism must be distinguished from racial separateness and segregation. As an issue of concern, racial separateness was debated in U.S. Baptist organizations from the beginning of the 20th century. Some, like the **National Baptist Convention, U.S.A.**, wanted to maintain a separate identity but also receive funds and maintain fraternal relations with white Baptists. Others, like the **National Baptist Convention of America** (1915), desired a limited form of cooperation with Southern Baptists, but set up their own educational and publication ventures. Still others, like the Virginia Baptist State Convention (black) wanted to be entirely independent and self-supporting. Black solidarity among Baptists was proclaimed from many important pulpits, including Olivet in Chicago, Ebenezer in Atlanta, Abyssinian in New York, First Baptist (Capitol Hill) in Nashville, and Shiloh in Washington, D.C.

Elsewhere in Baptist circles, racial issues have been focused on other racial groups. In Australia, for instance, while as early as the 1840s Baptists reached out to the Aboriginal population, it was not until a century later that Baptists joined other Australian **evangelicals** in evangelizing Aborigines. Following an uneven response to Aboriginal land claims, settlement policies, and citizenship issues in the 1940s and 1950s, Australian Baptists in 2000 committed themselves to reconciliation and becoming more sensitive to Aboriginal spirituality. Graham Paulson, the first Aboriginal to be ordained a Baptist minister (1968), helped to organize the Aboriginal and Islander Baptist Council of Australia, after 1997 called the National Indigenous

Training Association. In neighboring New Zealand, missionary work among the Maoris commenced in 1886, languished shortly after, and was restarted in 1955 to become a department of the Baptist Union of New Zealand. Similarly, the Chinese communities in the western United States and Canada that had been created from the mid-19th century around railroad construction and fishing industries were targets for missionary work, sometimes being referred to as the "Oriental (or Chinese) problem." Baptist missionaries in China, **Japan**, and **Korea** were far more responsive to Oriental traditions and customs than were Baptists in the homelands of North America, where there was almost exclusive segregation of the races except at the associational levels. Baptists in the United States were about evenly divided in editorial opinion about various pieces of national legislation that sought to curtail immigration.

With the rise of the **fundamentalist** movement, which asserted a 19th-century social view, numerous Baptists gravitated toward fundamentalist churches that protected certain family values, segregated education, and banned interracial relationships. In the U.S. South and the Middle Atlantic states during the 1960s, fundamentalist Baptist churches often started congregationally based primary and secondary schools that were not open to nonwhites. Attendance by blacks in Baptist **Bible colleges** until the 1990s was rare. One searches in vain in the proceedings of many **conservative** evangelical white Baptist groups for any statements on racial issues well into the 21st century.

By the mid-20th century, however, Baptists with progressive ideas on race were emerging across the denomination in North America. **Howard Thurman**, one-time chaplain at Howard University and Boston University, created in 1944 the Church for the Fellowship of All Peoples in San Francisco, California, to become the first truly multiracial congregation in the United States. **Leon Sullivan**, a Philadelphia Baptist minister, became an international antiapartheid advocate in the 1970s and 1980s. **Adam Clayton Powell, Jr.,** pastor at Abyssinian Baptist in New York, became the voice for racial solidarity and community development in Harlem, and later in the U.S. Congress. From the 1950s, Kelly Miller Smith produced a new sense of community in Nashville, Tennessee, while prominent black Baptist **pastors, Joseph H. Jackson** (Chicago), Gardner C. Taylor (New York), Ralph Abernathy (Atlanta), and, later, Jesse Jackson

(Chicago), James Forbes (New York), and Al Sharpton (New York) worked to equalize opportunities for persons regardless of color from 1950 to the present.

Following the lead of his mentors—notably **Benjamin Mays**, George Washington Davis, and Mordecai Johnson—**Martin Luther King Jr.** forever changed the face of understanding race, and because King was a Baptist minister, his impact was wide among the denomination. King came to personify not only civil rights but a colorless society and vision for the churches that he called "the beloved community." The American Baptist Convention quickly embraced his struggle, making grants to the Southern Christian Leadership Conference and often supporting clergy and laity who marched in his demonstrations. King's address, "Paul's Letter to American Christians," preached at the American Baptist annual convention in 1964, electrified many in the denomination. Two American Baptist–related theological schools, Crozer Theological Seminary in Chester, Pennsylvania, which King attended, and Colgate-Rochester Divinity School in Rochester, New York, developed social action programs and named chairs in King's honor in the interest of improved race relations. Their student bodies exemplified the integration of races in Baptist training for ministry. In England, the central building of the Northern Baptist College in Manchester was named the Luther King House in honor of the American civil rights leader. Ironically, King has not enjoyed the attention he might have among Southern Baptists in the United States, and for many years the support for King in the National Baptist Convention, U.S.A., was tepid under the auspices of President **Joseph H. Jackson**. Following King's assassination in 1968, his widow, Coretta Scott King, carried forth his principles of racial justice from the King Center in Atlanta. Among the U.S. white Baptist community, those working energetically for racial desegregation and civil rights included Edwin Dalglish, Foy Valentine, Henlee Barnette, Carlyle Marney, Harvey Cox, Jitsuo Morikawa, and **Jimmy Carter** and **Billy Graham**.

The high-water mark of Baptist engagement of racial issues in black-white context came at the International Summit on Baptists against Racism and Ethnic Conflict, held at Atlanta, Georgia, in 1999. Under the auspices of the Baptist World Alliance, this group of leaders produced the "Atlanta Covenant," wherein they called for racial justice, economic development, a new orientation to mission, and a decade (2000–2010) to promote racial justice.

RAMM, BERNARD LAWRENCE (1916–1992). American Baptist theologian, born at Butte, Montana. Earning degrees from the University of Washington, the Eastern Baptist Theological Seminary, and the University of Southern California (Ph.D.), Ramm was trained in the sciences and adapted his scientific methods to **theology**. As part of his extended seminary studies, he did graduate work at the University of Pennsylvania. Overseas, he studied theology at Basel and the Near Eastern School of Theology in Beirut. He taught various subjects at the Bible Institute of Los Angeles and the Eastern Baptist Theological Seminary, philosophy at Bethel College and Seminary, religion at Baylor University, and systematic theology at the American Baptist Seminary of the West at Covina. With **Carl F. H. Henry** and **Edward J. Carnell**, Ramm was considered one of the original neo-evangelical theologians, especially with his interest in **ecumenical** dialogue and responding to challenging questions of scientific verification. He studied with Karl Barth and was one of Barth's major interpreters among English-speaking readers. Among **evangelicals**, Ramm was critical of literalistic interpretations of scientific data in Genesis as well as scholastic arguments for the existence of God. He was convinced that without faith, knowing God was unattainable. Ramm's 27 published works include *A Christian View of Science and Scripture* (1955), *Protestant Biblical Interpretatioin* (1956), and *After Fundamentalism* (1983).

RAND, SILAS TERTIUS (1810–1889). Canadian Baptist minister and missionary, born at Cornwallis, Nova Scotia. He was self-taught, excelling in languages, including Latin, Greek, Spanish, French, German, and Italian. A bricklayer by trade, Rand became interested in Indian languages and mastered Mohawk, Micmac, and Malecite. He embarked upon a pastoral **ministry** among several Baptist churches at Parrsboro, Horton, Liverpool, and Windsor, Nova Scotia from 1834 to 1847. His fascination with Indian cultures led him to declare himself a **missionary** to the Micmacs, and the formation of the Micmac Missionary Society, an overtly anti-Catholic organization, resulted. His personal disinclination to rely on denominational resources and his adoption of Plymouth Brethren theology, followed by his public denunciation of the Baptist denomination, led to his being excommunicated from the Hantsport Baptist Church in 1872. Rand came to rely on Brethren leader George Müller's (1805–1898) plan of "begging" for funds, and these were never sufficient. He wrote a Micmac dictionary (1888), prepared a Micmac translation of the **Scriptures** (1875), and wrote a collection of Indian legends (1894), the latter a credit to his lifelong cultural interests. In 40 years of **evangelization** of the heavily Roman Catholic tribe, Rand made only one convert.

RAND, THEODORE HARDING (1835–1900). Canadian Baptist educator, born at Canard, Nova Scotia. He was educated at Acadia College and took up a career in education. A public school teacher, Rand advocated the establishment of nonsectarian, state-supported schools in Nova Scotia. As a superintendent of schools, he introduced the theories of Horace Mann (1796–1859) and Egerton Ryerson (1803–1882), and he began the *Journal of Education* in 1866 to trumpet his ideas. An indefatigable worker, Rand put in place a licensing system for teachers, uniform standards across the province, and a grading system for student progress. Deposed in 1870 from the Nova Scotia position for political reasons, he moved to New Brunswick, where he provided the same innovations in a similar role.

Also active in Baptist church life, Rand was twice elected president of the Maritime Baptist Convention, and he recommended that Maritime and Ontario Baptists cooperate in **theological** education. He held the chair in education at Acadia, the first of its kind in Canada, until he accepted a professorship in apologetics, ethics, and didactics at Toronto Baptist College in 1885. Senator **William McMaster** and principal **John Castle** relied heavily on Rand's reputation to secure a charter for their new Christian university. At length, Rand became chancellor of McMaster University (successor to Toronto Baptist College) in 1892 and designed its curriculum, particularly advocating the arts. Rand had a wide-ranging literary interest and produced *A Treasury of Canadian Verse with Brief Biographical Notes* (1900).

RANDAL, BENJAMIN (1749–1808). **Freewill Baptist** evangelist and church planter, born at New Castle, New Hampshire. Randal had various occupations in his early career, including sailmaker and seaman. In 1770, he was converted under the preaching of George Whitefield (1715–1770), and over the next 10 years, he moved to a full-time **evangelistic ministry** of his own. Randal came to Baptist principles from a plain reading of **Scripture** and was also influenced by the work of Nova Scotia evangelist **Henry Alline**. In 1777, he began preaching regularly at New Durham, New Hampshire, from which he gathered a congregation that was formally established by covenant in 1780. He itinerated across the northern stretches of New England, establishing in 1783 a quarterly meeting system and in 1792 the first yearly meeting.

Randal described his theological position as "free grace, free will, and free communion," all three principles derived in response to the prevailing Calvinism in the New England Congregationalist order. He was influenced in his position by Edward Lock of Gilmanton, New Hampshire, and Tozier Lord of Barrington, New Hampshire, both earlier Baptist opponents of Calvinism. When confronted in 1779 by Regular or Calvinistic Baptists, Randal dismissed their position and had little fellowship with that group, claiming to be "owned by God." He was a tireless preacher and exhausted himself itinerating through the Freewill Baptist Connexion, which he largely founded.

RANTERS. In the first half of the 17th century in English religious development, a number of radical sects grew up in defense of free interpretation of **Scripture** and in opposition to any form of religious establishment. Among these were the Ranters, pejoratively so called because of their blasphemous public behavior and seemingly careless statements of doctrine. Essentially a movement of migratory, dispossessed craftsmen, Ranters lacked any spokesman or organization, some preferring simply to be known as "My one flesh." Positioned somewhere on a continuum between **Seekers** and Quakers, Ranters often equated themselves with God; frequented ale-houses, where they sang blasphemous songs; publicly flaunted their misdeeds; and used tobacco to heighten their spiritual awareness. Some Baptists became Ranters or vice versa, while others were accused of having a ranting spirit or "being a loose person like a Ranter." *See also* DIGGERS; LEVELLERS; SEEKERS.

RAUSCHENBUSCH, WALTER (1861–1918). American German Baptist theologian and educator, born at Rochester, New York. The son of a German Baptist pioneer church planter and educator, Walter was educated at the Evangelische Gymnasium at Gutersloh, Westphalia; the University of Rochester; and Rochester Theological Seminary. His seminary mentors were Howard Osgood (1831–1911) and **Augustus H. Strong**. After graduation, Rauschenbusch went to the pastorate of Second German Baptist Church on New York City's West Side. There in "Hell's Kitchen," he developed advanced social theories and interacted with prominent reformers and theologians, including Henry George (1862–1916) and Richard Ely (1854–1943). In 1892, he, Samuel Zane Batten, and Leighton Williams (1855–1935) formed an international movement called the **Brotherhood of the Kingdom**, devoted to progressive Christian social thought, which came to be known as "social Christianity," or the "**social gospel**."

In 1897, Rauschenbusch took a faculty position at Rochester Seminary in the German Department, where he taught undergraduate courses and New Testament. In 1902, he became the Pettengill Professor of Church History in the English Department of Rochester Theological Seminary. Through the years of his professorship, he wrote extensively on social Christianity and Baptist identity. Among his outstanding works are *Christianity and the Social Crisis* (1907), *The Theology of the Social Gospel* (1917), and *For God and the People: Prayers for the Social Awakening* (1910). The outbreak of World War I crushed Rauschenbusch's plan for a better, peaceful kingdom under the righteous rule of God, and his health failed. Long hampered by profound deafness, he was greatly beloved by his students and colleagues, notably his lifelong friend, Augustus Hopkins Strong. *See* SOCIAL GOSPEL.

REEKIE, ARCHIBALD BROWNLEE (1862–1942). Canadian Baptist minister and missionary, born at Armow, Ontario. He was a farmer for several years and then returned to complete his education at Woodstock College and McMaster University. While still a student, Reekie studied the possibilities of a mission to **Bolivia** and convinced the Baptist Convention of Ontario and Quebec Foreign Mission Board to commence a work there. In 1897, he became the pioneer Protestant **missionary** to Bolivia, settling first at Oruro and later at Cochabamba and La Paz. Reekie used an educational approach to mission and began a school, which bears his name, in Oruro. He was influential in the development of a **liberal** policy toward Protestantism in Bolivia and served in the country until 1921. For a short time in 1917–1918, he served in **Cuba** for the **American Baptist Home Mission Society**. After missionary service, Reekie was **pastor** at several small congregations in southern Ontario.

REFORMED BAPTIST ALLIANCE (RBA). Influenced by the **holiness movement**, particularly as advanced by Phoebe Palmer (1807–1874), several Baptist congregations in the Canadian Maritime Provinces withdrew from the Free Christian Baptist Conference and formed an alliance of holiness-oriented churches. When the majority of Free Christian Baptist elders in New Brunswick and Nova Scotia refused to accept the doctrine of "instantaneous entire sanctification" and called for discipline of ministers who held this position, 75 "delegates" from New Brunswick, Nova Scotia, and Maine met at Main Street Free Baptist Church in Woodstock, New Brunswick, on 1–3 November 1888, to organize the Reformed Baptist Denomination of the Dominion of Canada, popularly called the Alliance. The terminology "reformed" was used in the sense of "reformulated," rather than referring to any association with the Calvinistic churches of the Reformation. Among the original leaders of the Alliance were James E. Drysdale (1834–1914), William Kinghorn (1823–1893), W. B. Wiggins (1849–1924), Elisha Cosman (1835–1925), and Benjamin N. Goodspeed (1835–1922).

The RBA was incorporated in 1894. In 1889, a periodical began, the *King's Highway*, which was published through 1967. Over the years, Reformed Baptists held to "**Bible** holiness," congregational **polity**, open communion, **Arminian** theology, and believer's **baptism** by immersion. By the 1950s, many were unhappy with the terminology "reformed" because it connected in some minds with a Calvinistic theology; the principal doctrinal point became holiness perfectionism. Institutional developments included a college called the Holiness Bible Institute in Woodstock, New Brunswick (1936) (later renamed Bethany Bible College), Yarmouth, Nova Scotia, and then Sussex, New Brunswick (1959); a Sunday School association; a home mission board; and foreign missions in Natal and the Transvaal in **South Africa**. In 1968, the RBA merged with the Pilgrim Holiness Church and Wesleyan Methodists to form the Wesleyan Church. *See also* FREEWILL BAPTISTS.

REFORMED BAPTIST MISSION SERVICES. Founded in 1985 as part of the Reformed Baptist movement in the United States and **Canada**, Reformed Baptist Mission Services supports missionaries in six countries, including **Colombia**, **France**, **Israel**, **Jamaica**, **Kenya**, and the United Kingdom. With heaquarters in Carlisle, Pennsylvania, it publishes *Missionary Update*.

REFORMED BAPTISTS. One of the recent smaller bodies of Baptists in the United States, the Reformed Baptists emerged about 1950 and coalesced in the 1970s. In general, Reformed Baptists revere the Puritan tradition and consider the 17th century a classic period in Baptist development. Energized by the Banner of Truth Trust, an English Calvinistic organization that promotes the republication of Calvinist writers like A. W. Pink (1886–1952), the classic works of **John Gill** and **Charles H. Spurgeon,** and the publication *Reformation Today*, pastors of existing **evangelical** Baptist congregations and newly planted churches have joined the movement. Many Reformed Baptists reckon the starting point in the call of Henry Mahan, **pastor** of Thirteenth Street Baptist Church in Ashland, Kentucky, for a Sovereign Grace Bible Conference in 1954. Later conferences were held in Carlisle, Pennsylvania; Pine Bluff, Arkansas; and Pasadena, Texas. In 1967, Reformed Baptist churches in Pennsylvania and New Jersey formed the Reformed Baptist Association and in 1985 the Reformed Baptist Mission Services.

Two streams have clearly emerged from the original movement. In the 1960s, several Reformed Baptists followed Carlisle, Pennsylvania, pastor Walter Chantry, a graduate of Westminster Theological Seminary who held conferences on various themes of Reformed interest. His following adopted the Philadelphia Baptist Confession of Faith as its standard, and eventually 10 congregations formed a regional association in Pennsylvania, New Jersey, and Delaware. The second group, calling themselves "Sovereign Grace Baptists," broke from the older Reformed Baptist body in 1980, preferring the First London Confession (1644) to the Second London Confession. They are critical of covenant theology, they are less puritanical in ethics, and their churches reflect the regions of the South and West rather than the Northeast. Leaders among the Sovereign Grace group include Jon Zens, the editor of *Searching Together*, successor to *Baptist Reformation Review*; Donald Moffatt; and Norbert Ward. Gary Long, a pastor in Springfield, Missouri, has made a major impact among Sovereign Grace Baptists and beyond through his publishing ministries, the Particular Baptist Press. Long was the catalyst behind the 2007 Baptist History Celebration in Charleston, South Carolina, involving most major Baptist groups in North America and commemorating the establishment of the Philadelphia Baptist Association (PBA) in 1707.

Reformed Baptists usually avoid entanglements with mainstream Baptists and, in particular, certain **Arminian** groups. Most of the churches emphasize sovereign grace and particular election, and several practice multiple eldership rather than singular pastorates. The Reformed Baptist movement has been influenced by hyper-Calvinistic non-Baptist groups, notably Orthodox Presbyterians trained at Westminster Theological Seminary at Chestnut Hill, Pennsylvania, and Bible Presbyterians associated with Faith Theological Seminary in Elkins Park, Pennsylvania. The PBA has distant relations with the **Continental Baptist Association**.

As of 1995, there were over 100 congregations scattered across the United States, united by the **Reformed Baptist Mission Services** and the periodical *Baptist Reformation Review* (1972–), a publication that it shares with the Continental Baptists.

REGULAR BAPTISTS. *See* GENERAL ASSOCIATION OF REGULAR BAPTIST CHURCHES.

RELIGIOUS LIBERTY. A fundamental earmark of Baptist identity from the beginnings of the movement. Prior to the advent of Baptists per se, **Anabaptist** writers in England asserted their rights to **freedom of conscience**. For instance, Hendrik Terwoort (fl. 1550–1570), a Flemish Anabaptist, was burned at Smithfield in June 1575 for his religious convictions, according to Van Braght's *Martyr's Mirror*. Likewise, Anabaptists were accused in 1589 of holding the erroneous opinion that the civil power should not hinder their preaching. The concern for religious liberty was thus firmly planted in English culture at the seedtime of the Baptist movement.

A concern for religious liberty grew out of circumstances in which English **Nonconformists** found themselves at the turn of the 17th century. Early in the reign of King James I, Separatists realized that the Crown and the Established Church were formidable obstacles to the free expression of biblical Christianity and the propagation of their faith. Moreover, their desire to avoid the **sacraments** drew the wrath of the Anglican Church and stern measures were taken to bring about conformity. As the first Separatist-Baptistic congregation emerged under the leadership of **John Smyth**, many Separatists fled to Holland to avoid imprisonment and the loss of their property; Smyth and his small congregation did likewise and settled in Amsterdam. Able to discuss their views in greater liberty, they were still confined to the frame of reference of the Mennonites, with whom they boarded and worshipped. Smyth would write in his **confession of faith** that "Christ alone is the King and Lawgiver of the Church and the conscience." At length, in 1609, one faction of this group under the leadership of **Thomas Helwys** decided to return to England and face the consequences. This led to Helwys's publication of the first tract in the English language to advocate complete religious liberty, *A Mistery of Iniquity*. Helwys argued in cogent terms that the king had no right to abuse his subjects, who were in spiritual matters required to abide by a higher law. Further, Helwys stated, persecution did not accomplish its objective, and finally, he made the classic assertion that "God alone is Lord of the conscience." For his accomplishment, Helwys was imprisoned and likely died there.

A second generation of those advocating religious liberty, beginning in the 1620s, is evident in the writings of **Leonard Busher**, a leader among the **General Baptists**. Busher took a slightly different tack, demonstrating first that **Scripture** never grants permission to use physical coercion in spiritual matters. He affirmed that "Christ hath given no such weapons to the Church." Rather, erring persons were to be disciplined and non-Christians were to be evangelized. Moslems, Busher reminded his readers, were more tolerant than some Christians.

By mid-century, English Baptists were clearly the leading spokesmen for religious liberty. The General and **Particular Baptists** held this truth in common. In the First London Confession of Faith (1644), there was found the following bold statement among the emerging Particular Baptists concerning religious liberty: "Concerning the worship of God; there is but one lawgiver . . . which is Jesus Christ. . . . So it is the magistrate's duty to tender the liberty of men's consciences." This position was to include all persons, regardless of religious affiliation: Protestants, Catholics, Turks, infidels, and so forth.

The third major theoretical base for the Baptist position on religious liberty was laid by the English and later Anglo-American thinker **Roger Williams**, a short-term leader more appropriately identified with the Separatists and later the **Seekers**. In his book *The Bloudy Tenent of Persecution* (1644), Williams recounted the instances of persecution of true believers in England and New England and demonstrated the futility of using force to achieve religious ends. He argued that there was a wall of separation between the church and the Crown that must not be violated by the state. Williams was oft quoted, particularly by Baptists in the American colonies.

The issues surrounding religious liberty were rejoined in the American colonies, and Baptists were again in the vanguard. The Standing Order establishment of New England was intolerant of the kind of dissent that the Baptists posed. They were especially antagonized by the Baptist refusal to practice the **sacrament** of infant **baptism**. Names like **William Screven**, Roger Williams, **Henry Dunster**, and **Obadiah Holmes** all evince the Baptist penchant in 17th-century New England for religious freedom. The theoretical case followed the pattern of the English Baptists, and the course of events in the colonies closely paralleled those in England. When the Toleration Act in 1689 was passed, Baptists in New England used this achievement to call for toleration in their own situation.

During the 18th century, Baptists fanned out through the Middle Colonies and the South, and they stood firm in their claim for religious liberty. In Pennsylvania and the Jerseys, they enjoyed complete freedom based on Quaker constitutional provisions. In Virginia and the Carolinas, intense persecution set in from the Church of England, which desired to silence the preaching of Baptists. It was left to leaders like **Isaac Backus**, **James Ireland**, and **John Leland** to make the particular case for **separation of church and state**, a corollary to religious liberty. With the winning of independence and the creation of the U.S. Constitution and Bill of Rights, religious liberty was formally achieved in the United States. Many historians credit John Leland in particular for the contribution of this doctrine to the Constitution. *See also* SEPARATION OF CHURCH AND STATE.

The 19th century saw yet another shift in the meaning and force of religious liberty among Baptists. As the great efforts were undertaken in world mission, Baptists moved their focus to advocating religious liberty as part of the missiological apologetic. **Burma** became the first battleground where Baptists called upon the government to recognize religious freedom. In **Liberia**, Baptists faced hostile insurgents and contended for a free state. In Europe, under the leadership of **Johann Gerhard Oncken**, Baptists called upon Lutheran authorities to grant the right of assembly and propagation of the faith. And in Latin America, Baptists became part of the "**evangelical** movement," favoring the ideals of a free church in a free state. Much of this ideology was transplanted from the American political experience. By the end of the century, Baptists were taking credit for having given to the world a precious gift of religious liberty.

In the United States, a curious set of circumstances led **liberal** Baptists to rediscover the heritage of religious liberty. In the 1940s, when the Franklin Roosevelt Administration advocated recognition of the Vatican for purposes of foreign affairs, Baptists in the United States protested loudly and issued the **American Baptist Bill of Rights**. Later, as **fundamentalism** sought to deprive more liberal theologians of their right of free expression, Baptists again sounded the chord of religious liberty, particularly **soul liberty**. *See also* LIBERAL TRADITION.

In the last decades of the 20th century, Baptists in the United States were divided on the relevance of religious liberty. **Conservative** and fundamentalist Baptists prefer to emphasize strict adherence to biblical authority and mandate confessions of faith; this retards the growth of pluralism and heterodoxy. Others emphasize complete freedom of conscience and maintain that nothing whatsoever should dictate to the human conscience, save the guidance of the Holy Spirit. The primary advocates of religious liberty among North American Baptist communities are the Baptist Joint Committee on Religious Liberty (formerly the **Baptist Joint Committee on Public Affairs**) and the **Baptist World Alliance,** both based in the Washington, D.C., region.

In the early 21st century, there continue to be concerns for religious freedom, some with implications for the Baptist family. In **Belgium**, Baptists are still classified as a cult; in **Romania** and **Bulgaria**, Baptist **pastors** have been imprisoned and churches closed; and in Saudi Arabia, small congregations of Baptists are denied the right to have churches and are harassed when they meet in homes.

When Baptists create a biblical warrant for religious liberty the most frequently referenced passages are Galatians 5:1 and 2 Corinthians 3:17. *See also* HUMAN RIGHTS, BAPTISTS AND.

RESURGENTS, SOUTHERN BAPTIST. Terminology applied to those leaders among **Southern Baptists** (SBC) of a **conservative evangelical** or **fundamentalist** theological orientation who transformed the organizational structures and seminaries of the SBC into their control between 1980 and 2000. The term "resurgent" indicates a return, or a "comeback," to former theological and social beliefs like biblical inerrancy, anti-evolution, and male-dominant family and church cultures that would have characterized Southern Baptists in the first half of the 20th century. The first wave of resurgents included W. A. Criswell, **Paul Pressler**, **Paige Patterson**, and **Clark Pinnock**. Later, Charles Stanley, Jerry Vines, **Adrian Rogers**, and Bailey Smith, all prominent SBC pastors, took up the emphases as presidents of the SBC. Among theological educators, Paige Patterson and Albert Mohler were champions of the restoration of theological integrity, as they have identified it, to the SBC seminaries. A highwater mark of the resurgency was the adoption by the SBC national convention in 2000 of the **"Baptist Faith and Message,"** the doctrinal statement that collects all of the fundamentalist agenda in an official confessional vehicle. While not a member of the Southern Baptist family until late in his ministry, **Jerry Falwell** of Lynchburg, Virginia, was an inspiration to the Southern Baptist resurgents.

REVIVALS, REVIVALISM. Revivals have been an important component of Baptist experience since the 17th century in Great Britain and North America, primarily in the latter. The term "revival" technically applies to a renewal of Christian experience, based upon biblical passages such as 2 Kings 23:21–25, Psalm 51:10, Matthew 12:20–24, and Revelation 2:5. In North American and British usage, "revival" applies first to a period of intense religious interest, for instance, in a single congregation, and also to a spiritual awakening in a region or country over a prolonged period of time.

Early in their history, English Baptists exhibited a revivalistic impulse, for instance, in the 1640s when **Thomas Lambe** of London held open church meetings and called people to repentance. Lambe also conducted itinerant preaching tours in Gloucestershire and trained others in this style of conversionist **evangelism**. **General Baptist messengers** in the latter 17th century also helped to renew congregations on a visiting basis. In the 18th century, Baptists followed general evangelical patterns in periodically looking for renewal in their congregations, a greater sense of personal godliness, and congregational vitality. In many cases, this renewal was associated with evangelism and church planting, because the revivals were the result of itinerant preachers in often remote areas. In **Wales**, leaders like **Vavasor Powell** traveled widely in this regard, as did **Dan Taylor** in England, and much renewal was the result.

In the American colonies, **Isaac Backus** and **Elias Smith** exemplified the revival tradition in the North; **Morgan Edwards** in the Middle Colonies; and **Shubael Stearns**, **John Leland**, and **Daniel Marshall** in the South. **David George** popularized the revival among **black Baptists** in South Carolina and later in Nova Scotia. In the Canadian Maritime Provinces, **Henry Alline** preached the New Light emphases as did **Joseph Dimock**. Their primary method was preaching convictional sermons in public places (usually not in meetinghouses) accompanied by prayer, and allowing for overt responses from their audiences. Home visitations of possible candidates typically preceded actual preaching events.

In the 19th century, the fruits of **Second Great Awakenings** leaders like Charles G. Finney (1792–1875) among the Presbyterians with their "New Measures" had an impact upon American and British Baptists. In the United States, men like **Jacob Knapp** moved from city to city employing means that included protracted meetings, altar calls, mass **baptisms**, and invitations to participate in social reforms such as the **temperance** crusade. In **Canada**, **Harris Harding** exemplified the fervor of the Second Awakenings. At length, in the

1880s, under the influence of the Keswick movement and the Niagara Bible Conferences, Baptists became sympathetic to crusades and conferences for personal renewal; these were led by **pastors** like **A. J. Gordon** and disciples of Dwight L. Moody (1837–1899). This New Measures style of revival meeting was translated to Britain in the **ministry** of **Charles Roe**, who in 1849 invited Finney to Britain to establish the "revival system." **Thomas Pulsford** held protracted meetings on the American model and employed many of Finney's strategies in his itinerant missions with the **Baptist Home Mission Society** in the 1840s. Sometimes Pulsford conducted two services a day, every day for several weeks.

In the 20th century, Baptists regularly responded to the revivalist impulse in mass meetings and within the congregation. The mass appeal of Billy Sunday (1862–1935) and **Billy Graham** swept up many Baptists in large protracted crusade meetings. Graham, himself a Baptist, often addressed significant Baptist gatherings like the **Southern Baptist Convention** and the **Baptist World Alliance** (BWA), thus reinforcing the symbols of the revival. International figures like Billy Kim of **Korea** and Nilson Fanini (1932–) of **Brazil** have itinerated broadly in the BWA circles as revivalists/**evangelists**. Within the local congregation, many Baptists frequently schedule one- or two-week revival services, usually inviting a guest preacher to follow a theme of personal renewal and invite people to make a public response. This phenomenon is popular in the Southern Baptist tradition, among **black Baptists**, and many of the **conservative evangelical** Baptist groups in the United States. A small number of Pentecostal **Freewill Baptists** in the United States encourage a second overt work of grace, "entire sanctification," at revival services.

Typically the elements of a Baptist revival service are uplifting congregational singing, personal testimony reports of God's work in individual lives, a season of prayer, a convictional sermon emphasizing personal experience, and an invitation to public profession of faith, rededication of one's life to Christ, or the opportunity to surrender one's life to Christian service. A key element at the conclusion of the service is the singing of a hymn of commitment or invitation, several of which have been written for the purpose: "Pass Me Not, O Gentle Saviour," "Almost Persuaded, Now to Believe," "Just as I Am, without One Plea," and "I Surrender All." The revivalist who holds meetings that result in numerous decisions quickly gains a reputation for this **ministry** and may embark upon a full-time ministry of evangelism or revivalism, thus making the role a permanent category of the Baptist ministry. *See also* BAPTIST REVIVAL FELLOWSHIP; NEW LIGHT BAPTISTS.

REYNOLDS, HERBERT HAL (1930–2006). Texas Baptist educator and statesman, born at Frankston, Anderson County, Texas. He was educated at Trinity University in San Antonio and received graduate degrees at Baylor University. Reynolds received the first doctorate in psychology awarded by Baylor University. Following four years of active duty in the United States Air Force, he taught air science and psychology at Baylor and returned to the military to do research in the aeromedical field at the national laboratory in Alamagordo, New Mexico. There he became chief of the comparative psychology program and, later, a leading biomedical research scientist in the U.S. space program. He traveled widely in Europe and the British Isles and was a consultant to the General Dynamics Corporation. In 1968, he was named the inaugural commander of the United States Air Force Human Resources Laboratory in San Antonio. Soon after, he retired and took the position of senior vice president of Baylor University under President Abner McCall. He became a key figure in restructuring the administration of Baylor, serving also as provost and treasurer, and was elected president in 1981. Under Reynolds's leadership, Baylor became an internationally renowned university, the largest Baptist school in the world. Upon his retirement in 1995, he became chancellor and was active in Texas Baptist life, sponsoring the theological moderate cause as the **fundamentalist** takeover of Baptist schools and the **Southern Baptist Convention** took place. Reynolds's great contribution to Baptist affairs occurred when he spearheaded the state charter revision process at Baylor, thus ensuring that the university would be related to Baptists but not controlled by the fundamentalist resurgency. His charitable foundation, set up with his wife, Joy, supported the growth of new Baptist organizations, notably **Texas Baptists Committed** and **Mainstream** Baptists.

RHYS, MORGAN JOHN, SR. (1760–1804). Welsh Baptist minister, born at Llanbradach. He was educated in a school kept by David

Williams, an Independent minister of Watford; later, he attended Bristol Baptist Academy and was ordained a Baptist minister at Penygarn, Pontypool, in 1787. As a young pastor, Rhys adopted radical reform positions opposing **slavery** and welcoming the French Revolution as a democratic movement. Rhys, in fact, in 1791 took a trip to **France** to visit the site of the Bastille. Very much a supporter of America as a "promised land," Rhys advocated setting up a democratic republic, and this drew criticism to the cause of **Nonconformists**. In 1794, Rhys and a company of Welsh Baptists emigrated to Pennsylvania, where he made the acquaintance of **William Rogers** and Benjamin Rush (1746–1813) of Philadelphia. Eventually, Rhys purchased a substantial tract of land, which he named "Cambria," and settled a colony. His last settlement was in Somerset County, Pennsylvania, where he died. In **Wales**, Rhys was a promoter of **missions** and **Sunday Schools**, as well as a plan for day and night classes. Rhys expressed his **antislavery** views in an early pamphlet among the American Baptist community, *Letters on Liberty and Slavery* (1798).

RICE, JOHN RICHARD (1895–1980). Southern and, later, **Independent Baptist** evangelist, born in Cooke County, Texas. He was educated at Decatur Baptist College, Baylor University, Southwestern Baptist Seminary, and the University of Chicago. For two years (1920–1921), Rice taught English and was a football coach at Wayland Baptist College in Plainview, Texas. In 1923, he was **pastor** of the Shamrock, Texas Baptist Church, but under the influence of **J. Frank Norris**, he withdrew from the **Southern Baptist Convention** and embarked on a career as full-time **evangelist**. From 1932 to 1940, he was pastor of the Fundamentalist Baptist Tabernacle in Dallas, Texas, a congregation he started. Having begun a newspaper, the *Sword of the Lord*, in 1934, he devoted himself full time to editorial responsibilities in 1940 and built the paper into a widely read platform for militant **fundamentalist** opinion. In 1955, Rice moved to the Chicago area, where he started Calvary Baptist Church in Wheaton, Illinois; four years later, he began the "Voice of Revival," a radio **ministry**. Rice moved to Murfreesboro, Tennessee, in 1963 and established the Sword of the Lord Foundation. He also became active in the **Southwide Baptist Fellowship** and related to Bob Jones

University. His citywide crusades across four decades drew large crowds to his open air and stadium preaching from Buffalo, New York, to Moncton, New Brunswick. He was the author of over 200 books, the most famous of which was based on his sermon, "What Must I Do to Be Saved?" (1949), which is said to have sold 32 million copies. His other titles include *Bobbed Hair, Bossey Wives, and Women Preachers: Significant Questions for Honest Women Settled by the Word of God* (1941) and *Amusements for Christians* (1955).

RICE, LUTHER (1783–1836). American Baptist missionary and denominational leader, born at Northborough, Massachusetts. He graduated from Williams College and Andover Theological Seminary a Congregationalist. Fresh from seminary, Rice joined the entourage of **Adoniram Judson** and others who persuaded the American Board of Commissioners for Foreign Missions to give him an appointment as a single missionary to the East. Rice was commissioned at Salem Tabernacle on 19 February 1812 and sailed for **India**. En route, he shifted to Baptist principles and was baptized by **William Ward** at Serampore. Rice took Judson's advice to return to the United States and build up the **missionary** enterprise among Baptists. This he did with singular devotion for the next two decades. Rice persuaded the Baptist leaders to expand the idea of **associations** to create a national **convention**, and he worked with **Richard Furman** and **William Staughton** to create a national collegiate and theological institution and denominational center at Washington, D.C., the nation's new capital. Rice overextended himself in support of Columbian College and was caught in a difficult debt situation. An investigation was called for in 1826, which essentially exonerated Rice, but reduced his sphere of influence. He lost leadership to the New England interests and after 1827 was solely the agent for the college, itinerating mostly in the southern states where he died. In 1814, Brown University conferred the honorary master of arts degree upon Rice.

RICHARD, TIMOTHY (1845–1919). English Baptist missionary to **China**, born in FfaldyBrenin, Carmarthenshire, **Wales**. He studied at Haverfordwest College (where he won the Hebrew prize) and was appointed in 1869 by the **Baptist Missionary Society** to **China**. He served first at Shanghai, then Chefoo and Chi'ing Chou-fu. Much influenced by J. Hudson Taylor (1832–1905), Richard desired to move into the interior of China, beyond Western influence; in 1874, he gathered the first church in Shantung Province. During the great famine of 1876–1877, Richard became a household name for his relief efforts, which he summarized in a fourfold plan: famine relief, teaching Christian civilization, introducing new industries, and teaching spiritual truths. Richard founded Whitewright Institute in Sinan on these principles. At the Exeter Hall meetings in 1885, he stressed the social aspects of missionary work, which changed profoundly the direction of the **evangelical** community. From 1900 to 1910, Richard was the first chancellor of the Western University in Tai-yuan-fu, which he modelled on London University. During furloughs back in Britain and Europe, he participated in Welsh revival meetings and advocated an International Federation of Nations, disarmament, and a Peace Conference at Lucerne; he was also present at the Edinburgh Conference of 1910. In 1905, he was elected general secretary (in Shanghai) of the China Literature Society, which he served until 1914. Richard was one of the most highly honored Baptists of the new century, receiving degrees from Brown University (1895) and the University of Wales (1907), plus the Order of the Double Dragon from the Chinese government (1907). Richard collected his biographical experiences in *Forty-Five Years in China, Reminiscences* (1916).

RICHARDS, HENRY (1851–1928). English and American Baptist missionary, born in Somersetshire, England. With a Church of England upbringing, he worked for his father during his youth. He affiliated with the Congregationalists and then the Baptists, among whom he preached for a time. Alfred Tilly (1821–1905), a Baptist minister and founder of the Livingstone Inland Mission, recruited Richards for that mission, which prompted Richards to take studies in medicine at Harley College. In 1879, Richards arrived in the Congo River region in Africa; in 1884, the Livingstone Inland Mission was transferred to the **American Baptist Missionary Union** and Richards continued in the new relationship. About 1886, following an intense study of the New Testament, Richards was involved in a remarkable conversion experience among the Bantu peoples: more than 1,000 people accepted the Christian message at Banza Manteke in August

1886, becoming known as the "Pentecost on the Congo." With the financial and prayer support of **Adoniram J. Gordon** in Boston, Richards superintended the establishment of evangelical work in the upper Congo area and the construction of the **mission** station. His study of Congolese languages led to an important classification scheme.

RILEY, WILLIAM BELL (1861–1947). American Baptist minister and **fundamentalist** leader, born in Greene County, Indiana. He was educated at Hanover College and Southern Baptist Theological Seminary and served pastorates in Kentucky, Indiana, and Chicago (1883–1897). In 1897, Riley became **pastor** at First Baptist Church, Minneapolis, Minnesota, where he served until 1947. In this role, he won many converts to the church and drew national attention for his scorn of **liberal** theology and the Northern Baptist Convention (NBC). He openly opposed Darwinism and tried to convince the NBC to adopt the New Hampshire Confession of Faith. His services were characterized by **evangelism**, popular music, and a "hymn of invitation." In his **ministry** in Minnesota, Riley estimated that 7,000 people had joined his church. As a fundamentalist organizer, he started the World's Christian Fundamentals Association, the Northwestern Schools, and a charitable foundation that was to rival the generosity of **John D. Rockefeller**. His chosen successor was a young evangelist from North Carolina, **Billy Graham**. Among Riley's numerous published works were *The Perennial Revival, A Plea for Evangelism* (1904), *The Menace of Modernism* (1917), and *The Conflict of Christianity with Its Counterfeits* (1940).

RIPPON, JOHN (1750–1836). English Baptist minister, hymnist, and editor, born at Tiverton, England. He was educated at the British Academy and entered the Baptist ministry in the early 1770s. Rippon succeeded the eminent **John Gill** as minister at Carter Lane Church in London and became a premier minister of the denomination. He edited the *Baptist Annual Register* (1790–1802), which did much to unite Baptists on both sides of the Atlantic. He is remembered for his popular *Selection of Hymns from the Best Authors* (1787), which made him a comfortable income, as well as for his history of Bunhill Fields, the **Nonconformist** burial ground in London. Rippon was appreciated in the American colonies for his support of the independence movement; Brown University conferred on him the degree of A.M. in 1784 and the D.D. in 1792.

ROBERT, HENRY MARTYN (1837–1923). American soldier and engineer, born at Robertville, South Carolina. Educated at the U.S. Military Academy at West Point, Robert was promoted through the ranks to brigadier general and chief of engineers. Before and following the Civil War, he taught at West Point and chaired the Department of Practical Military Engineering. During the war, Robert designed the defenses of Washington and Philadelphia and afterward the causeway and seawall for Galveston, Texas. As a member of Second Baptist Church, Germantown, Pennsylvania, he took an interest in parliamentary procedure and wrote a summary, which became a household manual for due process in organizations. *Robert's Rules of Order* (1876) were widely adopted as the standard manual in Baptist and other churches in the United States. Heavily suggestive of Baptist **polity**, *Robert's Rules* give priority to the rights of the membership of the organization.

ROBERTSON, ARCHIBALD THOMAS (1863–1934). Southern Baptist minister and educator, born at Chatham, Virginia. Robertson was educated at Wake Forest College and Southern Baptist Theological Seminary and held the position of professor of New Testament at Southern Baptist Seminary for 44 years. He concentrated his studies on Greek grammar and produced 45 books, including a *Harmony of the Gospels* (1922), *A Grammar of the Greek New Testament in Light of Historical Research* (1914), and *Word Pictures in the New Testament* (1930–1933). Robertson's stature as a Greek scholar was matched by few; his advocacy of an international Baptist conference led in large part to the establishment of the **Baptist World Alliance** in 1905.

ROBERTS-THOMSON, EDWARD (1909–1987). New Zealand and Australian Baptist minister and theological educator, born in Worthing, Sussex, England. He was educated at the Baptist College of Victoria (1932–1935) and completed his B.A. in theology at Bristol Baptist College in 1937. He served the Baptist church at Hobart,

Tasmania (1940–1944) before taking a commission as an Air Force chaplain in World War II. Following his military service, Roberts-Thomson served the Brunswick Baptist Church in Melbourne, **Australia**, through 1952. In 1953, he was installed as the principal of the New Zealand Baptist College, which he served through a period of impressive growth in enrollment. In 1961, Roberts-Thomson moved to become principal of the Baptist College of New South Wales, and there he encountered administrative resistance to his directions and policies, although achieving wide attention for his scholarship. He resigned from the college in Sydney in 1964 to serve a Presbyterian parish at South Turramurra from 1965 to 1973, where he found greater opportunity for **ecumenical** witness. Much influenced by the baptismal studies of Oxford scholar **H. Wheeler Robinson**, Roberts-Thomson published his Bristol Baptist College thesis as *Baptists and the Disciples of Christ* (1951), and a work he prepared for the doctor of divinity degree at Melbourne College of Divinity was published as *With Hands Outstretched: Baptists and the Ecumenical Movement* (1962). In an era of Australian indifference to ecumenism, Roberts-Thomson was a leading ecumenical scholar and statesman who favored full Baptist participation in the World Council of Churches.

ROBINSON, EZEKIEL GILMAN (1815–1894). American Baptist minister and educator, born at Attleborough, Massachusetts. He was educated at Brown University and Newton Theological Institution, after which he was **pastor** of the Baptist church in Norfolk, Virginia (1842–1845). During his Norfolk ministry, Robinson took a leave to serve as chaplain at the University of Virginia. In 1845–1846, he was pastor at Cambridge, Massachusetts, adjacent to Harvard College. In 1846, he accepted the professorship in biblical interpretation at Western Baptist Theological Seminary in Covington, Kentucky, leaving in 1850 to serve the Ninth Street Baptist Church in Cincinnati, Ohio. Robinson became an illustrious name among Baptists and was elected professor of **theology** at Rochester Theological Seminary in 1853, where he served for two decades. Among his students was **Augustus Hopkins Strong**. In 1872, having served Rochester as president from 1868, Robinson became president of Brown University, where he served until 1889. Having retired from Brown, he taught apologetics and ethics at the University of Chicago from 1892 to

1894. His published works include *The Relationship of Christianity to Ethics* (1883) and *Christian Evidences* (1895). In 1882, Robinson was the first Baptist to deliver the prestigious Lyman Beecher Lectures at Yale University.

ROBINSON, HENRY WHEELER (1872–1945). English Baptist minister born at Northampton. As a youth, he worked for a leather merchant and attended extension lectures at Cambridge University. Robinson studied at Regent's Park College in London and graduated from Edinburgh University with an M.A. in classics and philosophy. Later, he studied theology under the esteemed Andrew M. Fairbairn (1838–1912) at Mansfield College, Oxford University, and at the Universities of Strassburg and Marburg. Robinson served two churches, Pitlochry (1900–1903) and St. Michaels, Coventry (1903–1906), before joining the faculty at Rawdon College in 1906, where he lectured in church history, doctrine, philosophy, and New Testament for 14 years. His scholarship and service to the denomination increased considerably while he was at Rawdon, serving on several boards and committees. In 1920, Robinson became principal of Regent's Park College and devoted his efforts to relocating the school to Oxford University, a process completed in 1928–1940. Robinson thus opened the possibility of a Baptist foundation in an ancient university. A well-written scholar, he published the *Century Bible Commentary on Deuteronomy and Joshua* (1907), *The Faith and Life of the Baptists* (1927), *The Christian Experience of the Holy Spirit* (1928), and *Redemption and Revelation* (1942). A prize-winning student at Oxford, Robinson was also awarded the Burkitt Medal for Biblical Studies by the British Academy in 1944. He was president of the Society for Old Testament Study in 1929 and president of the Baptist Historical Society from 1921 to 1945.

ROBINSON, ROBERT (1735–1790). English Baptist minister, born at Swaffham, England. He received an excellent education in grammar school, but upon the death of his father, Robinson was apprenticed to a trade in London. He heard George Whitefield (1714–1770) preach and was eventually converted and joined Whitefield's circle as a protégé. He adopted Baptist sentiments in the late 1750s and began preaching among the churches. Robinson was called to the

Baptist Church at Cambridge and remained their **pastor** from 1761 to 1783. His preaching drew large crowds and required a new meetinghouse to accommodate 600 persons. Toward the end of his career, Robinson adopted Unitarian views, and this caused a decline in his influence among Baptists. He is best remembered for his *History of Baptism* (1790) and *Ecclesiastical Researches* (1792), as well as for hymns that he composed, likely including "Come Thou Fount of Every Blessing."

ROCKEFELLER, JOHN DAVISON (1839–1937). American industrialist and Baptist philanthropist, born at Richford, New York. Educated in public schools, he started his career as a clerk and cashier in Cleveland, Ohio. In 1862, Rockefeller entered the oil business, which through wise mergers eventuated in the 1873 creation of the Standard Oil Company; by the 1890s, the company controlled three quarters of the oil production and related industries in the United States. In 1896, Rockefeller retired from active work in oil and devoted his life to philanthropy, establishing in 1913 the Rockefeller Foundation, which was largely the work of **Frederick Gates**.

Rockefeller's religious leanings began with participation in the Erie Street Baptist Church, Cleveland, Ohio, where he was baptized in the 1850s. Later, he helped to construct the 1869 edifice for Euclid Avenue Baptist Church in Cleveland, known popularly as "Rockefeller's Church." He served as **Sunday School** superintendent for 60 years, and the family attended the church **prayer meetings** and socials; among Mrs. Rockefeller's students was Charles Evans Hughes (1862–1948). Rockefeller gave generously to Spelman College and Atlanta University, Rochester Theological Seminary, Brown University, and the Riverside Church in New York City, which he helped to create for the ministry of **Harry Emerson Fosdick**. Large gifts to the Northern Baptist and **Southern Baptist** pension and annuity boards led to retirement funds for Baptist ministers. In the 1890s, with **William R. Harper**, he established the University of Chicago as a premier modern research university for the United States. Because of Rockefeller's frequent generosity to Northern Baptists, **conservative** elements in the Northern Baptist Convention were often critical of his perceived control of convention policies, but this did not daunt his work.

ROE, CHARLES HILL (1800–1873). English and later American Baptist minister and evangelist, born in King's County, **Ireland**. Early in his life, Roe was converted through the Irish Baptist Mission, and he determined to be a Baptist minister; he studied with **William Steadman** at Bradford and married Steadman's daughter. After studies, Roe served the church at Middleton-in-Teesdale from 1824 to 1835. In 1834, he became secretary of the **Baptist Home Mission Society**, and there he exercised his considerable skills as a fund-raiser and **revivalist** among the churches of the **Baptist Union**. He became **pastor** of Heneage Street Baptist Church in Birmingham from 1841 to 1851; during this time (1849), Charles Finney (1792–1875) visited England and held revival meetings in Roe's church. Admiring Finney's revival methods, Roe decided to emigrate to America, and in 1851 he settled at Belvidere, Illinois, following brief periods at Milwaukee, Wisconsin, and New York City. In 1861, Roe became chaplain of a U.S. Army regiment and later superintendent of educational work among the freedmen. An ardent abolitionist, Roe protested the British support of the Southern cause during the American Civil War. In 1858, he became a founder of the first University of Chicago, taught there for two years, and served as secretary-treasurer of the university. Roe's autobiography, *A Minister's Life* (1900), provides much data on the transition from Victorian British Baptist life to the Progressive Era in the United States.

ROGERENES. A colonial New England sect that arose in support of the teachings of James and **John Rogers**, at one time members of the Baptist Church at Newport, Rhode Island. In Great Neck, New York, a Rogerene congregation was organized in 1674 around the principles of honoring the Sabbath on Saturdays, believer's **baptism**, nonresistance, and a healing **ministry** for the sick. The Rogerene church was opposed to formal prayers and conducted itself like a Quaker meeting. John Rogers, however, denied that his church was Quaker in orientation, doubtless to avoid the stigmas attached to that group. The Rogerenes practiced some outlandish behavior among the other Baptists, such as appearing unclothed in public to affirm their freedom in **Christ**. No evidence of their existence beyond Rogers's ministry survives. Their presence on the colonial religious scene, however, did lend credence to the adversarial case that claimed some Baptists were extreme sectarians.

ROGERS, ADRIAN (1931–2005). Southern Baptist minister, born at West Palm Beach, Florida. He was educated at Stetson University and New Orleans Baptist Theological Seminary. Rogers served three primary pastorates: Fellsmere, Florida; Fort Pierce, Florida; and Bellevue in Memphis, Tennessee. Following the reputation of preachers like **R. G. Lee**, at Bellevue Baptist, Rogers led in a membership growth surge that reached 27,000 members and was the driving force behind the establishment of Mid-America Baptist Seminary. Rogers's election to the presidency of the **Southern Baptist Convention** in 1979 marked the beginning of the resurgence movement. He was one of the most beloved **conservative evangelicals** and/or **fundamentalists** of his era, three times elected Southern Baptist Convention president (1979–1981; 1986–1988) and a friend of evangelist **Billy Graham**. Rogers chaired the influential revision committee of the "**Baptist Faith and Message**" (2000).

ROGERS, JOHN (1648–1721). Baptist minister born at New London, Connecticut. Little is known of his early years, except that his father was a well-to-do baker. In 1674, while visiting Newport, Rhode Island, John encountered the **Seventh Day Baptists** and was converted to their principles. Shunned by his family for this new direction, he relocated to Long Island where at Great Neck he organized a church. His principles included Sabbatarianism, believer's **baptism**, and open membership for Negroes. Eschewed by other Christians, the group came to be called "**Rogerenes**" and gained a reputation for literalistic interpretation of the Bible. Rogers was imprisoned in 1694 for blaspheming Governor Gurdon Saltonstall (1666–1724) of Connecticut. Concerned for those in need, he died of smallpox while in Boston caring for those stricken with the disease. Rogers's publications include *A Description of the True Shepherds of Christ's Flock and Also of the Antiochristian Ministers* (1695?) and *Epistle to the Church of Christ Call'd Quakers, and to the Seventh Day Baptists* (1705).

ROGERS, WILLIAM (1751–1824). American Baptist minister and military chaplain, born at Newport, Rhode Island. He was the first student in the College of Rhode Island under **James Manning**. In 1770, Rogers was baptized at Newport and two years later became **pastor** at First Baptist Church, Philadelphia. Among his adherents was the celebrated physician, Dr. Benjamin Rush (1746–1813). In 1775, Rogers was named chaplain to the Pennsylvania regiments in the Revolution, and he served in that capacity until 1780. George Washington (1732–1799) knew Rogers well and esteemed his work. In addition to his pastoral work, he taught oratory and belles lettres at the University of Pennsylvania. For two years, 1816 and 1817, Rogers served as a delegate to the Pennsylvania State General Assembly. He was elected a vice president of the **General Missionary Convention** and was one of the architects of the American Baptist national organization. In 1814, Rogers joined with others of the **Baptist Board of Foreign Missions** (BBFM) in opposing appointments of single women missionaries, and in protest he dissociated himself from the BBFM for a time. Rogers's journal (1879), written while he served with the expedition of General John Sullivan (1740–1795) in 1779, provides a unique insight into the defeat of the Six Nations Indian confederacy.

ROGER WILLIAMS FELLOWSHIP (RWF). A **voluntary association** of Baptists in the United States dedicated to "fellowship, freedom, and faith" in honor of **Roger Williams**. Founded in 1935 at the annual meeting of the Northern (American) Baptist Convention (NBC) in Colorado Springs, Colorado, the fellowship was made up of **pastors** of the younger generation who felt the need for open, free, and creative discussion of theological ideas and denominational issues. There was a sense of urgency in the midst of renewed **fundamentalist** reaction to perceived modernist tendencies in the NBC. From the beginning there have been no theological requirements for membership, and persons of varying theological perspectives have been members. Beginning in 1952, a three-day conference was held at the University of Chicago with the faculty and trustees of the Baptist Theological Union; in the 1980s, this institutional context was transferred to Colgate Rochester Divinity School in Rochester, New York. The RWF has intermittently published *Baptist Freedom* since 1944. Generally speaking, the RWF articulates a theologically **liberal**, socially active perspective within the **American Baptist**

Churches in the U.S.A., although in recent years, some wings of the **Southern Baptist** tradition have expressed interest. Prominent members over the years include Gordon **Poteat** (1891–1986), Dores R. Sharpe (1886–1981), Wilbur E. Saunders (1894–1979), H. Otheman Smith (1901–1971), and Gordon Torgerson (1916–2007).

ROMANIA. In addition to an appreciation for early **Anabaptist** influences in their history, there are four roots of the Baptist movement in what is now Romania. In 1845, Karl Scharschmiedt (1820–?), a disciple of **J. G. Oncken**, baptized converts near Bucharest. Russian Baptist immigrants from **Ukraine** began a congregation at Cataloi in 1862. Constantin Adorian, a graduate of the seminary in Hamburg, started several churches in the vicinity of Bucharest and Dobrogea. More than 100 Hungarian-speaking churches were started in Transylvania between 1871 and 1910 (where Baptists are referred to as "Repenters"), and in the region of Bessarabia in 1912, a congregation was started at Cetatea Alba (Akkerman), which led to the establishment of the Bessarabia Baptist Convention.

Baptists received official government recognition in 1905 and formed a union in 1919; by 1940, the All Romanian Union of Baptist Churches was established. A theological school was started in 1921, with assistance from U.S. **Southern Baptists**, who accepted responsibility for mission in Romania as of the **London Conference of 1920**. In recent years, Romanian Baptists have also been influential in establishing ethnic congregations in **Serbia**, later Yugoslavia, beginning in 1931. In 1988, the **Association of Baptists for World Evangelism** began a **mission** in Romania; the **Baptist Bible Fellowship** started its work in the country in 1990; and in 1991, the **Conservative Baptist** Foreign Mission Society opened a mission at Oradea.

As of 2006, there were 1,722 churches and 98,672 members in the Uniunea Bisericilor Crestine Baptists din Romania, and 232 churches and 8,632 members in the Conventia Bisericilor Crestine Baptiste Maghiare Din Romania. The Romanian Baptist Union publishes a periodical, the *Christian Guide*.

ROSTAN, CASIMIR (1774–1833). French scientist, diplomat, and Baptist missionary pastor, born at Marseilles, **France**. Rostin was educated at the College of Tournon and joined his father's mercantile business. He continued to study Oriental languages, natural sciences, and archaeology, and this led to an extensive tour to the eastern Mediterranean in 1792–1798. He became devoted to the cause of Greek nationalism and was instrumental in proclaiming political liberty among the Greek islands at Ithaca in 1798. Frustrated in his attempts to secure a position in the government service, Rostan returned in 1799 to Marseilles, where he became professor of botany and natural history at the Botanical Gardens; he also edited a religious and philosophical journal and became city archivist, owing to his erudition.

Rostan was converted to **evangelical** Christianity and attached himself to the Society of Christian Morals, where he again developed an interest in **Greece**. In 1825, he served in Havana, **Cuba**, as French Consul, after which he went to the United States in 1827. He became a minister, supported the revivalist tradition, and was involved with missionary societies while in the United States. In 1832, Rostan returned to Paris and began an evangelical church, which was supported by the Society of Christian Morals and the **American Baptist Board of Foreign Missions** as one of its first forays into European missions.

ROUMANIAN BAPTIST ASSOCIATION OF AMERICA. The first Romanian Baptist congregation in the United States was formed in 1910 in Cincinnati, Ohio, largely of recent immigrants from Europe. Within three years, eight small churches in Illinois, Indiana, and Ohio formed at Cincinnati the Roumanian Baptist Association to further cooperation and mission work among themselves. The association was a simple **voluntary** union that published *Crestinus* (the *Christian*) from 1913. At its peak of organization, the association included about 20 congregations and 1,200 members. In 1940, the association joined temporarily with the Northern Baptist Convention.

ROUSSY, LOUIS (1812–1880). French **evangelical** missionary and later Canadian Baptist minister, born at Vevey, **Switzerland**. His parentage was Huguenot, and as a young man, Roussy was apprenticed as a mason. He engaged in work as a **colporteur** in **France**, and in the 1830s, he served as a **missionary** for the Lausanne Institute. In

1835, **Henriette Feller**, a co-laborer in the institute, invited Roussy to accompany her to a mission among the French of Quebec. First at Montreal and later at Grande Ligne, Roussy and Feller planted the first Protestant congregation in French-speaking Canada, out of which grew the Grande Ligne Mission and School. He superintended the construction of the school and mission buildings in 1840 and baptized new converts to the mission. Essentially **pastor** or preacher at the Grande Ligne congregation, 1837 to 1880, Roussy was baptized in 1847 and enabled the Grande Ligne Church to affiliate with the Baptists in 1849. He continued to evangelize in Quebec and plant new congregations until his death.

ROWLEY, HAROLD HENRY (1890–1969). British Baptist missionary and biblical scholar, born at Leicester. He completed a B.A. in theology at Bristol, then a B.D. at London University and finally a B.Litt. at Mansfield College, Oxford, under the renowned linguistic scholar G. Buchanan Gray. Rowley was much influenced by early pastors **F. B. Meyer** and W. Y. Fullerton, the latter who went on to serve with the **Baptist Missionary Society** (BMS) and was familiar with China. After a year of work for the Young Men's Christian Association in Egypt and service in a Baptist church in Somerset, Rowley was appointed an educational missionary to China by the BMS in 1922. He taught Old Testament at Shantung University until 1929, when questions arose about the religious orientation of that school. In 1930, Rowley became lecturer in Semitic languages at University College, Cardiff (joining the well-known Baptist T. H. Robinson [1881–1964], and in 1935, he became a professor in Old Testament at the University College of North **Wales**. From 1945 to 1959, he was Professor of Semitic Languages and Literature at University of Manchester and a leading international biblical theologian. He thus joined a department in which the Methodist A. S. Peake had taught, and he was a colleague of T. W. Manson, thus forming an illustrious trio of 20th-century Manchester **Bible** scholars. Rowley was the author of over 30 books, the most outstanding of which were *The Relevance of the Bible* (1944) and *The Unity of the Bible* (1953). His Oxford thesis, "The Grammar and Vocabulary of the Aramaic in the Old Testament," helped to establish the Second Century date for the book of Daniel. In 1957, Rowley served as president of the **Baptist Union of**

Great Britain and Ireland and was active in recruiting university students to Christian work.

RUSHBROOKE, JAMES HENRY (1870–1947). British Baptist minister and denominational leader, born at Bethnal Green, England. Baptized by **John Clifford**, Rushbrooke was educated at Midland Baptist College and London University, after which, on a Pegg Scholarship, he studied at the University of Berlin, where he greatly admired Adolf von Harnack (1851–1930). In 1902, he commenced a pastorate at St. Mary's Gate Baptist Church in Derby, which he served until 1907. Thereafter he was **pastor** at Archway Road, London (1907–1910), and Hampstead Garden Suburb Free Church (1910–1920), a new congregation that brought together Baptist and Congregational elements. In 1919, Rushbrooke was selected to conduct a nine-week tour of postwar Europe for the **Baptist World Alliance** (BWA); this was owing to his familiarity with Europe and his ability to speak German fluently. In 1920–1925, the **London Conference** appointed him commissioner for Europe, which involved supervision of relief, development, and **mission** for the united Baptist community. Rushbrooke became vice president of the BWA in 1926, and from 1926 to 1939, he served as general secretary of the organization. During the war years, from 1939 to 1945, as president of the BWA, Rushbrooke made several trips on behalf of the Baptist community, personally uniting the denominational family. Rushbrooke's publications give evidence of his critical role in the making of an international Baptist identity: *Baptist Work in Europe* (1920), *Baptists as Champions of Religious Freedom* (1938), and *Baptist Reconstruction in Europe* (1945).

RUSSELL, DAVID SYMME (1916–). British Baptist minister, educator, and administrator, born in Whitburn, **Scotland**. He was educated at Rutherglen Academy; the Scottish Baptist College; Trinity College in the University of Glasgow; and Regent's Park College, Oxford University, where he specialized in pseudipigraphical works in biblical studies and earned a D.Phil. At Oxford, Russell studied under the renowned Old Testament authority, **H. Wheeler Robinson.** Russell served congregations in Berwick-upon-Tweed and Oxford, during his graduate studies, and later, Church Road Baptist Church in London

(1945–1953), after which he became principal of Rawdon Baptist College in the north of England. He was instrumental in the merger of Rawdon and Manchester Baptist Colleges, and he served as co-principal of the new Northern Baptist College for three years, 1964–1967. In addition to his administrative responsibilities, Russell soon became a well-known lecturer and author in apocalyptic literature. In 1967, he was elected general secretary of the **Baptist Union of Great Britain and Ireland** (BU), a post he held until 1982. He presided over many changes in the life of the churches and the BU, including the stormy session of the annual assembly in 1971, when **Michael Taylor** delivered an address that raised troubling Christological questions that distressed many **evangelicals**. Two defining groups in the BU during Russell's service were the **Baptist Revival Fellowship** and the **Baptist Renewal Group**. Russell was widely traveled in Eastern Europe and Asia with the European Baptist Federation, and representing the BU, he served on commissions of the World Council of Churches, the **Baptist World Alliance**, and the Human Rights Programme of the European Council of Churches. The author of 14 books, Russell is best known for *The Method and Message of Jewish Apocalyptic* (1964) and *The Old Testament Pseudipigrapha* (1987).

RUSSIA. European Baptist pioneer **J. G. Oncken** first visited Russia in 1864. He interceded on behalf of persecuted **evangelicals** in the south of Russia and planned a missionary venture into Russia. The first recorded **baptism** in what is now Russia occurred in the Kura River in August 1867 among the Molokans, an evangelical, non-sacramental sect in the country. Nikita Voronin (1840–1905) was the leader of this group, which called itself "baptist" because of their open professions of faith by baptism. Vasili G. Pavlov (1854–1924) was another leader of a pietistic group in Tiflis; he was baptized by Voronin and became a patriarch of the Baptist movement in Russia. As early as 1855, there was a German Baptist congregation in St. Petersburg, and by the turn of the 20th century, there were four language groups in the Baptist community in St. Petersburg: German, Estonian, Lettish, and Swedish. Several aggressive Baptist congregations also arose in the Caucasus region in Taurida, Samara, Astrakan, Tiflis, and Mihilev. Still other congregations were located in Kiev, Rostov, and Moscow. On 1 May 1884, a Russian Baptist Union was formed at Novo Vasil'evka, largely the initiative of Germans living in Russia, but with solid Russian leadership.

Another important pioneer was **Ivan S. Prokhanov**, who was associated with the early Baptists in St. Petersburg and who came to lead that part of the movement known as the evangelical Christians. In 1888, Prokanov went to St. Petersburg as a student and developed a dissenter renewal among some Orthodox Christians. Early in his career, Prokhanov developed a strategy of uniting Russian evangelicals (Baptists and others) as an alternative Christian movement to the Orthodox Church. Prokanov spearheaded a plan for a Baptist College (which the fall of the Czarist regime precluded), and he helped to organize in 1909 the first Russian Evangelical Christian Conference.

Elsewhere in the Russian Empire, other religious forces helped shape the Baptist tradition. In **Ukraine**, it was the **Stundist** movement that gave birth to many of the first Baptist congregations in the 1880s. Stundists were an indigenous Pietistic baptizing group that met clandestinely apart from the Orthodox liturgical services. Later, Col. Vasilii Pashkov, Johann Wieler, and Ivan Kargel would be especially influential in bringing together Stundists and other dissenters into the diverse Evangelical movement in Russia and Ukraine.

By 1914, the two groups, All-Russian Baptists and the Evangelical-Christians, numbered over 100,000 members, even under intense persecution by the government. During the 1920s, Baptists and other evangelicals enjoyed a period of relative freedom and new churches, Bible study institutes, and communities were started. Several communal experiments were attempted, notably the one at Astrakhanka, that collapsed in the poor harvest of 1924. One such scheme involved Ivan Prokhanov's 1926–1927 plan for a Christian commune in Siberia. Other advances during this era included a Baptist Congress at Moscow in 1926, at which 365 candidates were publicly baptized in the Moscow River, and in 1927, a Russian **Bible** was printed in Leningrad and a theological seminary was opened in Moscow with Ivanov-Klishnikoff as rector. In 1929, the seminary was closed and its leaders sent to Siberia.

Despite persecution under Joseph Stalin (1879–1953) in the 1930s and 1940s, during which time many churches were closed and the numbers of Baptists significantly decreased, Baptist growth resumed in the post-Stalinist era in Russia and the Soviet Union, totaling perhaps as many as 3,000 churches and a half million members. In 1944, a major union occurred of the Baptists and Evangelical Christians; in 1945, the Union of Christians of Evangelical Faith, a Pentecostal **association**, joined to create the All-Union Council of Evangelical Christians-Baptists (AUCECB). In the late 1940s, however, many of the former Pentecostal churches dropped out of the union. A fourth component in the history of the AUCECB, the Mennonite Brethren, was also added in 1963. The final remnants of the German Baptist Union in Russia were absorbed into the AUCEB in the 1950s.

With the disintegration of the Soviet Union in 1991, a Baptist seminary was started in Odessa and a second theological program at Moscow began in 1993. A magazine, *Bratski Vestnik* (*Brotherly Herald*), has been published since 1945. Other Baptist efforts in Russia include the U.S. **Baptist General Conference**, which had a mission in Siberia from 1922 to 1946.

In a context of isolation caused by persecution and ostracism, a number of Baptist pastors and congregations in the 1940s refused to join the formation of the AUCECB. Two primary groups, the Prokofievites and the Initsiativniki, or Action-group, coalesced to form a separatist movement known as the Council of Churches of the Evangelical Christians and Baptists in 1965. This body of "pure" Baptists and like-minded evangelicals opposed centralization of authority in the AUCECB, government registration of churches, and what they perceived to be a lessening of evangelistic interests. Leaders associated with various wings of this movement, sometimes described as the nonregistered, or "underground," Baptists, include Alexei F. Prokofviev (1915–), Gennadi K. Kryuchkov (1926–), and **Georgi Vins**. Worldwide attention was drawn to the group because of Vins's persecution by the Soviet authorities in the 1960s and 1970s, and the intervention of Baptist U.S. president **Jimmy Carter** in the late 1970s. In 1969 and later, several of these congregations were reconciled to the AUCECB. In recent years, the Initsiativniki have been associated with Donetsk Christian University in Donetsk, Ukraine, in which the president and some of the faculty are associated with this movement.

With the reordering of Baptist life after the organizational demise of the All Union Council of Evangelicals-Baptists in the Soviet

Union in 1992, mainstream Russian Baptists reconstituted themselves as the Soyuz Yevangel'skikh Khristian-baptistov Rossiyskoy Federatsyi (Union of Evangelical Christians-Baptists of the Russian Federation). This body conducts denominational business and **mission** from headquarters in Moscow and relates to the European Baptist Federation, the Euro-Asiatic Federation of Evangelical Christians-Baptists, and the **Baptist World Alliance**. In 1992, the **Conservative Baptist** Foreign Mission Society opened a cooperative mission with Peter Deyneka Russian Ministries and the Evangelical Alliance Mission, and the **Baptist Bible Fellowship** opened a mission in Russia in 1993.

As of 2006, there were 1,309 churches with 80,000 members affiliated with the Soyuz Yevangel'skikh Khristian-baptistov Rossijskoy Federatsi, and 231 churches with 16,530 members in the Euro-Asian Federation of Christians Baptists Union. The Soyuz Yevangel'skikh embraces five major regions, each headed by a vice president of the Soyuz, as well as local associations that are headed by superintendents. Many of the associational superintendencies are shared positions with pastoral ministries. Presently, there are four theological schools in Russia: Irkutsk, Moscow (four), and Volgograd.

RUSSIAN–UKRAINIAN EVANGELICAL BAPTIST UNION, U.S.A. (RUEBU). Founded in 1919 in Philadelphia, Pennsylvania, the Russian–Ukrainian Baptist Union united many of the immigrant churches in the United States and lends support to churches and projects in **Russia, Belarus**, and **Ukraine**. Originally, there were 20 congregations in the United States and **Canada**, located mostly in the Northeast and Great Lakes regions. Headquartered in Ashford, Connecticut, since 1952 and also in Union, New Jersey, with close ties to the **American Baptist Churches** and the **Baptist World Alliance**, the RUEBU includes 24 churches and 1,200 members. The RUEBU publishes *Sower of Truth* (1919–) and *Evangelical Baptist Herald* (1952–), formerly the *Pilot* (1934–1952), together the oldest Russian language religious magazines in print. As of 2006, there were 20 churches with 1,400 members affiliated with the RUEBU.

RWANDA. Danish Baptists pioneered mission work in what became Rwanda in 1938. In 1977, **Southern Baptist** missionaries entered

Rwanda and began work at Kigali. The **Conservative Baptist** Foreign Mission Society also established its **mission** at Kigali in 1965 and later established the Association des Eglises Baptistes du Rwanda.

As of 2006, there were 184 churches and 256,338 members affiliated with the Association des Eglises Baptistes du Rwanda, 120 churches with 257,613 members affiliated with the Union des Eglises Baptistes du Rwanda, and 115 churches with 30,015 members affiliated with Community of Christian Churches. Presently, there are nine Baptist-related theological schools or colleges in Rwanda: Bugesera, Butare (three), Gisenyi, Kigali (three), Nyabisindu, Nyantanga, and Ruhengeri.

RYLAND, JOHN (1753–1825). English Baptist minister and educator, born at Warwick, England. Ryland was self-taught in the classics, and as a prodigy, he taught in his father's school at age 15. Beginning in 1771, he assisted his father in the Northampton Church, ultimately becoming sole **pastor** in 1786. In 1793, he was called to be pastor of the Broadmead Church in Bristol and the president of the academy there. From 1815 to 1825, he was secretary of the **Baptist Missionary Society**, which he helped to found. A Calvinist devoted to the position of American Congregationalist theologian/pastor Jonathan Edwards (1703–1758), Ryland inveighed against perceived Pelagianism and antinomianism. He was credited with being a principal force in the **revival** of the churches in the West Country and the upgrading of Bristol Academy to college status at the turn of the 19th century. He was a well-known Oriental scholar and was fond of natural history. Ryland's published works, which include *Advice to Students of Divinity* (1770), *The Difficulties of the Christian Ministry and the Means of Surmounting Them* (1802), and *The Practical Influence of Evangelical Religion* (1819), give evidence of his concern for ministerial training and spiritual nurture. Brown University in Rhode Island conferred on Ryland the doctor of divinity degree in 1792.

RYLAND, JOHN COLLETT (1723–1792). English Baptist minister, born at Bourton-on-Water, England. Ryland was a consistent Calvinist who exemplified the **Particular Baptist** tradition. He studied at Bristol Baptist Academy under **Bernard Foskett** and served congregations at Warwick, Northampton, and Enfield. He also managed schools in these villages. Ryland is best remembered as a gruff Calvinist delegate at the annual meeting of the Northamptonshire Baptist Association in 1792 who accused **William Carey** of enthusiasm and silenced his proposal about **missionary** endeavors. **Robert Hall** was terrified of Ryland when, as a child, Hall was admitted to Ryland's academy at Northampton. Ryland was considered ahead of his time in supporting the American War for Independence, a position for which Brown University rewarded him the honorary doctor of divinity degree in 1769. Ryland was one of the most widely published Baptists of his era, producing over 50 works, including *List of Baptist Churches in Great Britain* (1753), *A Contemplation on the Insufficiency of Reason* (1775), *The Preceptor, or General Repository of Useful Information* (1775), *An English and Greek Grammar* (1777), and *A Body of Divinity in Miniature* (1791).

– S –

SACRAMENTS. *See* BAPTISM; LORD'S SUPPER.

SAKER, ALFRED (1814–1880). English Baptist missionary, born in Borough Green, Wrotham, England. In his youth, Saker worked at the Devonport Dockyard and was active in the local Baptist church. Inspired by stories of Africa and the **mission** of **William Knibb**, Alfred and his wife, Helen Jessup, offered themselves for service with the **Baptist Missionary Society** (BMS). They sailed in 1843, stopping briefly in **Jamaica**, where they met Knibb, and landing finally on the island of Fernando Po, West Africa, in 1844. In 1845, he began work among the Dualla tribe on the mainland in **Cameroon**; he learned the language and ultimately translated the **Scriptures** into Dualla (1872). Despite the odds against Europeans surviving in the African tropical climate, Saker believed the British should colonize Cameroon as an entry to the interior of Africa, and he set about to create a religious colony at Victoria. He preached, built churches and schools, and advocated the mission to a reluctant BMS board in London over the next three decades. From the coast, he created settlements well into the interior and established a firm footing for British

Baptist African missions. Saker became a virtual administrator of the territory, arbitrating tribal disputes, and influencing a number of later Africa missionaries, including **George Grenfell**. Saker's publications include a *Grammatical Elements of the Dualla Language* (1855), *Dualla Hymnbook* (1859), and translations of the **Bible** into Dualla (1872–1882).

SAMPEY, JOHN RICHARD (1863–1946). Southern Baptist minister and educator, born at Fort Deposit, Alabama. He was educated at Howard College and Southern Baptist Theological Seminary. Upon graduation from seminary, Sampey was selected by **John A. Broadus** to assist him in teaching New Testament and homiletics. Later he studied Hebrew under **William Rainey Harper** at the University of Chicago, and he adopted Harper's "inductive method." Eventually, he held the chair in Old Testament and taught as many as 7,000 students in English and Hebrew. He authored textbooks in Old Testament and was editor of the Uniform **Sunday School** Lesson Series for 40 years, which influenced thousands of lay students in scores of Protestant denominations. In 1928, Sampey followed **E. Y. Mullins** as president of Southern Baptist Theological Seminary, and in the course of his 13 years in that office, he liquidated the seminary's debt. In 1935, Sampey served as president of the **Southern Baptist Convention**, and later in the decade, he represented Southern Baptists at the Conference on Faith and Order and the Conference on Life and Work of what would become the World Council of Churches. Sampey was widely published, and a chair in Old Testament at Southern Baptist Theological Seminary was named in his honor. He was the author of several significant works, including *Syllabus for Old Testament Study* (1903), *The Heart of the Old Testament* (1908), and *The International Lesson System* (1911).

SANDEMANIANS. Term used to designate followers of Robert Sandeman (1718–1771), the son-in-law of **John Glas**, a Scottish **dissenter**. A native of Perth, **Scotland**, Sandeman brought to London the ideas of recovering primitive Christianity, and this created distress in the greater Baptist community in the 1760s. In 1764, he moved to Boston and planted several Sandemanian meetings, notably in Boston, Portsmouth, New Hampshire, and Danbury, Connecticut, where Sandeman died and was buried. Two congregations in New England were known to have absorbed the Sandemanian position: Stratfield, Connecticut, and Chelmsford, Massachusetts.

Among the Sandemanian principles were literalistic interpretation of **Scripture**, multiple ruling **elders** of a congregation, unpaid clergy, celebrating the **Lord's Supper** each Lord's Day, **foot washing**, and contempt for an educated ministry and proselytizing. Some Sandemanian gatherings were said to reject the practice of family prayer. Sandeman often spoke of faith as an intellectual assent and rejected the necessity of spiritual conversion. Some of Sandeman's followers held that the atonement of **Christ** as an external act of God's grace was sufficient to human salvation. **Isaac Backus** wrote a polemic against Sandeman's teachings in 1767, and **Andrew Fuller** published in 1810 a major treatise in opposition to Sandemanianism. Sandemanianism lost out among American Baptists who preferred to emphasize heartfelt religious experience over legalistic formulations of Calvinism.

SAUNDERS, EDWARD MANNING (1829–1916). Canadian Baptist minister and historian, born at Tremont, Nova Scotia. A graduate of Acadia College, he served pastorates at Berwick and Halifax, Nova Scotia (1867–1881). In 1881, Saunders resigned from Granville Street Baptist Church, Halifax, to edit and publish the *Christian Visitor*, the principal Baptist paper in the Maritime Provinces. He published a *History of the Baptist Churches of the Maritime Provinces*, long considered a standard. Saunders based much of his work on the earlier unpublished manuscript of **John M. Cramp**.

SAUNDERS, JOHN (1806–1859). English missionary and Australian Baptist minister, born in London, England. A member of **Edward Steane**'s Baptist church at Cold Harbor Lane, Camberwell, Saunders studied for a career in the law but felt called to missionary service. He studied at the University of Edinburgh, devoting some of his time to itinerant preaching. During the early 1830s, he planted churches at Mason Court and Ball's Pond and served an existing congregation at Shacklewell, all three near London. In 1834, he applied to the **Baptist Missionary Society** and was referred to a group in **Australia** that was seeking a minister. Saunders and his wife, Elizabeth, arrived at

Sydney, New South Wales, and in 1835 began preaching services at South Head Lighthouse and later at Court House Room. In 1836, this meeting became the Bathurst Street Baptist Chapel, the first congregation of the Baptists in Australia. From this strategic point, Saunders conducted **evangelistic** tours and helped to form several of the other churches in what became the New South Wales Baptist Association. Saunders is remembered as the first Baptist missionary to Australia.

SAVANNAH RESOLUTIONS. A series of resolutions presented on 13 May 1861 to the annual meeting of the **Southern Baptist Convention** (SBC) in Savannah, Georgia. In the midst of the secessionist movement to form the Confederate States of America, a Special Committee on the State of the Country was established to make appropriate recommendations to the Baptist churches of the southern states. **Richard Fuller** of Baltimore, Maryland, a state that had not yet seceded, made the report, which included nine resolutions disclaiming blame for dissolution of the Union, approving of the formation of the Confederacy, and accusing the U.S. government of "lawless terror in the North." Other resolutions included an injunction to prayer and an observance of a day of humiliation, fasting, and prayer in the month of June. The resolutions were signed by 10 leading pastors, including Richard Fuller, **James B. Taylor**, **R. B. C. Howell**, and Basil **Manly** Sr., and transmitted to the Confederate Congress at Montgomery, Alabama. The Savannah Resolutions became a statement of rebellion in the North, and Fuller was especially vilified for his part in the process. As president of the SBC he was targeted by Northern sympathizers, and the 1861 SBC delegates therefore offered their collective prayers for his safety.

SCARBOROUGH, LEE RUTLAND (1870–1945). Southern Baptist evangelist, pastor, and educator, born at Colfax, Louisiana. Scarborough was reared in hardship in frontier Texas in a cowboy society where his father was a Baptist minister. His education included bachelor's degrees from Baylor and Yale universities, plus additional work at Southern Baptist Theological Seminary. Upon completion of his studies, he served as **pastor** at First Baptist, Cameron (1896–1901), and First Baptist, Abilene, Texas (1901–1908). Scarborough was in great demand as an evangelist and came to prominence in the Texas Baptist Convention and the **Southern Baptist Convention** (SBC). In 1919, he was director of the convention-wide $75 Million Campaign, following which he held strategic positions in the Baptist General Convention of Texas and became president of the SBC, 1939–1940. He was named to the first chair of **evangelism** at Southwestern Baptist Theological Seminary in 1908 and then president at Southwestern (1914–1945) during its period of greatest growth. In 1936, he made an evangelistic tour of South America for the **Foreign Mission Board** and drew international attention to his gifts. Scarborough was the author of over 30 books, among which are *Christ's Militant Kingdom* (1924), *How Jesus Won Men* (1926), and *A Modern School of the Prophets* (1939). He was awarded the honorary doctorate by Baylor and Union Universities.

SCHMIDT, NATHANIEL (1862–1939). American Swedish Baptist educator, born at Hudiksvall, Sweden. He was educated at the University of Stockholm and Colgate University, where he received an M.A. degree. His mentor at Colgate was **Ebenezer Dodge, a liberal** and irenic theologian. After a brief return to **Sweden**, Schmidt was **pastor** of the Swedish Baptist congregation in New York City, 1887–1888. Colgate invited Schmidt back to teach languages in 1888, and in 1891, at 29 years old, he was given a professorship in Semitic languages and literature in view of his attainments in scholarship. He began and edited the seminary's scholarly journal in 1892.

During the 1890s, Schmidt brought concern to the faculty and trustees for his application of scientific principles to biblical interpretation. Ultimately accused of holding Unitarian views and weakening the confidence of young seminarians in the authority of **Scripture**, Schmidt was dismissed from the faculty at Colgate in 1896. **Jacob Schurman** immediately offered him an endowed chair in Semitics at Cornell University. He became one of America's most distinguished scholars at Cornell through his retirement in 1932. His major works include *The Prophet of Nazareth* (1905), in which he asserted that Jesus did not claim to be the Messiah, and *The Coming Religion* (1930), in which he advocated new religious ideals—free, ethical, and scientific as well as devoid of creeds and dogma. He also authored 1,500 encyclopedia articles. Schmidt was president of the

Society of Biblical Literature in 1914 and the Jewish Institute awarded him the degree D.H.L. in 1931.

SCHURMAN, JACOB GOULD (1854–1942). Canadian and later American Baptist educator, born at Freetown, Prince Edward Island. Raised in a Baptist home, Schurman was educated at Prince of Wales College, Acadia College, and the University of London, where he completed his B.A. with first-class honors. For a time, he studied religion and moral philosophy at Manchester New College under James Martineau (1805–1900), and then he studied concurrently at the University of Edinburgh, where he earned a D.Sc., and the University of London, where he took an M.A. He studied further in **Germany** at the Universities of Heidelberg, Berlin, and Göttingen. In 1880–1882, Schurman taught English at Acadia College and then moved to Dalhousie University (1882–1886), also teaching literature and metaphysics. Returning to the United States, in 1886 he took a position at Cornell University and developed a close friendship with Henry W. Sage (1814–1897), who endowed a chair in Christian ethics and mental philosophy, which Schurman occupied. In 1890, Schurman was named dean of the Sage School of Philosophy, which included many of his students in what would become known as the "Cornell School" of philosophy. Schurman was president of Cornell from 1892 to 1920, during which time he developed a prestigious university and pioneered women faculty appointments, racial equality in student life, and state support for certain programs. Even before his departure from Cornell, he followed orthodox Republican politics and was rewarded with a string of diplomatic posts: chaiman of a **Philippines** Commission (1899–1900); minister to **Greece** and Montenegro (1912–1913); ambassador to **China** (1921–1925); and ambassador to Germany (1925–1930). Shurman was the author of numerous books on foreign policy and philosophic subjects, the most important being *Kantian Ethics and the Ethics of Evolution* (1881) and *Agnosticism and Religion* (1896).

SCOTCH BAPTISTS. Term applied to those Baptist churches in **Scotland** that were a native outgrowth of reactions to the Church of Scotland and its offspring. Also known as "Scots" Baptist gatherings, these churches are distinguished from the English Baptist churches of Scotland.

In the early 1760s, various leaders of the Anti-Burgher section of the Session Church met to discuss articles of church government and **polity**. Among them were Robert Carmichael (d. 1774) and **Archibald McLean**, who had been associated for a time with the **Glasite** movement in Glasgow. They agreed that **baptism** was for believers only. Soon after, Carmichael moved to Edinburgh to be the **pastor** of an Independent church there. In 1765, Carmichael withdrew from the Independent church and formed a small congregation at the historic Mary Magdalene Chapel in the Cowgate. Carmichael applied to **John Gill** of London to be baptized, and this occurred at the famous **baptistery** at the Barbicon on 9 October 1765 in the public company of about 600 people. The "mother church" of the Scotch Baptists was thus formed the following November at Edinburgh. After Carmichael's death in 1779, Archibald McLean became the principal figure in the evolution of the movement.

Among the doctrinal and polity standards that McLean had derived from the Glasites or achieved from his own **Bible** study were strict communion, a plurality of **pastors**, a body of **deacons**, celebration of the **Lord's Supper** every Lord's Day, the Agape or **Love Feast**, public prayers, and contributions to the poor. Unanimity in decision making and marriage only among Christians were also practiced. From the Glasites, the Scotch Baptists held to the absolute independence of each congregation.

As the movement spread throughout Scotland and into northern England, various splits occurred. In the 1790s, the Scotch Baptists worked closely with the **revivals** begun by the **Haldane** brothers. James Haldane was baptized in 1808, and for a time the **Haldanite tradition** moved upon Baptist principles. The Haldanes, however, were more tolerant on the question of baptism than were the Scotch Baptists, and rifts occurred among the Haldane churches. Eventually, some of the congregations permanently joined the Scotch Baptists, while others pursued an independent tradition, which would later be associated with the Campbellite movement.

In Canadian Baptist heritage, the term "Scotch Baptist" has a slightly modified usage. As Haldanite Baptists emigrated to Upper and Lower **Canada** in the first two decades of the 19th century, some were referred to as "Scottish" Baptists and settled in the Ottawa Valley among the other Baptist churches. Some of these congregations evolved into the mainstream community, notably behind the leadership of men like **John Gilmour**. Others, however, moved in a more Glasite direction and came under the influence of the Campbellite movement in the United States. Eventually these churches joined the Disciples of Christ denomination and were referred to at an interim stage as "Scotch Baptists." *See also* CAMPBELL, ALEXANDER; SCOTLAND.

SCOTLAND. The Baptist movement in Scotland is the result of Baptist witness from England during the Commonwealth era (1648–1660) and indigenous growth. The earliest churches, composed of mostly English folk, were Leith (1652), Cupar (1652), and Perth (1653). These churches were formed from Baptists serving in English regiments during the Cromwell occupation. Indigenous Scottish Baptist life is dated from the Keiss church, founded in 1750 by Sir William Sinclair. Two streams of indigenous Scottish Baptists were prominent: the first composed of dissenters from the Church of Scotland, Independents, Old Scots, **Glasites**, and Bereans (sometimes referred to as Scotch Baptists), and the second composed of those involved in the **Haldanite** movement. The first Scottish Baptist Association dates from 1835; it was known as the Baptist Union of Scotland after 1843 until it lapsed in 1856. The current Baptist Union of Scotland dates from 1869 and includes ministerial funds, auxiliary associations, a women's organization, and district associations. The Home Mission Society, which focused upon work in the "Highlands and Islands," was formed in 1827 and amalgamated with the union in 1928. Since 1872, the union has been affiliated loosely with the **Baptist Union of Great Britain and Ireland** (BU) in fund-raising schemes, a common ministerial listing, and membership in the British Council of Churches. When the BU adopted its Declaration of Principle in 1904, the Baptist Union in Scotland followed with adopting the statement. Prominent English Baptists like **Alexander Maclaren** (himself a Scot) and **Charles H. Spurgeon** had a particular interest in advancing missions in Scotland. However, in 1967 in an expression of independence from the BU, the Scottish Baptist Union was admitted to the **Baptist World Alliance** as an independent member.

The doctrinal stance of the early Scottish Baptists was historically similar to that of the English **Particular Baptists**: in 1653, a Scottish version of the 1644 London Confession was produced. Owing to the irregularity of educational opportunities within the Baptist Union in Scotland, prominent Scottish Baptists have received theological educations at Presbyterian divinity halls like St. Andrews or New College, Edinburgh, or in the English Baptist colleges at Rawdon, Manchester, or Stepney. Noteworthy among the recent general secretaries of the Baptist Union of Scotland have been George M. Hardie (1952–1966), Andrew D. MacRae (1966–1980), and Peter Barber (1980–1991), all evangelical in orientation.

As of 2006, there were 176 churches with 13,769 members affiliated with the Baptist Union of Scotland. Scottish Baptist theological education began with the **Haldane** School at Granton-on-Spey, the principal Baptist theological college of the union has operated at Glasgow since 1894, plus another independent school, the Dunoon Baptist College, that trained **evangelists** and **missionaries** 1893–1915. The union publishes the *Scottish Baptist* magazine (1875–). The U.S. **Baptist Bible Fellowship** opened a mission in Scotland in 1983.

SCREVEN, WILLIAM (1629–1713). English businessman and colonial American Baptist **pastor**, probably born in Somerset, England. Little is known of his background, except that it is assumed that one of the reasons he emigrated to the colonies was to escape religious difficulty. In the region of northern coastal Massachusetts (present-day southern Maine), Screven operated a trading business that eventually extended to southern Carolina colony. Convinced of a Baptistic position sometime in 1681, Screven declined to have his child baptized in the Kittery Congregational Church. He traveled to Boston to confer with the Baptist Church there, and he was licensed to the **ministry** in January 1682. Returning to his home at Kittery, he formed a congregation and immediately drew the ire of authorities. Before the York County civil authorities, Screven maintained that infant **baptism** was an **ordinance** of the devil, and he was sent to jail for his assertion. Upon release, he and his family and the friends who joined him in the congregation he had organized, moved to the Cooper River about 1696, near what became Charleston, South Carolina. There they joined a small, mostly **General Baptist** congregation, which had been constituted about a decade previously. Screven's descendants thus became the seed of the First Baptist Church of Charleston and, by extension, the first Baptist congregation in what is now the southern United States.

SCRIPTURE, AUTHORITY OF. A basic Baptist tenet is a firm conviction that the final authority in determining faith and practice is Scripture. Baptists have universally described Scripture as the Word of God, which is revealed to the church in order that God's people may know God's will. Baptists also understand that within a body of believers, Scripture is a guide and comfort for new life in **Christ**. In the 17th-century context, Baptists rejected the authority of ecclesiastical structures, especially the Church of England. Later, Baptists likewise moved away from the presbyterial system while empowering their own **associations** for specific tasks. More important were the canonical Scriptures of the Old and New Testaments, which were variously described as "sufficient," "infallible," "perfect," "divinely inspired," "without error," and "the final authority." **Polity** manuals, theological treatises, and personal narratives all evince a Baptist understanding of Scripture as specifically relevant and applicable in people's lives as well as the corporate congregation. In each of the **confessions of faith**, countless Scripture references, notably 2 Timothy 3:15–17 and 2 Peter 1:19–20, are used to buttress theological assertions.

Baptist respect for the authority of Scripture led the denomination to take a premier role in the translation and distribution of Scriptures in the 19th century. Baptists helped to form the British and Foreign Bible Society in 1804 and the American and Foreign Bible Society in 1816. Baptist **missionaries**, such as like **William Carey**, **Adoniram Judson**, and **William Dean**, pioneered the translation of Scriptures in the missionary context. In a controversial movement in the American Bible Society, it was Baptists who started new **Bible** associations to promote certain translations of the Bible, notably the American Bible Union in 1850. Baptist scholars and educators also produced a number of Bible commentaries and thematic studies of the Bible through both denominational and other publishers.

In the later 19th century, German higher criticism had influence in biblical studies and theology at key northern Baptist seminaries in the United States, notably Colgate, Rochester, Newton, Crozer, and the University of Chicago, and noticeably at smaller schools, including Southern Baptist Theological Seminary and Cobb Divinity School. At the University of Chicago, under the direction of **William Rainey Harper**, the critical approach was dominant. This caused a widespread reaction among churches over modernistic teachings that were perceived to reduce the authority of Scripture. The result was the birth of **fundamentalism**, which holds as its key doctrine an unassailably inerrant Bible. New schools grew up to train leaders along these lines, for instance, Northern Baptist Theological Seminary in Chicago, a response to the University of Chicago, and the Eastern Baptist Theological Seminary, a reaction to Crozer Theological Seminary. Eventually, this same phenomenon occurred in the **Southern Baptist Convention**, where Southern Baptist Theological Seminary and others were deemed to be "**liberal**" on the matter of Scriptural authority, and other institutions emerged to protect the authority of the Bible. In Canada, at McMaster University, the influx of critical thinking led to the establishment of the hyper-orthodox Toronto Baptist Seminary.

The overall Baptist community in North America has often become badly divided over the meaning and use of Scripture. Wide divergence exists in the denomination over the issue of authority, sometimes giving the impression that liberal thinkers are closer to mainstream Protestants and **evangelical**/fundamentalists are closer to Independent, orthodox Presbyterian, and Brethren groups. *See also* BIBLE.

SEARS, BARNAS (1802–1880). American Baptist minister and educator, born at Sandisfield, Massachusetts. He was educated at Brown University and Newton Theological Institution. In 1828–1829, Sears was **pastor** at First Baptist, Hartford, Connecticut, but resigned for health reasons to take a faculty position teaching biblical theology at Hamilton Literary and Theological Institution in Hamilton, New York. The leading member of the Hamilton faculty, he took a study leave to travel in Europe in 1833, making the acquaintance of numerous church leaders and theologians, including professors August Tholuck (1799–1877) and Wilhelm Gesenius (1786–1842) at Halle and Julius Müller (1801–1878) at Berlin. In 1834, he baptized **J. G. Oncken**, the Baptist apostle to Europe. Upon his return in 1835, Sears took the chair in Christian Theology at Newton Theological Institution, in 1839 becoming president of the seminary. He served as president of the Massachusetts Education Board from 1848 to 1855, during which time the "town system" was developed. Upon the resignation of **Francis Wayland**, Sears became president of Brown University in 1855, a position he held concurrently with the professorship in philosophy and Christian evidences through the Civil War. In 1867, he accepted the secretaryship of the George Peabody Fund and in this role traveled widely in the southern states during Reconstruction. He advocated the development of public school systems in each state and took special interest in the creation of "normal" schools for teacher training. Sears was the author of a variety of books, including *Life of Luther* (1849) and *Objections to Public Schools Considered* (1875).

SECOND GREAT AWAKENINGS. Term applied to the series of religious renewals that occurred in the United States from about 1800 to 1835–1840. The initial phase erupted at Cane Ridge, Kentucky, in 1800 where outdoor camp meetings, primarily among the Presbyterians, produced general religious awakenings in the Appalachian Mountain region. Another phase took place at Yale College, New Haven, Connecticut, in the first decade of the new century where Timothy Dwight (1752–1817), a Congregationalist, spearheaded a renewal on that campus. Other manifestations included the ministry of Charles G. Finney (1792–1875), a Presbyterian, in upstate New York and throughout New England and the Western Reserve region in Ohio. Finney was particularly responsible for the "New Measures," a collection of behavior-modifying strategies such as the anxious bench, the altar call, protracted meetings, naming sinners, and seasons of prayer.

Baptists were caught up in the general religious enthusiasm in mostly indirect ways. Part of the awakening was channeled through new **voluntary** societies for **missions**, education, and humanitarian concerns; Baptists followed the patterns set by others and created numbers of these societies. Some of the leaders in these awakenings were local church pastors, such as **William F. Broaddus** of Virginia, who in 1831–1833 adopted the New Measures, preached widely in his **association**, and created a new congregation around the **revival** techniques. There were also Baptist **evangelists** who itinerated widely, preaching on ultraistic themes and claiming extraordinary results; these included **Jacob Knapp**. **Freewill Baptists** like **David Marks** were involved in the Second Great Awakenings as they planted new congregations throughout the United States and **Canada** and experimented with social and moral reform causes. *See also* REVIVALS; VOLUNTARISM.

SEEKERS. During the first half of the 17th century in English religious developments, a number of sects arose from a free interpretation of **Scripture** and in opposition to any form of establishment. Among these were Baptists, Quakers, **Ranters**, **Levellers**, **Familists**, and **Diggers**. The Seekers, whose name was loosely applied to people in search of the truth, questioned the value of the **sacraments**, churches, ministers, and organized worship. Many felt the end of the world was near and advocated radical social policies like poor relief, heavier taxation of the rich, identification of the saints with the poor, and abolition of ministers. William Erbury (1604–1654) was acclaimed the champion of the Seekers; he taught the universal redemption of mankind and that the fullness of the Godhead would be manifested in the saints. A number of disillusioned Baptists went over to the Seekers at least for a time, including **Roger Williams**. *See also* DIGGERS; LEVELLERS; RANTERS.

SEMPLE, ROBERT BAYLOR (1769–1831). American Baptist minister and historian, born at Rosemont, Virginia. He pursued a career in school teaching and studied law, before turning to **ministry** in 1789. He was ordained in 1790 and called to the Bruington (Virginia) Baptist Church, which he served to his death. Semple was an advocate of **missionary** endeavor, **education**, and associationalism. He was the first president of the Baptist General Association of Virginia in 1823 and president of the **General Missionary** (Triennial) **Convention** in 1820. A close friend of **Luther Rice**, Semple was a promoter of the national Baptist movement and adroitly maneuvered

Virginia churches in that direction. His book, *The Rise and Progress of Baptists in Virginia* (1810), contains much primary source material and follows the pattern of historical writing set by Joshua Thomas, **Morgan Edwards** and later by **David Benedict**. Brown University awarded Semple an honorary A.M. in 1814 and the doctor of divinity in 1824.

SENEGAL. In 1962, **Conservative Baptists** from the United States opened a mission at Thies, a coastal city, Diourbel, and Dakar. In 1969, the **Southern Baptists** appointed their first missionary to Senegal, Farrell Runyan, who settled at Dakar. Work is much controlled by government restriction.

As of 1995, there were two congregations and about 100 members associated with the Mission Baptiste du Sénégal.

SEPARATE BAPTISTS. A movement of churches and ministers associated initially with the first **Great Awakening** in the American colonies, particularly the South. In New England, the Separate movement was popularly known as **New Light Baptists.** As the **revivalists** itinerated in the New England and the Middle Colonies, beginning in 1740, congregations emerged around tighter standards of church membership, the reassertion of sovereign grace, evidence of conversion, and **evangelism**. Some churches of a separate kind resulted from separating from older Congregational churches, while others sprang up around the **ministry** of younger preachers. By the late 1740s, leaders like **Isaac Backus** were persuaded to adopt Baptist principles and many of the Separates became Separate Baptists, because they practiced believer's **baptism** and other Baptistic ideas. These churches stressed a pure church, they practiced the **associational** principle, held in priority the work of the Spirit, engaged in preaching, and emphasized evangelism. Most held to closed communion and high ethical expectations. The term "separate" came from their desire to be separate from churches and Christians who practiced open communion and more **liberal** standards of Christian faith and conduct.

Although the Separate Baptists initially had difficulties with Regular Baptist organizations, a learned ministry, and the **General Baptist** position, they gradually moved toward the mainstream and by

1787 in Virginia and 1801 in Kentucky were assimilated into the Regular, Calvinistic family. Several of the New England Separates moved to the southern states, notably **John Leland** and **Shubael Stearns**, to carry the Separate emphases to that region. Among the leaders of the southern Separate Baptists were **James Ireland** and **John Taylor**, the latter eventually becoming anti-missionary in his views. Those churches, particularly in Kentucky, that remained out of the Regular Union of 1801 gradually evolved into the General Association of Separate Baptists in Christ (1912). *See also* GREAT AWAKENING; NEW LIGHT BAPTISTS.

SEPARATION OF CHURCH AND STATE. Part of the sociopolitical outlook of Baptists from their beginning was a doctrine of the separation of church and state. In some places, this has been more aggressively pursued than elsewhere.

In the first half of the 17th century, Baptists found themselves labeled "**Nonconformists**" in the context of a state and Established Church, the Church of England. Under the policies of King James I (1603–1625), Charles I (1625–1649), Church of England Archbishop Laud, the Presbyterian Westminster Assembly, or the later Restoration monarchs King Charles II (1660–1685) and King James II (1685–1689), the interests of the state and the church were unhealthfully wed, from a Baptist perspective. To no one's surprise, therefore, Baptist writers came down on the "separateness" of the two spheres, the civil and the spiritual. **Roger Williams** was perhaps the first to develop the metaphor of a "wall of separation." By this he meant that there are two distinct spheres of influence, the civil and the spiritual, which should be maintained constitutionally and kept practically separate. In later English Baptist development, Baptists struggled to achieve toleration and advocated a completely **voluntary** system of church relationships. They contented themselves with influencing government policy through coalitions with other Nonconformists, notably the **Three Dissenting Denominations**, later the Dissenting Deputies, or their own elected members of Parliament and other government appointments.

An important contribution distantly related to the Baptist movement was made by **John Glas**, a Scotsman who favored an entirely voluntary system of church support and membership. While considered quite radical in his era, Glas influenced major Baptist thinkers as well as the Christian Church/Disciples of Christ, begun by **Alexander Campbell**. Outside the Baptist movement can be noted the work of Thomas Chalmers (1780–1847) in **Scotland**, who also made the case for dismantling established churches in Britain.

In the American colonies, a similar distrust of governments ensued with the colonial establishments, the Standing Order Congregationalists in New England, and various shades of Anglicanism in the South. Taxation, licensing, and other attempts of colonial governments to intrude in personal and congregational religious experience forced Baptists to take the position that the state should not be allowed to interfere in the life and work of the church. **Isaac Backus** and **John Leland** were leading proponents of the separation ideal in the 18th century. Through the Massachusetts delegation to the Constitutional Convention, Backus proposed a dissolution of the principle of established churches supported by the states. Leland likewise influenced his friend James Madison (1751–1836), and perhaps Thomas Jefferson (1738–1826), to include in the Bill of Rights a clear guarantee that "Congress shall make no laws concerning an establishment of religion." The separation of church and state was thus guaranteed in the United States by constitutional amendment. Baptist groups, notably the **Baptist Joint Committee on Religious Liberty** (formerly Public Affairs), are vigilant on government policies, lest the wall be breached.

Issues that cause debate in the United States are religious exercises in schools, government surveillance over unorthodox religious groups, Sunday "blue laws," the civic role of ecclesiastical persons, taxation of both personal income and church property, and the use of language about God in official national symbols. Most Baptists in the United States generally believe Christians have a responsibility under God to advocate Christian ideals and biblical faith in the making of public policy. This advocacy takes the form of supporting political candidates, campaigning for referenda issues, critique of public policy, and of course exercise of personal franchise. In the later decades of the 20th century, some **fundamentalistic** Baptists in the United States held that there should be clear political advocacy and even political pressure groups and parties (i.e., the Moral Majority) dedicated to biblical ideals. *See also* RELIGIOUS LIBERTY; VOLUNTARISM.

SERAMPORE MISSION. Serampore in the state of Danish **India** was the beginning point of Baptist missionary activity in India. From 1795 to 1816, the "Serampore Trio" of **William Carey**, **William Ward**, and **Joshua Marshman** superintended a major station for the **Baptist Missionary Society** (BMS) in England. In 1816, a schism in the administration of the Serampore work occurred, with the result that the BMS gave up its support and the mission was independent until 1854 when it was reunited with the BMS. In the years of its independency, the Serampore Mission conducted an extensive translation work and **evangelism** into Assam and Meghalaya. Krishna Chandra Pal, Carey's first convert, was instrumental in 1813 in the conversion of four Sepoys, one from Assam, the others from Khasia. In the 1820s, Serampore influence reached into the Manipur region with a New Testament translation. At Guwahati, the mission opened a school in 1829 for Lower Assam. In the 20th century, the historic school property became headquarters for the Council of Baptist Churches in Northeast India and the site of the Guwahati Medical College Hospital. Through its various stages, the Serampore Mission became a Baptist focal point for evangelical advancement in northeast India.

SERBIA AND MONTENEGRO. The center of Baptist life in Serbia has been Novi Sad in the Vojvodina region, where Heinrich Meyer (1842–1919), a German Baptist missionary who had worked in **Hungary**, established the first church in 1875. In 1898, Peter Lehotsky (1873–1956) began a congregation in Belgrade, also in the German tradition. The Romanian Baptists began an ethnic church at Straza in 1924 and a Slovakian ethnic minority church started at Backi Petrovac in 1897. As early as 1938, American Southern Baptists also commenced missionary work in Belgrade. A theological school started in Belgrade in 1940; closed during the war; reopened at Zagreb, Croatia, in 1954; moved to Daruvar in 1955; and finally settled in Novi Sad in 1957. Beginning in 1922, the Serbo-Croatian Conference included Germans, Slovaks, and Hungarians, and later this ethnic combination comprised the Baptist Union of Yugoslavia (officially recognized in 1926) until World War II.

Following the civil war of 1991 and more recently in 1995, Serbian Baptists have been constituted in two unions: roughly located among churches in the north is Savez Baptisticakih Crkava u Srbiji (Union of Baptist Churches in Serbia, offices in Belgrade), and Savez Evanvjeoskih Crkava Baptista (Union of Evangelical Christians-Baptists in Yugoslavia, offices in Vrnjacka Vanja), concentrated in the south. The northern union is multinational, while the southern union is mostly Serbian.

Serbian Baptists in Belgrade helped to establish the Baptist churches in Macedonia, beginning in 1936.

As of 2006, there were 52 churches with 2,029 members affiliated with the Savez Baptisickih Crkava u Srbiji, and 14 churches with 685 members in the Baptist Union of Evangelical Christians in Serbia and Montenegro. There is a theological school in Novi Sad. *See also* MACEDONIA.

SEVENTH DAY BAPTISTS (SDBs). Seventh Day, or Sabbatarian, Baptists first appeared in the mid-17th century English context of rapid **Nonconformist** development. British Baptist historian **William T. Whitley** and others believe that Sabbatarians emerged from the biblical literalism associated with groups such as the **Fifth Monarchists**. Early Sabbatarian writers include James Ockford, William Saller (fl. 1640–1680), and Thomas Tillam (fl. 1635–1670). Whatever their origin was, the first congregation can safely be identified as the Mill Yard Church (c. 1653). Both **General** and **Particular Baptists** crossed over to be involved as SDBs, and the movement included a number of prominent people, such as **Francis Bampfield** and Dr. **Peter Chamberlen**. By 1730, the SDB movement was essentially defunct in England, with only a few scattered congregations left by the 20th century. Among the reasons for the decline are reliance upon personal endowments rather than congregational stewardship, a lack of organized fellowship, employment of first-day Baptist ministers, and crossover of SDB members to first-day congregations.

In the United States, however, there is an ongoing history for the group. In Newport, Rhode Island, in 1671 a schism grew up among the Regular Baptist churches over the Sabbath, and a separate congregation was started by Seventh Day advocates. From this beginning, a chain of churches in New Jersey, New York, Rhode Island, and the upper Midwest evolved later to constitute a Yearly Meeting, which became the Seventh Day Baptist General Conference, formed in 1802. Five associations were formed in 1835: Eastern, Central, Western, Northwestern, and Southeastern. In 1843, the Seventh Day Baptist Foreign Mission Society was founded and it maintained a field in **China** until 1950, when, due to closure of the field, missions were focused in **Burma, Poland, Malawi**, and **Mexico**. The Seventh Day Baptist Publication Society produced sabbatarian literature and the Education Society, originally located at Alfred, New York, has provided support for candidates for the **ministry**. Centers of the movement include Alfred, New York, where there was a university related to the SDBs, and Salem, West Virginia, where a second school exists, Salem College. In 1965, six national conferences plus the General Conference of Seventh Day Baptists in the United States formed the Seventh Day Baptist World Federation. The federation provides increased communication, stimulates fellowship, and promotes evangelism and special projects.

American SDBs have a long **ecumenical** heritage, including membership for several years in the National Council of Churches (1905–1973) and the World Council of Churches (1948–1976); in 1963, merger with the American Baptist Convention was discussed but later rejected in the 1970s. The denomination in the United States has also taken various moral positions on issues such as **peacemaking**, race relations, **separation of church and state**, and **human right** to life.

The SDB national headquarters is in Janesville, Wisconsin (which includes the Historical Society), and the conference publishes the *Sabbath Recorder* (1844–).

As of 2006, there were 70 churches and 3,400 members belonging to the Seventh Day Conference in the United States and **Canada**. *See also* SOLITARY BRETHREN.

SEXUALITY, BAPTISTS AND. Over the course of four centuries, Baptists have been traditionalist on the matter of human sexuality, namely, defining marriage as the union of a man and a woman and interpreting the **Bible** as supporting heterosexual, monogamous, life-long relationships. This is evident from confessional documents, although individual instances of homosexual behavior can be identified, such as was alleged in the life of Andrew Gifford (1700–1784) of Bristol and, later, London, England. This began to change, however, with the public legislation and Christian organizational responses in North America that recognized gay/lesbian relationships and/or same-sex unions. In the United States, the **Alliance of Baptists** has taken a strong position in support of full marriage equality for all citizens and "laments the denigration of gay, lesbian, and transgender sisters and brothers," while the **Cooperative Baptist Fellowship** states that it does not condone or affirm homosexual practices nor appoint staff persons or missionaries who are practicing homosexuals. The **Southern Baptist Convention** has remained aggressively heterosexual and monogamous in outlook, while the **American Baptist Churches** have produced somewhat conflicting statements: in 1992, a general board resolution stated that homosexual lifestyle was incompatible with Christian teaching; the following year, a second resolution came forth that called for dialogue, and still later, a Commission on Denominational Unity further recognized diversity in the denomination on these matters and "called for study, prayer, and achieving common ground." Within the American Baptist context is the Association of **Welcoming and Affirming Baptists** and the voice of Tony Campolo, who has asserted that a monogamous, committed relationship among gay persons is morally preferable to many heterosexual marriages.

In **Canada**, when the Liberal Party Governmnent led by Prime Minister Jean Chretien passed Bill C-38 in 2005, recognizing that traditional definitions of marriage violated the *Charter of Rights and Freedoms*, Convention Baptists debated the issues and took a clear position against same-sex unions. Typical was the policy of the Baptist Convention of Ontario and Quebec (BCOQ), where in 2003, the BCOQ resolved in council that ministerial registration to perform marriages could be revoked and that **pastors**, chaplains, and counselors were not to officiate at same-sex marriage ceremonies. In support of their position, BCOQ officers offered the biblical foundations from Genesis, St. Matthew, and the Epistle to the Ephesians; the BCOQ has also called upon its churches to demonstrate Christian love for those involved in the practice of homosexuality. Similar positions were passed in the eastern and western Baptist conventions/unions. In the Maritime Convention, a minority position has been declared by some congregations that such sanctions to revoke ministerial credentials violate the cherished Baptist positions on liberty of conscience and the autonomy of local churches. The **Fellowship of Evangelical Baptists** likewise practice and recognize only heterosexual, monogamous marriages.

Australian Baptists have debated issues focused upon homosexuality in two eras, the 1960s and the 1990s. In the earlier period, newspaper editorials led to seminars across the country in Baptist circles about the nature of homosexuality; whether it is an illness or acquired preference. The consensus was that more discussion should occur among the churches, but disdain for homosexual behavior or recognition remained strong. In the 1990s, as various states in **Australia** moved to de-criminalize homosexual behavior as a matter of public policy, Baptists debated the consequences and stood with conservative politicians in opposition to decriminalization, while also not wishing to exclude homosexual persons from the care of churches. The universal stance remained to be disinclined toward homosexuality on the basis of its condemnation in **Scripture**. In 1998, after a balanced discussion on the matter of recognizing homosexual candidates for ministry, the Baptist Union of Victoria concluded not to ordain persons who engage in homosexual practice.

SHAKESPEARE, JOHN HOWARD (1857–1928). English Baptist minister and denominational leader, born in Leicestershire. Shakespeare was educated at Regent's Park College and the University of London. In 1898, he became secretary of the **Baptist Union** (BU), and in that role for the next three decades, he became the leading force of the ecclesiastical organization of British Baptists as a denomination. Shakespeare began the Twentieth Century and Sustentation Funds, superintended the building of Baptist Church House in London, and organized the Baptist **ministry** according to credentials with the BU. He also was instrumental in establishing the system of superintendency in 1916. Shakespeare was an advocate in 1905 of the **Baptist World Alliance** and later of a union of all the Free Churches in Great Britain. Shakespeare's published works give evidence of his **ecumenical** orientation: *Baptist and Congregational Pioneers* (1905), *The Free Churches and the National Life* (1910), and *The Churches at the Crossroads* (1918).

SHATTERED BAPTISTS. A term used by Quaker founder George Fox (1624–1691) to describe a community of Baptists he encountered in 1648 in Nottinghamshire. According to entries in Fox's *Journal*, he was practicing his trade in Mansfield, and he came in contact with Baptists in Nottingham who had lost their spiritual life and scattered. He referred to them as "shattered Baptists" and found two types: one group continued to meet on Sundays "to play at shovelboard and to be merry," the other was a group of Separatists whom Fox considered to be a "tender people." Significantly, **Elizabeth Hooten**, who later became a leading Quaker, was among the second group. Fox found many followers among the shattered Baptists and he organized some under the new name "Children of the Light." Among those who played games on Sundays, Rice Jones (fl. 1650–1658) was a Nottingham Baptist leader who joined the Children of the Light for a time, but "returned out of the light to dark imaginations" thereafter. Jones became an adversary of Fox and in 1654 influenced many of the former Baptists among Fox's new group to rejoin Jones and later the **Ranter** movement, thus causing the first schism among the Quakers.

SHIELDS, THOMAS TODHUNTER (1873–1955). Canadian Baptist minister, born in Bristol, England. The Shields family emigrated to **Canada** in the 1880s, where the father was a Primitive Methodist preacher who taught his children **theology** and biblical subjects. Thomas entered the **ministry** in the Baptist Convention of Ontario and Quebec (BCOQ) and from 1894 to 1910 served several small congregations at Florence, Delhi, Dutton, and Hamilton before accepting the call from the prestigious Jarvis Street Church in Toronto. From the beginning, Shields attacked what he perceived to be the evidences of **liberal** theology in the BCOQ, mostly centered on McMaster University. Between 1919 and 1921, he organized the Canadian wing of the **Baptist Bible Union** and became a symbol for emerging Canadian **fundamentalism**. In a major rift with the BCOQ in 1925, Shields left, forming a separate newspaper (the *Gospel Witness*), seminary (Toronto Baptist Seminary), and denominational organization (the Regular Baptist Missionary and Education Society). With **William Bell Riley** and **J. Frank Norris**, Shields built a North American fundamentalist empire; in 1927, he took control of Northern Baptist–related Des Moines (Iowa) University, hoping to operate it as a Baptist fundamentalist institution. This plan failed, and for the remainder of his career, Shields focused his efforts on his pulpit ministry and Toronto Baptist Seminary. Shields's publications include *The Plot That Failed* (1937) and *Russellism or Rutherfordism?* (1942).

SHOUTER BAPTISTS. A group of Baptists in **Trinidad and Tobago**, St. Vincent, and **Jamaica** whose forms of worship draw upon vivid African styles. Traced from Yoruba tribe slaves brought to the islands from Africa, the Shouters' worship involves hand clapping, chanting, shouting, pouring of lotion, and bell ringing. The hand clapping and chanting are believed to be substitutes for drums and shac-shacs in the African custom. In the 19th century on several of the West Indies islands, Africans were persecuted for their often-disruptive worship practices. They were called "Shakers," and they were frequently prohibited from worship by law, as in 1912 on St. Vincent. As a result, the Shakers held worship in secret and met in huts. In Trinidad and Tobago, this same tradition was called "Shouter" or "Spiritual Baptists," and in 1917, such worship was outlawed. In 1951, the ordinance banning the Shouters was repealed, and the Shouters have come to associate with charismatic groups in the United States. The theological beliefs of the Shouters are similar to other Baptists, with the addition of articles that define the connections between Yoruba dances and music and New Testament spirituality.

SHUCK, JEHU LEWIS (1812–1863). American, and later Southern, Baptist missionary, born in Alexandria, Virginia. He was educated at Virginia Baptist Seminary (later Richmond College) and was appointed with his wife, Henrietta Hall (1817–1844), by the **Baptist Board for Foreign Missions** (BBFM) for work with the Chinese. He was a protege of **William Dean**, first Baptist **missionary** to the Chinese and was sent initially to Macao near Canton. A misunderstanding over their financial support in the beginning of their mission soured the Shucks' relationship with the BBFM and nearly cost them their assignment. In 1842, they moved to **Hong Kong** when it was opened to the West. There Henrietta opened a school and Lewis preached at a local bazaar, with much success. In 1845, Shuck wrestled with his relationship to the BBFM and the news that a new Southern Baptist Board would be formed. He ultimately allied himself with the **Southern Baptist Convention** and became its first missionary. His former colleagues, still under the patronage of the national board, shunned his decision. In 1852–1853, Shuck was accused of moral laxity and withdrew from the **China** field. He settled in California, where he worked in the immigrant Chinese community and started a church among the English-speaking settlers in Oakland under the auspices of the Home Mission Board. In 1840, Shuck published *Portfolio Chinensis*, a collection of important Chinese state papers.

SIAM. *See* THAILAND.

SIERRA LEONE. David George, the famous American and, later, Canadian **black Baptist** missionary, established a Baptist presence at Freetown in 1792. Three years later, the **Baptist Missionary Society** from Great Britain established a work, but withdrew shortly afterward. George R. Thompson and J. J. Brown, who had been ordained in 1853 at Freetown by T. J. Bowen (1814–1875) of the Southern Baptists, came under support of the **Foreign Mission Board** in 1855, but the mission was hampered by shortage of funds. For many years, Jamaican Baptists contributed generously to the small Baptist community in Sierra Leone. In 1964, the Nigerian Baptists entered the country and established a church at Bumbuna. This was followed by the European Baptist Missionary Society in 1966. In 1974, delegates of the Nigerian Mission, the European Mission, and the Bassa Baptist Church met in Mambolo to create the Baptist Convention of Sierra Leone. Finally, in 1984, U.S. **Southern Baptists** in their own right established a mission in Sierra Leone. The **Baptist Bible Fellowship** opened a mission in Sierra Leone in 1997.

As of 2006, there were 101 churches and 9,015 members affiliated with the Baptist Convention of Sierra Leone.

SIMMONS, WILLIAM J. (1849–1890). American **black Baptist** minister and educator, born at Charleston, South Carolina. He was born into slavery but raised a free man in Pennsylvania and New Jersey. He served in the 41st U.S. Colored Troops during the Civil War and then turned to study for the Baptist ministry. Following education at Madison University and Howard University, he was a school-teacher in Washington, D.C., and Ocala, Florida, and a **pastor** in Lexington, Kentucky (1879–1880). He took a faculty position at the Kentucky Normal and Theological Institute, a school sponsored by the **American Baptist Home Mission Society** (ABHMS). The ABHMS in 1887 appointed Simmons superintendent of their work in the South, which gave him the opportunity to travel extensively in the region. Sensing an opportunity, in 1886 he organized a meeting of black leaders under the motto "God, My Race and Denomination" to discuss possible organization; the result was the formation of the American **National Baptist Convention**, with Simmons as the first president. During the remainder of his career, he advocated Negro progress, the liberation of black women and he assailed white supremacy. In 1891, following Simmons's death, the Kentucky Normal Institute was renamed Simmons University.

SINGAPORE. The first Baptists in Singapore came through Malaya from Swatow, China, in 1905. The earliest congregation worshiped on an **ecumenical** basis until Lim Kian Tong, an educator from China, visited Singapore and urged the Baptists to constitute their own church. The first congregation was called the Overseas-Chinese (Swatow) Baptist Church of Singapore and it opened in 1937. Likewise in 1949 a church was organized among the Cantonese peoples living in Singapore. In 1951 U.S. **Southern Baptist** mission work began and the **Baptist Bible Fellowship** (BBF) opened a mission in 1970, the **Conservative Baptist** Foreign Mission Society (CBFMS) in 1983, and more recently the **Association of Baptists for World Evangelism** (ABWE) commenced a mission in 1992.

As of 2006, 30 churches and 6,939 members were affiliated with the Singapore Baptist Convention.

SIX PRINCIPLE CALVINISTIC BAPTISTS. In (U.S.) colonial New England and the Middle Colonies, there were Calvinistic Baptists who followed the basic tenets of the Westminster Confession (1646) but who also practiced the "sixth principle"—the **laying on of hands**. Among the churches who espoused this position were Providence, Rhode Island, (after 1730); Wallingford, Connecticut;

and perhaps North Kingston, Rhode Island. These congregations, recognizing the validity at least on a voluntary basis of the laying on of hands, attended the General Six Principle Baptist Association as fraternal delegates. In the Middle Colonies, Welsh Baptist congregations and some English-speaking churches, like Great Valley in Pennsylvania, were Calvinistic but practiced imposition of hands at membership. *See also* FIVE PRINCIPLE CALVINISTIC BAPTISTS; GENERAL BAPTISTS.

SKOGLUND, JOHN EGNAR (1912–2005). American Baptist missionary, pastor, and educator, born at San Diego, California. He was educated at the University of California at Berkeley (B.A.), Berkeley Baptist Divinity School (M.A., B.D.), and Yale University (Ph.D.), where he received the doctorate in theology and philosophy. From 1947 to 1954, Skoglund served as a missionary to students in the **Philippines**, **China**, and **Hong Kong** with the **American Baptist Foreign Mission Society** (ABFMS). During that time, he was also foreign secretary for the ABFMS. An accomplished theological educator, Skoglund taught **theology** at Central Baptist Seminary in Kansas City (1938–1940) and from 1959 to 1977 was **Cornelius Woelfkin** Professor of Preaching at Colgate Rochester Divinity School; later, he was professor of Christian worship at the American Baptist Seminary of the West (1977–1981), and Chung Chi College (Hong Kong) and Hong Kong Baptist Seminary (1981–1982). **Pastor** at First Baptist Church of Seattle, Washington (1954–1958), Skoglund was a longtime member of the Faith and Order Commission of the World Council of Churches (1954–1973) and the General Board of the National Council of Churches during an era when American Baptists fully embraced the **ecumenical** movement. His *Worship and the Free Churches* (1965) and *Manual of Worship* (1968; rev. 1993) were used widely among Baptist ministers and seminary students in the latter half of the 20th century, and his orientation was suggestive of a larger ecumenical vision for Baptists and a more liturgical style of worship for Free Churches. Skoglund's ecumenicity was also realized in congregational life, where he served churches in the Methodist tradition in Hong Kong and England and also in the Church of South **India**.

SLAVERY, AMONG BAPTISTS. Even with a demonstrated record on **religious liberty** and **human rights** from their origins in the 17th century, Baptists have from time to time countenanced economic systems which involve human servitude; Baptists have also been slaveholders. For instance, in **Jamaica, William Knibb** reported that Baptists owned slaves. In the development of Baptist churches in the colonial southern United States, Baptist plantation owners employed field slaves and Baptist farmers and artisans employed household slaves and semiskilled slaves. The segregation of slaves according to race is evident in Baptist churches, notably in Virginia and South Carolina, where prominent **pastors** of white congregations, like **Jeremiah B. Jeter** and **Richard Fuller**, preached either to slaves in the balconies of their churches or to slave congregations in their cities and towns. Fuller later attempted to justify the slave system on biblical and humanitarian grounds in a famous written exchange with **Francis Wayland** of New England. Other southern slaveholders, like **William H. Brisbane**, manumitted their slaves and became ardent abolitionists. From at least 1755 at the plantation of William Byrd III (1728–1777) in Virginia, a slave community was noticed in the greater Baptist tradition; the Baptist faith was attractive to freed slaves for its organizational simplicity and emphasis upon Christian experience. Former slaves achieved many results in the Baptist **ministry** or **missionary** service, notably **David George, Lott Carey, Richard H. Boyd**, and **William J. Simmons**. The slave experience in many emancipated black leaders' experiences provided a rationale for the development of separate **black Baptist** organizations and churches, in part to exercise authority and leadership within the black community. *See also* ANTISLAVERY, AMONG BAPTISTS; RACE, BAPTISTS AND.

SLAVIC MISSIONARY SERVICES. Founded in 1933 in the Baptist tradition, Slavic Missionary Service engages in **Bible** and literature distribution, broadcasting, and support of national workers, particularly in the Commonwealth of Independent States and **Ukraine**. Its headquarters are located in South River, New Jersey.

SLOVAK REPUBLIC. The first practitioners of believer's **baptism** were doubtless connected with the **Anabaptists—Balthasar Hubmaier** sought refuge in Slovakia in the 16th century. The modern Baptist movement is connected with Baptist missions in the

Austro-Hungarian Empire and particularly with Bohemia, later the **Czech Republic**. The pioneer was August Meereis (b. 1847), a **colporteur** of the British Bible Society working in eastern Bohemia. An early baptism took place in 1877 at Brandys, a place associated with Comenius. Meereis founded at Kezmarok-Vavrisovo a Slovak-German Baptist congregation in 1888. A second church was formed at Chvojnice in western Slovakia. From 1898 to 1901, the Slovak Baptist congregations were related to the Austro-Hungarian Baptist Union, with the Slovak churches gravitating to Vienna or Budapest for support.

Work following World War I was characterized by missions from the Northern Baptist Convention and the **Baptist Missionary Society**; in 1919, the churches in Slovakia entered a relationship with the Czechs called the Czechoslovak Baptist Union, which lasted until 1992 when the Slovak Republic emerged as an independent nation. In addition to the indigenous work, **Baptist Mid-Missions** from the United States established a mission in Kosice in 1946 and later one at Stitnik. In 1995, the **Association of Baptists for World Evangelism** commenced a mission in Slovakia.

As of 2006, there were 20 churches and 1,970 members related to the Bratska Jednota Baptistov Rada V SR. Offices of the Union are located in Bratislava.

SLOVENIA. Prior to 1993, Baptist churches in Slovenia were part of the Savez Evandeoskih Hriscana-Baptista SR Jugoslavija (Baptist Union of Yugoslavia). That year, with political independence, the Zveza Baptisticnih Cerkava v Republiki Sloveniji (Slovenian Baptist Union) was formed. In 1991, the **Conservative Baptist** Foreign Mission Society opened a mission to Slovenia, focusing on refugee work and church planting in Ljubljana.

As of 2006, there are seven churches with 160 members affiliated with the Zveza Baptisticnih Cerkava v Republiki Sloveniji.

SMITH, ELIAS (1769–1846). American Baptist minister and editor, born at Lyme, Connecticut. He was raised in a **New Light** home and underwent a protracted conversion experience of his own. From 1787 to 1802, he itinerated as an **evangelist**, sometimes critical of the growing formalism among the Baptists. He was **pastor** at Woburn,

Massachusetts, and later began to gather **independent** congregations among New England's working classes. The Baptists disfellow-shipped Smith in 1804, and he bitterly attacked the Baptists as un-scriptural and overly confessional. He referred to his church as a "Christian Church" and served at Portsmouth, New Hampshire (1802–1808). Beginning in 1808, Smith published a religious news-paper, the *Herald of Gospel Liberty*, said to be one of the oldest in the United States. After 1815, when he adopted **Universalist** views, he won much acclaim among Unitarians and Universalists for his advo-cacy of **religious liberty**. His autobiography, *The Life, Conversion, Preaching, Travels and Sufferings of Elias Smith* (1816), was a vivid critical description of New England Baptists at the turn of the 19th century.

SMITH, GERALD BIRNEY (1868–1929). American Baptist minis-ter, educator, and theologian, born at Middlefield, Massachusetts. Smith was educated at Brown University and Union Theological Seminary, and as an exceptional student, he studied at the universi-ties of Berlin, Marburg, and Paris. In 1900, he began a lifelong teach-ing career at the University of Chicago, where he taught theology and ethics. Smith was greatly influenced by the work of German theolo-gians Albert Ritschl (1822–1889) and Johann W. Hermann (1846–1922). He emphasized religious experience over biblical con-tent as the basis for **theology**. One of the foremost members of the Chicago School with **Ernest D. Burton** and **Shailer Mathews**, Smith attempted to blend the results of scientific investigation with critical theology. In his need to move away from authoritarian reli-gion, he came to advocate an empirical approach, and he refused to write a systematic theology, in view of changing contexts. His schol-arship won international renown with such titles as *Practical Theol-ogy* (1903), *Social Idealism and the Changing Theology* (1913), and *The Principles of Christian Living: A Handbook of Christian Ethics* (1924). Smith was the editor of the *American Journal of Theology* (1909–1920) and the *Journal of Religion* (1921–1929).

SMITH, HEZEKIAH (1737–1805). American Baptist minister and chaplain, born at Hempstead, New York. Smith graduated from Hopewell Academy and the College of New Jersey, one of the first to be given a Baptist education in the colonies. In 1762, he began an itinerant ministry, keeping an extensive journal throughout the Revolutionary era. He settled in Haverhill, Massachusetts, where he gathered a church in 1764. During the Revolution, he identified with the Patriot cause and held the Revolution to be an act for the salvation of America. In 1777, the Continental Congress appointed him a chaplain to the Army of the United States, and he served with distinction in several campaigns. In later years as **pastor** at Haverhill, he was an advocate and founder of the Massachusetts Baptist Missionary Society. Smith published a tract on believer's **baptism** (1766), which became an important resource in the New England Baptist community.

SMYTH, JOHN (fl. 1586–1612). Separatist and, later, English Baptist minister, born possibly at Sturton. He graduated from Christ's College, Cambridge, about 1590, having studied under the Puritan scholar **Francis Johnson** (1562–1618). Smyth was a fellow in Christ's College in 1594, after which he was ordained by the Bishop of Lincoln. In 1598, he was married, left Cambridge, and took a city lectureship in Lincoln, a popular outlet for ministers of Puritan sympathies. His sermons offended the wrong people, and he practiced medicine for a time. About 1606, Smyth left the Church of England and became a Separatist in Gainsborough, where he served a congregation as **pastor**. At length the authorities bore down upon the congregation, and Smyth and a prominent lay leader, **Thomas Helwys**, fled with much of the membership to Amsterdam. In Amsterdam, Smyth wrote on the nature of the church and **ministry** and ultimately led his part of the emigrant flock to closer cooperation with the Mennonite congregation at the Singelkerk.

In 1609, Smyth and his congregation concluded that infant **baptism** was erroneous, and Smyth baptized himself in order to begin a new gospel order of believers; this earned him the derisive title "sebaptist," meaning "self-baptizer." He then baptized Helwys and others, likely by pouring, in the Mennonite tradition. Feeling ostracized by the Christian community for his audacious act, Smyth opened negotiations with the Waterlander Mennonites and moved toward full inclusion in their fellowship. This in turn offended Helwys, and a rift occurred between the two friends and within the congregation. Smyth apparently had adopted a more **Arminian** stance and took a radical stand on the matter of **religious liberty**. He wrote four important books and a significant **confession of faith,** which defined the earliest Baptists. He remains the parent of modern Baptists and the first Englishman to pen a case for full religious liberty. Smyth died in Amsterdam and was buried at the Nieuwkerk.

SOCIAL GOSPEL MOVEMENT. In the decades following the American Civil War (1861–1865), numerous writers addressed the social concerns raised by urbanization and industrialization. Among the leading voices was **Walter Rauschenbusch**, a Baptist of New York City and later Rochester, New York, who wrote passionately in advocating a Christian response to these problems. He defined social Christianity in terms of the earthly Kingdom of God, which should be the righteous rule of God in all human affairs. His theological treatises formed some of the most significant literature of the growing movement, which included social theorists, seminary professors, **pastors,** and denominational leaders. A new and broader doctrine of the church helped to redefine the mission of God's people: to witness in public affairs, advocate changes in the social and economic order according to the principles of Jesus, and seek justice on an international plane. Of particular interest to those in the social gospel movement were abusive labor practices involving women and children, the right of collective bargaining, improved urban housing, better treatment of immigrants, and an end to military action as a means of settling disputes. Among Baptists in the United States, the Northern Baptist Convention pioneered the establishment of a Social Service Commission in 1910, headed by Samuel Zane Batten (1859–1925). **Thomas Clement Douglas** in western **Canada**, a distant disciple of the Rauschenbusch movement, applied the principles of the social gospel to Canadian welfare politics.

While the social gospel movement ushered in many useful innovations in understanding the task of the church, it also created much division. Frequently misunderstood as "socialism," it drew the wrath of ardent capitalists and individualists. **Fundamentalists** derided the social gospel as a modernist substitute for personal **evangelism**, and the two were often seen as mutually exclusive. The major proponents of the social gospel prior to World War I tended to be associated with various new theological systems, including idealism, pragmatism, and modernism; the influence of German theologians, notably Albert Ritschl (1822–1889), was paramount. The Baptist educational centers of the movement were Rochester Theological Seminary, Crozer Theological Seminary, and the University of Chicago Divinity School.

"SOFT POLICY" BAPTISTS. *See* BAPTIST WORLD MISSION.

SOLITARY BRETHREN. A colony of Baptistic Christians founded in 1721 by **Johann Conrad Beissel** at Mill Creek, Pennsylvania. Later, the colony was reconstituted at Ephrata near Lancaster, Pennsylvania. Beissel organized his followers around a celibate male order, the Brotherhood, and a virginal woman's order called the Sisterhood. Men and women were housed in separate monastic halls and practiced strict **discipline** and a type of mystical prayer life. Women were veiled in drab cloaks so as to obscure images of their humiliating sexuality, and both sexes engaged in various crafts—including book making, learned from the eminent Christopher Sower (1693–1758)—and illumination of manuscripts. The worship chapel was the largest in the colony in the early 18th century. Nightly, the members of the order would process about the Ephrata grounds singing hymns led by Beissel. He required strict written confessions of spiritual accountability of all members. Sabbatarian and practicing believer's **baptism**, the group was also known as the German Seventh Day Baptist Brethren and derisively as "Beisselianer." The colony eventually declined with the death of Beissel in 1768. *See also* GERMAN BAPTIST BRETHREN.

SONSHIP CONTROVERSY. Within the **Strict Baptist** movement in Great Britain, beginning in the 1860s, a rancorous debate opened over the nature of Jesus **Christ** as the Son of God. In 1861, **Joseph Philpot,** in his newspaper the *Gospel Herald*, called attention to what he felt was a pernicious error concerning the true sonship of Jesus. Philpot took the position that Jesus was eternally the Son of God, and only as the Son of God could he rightly be a mediator between God and man. Others, following Charles W. Banks (1806–1886), held that rather than an eternal characteristic, the sonship of Jesus lies in his complexity and is the result of the incarnation, not as part of his absolutely divine nature. The limited view of the sonship of Christ was first articulated at Zoar Chapel, Great Alie Street, in East London about 1859–1860. An editorial war ensued between the *Gospel Standard* Baptists and those who followed Banks in the *Earthen Vessel*, later called the *Gospel Herald* Baptists. *See also* STRICT BAPTISTS.

SOUTH AFRICA. William Miller (1779–1856), a Baptist emigrant from England, founded a congregation at Grahamstown in 1822–1823, and this became the initial Baptist work in South Africa. Another pioneer was Moses H. Bixby (1827–1901), a missionary of the **American Baptist Missionary Union** who stopped in Capetown en route to **Burma** and gathered the first Baptist congregation in that city.

In the late 1850s, German settlers emigrated to South Africa, and a number of German Baptists, influenced by **J. G. Oncken**, were among them. Small scattered congregations were founded, 1858–1861, and with the arrival in 1867 of Carl H. Gutsche (1845–1926), a protégé of Oncken, greater unity was achieved and an **association** of the German churches was formed in 1870. The Afrikaanse Baptiste Kerk began in 1886 in the Orange Free State at Sugarloaf (later Cornelia), comprised of Dutch-speaking Baptists.

In 1877, the Baptist Union of South Africa was formed, uniting many of the different cultural communities. In 1878, the **American Baptist Foreign Mission Society** began a mission in Natal. The South African Baptist Missionary Society (1892) assumed evangelization and church development among black communities. This work included Transkei, Natal, Transvaal, and the Orange Free State, among others. In 1927, the first black church was founded, the Bantu Baptist Church, which became part of the Baptist Convention of South Africa (1966). Several of these congregations have subsequently left the convention and joined the Baptist Union of Southern Africa.

In a collaborative arrangement, **Southern Baptists** entered the homeland areas in 1977. That same year, American Baptists signed a collaborative agreement with the **Baptist Missionary Society** to conduct work in the country. The **Association of Baptists for World Evangelism** created a mission in South Africa in 1980, and the same year the **Baptist Bible Fellowship** opened a mission in South Africa. In 1906, a **Seventh Day Baptist** church was established in South Africa.

As of 2006, there were 495 churches and 49,554 members in the Baptist Union of South(ern) Africa; 150 churches with 22,000 members affiliated with the Baptist Convention of South Africa; 13 churches and 2,300 members affiliated with the Baptist Mission of South Africa; and 26 churches with 3,500 mermbers affiliated with the Baptist Association of South Africa. As the result of the demise of apartheid, in 1996 the Baptist Union of Transkei, which had been formed in 1980, was dissolved. In 1951, the Baptist Theological College of Southern Africa opened, and there are presently schools located at Debenek, Johannesburg, Kempton Park, Menlo Park, and Randburg. The *South African Baptist* has been published since 1894 (later known as *Baptists Today*).

SOUTHERN BAPTIST CONVENTION (SBC). The largest organization of Baptists in the world (U.S. based), formed at Augusta, Georgia, on May 8, 1845. Symbolically, its "mother congregation" is First Baptist, Charleston, South Carolina, the oldest in the American South, formed in 1682 in Kittery, Maine. Ostensibly, the reason for the separation of the SBC from the **General Missionary** (Triennial) **Convention** was the **slavery** issue, whereby the northern-dominated mission societies declined to support slaveholding interests. In fact, a different **polity** and more unified theological tradition characterized the southern churches long before the schism.

In the original articles of incorporation, a unified body called the "convention" superintended two boards, one for foreign missions, the second for domestic missions. In 1847, a Southern Baptist Publication Society was formed and endorsed by the SBC without being integral to it. Also related to the SBC was a Bible Board, established in 1851, and an Indian Mission Board, which was later combined with the Domestic Mission Board in 1855. An initial attempt at a **Sunday School Board** in 1863 was aborted, and the assets were turned over to the Domestic Board after a decade. The outbreak of the Civil War decimated the work of the SBC and its agencies, and following the war, competition resumed with the northern Baptist societies.

During Reconstruction, numerous leaders held out the possibility that reunion with northern Baptists might take place. At the same time, however, signs revealed separation was permanent. In 1888, the Woman's Missionary Union, auxiliary to the SBC, was formed. In 1898, a comity conference was held at **Fortress Monroe**, Virginia, where the northern Baptist societies agreed to separate territorial spheres of mission work. A third major event was the recreation in 1891 of the Sunday School Board, signaling final separation with the **American Baptist Publication Society**. The Southern Baptist Theological Seminary, reborn after the war, also did much to establish Southern Baptist leadership for the SBC.

In the first decades of the 20th century, Southern Baptist identity was greatly strengthened. New state conventions were formed across the southwestern states, new schools were formed in Texas and Louisiana, and a Laymen's Missionary Movement was begun in 1907. Denominational solidarity was further strengthened when the Relief and Annuity Board was made a part of the national convention in 1918 and well in excess of $75 million were raised to commemorate the 75th anniversary of the SBC in 1920. That same year, the membership of the SBC surpassed 3 million with over 27,000 churches.

In 1925, a confessional statement, the "**Baptist Faith and Message**" (based on the New Hampshire Baptist **Confession of Faith** of 1833), was adopted by the SBC, thus defining the theological stance as "progressive conservatism." The theological consensus achieved by **E. Y. Mullins** and others allowed for an unprecedented stewardship effort each year, known after 1925 as the Cooperative Program because of its linkages of national boards, **associations**, state **conventions**, and local congregations.

Following World War II, Southern Baptists surged ahead in virtually every area of work. The **Foreign Mission Board** expanded into every continent of the world, establishing national conventions, seminaries, and ties with the SBC. In North America, the migration of southern Americans called for new southern-style churches outside the traditional South. Home missions were conducted in California, the Pacific Northwest, the Great Plains, the upper Middle Atlantic States, and New England. By the 1970s, Southern Baptists entertained goals of an SBC congregation in every county in the United

States. To provide leadership for the new congregations, two seminaries were expanded to six and a seminary extension department was established for the northern "territories." The new seminaries included Southeastern Baptist Theological Seminary in North Carolina, an outgrowth of Wake Forest College; New Orleans Baptist Theological Seminary, an upgrading of the Baptist Bible Institute; Midwestern Baptist Theological Seminary in Kansas City, Missouri, to offset the schism at American and Southern Baptist-related Central Baptist Seminary in Kansas; and Golden Gate Baptist Theological Seminary in Mill Valley, California, to establish a beachhead in the far West.

The last decades of the 20th century witnessed growth, as in the "Bold Mission Thrust" campaign, whereby a combined effort by all Southern Baptists sought to present the gospel to every person in the period A.D. 1978 to A.D. 2000. However, severe tensions and schism erupted in the SBC over the ordination of **women**, tolerance for homosexuality, and perceived theological **liberalism**, offset on the **conservative** side by authoritarian pastoral and executive leadership. Resurgent **fundamentalism** has divided seminaries and universities from state conventions. A battle for the presidential control of the national convention has led to a series of symbolically conservative elected officers, notably Charles Stanley (1932–) of Atlanta, Georgia, and **Adrian Rogers** of Memphis, Tennessee, and a radical reorganization of the boards and agencies of the SBC. Coalescing around Southern Baptist Seminary, from 1982, is a group of Calvinistic fundamentalists called **Founders Ministries**.

In the 1980s, two major **voluntarist** organizations have emerged to challenge the direction of the SBC, the Southern Baptist Alliance (1986), later the **Alliance of Baptists**, and the **Cooperative Baptist Fellowship** (1991). New educational ventures have also emerged in the moderate and progressive wings, notably new theological schools at Birmingham, Alabama; Richmond, Virginia; Macon, Georgia; Winston Salem, North Carolina; and Waco, Texas. Richmond, Averett, Wake Forest, Baylor, Stetson, Furman, Belmont, and Mercer universities, plus Meredith, William Jewell, and Georgetown colleges, have also changed their charters to distance themselves from the fundamentalist directions of the national convention.

As of 2006, the SBC comprised 41 state conventions; 1,200 associations; 42,000 churches; and over 16 million members. Currently, there are 50 colleges or universities affiliated with the SBC or its state organizations, six theological seminaries sponsored by the SBC, and five independent theological schools that are Southern Baptist in perspective and support. Through its mission boards, the SBC supports 5,000 field workers and 34,000 volunteers in 153 nations and 2,000 people groups internationally, and 5,000 home missionaries in the United States and its territories. *See also* FOREIGN MISSION BOARD; FOUNDERS MINISTRIES; SUNDAY SCHOOL BOARD, SOUTHERN BAPTIST CONVENTION.

SOUTHWIDE BAPTIST FELLOWSHIP (SBF). A loosely connected coalition of **fundamentalist** Baptist churches in the American southeastern states. The SBF was organized in 1956 at Highland Park Baptist Church in Chattanooga, Tennessee. It began with 147 charter members and accepts those who subscribe to its fundamentalist, premillennial doctrinal statement and pay two dollars per year. Among those active in the early years were **John R. Rice** and Lee Roberson (1909–2007), **pastor** of a 33,000-member church in Chattanooga. The SBF relates to Tennessee Temple Schools and Bob Jones University for religious education and **theological education**; the publication most closely associated with the churches is the *Sword of the Lord*, which Rice began in 1934. The SBF has a particular interest in contending with neo-evangelicalism, which many feel is infiltrating the ranks of historic fundamentalism. The principal outreach of the SBF is through occasional pastor's conferences and a website.

SPAIN. Baptist work in Spain is traced to the evangelistic ministry of **William Knapp**, first an independent Baptist, then a missionary of the **American Baptist Missionary Union**. Knapp baptized numerous candidates and organized a church at Madrid in 1870. Later, he began a church at Alicante, baptizing candidates in the Mediterranean Sea. Knapp was forced to leave the country in 1876. Later, in 1880, a Swedish Baptist missionary, **Eric Lund**, began a literature and translation **mission** in Barcelona, which he led until 1900; this was followed by the **Baptist General Conference of America** (Swedish-American), which sponsored a Spanish mission from 1914 to 1922, when it was transferred to the U.S. Southern Baptists. An independent Baptist work was carried on in Spain 1913–1921 by Gustavo Vickman from the United States. Subsequently, **Northern** and **Southern Baptists** in the United States agreed in 1920 (the **London Conference**) that the Spanish mission field should be administered by the **Southern Baptist Convention**. Spanish Baptists publish *El Eco de la Verdad* (*The Voice of the Truth*) (1892–). In addition to the indigenous work, the **Association of Baptists for World Evangelism** began a mission in 1968, the **Baptist Bible Fellowship** opened a mission in Spain in 1970, **Baptist Mid-Missions** from the United States established its work at Madrid in 1980, and the **Conservative Baptist** Foreign Mission Society opened a mission to Spain in 1984.

As of 2006, there were 88 congregations and 9,550 members in the Unión Evangelica Bautista Española. Presently, there is a theological school located in Alcobenas.

SPANISH WORLD GOSPEL MISSION. Mission founded in 1959 by F. D. Toirac, a Cuban who served as a missionary to **Haiti**. The mission is Baptistic in doctrine, in an independent Baptist tradition. It supports **mission** work in eight countries with about 20 missionaries. The headquarters are located in Winona Lake, Indiana, and it publishes *El Camino* (*The Highway*).

SPILSBURY, JOHN (1593–1668). English Baptist minister, originally a cobbler at Aldersgate in London. Spilsbury was the first of many in the **Particular**, or Calvinistic, Baptist tradition who influenced many churches with his view that **Christ** died for his elect only. He was pastor of the first Calvinistic congregation, located in London, where he remained from 1638 to 1656. Henry Cromwell (1628–1674) regarded Spilsbury highly and tried to induce him to go to **Ireland** to quiet the Baptists there. Instead, Spilsbury left the London church to serve at Wapping. He is remembered as the pioneer Particular Baptist, likely one of the principal authors of the first London **Confession of Faith** (1644). His publications include some of the earliest defenses of **baptism**: *A Treatise Concerning the Lawfull Subject of Baptisme: The Baptizing of Infants Confuted* (1643) and *Heart Bleedings for Professors Abominations* (1650).

SPONTANEOUS BAPTISM. *See* BAPTISM.

SPURGEON, CHARLES HADDON (1834–1892). English Baptist minister, born at Kelvedon, Essex. Spurgeon lacked formal postsecondary education but was well read in the Puritan classics. He was converted at age 16 in a Methodist meeting and joined a Congregationalist church in Newmarket. Following his transfer to Baptist principles, at 20 he was called to serve John Rippon's church at Carter Lane. Following a move to New Park Street, Spurgeon developed a city-wide reputation as a great preacher and crowds thronged to hear him. Eventually, the congregation erected the Metropolitan Tabernacle (at a cost of £30,000) where he was **pastor** until his death. At one service in the Crystal Palace, Spurgeon preached to over 23,000 people. He led his church to establish Pastor's College (1856) and other **voluntary** enterprises, including Stockwell Orphanage (1866). A strict Calvinist, Spurgeon was critical of modernistic tendencies in the **Baptist Union of Great Britain and Ireland** (BU). In the 1880s, he wrote in his paper, the *Sword and Trowel*, of the BU's decline at "breakneck speed," which became known as the **Downgrade Controversy**. This brought him into immediate and public controversy, particularly with **John Clifford**, a **General Baptist** who led the BU.

Spurgeon's sermons were widely published as were hundreds of editions of devotional works. With **John Bunyan**, Spurgeon was one of the most widely published British Baptists of all time. Having attained an international reputation, Spurgeon ended his career alienated from the mainstream family of British Baptists. *See also* CONTINENTAL BAPTISTS; SPURGEONIC BAPTISTS.

SPURGEONIC BAPTISTS. A tradition of congregations and pastors in the Baptist family of Great Britain who associate themselves with **Charles Haddon Spurgeon** and his ministries. Beginning in the 1860s and reaching an apex in the **Downgrade Controversy** of the 1880s, a significant number of **Baptist Union of Great Britain and Ireland** congregations and some **Strict Baptists** identified with the Calvinistic and Puritan emphases of Spurgeon's theology. Many were subscribers to his paper, the *Sword and Trowel*, while others attended his ministerial meetings or supported one or more of his benevolent causes. Those men who attended or graduated from his Pastor's College, even after his death, were identifiably in the "Spurgeonic tradition."

SRI LANKA. Baptist mission entered Ceylon as an extension of the **Baptist Missionary Society** mission in Bengal under **William Carey**. **James Chater** went to Colombo in 1812 and experienced meager conversion results. At the ancient capital of Kandy, there developed a strong center of Baptist work. A Baptist Union in Ceylon was founded in 1895. Other Baptist groups entered the field in the 20th century: in 1989, the **Baptist Bible Fellowship** opened a mission in Sri Lanka.

As of 2006, there were 22 churches and 4,011 members associated with the Sri Lanka Baptist Sangamaya. Presently, there are two Baptist-related schools in Sri Lanka: Colombo and Pilimatalawa.

STAGG, FRANK (1911–2001). Southern Baptist theologian and educator, born at Eunice, Louisiana. He was educated at Louisiana College (B.A.) and Southern Baptist Theological Seminary (B.D., Th.M. Ph.D.). He also did further study in New Testament at Union Theological Seminary in New York, the University of Edinburgh, and University of Basel in Switzerland. Stagg was professor of New Testament at New Orleans Baptist Theological Seminary (1945–1964) and at Southern Baptist Seminary (1964–1982). At Southern, he held the James Buchanan Harrison Chair and was senior professor 1977–1982. Stagg was considered by Southern Baptist moderates to be one of their most distinguished thinkers, given his advocacy of civil rights, gender equality, **ecumenism**, and antiwar stances in the Vietnam and Gulf War eras. Among his many publications are *New Testament Theology* (1976) and *The Doctrine of Christ* (1984).

STAUGHTON, WILLIAM (1770–1829). English and American Baptist minister, born in Coventry. Baptized by **Samuel Pearce**, he was educated at Bristol Baptist College and was considered to succeed **John Ryland** at Northampton. An able preacher, Staughton was present at the organizing meeting of the **Baptist Missionary Society** at Kettering and held great promise as a leader in the denomination. His interest in emigration to America was strong, and he left England for Georgetown, South Carolina, in 1793. Staughton served the church there until 1795, when he moved to the Baptist church in Bordentown, New Jersey, and then to Jacobstown and Burlington, New Jersey, where he remained until 1805. That year he became **pastor** at First Baptist, Philadelphia, which he served until 1811, when he formed a new congregation, the Sansom Street Baptist Church in Philadelphia. While at Sansom Street, he built a new building, which was advanced architecturally for the era; he resigned in 1823 to become president of Columbian College (later George Washington University) in Washington, D.C.

Staughton had a lifelong interest in **higher education**: while in Bordentown, he also served as principal of a seminary, and in 1811 in Philadelphia, he opened a theological school at his home, which became the first such school of the Baptists in the United States. For six years he was the president of the Baptist attempt at a national university in Washington, D.C., and after a brief stay in Philadelphia, Staughton accepted the presidency of Georgetown College in Kentucky, the oldest Baptist institution west of the Appalachian mountains. While en route to take up his responsibilities, Staughton died. He was the first secretary of the **Baptist Board of Foreign Missions** and, with **Luther Rice**, gave shape to the national organization of Baptists. In 1798, at an early age, Princeton College awarded him an honorary doctor of divinity degree. Staughton's published works include a number of sermons, *The Baptist Mission in India* (1811), *A Compendius System of Greek Grammar* (1813), and an edition of *The Works of Virgil* (1825). *See also* THEOLOGICAL EDUCATION.

STEADMAN, WILLIAM (1764–1837). English Baptist minister and denominational leader, born in Yorkshire. A graduate of Bristol Baptist College, he took the pastorate at Broughton, then moved to Bradford in 1805. There he became the president of the Baptist Academy and a founder of the Northern Education Society. For over 30 years, Steadman managed the affairs of the academy, was **pastor** of a vital congregation, and busied himself in developing the Baptist denomination in the North. In 1809, he established the Baptist Itinerant Society to aid in establishing churches required by the growth of the Industrial Revolution; the academy specialized in a training pattern that emphasized the students' engagement in church planting and evangelism—"**evangelism** steadied by education." Steadman also helped to rally the churches of the north of England to the support of the **Baptist Missionary Society** and the **Baptist Union**, in whose interests he traveled widely. Steadman's published works include a dozen sermons on devotional and educational topics.

STEANE, EDWARD (1798–1882). English Baptist minister, born at Oxford, England. He studied at Bristol Baptist College and later at the University of Edinburgh, graduating in 1821. Steane became **pastor** at Camberwell in 1823 and served until 1853, when he became co-pastor with John Burnet. Although frequently ill, he served the Baptist denomination in a number of significant posts, including co-secretary of the **Baptist Union** with **John H. Hinton**, a member of the General Committee of the **Baptist Missionary Society**, editor of the *New Selection Hymnbook*, and one of the founders of the Bible Translation Society, formed in opposition to the British and Foreign Bible Society. Steane was a keen promoter of the formation of the Evangelical Alliance and was editor of its journal. In 1862, although removed from pastoral work, he retained the title in his congregation. Among his published works are *Christ, the First Fruits of the Resurrection* (1833), *The Religious Condition of Christendom* (1851), and *The Doctrine of Christ, Developed by the Apostles* (1872).

STEARNS, SHUBAEL (1706–1771). American Baptist minister, born at Boston, Massachusetts. The early life of Stearns is without detail, except that he was caught up in the **New Light** Congregationalist movement at the time when many were converting to Baptist principles. Baptized by Wait Palmer (fl. 1740–1780), the **pastor** of First Baptist Church, North Stonington, Connecticut, Stearns and his brother-in-law, **Daniel Marshall**, went south in 1754 and conducted itinerant **evangelism**. The result was the gathering of several churches in central North Carolina, which later became the Sandy Creek Association. Stearns considered himself a **Separate Baptist**, emphasizing believer's **baptism**, experiential conversion, and strict adherence to biblical lifestyle. **Morgan Edwards** reported in his travels that Stearns had collected a following of almost 600 people in Carolina colony.

STENNETT FAMILY. A family of Baptist ministers in England who enjoyed great distinction over four generations. Edward Stennett (d.

1705) was a clergyman during the Puritan Revolution who suffered great persecution, preaching at Abingdon, Wallingford, and Pinner's Hall, London. His persecution stemmed from participating in the Civil War on the side of Parliament and his violation of the **Clarendon Code** during the Restoration. Early in his life, he developed Sabbatarian tendencies and was instrumental in 1670 in establishing the first **Seventh Day Baptist** Church in the American colonies.

Joseph, Edward's brother (1663–1713), born at Abingdon, was a Seventh Day Baptist who preached at the Pinner's Hall Church on Saturdays and elsewhere among the **Particular Baptists** on Sundays. A poet and Hebrew scholar, he frequently defended Baptist beliefs and was well received by the Royal Family. He published five volumes of essays and sermons, as well as influencing positively the singing of contemporary hymns in the **Nonconformist** community.

Joseph's son, Joseph (1692–1758), was **pastor** of the Seventh Day Baptist Church at Mill Yard, Goodman's Fields, in London from 1720 to the 1750s. He also served first-day congregations in Exeter and was pastor of the church at Little Wild Street in London, a Seventh Day minister in a **Particular Baptist** congregation. On behalf of the **Three Dissenting Denominations**, he presented an address to King George II that pleased the king greatly on his return to England in 1745. Joseph authored eight works and was given the doctor of divinity degree by the University of Edinburgh.

Joseph's son, Samuel (1727–1795), was born in Exeter. He was a language scholar and person of high social standing. Following his father, Samuel served the Little Wild Street Church for 47 years. The University of Aberdeen conferred upon him the doctor of divinity degree in 1763. Like his forbears, he enjoyed a wide political influence in addressing the concerns of **dissenters**. Samuel was also the author of scores of devotional and doctrinal works and numerous hymns, including "Majestic Sweetness Sits Enthroned" and "On Jordan's Stormy Banks," both favorites of generations of Baptists.

ST. HELENA AND ASCENSION ISLAND. Baptist life on St. Helena dates from the early 19th century when **Adoniram Judson** landed there in 1850 for a brief time. Baptist church development began in the 1880s as part of the care of Baptists in **South Africa**, largely influenced by the **Baptist Missionary Society**. As of 2001, there was a small Baptist community of one church with about 75 members on St. Helena.

STILLMAN, SAMUEL (1737–1807). American Baptist minister, born at Philadelphia, Pennsylvania. At an early age, Stillman moved to Charleston, South Carolina, and was tutored privately. Converted under the ministry of **Oliver Hart**, he also received his **theological education** under Hart as a personal mentor. In 1759, he was ordained an **evangelist** and assumed the pastorate at James Island, South Carolina. While on a tour of the Northeast, he received the A.M. degree from the College of Philadelphia and the next year an honorary degree from Harvard College. In 1761, he moved to the Baptist church at Bordentown, New Jersey, and in 1763, he became James Bound's (fl. 1760) assistant at Second Baptist, Boston, Massachusetts. In 1765, Stillman succeeded Jeremiah Condy (fl. 1750–65) at First Baptist, Boston, where he remained until his death. For 42 years, Stillman was the leading Baptist minister in New England, if not the United States. He was a prime mover in the organization of the Massachusetts Baptist Missionary Society, the foremost preacher at **ordinations** and for election sermons in the region, and well respected among other denominations. Stillman's published works include over 30 sermons.

STINSON, BENONI (1798–1869). American Baptist minister, born at Montgomery County, Kentucky. In 1816, he experienced a call to **ministry** and served churches in the Wabash Association. He found the doctrinal standards of the Association rigidly Calvinistic, and he formed a new congregation on the general atonement principle. At one point, Stinson considered joining the **Freewill Baptists,** but he disliked their connectionalism. By 1824, a following, called "Stinsonites," formed a new **association**, the Liberty Association of **General Baptists**, a forerunner of the **General Association of General Baptists**. Stinson himself served the Liberty Baptist Church of Howell, Indiana, for 46 years (1823–1869).

STINTON, BENJAMIN (1677–1719). English Baptist minister and historian, born in London. He was educated in a grammar school and learned several languages, becoming a schoolteacher. In his early years, Stinton did translation work and wrote hymns. In 1704, he was persuaded to become the **pastor** at Horsley-down Baptist Church, which he served to his death. Stinton became a significant Baptist leader beyond the local church, serving as a delegate to the **Particular Baptist** Assembly in 1692, and organizing in 1713 a Baptist ministerium at the Hanover **Coffeehouse**, which became the denomination's link with the **Three Dissenting Denominations**. Stinton reached across theological lines to include **General Baptists**, and he was respected among Congregational and Presbyterian **Nonconformists**. In 1717, he participated in a public debate with illustrious dissenters on a point of baptismal theology, and he helped to found the Particular Baptist Fund in the same year. A collector of Baptist historical materials, Stinton was assigned the task of preparing a history of the Baptists, which he diverted to a history of **baptism**. The task and his collected materials eventually devolved upon his son-in-law, **Thomas Crosby**. Stinton's records are the primary sources for the historical beginnings of the Particular Baptists. In 1730, Stinton published *A Short Catechism*, reprinted in several later editions.

STOW, BARON STEUBEN (1801–1869). American Baptist minister and denominational leader, born at Croydon, New Hampshire. He was among the first to register at Columbian College, the new Baptist university in the nation's capital, from which he graduated; the failure of the college, however, was a sore point to Stow, and he blamed **Luther Rice** for its demise. This led ultimately to his service on a committee of investigation of Rice's conduct in 1826. Stow served churches in Portsmouth, New Hampshire, and Boston, Massachusetts, becoming an influential spokesman for New England–style organizations. In the Boston context, he supported **revival** meetings in 1838 and 1842, part of a city-wide awakening; his pastoral ministry included over 1,500 sermons and 25,000 miles of travel. Stowe was one of those asked to prepare a draft of a new organization for the **General Missionary Convention** in 1845 after the **Southern Baptist** delegates departed. His plan won, emphasizing the powers of the executive committee, and he was largely responsible for eliminating the debt of the old convention. Stow was a principal correspondence link with Baptists in Great Britain, each year composing data and opinion for their annual yearbook entries on American Baptists. His publications include *The Efficiency of*

Missions (1838), *The Psalmist: A New Collection of Hymns for Use in Baptist Churches* (1843), and *The Missionary Enterprise* (1846).

STOWE, PHINEAS (1812–1868). American Baptist minister and missionary, born at Milford, Connecticut. He studied at New Hampton Literary and Theological Institute and served the South Danvers, Massachusetts, Baptist Church for two years, 1843–1845. Out of this **ministry** came a concern for seamen, and at the Mariner's Exchange in Boston, he formed a general purpose mission that focused on **evangelism**, personal care, education, and worship. This expanded into a Soldiers Home and ministries to prostitutes. His entire scheme was to become the Boston Baptist Bethel Society (1845), the term "Bethel" applying to the seamen's missions. Stowe's work in Boston became a model for other city missions in mid-19th-century America. He was the author of *Ocean Melodies and Seamen's Companion* (1849).

STRATON, JOHN ROACH (1875–1929). Southern and American Baptist minister and educator, born at Evansville, Indiana. He attended Mercer University and studied for two years at Southern Baptist Theological Seminary. For short terms, he taught oratory at Mercer and Baylor Universities, but then turned to the pastoral **ministry**. He successively served churches at Louisville, Kentucky (1900–1903); Hubbard City, Texas (1903–1905); Chicago, Illinois (1905–1908); Baltimore, Maryland (1908–1913); Norfolk, Virginia (1914–1917); and New York City (1918–1929). Straton employed sensational methods (colorful language and name calling) and was considered one of the strictest **fundamentalists** of his era.

Straton's primary circle of influence was the Fundamentalist League of Greater New York City for Ministers and Laymen, which he founded in 1922. He was active in organizing fundamentalists in the Northern Baptist Convention (NBC), (1920–1926), ultimately withdrawing his church, Calvary Baptist in New York City, from the NBC in 1926. Confrontational in style, Straton began the first regular religious broadcast in New York City (on station WQAO) and held tent meetings about the region. He confronted prostitution districts in East Coast cities, evolutionary teachings in Northern Baptist schools, and wealthy Baptist laymen like **John D. Rockefeller**, who supported what Straton termed "**liberal** causes." In 1928, Straton purchased a hotel in Ocean Grove, New Jersey, to operate a **Bible** conference, but after only a short time it burned down, the result of arson. An opponent of the **social gospel**, the liquor traffic, and Alfred E. Smith (1873–1944), the Democratic candidate for president, Straton favored woman's suffrage as a vehicle to increase the political power of his fundamentalist agenda. His published works include *Ragtime Religion* (1899), *The Menace of Immorality in Church and State: Messages of Judgement* (1920), and *Fighting the Devil in Modern Babylon* (1929). *See also* LIBERAL TRADITION.

STRICT BAPTISTS (SB). A movement among English **Particular Baptists** of the late 18th and early 19th centuries that stressed **conservative**, high-Calvinistic doctrines and practice. In response to the perceived antinomianism and open communionism of the era and Baptist leaders such as **Robert Hall** and **Andrew Fuller**, certain Baptist ministers called for strict adherence to the faith. In the 1820s, fellowship among churches and **pastors** was divided in the Norfolk and Suffolk Associations between supporters of George Wright (1789–1863), a strict Calvinist, and Cornelius Elvin (1797–1873), an open communionist. Another early leader was **William Gadsby**, who was followed by Joseph Tiptaft (1803–1864), Charles W. Banks (1806–1886), and **Joseph C. Philpot** in a strict, Calvinistic Baptist persuasion. Most of these pastors refused to accept "Fullerism" as a subtle concession to general atonement and, worse, perceived rising **Universalism**, and they remained outside the regular associational life and membership in the **Baptist Union of Great Britain and Ireland**. Gadsby began publication of *The Gospel Standard, or Feeble Christian's Support* in 1835, which greatly united the emerging Strict Baptist churches. Those following the position of Gadsby came to be called "Gadsbyites." *See also* FULLER, ANDREW.

Strict Baptists formed their own association in the Suffolk and Norfolk Strict Association (1829), the first such group to be called "Strict." In 1841, the Strict Communion Society was formed in London and evolved into the Baptist Evangelical Society, supporting missionary activity in **Germany** and **Denmark** and an educational institution, the Manchester Baptist College. In 1852, the London

Strict Baptist Association was formed, becoming the Metropolitan Association of Strict Baptist Churches (1871) in the London region.

Schisms over the degree of hyper-Calvinism and Christological issues occurred with one branch following Philpot known as the *Gospel Standard* Strict Baptists; a second branch following John Stevens of London, dubbed the "Preexisterians" because they held that Christ's human soul existed before the Incarnation; and a third branch following Banks and his paper, the *Earthen Vessel* (later united with the *Gospel Herald*), which was open to discussion of doctrinal matters with other Baptists and considered by some open to error. Beginning in 1861, the *Gospel Standard* Strict Baptists engaged in a divisive disagreement with the *Earthen Vessel* Strict Baptists over the **Sonship Controversy**. At length defined as Separatists on doctrinal matters, the *Gospel Standard* Baptists in 1870 asserted a name for themselves, "The Living Family," in contrast with all other churches, which constituted the "Congregation of the Dead." In contrast, the *Earthen Vessel* Strict Baptists characterized themselves as "full, faithful, free grace, old-fashioned New Testament followers of Jesus." In more recent history, the generic term "Strict Baptist" has applied to at least three divisions, with the *Gospel Standard* group maintaining its sole claim to the historic Strict position. Certain segments of the Strict Baptists have had relations with the Old School, or **Primitive**, **Baptists** in the United States, who share a similar doctrinal ethos. In the early years of the Strict Baptist movement, the churches were characterized by plain dress, no instrumental music, and no ministerial titles such as "reverend." Strict Baptists commonly referred to Union Baptists as "amalgamated and aristocratic," meant in a pejorative sense.

In the later 20th century, one branch of the Strict Baptists, which includes many of the churches and four associations, has since 1961 taken the name "Grace Baptists," united by congregational freedom and several cooperative agencies. This contemporary movement supports the Grace Baptist Assembly (the annual gathering), Grace Baptist Mission (formerly the Strict Baptist Mission), four regional **associations**, a women's organization, a **Sunday School** association, a youth fellowship, a publishing house called Grace Publications Trust, and a monthly paper called *Grace*. Among their many objectives, the Grace associations seek to support the historic local churches against closure and dwindling resources. The "Gadsbyites," supporting the *Gospel Standard* publication, constitute a separate group, and a third segment of Strict Baptists for many years rallied around the publication, the *Christian's Pathway*, published 1895–1969 at London. That branch continued energetically to promote the old theological distinctives. The terminology "Strict Baptist" remains in a historical society and a trust and pension fund.

As of 2005, there were about 700 churches and approximately 20,000 members and adherents in the Strict Baptist connection, regionally organized in three associations: Kent, Norfolk, and Suffolk and the Metropolitan Area. *Grace Magazine* (1970–), whose predecessors were the *Gospel Herald* (1833–1970) and the *Free Grace Record* (1920–1970), is published at Surrey and there is a Sovereign Grace Union in Swanwick.

STRONG, AUGUSTUS HOPKINS (1836–1921). American Baptist minister and educator, born at Rochester, New York. He was educated at Yale College and was one of the first graduates of Rochester Theological Seminary. For a time, he followed the career of his father in newspaper writing, later turning to pastoral ministry at both Haverhill, Massachusetts, and First Baptist, Cleveland, Ohio, from 1865 to 1872. At Cleveland, he met **John D. Rockefeller**, who almost persuaded Strong to head up a revised University of Chicago. Instead, Strong became the president of Rochester Theological Seminary and taught systematic theology there for 40 years. He became the leading American Baptist **theologian** of his era, and his popular *Systematic Theology* (1907) was used by scores of Baptist professors and students as a statement of orthodox Baptist beliefs. Strong led Rochester Seminary into becoming a premier theological school of the Northern Baptists, attracting a distinguished faculty and a large endowment from donors such as Rockefeller and John Jay Jones (1831–1904). Strong's impressive list of publications includes *Philosophy and Religion* (1888), *The Great Poets and Their Theology* (1898), *Christ in Creation and Ethical Monism* (1899), and *A Tour of the Missions* (1918).

STUNDISM. A religious movement in Imperial **Russia** that led to the development of the Baptist movement in that country and **Ukraine**.

The term (from the German *stunde*, meaning "hour") seems to have appeared first in Odessa about 1867 to denote Christian believers who followed a pietistic lifestyle, including small group **Bible** study, other pietistic practices of the early church, and a sober lifestyle. Its early leaders were Mikhail Ratushnyi (1830–1911) of Osnova and Ivan G. Riobashapka (1832–1902) of Liubomirka. About 1869, Efim Tsymbal (d. 1880) led many Stundists to accept water **baptism**, and in 1872, the movement split into two factions. The Novo-Stundists organized a congregation at Kosiakovko, which became the first Baptist church in Ukraine. The term "Stundism" became synonymous with undesirable sectarianism, and in 1894, Stundism broadly applied was outlawed by the Ministry of Internal Affairs of Russia.

ST. VINCENT. Baptist Mid-Missions from the United States established a mission on the island in 1947 at Arnos Vale. The mission also serves churches on St. Lucia.

SUCCESSIONISM. Term applied to the attempt by some Baptist historians to trace the development of Baptists back through the ages in an unbroken line, or "succession," to roots in the New Testament. In this tradition, each congregation grows out of another and is formed by the authority of another. Among those who espoused this position were **David Benedict** (1813), G. H. Orchard (1838), **James R. Graves** (1855), **John T. Christian** (1896), W. B. Jarrel (1894), and D. B. Ray (1949). Refutation of the successionist theory began with **Henry C. Vedder** (1892), **William H. Whitsett** (1896), **Albert H. Newman** (1899), and most recently, W. Morgan Patterson (1969). While many still hold to the theory, it has for the most part been dismissed by serious historians. Many editions of the book *The Trail of Blood* (1931) by **J. M. Carroll** carry an illustrated historical successionist chart, and this has led to the popular epithet "Trail of Blood" applied to successionism. *See also* LANDMARKISM; LOCAL CHURCH PROTECTIONISM.

SUDAN. Baptist missionary work in Sudan commenced in 1893 as part of the Sudan Interior Mission. In recent years, governmental restrictions and the heavy Islamic population have made missions difficult; however, the civil wars in 1983–2005 were devastating in their impact, ultimately dividing the Christian community. In 1980, **Southern Baptists** began a medical and agricultural **mission** project growing from their work in Ethiopia, but this was withdrawn to Kenya in 1984. Several Baptist missions attempted church establishment, and the result was scattered congregations that became part of the **evangelical** Christian community. In 2008, the two divisions of Baptist life were reunited, comprising 225 congregations and about 40,000 members. About 5 congregations with 458 members are affiliated with Baptist International Missions (U.S.).

SULLIVAN PRINCIPLES. In the 1970s and 1980s, many North American Christians became sensitive to the racial segregation policy of the government of **South Africa**, known as apartheid. Some organizations in the United States, notably the **American Baptist Churches in the U.S.A.**, took steps to influence the government of South Africa, and one strategy was the adoption of the "Sullivan Principles." Named for the Reverend Leon Sullivan (1922–2001), **pastor** of Zion Baptist Church in Philadelphia, Pennsylvania, the six principles involved nonsegregation of races, fair employment practices, pay equity, training programs for black employees, and appointment of more black supervisors and managers in businesses. Underlying the principles were assumptions that economic pressure would eventuate in social changes. The American Baptist Churches General Board in June 1981 agreed to investigate banking and investment procedures and evaluate the ethical and moral bases of all involvements of companies representing the denomination's interests in South Africa, in addition to adopting the Sullivan Principles at the same time.

SUNDAY SCHOOL BOARD, SOUTHERN BAPTIST CONVENTION (BSSB). Several attempts were made to establish a publishing house and Sunday School organization from the beginning of the **Southern Baptist Convention** (SBC) in 1845 through the 1870s. First was the Southern Baptist Publication Society (1847–1863), which was charged with producing literature indigenous to the South. Next came the Bible Board (1851–1863), which circulated **Bibles** across the South but soon came under **Landmarkist** influences. Third was the founding of the Southern Baptist Sunday School Union in 1857, which was decidedly under Landmark control and the result of efforts made by **James R. Graves**. These early organizations floundered due to competition or because of the Civil War. Following the war, several attempts were again made to create a southern publishing organization, notably with the inclusion of publication in the work of the Domestic and Indian Mission Board. Competition from the **American Baptist Publication Society**, however, again outdistanced the efforts of Southern Baptists.

It was in 1885 that **Isaac T. Tichenor** in the Home Mission Board called for a committee to provide **Sunday School** literature for the churches. Three years later the Sunday School Board was established by vote of the SBC. It began a denominational publishing business and aggressive outreach to the churches. Between 1901 and 1919, the BSSB developed a strategy to make the Sunday School a primary facilitator of **evangelism**, and this emphasis marked its genius. In 1917, the Baptist Young People's Union came under the aegis of the BSSB. From 1935 through the 1950s, the sales of the BSSB reached unprecedented levels and financially carried a good deal of the mission program of the convention. In 1916, the BSSB was requested to develop a historical program for Southern Baptists, and this eventually led to the development of the E. C. Dargan Library and to the establishment of the separate Historical Commission in 1951. Growth in Sunday Schools slowed in the 1960s, and the Baptist Training Union program declined dramatically in the same era. To complicate matters further, controversy arose in the publishing house related to the board in the 1970s, Broadman Press, over perceived **liberal** tendencies in producing **Bible** commentaries. Change in leadership and a renewed emphasis upon biblically centered material maintained the status of the BSSB as the largest producer of Baptist-related educational materials in the world. Also related to the BSSB are regional Baptist Book Stores; the Baptist Conference Centers at Ridgecrest, North Carolina, and Glorietta, New Mexico; and the purchase of the Holman Bible Company. The world headquarters of the BSSB are in Nashville, Tennessee. *See also* AMERICAN BAPTIST PUBLICATION SOCIETY; SUNDAY SCHOOLS.

SUNDAY SCHOOLS. The idea of Sunday, or Sabbath, school education emerged from a concern for the poorer and working-class children of England in the late 17th century. Charity schools were operated under the auspices of Christian leaders in the late 17th century. In the 1780s, Robert Raikes (1735–1811) and **William Fox** pioneered a system of schools that held classes on the only free day of the week, Sunday. The purpose of Sunday Schools included inculcation of literacy, manners, and religious instruction.

Baptists were at the forefront of Sunday School development in the United States as well. In Philadelphia, Pennsylvania, the First Day Society was organized in 1791; the first Sunday School in New York was opened in 1803. Baptists became directly interested in the movement in 1826 when the **General Missionary Convention** urged American Baptists to develop Sunday Schools. In 1839, the Hudson River New York Baptist Association recommended the creation of an American Baptist Sunday School Union, based on the model of the New England Sabbath School Union, an **ecumenical** venture. This in turn led to the inclusion of the term "Sunday School" in the new charter of the **American Baptist Publication Society**, and it became the primary advocate of Sunday Schools among Baptists in the United States for the remainder of the 19th century. Southern Baptists, also sensing the importance of Sunday Schools, established in 1857 a Southern Baptist Sunday School Union, to be followed by a Board of Sunday Schools in 1863. What later became the Baptist **Sunday School Board** in 1891 developed into the largest producer in the world of program materials and literature for all ages. The Broadman Press was established by the Sunday School Board in honor of the first secretary, **John A. Broadus**, and the first president, Basil **Manly** Jr. (1825–1892).

Among many Baptists, Sunday School is not only a forum for **evangelism** of children and youth but also a regular setting for Christian nurture and **Bible** study for persons of all ages. Many Baptist groups administer "graded lesson plans" that correspond to school grades and have a regular development of Bible content instruction. Others follow the Uniform lesson series, which follows a Protestant lectionary series of lessons. Typically, the Sunday School meets either just prior to the morning worship service or during the last portion of the service.

SURINAME. In 1888, the initial Baptist presence was established in Suriname by Solomon Bromet, a national of the country trained in

England. The congregation he commenced became an interdenominational work. Much later, **Southern Baptist** mission in Suriname began in 1971 at Paramaribo as an outgrowth of work in Trinidad. Baptist membership involves not only the Dutch community but also East Indian peoples living in Suriname. The United Baptist Church, a Baptist **association**, was formed around the main Baptist community.

As of 2001, there were approximately two churches with about 600 members affiliated with the United Baptist Church of Suriname.

SUTCLIF, JOHN (1752–1814). English Baptist minister, born at Hebden Bridge, England. Sutcliff was educated at Bristol Academy under **Dan Taylor** and **John Fawcett**. Sutcliff served briefly at the Baptist Church in Shrewsbury and Cannon Street Baptist Church in Birmingham in 1774. He entered his long **ministry** at Olney in 1775. It was Sutclif who sent **William Carey** into the ministry and who was a prime mover in the establishment of the **Baptist Missionary Society**; he was present with Carey and **Andrew Fuller** and preached at the 1791 Northamptonshire Association meeting at Clipstone. Sutclif developed the idea of auxiliary societies in distant regions in support of the central society itself. He was a close confidant of Fuller and was remembered for his cautious attitudes. Among those who exerted theological influences on Sutclif was John Newton (1725–1807), who helped him to moderate his Calvinistic perspective. Sutcliff's publications include *First Principles of the Oracles of God* (1789), a widely used catechism for children.

SUTTON, AMOS (1802–1855). English Baptist missionary, born at Sevenoaks, Kent. He entered the New Connexion of **General Baptists** and became, in 1824, a missionary of the General Baptist Missionary Society to **India**. His appointment sent him to Calcutta, but he settled at Cuttack in Orissa State. Due to ill health in 1832, Sutton traveled to the United States, where he came in contact with the **Freewill Baptists** and helped them form the Freewill Baptist Foreign Mission Society in 1832, becoming their first missionary. He returned to be **pastor** of the church at Cuttack in 1836–1847. Returning again to England in 1847–1850, he was pastor of the General Baptist church at Dover Street, Leicester, after which he went out a third time to Cuttack in Orissa. Sutton had a remarkably prolific publishing career, including a translation of the New Testament into Oriya (1845), *A Narrative of the Mission to Orissa* (1833), *Oriya Grammar* (1840), *Oriya Dictionary* (1843), and *Elements of Natural Philosophy* (1843).

SWAN, JABEZ SMITH (1800–1884). American Baptist evangelist, born at Stonington, Connecticut. Called to preach in 1822, he studied at Hamilton Literary and Theological Institution (later Madison University). He was ordained an **evangelist** in 1827, but settled at Norwich, New York, in 1830. Over the next 30 years, Swan moved from church to church and conducted several successful evangelistic and protracted **revival** meetings. His labors in revival were especially noteworthy in Preston, New York (1837); Mystic Bridge and New London, Connecticut (1842–1843); Albany, New York (1848); and Providence, Rhode Island (1858), after which he served as **pastor** at Huntingdon Street, New London, Connecticut. For alternative years, he was state Baptist evangelist in Connecticut and New York and one of the greatest exponents of the **Second Great Awakenings**. His biography, *The Evangelist* (1873), became a textbook of revival techniques.

SWAZILAND. Baptist witness in Swaziland began early in the 20th century with missionary efforts by the **Southern Baptists** and the **National Baptist Convention, U.S.A**. Beginning in 1983, Southern Baptists focused their efforts among refugees from Mozambique and Angola.

As of 2001, there were 11 churches with 500 members in the Baptist community in Swaziland associated with the Southern Baptist Mission.

SWEDEN. Baptist life in Sweden is one of the oldest and strongest families in Europe. The first congregation dates from 1854, when two furriers started a work at Stockholm. **Anders Wiberg**, who had been baptized by **F. O. Nilsson**, became **pastor** of the church in 1856 and led in the dramatic development of the sect in Sweden. In 1857, a union was formed and soon thereafter cordial relations were established with German leaders. A theological seminary named Betelseminariat was opened near Stockholm in 1866, and it did much to foster leadership for over a hundred churches. In 1889, the Swedish Union organized a missionary society, which sponsored domestc missions and overseas efforts in **Spain**, **Russia**, Asia, and Africa. The Svenska Baptistsamfundet publishes *Vecko-posten* (*Weekly Post*) (1868–).

A major rift occurred among Swedish Baptists in 1892–1907, when a mission work was started at Örebro, an industrial town. The rift initially occurred over influences of the "New Movement," a type of Pentecostalism. Those associated with the mission under the leadership of John Ongman (1855–1931) were ardent supporters of **women** preachers, foreign **missions**, and **revivalism**. Ongman was independent in his attitude and started his own **theological** school. In the 1930s, differences again arose over central organization, Pentecostal gifts, and **liberal** theology. In 1936, a formal split occurred as the Filadelfia Church in Örebro left the union. Thus far, the Örebro Association has remained separate not only from the Baptist Union but also from the **Baptist World Alliance**. It publishes *Missions Banneret* (Banner of Missions) (1920–).

For all Baptists in Sweden, an artistic treasure is the mural painting *The Baptists*, completed in 1886 by Baron Gustaf Cederstrom. It depicts an outdoor group baptismal scene on Lake Malaren near Uppsala. Originally displayed in Paris as *Midsummer Night in Sweden*, the painting reveals the painful personal transition from the established church to a **believer's church** relationship, as well as the stigma attached to Swedish dissenters in the 19th century. The painting is on display at Betelseminariat near Stockholm.

As of 2006, there were 226 churches and 17,247 members affiliated with the Baptist Union; 362 churches with 33,000 members affiliated with the Örebro Mission; 12 churches with 1,241 members affiliated with the Free Baptist Union; and 767 churches with 44,000 members in other Baptist communities. The **Baptist Bible Fellowship** opened a mission in Sweden in 1985. Presently, there are two Baptist-related theological studies programs in Sweden: Betelseminariat and the Stockholm School of Theology.

SWITZERLAND. There are two classes of Baptists in Switzerland: those who are the result of **J. G. Oncken**'s **mission** and those who practiced believer's **baptism** since the Reformation. Oncken visited

Switzerland in 1847 and baptized several at Hochwart. By 1849, there was a church in Zurich, from which came congregations at St. Gall and Thurgau. A second group, the Wiedertaufer, began in Zurich and is not formally related to the mainstream Baptist movement. The Bund der Baptistgemeinden in der Schweiz was formed in 1923. From 1949 to 1996, the **Southern Baptist**–founded theological school at Rüschlikon (Zurich) was a center of European Baptist life and education. When the Swiss government immigration policies made it difficult and expensive to maintain the student body and faculty from outside Switzerland, the seminary relocated to Prague, the **Czech Republic**. The **Baptist Bible Fellowship** opened a mission in Switzerland in 1987.

As of 2006, there were 10 churches and 1,187 members affiliated with the Bund der Baptistgemeinden in der Schweiz. The Bund der Baptistgemeinden publishes *Gemeindbote* (*Church Notes*) (1954–).

***SWORD AND TROWEL* BAPTISTS.** *See* CONTINENTAL BAPTISTS.

SYRIA. In 1948, the first Baptist witness in Syria was undertaken by the American Evangelical Mission, which was reorganized in 1955 to become the Syrian Baptist Mission, Inc. In 1957, this work was assumed by **Evangelical Baptist Missions**. Organized in 1983, the Baptist Convention of Syria has four churches with 150 members.

– T –

TAIWAN. Baptist work in Taiwan results from the displacement of Baptist missionaries from mainland **China** after the Communist revolution in 1949–1953. The **Southern Baptists** have built extensively in Taiwan, organizing the Chinese Baptist Convention in 1954. In addition to the larger Baptist work in Taiwan, the **Baptist Bible Fellowship** began a mission there in 1946, the **Conservative Baptist** Foreign Mission Society in 1952, and **Baptist Mid-Missions** from the United States established its mission in 1972. At Hsilo is located the Taiwan Conservative Baptist Theological College, founded in 1957.

As of 2006, there were 197 churches and 22,767 members affiliated with the Chinese Baptist Convention, and about 25 churches with 1,691 members in the Conservative Baptist Association in Taiwan. There is a theological school located at Taipei related to the Southern Baptist mission work.

TAJIKISTAN. *See* MIDDLE or CENTRAL ASIA.

TANGANYIKA. *See* TANZANIA.

TANZANIA. In 1964, the former states of Tanganyika and Zanzibar were united as Tanzania. Baptists entered Tanzania from **Nigeria** under the sponsorship of the Southern Baptist **Foreign Mission Board**. Work began in 1956 at Dar es Salaam, and at Arusha a theological school opened in 1962. For a time, Tanzania was part of the East Africa Baptist Mission; from the first **association** in 1960 has evolved the Baptist Convention of Tanzania (1971). The **Baptist Bible Fellowship** opened a mission in Tanzania in 1988.

As of 2006, there were 3,100 churches and 489,000 members affiliated with the Baptist Convention of Tanzania.

TAYLOR, ADAM (1768–1833). English Baptist schoolmaster and historian, born at Halifax, England. The son of a coal miner and General Baptist minister, and the nephew of **Dan Taylor**, Adam was a schoolteacher in London for most of his career. He edited the *General Baptist Repository* (1810–1822) and wrote extensive biographies of his father and uncle. His *History of the English General Baptists* (1818) was the next attempt after **Thomas Crosby** to write the history of the denomination in England. Taylor separated the **General** theological stream of Baptists from the **Particular** or Calvinistic Baptists, which Crosby had intermingled.

TAYLOR, DAN (1738–1813). English Baptist minister and denominational leader, born at Sour Milk Hall, Northowram. Taylor was the son of a miner. He was raised an Anglican and joined the Methodists in 1757. Taylor read theology and studied the **Bible** as he itinerated and worked as a schoolteacher. He differed with Wesley on **discipline** and, after reading a history of **baptism**, converted to the Baptists, being baptized by a **General Baptist** in Nottinghamshire. For a time, Taylor joined the existing General Baptists but was critical of their spiritual laxity and particularly their doctrine of **Christ**; in 1770, he formed the New Connexion of General Baptists, characterized by **evangelical** zeal and connectionalism. Taylor's leadership and **revivalistic** techniques led to the establishment of numerous churches, a **missionary** society, **Sunday Schools**, and various funds. Taylor continued fellowship with the Old General Baptists, reporting to their assembly as the representative of the Leicestershire Association and **pastor** of Church Lane, Whitechapel. He also served as the principal of the General Baptist academy. Taylor's many published works include *Fundamentals of Religion in Faith and Practice* (1775), *A Humble Essay on Christian Baptism* (1776), *The Reality and Efficacy of Divine Grace* (1787), *An Antidote against Deism* (1819), and *The Christian Religion: Its Leading Principles, Practical Requirements, and Experimental Enjoyments* (1844).

TAYLOR, JAMES BARRETT (1804–1871). Southern Baptist denominational leader, born in Lincolnshire, England. At an early age, Taylor's parents emigrated to the United States, settling in New York City. After relocating to Christiansville, Virginia, he declared his call to **ministry** and studied under a local tutor. In 1826, he was commissioned a **missionary** by the Virginia General Association, and during one of his tours, he met **Jeremiah Jeter**, whose influence on Taylor's life was profound. Taylor was offered the pastorate of Second Baptist Church in Richmond, which he served from 1826 to 1839. Following pastoral ministry, he was chaplain to the University of Virginia and was a principal founder of Virginia Baptist Seminary, later the University of Richmond. In 1846, when the **Southern Baptist Convention (SBC)** formed its **Foreign Mission Board**, Taylor was chosen the first corresponding secretary. In that role for the remainder of his career (through 1872), he built an overseas program for the SBC and personally supervised appointments and efforts to raise support. During the Civil War, he traveled throughout the South as a chaplain and sought to interpret the impact of the war on the overseas missionaries. During the period of Reconstruction, Taylor favored reconciliation with the Baptist churches of the North, and he opened a significant correspondence with **Baron Stowe**, the secretary of the

American Baptist Missionary Union. Taylor's published works include *Lives of Virginia Baptist Ministers* (1837, 1859), *Memoir of Rev. Luther Rice* (1840), and *Restricted Communion; Or Baptism an Essential Prerequisite to the Lord's Supper* (1849).

TAYLOR, JOHN (1752–1835). American Baptist preacher and writer, born in Fauquier County, Virginia. Taylor was not formally educated, but he was baptized by **James Ireland**, a Virginia **Separate Baptist**, and became an itinerant frontier preacher. He first served churches in the Shenandoah Valley, later moving to Kentucky, where he served eight churches in a decade. Taylor is best remembered for his book *Thoughts on Missions* (1819), in which he was the fountainhead of the anti-missionary movement. He denounced **Luther Rice** and opposed missionary **associations** and societies. Later in life, Taylor is said to have regretted his earlier stances, but his book continued to be definitive of that movement. His other major work, *History of Ten Baptist Churches* (1823), is an important autobiographical account of frontier Baptist life.

TAYLOR, MICHAEL HUGH (1936–). British Baptist minister, educator, and activist, born at Northampton. He was educated at Manchester University (M.A., B.D.) and Union Theological Seminary in New York (S.T.M.). At Manchester, he emphasized comparative religions and modern theology, and at Union he was much influenced by Reinhold Niebuhr and John Bennett. He served Baptist pastorates at North Shields (1960–1966) and Hall Green, Birmingham (1967–1970). The 1969 recipient of a Fulbright Travel Fellowship, in 1970 Taylor was slated to teach at Serampore College in **India**, but the political situation there prevented his taking up the opportunity. From 1970 to 1985, he was principal of Northern Baptist College in Manchester, leading in the development of an Alternative Pattern for Training Ministers, a program designed for **pastors** in Lancashire and Yorkshire while they served in the fields. During that time, he was also an adjunct lecturer at the university in **theology** and ethics, and he encouraged the college to cooperate in **ecumenical** education. He served on the World Council of Churches Commission on Theological Education, 1972–1991.

In 1971, Principal Taylor became involved in a major controversy in the **Baptist Union** (BU) following a theological address he gave at the annual assembly that year. At the request of Regent's Park College principal, G. Henton Davies, Taylor was asked to speak to the topic, "The Incarnate Presence: How Much of a Man Was Jesus Christ?" In his remarks, Taylor took issue with the historic creedal formulae about the person of **Christ**, asserting that he must stop short of saying categorically that Jesus is God, because it sounded like a contradiction to him. Instead, Taylor understood Jesus to have cooperated with God and responded to God in an extraordinary way as a man. This address caused quite a stir among **evangelicals** in the BU and precipitated what has been called the "Christological Crisis." Numerous churches threatened to sever ties with the BU, at least one prominent educator resigned from the BU council, and a division among pastors arose between members of the Baptist Revival Fellowship and the Baptist Renewal Fellowship. Taylor's address came to be seen as the watershed from which the BU became more doctrinally sensitive and decidedly more evangelical in its selection of leaders.

Taylor resigned from Northern in 1985 to become director of Christian Aid, a prominent charity in Great Britain. In his 12-year term of service, he led in the significant extension of the organization, especially focused on Africa. In working to change structures, Christian Aid was a leading organization in the South African Coalition against apartheid, and Taylor presided over the Jubilee 2000 Debt Campaign. He was also a resource to World Bank policies on indebtedness. In 1997, he moved to be president of Selly Oak Colleges in Birmingham, where he negotiated the federation of the 11 colleges into the University of Birmingham. In 2000, the University of Birmingham created an academic chair for Taylor in social theology, which has allowed his continued involvement in projects relating to religion and development in **Tanzania** and **Nigeria**. Among his published works are *Learning to Care* (1983) and *Christianity and the Persistence of Poverty* (1991).

TEMPERANCE, BAPTISTS AND. The temperance movement was a multiplicitous approach to public drunkenness and immoral behavior; the movement ranged from those who exercised restraint in social consumption of alcohol to total abstinence. Total abstainers have always been in the numerical minority even among most **evangelical** religious groups.

For the most part, mainstream Baptists have reflected cultural patterns commensurate with their socioeconomic status. The use of alcoholic beverages represents changing patterns in light of larger social trends. In the 17th century, English and North American Baptists doubtless drank wine at meals and on social occasions. This is attested to in the identification of Baptists in the working-class community and in the use of wine in the celebration of the **Lord's Supper**. Further, some Baptist laymen were involved in the production of beer, like **William Kiffin**. It is historically invalid to argue that these beverages were not commonly found in households and in social interaction, as with other **Nonconformist** groups. Less likely was serious consumption of spirituous liquors, largely because of price and availability. Baptist ministers and merchants are known to have imbibed brandy, scotch, and cordials on social and ecclesiastical occasions. Extant sermonic literature and **associational** records do not indicate widespread prohibitory injunctions before 1800.

In the first two decades of the 19th century, Christian moral behavior evolved to lifestyle expectations that cast a serious doubt on the consumption of alcohol. Many Christian churches fostered prejudices against alcohol based on its effect upon family and relationships when used to excess. As the temperance crusade was launched, leadership came from evangelical denominations such as the Methodists, and to a lesser extent the Baptists. In England, for instance, in the 1830s, Baptist ministers became involved in the moderation movement, notably James Jackson of Hebden Bridge in Yorkshire, who toured widely and founded numerous local temperance societies. By the 1840s, Francis Beardsall (1799–1842) argued that only nonalcoholic wine should be used in the **ordinances**, and in 1847, Jabez Tunnicliff (1809–1866) founded at Leeds the **Band of Hope** organization for children associated with the temperance cause. By the 1880s, many associations had temperance chapters, and the Baptist Total Abstinence Association was nationally organized in 1874, although its membership and resources were quite limited. Baptists in **Wales** have taken a dim view of intoxicating beverages; no less than **Christmas Evans** spoke at rallies in the 1830s on the subject of the drink, and 19th-century Welsh associations admonished members not to go to taverns on the Sabbath. As late as 1905, British Baptist leader **J. H. Shakespeare** delivered an address to the **Baptist World Alliance** on the merits of temperance, indicating a continuing commitment to the cause.

In the United States, it was Lyman Beecher (1775–1863), a Congregationalist **theologian**, who led the crusade against drink, beginning in the 1820s. His six sermons on intemperance in 1825 catalyzed the evangelical moral crusade and were reprinted for many generations. At length, many local societies were formed that called for making a pledge of abstinence. These efforts were only modestly successful among Baptists; however, a number of associations issued letters calling for temperance. In 1840, a new phase of the movement emerged in the Washingtonian societies, which pledged total abstinence. Baptists involved included evangelist **Jacob Knapp** and Virginia **pastor William F. Broaddus**. Many local churches joined the Sons of Temperance movement, and some associations in Virginia required a "test" to establish absolute abstinence from imbibing any intoxicating liquor.

By the 1860s, with the advent of the technology to produce unfermented grape juice commercially, Baptist ministers like Abraham Coles (1813–1891) took the position that the term translated "wine" in the New Testament meant unfermented wine. Although leading **Bible** scholars took exception with this viewpoint, such as **Alvah Hovey** of Newton Theological Institution, most churches soon adopted grape juice in the **Lord's Supper** and a disinclination to admit to social uses of alcohol.

In the **social gospel** movement at the turn of the 20th century, Northern Baptist leaders such as **Shailer Mathews** and Samuel Zane Batten (1859–1925) advocated temperance on a scientific platform. Southern Baptists were publicly and vehemently teetotal, partly in response to the fiery attacks on "demon rum" by **fundamentalists** like **J. Frank Norris**. Norris railed against those who failed to perceive the effects of drinking and preached a famous sermon on "Hebrew, Shebrew, the World Is Going to Hell with Home Brew." (This was in contrast to the reputation of Southern Baptist Seminary theologian **James P. Boyce**, who had a renowned wine cellar and died of gout!) The ranks of those who called for closure of saloons and temperance for spiritual and medical reasons included nationally recognized leaders like George B. Cutten (1874–1962), president of Colgate University in 1942, and **Harry Emerson Fosdick**, who thought the merits of temperance outweighed the freedom to consume in an era of Prohibition.

Popularly speaking, during the 21st century, the majority of Baptists in the United States abstain from alcoholic consumption, but many are not openly critical of social drinking. Support for a temperance position is found in the words of a popular covenant (1836), "We will abstain from the use of intoxicating beverages." In Europe, social drinking is common among Baptists; in Latin America and Eastern Europe, alcoholic consumption can be associated with a more permissive lifestyle and the Roman Catholic tradition, thus it is not encouraged. In the missionary context, particularly where **Southern Baptists** and other **conservative** evangelical Baptists are located, abstinence is the norm both for the missionaries and usually the indigenous communities they serve.

TEXAS BAPTISTS COMMITTED (TBC). An influence group in the **Mainstream** Baptist organizational family in Texas that promotes historic Baptist principles and the work of the Baptist General Convention of Texas. TBC was founded in 1989 by leaders across the state, including **Herbert Reynolds**, John Baugh, Phil Strickland, Richard Jackson, Bill Bruster, David Currie, Robert Sloan, and Charles Wade, all of whom for various reasons were concerned about the **Southern Baptist resurgent** takeover of **Southern Baptist Convention** agencies, institutions, and state conventions. The organization is visible through print and Internet media as well as an annual meeting in conjunction with the Baptist General Convention of Texas. As a theologically moderate coalition, TBC advocates Texas Baptist **ministry** and **mission** as a **voluntary association**, principles of biblical **evangelism**, cooperation in missions, **religious liberty**, soul freedom, and organizational accountability. In general, the group has opposed the continued participation of the Baptist General Convention of Texas in Southern Baptist programs. It is linked with other moderate groups through the **Cooperative Baptist Fellowship** and the Mainstream Baptist network. Since 1993, TBC has published *Newsletter* and in the last decade, the website *Rancher's Rumblings*.

David Currie, a former Texas Baptist **pastor**, is executive director and the organization is headquartered in San Angelo, Texas.

THAILAND. Baptists began missionary work in Siam (Thailand) as an outgrowth of the **American Baptist** mission in **Burma** (Myanmar). In 1833, John Taylor Jones (1802–1851) established the first congregation at Bangkok; in 1835, **William Dean**, another American Baptist missionary, established the first Chinese Baptist Church in Bangkok. Although numerous missionaries were appointed to Siam, most left and went to one of the **China** fields. This caused the Siamese work to languish, and American Baptists withdrew from the field in 1914.

The Chinese Baptist churches date their organization from William Dean in 1837 and many years later, in 1959, formed the Pakh District Church of Christ. The Lahu Baptist Convention of the 18th District was organized in 1901; the Karen Baptists of the 19th District formed an **association** in 1954, and the Thailand Baptist Churches Association in the 16th District organized in 1989. With the closing of the Chinese field in 1949–1954, Siam became an important staging area for missions to China, and since the 1940s, American missionaries again have begun work permanently in Thailand. The Thailand Baptist Missionary Fellowship was formed in 1974 to coordinate the work of the American and **Australian** Baptists in the country; **Swedish** Baptists joined in 1976, and the **Baptist Missionary Society** of Great Britain entered the arrangement in 1986. The **Baptist Bible Fellowship** opened a mission in Thailand in 1983, and the **Association of Baptists for World Evangelism** began a mission to Thailand in 1992, which includes 11 churches with about 300 members. Baptist International Missions (U.S.) relates to 3 churches with over 200 members. There is a Baptist theological school at Chiang Mai.

THEOLOGICAL EDUCATION. Theological education, strictly speaking, applies to the training of ministers; among Baptists it has also applied to education for missionaries, educators, and lay training.

The first school for ministerial training was Bristol Academy in England. The roots of this school are found in the Edward Terrill Trust, established in 1679 to support the **pastors** of Broadmead

Baptist Church, Bristol, in mentoring candidates for **ministry**. Bristol Baptist Academy was started in 1720, became a college in 1770, and affiliated with the University of Bristol in 1909. In 1787, the **General Baptists** founded Midlands College at Nottingham; in 1919, this school merged with Rawdon College.

Other schools in the British Baptist family were formed in the early 19th century. In the North, **William Steadman** pioneered the development in 1804 of an academy (which became Rawdon College) to train ministers for the churches of Lancashire and Yorkshire. Partly in response to the advance of the Baptists of the North, London Baptists founded the Theological College at Stepney in 1810, later to become Regent's Park College in Oxford. At Croydon, **Charles H. Spurgeon** started the Pastor's College (later known as Spurgeon's College) in 1856. Closed communion Baptists in the North formed in 1866 a college at Bury, later the Manchester Baptist College, which in 1964 merged with Rawdon College to become the Northern Baptist College at Manchester. Related to Spurgeon's College was the establishment in 1892 of the Irish Baptist Theological College by Hugh D. Brown (1858–1918) at Belfast, later transferred to Dublin.

Baptist theological education in **Scotland** dates from the early 19th century. The Haldanes operated theological schools from 1797 to 1806, producing most of the domestic missionaries of that era. In 1820, **Robert Haldane** permanently established classes at Grantown-on-Spey. In 1837, the Baptist Academical Society for Scotland was formed, and a year later, Francis Johnstone (1810–1880) began the Baptist Theological Academy of Scotland, first at Cupar, then at Edinburgh. In 1894, a second attempt to start a college was made with the establishment of the Baptist Theological College in Glasgow. It continues to the present.

In **Wales**, there has been a significant interest in the training of ministers. An academy at Trosnant was started in 1734 by John Griffiths. The first college was opened at Abergavenny in 1807. Subsequently, colleges appeared at Pontypool (removed from Abergavenny in 1836), Haverfordwest (1839), and the Coleg Bartolomeus at Llangollan (1862); Pontypool College moved to Cardiff in 1893; the Baptist College at Haverfordwest moved to Aberystwyth in 1894 and closed in 1899. Following a major study in 1892, the number of colleges in Wales was reduced to two: Bangor in the North and, by 1899, Cardiff in the South.

In the extended British educational tradition are the Baptist schools in **Australia** and **New Zealand**. Australian Baptists maintain five colleges: Baptist Theological College of Victoria (Whitley College, 1891), Queensland Baptist Theological College (1904), Baptist Theological College of New South Wales (Morling College, 1916), Baptist Theological College of South Australia (Burleigh College, 1952), and Baptist Theological College of Western Australia (1963). Several of these colleges have some type of relationship with a local university. In New Zealand, there is one institution: the Baptist Theological College of New Zealand, at Auckland.

In North America, the first strategy of ministerial training involved being mentored by a senior pastor. This was popular in New England and the South, illustrated best in the life of **Samuel Stillman**, who was mentored by **Oliver Hart**. Later as the need grew, five basic institutional models of ministerial education have been employed. In 1764, Baptists of the **Philadelphia Baptist Association** led in establishing the College of Rhode Island, which offered a classical undergraduate university degree; this model was sufficient for several generations of select ministerial leadership, most of whom served eastern, urban congregations.

A second model was the school created by **William Staughton** in his home in Philadelphia in 1807, largely on the example of Bristol Baptist College in England, his alma mater. This model did not have a long history in the United States due to competition from leading schools in other denominations and the institutional progress of **higher education**. Staughton himself was persuaded to abandon the concept for the literary and theological school model (see below).

The third model was employed in the period 1830–1850, the manual labor "institute." Popular among many denominations, particularly in rural southern states, this concept involved students on an agricultural farm who attended lectures and enjoyed both practical and theoretical education. The cost of students was kept to a minimum, they being allowed to work for expenses, and it was generally considered to be a physically healthful approach to secondary and collegiate studies. Owing to the sponsorship of Baptist state organizations, theological subjects and religious exercises characterized instruction in the institutes. The manual labor model was used in Virginia (Richmond College, pre-1840), Indiana (Franklin College, 1837), North Carolina (Wake Forest College, 1834), Georgia (Mercer University, 1833), and South Carolina (Furman University, 1837). This model was quickly superceded by the literary and theological model, owing to the limit of students on a farm and the limitations of faculty, curriculum, and financial resources, which came mostly from urban areas.

A fourth major model was the literary and theological school (L&T) combination. Baptists in Maine followed this path first when they established Maine Literary and Theological Institution at Waterville in 1813. The idea called for a basic arts curriculum maintained in conjunction with a theological program taught by one or two professors. This was the model employed in Hamilton Institution, New York (1819); Columbian College, Washington, D.C. (1821); Granville Literary and Theological Institution, Ohio (1831); Michigan and Huron Institute, Michigan (1833); and Rock Springs Seminary, Illinois (1827). After a decade or so of the combined program, under pressure from the Andover model, most of the L&T schools placed their emphasis upon the arts curriculum and either closed the theological program (Colby, Columbian) or made it an independent department (Madison/Colgate).

The fifth model was the post-undergraduate theological seminary pioneered by Massachusetts Baptists at Newton Theological Institution, founded in 1825. Newton's curriculum was based on Andover Theological Seminary (Congregationalist) and rested on the assumption that candidates for the ministry would first complete a baccalaureate degree. Other institutions that followed this pattern include the transformed Theological Department of Madison University (later Colgate, 1835), Rochester Theological Seminary (1850), Southern Baptist Theological Seminary (1859), Crozer Theological Seminary (1867), Cobb Divinity School of Bates College (1870), and the Divinity School of the University of Chicago (1892).

In the 20th century, Baptist theological education in the United States followed one of two streams: a denominational expansionary pattern or a pattern based on a theological **confession**. Those which were established to meet expanding needs of a particular group include North American Baptist Seminary (1851/1949), Bethel Theological Seminary (1871), Southwestern Baptist Theological Seminary (1909), Berkeley Baptist Divinity School (1912), Norwegian Baptist Theological Seminary (1913), New Orleans Baptist Theological Seminary (1947), Southeastern Baptist Theological Seminary (1950), Midwestern Baptist Theological Seminary (1959), and Golden Gate Baptist Theological Seminary (1954). Those for which a theological tradition was important are Northern Baptist Theological Seminary (1913), the Eastern Baptist Theological Seminary (1925), Western Conservative Baptist Seminary (1928), California Baptist Theological Seminary (1948), Denver Conservative Baptist Seminary (1953), Mid-America Baptist Theological Seminary (1972), Liberty Baptist Seminary (1973), and Beeson Divinity School (1988). Several factions in a more progressive theological tradition have established theological schools or faculties at Richmond, Virginia, Baylor University in Texas (1994), Mercer University in Georgia, and at Campbell University and Wake Forest University in North Carolina.

In **Canada**, the L&T model was followed at Acadia University, New Brunswick Seminary (closed in 1872), and in the first generations at McMaster University. In 1957, McMaster shifted to an exclusively postgraduate model, as it recognized American theological school models; 10 years later, Acadia made the same transition to a predominantly graduate-school level of instruction. The other Baptist theological schools, Carey Theological College, Edmonton Baptist Seminary (North American Baptist Conference), Canadian Southern Baptist Seminary, Heritage Baptist Seminary, and Associated Canadian Theological Schools (related to the Baptist General Conference, Fellowship Baptists, the Evangelical Free Church in Canada and Pentecostal Assemblies of Canada), all emphasize postgraduate level degrees, while some make provision for undergraduates.

Basically, the curriculum of most graduate Baptist theological schools includes instruction in biblical studies; theology; church history; sometimes ethics and sociology; practical areas such as preaching, counseling, religious education; and pastoral care. Attention is given to internships, usually referred to as field education.

Programs specifically designed for those in ministry other than pastors include religious education, music, and **missions**. Originally a project of the Women's Missionary Union, the **Carver** School of

Missions and Social Work (1905) was merged with Southern Baptist Seminary in 1962.

Among several **conservative evangelical** and **fundamentalist** branches of the Baptist family, a **Bible college** model is followed. The first of these was the **Freewill Baptist** Biblical School founded in 1840 at Whitestown, New York. A major impetus in the Bible college tradition occurred in the establishment of Gordon Bible and Missionary Training School (1889). Later institutions include Baptist Bible College, Clark's Summit, Pennsylvania (1931); Baptist Bible College, Springfield, Missouri; Bible Baptist Seminary, Arlington, Texas; Faith Baptist Bible College, Ankeny, Iowa (1968); Grand Rapids Baptist Bible College and Theological Seminary, Grand Rapids, Michigan (1954); and the Baptist University of America, Doraville, Georgia (1975). Among Freewill Baptists in the southern United States, Bible colleges characterized the training of ministers, particularly the Freewill Baptist Bible College (1942). The curricula of these schools follows an English Bible survey pattern, usually some form of **dispensationalist** theology, and practical courses such as **evangelism**, preaching, missions, and Christian education. Student involvement in church service and/or missions is usually expected.

Baptists in Europe also have an ancient tradition of theological education. The first seminary, Betelseminariet, opened at Stockholm, Sweden, in 1866. Later, German Baptists, influenced by **J. G. Oncken**, started a seminary at Hamburg in 1880, which is now located at Elstal. National institutions at Tallinn, **Estonia**; Budapest, **Hungary**; and Warsaw, **Poland**, all emerged in the early mission advance of the Baptist movement in Europe. Small theological faculties exist at Tollose, **Denmark**; Stabekk, **Norway**; and Novi Sad, **Serbia**. **Southern Baptists** from the United States began in 1949 the Baptist Theological Seminary at Rüschlikon (later removed to Prague, Czech Republic), **Switzerland**, to serve the international English-speaking needs of the entire European community. Following the political transition in the Soviet Union in 1991, Baptists opened a seminary at Odessa, **Ukraine**, in 1992 and in Moscow, **Russia,** in 1993.

In Asia, primary theological colleges exist at Serampore, Andhra Pradesh, Jorhat, Ramapatnam, and Bangalore, **India**; **Hong Kong**; Manado, **Indonesia**; and Chiang Mai, **Thailand**. *See also* BIBLE COLLEGES; EDUCATION.

THEOLOGY AND THEOLOGIANS, BAPTIST. Contrary to popular opinion that Baptists have no particular theology, an identifiable set of theological traditions has emerged in the denominational family, and there is a wide variety of theologians who work within a generally Baptistic perspective.

Sources of Baptist Theology. Essentially, there are three historic sources of Baptist theological understanding: **confessions of faith**, pastoral or popular theologians, and academic or systematic theologians. The confessions of faith, dating from the first decade of the 17th century and the beginnings of the Baptist movement, reflect consensus among **pastors** and laymen about theological beliefs on God, the church, the **Bible**, the **ordinances**, Jesus Christ, salvation, humanity, and ethics, to mention the major categories of treatment. The purpose of confessions of faith was often to defend Baptists against false charges or to articulate one's theological position, a technique borrowed from the Reformers and more directly from the Puritans. Among the outstanding Baptist contributors to confessions are **William Kiffin**, **Hanserd Knollys**, **Benjamin Keach**, **J. Newton Brown**, and **Herschel H. Hobbs**. The theological content of confessions of faith continues to be a resource of doctrinal understanding, particularly among **conservative evangelical** Baptist groups.

From the middle of the 17th century, pastors and leaders have been a source of theological statement for Baptists. Sermons and theological treatises published far beyond the original setting create a breadth of influence for such writers. English pastors such as **John Gill**, **Thomas Grantham**, **Robert Hall**, **Andrew Fuller**, **Charles H. Spurgeon**, and **Alexander Maclaren** typify this contribution, as do North Americans like **Thomas Baldwin**, **George Dana Boardman**, **Edward Judson**, **T. T. Shields**, **Harry Emerson Fosdick**, **Martin Luther King Jr.**, and **Howard Thurman**.

Perhaps the most influential group of theologians, however, have been the academic or systematic theologians, in part because of their classroom and published authority, in part because of the reinforcement of their work in references and citations. Among the outstanding academic theologians have been, in Britain, **Dan Taylor**, **Frederick W. Gotch**, **H. Wheeler Robinson**, **Ernest Payne**; in North America, **Francis Wayland**, **W. N. Clarke**, **A. H. Strong**, **E. Y. Mullins**, **D. C. Macintosh**, and the **Chicago School**.

The Evolving Content of Baptist Theology. In the 17th century, the earliest Baptist theologians reacted against the prevailing trends both of determinism of Calvinistic thought and high church sacramentalism. The **General Baptists** built their theology upon an openness on the issue of the application of **Christ**'s redeeming work. They held a strong view of the authority of **Scripture**, doubtless derived from the Puritans and later Separatists. The **Particular Baptists**, in contrast, were consistent Calvinists who adopted most of the tenets of the Westminster Confession of Faith with its emphasis upon the nature of redemption of an elect body of the faithful. Holding also to a freedom of conscience, Particular Baptists sought to align themselves theologically with Presbyterians and Congregationalists in the greater Reformed tradition. The most frequently articulated doctrines of the first and second generations of Baptist theologians were church, ordinances, and redemption. Both major divisions of the 17th-century Baptist family developed a peculiar ecclesiology, holding the local congregation as the essence of the visible church, from which their understanding of the **sacraments**/ordinances, the **ministry**, and **mission** were derived.

The 18th-century Baptist community on both sides of the Atlantic Ocean wrestled with the theological meaning and implications of **revivalism**. Many of the older tradition of strict Calvinists, including John Gill and **John Brine**, abhorred what they called "**Arminian**," or worse yet, "Antinominan" thinking. Both men were influenced by English high-Calvinist theologians Richard Davis (1658–1714), Tobias Crisp (1600–1643), and Joseph Hussey (1660–1726). On the other hand, by mid-century, younger thinkers such as Andrew Fuller, **John Collett Ryland**, **John Ryland Jr.**, and **Robert Hall** of Arnesby argued for a loosening of determinism and a recognition of the church's responsibility to work for the conversion of sinners. John Ryland was an important bridge between the Old School and the new emphases, having been influenced by John Newton (1725–1807). Another key figure, Dan Taylor, was influenced by the Wesleys, and joined the "Arminianized" Baptists in England to revitalize the General Baptist movement. To add variety to the English Baptist scene, **William Vidler** and **Elhanan Winchester** sought an outer edge in **Universalist** thought, while still claiming other Baptistic distinctives.

Early in the 19th century, the less compromising Calvinists gradually organized themselves in defense of a Puritan style of Calvinism, led by men like Charles H. Spurgeon, **Joseph C. Philpot**, and **William Gadsby**. In the United States, the **Primitive Baptists** and some Old School orders followed a Calvinistic tradition, without the leadership of an educated theologian. Outstanding pulpiteers like Alexander Maclaren, **Richard Fuller**, **John A. Broadus**, **A. J. Gordon**, **Russell H. Conwell**, **George W. Truett**, E. Y. Mullins, **W. J. Simmons**, and **Adam Clayton Powell Sr.** helped to give shape to Baptistic theological discourse as warm-hearted religious experience.

Beginning in the mid-19th century, new patterns of Baptist theology emerged in Britain and the United States. Biblical scholars gradually informed their Baptist constituency of more critical questions impinging upon traditional views of the authority of the **Bible**. Included in this group were **Frederick W. Gotch** and **S. H. Green** in Britain and **C. H. Toy** and **Nathaniel Schmidt** in the United States. Missionaries and theological professors like **John E. Clough** and **Shailer Mathews**, following the interaction with other Christian and non-Christian traditions, gave sanction in some circles to a more universal view of God and an evolutionary perspective on theological doctrine.

In response to these "modernistic" trends, some Baptists moved to defensive positions around classic doctrinal statements about the Bible, church, Christian experience, and the finality of the work of Jesus Christ. Men such as A. J. Gordon and **Henry G. Weston** took an uncompromising stand on the issues. Some of the more **liberal** Baptists attempted to have editorial dialogue with the more **conservative** thinkers in an attempt to explain their new social science understandings of doctrine in traditional terms. Among this group were **William Newton Clarke**, Harry Emerson Fosdick, **George Burman Foster**, **Gerald B. Smith**, **Henry Clay Vedder**, and Douglas Clyde Macintosh. Clarke, Fosdick, and Foster emphasized experience in religious understanding, while Smith and Macintosh stressed an empirical basis for theology. These pioneers of the "New Theology" were met often with an uncompromising strident attack from traditionalist pulpit theologians, including **John Roach Straton**, **J. Frank Norris**, **J. C. Massee**, T. T. Shields, **W. B. Riley**, John R. Rice, and **G. B. Vick**.

In the 20th century, Baptist theology was predictably divided between those with a high view of the divine inspiration of Scripture, those who sought to reformulate theology in terms of social trends and scientific modernism, and those who ultimately took more radical approaches. As the century began, A. H. Strong, **Alvah Hovey**, E. Y. Mullins, and **W. T. Connor** ruled supreme in the theological schools, Strong evolving in view of scientific advances he needed to account for. That magisterial position of the "Baptist schoolmen" was broadened with Baptists who came to teach in other denominations' schools or ecumenical centers. A list of more contemporary Baptist theologians is characterized by great variety. They include **Carl F. H. Henry**, **George Beasely-Murray**, **Dale Moody**, Millard Erickson (1932–), Samuel Mikolaski (1923–), **Clark Pinnock** (1937–), James Leo Garrett (1925–), James W. McClendon (1924–2000), and Stanley Grenz (1950–2005), who have each indirectly or explicitly reinforced traditional baptistic interpretation (with unique differentiating points).

At the same time, Harvey Cox (1929–), William Hamilton (1924–), W. Kenneth Cauthen (1930–), Howard Thurman, Henry Mitchell (1919–), **Michael Taylor** (1936–), **Carlisle Marney**, Erich Geldbach (193 –), Thorwald Lorenzen (1936–), William Brackney (1948–), and Paul Fiddes (1950–), to name a few, have moved far afield of any traditional Baptist evangelical or strictly denominational agenda. They have emphasized postmodern thought (Grenz), radical theology (Hamilton, Cox), process theology (Cauthen), civil rights (Howard Thurman), environmental concerns (Brackney), ecumenical theology (Geldbach, Fiddes, Brackney), **human rights** (Lorenzen, Brackney), and new perspectives on Trinitarian thought and the role of covenants in the Free Church tradition (Fiddes). Perhaps the widest departure from traditional Baptist thinking was that of William Hamilton, an advocate of the "Death of God" movement in radical theology.

New fields such as ethics, historical theology, biblical theology, philosophical theology, and pastoral theology have produced numerous Baptist writers and theologians in the broadest sense of the term, working out systems of theological reflection in their respective disciplines; these include **Wayne Oates**, psychology; **Edward J. Carnell**, apologetics (1919–1967); Paul Simmons, ethics (1936–);

George Eldon Ladd, New Testament (1911–1982); Frank Stagg, biblical theology (1911–2001); and John Jonsson, missions (1925–). Many of those on both sides of the spectrum probably value their identity as "Baptist" theologians less than their conversancy with other evangelicals or social activists.

The Consensus of Baptist Thought. What characterizes historic Baptist theology? The majority of all Baptists emphasize Christian experience; the authority, if not plain interpretation, of Scripture; and the primacy of the local congregation in their determination and articulation of Christian doctrine. Whether conservative or liberal in outlook, Baptists of all kinds affirm liberty of conscience and freedom of expression as essential to their faith. **Separation of church and state** are widely held also, except among **fundamentalistic** Baptists in the United States, who have a concern for influencing public policy with religious ideals and ethical standards. From these central theological tenets there is very wide differentiation on matters such as the sacraments/ordinances, the kingdom of God, evangelization and missions, human rights, Christology and the Holy Spirit, and "last things." Typically, most Baptists are biblicists, Trinitarian, Christocentric, evangelical, experiential, and mildly Calvinistic and mildly sacramentarian in theological perspective. Their doctrine of the church is local in emphasis, and one's freedom of personal religious opinion and expression is jealously guarded.

Baptist theology may be summarized as follows:

A BAPTIST QUADRILATERAL

Scripture

Freedom   CHRIST   Mission

Experience

THOMAS, JOHN (1760–1801). English Baptist surgeon and missionary, born at Fairford, England. He studied medicine and qualified as a surgeon in 1780. In 1783, he became a ship's surgeon, associated with the East India Company, and traveled to Calcutta, **India**. There he found no European Christians willing to worship with him and he advertised for those who would help to form a church. He returned to London in 1785 and became associated with the Baptist Church at Little Wild Street in London. When he returned to Calcutta in 1786, Thomas organized a congregation and recognized the great need for gospel work in Bengal. Returning again to Britain in 1792, he made the acquaintance of **William Carey** and convinced Carey and the newly formed Particular **Baptist Missionary Society** to accept Bengal as their initial field. Thomas is thus rightly credited with focusing English Baptist missionary attention upon India. Thomas completed a Bengali translation of most of the New Testament, Psalms, and Prophets by 1795.

THOMAS, JOSHUA (1719–1797). Welsh Baptist minister and historian, born at Caio, Carmarthenshire, Wales. He was self-educated as a farmer who, at first, was encouraged by the Baptist church at Leominster to preach, and after several years of supply preaching in the vicinity of Hay-on-Wye in Brecknockshire, he was ordained in 1749. In 1754, Thomas was called to the pastorate at Leominster, which he served for 43 years. In addition to being a model **pastor**, he collected historical materials on the Welsh Baptists and published eight historical works, two devotional tracts, and seven theological treatises. Among his most outstanding works are *Materials for a History of the Baptist Churches in the Principality* (1784), which was influenced by the work of **Morgan Edwards** in the United States, and *Ecclesiastical History of Wales* (1779). Thomas also supplied historical sketches for **John Rippon** and numerous obituary notices. He was recognized as a principal apologist for the **Particular Baptist** cause and the broader community of Baptists in Britain and America.

THREE DISSENTING DENOMINATIONS. Following the Act of Toleration, Baptists, like other English dissenters, began to expand their horizons and express their political opinions. The first concerns were for recognition of the church and **ministry** and later for benefits enjoyed by the Establishment. In 1714, **Benjamin Stinton** began to gather London ministers at a **coffeehouse** for discussion of common needs and goals. By 1723, this became what was later referred to as the Baptist Board. Beginning in 1727, similar Presbyterian and

Congregational bodies joined with the Baptist Board to address common political concerns and provide an ongoing list of dissenting ministers and congregations. Meeting collectively at least annually, they came to be known as the Three Dissenting Denominations, later as the Dissenting Deputies.

THURMAN, HOWARD (1900–1981). American **black Baptist** minister, born at Daytona Beach, Florida. He was educated at Morehouse College and Rochester Theological Seminary and served Mt. Zion Baptist Church in Oberlin, Ohio, 1926–1929. In 1929, he began a distinguished career in **higher education**, becoming professor of religion and director of religious life at Baptist-related Morehouse and Spelman Colleges in Atlanta, Georgia. In 1932, Mordecai Johnson (1890–1976) invited Thurman to become dean of the chapel and professor of Christian **theology** at Howard University in Washington, D.C., where he served until 1944. Influenced by the thought of Mahatma Gandhi (1869–1948), Thurman and Alfred G. Fisk started the Church for the Fellowship of All Peoples in 1944 in San Francisco, California, which became a model of interracial and **ecumenical** cooperation. From 1953 to 1965, Thurman served as Dean of Marsh Chapel and Professor of Spiritual Resources and Disciplines at Boston University in Massachusetts. He was one of the best-known speakers and social prophets of his era and devoted his retirement years to the establishment of the Howard Thurman Educational Trust to encourage intercultural understanding and support for black colleges. Among Thurman's many published works are *Jesus and the Disinherited* (1949), *The Creative Encounter* (1954), and *The Search for Common Ground* (1971).

TICHENOR, ISAAC TAYLOR (1825–1902). Southern Baptist minister and denominational leader, born in Spencer County, Kentucky. He was not formally educated and began to preach at an early age, earning the epithet "boy orator of Kentucky." He served as a **missionary** for the American Indian Mission Association (1847), later becoming a **pastor** at Columbus, Mississippi (1848–1850), and First Baptist, Montgomery, Alabama (1852–1867). During the American Civil War, Tichenor served as a sharpshooter under General Braxton Bragg (1817–1896), at the same time serving as a missionary/chaplain. In

1867, he was president of the Montevallo Coal Mining Company in northern Alabama, which was responsible for discovering the vast coal reserves near what became Birmingham. For a time, he was president of Auburn Agricultural and Mining College (1871), and in 1872, he was elected president of the **Southern Baptist** Home Mission Board, which he served for 17 years. In the latter post, he completely reorganized Southern Baptist work, expanded it to the Caribbean, and offset the advance of the **American Baptist Home Mission Society** following the Civil War.

TIMPANY, AMERICUS VESPUCIUS (1840–1885). Canadian and American Baptist missionary, born at Vienna, Ontario. He was educated at Canadian Literary Institute and was influenced by **R. A. Fyfe**. As the Canadian churches had no overseas agency as yet, Timpany was appointed by the **American Baptist Missionary Union** to work in **India** in 1868. He began ministry with the Telugus and witnessed a large increase of converts from 1868 to 1872. He began the Ramapatam Theological Seminary in 1872 and organized the American Baptist Telugu Conference. While on furlough in 1876–1878, he and his wife, Jane Bates, toured **Canada** and raised support for the newly established Canadian Baptist Missionary Society and they began publication of *The Missionary Link*. Support for the Timpanys shifted to the Canadian society, and when they returned to India, a new field was opened for Canadians at Cocanada. His duties included practicing medicine, translating **Scripture**, and working in the municipal government. Timpany's death caused quite a sensation among the Canadian churches and helped to solidify their efforts. Timpany published the extensive *Compendium of Theology* in Telugu (1877).

TOGO. The first Baptist church in Togo was organized at Lomé, and it was initially related to the Baptist Convention of **Ghana** and the presence of traders from Nigeria. In 1959, the **General Baptist** Missionary Society in the United States began a **mission**. In 1967, the Baptist Association of Togo was formed, and this evolved into the Baptist Convention of Togo in 1988, jointly supported by the **Southern Baptists** and the **National Baptist Convention, U.S.A.** In 1973, the **Association of Baptists for World Evangelism** began a mission in Togo.

As of 2006, there were 519 churches and 31,673 members affiliated with the Togo Baptist Convention Baptiste Togolaise, formerly the Association Baptiste Togolaise. Presently, there is a Baptist-related theological school at Lomé.

TOLBERT, WILLIAM (1913–1980). Liberian Baptist political leader and minister. He was born at Bensonville, **Liberia**, and educated at Liberia College (later the University of Liberia). Tolbert entered public service in the Treasury Office and later served eight years in the Liberian House of Representatives. In 1951, he was elected vice president of Liberia, a post that included presidency of the country's Senate. He was reelected to that office in 1953, 1955, 1959, and 1963. In 1971, on the death of President Tubman, Tolbert became president of Liberia, to which post he was subsequently reelected.

His involvement with the Baptist community was lifelong. In 1953, he became **pastor** of Zion Praise Baptist Church in Bensonville, and in 1956, he founded Mount Sinai Baptist Church in the Tondee District, which he co-pastored with the Bensonville Church. In 1958–1965, he served as president of the Liberian Baptist Missionary and Education Convention, Inc., and vice president of the **Baptist World Alliance** (BWA) in 1960–1965. At the 11th Baptist World Congress meeting in Miami Beach, Florida, in 1965, Tolbert was elected president of the BWA, which he served until 1970. Tolbert was assassinated in Liberia in 1980, becoming both a political and religious martyr.

TORBET, ROBERT GEORGE (1912–1995). American Baptist educator and historian, born at Spokane, Washington. He was educated at Wheaton College (Illinois), the Eastern Baptist Theological Seminary, and the University of Pennsylvania, where he received the Ph.D. degree. He taught church history at Eastern Seminary from 1944 to 1952, after which he was a senior staff editor and later director of educational services at the American Baptist Board of Education and Publication. In 1958, Torbet became dean at Central Baptist Theological Seminary in Kansas City, Kansas, where he led in establishing its accreditation. His final post was as associate general secretary for **ecumenical** relations of the American Baptist Convention from 1967 to 1977. In this role, he was a leading force in the

1972 Lima meetings of the World Council of Churches' recognition of the place of believer's **baptism**. Torbet wrote major textbooks on the **Philadelphia Baptist Association** (1944), general Baptist history (*A History of the Baptists*, 1950), and the **American Baptist Foreign Mission Society** (1955). For the latter half of the 20th century, Torbet's Baptist history was the common textbook in the denomination.

TOY, CRAWFORD HOWELL (1836–1919). Southern Baptist minister and educator, born in Norfolk, Virginia. Educated at the University of Virginia and Southern Baptist Theological Seminary, he taught at Albemarle Female Institute and Richmond College. During the Civil War, Toy was a Confederate chaplain and was captured at Gettysburg. While in prison, he taught Italian and organized a Glee Club. Following the war, Toy returned to teaching languages and philosophy at the University of Alabama and Furman University. In 1869, he assumed the chair in Old Testament at Southern Baptist Seminary where he was highly regarded. In the 1870s, however, he opposed the **Landmarkist** teachings of **James R. Graves** and adopted German higher critical views of the **Bible**. In 1879, Toy was forced to resign because his views of the Bible were held to be incompatible with the doctrinal statement of the seminary. Shortly thereafter, he went to Harvard College as the Hancock Professor of Semitics. The president of Harvard remarked of Toy's appointment that "Harvard Divinity Faculty now had an American heretic in its ranks." Toy built a strong reputation at Harvard in Semitic languages and Old Testament studies based on German documentary hypothesis theories. His great interest was in the application of comparative religions methodologies, which he pioneered among American theological educators. For a time, he carried on a close relationship with **Charlotte Moon**, a missionary to **China**. Miss Moon, upon reading Toy's views, decided to end the romance. Toy published commentaries on Proverbs (1899) and Ezekiel (1899), plus the books *Judaism and Christianity* (1890) and *Introduction to the History of Religions* (1913).

TRAIL OF BLOOD. *See* SUCCESSIONISM.

TRASKITES. A 17th-century English Nonconformist group that followed the teachings of John Traske (1585–1636). Originally a Puritan ordained by the Bishop of Salisbury, Traske became a popular preacher in Devon, Ely, and later London. Among his extraordinary views, he adopted the teaching of the Sabbath as a day of rest and blessing and became known as a religious radical. He drew a large following, known pejoratively as "Traskites," who spread through the country with Judaical teachings. Their doctrines and practices included observance of the old Sabbath, differentiating meats, sinless perfectionism, the equation of the Old Testament priest Melchizedek as the Holy Spirit, and the keeping of the Feast of Passover. Traske himself categorized all men in one of three states: nature, repentance, and grace, the latter of which was the "Holy City of sinlessness." Some Traskites turned to Antinomianism and **Familism**; Traske himself was given a severe sentence in 1618 involving a fine, whipping, the pillory, and banishment from **ministry** for his Judaical teachings. In the late 1620s, he joined the Separatist congregation in London, identified with **Henry Jacob** and **John Lathrop**. Although there is no evidence that Traske ever adopted Baptistic views, his Sabbatarian thought was a forerunner of that found in the **Seventh Day Baptist** movement associated with Mill Yard Church in the 1650s, and his wife, Dorothy (c. 1585–1645) bridged the early development of Sabbatarian thought with the development of later practicing congregations. Some Seventh Day Baptist historians claim Traske as their earliest exponent. *See also* SEVENTH DAY BAPTISTS.

TRIENNIAL CONVENTION. *See* GENERAL MISSIONARY CONVENTION OF THE BAPTIST DENOMINATION IN THE UNITED STATES OF AMERICA FOR FOREIGN MISSIONS.

TRINIDAD AND TOBAGO. Baptist history in Trinidad and Tobago began during the Napoleonic Wars as many freed slaves emigrated to the islands. Among these were Baptists, who formed the first church in 1816. As the work grew, it caught the attention of the **Baptist Missionary Society** (BMS), which began support of a mission at Port of Spain in 1843. **E. B. Underhill**, secretary for the BMS, visited Trinidad in 1859 and noted the extraordinary overt, excited behavior in worship. This style of worship coalesced in the "Spiritual," or "**Shouter,**" Baptists. In the 1890s, the BMS gradually withdrew its missionaries in favor of an indigenous leadership; the Baptist Union of Trinidad was formed in 1854. Much fragmentation occurred within the Baptist community, such as in 1890 when the St. Paul's Independent Baptist Missionary Society was formed. This evolved into the Independent Order of Baptists (1900), the Independent Baptists Missionary Union (1944), the Independence Baptist Mission Churches, Inc. (1966), and finally a split in 1986, which generated the Independent International Baptist Church of Trinidad and Tobago, which has ties to the **Southern Baptist Convention**, the **National Baptist Convention, U.S.A.**, and the **National Baptist Convention of America**. In more recent years the BMS has returned to support work in Trinidad (1946), and Southern Baptists launched a mission in 1970–1976, but withdrew from direct cooperation with the Baptist Union of Trinidad, preferring the independent movement and an umbrella organization called the Caribbean Baptist Fellowship.

As of 2006, there were 24 churches and 3,300 members affiliated with the Baptist Union of Trinidad and Tobago; 9 churches with 860 members affiliated with the Baptist Convention of Trinidad and Tobago; 12 congregations and 2,500 members affiliated with the Orthodox Baptist Churches (an independent group); and 18 churches with 2,400 members affiliated with the Evangelical Baptist Association.

TRUETT, GEORGE WASHINGTON (1867–1944). Southern Baptist minister, born at Hayesville, North Carolina. Educated at Baylor University, he founded Hiawasee Academy in 1887 and returned in 1892 to Baylor as financial secretary to President **B. H. Carroll**. In 1893, Truett became **pastor** at East Waco, Texas, and in 1897 at First Baptist Church in Dallas, Texas. Under Truett's **ministry**, which lasted for 47 years, First Baptist in Dallas became the center of Baptist life in the state and one of the largest congregations in the Baptist world. Truett is credited with great preaching, which increased the membership in Dallas tenfold while he was pastor. He was president of the **Southern Baptist Convention** in 1927–1930 and of the **Baptist World Alliance** in 1935–1940. President Woodrow Wilson invited Truett to preach to American troops in Europe in 1918, and the next year, Truett was a leading spokesman of the $75 Million Campaign among Southern Baptists. In May 1920, he preached his memorable sermon "Baptists and **Religious Liberty**" on the steps of the U.S.

Capitol to 15,000 people gathered there. The most memorable of Truett's sermons were published as *A Quest for Souls* (1917).

TRUMAN, HARRY S. (1884–1972). Baptist layman and 33rd United States president, born at Lamar, Missouri. Truman worked on his father's farm and later in a haberdashery business. He served in the National Guard and in the United States Army, where he led an artillery regiment in World War I. In 1922, he was elected a county judge, and owing to his lack of legal training, he studied at Kansas City Law School. In 1934, he was elected to the U.S. Senate, and in 1944, he found himself a compromise Democratic candidate as vice president with Franklin Roosevelt. Upon Roosevelt's death in 1945, Truman succeeded to the presidency. He was reelected president in 1948.

Mr. Truman was the heir of a long line of Kentucky Baptists and was baptized in the Little Blue River by the **pastor** of Benton Boulevard Baptist Church in Kansas City, Missouri. As a Baptist, Truman was a lifelong member of Grandview Baptist Church in Grandview, Missouri, south of Kansas City. During his presidency years, he frequently attended First Baptist Church in Washington, D.C. because he liked the plain folk treatment accorded him there by the pastor, Edward Hughes Pruden. Upon his return to private life in Independence, Missouri, in 1953, President Truman was not an active church member. His funeral was conducted by an Episcopal priest (Mrs. Truman was of that persuasion), during which the minister at First Baptist, Independence, Harold Hunt, Truman's neighbor, read a prayer. Truman often irritated Baptists because of his off-color language, sporadic church attendance, and his membership in the Freemasons, which he joined in 1909. He preferred the King James Version of the **Bible** and was drawn to Jesus' Sermon on the Mount.

TUNKERS. *See* BAPTIST (THE NAME); GERMAN BAPTIST BRETHREN.

TUPPER, CHARLES, SIR (1821–1915). Canadian medical doctor, political leader, and Baptist layman, born at Amherst, Nova Scotia. He was the son of a Baptist minister and first pursued a career in school teaching. He trained locally as a physician, later graduating from the Royal College of Surgeons of the University of Edinburgh.

He practiced medicine most of his life, becoming the chief medical officer of the City of Halifax. At the invitation of fellow Baptist James W. Johnston, Tupper entered politics as a Conservative in the Nova Scotia Legislature in 1855, an opponent of Joseph Howe. To reach a majority government, Tupper successfully courted the Roman Catholics in Nova Scotia. He rose to prominence as premier 1864–1867 and led Nova Scotia into Confederation, becoming a "Father of Canadian Confederation." From 1883 to 1895, he was Canadian high commissioner to the United Kingdom, also holding a number of cabinet responsibilities, bringing British attention to his emerging country's needs. Tupper was a member of the British Privy Council 1871–1914 and was knighted in 1907. In 1896, he became the sixth prime minister of Canada, serving from May–July that year, the shortest term (69 days) of a Canadian prime minister. Tupper was a strong advocate of a national railroad system, canals, a transatlantic cable, and the exploitation of Canada's rich mineral resources. As prime minister, he was defeated by Wilfred Laurier, and when Tupper refused to cede the election, Lord Aberdeen removed him from office. Tupper was a colorful character, and his Baptist temperance heritage languished under the influence of Scottish whiskey during his medical studies in Edinburgh, and he had a reputation as a womanizer. He married an Anglican, Frances Morse, and raised his family in that church. Yet, he was known to attend Baptist meetings when traveling, and he made large contributions of money to Baptist churches and projects. When criticized by his fellow Baptists for not recognizing their cause, he appointed **Theodore Harding Rand** of Upper Canard, Nova Scotia, the first superintendent of schools in Nova Scotia. When in Ottawa, Tupper attended First Baptist Church and contributed a large sum to the construction of their building.

TUPPER, HENRY ALLEN (1828–1902). Southern Baptist minister and denominational leader, born in Charleston, South Carolina. He was educated at Madison University (later Colgate) and served pastorates at Graniteville and Washington, Georgia (1853–1872). During the American Civil War, Tupper served as a chaplain to the Confederate Ninth Georgia Volunteers Regiment, earning the nickname "the Fighting Parson," although he never carried a weapon. In 1872, he was elected corresponding secretary of the Southern Baptist **Foreign Mission Board** (FMB).

A lifelong mission enthusiast, Tupper raised large sums of money while a **pastor** for the Southern Baptist foreign mission enterprise and was a natural choice to succeed **James B. Taylor**. He reorganized the FMB into committees for various fields and expanded the outreach of **Southern Baptists** overseas in **Mexico**, **Brazil**, **Nigeria**, and **Japan**. At home, he encouraged the establishment of support groups in each of the state **conventions**. One of Tupper's most outstanding achievements was the appointment of the first **women** missionaries; during his tenure, the Woman's Missionary Union was organized in 1888. He also involved the FMB in the **ecumenical** Foreign Mission Conference of North America in 1892. The author of two books on the history of Southern Baptist foreign missions, Tupper ended his career as an instructor in biblical studies at Richmond College. Among Tupper's published works on missions is *A Decade of Foreign Missions 1880–1890* (1891).

TURKEY. Baptist work in Turkey is meager, due to extreme government restrictions. **Southern Baptists** have one congregation of approximately 100 members at Ankara, and Canadian Baptists employ missionaries indirectly in Turkey.

TURKMENISTAN. The Baptist movement in the Asian republic of Turkmenistan is an outgrowth of Russian missionary endeavor, in large part since the downfall of the Soviet Union in 1992. Support for new church development is provided by the Euro-Asian Baptist Federation and the **European Baptist Federation**.

As of 1995, there were three churches with about 100 members in the Baptist community in Turkmenistan. *See also* MIDDLE ASIA.

TURKS AND CAICOS ISLANDS. Baptist missions in these islands began with visits from **Jamaica**, the **Bahamas**, and **Trinidad and Tobago**. The Jamaican Baptist Union sent workers to Turks in 1849 and three historic congregations emerged from that effort. The Southern Baptist **Foreign Mission Board** began work here in 1982 at the invitation of the Jamaica Baptist Union. Also, **fundamentalist**

Baptists from the United States have a small missionary work in the islands.

As of 2006, there were 13 congregations with 3,600 members that form an association historically related to the Jamaica Baptist Union; 2 churches with 300 members called the Spiritual Baptists; and 1 congregation of about 50 members related to the Baptist Bible Fellowship in Turks and Caicos Islands.

– U –

UGANDA. Baptist work in Uganda may be traced to 1956 when Southern Baptists began to plan for a mission in the country. However, before that happened, the **Conservative Baptist** Foreign Mission Society began a mission in Uganda in 1961, with a center at Kampala. **Southern Baptists** officially began work at Kampala, Mbale, and Masindi. In 1970, the Baptist Convention of Uganda was organized; later, during 1982, this became the Baptist Union of Uganda. During the civil unrest and war of 1979 and after, Conservative Baptist and Southern Baptist **missionaries** worked among the refugee communities.

As of 2001, there were 566 churches and 22,000 members affiliated with the Baptist Union of Uganda. A smaller body, the Association of Baptist Churches, relating to Conservative Baptists (U.S.), had 60 congregations with about 5,000 members.

UKRAINE. The Baptist movement in Ukraine was introduced via **J. G. Oncken** about 1869. That year, he participated in the ordination of a Mennonite, which led to the **baptism** of Ivan Riaboshapka (fl. 1870), a blacksmith, in that same year. Baptist life in this region of the Russian Empire was closely allied with **Stundism**, an **evangelical**, pietistic sect. The growth of first Stundist and, later, Baptist congregations was remarkable, beginning with the church at Kosiakovko in 1875. After 1884, when the Russian Baptist Union was formed, steps toward more formal organization of Baptist churches and regional life took place in Ukraine. The Baptist church in the capital city, Kiev, was founded in 1886. At the signing of the Treaty of Brest-

Litovsk in 1918, the Ukrainian congregations adopted a constitution for the All-Ukrainian Union of Baptists and commissioned a periodical. Growth was phenomenal, and by 1921, there were 2,000 churches in Ukraine. In 1922–1925, Ukrainian leaders recognized that they were better served by the Russian Union, and the All-Ukrainian Union of Associations became a department of the Russian Union, with offices in Kharkov. Fourteen territorial units, or raiony, were set up at that time. In 1929, growth was halted as the Russian president, Stalin, closed all of the territorial unions, and the churches participated once again in the Russian Union and, after 1944, in the All-Union Council of Evangelical Christians-Baptists. With the dismantling of the Soviet Union in 1991–1992, and the subsequent reorganization of the All-Union Council of Evangelical Christians-Baptists in 1993, the main body of Baptists in Ukraine reorganized themselves in 1993 as Soyuz Yevangel'skikh Khristiyan-Baptistiv Ukraini (Union of Evangelical Christians-Baptists of Ukraine). The union has published *Baptist Ukrainy* (Ukrainian Baptist) (1918–). In 1992, the **Conservative Baptist** Foreign Mission Society began a mission in Ukraine, focused at Rovno and Donetsk. In 1993, a second group of Baptists in Ukraine emerged from what had been the illegal, unregistered, underground congregations for over two decades, Bratstvo Nzaleznykh Cerkov ta Misiy Evangelskikh Khristian-Baptistiv Ukrainy (Brotherhood of Independent Baptist Churches and Ministries of Ukraine). This group is headquartered at Kiev.

As of 2006, there were 130 churches and 11,150 members affiliated with Bratstvo Nezaleznykh Cerkov ta Misiy Evangelskikh Khristian-Baptistiv Ukrainy, and 2,863 churches with 151,030 members affiliated with the Soyuz Yevangel'skikh Khristiyan-Baptistiv Ukraini. Presently, there is a theological seminary located at Odessa.

UNDERHILL, EDWARD BEAN (1813–1901). English Baptist layman and denominational leader, born at Oxford. Not of robust health, he chose not to study for the **ministry**, received no university education, and entered business for over a decade. His marriage to the daughter of the Oxford University printer gave him the opportunity to observe scholarly publishing and the literature of the Oxford movement. In 1843, he moved to a retreat in Gloucestershire, became a collector of books, and wrote on the defenses of **evangelical** Christianity, also editing the *Baptist Record*. In 1849, Underhill became one of the two principal secretaries of the **Baptist Missionary Society**, his portfolio becoming the foreign fields. Between 1854 and 1857, he toured **India**, Ceylon, and **China**; in 1859, the West Indies; and in 1869, **Cameroon**, the first secretary to visit personally the fields. Underhill was first among historians of British Baptists in the mid-19th century, publishing notes on many original sources and organizing the **Hanserd Knollys** Society in 1845. He served as chair of the **Baptist Union of Great Britain and Ireland** from 1849 to 1876. In 1875, the University of Rochester (U.S.) conferred upon him the LL.D. degree. Through his editorial labors with the Hanserd Knollys Society, Underhill published numerous editions of Baptistiana, including *Struggles and Triumphs of Religious Liberty* (1851) and biographies of James Phillippo (1881), **Alfred Saker** (1884), and John Wenger (1886). His thorough account of *The Tragedy of Morant Bay* (1895) won him much international acclaim, and his *Confessions of Faith and Other Public Documents* (1854) was the first published collection of Baptist historical documents to emerge.

UNDERWOOD, ALFRED CLAIR (1885–1948). English Baptist missionary and historian, born at Leicester, England. He was educated at Oxford and London Universities and was appointed under the **Baptist Missionary Society** in 1911 to teach church history at Serampore College in **India**. In 1920, he returned to England, where he became president of Rawdon College and taught church history there. He retired from the principalship of Rawdon in 1940. Underwood wrote a history of Serampore College, but is best known for his *History of the English Baptists* (1947). His lesser-known works include *Conversion: Christian and Non-Christian, A Comparative and Psychological Study* (1925), and *Shintoism: The Indigenous Religion of Japan* (1934).

UNION BAPTISTS. *See* BAPTIST UNION OF GREAT BRITAIN AND IRELAND.

UNION BAUTISTA LATINA AMERICA (UBLA)/BAPTIST UNION OF LATIN AMERICA. Union formed in 1976 as part of the regional development within the **Baptist World Alliance** (BWA).

The Union Bautista Latina America (Baptist Union of Latin America) was created by the major Baptist conventions/unions of South and Central America. A structural reorganization took place in 1982. The purpose of the UBLA is to promote cooperation within the affiliated organizations for **mission**, education, and **evangelism** in the region, and to advance the purposes of the BWA. An executive secretary administers the programs of UBLA and a board of directors sets policy. The UBLA holds an assembly every three years.

UNITED ARAB EMIRATES (U.A.E.). Baptist presence in this nation is small. As a result of **religious liberty** policies and the large numbers of expatriates and immigrant workers living in the U.A.E., Baptist witness has been conducted indirectly since 1993. Currently, there are pastoral appointments serving in international congregations, which include Filipinos and Indian workers.

UNIVERSALISM, AMONG BAPTISTS. Universalism, or the belief in universal salvation for all people as the "elect," in contrast with the traditional Calvinistic position that only a few whom God ordains will be "elected," became a contentious issue problem for Baptists on both sides of the Atlantic at the turn of the 19th century. In the United States, Universalism, as well as Unitarianism, was a noticeable position among **liberal** clergy in the Congregationalist churches, especially in eastern Massachusetts in reaction to the excesses of the **Great Awakening**. In 1770, John Murray (1741–1815), an English preacher, arrived in New Jersey and began circulating Universalist teachings. Within 20 years, a significant number of congregations in New England adopted Universalist theology and a national convention was held in Philadelphia in 1790. The most prominent Baptist to join the movement was **Elhanan Winchester**, who announced his profession to universal restoration and caused an uproar in the **Philadelphia Baptist Association** and his church, First Baptist of Philadelphia. Winchester developed a Universalist "**confession of faith**," which involved a belief in the revelation of the **Bible**, the certainty of eventual salvation, and a moral imperative for good works. This became a standard for the development of Universalism in England and the United States. Universalist thought proceeded in two basic directions: ultra-Universalism, which rejected all future punishment (as advocated by Hosea Ballou), and restorationism, which held that limited punishment was part of the divine plan (as taught by **William Vidler**).

Generally, Universalism was considered theologically **conservative** in contrast with Unitarianism, in that it acknowledged the authority of the Bible and the centrality of Jesus and his atonement. Universalist thinking was productive of schism among Baptists: William Vidler's announcement of Universalist theology split his congregation at Battle and signaled the virtual collapse of the **General Baptist** movement in England, and Winchester's action sorely divided the most prestigious Baptist congregation in Philadelphia and drove the intellectual classes away from the Baptist movement. While the Universalist position among Baptists waned by the 1830s, from time to time **evangelicals** have called attention to Universalist tendencies in certain clergy, which is usually a sign of unacceptable liberal or heterodox thinking.

UPHAM, EDWARD (1710–1797). American Baptist minister, born at Malden, Massachusetts. He graduated from Harvard College, one of the best educated Baptist clergymen of his era. In 1738, he was called to be **pastor** at the Baptist Church in West Springfield, Massachusetts, which he served for 10 years. In 1748, he moved to the Baptist Church at Newport, Rhode Island, where he served until 1771. Upham's relocation to Newport was problematic, because his congregation at West Springfield refused to grant him a letter of dismission, and he was never **ordained** or, rather, installed formally in Newport. In 1764, he was an advocate of the founding of the College of Rhode Island and served as one of its first trustees. When a vote on the relocation of the college was taken in 1770, Upham voted in favor of the Providence site, and this stirred great opposition against him from organized labor in Newport. He was forced to resign, and he returned to West Springfield, where for the next 20 years he led a campaign against the religious taxation of his members. Upham was theologically **Arminian**, in contrast with the prevailing Calvinism of his contemporaries, and he was often classed as an Old Light opponent of the **Great Awakening**. **Isaac Backus** considered Upham's doctrine of grace to be "unclear."

UPLAND BAPTISTS. A term used in early 19th-century Canadian Maritime Baptist life to designate those church members who professed to be convinced of the duty of believer's **baptism**, without actually ever being baptized. They practiced mixed communion with tolerant immersed believers, the latter expecting an eventual spiritual change toward believer's baptism. Many of the baptized persons were so fully convinced of the propriety of mixed communion over strict enforcement of believer's baptism that they appeared to sanction the neglect of Upland Baptists by admitting them to the same church privileges they enjoyed. Eventually, those advocating closed communion won the debate over church membership privileges and **associational** membership so that the Upland Baptists disappeared by 1800. The term "Upland" referred to their location inland from the sea.

URUGUAY. In 1911, Argentine Baptists began mission work in Uruguay as part of the Mision Bautista del Rio Plata. Jaime and Lemuel Quarles opened a church at Montevideo in 1911. The Convención Bautista del Uruguay was organized in 1948, and in 1954, the Uruguayan Mission was separated from the Argentine work. A seminary, El Instituto Teologico Bautista, was opened at Montevideo in 1955. The **Baptist Bible Fellowship** commenced a **mission** in 1958, and more recently, in 1990, the **Association of Baptists for World Evangelism** began a mission in Uruguay. In 1995, the **Conservative Baptist** Foreign Mission Society began a mission in Uruguay.

As of 2006, there were 133 churches and 5,700 members affiliated with the Convención Bautista del Uruguay.

UZBEKISTAN. *See* MIDDLE ASIA.

– V –

VALDER, HANS (1813–1899). Norwegian and American Baptist **pastor** and **missionary**, born at Ryfylke, **Norway**. Early in his life, Valder was a schoolteacher and farmer. He emigrated to the United States in 1837 and helped to organize Norwegian settlements in

Illinois. He converted from his Lutheran faith to that of a Baptist persuasion about 1841. In August 1844, Valder became the first ordained Norwegian Baptist in the world. Four years later, he became the first Scandinavian missionary of the **American Baptist Home Mission Society**, a role he held for two years. Valder became active in other **voluntary** associations and moved to Minnesota, where he entered politics and eventually became a Methodist.

VARDAMAN, JEREMIAH (1775–1842). American Baptist minister and evangelist, born in Wythe County, Virginia. Lacking any formal education, Vardaman was a rugged frontiersman and traveled widely in the West, moving to Kentucky in 1779. His faith was quickened in 1792 under the **ministry** of a blind **evangelist**, Thomas Hansford, and Vardaman entered the full-time ministry himself. He served churches at Cedar Creek (1802–1810) and David's Fork (1810–1830), Kentucky, and organized other later leading congregations at Bardstown, Lexington, and Louisville, and at Nashville, Tennessee. He was the pioneer preacher in Missouri and helped to organize the Missouri Baptist Convention. It is believed Vardaman was instrumental in converting over 8,000 persons to the Christian faith.

VASSAR, MATTHEW (1792–1868). American Baptist industrialist and philanthropist, born at East Tuddingham, County of Norfolk, England. Emigrating to the United States in 1796, Vassar later worked in the business of his father and also at a tannery in Newburgh, New York. In 1810, he returned to his father's brewery and ultimately assumed control of it, rebuilding after a fire, at Poughkeepsie, New York. Milo P. Jewett (1808–1882), a well-known educator, persuaded Vassar to endow a college for **women**, and this he did in 1861. Vassar College was influenced also by the thought of Martin Brewer Anderson (1815–1890), president of the Baptist-related University of Rochester. Although the college was listed among the Baptist-related schools for a time, Vassar was categorically opposed to any formal religious affiliation or doctrinal test, and it became essentially a nonsectarian, high-caliber women's college. Mr. Vassar's religious beliefs are detailed in *The Autobiography and Letters of Matthew Vassar*, edited by Elizabeth Haight (1916).

VEDDER, HENRY CLAY (1853–1935). American Baptist minister and historian, born at DeRuyter, New York. He was educated at the University of Rochester (B.A., M.A.) and Rochester Theological Seminary. Following seminary, he joined the staff of the *Examiner* in New York, which ultimately he edited, along with the *Baptist Quarterly Review* (1885–1892). In 1894, he went to Crozer Theological Seminary, where he served as church history professor until 1926. Vedder began his career as a **conservative** thinker, but after about 1910, he advocated a "new" church history, by which he meant a greater appreciation for socialism, evolution, and pragmatism. Vedder desired a modification of Christianity to address the excesses of capitalism, and like those in the **Chicago School**, he embraced the theory of evolution as a tool for better understanding the Christian faith. He grew to become one of the chief targets for those in the early **fundamentalist** movement, publishing *The Fundamentals of Christianity* (1922). His historical works were groundbreaking and included *A History of Baptists in the Middle States* (1898), *Balthasar Hubmaier: The Leader of the Anabaptists* (1905), *A Short History of the Baptists* (1907), and *A Short History of Baptist Missions* (1927).

VENEZUELA. In 1925, the first Baptist missionaries entered Venezuela under the sponsorship of **Baptist Mid-Missions**; they established a mission at El Collao in 1927, with later stations at Tucupita, San Felix, and El Palmar. Following initial exploration in 1945 by **Southern Baptists** in Colombia, Julio Moros, who had begun a church at Barranquilla, started a congregation in Caracas in 1946. Three years later, several of the early congregations affiliated with the Convención Colombo-Venezol, and in 1951, a separate Convención Bautista Nacional was formed. The **Baptist Bible Fellowship** opened a **mission** in Venezuela in 1966, and the **Conservative Baptist** Foreign Mission Society began its mission in the country in 1986, centered in Caracas. In 1956, the Instituto Teológico opened at Los Teques.

As of 2006, there were 430 churches and 53,000 members affiliated with the Convención Bautista Nacional de Venezuela. The Convención Bautista publishes *Luminar Bautista* (*Baptist Light*) (1952–).

VICK, GEORGE BEAUCHAMP (1901–1975). American Indepen-
dent Baptist minister and educator, born at Russellville, Kentucky.
With no formal education, Vick worked on the Louisville and
Nashville Railroad (1918–1920) and later the Fort Worth and Denver
Railroad (1920–1924). While in Ft. Worth, he joined First Baptist
Church and became interested in Sunday School **ministry** with
J. Frank Norris. Beginning in 1932, he served Norris for six years
and then went to work for Wade House as a song leader in his **revivals**. Later in this period, Vick worked for other traveling **evangel-
ists**, including **Mordecai Ham**. In 1936, he again joined Norris as associate **pastor** in the Temple Baptist Church in Detroit, Michigan.
Later as co-pastor in Detroit, he led in building a large congregation,
averaging over 3,000 in **Sunday School**. In 1948, Norris invited Vick
to become president of the Fundamental Bible Baptist Seminary in
Texas, a school under Norris's control. At length, Vick and Norris disagreed on administrative matters in 1950, and Vick separated from
Norris's church and educational institutions and formed a movement
with other sympathetic pastors, the **Baptist Bible Fellowship**. He
was the founder of the Baptist Bible College in Springfield, Missouri
(1950–1975) and an ardent advocate of Baptist **fundamentalism**. A
sample of Vick's writing is found in *Soul-Winning Sermons* (1958).

VIDLER, WILLIAM (1758–1816). English Baptist and, later, Unitarian minister, born at Battle, England. Apprenticed as a bricklayer, he
was raised in the Church of England but became an Independent.
About 1816, he began to preach and joined the Baptists under
Thomas Purdy at Rye. In 1780, he was baptized and ordained and
started a congregation at Battle. To secure funds for a building, he
traveled among the Baptists and other dissenters in 1791 and was
drawn to **Arminian** Baptists and Universalists. Under the influence
of Richard Wright (1764–1836), a Unitarian preacher, Vidler professed **Universalism** in 1792 and this split his church at Battle; he
joined the recently emigrated American Universalist, **Elhanan Winchester**, at Artillery Lane in London in 1794 as an associate pastor
and when Winchester returned to the United States, Vidler served
both the London Church and his congregation at Battle 1794–1796.
From 1796 to 1815 he served at Parliament Court as well as managing a bookseller's shop and publishing a periodical, *The Universal*

Theological Magazine. In 1801, Vidler was admitted to the **General Baptist** Assembly, an action that offended the **evangelical** General Baptists and prompted the withdrawal of **Dan Taylor**. The next year, Vidler announced his transition to Unitarianism and he became active in the broader organization of English Unitarianism, serving the Unitarian Fund and writing numerous tracts in defense of his position. He wrote a biography of Elhanan Winchester and, in a series of letters to **Andrew Fuller** in 1803, he defended universal restoration. Vidler's theological perspective is found in *God's Love to His Creatures Asserted and Vindicated* (1799) and *Letters to Mr. Fuller on the Universal Restoration* (1803).

VIETNAM. Baptist witness in Vietnam was late in commencement and followed American military presence. Southern Baptists began missionary work in Saigon in 1959, the first missionary being Herman Hayes (1928–1997). **Hong Kong** Baptists also sponsored a **mission** among the Chinese, beginning in 1968. The **Baptist Bible Fellowship** opened a mission in Vietnam in 1971.

As of 2001, there were 50 congregations with about 7,000 members related to the Viet Nam Baptist Church, which has been affiliated with the **Southern Baptist Convention** since 1954.

VINS, GEORGY PETROVICH (1928–1998). Russian Baptist minister and leader, born in Siberia of American **missionary** parents. He moved to Kiev at an early age and was trained as an engineer. In Kiev, Vins became involved in the Baptist movement, ultimately the **pastor** of a congregation. During the religious persecution of Christians under Soviet Premier Nikita Khrushchev, Vins founded a breakaway congregation and met in a forest outside Kiev. In 1965, he became general secretary of a council of churches and openly opposed government suppression of religion. He was tried and sentenced to three years in prison, and after similar events in 1974, he was again sentenced to a labor camp for five years and then internal exile. The world rallied to Vins' plight, including the World Council of Churches, prominent Baptists, and Andrei Sakharov. With the urging of U.S. president **James Carter**, in 1979 Vins was involved in a secret prisoner exchange that brought him and eventually his family to the United States. In 1990, Soviet president Mikhail Gorbachov lifted the ban on Vins, and he was able to return to **Russia** to preach and travel. Vins' career was often played out in contrast to the registered Baptist movement in Russia, which Vins thought was infiltrated by Communists.

VOLUNTARISM. Term applied to the impulse among Christian individuals to engage in benevolent works and belong to various sorts of **associations** of a **missionary** or service character. In the Old and New Testaments, there is abundant evidence of the voluntary impulse, for instance, in the offerings brought before the Lord (Exod. 35:4–29) and in the way early disciples followed Jesus (Luke 5:1–11). The gospel itself has been interpreted as an invitation that calls forth a voluntary response. In the early church, various acts of charity characterized the Christian movement; during the medieval period, associations, orders, and itinerants went about conducting charitable and reforming ministries and missions.

It was during the Reformation that Protestant groups engaged in renewal movements, which, though originally voluntary, became denominations. The Pietists, followed by Puritans and Anglicans, formed prayer groups, missions, funds, publishing concerns, and academies on the basis of voluntary associations. Thomas Chalmers (1780–1847), a Presbyterian leader of the Free Church movement in Scotland, advocated a voluntary system of Christian and humanitarian works. **Valentine Wightman**, a colonial American Baptist, made a case for the New Testament basis for a voluntary support of the **ministry**, which did much to establish the principle in New England. The later half of the 18th century saw English Baptists leading the voluntarist movement in forming associations for missions, **education**, and care of persons with special needs. During the 19th century, the **evangelical** movement in the United States, Great Britain, and Western Europe forged most of its missionary work as voluntary associations. Entire segments of the Baptist denomination were constructed as voluntary associations, later to be restructured in bureaucratic patterns. The "society" model was especially popular among American Baptists and British Union Baptists. More recently, **black Baptists** in the United States have followed a voluntary organizational pattern, as witnessed not only in their ecclesiastical bodies but also in their reform associations, such as the Montgomery Improvement Association and the Southern Christian Leadership Conference. **E. Y. Mullins**, a professor at Southern Baptist Seminary, made a significant contribution to the development of voluntarist thought among Baptists in the 20th century, with his advocacy of soul competency and the principle of the autonomy of local churches.

Voluntary organizations are usually characterized by volunteer personnel, support through voluntary donations, and democratic decision making. Such associations have become a leading characteristic of American religious tradition, regardless of denomination. *See also* ASSOCIATIONS, BAPTIST.

VOSE, GODFREY NOEL (1921–). Australian Baptist minister and theological educator, born at Perth, Western **Australia**. Early in his career, Vose worked for the Commonwealth of Australia and served in the Air Force during World War II. He was educated at the University of Western Australia (B.A., B.Ed.); the Baptist Theological College of New South Wales, which resulted in a licentiate from Melbourne College of Divinity; and later at Northern Baptist Theological Seminary in Chicago, Illinois (Th.M.). Ultimately, he earned a Ph.D. in religion at the University of Iowa. Vose was **pastor** at East Freemantle Baptist Church (1951–1956), Garfield Park, Chicago (1959–1960), and Downey, Iowa (1960–1963). From 1963 to his retirement in 1991, Vose devoted his energies to founding and administering the Baptist Theological College of Western Australia. In that role, he rose to prominence nationally as president of the Baptist Union of Australia (1975–1978) and internationally as chair of the Study and Research Division of the **Baptist World Alliance** BWA) (1980–1985) and president of the BWA from 1985 to 1990. Within Baptist circles, Vose was an advocate of research and scholarship, and he encouraged a number of younger scholars to be involved in the world family of Baptists. He has served as a board member of **ecumenical** and evangelical organizations like the United Bible Societies and Scripture Union. Among his publications are *The Authority and Relevance of the Bible in the Modern World* (1983) and *A Glimpse of Baptist Roots* (1985). Since 1993, Vose has served as pastor of Parkerville Baptist Church, a congregation he helped to start. In 2008, the Baptist Theological College of Western Australia was renamed Vose Theological College in honor of its founder.

– W –

WALES. Baptist preaching in Wales was conducted by individuals early in the 17th century, the first churches possibly established in the Olchon Valley in 1633. Yet other evidence suggests that early Baptist work was established at Llanfaches in 1639, at Llan-hir in 1646, and among soldiers in Cromwell's army preaching in Radnorshire and Breconshire in 1646–1648. Under the Act of 1650 for the Better Propagation of the Gospel, the first Baptist preachers of clear record entered Wales on preaching **missions**; they included **Vavasor Powell**, **John Myles**, Jenkin Jones, Thomas Evans, and William Thomas. The influence of John Myles was primary in creating Calvinistic, closed-communion congregations. Myles was also instrumental in forming the first association among the churches he helped to found.

Welsh Baptists followed the English example of **voluntary** associations for mission and education, and cooperated with the English **Baptist Missionary Society**. English-speaking **associations** of Welsh Baptist churches were formed in Monmouthshire (1857), Glamorgan (1860), and Carmarthenshire (1860), and an English Union in North Wales was established in 1879, which eventually affiliated with the Lancashire and Cheshire Association in 1912. Most of the English-language congregations also associated with the Welsh Baptist Union since 1866. Many of the congregations have belonged jointly to the Welsh Union and the **Baptist Union of Great Britain and Ireland**, though relations between the two bodies have not always been smooth. One of the characteristic features of Welsh Baptist life was the **Nonconformist** chapels built of fieldstone and simple interiors, notably at Rhydwilym (1701) and Hengoed (1710). Separate efforts in launching a home mission to plant Welsh-speaking congregations date to the early years of the 19th century among the associations; formally, a Home Mission Society was established by the Welsh Baptist Union in 1895, only to suffer poor funding and foreclosure by 1914.

As of 2006, the Undeb Bedyddwyr Cymru included 447 churches and 15,871 members. The periodical, *Seren Cymru* (*Star of Wales*), has been published since 1866, and there are currently two theological colleges, one at Cardiff, the other at Bangor (see **Theological Ed-**

ucation). The **Baptist Bible Fellowship** opened a mission in Wales in 1982.

WALLER, JOHN (1741–1802). **Southern Baptist** preacher, born in Spotsylvania County, Virginia. Originally planning a career in the law, Waller unsuccessfully tried several vocations. In 1767, he was converted by the testimony of a Baptist minister, Lewis Craig, and Waller became a traveling **evangelist**. He was frequently imprisoned—once for a month and a half—and wrote denouncing his treatment. Called "fighting Jack Waller," he was a powerful advocate for **religious liberty** in Virginia, yet an erratic preacher among the Baptists. In the 1780s, Waller adopted **Arminian** theology and a Wesleyan polity, which caused other Baptists to avoid contact with him. He became a self-proclaimed Independent Baptist for a time, until returning to Calvinistic views. His evangelistic **ministry** produced 2,000 converts, and he constituted 18 churches, mostly in the tidewater region.

WALLIN, BENJAMIN (1711–1782). English Baptist minister, born at Southwark, London. The son of Edward Wallin (1678–1733), a Baptist minister, Benjamin was crippled from birth. He was educated by a mentor, John Needham (d. 1743), the Baptist **pastor** at Hitchin, Hertfordshire. Wallin became the pastor at Maze Pond Baptist Church, a 1691 break-off congregation from Horsely-down Church on the matter of not allowing singing in worship. He remained in this church for 27 years, one of the longest tenures in the century. One of Wallin's distinctives was that he may have enjoyed the longest **ordination** service ever conducted among English Baptists—four hours and 15 minutes—in 1741. **John Gill** presided over the service, which involved 16 ministers. Wallin was both a scholarly and a devotional writer, among the leading hymnist-poets of the era. Among his published works are *The Folly of Neglecting Divine Institutions* (1758), *Lectures on Primitive Christianity* (1768), and *Scripture-Doctrine of Christ's Sonship* (1771).

WARD, JOHN (1679–1758). English Baptist layman and educator, born in London. Ward served in the Navy Office and then as a schoolmaster.

In 1720, he became a professor of rhetoric at Gresham College, where he taught for the remainder of his career. An officer in the Royal Society, he was a founding trustee of the British Museum. Ward published several books and was awarded an honorary doctorate by the University of Edinburgh. He designed the fireworks display in 1748 to celebrate the Peace of Aix-la-Chapelle.

WARD, WILLIAM (1769–1823). English Baptist missionary, born at Derby. He served an apprenticeship as a printer and for a time was a newspaper editor. In 1796, Ward was converted and joined the Baptist church at Hull. Hearing of the **Baptist Missionary Society**'s interest in a printer, he offered himself for service in **India**. He published a major work on the Hindus and became a valued companion in the "Serampore Trio" with **William Carey** and **Joshua Ward**. Ward was the first missionary to return from the East, and he visited Holland and the United States, raising money for Serampore College, 1819–1821. He returned to India where he died. Ward's published works include *Farewell Letters to a Few Friends in Britain and America on Returning to Bengal in 1821* (1821) and *Brief Memoir of Krishna-Pal, the First Hindoo in Bengal Who Broke the Chain of Caste by Embracing the Gospel* (1822).

WASHINGTON, BOOKER TALIAFERRO (1856–1915). American **black Baptist** leader and educator, born a slave on James Burroughs's plantation in Hale's Ford, Virginia. He was called "Booker" because of his studious habits. He studied at Hampton, Virginia, and later at Wayland Seminary in Washington, D.C. In his early career, Washington pursued several trades, including masonry and teaching. In 1881, he was selected to head up a new Negro Normal School at Tuskeegee, Alabama, which evolved into Tuskeegee Institute. Upon the death of Frederick Douglass (1817–1893), Washington became the preeminent black leader of the era, until the rise of the National Association for the Advancement of Colored People. He favored education and training as a means to improve the social status of blacks, a position that W. E. B. Dubois (1868–1963) and others criticized because it denied the Negro of inherent civil rights. He was influenced early in his life by Baptists and was educated in a Baptist school, though his theology was said to be much inclined toward Unitarianism. He was one of the most honored persons of his era, receiving a degree from Harvard in 1891. Washington is the author of *Up from Slavery* (1901) and *The Story of the Negro* (1909).

WAYLAND, FRANCIS (1796–1865). American Baptist minister and educator, born in New York City. Wayland graduated from Union College (Albany, New York), then studied medicine, and finally turned to theological studies at Andover Theological Seminary. His first pastorate was First Baptist, Boston, which he served in 1821–1826 with some difficulty in pastoral work. He turned to teaching at Union College and after one year was elected president of Brown University. Wayland also taught moral philosophy at Brown and authored a popular textbook of the era. An influential denominational leader, Wayland reshaped American Baptist **polity** along the lines of **voluntary** societies rather than a strong national **convention**. President of the **General Missionary Convention** and chair of the **Baptist Board of Foreign Missions**, Wayland was the most visible leader of Baptists in the North. During the 1840s, he engaged in a series of debates on the subject of **slavery** with **Richard Fuller** of South Carolina; Wayland took the position that modern Christians must take a moral stand even on those issues that **Christ** recognized but did not change. In the U.S. presidential campaign of 1860, Wayland was a prominent New England supporter of Abraham Lincoln (1809–1865). He was one of the most widely published writers of his era, with his works including *The Elements of Moral Science* (1835), *The Elements of Political Economy* (1837), *Domestic Slavery Considered as a Scriptural Institution* (1845), *The Memoir of the Life and Labors of Adoniram Judson* (1853), *The Elements of Intellectual Philosophy* (1854), and *Notes on the Principles and Practices of Baptist Churches* (1827). His sermon, "The Moral Dignity of the Missionary Enterprise" (1823), became a definitive tract in the American **evangelical** tradition. *See also* VOLUNTARISM.

WEBB, MARY (1779–1861). American Baptist missionary organizer, born at Boston, Massachusetts. From childhood she suffered from a crippling disease and was confined to a wheelchair. Influenced by her **pastor, Thomas Baldwin** at Second Baptist Church in Boston, she took an interest in **missions**. In 1800, Webb organized what became the first woman's missionary society in the United States, the Boston Female Society for Missionary Purposes. Originally an inter-denominational society, Webb's organization was based on the Massachusetts Baptist Missionary Society, which her pastor helped to found. In time, the society became exclusively Baptist and was a model for each state. Webb guided the Boston Female Society into not only support of overseas missions but also direct involvement in work with widows, children, and Jewish persons.

WELCH, JAMES ELY (1789–1876). American Baptist missionary, born near Lexington, Kentucky. As a frontiersman, he lacked formal education, except study with **William Staughton** at his school in Philadelphia. Welch was appointed as one of the first domestic **missionaries** of the **Baptist Board of Foreign Missions** in 1817 to work with the Indian tribes in the Mississippi Valley. En route to their field at St. Louis, Welch and his wife organized a number of local missionary societies in the Ohio Valley. He started the first Baptist Church in St. Louis and a school, which became a model for later development. When his appointment with the Baptist Board expired, he worked for the American **Sunday School** Union. It was Welch's influence that caused the Baptists to conduct their Indian missions on or near tribal lands rather than in white settlements.

WELCOMING AND AFFIRMING BAPTISTS, ASSOCIATION OF. With changing attitudes toward various aspects of human sexuality, scattered Baptists in the gay, lesbian, and bisexual communities in the United States began in the 1980s to express their **sexuality** as church members and some as ordained clergy. This was initially met with strong antagonism, mostly from the **evangelical** community, and distress among the leadership of the **American Baptist** regional and national organizations. The issue of homosexuality exploded in the American Baptist community in 1991 at the Charleston, West Virginia, Biennial Meeting, where American Baptists Concerned (a support group for gays and lesbians) attempted to display its materials at the national gathering. Stiff opposition to their presence emerged and a Statement of Concern was adopted at that Biennial Meeting repudiating homosexual lifestyle, marriage, or **ordination** and the establishment of gay churches or caucusses. The next formal step was taken at the American Baptist General Board Meeting in the fall of 1992, when that body voted "to affirm that the practice of homosexuality is incompatible with Christian teaching." A second resolution called for dialogue on issues of sexuality and acknowledged that there is a variety of understandings throughout the denomination about homosexuality; a plea was also issued to respect the individual integrity of persons within the denomination as the issue of homosexuality was engaged.

At the Biennial Meeting in Charleston, a group of **pastors** agreed to form an association and in 1993 the Association of Welcoming and Affirming Baptists was formed to offer support for gay and lesbian people's membership and to provide a forum for better understanding of matters from sexuality to **disfellowshipping** churches in the denomination. As pastors and churches have announced their intention to join the association, national gatherings have been held and a newsletter, the *Inspiriter* (1996–), has begun publication.

As of 2007, 69 congregations were affiliated with the Association of Welcoming and Affirming Baptists.

WEST VIRGINIA FUNDAMENTAL BAPTIST MISSION. Among the hundreds of Baptist congregations in the state of West Virginia, many were sympathetic to the **fundamentalist** movement in the 1920s and 1930s. At Charleston, West Virginia, in January 1944, the West Virginia Fundamental Baptist Mission was founded for the purpose of organizing Baptist churches and supporting feeble congregations. The mission was guided by the principles of local church autonomy and self-support of **missions**. In May 1950, the West Virginia Fundamental Baptist Mission merged its programs into the **Fellowship of Baptists for Home Missions**.

WESTERN BAPTIST MISSION. Pastors of the California State Association of Regular Baptists formed in 1942 the Pacific Home Mission of Regular Baptists, later known as the Western Baptist Mission. The objects of the domestic **mission** were to hold **Bible** conferences and **evangelistic** meetings, and also to assist needy churches in their building programs. The region of interest was the far western United States. In November 1949, the Western Baptist Mission merged its efforts with the **Fellowship of Baptists for Home Missions**.

WESTON, HENRY GRIGGS (1820–1909). American Baptist minister and educator, born at Lynn, Massachusetts. He was educated at Brown University and Newton Theological School. Owing to poor health, he traveled to the west and served as a missionary **pastor** in Washington, Illinois, accepting the church at Peoria in 1846. In 1859, Weston became pastor of Oliver Street Baptist Church, New York City, where he served for nine years. In 1868, he was named president of Crozer Theological Seminary in Upland, Pennsylvania, where he served for 40 years, the longest tenure of an American Baptist seminary administrator. Weston built Crozer into a premier theological faculty and library, strongly related to the **Philadelphia Baptist Association** community. In scholarly terms, Weston specialized in the interpretation of the Gospels and was a widely regarded teacher of the **Bible**. He was a close friend of Dwight L. Moody (1837–1899) and served as an associate editor of the first edition of the Scofield Reference Bible, published in 1909. Weston was president of the **American Baptist Missionary Union** in 1872–1873 and editor of the *Baptist Quarterly* from 1869 to 1877. With **Augustus Hopkins Strong** at Rochester and **Alvah Hovey** at Newton, Weston was part of an educational triumvirate that built an outstanding network of theological schools for the Baptist community in the northern United States. Among Weston's published works were *Outline of Ecclesiology* (1895) and *Matthew: The Genesis of the New Testament: Its Purpose, Character, and Method* (1900).

WHITE, BARRINGTON RAYMOND (1934–). English Baptist minister and historian, born in the County of Kent. He graduated with an honors degree in **theology** from Queens College, Cambridge, and completed the D.Phil. at Regent's Park, College, Oxford, under Norman Sykes, Geoffrey Nuttall, and Ernest Payne. Ordained a minister in the **Baptist Union**, he served Andover Baptist Church 1959–1963, after which he became tutor in ecclesiastical history at Regent's Park and in 1972, the 12th principal of the college. Under his direction, the college established itself as a leading center of Baptist graduate scholarship. He also taught as an adjunct lecturer at Southern and Southeastern Baptist Seminaries in the United States. White retired in 1999 for health reasons and since has been a Senior Research Fellow in Ecclesiastical History. White was president of the Baptist Historical Society from 1981 to 1993. He mentored a number of significant research degree students, including R. T. Kendall, Stephen Brachlow, Karen Smith, Richard Land, and Ken R. Manley. White's own 1961 doctoral dissertation, published as *The English Separatist Tradition: From the Marian Martyrs to the Pilgrim Fathers* (1971), was groundbreaking in that it largely dispelled any direct connection between Baptists and Anabaptists and established the origins of English Baptists in the **Puritan-Separatist tradition** of English dissent. His other major publication is *The English Baptists of the Seventeenth Century* (1983, 1996).

WHITE, CHARLOTTE HAZEN ATLEE (fl. 1815–1830). American and English Baptist missionary, born in Pennsylvania. Following the organization of the Baptist **General Missionary Convention** in 1814, the **Baptist Board of Foreign Missions** (BBFM) appointed a printer to assist the **Judsons** in **Burma**. Mrs. Charlotte White, a widow, volunteered her services and her personal property to go to Burma to care for the women and children. Against stiff pressure within the BBFM and a restrictive definition of "**missionary**," the BBFM appointed her the first Baptist **woman missionary** from the United States. She arrived in **India** in 1816; met and married a widower named Joshua Rowe (1781–1823), who was under the appointment of the British **Baptist Missionary Society**; and transferred to that society. As a missionary spouse, Mrs. Rowe conducted work among Indian women at Digah and planned to start a system of schools. She also published a Hindustani spelling book for children. When Joshua died in 1823, however, Charlotte returned to the United States and taught English, music, and drawing in an academy in Loundesboro, Alabama.

WHITLEY, WILLIAM THEOPHILUS (1861–1947). English and Australian Baptist minister and historian, born at Islington, London. He was educated at King's College, Cambridge, taking degrees in the arts and law. Later he graduated from Rawdon College and served a church at Bridlington in 1888–1891. In 1891, Whitley left for **Australia**, where he became the first principal of Baptist College of Victoria in Melbourne. He earned a doctor of laws degree at Melbourne University and became a lecturer at Queen's College, University of

Melbourne. In 1902, he returned to England and served congregations at Fishergate, Preston (1902–1917), and Droitwich (1917–1928). His literary contributions to Baptist historiography were enormous, producing editions of the *Works of John Smyth* and the *Minutes of the General Assembly of General Baptists*, and editing the *Transactions of the Baptist Historical Society*. He was a founder of the Baptist Historical Society in 1908. One of Whitley's most important theses was the linkage between the New Model Army and the establishment of the first Baptist **associations**. The Baptist Theological College of Victoria in Melbourne was renamed Whitley College in 1965 in his honor.

WHITSETT, WILLIAM HETH (1841–1911). Southern Baptist minister and educator, born at Nashville, Tennessee. He was educated at Union University and served in the Confederate army before pastoral **ministry** at Mill Creek, Tennessee, and Albany, Georgia. In 1872, he became professor of ecclesiastical history at Southern Baptist Theological Seminary, distinguishing himself as a writer and researcher. Whitsett wrote in 1895 that he believed Baptists borrowed the practice of believer's **baptism** from the Dutch **Anabaptists**, and he questioned the **Landmarkist** and **successionist** positions that there was an unbroken line of Baptists from the New Testament. This controversy cost him the presidency of the seminary, from which he had to resign in 1899. Thereafter, he taught at Richmond College and helped lead a successful drive to establish the **Baptist World Alliance**. He also believed in the universal church and helped establish the notion that early Baptists were part of a larger movement of English religious life. Among Whitsett's published works are *Origins of the Disciples of Christ* (1887), *A Question in Baptist History: Whether the Anabaptists in England Practised Immersion before the Year 1641?* (1896), and *Sidney Rigdon, Real Founder of Mormonism* (1918).

WIBERG, ANDERS (1816–1887). Swedish and American Baptist minister, born in Helsingland, **Sweden**. He was educated at the University of Uppsala and served for six years as a Lutheran **pastor**. He met **Julius Köbner** and **J. G. Oncken** and was drawn to the Baptist position. In 1852, he traveled to the United States to visit his exiled countryman, **F. O. Nilson**, who baptized him. Wiberg remained in the Midwest during 1853 as an itinerant minister in Iowa and Illinois. For two years in Philadelphia, he wrote tracts on Baptist doctrine for the **American Baptist Publication Society** (ABPS). Returning to Sweden in 1855, he began an extensive work of church planting, **evangelism**, and **education** in conjunction with the Brothers **Palmquist** (**Gustaf**, Johannes, Per). Under this central administration, Wiberg superintended the growth of the **Baptist Union** to 125 churches by 1861. During this period, Wiberg also served as a missionary of the ABPS and fostered the establishment of Betelseminariat, the first Swedish Baptist theological school. Wiberg's published work includes a classic study of **baptism**, *Christian Baptism Set Forth in the Words of the Bible* (1880?).

WIGHTMAN, VALENTINE (1681–1747). American Baptist minister, born at North Kingston, Rhode Island. Descendant of a line of Baptists who went back to the early 17th century, Wightman was ordained at North Kingston in the tradition of the **General** Six Principle **Baptists**. In 1705, he began preaching at Groton, Connecticut, and moved there two years later, without permission of the town selectmen. This move caused a stir and eventuated in a celebrated legal proceeding and fines levied upon Wightman. After several appeals, Wightman paid the fines and was admitted to the town, thus establishing the first permanent Baptist congregation in the colony of Connecticut. Wightman served the Groton church until 1747 and was instrumental in starting churches in Waterford and Wallingford and in New York City.

Wightman continued to be a leader among the New England Baptists. In 1727, he participated in a debate with John Bulkley on matters ranging from the proper subjects of **baptism** to an exposition of **voluntarism** in the support of ministers. He was frequently involved in **ordination** proceedings, notably of Nicholas Eyres (1691–1759) in 1724 and Ephraim Bound (c. 1719–1765) in 1743. He contended for hymn singing in worship services and for the **laying on of hands** according to Six Principle practices. As the **Great Awakening** gained momentum in the 1740s, Wightman was a leader among **New Light Baptists**, along with **Ebenezer Moulton** and Thomas Green (1699–1773).

WILLIAMS, GEORGE WASHINGTON (1849–1891). American **black Baptist** minister and political leader, born at Bedford Springs, Pennsylvania. During the Civil War, he enlisted in the Massachusetts Regiment and served along the Texas-**Mexico** frontier with distinction. He was denied a promotion to the regular army because of color. Following military service, Williams entered Howard University in Washington, D.C., and also became its groundskeeper. He then graduated from Newton Theological Institution and was ordained to the Baptist **ministry**. He served 12th Street Baptist Church in Boston (1875) and Union Baptist Church, Cincinnati, Ohio (1875–1879), before entering politics. President Rutherford B. Hayes (1822–1893) appointed Williams a commissioner of internal revenue, and Williams eventually won a seat in the Ohio legislature, 1879–1881. In 1885–1886, he served as U.S. minister to **Haiti**, and then he worked for the Belgian government in the **Congo**. He was the author of *The History of the Negro Race in America* (1883), a classic text. He died at Blackpool, England.

WILLIAMS, ROGER (c. 1603–1684). Anglican and Puritan/Separatist minister and, for a time, American Baptist pioneer, born at London, England. He was educated at Pembroke College, Cambridge University and served as a personal chaplain to Sir Edward Masham in 1627–1630. Dissatisfied with the state of the Church of England and denied his master's degree because he would not submit to the episcopacy, Williams emigrated to Massachusetts in 1630–1631 with his wife, Mary, and took the position of assistant **pastor** in the Congregationalist church at Salem. In New England, he raised questions about the magistracy, treatment of Indian land claims, and religious freedom, and this brought him into adversarial relations with the authorities. He was banished to England in 1635, and the following year he relocated to Narragansett Country (later Rhode Island), where he concluded a treaty with the Indians and organized a colony at Providence Plantations. Williams founded a small congregation in his home that was of a Puritan/Separatist bent in 1636.

In 1638, Williams embraced Baptist practices and assisted in transforming his fledgling congregation to become the first Baptist church in America, at Providence. At the suggestion of Catherine Scott, a sister of Anne Hutchinson, the celebrated Antinomian, Williams and about 20 others were baptized as believers. After only three to four months, however, Williams evolved to a more radical position, generally referred to as a "Seeker," and there is no record of his being involved with his former congregation thereafter. He wrote to John Winthrop Jr. (1605–1676) in 1649 that he believed Baptist practice "came nearer the first practice of our great Founder Christ than other practices of religions doe, & yet I have no satisfaction neither in the authority by which **baptism** is done nor in the manner." Williams observed from a distance the course of **John Clarke**'s work in the Newport Baptist church, and he was repulsed by the persecution of Baptists in the early 1650s, but he did not rejoin the sect. **Isaac Backus**, in the next century, resurrected Williams from oblivion among Baptists and created in him a champion of **religious liberty** and pioneer status for Baptists in the United States, which his contemporaries little accorded him. Among Williams's published works are *A Key to the Language of America* (1643); *The Bloudy Tenent, of Persecution for Cause of Conscience, Discuss'd in a Conference between Tryth and Peace* (1644); *The Bloudy Tenent Yet More Bloudy, By Mr. Cotton's Endeavour to Wash It White in the Blood of the Lambe* (1652); and *George Fox Digg'd Out of His Burrowes* (1676). *See also* ROGER WILLIAMS FELLOWSHIP.

WINCHESTER, ELHANAN (1751–1797). American Baptist minister, born at Brookline, Massachusetts. Self-educated, Winchester was an **evangelist** and then settled as **pastor**, initially at Welsh Neck, South Carolina (1775–1779), and then at First Baptist, Philadelphia, in 1780. While pastor in Philadelphia, he adopted a **Universalist** theology and was branded a heretic. Popular with a faction in the congregation, Winchester took a group to meet at the University of Pennsylvania after his emphases split the church. At length, he became a religious lecturer and traveled widely in Europe and the United States as a Universalist. In 1787, he settled in London, England, where he preached at Worship Street in the mornings and Glass House Yard in the evenings. While in Great Britain, he acquainted himself with several religious leaders, including John Wesley (1703–1791), who admired Winchester's **Arminian** theological tilt. He also lectured widely on prophetic themes. Apparently due to marital difficulties, Winchester left England abruptly in 1794 and returned to the United

States, where he lectured in Massachusetts and Connecticut. Winchester continued to be a colorful figure, spontaneously ordaining a young evangelist Hosea Ballou (1771–1852) to the ministry at a service in 1794 and writing against the deistical tendencies of Thomas Paine (1737–1809). He was a forceful **antislavery** writer, beginning in 1774. Ironically, for a radical thinker, he was also condemned for not adopting some of the new currents of thought. Among his important published works are *The Mystic's Plea for Universal Redemption as Held Forth* (1781), *The Universal Restoration Exhibited in a Series of Dialogues between a Minister and His Friend* (1788), and *A Plain Political Catechism Intended for the Use of Schools in the United States of America* (1796).

WINEBRENNER, JOHN (1797–1860). American Reformed **pastor** and leader, born at Walkersville, Maryland. He was educated at Dickinson College and determined to enter the **ministry** of the German Reformed Church. He became a student of Samuel Helffenstein (1775–1866), a Reformed pastor in Philadelphia, Pennsylvania, and developed a pietistic and revivalistic **theology**. Winebrenner served churches in Harrisburg and Cumberland County, Pennsylvania. His extreme **revivalistic** style, similar to Charles Finney's (1792–1875) New Measures, led to his dismissal from his Reformed congregation in 1828. He continued to itinerate and preach on themes of renewal throughout central Pennsylvania and Maryland.

In 1830, Winebrenner was rebaptized, and he took on a reputation of developing Baptist leanings. He rallied his substantial following into a new organization that he called the "Church of God," based upon a New Testament apostolic plan. Winebrenner's baptistic **polity** and theology spread to the Ohio Valley. In 1845, he organized a general eldership for the Church of God. Derogatorily referred to as "Winebrennerians," the sect sought to be faithful to biblical literalism, restoration of the primitive order, and social reforms such as **antislavery**. Winebrenner himself remained aloof from the Baptist tradition, publishing a paper, the *Gospel Publisher*, and engaging in various forms of reform, including **peace** and **temperance**. His movement, the Church of God, was often included in 19th-century listings of Baptistic groups, primarily because of their advocacy of believer's **baptism**.

WOELFKIN, CORNELIUS (1859–1928). American Baptist minister, born in New York City. He was educated at Colgate and Rochester Universities, after which he entered the pastoral **ministry**. Woelfkin served several congregations: First Baptist, Hackensack, New Jersey (1887–1892); North Jersey City (1892–1894); and Green Avenue Baptist, New York City (1894–1905). From 1905 to 1912, he served as Wyckoff Professor of Homiletics at Rochester Theological Seminary. Woelfkin's first commitment was to the pastorate, however, and he returned to New York City in 1912 as **pastor** at Fifth Avenue Baptist Church in 1912–1928. While in that role, he was a distinguished president of the **American Baptist Foreign Mission Society** in 1911. Woelfkin's chief monument was his substitute motion at the Northern Baptist Convention annual meeting in 1922 to make the New Testament the sole rule of faith and practice, which ultimately outmaneuvered the **fundamentalist** faction led by **William Bell Riley**. **Harry Emerson Fosdick**, a close friend of Woelfkin, delivered the eulogy at his funeral. Woelfkin was well-known for his sermon, "The Quest for Immortality" (1913), preached in the Brick Presbyterian Church in Rochester, New York. A professorial chair in preaching at Colgate Rochester Divinity School was instituted in the 1940s in honor of Dr. Woelfkin.

WOMEN, IN BAPTIST LIFE. From the earliest period of Baptist history in England, **women** have played a significant role in **ministry** and **mission**. Baptists have wrestled with biblical teaching on the appropriate roles for women in the church: a text that is perceived to limit the role of women is 1 Corinthians 14:34–35; those which have been used to heighten the appreciation of women are Joel 2:28–29, John 8:36, and Galatians 3:28.

Women in the 17th Century. Baptists were among the first of the **Nonconformist** community in 17th-century England to allow women to preach and engage in ministry within the congregations. Some historians believe that the openness to women in ministry was a trait of the Brownists during the Elizabethan era, which passed to the Baptist communities. Called "she-preachers" and "widows" (the latter in the biblical sense), women enjoyed many liberties not allowed elsewhere in the English Church and among dissenters. By the 1660s, however, the tide had changed and women were not as frequently found in congregational leadership roles. Doubtless this was the result of accommodation to the emerging mainstream Nonconformist consensus.

Among the early English **General Baptists**, **John Smyth** categorized women as part of the "private" sector of the congregation, in contrast with the "prophets." Smyth and **Thomas Helwys** allowed that women could serve as **deacons**; Helwys described the office of widow, which he defined as women over 60 years old. There is scant mention of women in the **Particular Baptist** tradition. Thomas Edwards (1599–1647), Presbyterian author of *Gangrena*, railed against women preachers, and such were known to be at Brasted, Westerham, and Bell Alley, London. (One of the problems noted of early General Baptist women preachers was long sermons; one woman was said to have preached for two hours.) A Mrs. Attaway among the General Baptists in the church at Coleman Street, London, was known as the "mistress of all the she-preachers." **Dorothy Hazzard** of Bristol, who discipled her husband, won acclaim for her leadership in the formation of Broadmead Church there. Additionally, six Nonconformist women preachers in Kent, Salisbury, and Cambridgeshire may have had Baptist leanings in the 1640s.

Later in the 17th century, there is evidence of separate women's organization within churches, as at **Benjamin Keach**'s church, where there was a separate **prayer meeting**. Women writers such as Katherine Sutton and Jane Turner, a **Fifth Monarchist**, made contributions to the growing literature of Nonconformity. **Ann Dutton** wrote and spoke widely and was well known for her composition of hymns. For the most part, however, at the outset of a new century, women were seated separately from men and deprived of most leadership positions in British Baptist congregations.

In the American colonies, there are isolated instances of women in significant leadership roles. Catherine Scott was among those who organized the first Baptist congregation at Providence, Rhode Island in 1638."

As early as the 1640s, **Deborah Moody** adopted Baptist principles in Massachusetts and encountered stiff opposition for her views. Rachel Scammon (fl. 1720–1730), also of Massachusetts, made several missionary forays into New Hampshire to distribute literature, which later led to the establishment of at least one congregation at

Salem. In the southern colonies, there is scant evidence of women, such as Martha Stearns Marshall (fl. 1750), being involved in **revival** meetings involving Baptists. Mary Savage was listed among **Freewill Baptists** as a "co-worker" in New England in 1791.

The role of women in Baptist life was greatly enhanced at the beginning of the 19th century. In Boston in 1800, **Mary Webb**, a crippled member of Second Baptist Church, organized the "mother society" of missionary support, from which both women's and broader missionary work among American Baptists stemmed. Later, with role models like the three wives of **Adoniram Judson**, women began to organize missionary groups and enjoy new roles outside the household circles. In Britain, societies of benefit to women and administered by women were common by 1850. Notably, in 1890, British Baptist **pastor F. B. Meyer** helped to form a Baptist Sisterhood in London: the Baptist Deaconess Home and Mission became the Order of Baptist Deaconnesses, imitating Lutheran and Methodist experience. The **Baptist Missionary Society** (BMS) in 1854 approved the work of missionary spouses among women's exclusive communities (zenanas) in **India**, and this led to the formation of the Ladies Association for the Support of Zenana Work in 1866, first woman's auxiliary to the BMS. The first official women missionaries in the British Baptist family were Emily Saker (1850–1932) and Carrie Comber (d. 1885), both commissioned in 1879 as single missionary workers in the zenana movement in **Cameroon**. In East Bengal, Australian missionary pioneer Ellen Arnold began a zenana mission that lasted 1882–1931, longest of any Australian missionary. By the conclusion of the century, in addition to the interdenominational organizations to which Baptist women contributed, there were 13 Baptist societies in the United States, 2 in Great Britain, and 5 in **Canada** focused on women's work.

Meanwhile, the lot of women in local congregational leadership also evolved. In the British **Baptist Union** (BU), the first woman to serve as pastor of a congregation was Edith Gates (1883–1962), who began her long ministry at Little Tew and Cleveley in 1918. The first husband-wife combination ministry was that of Maria Living-Taylor, who served a series of churches with her husband, beginning in 1922. Regent's Park College admitted a woman student, Violet Hedger (1900–1992), in 1923, and Bristol Baptist College registered its first woman candidate for ministry in 1937. Edith Gates, who served the churches at Little Tew and Clevely, won probationer status in 1922 and served as president of the Oxfordshire Association. Baptist lay-women in 1908 created the Baptist Women's Home Work Auxiliary, which evolved in the Baptist Women's League in 1910. Two women have served as presidents of the Baptists Union of Great Britain, Nell Alexander (d. 1986) in 1978 and the Reverend Margaret Jarman (1932–) in 1987. Related to the British Baptist family is **Australia**, where the **deaconess** movement put forth women in both congregational roles and more broadly in cities and specialized work form the 1860s. In the 1860s, the **Bible** Women's movement among the Baptists sent female workers into homes, where the ladies taught domestic skills, literacy, and care for the sick.

Baptist Women in North America. As with other denominations, North American Baptist women began to organize for missions. The first associations were prayer gatherings in homes. In 1800, one of these was made a formal society, the Boston Baptist Female Missionary Society, founded by Mary Webb in Second Baptist Church. This "mother society" became a model for Baptist women in the North and South. When the national **General Missionary Convention** and **Baptist Board for Foreign Missions** were formed in 1814, **Charlotte White** volunteered to go to **Burma**, prompting a debate over whether women should be allowed to serve as missionaries. In 1815, White was appointed and became the first single woman missionary in the denomination. Of course, each of the male missionaries appointed were married, and a case has been made that their spouses constituted de facto missionaries from the beginning of overseas work.

The major role of women in the first half of the century continued to be in support of missions. In 1847, in Sutton, Vermont, the Freewill Baptist Female Missionary Society was founded. In the Canadian Maritme Provinces, **Hannah Maria Norris** Armstrong organized numerous bands of missionary supporters in the early 1870s. At the same time, Baptist women in New England, under the leadership of Mrs. **Alvah Hovey**, formed the Woman's American Baptist Foreign Mission Society in 1871; the same year, a western states society was formed in Chicago. Not only did these organizations bring women together in local congregrations, they also increased the possibilities for women to engage directly in **ministry** as missionaries or administrators. In 1914, on the centennial anniversary of the recognition of **Ann Judson** in Burma, the two regional societies merged into the Woman's Baptist Foreign Mission Society. A similar story unfolded with women involved in domestic missions, the result becoming the Woman's American Baptist Home Mission Society (WABHMS), chartered in 1877 and made a national organization in 1909.

American Baptist women have been involved in some remarkable experiences. In the overseas context, Marilla Baker Ingalls (1828–1902) is an example. Baker was appointed with her husband to the Arracan field of the **American Baptist Missionary Union** (ABMU), but Lovell Baker died in 1858. The ABMU appointed Marilla to "independent work" due to her effectiveness as a teacher. Her tract distribution and outreach to Buddhists, in particular, antagonized local gangs and Buddhist leaders. At one point, a reward was placed upon her head for 10,000 rupees, but she was prevented from capture. It was said at her retirement that Baker influenced the conversion of 100 Buddhist priests to the Christian faith. Similarly, on the domestic front, a memorable set of events occurred in Kiowa Territory, Oklahoma, at the turn of the 20th century. **Isabel Crawford**, a missionary for the WABHMS, in 1905 supervised a celebration of the **Lord's Supper** at Saddle Mountain mission station in the absence of a local male pastor. She was judged to have acted contrary to WABHMS policy, she was reprimanded, and subsequently, she resigned from the board. Her action and later protest raised the consciousness of women in the northern Baptist family in the United States during an era of increasing women's rights recognition.

The **Southern Baptists** of the United States have responded to direct leadership of women more slowly. There are no examples of women in pastoral roles in the 19th century; however, Harriet Baker (fl. 1850) was appointed by the **Foreign Mission Board** (FMB) in 1851 to establish a school for female girls at Canton, **China**, thus becoming the first female appointment of Southern Baptists in missions. For many years after Baker's health failed, no further women were appointed. **Henry A. Tupper**, corresponding secretary of the FMB, profoundly changed this trend with the appointment of Lula Whilden (1846–1916) and Edmonia Moon (1851–1908) to China in 1873. The premier figure in Southern Baptist missions was **Charlotte Digges Moon**, appointed to China 1873–1912.

Southern Baptist women likewise organized themselves for missionary endeavor. In 1868, the first meeting of women in conjunction with the annual **Southern Baptist Convention** (SBC) session was held in Baltimore and led by Ann Baker Graves, the mother of R. H. Graves, a prominent missionary. Ten years later, a SBC committee recommended establishing state committees of women, and in 1888, the national Woman's Missionary Union was founded under the aegis of Annie Armstrong (1850–1938), following a stirring call from Lottie Moon of China.

Women among **black Baptists** in the United States have also been organized. Prominent since the 19th century have been local church groups of "matrons," who serve in an auxiliary role in programs, missions, and education. Women have served in executive leadership in the denominational bodies and as missionaries. Each of the national black Baptist organizations has a women's auxiliary.

Ordination of Women. **Ordination** of women has occurred in ever-increasing numbers since the latter half of the 19th century. A first step was taken in 1846 in the United States, when Ruby Bixby was licensed to the ministry by the Honey Creek, Iowa, Freewill Baptist Quarterly Meeting. The first recorded ordination of a Baptist woman at the local church level (in contrast with denominational credentials) occurred among northern Freewill Baptists with A. Gerry in 1869; among southern Freewill Baptists, in 1938, Lucy Wells, a member of the Eastern Conference, was ordained to the ministry by the denominational Examining Board. A **Seventh Day Baptist** woman, Experience P. F. Randolph (fl. 1850–1890) was ordained between 1880 and 1885 at the Hornellsville (New York) Seventh Day Baptist Church. At Fairfield, Connecticut, Frances Townsley was ordained by the local association in 1885. Susan Elizabeth Cilley Griffin (1851–1926) was the first woman to enjoy denomination-wide recognition for her ordination in the Elmira Heights (New York) Baptist Church, ultimately related to the Northern Baptist Convention.

While more rarely, Southern Baptists in the United States have also ordained women, beginning with Addie Davis of Watts Street Baptist Church, Durham, North Carolina, on 9 August 1964. The second Southern Baptist ordination of a woman occurred in 1971, when Shirley Carter was ordained at Kathwood Baptist Church in Columbia, South Carolina. The following year, however, under pressure, the church rescinded the ordination, the first such instance on record. In an unusual circumstance, Druecillar Fordham, an Amercan Baptist African American pastor at Christ Temple Baptist Church in New York City, took Southern Baptist affiliation in the Metro New York Association, creating a role for Carter as a Southern Baptist pastor. Over the next 15 years, over 50 Southern Baptist women were ordained to the gospel ministry. One of the most celebrated occurrences surrounding the recognition of the ordination of women involved Nancy Hastings Sehested (1951–). Ordained in 1981, Sehested was called in 1987 to be the senior minister at Prescott Memorial Baptist Church in Memphis, Tennessee. Once installed in that role, the church was **disfellowshipped** that year by the local Shelby County Baptist Association. In response to the growing frustration among women candidates for ministry and the need for mutual support, an alliance, the Southern Baptist Women in Ministry, was formed in 1983 as a support group for women in ministry of various kinds. As of 1995, there were 60 women pastors and 176 endorsed women chaplains relating to the Southern Baptist Home Mission Board.

Although the ordination of women in black Baptist churches has been rare historically until recently, there are noteworthy exceptions. Jennie Johnson (1867–1967) was apparently the earliest black woman to be ordained. She was a Canadian Free Baptist who, due to discrimination against women and blacks, was actually ordained at Galesville, Michigan, on 26 October 1909. Her ordination was certified by the General Conference of Free Baptists. Similarly, Rosetta O'Neal (1937–) of Detroit, Michigan, was ordained in 1975 and, serving a congregation in Windsor, Ontario, has been president of the Baptist Convention of Ontario and Quebec, 1998–1999. Among Americans, Ella P. Mitchell (1917–) was ordained at Allen Temple Baptist Church in Oakland, California, in 1978, and Suzanne Johnson Cook (1957–) was ordained at Oliver Street Baptist Church in 1982, a dually aligned American Baptist congregation in New York City. The first duly elected woman executive (or regional) minister among Baptists was Kathryn Baker (1939–), ordained in 1976, who served the American Baptist Churches of the Niagara Frontier (New York), 1985–1993. In central Canada, Muriel Spurgeon Carder (1922–) was the first Baptist woman ordained in 1948, while Mae Benedict Field (1906–1998) was first among the western Canadian

Baptists in 1959. In Australia, Marita Munro was the first Baptist woman ordained in 1978, followed by Marian Welford in 1979 and Susan Harris in 1984. In Tasmania, June Robertson was ordained in 1996. Outside the English-speaking Baptist family, several strides have been noted. Angelina Buensuceso became the first woman ordained in the **Philippines** Baptist community in 1980; in **Cuba**, Edna Garcia, Clara Rodes, and Xiomara Diaz were ordained in 1992 by the Fraternidad de Iglesias Bautistas, with 16 more women ordinations after 2000; **Brazilian** Baptists ordained Silvia Noguiera in 1999; and in **Mexico** Rebeca Lopez was ordained in 2000.

Women in Specialized Educational and Organizational Ministries. Noteworthy among the 20th-century rise of Baptist women in leadership are several "firsts," particularly in education. The initial steps were found among Baptists in the United States: Blanche Eliza Parks was appointed dean of women and instructor in Methods of Missionary Service in 1925 at Berkeley Baptist Divinity School, and Catherine H. Thompson was appointed instructor in missions at the Eastern Baptist Theological Seminary the same year. Northern Baptist Theological Seminary appointed Ruthella Rodeaver in Christian education in 1936. Later women appointments to previously all-male faculties were Martha Leypoldt in Christian education at Eastern Seminary in 1966, Phyllis Trible in Old Testament at Andover Newton Theological School in 1971, and Beverly R. Gaventa in New Testament at Colgate Rochester Divinity School in 1976. Dramatic change also came in the European Baptist family with the election of Birgit Carlson (1935–), who served as president of the **Swedish** Baptist Union, 1984–1995, the first female executive officer of a national organization of Baptists, and Ruth Lehotsky (1933–), the first woman theological school professor in Eastern Europe. In Australia, with 14 women ordained in Victoria State between 1991 and 2004, three women presidents were appointed in the Victoria Union: Winsome Abbott in 1985–1986; Gwyn Milne in 1997–1998; and Judy McMaster in 2001–2002. Milne was later elected the first woman president of the Baptist Union of Australia in 2003. Of parallel significance was the appointment of Marita Munro as a lecturer at Whitley College in Melbourne, the first woman to hold a position in an Australian Baptist theological college. In Canada, Lois A. Tupper (1911–) was appointed in 1968 as professor of Christian Ministry at

McMaster Divinity College, the first full-time female faculty member in any theological school. Other Canadian Baptist women in **higher education** include Joyce Bellous at McMaster Divinity College and Carol Anne Janzen at Acadia Divinity College, both in Religious Education; Patricia Fisher at Taylor University College (Leadership); and Barbara Mutch (Ministry) and Joyce Chan (Historical Studies) at Carey Theological College.

Recent Baptist Women in Leadership. In the past three decades, Baptist women have become prominent in executive leadership roles in European, North American, and Australian Baptist life. The Reverend Regina Claas, daughter of the former general secretary of the Baptist World Alliance, Gerhard Claas, assumed the role of General Secretary of the Union of Evangelical Free Churches (Baptist) in **Germany** in 2003. A watershed occurred among Baptist women in England in 1979 when questions arose over the role of the traditional Baptist Women's League and a new strategy, "Baptist Women's Work," came forth, similar to the Study on Women in Ministry among American Baptists in the same era. Both recognized that women experienced difficulty in obtaining their first pastorates. American Baptist influence favoring women in ministry planted an important seed in 1989 when David Scholer, a member of the American Baptist General Board and a theological educator, taught a course on "Women and Ministry in the New Testament" at Whitley College in Melbourne. A denominational task force in Australia was subsequently organized to pursue further questions related to women in ministry. Among the **American Baptist Churches in the U.S.A.**, Dr. Marsha Patton has served as executive minister of the Evergreen (Washington) Baptist Association since 2004, a key new region in the denomination. Dr. Molly Marshall-Green, aligned with the **Cooperative Baptist Fellowship**, has been president at Central Baptist Seminary in Kansas City, Kansas, a historically American Baptist school, since 2004. At the January 2009 meeting of the New Covenant Baptists, the Reverend Julie Pennington-Russell of Macon, Georgia, gave one of the major plenary addresses to over 10,000 delegates, and Dr. Pamela R. Durso, a Baptist historian, has served as associate executive director of the Baptist History and Heritage Society since 2006. The largest percentage of women in pastoral ministry and executive leadership remains in the American Baptist Churches in the U.S.A., with over 100 women serving in **National Baptist Convention, U.S.A.,** congregations as senior pastors. Baptist women in ministry in the United States have created a website, Baptist Women in Ministry, for mutual support, information on placement, and a speaker's bureau for women's concerns.

WOMEN'S MISSIONARY ORGANIZATIONS, BAPTIST. Baptist **women** have long been active in support of missions, and the ensuing organizations that they have formed provide an important international chapter in Baptist history. The patterns for organized women's work were set in the British and American Baptist communities in the late 19th century. From that period, and as a result of missionary advance itself, most Baptist conventions and unions worldwide have a women's auxiliary or missionary support organization of the historic patterns.

Overseas Missionary Work. The first organization that Baptist women joined was undoubtedly the Boston Bethel Missionary Society, formed by **Mary Webb** in 1800. Chapters or missionary bands soon followed in support of America's first missionaries, the **Adoniram Judsons.** Doubtless there were women who joined the **evangelical** movements in the 1830s, such as those formed in the wake of David Abeel's (1804–1846) challenge toward organized women in London in 1834. The first strictly Baptist general women's organization in North America was the **Freewill Baptist** Female Missionary Society, formed in 1847 in New Hampshire. Later, in 1861, the Woman's Union Missionary Society of America for Heathen Lands was formed of numerous Baptist supporters. The popularity of this endeavor led to the organization of American Baptist women in 1870–1871. In Newton Centre, Masachusetts, the Woman's Baptist Foreign Mission Society of the East was formed in April 1871, with the Woman's Baptist Foreign Mission Society of the West formed the following May in Chicago. A third society was formed in the Far West in 1874, the Woman's Baptist Foreign Mission Society of the Pacific Coast. These organizations prepared candidates to serve in various fields approved by the **American Baptist Missionary Union**, while also training a female administrative corps at home. Membership in these societies was kept at one dollar per year to include as many persons as possible. Women's work overseas through these three bodies came to include hospitals, schools, construction projects, and women's advocacy issues. In 1913, the societies from the East and West merged into the Woman's American Baptist Foreign Mission Society, which in 1955 was integrated into the **American Baptist Foreign Mission Society**, affiliated with the American Baptist Convention.

Other groups of Baptist women in the United States also organized in the period between 1880 and 1940. The largest of these was the Women's Missionary Union (WMU) of the **Southern Baptist Convention**, founded in 1888, largely in response to a plea from missionary to China, **Charlotte Moon**. By 1915, the WMU recorded 250,000 members in over 13,000 affiliated local and state organizations. The WMU has since 1887 superintended the annual Lottie Moon Christmas Offering, which accounts for a significant percentage of Southern Baptist missionary support. Likewise, the General Conference of the German Baptists in the United States in 1895 authorized the formation of a women's organization, and this became a reality in 1907 with Der Allgemeine Schwesternbund Deutscher Baptisten von Nord Amerika (the General Women's Union of German Baptists of North America). This organization paralleled for a few years the development of a German Baptist deaconess movement, formed in Chicago in 1897. Following the pattern, in 1932 the Women's Commission of the **Baptist General Conference** was organized in the Swedish Baptist community in North America.

Within the British Baptist Family, women's organization for support of overseas **mission** began in 1867 with the establishment of the Ladies Association for the Support of Zenana Work and Bible Women in **India**, as an auxiliary of the **Baptist Missionary Society** (BMS). Eventually this became a vehicle through which single female missionaries were appointed. In 1897, the Ladies Association became the Baptist Zenana Mission, which, after recommendations from the Edinburgh 1910 Conference, was incorporated in 1914 as the Women's Missionary Association of the BMS. By 1924, the association became a department within the BMS structure.

Similarly, **voluntary** women's **associations** of local and regional kinds in support of the **Baptist Union** (BU) and the **Baptist Home Mission Society**, became in 1908 the Baptist Women's Home Work Auxiliary, which in turn evolved into the Baptist Women's League in

1910. Eventually, a Women's Department of the BU was formed, and this coordinated with local church groups to coordinate fellowship among women. Desirous of greater integration in the life of the church as a whole, the formal organization and department evolved into the Baptist Women's Conference in the 1970s and the Baptist Women's Mission Network in the late 1980s. The organization disbanded in 1998.

Baptist women in **Canada** organized in the formative years 1880–1890. **Hannah Maria Norris** Armstrong in 1870 became the catalyst for organizing local societies in support of her plans to serve in India. In one summer, she founded 32 societies in the Maritime Provinces. Ultimately, the result of this work was the formation of the United Baptist Woman's Missionary Union of the Maritime Provinces in 1884. Similar organizations emerged to serve the needs of central Canada, the Women's Baptist Foreign Mission Society of Ontario (West) in 1876 and the Women's Baptist Foreign Missionary Society of Eastern Canada in the same year. In 1953, the separate entities merged as the Baptist Women's Missionary Society of Ontario and Quebec. As part of the national movement among Canadian Baptists in the 1940s, there was for a time after 1940 a consultative body called the Dominion Committee of the Affiliated Baptist Women's Missionary Societies of Canada, which involved all of the organizations across the country.

Domestic Missionary Work and Support. As noted earlier, the first woman's organization in the Baptist community was the Boston Society formed by Mary Webb. This group actually provided more support for home and urban projects than for overseas work. Gradually, as women became interested in missionary work, primarily encouraged by the heroism of women like the Judson wives, local and state societies were formed in Ohio, Illinois, Connecticut, and Michigan, which forwarded contributions to the **American Baptist Home Mission Society** (ABHMS). Matching the development of the women's foreign societies (see above), in 1877 a western woman's society (Chicago) was chartered and an eastern woman's society (Boston) was formed in 1878. These joined in 1910 as the Woman's American Baptist Home Mission Society (WABHMS). This organization, headquartered in Chicago, Illinois, trained and appointed women missionaries as teachers, nurses, friendship house workers, and urban workers in the United States and other fields of the ABHMS. In 1955, The WABHMS was integrated with the ABHMS and the headquarters was moved to Valley Forge, Pennsylvania.

WORLD BAPTIST FELLOWSHIP (WBF). In 1933–1934, **J. Frank Norris** and a collection of **fundamentalist** Baptist **pastors**, including C. P. Stealey in Oklahoma and Robert White in Texas, founded the Premillennial Baptist Missionary Fellowship to enjoy "no officialism, but abounding fellowship." The purpose was to receive and distribute funds for acceptable missionaries, as advertised in the *Fundamentalist*. For the WBF's first five years, local pastors presided over its business. In 1938, Norris took personal control of the WBF and renamed it the World Fundamental Baptist Missionary Fellowship, with headquarters in Chicago. The creed of the group was in harmony with the former **Baptist Bible Union**, with a militant opposition to modernism, Communism, and conventionism (the latter referring to the Southern and Northern Baptist conventions). Norris boasted that 300 pastors supported the fellowship as well as the related organizations, **China** Baptist Evangelization Mission, the East China Mission, the French Bible Mission, and the San Antonio Spanish Mission. In 1950, a serious division occurred in the fellowship, which led to the formation of the **Baptist Bible Fellowship**. To distinguish the group from the splinter faction, Norris changed the name to World Baptist Fellowship.

The major asset of the WBF was the theological school, founded in 1939 as the Fundamental Baptist Bible Institute and renamed in 1944–1945 the Bible Baptist Seminary. Norris died in 1952, amidst concerns over financial management and authoritarian control, and the leadership of the WBF evolved to Louis Entzminger (1878–1956), at first Norris's lieutenant and later professor of English Bible. In recent years, the number of congregations has grown less dramatically than other fundamentalist groups, and the **mission** program is limited. The "Arlington Schools" in Ft. Worth, Texas, include a high school and **Bible college**. About 1,000 churches cooperate in the fellowship; as a contemporary overseas mission agency, the WBF supports 135 missionaries in 25 countries, including South America, Europe, the Far East, and Central America. Since 1927, the WBF has published the *Fundamentalist* (formerly the *Fence Rail*, 1917–1921, and the *Searchlight*, 1921–1927).

WORLDWIDE NEW TESTAMENT BAPTIST MISSION. An independent, **fundamentalist** Baptist mission agency founded in 1971 by Bill Wingard (1934–), **pastor** of Calvary Baptist Church, New Bern, North Carolina. The purpose of the **mission** is to conduct **evangelism** and plant new churches on the New Testament model with strict adherence to a doctrinal position that emphasizes premillenial theology, the local church, and a separationist stance. As of 2007, there were about 80 missionary couples in 23 countries including Europe, Africa, **Australia**, Latin America, the Caribbean Islands, Micronesia, the United States, and **Canada**. An executive board of 10 pastors drawn mostly from eastern North Carolina operates the mission. Headquarters is located in New Bern, North Carolina.

WORSHIP IN BAPTIST TRADITION. Over the almost four centuries and the vast geo-cultural spread of Baptist principles, not to speak of the differentiation caused by local congregational styles, Baptist worship is highly variegated. Yet, some historical patterns do emerge.

From early English Baptist experience, the **General Baptists** seem to have followed principles first suggested by the se-Baptist **John Smyth**. In a typical service, the emphasis was upon spirituality in worship. **Scripture** was the ever-present resource for sermons, most often being understood in a literal sense. The dramas of the Old Testament were metaphorically applied to contemporary audiences, and the didactic literature of the New Testament epistles form the most frequently quoted passages in Baptist sermons. The life of **Christ** for most Baptist sermons sets an ethical expectation and the birth and passion narratives provide a rich theater at the appropriate occasions of the year. The preaching of the word, in contrast with the **sacramental** traditions, or those of a more mystical/illuminatory kind, tend to predominate in Baptist worship. It is taken for granted that one of the great assets of every believer-priest is the ability and insight to interpret Scripture for him or herself, and therefore every Baptist has the potential to be a preacher as well as to offer to God individual sacrifices of person, prayer, and possessions. The typical 17th-century Baptist worship service consisted of prayer, Scripture reading which was translated from the originals by the leader, exposition of the

Scriptures, and prophesyings. There was no singing, except perhaps in the manner of some prophesying.

Baptist worship in North America has moved in several streams over three centuries. In the **revivalistic** tradition, there are groups that prefer a strictly **evangelistic** approach wherein the services are geared to evangelistic sermons leading to an invitation to accept Christ as Savior or to consecrate one's life to God. There is much uplifting and convictional singing, often supported by a choir. An outgrowth of the revivalist tradition is found among **fundamentalists**, who stress dramatic preaching on doctrinal and ethical themes and invitations to join the church (following a weekly canvass of new member prospects), an act that is synonymous with adopting their views and lifestyle. While most of the typical fundamentalist Baptist service is given to preaching, there are choirs and the collection of an offering is emphasized to produce maximum response.

Yet other Baptists prefer a kind of didactic service of worship in which the focus is upon nurture, doctrinal emphases, and discipleship. Simple services of prayers, the collection of tithes and offerings, Scripture readings, and a 20- to 30-minute sermon, expository or thematic, illustrate this style. Such services close in hymns and prayers of service or dedication. The Liturgical Renewal Movement had a deep impact upon many Baptist congregations in the 1960s in Britain and North America; it stressed a theological basis for worship, a prominent place for the **Lord's Supper** (called Eucharist after the sacramental tradition), and active involvement of laity in worship, through Scripture, choral work, ritual, and offering.

In the 1970s and 1980s, in response to other denominations and traditions, Baptist congregations in **Canada** and the northern United States have absorbed elements of the charismatic and "praise and worship" traditions. These streams vary widely from singing adorational, repeating choruses (often projected on an overhead screen or wall, or printed on songsheets or in published booklets) to healing services and ecstatic utterances and words of prophecy being delivered and interpreted. The use of musical instruments has in many churches shifted from organs and pianos to guitars, musical synthesizers, and electronic keyboards. Clapping of hands, bodily movement, unscripted utterances, and dancing can be evident in these services, which seem to be reactions against formalism and/or perceived lethargy in the traditional styles. Typically, worship leaders and **pastors** dress informally, and there is no rigid structure to the service. Underlying this style is a sense of the presence of Christ in worship and the unity of soul, spirit, and body. A significant amount of time in these services is spent under the direction of a worship leader or team, after which a "teaching sermon" is given with ample time for overt behavioral responses.

Another continuing worship style is found typically in urban and upper middle-class Baptist congregations in the **Southern Baptist Convention**, many **American Baptist**, and Canadian Baptist churches. Modestly formal, the principal weekly worship service comprises a liturgy of a call to worship, hymns of adoration of God, consecration of self and dedication to God. Readings of Scripture from the Old and New Testaments, choral selections, a sermon that may draw upon a published lectionary, and a children's talk round out what amounts to about one hour of worship on Sunday mornings. There may be a choral and ministerial procession and recession, though these are becoming more rare.

Black Baptist worship in North America can be a unique experience. Preaching is the primary focus of the worship service, supported by choirs and enthusiastic congregational singing of songs and hymns, which often reflect the African American experience, such as "Go Down, Moses," "We Are Climbing Jacob's Ladder," "Go Tell It on the Mountain," and "He's Got the Whole World in His Hands." Among many churches, the preacher is considered a mouthpiece of God and speaks with great authority and power. Metaphorical language can predominate and dramatic gestures and voice modulation accompany the delivery of the sermon. There may be several sermons in a morning worship service in the black tradition.

Outside the Anglo-American patterns, there is diversification on familiar patterns. Across Europe, Baptists tend to be quietistic, placing much emphasis upon confessional preaching and ethics. Services run the familiar course of prayers, responses, and sermons. The celebration of the **ordinances**/sacraments is symbolic as a statement in contrast with Roman and Orthodox traditions. Choirs are a prominent feature of worship, especially in former Marxist countries, such as **Hungary**, **Poland**, and **Romania**; choral fests and traveling choirs have been an important social expression of the faith. Many services feature several sermons, not only from the pastors but also from **deacons**. African Baptists take delight in music and singing influenced by tribal idioms, and this constitutes a major part of worship that may last for several hours. In Latin America and the Caribbean, Baptist worship is vivid and charismatic, with an emphasis upon evangelistic preaching. For Asian Baptists, preaching has a didactic function, especially in view of the paucity in many locales of written Scriptures. The influence of **missionaries**, particularly American and British Baptists, has ensured that extemporaneous preaching is important, and singing of familiar hymns and gospel songs characteristic of the pietism and biblicism of historic Baptist tradition gives an international "sound" to Baptist worship.

In general, Baptist worship patterns reflect the overall culture and the particular social class and theological traditions of a congregation. It is not unusual to have "blended" worship of many styles in contemporary Baptist experience. *See also* MUSIC; PRAYER MEETING.

– Y –

YEMEN. The history of Baptist presence in Yemen is a remarkable story. Based on the experience of the health care provided by the **Southern Baptist** Hospital in Gaza, the Ministry of Health in Yemen in 1963 requested the Southern Baptists to begin a medical clinic in Yemen. In 1964, a clinic was opened at Taiz and a large hospital was subsequently begun at Jibla. Continuing Baptist presence in the country is related to medical and technical appointments.

YUGOSLAVIA. *See* BOSNIA; CROATIA; MACEDONIA; SERBIA; SLOVENIA.

– Z –

ZAIRE. *See* CONGO, DEMOCRATIC REPUBLIC OF.

ZAMBIA. Swedish Baptists were the first to plant a work in what was northern Rhodesia in 1892. Results of the **mission** included a theological institute. The South African Missionary Society established its work in 1913 at Kafulafuta. In 1957, the **Reformed Baptists** of **Canada** started a work that was transferred to the Wesleyan Church in 1968. **Southern Baptists** entered Zambia in 1905 and in 1974 helped establish the Baptist Convention of Zambia. A theological school was established at Lusaka in 1967. The **Conservative Baptist** Foreign Mission Society began a mission in Zambia in 1995.

As of 2006, there were 480 churches and 56,000 members affiliated with the Baptist Convention of Zambia, and 400 churches with 48,000 members in the Baptist Union of Zambia, which has ties to the **Baptist Missionary Society**.

ZIMBABWE. In 1913, the **Baptist Missionary Society** established its first church at Gweru, which evolved into the Association of Baptist Churches of Rhodesia in 1950. That same year, **Southern Baptists** began a mission at Gatooma, and this evolved into the Baptist Convention of Zimbabwe in 1981, composed mostly of indigenous churches.

As of 2006, there were 316 churches and 110,900 members affiliated with the Baptist Convention of Zimbabwe; 47 churches and 10,000 members affiliated with the United Baptist Churches of Zimbabwe; 38 churches and 3,500 members affiliated with the Baptist Union of Zimbabwe; and 45 churches with 7,000 members affiliated with the National Baptist Convention.

ZIONITIC BROTHERHOOD. A splinter group established in 1738 from the Ephrata Community formed by **Conrad Beissel**. Led by Gabriel Eckerling (also called Jotham) (d. 1757), the movement consisted of a blend of Egyptian Freemasonry, Rosicrucianism, and Baptistic practices. Eckerling became disenchanted with Beissel's leadership and established a mystical society at Coalico Creek in Lancaster County, Pennsylvania, where he became the first "Perfect Master," or Prior. The group's goal was to obtain physical and moral regeneration by practicing high ethical standards and mystical exercises. A subgroup of the **German Baptist Brethren**, the Zionitische Bruderschaft became indistinguishable from the larger group by the 19th century. Eckerling himself was captured by the French in western Pennsylvania/Virginia in 1757, and after being scalped and transported through Quebec to France, he died in a monastery.

Bibliography

Baptist bibliography has been a science from the 19th century in England to recent updating essays in the leading journals (especially *American Baptist Quarterly*, *Baptist History and Heritage*, and *Baptist Quarterly*). Because of the numerical size of the denomination as well as its geographical distribution, theological variety, and number of publication outlets, Baptist historical bibliography is expansive. There is a noticeable difference between those who write Baptist history as "Baptist historians" and those who investigate the Baptist contribution to the larger culture and theological trends. The former are typically found in theological schools and denominational posts, while the latter are in university positions, quite removed from congregational life or even an identity with Baptists. The one can be essentially apologetic, the other quite critical in a scholarly sense. With the elevation of Baptists in the public sphere in the United States and Canada, a number of scholars are interested in the Baptists as models of a Free Church or Congregational type of Christianity. An interest in Baptist contributions to political issue discussions or social movements in exhibited. Increasingly, recent Baptist historical writing in Britain is often tied to the task of advancing evangelical history. In developing Baptist national cultures, what has emerged is missionary history, biography, and institutional history, with little attention to social or theological analysis.

The bibliography that follows is not intended to be exhaustive, but selective. Many classic entries are included; every effort has been made to include recent publications.

CONTENTS

GENERAL REFERENCE

Baptist studies should be placed in the context of the larger categories of Christian religion and, for instance, in North America, the literature of American and Canadian religion. Biographical dictionaries, statistical analyses, handbooks, and encyclopedias are very useful resources. Old standard bibliographies, like Whitley and Starr, are still the beginning points for citations and are both available online.

Anderson, Gerald, editor. *Biographical Dictionary of Christian Missions*. New York: Scribner's, 1997.

Brierley, Peter, editor. *World Churches Handbook*. London: Christian Research, 1997.

Burgess, G. A., and Ward, J. T. *Free Baptist Cyclopedia: Historical and Biographical*. Boston, Mass.: Free Baptist Cyclopedia, 1889.

Cathcart, William. *The Baptist Encyclopedia*. 2 vols. Philadelphia, Pa.: Louis H. Everts, 1883.

Goldman, Minton F. *Global Studies: Commonwealth of Independent States and Central/Eastern Europe*. Guilford, Conn.: Dushkin Publishing Group, 1992.

Siewert, John A., and Kenyon, John A. *Mission Handbook: A Guide to USA/Canada Christian Ministries Overseas*. Monrovia, Calif.: MARC, 1993.

Sprague, William B. *Annals of the American Baptist Pulpit*. New York: R. Carter, 1860.

Starr, Edward C. *A Baptist Bibliography*. 26 vols. Rochester, N.Y.: American Baptist Historical Society, 1976.

Whitley, William T. *A Baptist Bibliography*. 2 vols. London: Carey Kingsgate Press, 1915–1922.

Wooley, Davis C., and May, Lynn E., Jr. *Encyclopedia of Southern Baptists*. 4 vols. Nashville, Tenn.: Broadman Press, 1971–1982.

PRIMARY SOURCE MATERIALS

Unfortunately, too little primary source material is available in a reliable form. Sourcebooks have limitations in that only partial selections are republished. Collections of confessional materials are readily available, as is a limited amount of American Baptist personal diaries, letters, and so forth, notably those of Isaac Backus. English Baptist resources from the 17th century are in print, though not readily available in North America.

Baker, Robert A., editor. *A Baptist Sourcebook, with Particular Reference to Southern Baptists*. Nashville, Tenn.: Broadman Press, 1966.

Brackney, William H., editor. *Baptist Life and Thought*. Valley Forge, Pa.: Judson Press, 1983; second edition, 1998.

Hayden, Roger, editor. *Baptist Union Documents, 1948–1977*. London: Baptist Historical Society, 1980.

———. *The Records of a Church of Christ in Bristol, 1640–1687*. Bristol: Record Society, 1974.

Hobbs, Herschel H. *The Baptist Faith and Message*. Nashville, Tenn.: Convention Press, 1971.

McGlothlin, William J. *Baptist Confessions of Faith*. Philadelphia Pa.: American Baptist Publication Society, 1910.

Underhill, Edward Bean. *Confessions of Faith and Other Public Documents, Illustrative of the History of the Baptist Churches of England in the 17th Century*. London: Haddon Brothers, 1854; repr. Kessinger Publishing Co., 2006.

White, Barrington R., editor. *Associational Records of the Particular Baptists of England, Wales, and Ireland to 1660*. London: Baptist Historical Society, 1974.

Whitley, William T., editor. *Minutes of the General Assembly of General Baptist Churches in England, with Kindred Records*. 2 vols. London: Carey Kingsgate Press, 1909–1910.

——, editor. *The Works of John Smyth, Fellow of Christ's College, Cambridge 1594–98*. 2 vols. Cambridge: Cambridge University Press, 1915.

BACKGROUNDS TO BAPTIST HISTORY

The researcher finds an increasing amount of material available in the area of backgrounds, in large part because a long-standing debate over the relationship of Baptists to Continental Anabaptists continues to draw attention. Exceptional recent work is available on John Smyth, John Robinson, and Francis Johnson. Secondary sources by B. R. White, Christopher Hill, Richard Greaves, and Michael Watts are excellent starting points. The African American tradition is entirely distinct.

Ball, Bryan W. *The Seventh-day Men: Sabbatarians and Sabbatarianism in England and Wales, 1600–1800*. Oxford: The Clarendon Press, 1994.

Brachlow, Stephen. *The Communion of Saints: Radical Puritan and Separatist Ideology, 1570–1625*. Oxford: Oxford University Press, 1988.

Brown, K. D. *A Social History of the Nonconformist Ministry in England and Wales, 1800–1930*. Oxford: The Clarendon Press, 1988.

Burrage, Champlin. *The Early English Dissenters in Light of Historical Research*. 2 vols. Cambridge: Cambridge University Press, 1912.

Coggins, James R. *John Smyth's Congregation: English Separatism, Mennonite Influence, and the Elect Nation*. Scottdale, Pa.: Herald Press, 1991.

Culpepper, K. Scott. "The Life and Work of Francis Johnson at Cambridge." Ph.D. dissertation, Baylor University, 2005.

Edwards, Thomas. *Gangraena; or A Catalogue and Discovery of Many of the Errours, Heresies, Blasphemies, and Pernicious Practices of the Sectaries of This Time. . . .* London: R. Smith, 1646.

Estep, William. *The Anabaptist Story*. Nashville, Tenn.: Broadman Press, 1963.

George, Timothy. *John Robinson and the English Separatist Tradition.* Macon, Ga.: Mercer University Press, 1982.

Greaves, Richard L. *Deliver Us from Evil: The Radical Underground in Britain, 1660–1663.* New York: Oxford University Press, 1986.

———. *The Puritan Revolution and Educational Thought: Background for Reform.* New Brunswick, N.J.: Rutgers University Press, 1969.

Hill, Christopher. *The World Turned Upside Down: Radical Ideas during the English Reformation.* London: Maurice Temple Smith, 1972.

Kliever, Lonnie D. "General Baptist Origins: The Question of Anabaptist Influence." *Mennonite Quarterly Review* 36:4 (October 1962): 291–321.

Krahn, Cornelius. *Dutch Anabaptism: Origin, Spread, Life and Thought (1450–1600).* The Hague: Martinus Nijhoff, 1968.

Littell, Franklin H. *The Anabaptist View of the Church: A Study in the Origins of Sectarian Protestantism.* Boston, Mass.: Starr King Press, 1958.

Mosteller, James D. "Baptists and Anabaptists." *Chronicle* 20:1 (January 1957): 3–27; 20:3 (July 1957): 100–114.

Nuttall, Geoffrey. *The Beginnings of Nonconformity.* London: J. Clark, 1964.

Orchard, G. H. *A Concise History of Foreign Baptists.* Nashville, Tenn.: Graves, Marks, 1855.

Parker, K. L. *The English Sabbath: A Study of the Doctrine and Discipline from the Reformation to the Civil War.* Cambridge: Cambridge University Press, 1988.

Payne, Ernest A. *The Anabaptists of the 16th Century.* London: Carey Kingsgate, 1949.

Sobel, Mechal. *Trabelin' On: The Slave Journey to an Afro-Baptist Faith.* Westport, Conn.: Greenwood Press, 1979.

Stassen, Glen H. "Anabaptist Influence in the Origin of the Particular Baptists." *Mennonite Quarterly Review* 36:4 (October 1962): 322–348.

Watts, Michael. *The Dissenters: From the Reformation to the French Revolution.* Oxford: The Clarendon Press, 1978.

White, Barrington R. *The English Separatist Tradition.* Oxford: Oxford University Press, 1971.

Whitley, William T. "Continental Anabaptists and Early English Baptists." *Baptist Quarterly* 2 (1924–1925): 27.

BAPTIST HISTORY-GENERAL STUDIES

For general surveys of Baptist life, one selects on the basis of national orientation. Robert Torbet's work is still reliable, H. L. McBeth writes from a southern United States perspective, and Leonard's work is stylized according to American themes. Older works like Thomas Armitage are available online.

Anderson, Justo. *Historia de los Bautistas*. 3 vols. El Paso, Tex.: Casa Bautista de Publicaciones, 1990.

Armitage, Thomas. *A History of the Baptists, Traced by Their Vital Principles and Practices from the Time of Our Lord and Savior Jesus Christ to the Year 1886*. New York: Bryan Taylor, 1887.

Brackney, William H. *The Baptists*. Westport, Conn.: Greenwood Press, 1988.

Leonard, Bill J. *Baptist Ways*. Valley Forge, Pa.: Judson Press, 1996.

McBeth, H. Leon. *The Baptist Heritage: Four Centuries of Baptist Witness*. Nashville, Tenn.: Broadman Press, 1987.

Thompson, E. Wayne, and Cummins, Daniel L. *This Day in Baptist History: 366 Daily Devotions Drawn from the Baptist Heritage*. Greenville, S.C.: Bob Jones University Press, 1993.

Torbet, Robert G. *History of the Baptists*. Valley Forge, Pa.: Judson Press, 1963.

Wardin, Albert W., editor. *Baptists around the World: A Comprehensive Handbook*. Nashville, Tenn.: Broadman and Holman, 1995.

BAPTISTS GROUPS—GEOGRAPHICAL

Africa

Historical work on Baptists in Africa is still in its infancy stages. Much of what is available is missionary history, culled from sending agency perspectives.

Atanda, J. A. *Baptist Churches in Nigeria, 1850–1950*. Ibadan: Author, 1988.

Batts, H. J. *The Story of a Hundred Years 1820–1920; Being a History of the Baptist Church in South Africa*. Capetown: Miller, 1920.

Coger, Dalvan M. "An Early Missionary Enterprise: The Baptists at Fernando Po, 1840–1860." *American Baptist Quarterly* 9:3 (September 1990): 158–166.

Hudson-Reed, Sydney. *History of the Baptist Union of South Africa*. Pietermaritzburg: South African Baptist Historical Society, 1977.

Jonnson, Jon N. "Baptists in Socio-Political Life in South Africa." *American Baptist Quarterly* 4:3 (September 1985): 4.

Maddry, Charles. *Day Dawn in Yoruba Land*. Nashville, Tenn.: Broadman Press, 1939.

Saunders, Davis L. "Baptists in East Africa: The Birth of Two Conventions." *Baptist History and Heritage* 6:4 (October 1971): 226–232.

Schneider, G. *A Graphic Portrayal of a Christian Mission at Work in the Cameroons*. Forest Park, Ill.: North American Baptist General Conference, 1957.

Stuart, Charles H. "The Lower Congo and the American Baptist Mission to 1910." Ph.D. dissertation, Boston University, 1969.

Valcarcel, S. J. *A Short History of Baptists in Sierra Leone, 1792–1984*. Bad Homburg, Germany: European Baptist Mission, 1984.

Asia, Australia, and New Zealand

Asian Baptist history is still in its missionary stages. The large need is for comprehensive work on India; here Frederick Downs' work is crucial as a beginning. There are several works on Australia, including Ken Manley's masterful two volumes.

Bollen, J. P. *Australian Baptists—A Religious Minority*. London: Baptist Historical Society, 1975.

Brown, B. S. *Baptized into One Body: A Short History of the Baptist Union of Australia*. Hawthorn: Baptist Union of Australia, 1987.

Cho, Timothy H. "A History of the Korea Baptist Convention, 1889–1969." Th.D. dissertation, Southern Baptist Theological Seminary, 1970.

Clough, John E. *From Darkness to Light: A Story of the Telugu Awakening*. Philadelphia, Pa.: American Baptist Publication Society, 1892.

Dean, William. *China Mission: A History of Missions of All Denominations among the Chinese, with Biographical Sketches of the Deceased*. New York: n.p., 1859.

Downs, Fred S. *The Mighty Works of God: A Brief History of the Council of Baptist Churches in Northeast India: The Mission Period 1836–1950*. Gauhati: Christian Literature Center, 1971.

Fenwick, Malcolm C. *The Church of Christ in Corea*. Seoul: Baptist Publications, 1967.

Gibson, Mary Ann. "Baptist Pioneers in Tasmania, Australia." *Chronicle* 11:3 (July 1948): 111–123.

Hughes, P. J. *The Baptists in Australia*. Canberra: Australian Government Publishing Services, 1996.

Manley, Ken R. *The First Australian Baptists*. Eastwood: Baptist Historical Society of New South Wales, 1981.

——. *From Woolloomooloo to "Eternity": A History of Australian Baptists*. 2 vols. Carlisle, Cumbria: Paternoster Press, 2006.

Moore, Richard K. *Baptists of Western Australia: The First Ninety Years, 1895–1985*. Perth: Baptist Historical Society of Western Australia, 1991.

Prior, Alan C. *Some Fell on Good Ground: A History of the Beginnings and Development of the Baptist Church in New South Wales, Australia, 1831–1965*. Sydney: Baptist Union of New South Wales, 1966.

Puthenpurakal, Joseph. *Baptist Missions in Nagaland*. Calcutta: Firma KLM, 1984.

Rogers, Lillie O., editor. *A History of Baptists in Malaysia & Singapore*. n.p., n.d.

Rubenstein, Murray. "American Evangelicalism in the Chinese Environment: Southern Baptist Missionaries in Taiwan, 1949–81." *American Baptist Quarterly* 2:3 (September 1983): 269–289.

Smith, Ebbie. "Baptist Advance in Indonesia." M.A. thesis, Fuller Theological Seminary, 1970.

Tegenfeldt, Herman. *A Century of Growth: The Kachin Baptist Church of Burma*. Pasadena, Calif.: William Carey Library, 1974.

Tonson, Paul. *A Handful of Grain: The Centenary History of the Baptist Union of New Zealand*. 4 vols. Wellington: New Zealand Baptist Historical Society, 1982.

Wa, Maung Shwe. *Burma Baptist Chronicle*. Rangoon: Board of Publications, 1963.

Canada

Canadian Baptists have had only one national historical survey (Harry Renfree) produced over two centuries. Most of the scholarship is regional and biographical. The Atlantic Baptists have slowly published primary sources useful to their revivalistic emphases, but these texts lack overall analysis. George Rawlyk's work dominates the Canadian and evangelical schools of interpretation.

Bentall, Shirley. *From Sea to Sea: The Canadian Baptist Federation, 1944–1994*. Mississauga, Ont.: Canadian Baptist Federation, 1994.

Bill, I. E. *Fifty Years with the Baptist Ministers and Churches of the Maritime Provinces of Canada*. Saint John, N.B.: Barnes and Company, 1880.

Brackney, William H. "Baptists in Canada." In *Baptist Streams*, edited by W. Glenn Jonas, pp. 206–226. Macon, Ga.: Mercer University Press, 2006.

Britten, Edward G. "A History of the Reformed Baptist Alliance of Canada." B.D. thesis, Acadia University, 1964.

Burnett, Frederick C. *Biographical Dictionary of Nova Scotia and New Brunswick Free Baptist Ministers and Preachers*. Hantsport, N.S.: Lancelot Press, 1996.

Ivison, Stuart, and Rosser, Fred. *The Baptists in Upper and Lower Canada before 1820*. Toronto, Ont.: University of Toronto Press, 1956.

Levy, George Edward. *The Baptists of the Maritime Provinces, 1753–1946*. Saint John, N.B.: Barnes-Hopkins, 1946.

Lewis, James K. *The Religious Life of the Fugitive Slaves and the Rise of Coloured Baptist Churches 1820–1865 in What Is Now Known as Ontario*. New York: Arno Press, 1980.

McCormick, Roland K. *Faith, Freedom, and Democracy: The Baptists in Atlantic Canada*. Moncton, N.B.: Four East Publishers, 1993.

McLaurin, C. C. *Pioneering in Western Canada: A Story of the Baptists*. Calgary, Alb.: Armac Press, 1939.

Renfree, Harry A. *Heritage and Horizon: The Baptist Story in Canada*. Mississauga, Ont.: Baptist Federation of Canada, 1988.

Saunders, Edward Manning. *History of the Baptists of the Maritime Provinces*. Halifax, N.S.: John Burgoyne, 1902.

Tarr, Leslie K. *This Dominion, His Dominion: The Story of Evangelical Baptist Endeavour in Canada*. Willowdale, Ont.: Fellowship of Evangelical Baptist Churches in Canada, 1968.

Zeman, Jarold K. *Baptists in Canada: Search for Identity amidst Diversity*. Burlington, Ont.: G. R. Welch, 1980.

Caribbean

The leading source on Baptist life in this region is Horace Russell's work on Jamaica, which is based upon an Oxford dissertation.

Hackshaw, John W. *The Baptist Denomination*. Kingston, Jamaica: Amphy and Bashana Memorial Society, 1991.

Ramos, Tomas Rosario. *Historia de los Bautistas de Puerto Rico.* Santo Domingo: La Convencion, 1979.

Russell, Horace O. *Foundations and Anticipation: The Jamaica Baptist Story: 1783–1892.* Columbus, Ohio: Brentwood Christian Press, 1993.

Sibley, Inez Knibb. *The Baptists of Jamaica, 1793–1965.* Kingston: Jamaica Baptist Union, 1965.

Symonette, Michael C. *Baptists in the Bahamas: An Historical Overview.* El Paso, Tex.: Baptist Spanish Publishing House, 1977.

Europe

Baptist scholarly studies are emerging from independent unions across Eastern and Western Europe. An important impetus is the Theological Teacher's Fellowship of the European Baptist Federation, plus the trickle of essays from the Seminary at Prague. Bernard Green's work, English Baptist in orientation, is informative of organizational developments.

Bednarczyk, Krzysztof. *Historia Zborow Baptystow w Polsce do 1939 roku.* Warszawa: Slowo Prawdy, 1997.

Bordeaux, Michael. *Religious Ferment in Russia: Protestant Opposition to Soviet Religious Policy.* London: Macmillan, 1968.

Corrado, Sharyl, and Pilli, Toivo, editors. *Eastern European Baptist History: New Perspectives.* Prague, Czech Republic: International Baptist Seminary, 2007.

Eden, David. *Svenska baptisterna in Finland historia, 1856–1931.* Vasa: 1930.

Eidberg, Peder. *The People Called Baptist.* Stabekk, Norway: Baptist Seminary, 1999.

Geldbach, Erich. *Freikirchen—Erbe, Gestalt, und Wirkung.* Göttingen: Vandenhoeck and Ruprecht, 2005.

Green, Bernard. *Crossing the Boundaries: A History of the European Baptist Federation.* Didcot: Baptist Historical Society, 1999.

Harrell, Norman L. "Beginnings of Baptist Work in Portugal, 1808–1928." M.A. thesis, Southern Baptist Theological Seminary, 1991.

History of the Evangelical Christian Baptists of the Soviet Union. Moscow: Union of Evangelical Christians-Baptists, 1989.

Hopper, John D. "Baptist Beginnings in Yugoslavia." *Baptist History and Heritage* 17:4 (October 1982): 28–37.

Hylleberg, Bent, and Jorgensen, Bjarne M. *Et kirkesamfund bliver til*. Omslag, Denmark: Henning Aardestrup, 1989.

Lehman, Joseph. *Geschichte der deutschen Baptisten*. Hamburg: Oncken Verlag, 1896.

Novotny, Joseph. *The Baptist Romance in the Heart of Europe (Czechoslovakia): The Life and Times of Henry Novotny*. New York: John Felsburg, 1939.

Parker, G. Keith. *Baptists in Europe: History and Confessions of Faith*. Nashville, Tenn.: Broadman Press, 1982.

Payne, Ernest A. *Out of Great Tribulation: Baptists in the USSR*. London: Baptist Union of Great Britain, 1974.

Rogaczewski, Jerzy P. "The Polish Baptist Identity in Historical Context." M.Div. thesis, McMaster University, 1995.

Rousseau, Georges J. *Histoire des Eglises Baptistes*. Paris: Société de Publications Baptistes, 1951.

Sanfilippo, P. *L'Italia Battista*. Rome: Unione Cristiana Evangelica Battista d'Italia, 1959.

Steeves, Paul D. "The Russian Baptist Union, 1917–1935: Evangelical Awakening in Russia." Ph.D. dissertation, University of Kansas, 1976.

Sundquist, Alfons. "The Baptist Movement in Finland." *Chronicle* 11:1 (January 1948): 3–16.

Trutza, Peter. "A Short History of Roumanian Baptists." *Chronicle* 5:1 (January 1942): 9–21.

Vojta, Vaclav. *Czechoslovak Baptists*. Chicago, Ill.: Czechoslovak Baptist Convention of America, 1941.

Wardin, Albert. "The Baptists of Bulgaria." *Baptist Quarterly* 34:4 (October 1991): 148–159.

Great Britain and Ireland

All Baptist studies rely upon strong scholarship in the British context. Secondary sources that are informed and useful are the Baptist Historical Series edited by Roger Hayden and Hayden's own book on the English Baptists. Recent monographs from Paternoster Press provide theological depth to the tradition. T. H. Bassett's work on Wales and Derek Murray's book on Scottish Baptists (supplemented with David Bebbington's essays) are key resources.

Bassett, T. M. *The Welsh Baptists*. Swansea, Wales: Ilston House, 1977.

Bebbington, David. *Baptists in Scotland*. Glasgow, Scotland: Union, 1988.

Briggs, John H. Y. *The English Baptists of the Nineteenth Century*. Didcot: Baptist Historical Society, 1994.

Brown, Raymond. *The English Baptists of the Eighteenth Century*. London: Baptist Historical Society, 1986.

Crosby, Thomas. *History of the Baptists*. 4 vols. London: Editor, 1738–1740.

Dix, Kenneth. *Strict and Particular: English Strict and Particular Baptists in the Nineteenth Century*. Didcot: Baptist Historical Society, 2001.

Evans, Benjamin. *Early English Baptists*. 2 vols. London: J. Heaton, 1862–1864.

Hayden, Roger. *English Baptist History and Heritage*. Didcot: Baptist Union of Great Britain, 2005.

Ivimey, Joseph. *History of the Baptists*. 4 vols. London: I. T. Hinton, 1811–1830.

Murray, Derek B. *The First Hundred Years: The Baptist Union of Scotland*. Glasgow: Baptist Union of Scotland, 1969.

———. "The Scotch Baptist Tradition in Great Britain." *Baptist Quarterly* 33:4 (December 1989): 186–198.

Paul, S. F. *Historical Sketch of the Gospel Standard Baptists*. London: Gospel Standard Publications, 1945.

Payne, Ernest A. *The Baptist Union: A Short History*. London: Carey Kingsgate Press, 1958.

Randall, Ian M. *The English Baptists of the 20th Century*. Didcot: The Baptist Historical Society, 2005.

Sellers, Ian, editor. *Our Heritage: The Baptists of Yorkshire, Lancashire, and Cheshire, 1647–1987*. Leeds: Yorkshire Baptist Association, 1987.

Shepherd, Peter. *The Making of a Modern Denomination: John Howard Shakespeare and the English Baptists, 1898–1924*. Carlisle, Cumbria: Paternoster, 2001.

Taylor, Adam. *History of the General Baptists*. 2 vols. London: T. Bore, 1818.

Thompson, Joshua. *Century of Grace: The Baptist Union of Ireland, a Short History, 1895–1995*. Belfast: Baptist Union of Ireland 1996.

Underwood, A. C. *A History of the English Baptists*. London: Carey Kingsgate Press, 1947.

Ward, W. R. "The Baptists and the Transformation of the Church 1780–1830." *Baptist Quarterly* 35:4 (December 1973): 167–184.

White, B. R. *The English Baptists of the Seventeenth Century*. Didcot: Baptist Historical Society, 1983.

Whitley, William T. *A History of British Baptists*. London: Charles Griffin, 1923.

Latin America

Much more secondary literature needs to be forthcoming from Latin American Baptists. There are not yet any publications of original sources, nor any overall surveys of the region. The narrative has to be recovered from mission histories.

Actas da Convencão Baptista Brasileira. 2 vols. Rio de Janeiro: Archivos de la Convencion, 1967.

Actas de la Union Bautista de Chile. 2 vols. Santiago: Archivo del Seminario, 1921, 1967.

Brackney, William H. *Bridging Cultures and Hemispheres: The Legacy of Archibald Reekie and Canadian Baptists in Bolivia*. Macon, Ga.: Smyth and Helwys, 1997.

Crabtree, A. R., and de Mesquita, Antonio N. *Historia dos Batistas do Brasil*. 2 vols. Rio de Janeiro: Cas Publicadora Batista, 1937–1940.

Loredo, Ignacio. *Un hombre, Un pueblo: Los Bautistas Argentinos a cien anos de la llegada de Pablo Besson*. Buenos Aires: Casa Bautista de Publicaciones, 1981.

Mesquita, Antonio Neves de. *Historia dos Batistas em Pernambuco*. Recife: Tipografia do CAB, 1930.

Nacho, Arturo. *Un siglo de evangelización: 100 anos de la Obra Bautista en Bolivia*. Cochabamba, Bolivia: Comisión de Historia de la Union Bautista Boliviana, 1998.

Patterson, Frank W. *A Century of Baptist Work in Mexico*. El Paso, Tex.: Baptist Spanish Publishing House, 1979.

Pitts, William L. "Baptist Beginnings in Brazil." *Baptist History and Heritage* 17:4 (October 1982): 4–16.

Rodriquez, J. M. *Los Bautistas en las republicas del plata*. Buenos Aires: Junta Bautista de Publicaciones, 1930.

United States

Works on Baptist development in the United States abound over 200 years, from Morgan Edwards to recent surveys by Brackney and Leonard. Each of the sub-denominational groups has its own narrative, many of which bring details through the 1980s. The leading models of U.S. Baptist history are William McLoughlin (*New England Dissent*), James Washington (*Frustrated Fellowship*), and Don Sandford (*A Choosing People*).

Anderson, Donald E. *The 1960s in the Ministry of the Baptist General Conference.* Evanston, Ill.: Harvest Publications, 1961.

———.*The 1970s in the Ministry of the Baptist General Conference.* Arlington Heights, Ill.: Baptist General Conference, 1981.

Armstrong, O. K., and Armstrong, Marjorie. *The Indomitable Baptists: A Narration of Their Role in Shaping American History.* New York: Doubleday, 1967.

Backlund, J. O. *Swedish Baptists in America.* Chicago, Ill.: Conference Press, 1933.

Backus, Isaac. *A History of New England with Particular Reference to the Denomination of Christians Called Baptists.* Newton, Mass.: Backus Historical Society, 1871.

Barnes, William W. *The Southern Baptist Convention, 1845–1953.* Nashville, Tenn.: Broadman Press, 1954.

Baxter, Norman A. *History of the Freewill Baptists: A Study in New England Separatism.* Rochester, N.Y.: American Baptist Historical Society, 1957.

Benedict, David. *A General History of the Baptist Denomination in the United States and Other Parts of the World.* New York: Lewis Colby, 1848.

Bitting, W. C. *A Manual of the Northern Baptist Convention, 1908–1918.* Philadelphia, Pa.: American Baptist Publication Society, 1918.

Bone, John S. *"The Better Maintenance of the Ministry": The First Seventy Five Years of the Ministers and Missionaries Benefit Board.* New York: Ministers and Missionaries Benefit Board, 1987.

Booth, William D. *The Progressive Story: New Baptist Roots.* Nashville, Tenn.: PNBC, 1981.

Brackney, William H. *Baptists in North America: An Analytical History.* Oxford: Blackwell Publishers, 2006.

Bradley, Lasserre, Jr. *A Brief History of Primitive Baptists.* Cincinnati, Ohio; Baptist Bible Hour, 2007.

Burkitt, Lemuel, and Read, Jesse. *A Concise History of the Kehukee Baptist Association from Its Original Rise Down to 1803.* Philadelphia, Pa.: Lippincott, Grambo and Co., 1850.

DiDomenica, Angelo. *Protestant Witness of a New American*. Philadelphia, Pa.: Judson Press, 1956.

Dodd, Damon C. *The Freewill Baptist Story*. Nashville, Tenn.: National Association of Freewill Baptists, 1956.

Duggar, John W. *The Baptist Missionary Association of America*. Texarkana, Tex.: Baptist Publishing House, 1988.

Durso, Pamela R. *A Short History of the Cooperative Baptist Fellowship Movement*. Brentwood, Tenn.: Baptist History and Heritage Society, 2006.

Fisher, Miles Mark. *A Short History of the Baptist Denomination*. Nashville, Tenn.: Sunday School Board, 1933.

Fitts, Leroy. *A History of Black Baptists*. Nashville, Tenn.: Broadman, 1985.

Fletcher, Jesse C. *The Southern Baptist Convention: A Sesquicentennial History*. Nashville, Tenn.: Broadman and Holman, 1994.

Glover, Conrad E., and Powers, Austin T. *The American Baptist Association, 1924–1974*. Texarkana, Tex.: Bogard Press, 1979.

Goen, Clarence C. *Revivalism and Separatism in New England, 1740–1800: Strict Congregationalists and Separate Baptists in the Great Awakening*. New Haven, Conn.: Yale University Press, 1962.

Hassell, Cushing B. *History of the Church of God, From the Creation to A.D. 1885, Including Especially the History of the Kehukee Primitive Baptist Association*. Middletown, N.Y.: Gilbert Beebe's Sons, 1886.

Hubbard, Kenneth. "The Southwide Baptist Fellowship." Th.D. dissertation, Southwestern Baptist Theological Seminary, 1968.

Jackson, Joseph H. *A Story of Christian Activism: The History of the National Baptist Convention, USA, Inc*. Nashville, Tenn.: Townshend Press, 1980.

Jordan, Lewis G. *Negro Baptist History, USA*. Nashville, Tenn.: Sunday School Publishing Board of the National Baptist Convention, 1930.

Lambert, B. C. *Rise of Antimission Baptists*. New York: Arno Press, 1980.

Latch, Ollie. *History of the General Baptists*. Poplar Bluff, Mo.: General Baptist Press, 1972.

Leonard, Bill J. *Dictionary of Baptists in America*. Downer's Grove, Ill.: Intervarsity Press, 1994.

———.*God's Last and Only Hope: The Fragmentation of the Southern Baptist Convention*. Grand Rapids, Mich.: Wm. B. Eerdmans, 1990.

McLoughlin, William G. *New England Dissent: Baptists and the Separation of Church and State, 1630–1833*. 2 vols. Cambridge, Mass.: Harvard University Press, 1971.

Miller, Terry E. "Otter Creek Church, Indiana: Lonely Bastion of Daniel Parker's Two-Seedism." *Foundations* 18:4 (October 1975): 358–376.

Montgomery, D. B., editor. *General Baptist History*. Evansville, Ind.: Courier Co., 1882.

Newman, Albert H. *A History of Baptist Churches in the United States*. Philadelphia, Pa.: American Baptist Publication Society, 1898.

Olson, Adolf. *A Centenary History, as Related to the Baptist General Conference of America*. Chicago, Ill.: Baptist Conference Press, 1952.

Parry, Pam. *On Guard for Religious Liberty: Six Decades of the Baptist Joint Committee*. Macon, Ga.: Smyth and Helwys, 1996.

Pelt, Michael R. *A History of Original Free Will Baptists*. Mount Olive, N.C.: Mount Olive College Press, 1996.

Pelt, O. D., and Smith, R. L. *The Story of the National Baptists*. New York: Vantage Books, 1960.

Perrigan, Rufus. *History of Regular Baptists and Their Ancestors and Assessors*. Hayes, Va.: Privately Published, 1961.

Pius, Nathaniel H. *An Outline of Baptist History*. Nashville, Tenn.: National Baptist Publishing Board, 1911.

Rentz, James, editor. *What Hath God Wrought? Sixty Years of Christian Stewardship, 1901–1961*. Chicago, Ill.: Baptist Mission Union of America, 1961.

Rogers, Albert N. *Seventh Day Baptists in Europe and America*. 3 vols. Plainfield, N.J.: Seventh Day Baptist Publishing House, 1972.

Rogers, John B. *The Rogerenes: Some Hitherto Unpublished Annals Belonging to the Colonial History of Connecticut*. Boston, Mass.: Stanhope Press, 1904.

Rosenburg, Ellen M. *The Southern Baptists: A Subculture in Transition*. Knoxville: University of Tennessee Press, 1989.

Sachse, Julius F. *The German Sectarians of Pennsylvania, 1708–42: A Critical and Legendary History of the Ephrata Cloister and the Dunkers*. Philadelphia, Pa.: Stockhausen, 1899.

Sandford, Don A. *A Choosing People: The History of Seventh Day Baptists*. Nashville, Tenn.: Broadman Press, 1992.

Stianson, Peter. *History of the Norwegian Baptists in America*. Philadelphia, Pa.: American Baptist Publication Society, 1939.

Sweet, William W. *Religion on the American Frontier: The Baptists*. New York: Henry Holt and Co., 1931.

Taylor, Wilburn S. "World Baptist Fellowship." *Quarterly Review* 19:2 (April 1959): 35–39.

Torbet, Robert G. *Baptists North and South*. Valley Forge, Pa.: Judson Press, 1964.

Washington, James Melvin. *Frustrated Fellowship: The Black Baptist Quest for Social Power*. Macon, Ga.: Mercer University Press, 1985.

Wood, James E., editor. *Baptists and the American Experience*. Valley Forge, Pa.: Judson Press, 1976.

Woolley, Davis C., editor. *Baptist Advance: The Achievements of the Baptists of North America for a Century and a Half*. Nashville, Tenn.: Broadman Press, 1964.

Woyke, Frank H. *Heritage and Ministry of the North American Baptist Conference*. Oakbrook Terrace, Ill.: North American Baptist Conference, 1979.

BAPTIST MISSIONS

So much of Baptist history began as missionary outreach in various locations. The genre is thus important for identifying pioneering persons and ideals. Yet mission history tends to be either institutional (if of a board or agency) or a first step in historical interpretation from a colonialist perspective. Older works like Howard Malcolm's *Travels* contain much useful material. Brian Stanley's history of the Baptist Missionary Society (U.K.) is a model of scholarship.

Adams, C. C., and Talley, Marshall A. *Negro Baptists and Foreign Missions*. Philadelphia, Pa.: Foreign Mission Board of the National Baptist Convention, 1944.

Allen, Catherine B. *A Century to Celebrate*. Birmingham, Ala.: Women's Missionary Union, 1987.

Anderson, Courtney. *To the Golden Shore: The Life of Adoniram Judson*. Boston, Mass.: Little, Brown, 1956.

Ball, G. B. "The Australian Baptist Mission and Its Impact in Bengal." M.A. thesis, Flinders University, 1978.

Barnes, Lemuel C., editor. *Pioneers of Light: The First Century of the American Baptist Publication Society, 1824–1924*. Philadelphia, Pa.: American Baptist Publication Society, 1924.

Beers, G. Pitt. *Ministry to Turbulent America: A History of the American Baptist Home Mission Society, Covering Its Fifth Quarter Century, 1932–1957*. Philadelphia, Pa.: Judson Press, 1957.

Brumberg, Joan J. *Mission for Life: The Dramatic Story of the Family of Adoniram Judson*. New York: Free Press, 1980.

Carey, William. *An Enquiry into the Obligation of Christians to Use Means for the Conversion of the Heathens*. Leicester: T. Dicey, 1792.

Cauthen, Baker J. *Advance: A History of Southern Baptist Foreign Missions*. Nashville, Tenn.: Broadman Press, 1970.

Commons, Harold T. *Heritage and Harvest*. Cherry Hill, N.J.: Association of Baptists for World Evangelism, 1981.

Cox, F. A. *History of the English Baptist Missionary Society from 1792 to 1842, to Which Is Added a Sketch of the General Baptist Mission*. London: T. Ward, 1842.

Estep, William R. *Whole Gospel, Whole World: The Foreign Mission Board of the Southern Baptist Convention, 1845–1995*. Nashville, Tenn.: Broadman and Holman, 1995.

Fellowship of Baptists for Home Missions. *Two Decades of Home Missions 1940–1960*. Elyria, Ohio: Fellowship of Baptists for Home Missions, 1960.

Finzel, Hans, editor. *Partners Together*. Wheaton, Ill.: Conservative Baptist Foreign Mission Society, 1993.

Freeman, Edward A. *The Epoch of Negro Baptists and the Foreign Mission Board, National Baptist Convention USA, Inc.* Kansas City, Kans.: Central Seminary Press, 1953.

Gammell, William. *A History of American Baptist Missions*. Boston, Mass.: Gould, Kendall, and Lincoln, 1849.

Harvey, William J. *Bridges of Faith across the Seas*. Philadelphia, Pa.: National Baptist Convention, 1989.

Hervey, G. W. *The Story of Baptist Missions*. St. Louis, Mo.: Barnes, 1886.

Hopewell, William J. *The Missionary Emphasis of the General Association of Regular Baptist Churches*. Chicago, Ill.: Regular Baptist Press, 1963.

Kverndal, Roald. *Seaman's Missions: Their Origin and Early Growth*. Pasadena, Calif.: William Carey Library, 1986.

Malcolm, Howard. *Travels in Southeastern Asia: Embracing Hindustan, Malaya, Siam, and China, with Notices of Numerous Missionary Stations*. Boston, Mass.: Gould, Kendall, and Lincoln, 1839.

Marshman, Joshua. *Brief Memoir Relative to the Operations of the Serampore Missionaries*. London: Parbury, Allen and Co., 1827.

McKivigan, John R. "The American Baptist Free Mission Society: Abolitionist Reaction to the 1845 Baptist Schism." *Foundations* 21:4 (October 1978): 340–355.

McLoughlin, William G. *Cherokees and Missionaries, 1789–1839*. New Haven, Conn.: Yale University Press, 1984.

Means, Frank K. *Advance to Bold Mission Thrust: A History of Southern Baptist Foreign Missions, 1970–1980*. Richmond, Va.: Foreign Mission Board of the Southern Baptist Convention, 1981.

Padelford, Frank W. *The Kingdom in the States: A Study of the Missionary Work of State Conventions*. Philadelphia, Pa.: Judson Press, 1928.

Potts, E. Daniel. *British Baptist Missionaries in India, 1793–1837*. Cambridge: Cambridge University Press, 1967.

Puthenpurakal, Joseph. *Baptist Missions in Nagaland*. Calcutta: Baptist Press, 1984.

Redman, J. *The Light Shines On: The Story of the Missionary Outreach of the Baptist People of Australia, 1882–1982*. Hawthorne: Australian Baptist Mission Society, 1982.

Rutledge, Arthur B. *Mission to America: A Century and a Quarter of Southern Baptist Home Missions*. Nashville, Tenn.: Broadman Press, 1969.

Slaight, Lawrence T. *Multiplying the Witness: 150 Years of American Baptist Educational Ministries*. Valley Forge, Pa.: Judson Press, 1974.

Sparkes, Douglas C. *The Home Mission Story*. Didcot, England: The Baptist Historical Society, 1995.

Stanley, Brian. *The History of the Baptist Missionary Society, 1792–1992*. Edinburgh: T and T Clark, 1992.

Strong, Augustus H. *A Tour of the Missions: Observations and Conclusions*. Philadelphia, Pa.: Griffith and Rowland Press, 1918.

Strong, Polly. *Burning Wicks: The Story of Baptist Mid-Missions*. Cleveland, Ohio: Baptist Mid-Missions, 1984.

Talley, Marshall A. *Negro Baptists and Foreign Missions*. Philadelphia, Pa.: Foreign Mission Board of the National Baptist Convention, 1944.

Tidball, Derek J. "Evangelical Nonconformist Home Missions, 1796–1901." Ph.D. dissertation, University of Keele, 1981.

Titterington, Sophie B. *A Century of Baptist Foreign Missions*. Philadelphia, Pa.: American Baptist Foreign Mission Society, 1891.

Torbet, Robert G. *Venture of Faith: The Story of the American Baptist Foreign Mission Society and the Woman's American Baptist Foreign Mission Society 1814–1954*. Philadelphia, Pa.: Judson Press, 1955.

Tupper, Henry A. *The Foreign Missions of the SBC*. Philadelphia, Pa.: American Baptist Publication Society, 1880.

Underhill, Edward B. *The Tragedy of Morant Bay: A Narrative of the Disturbances in the Island of Jamaica in 1865*. London: Alexander Shepheard, 1895.

Wayland, Francis. *The Moral Dignity of the Missionary Enterprise*. Boston, Mass.: James Loring, 1824.

White, Charles L. *A Century of Faith*. Philadelphia, Pa.: Judson Press, 1932.

Wright, Mary E. *The Missionary Work of the Southern Baptist Convention*. Philadelphia, Pa.: American Baptist Publication Society, 1902.

BAPTIST THEOLOGY AND BELIEFS

Aldwinckle, Russell. *More Than Man: A Study in Christology*. Grand Rapids, Mich.: Wm. B. Eerdmans, 1976.

Ashmore, William. *Outline of Theology for Chinese Students*. Yokohama, Japan: Author, 1900(?).

Boyce, James P. *Abstract of Systematic Theology*. Baltimore, Md.: H. Wharton, 1887.

Brackney, William H. *A Genetic History of Baptist Thought, with Reference to Britain and North America*. Macon, Ga.: Mercer University Press, 2005.

———. *A Capsule History of Baptist Principles*. Atlanta, Ga.: Baptist History and Heritage Society, 2009.

———. "Thomas Grantham, Systematic Theology, and the Baptist Tradition." In *Biblical Criticism to Biblical Faith*, pp. 199–216. Macon, Ga.: Mercer University Press, 2007.

Bush, L. Russ, and Nettles, Tom J. *Baptists and the Bible: The Baptist Doctrines of Biblical Inspiration and Religious Authority in Historical Perspective*. Chicago, Ill.: Moody Press, 1980.

Butler, John J. *Natural and Revealed Theology*. Dover, N.H.: Freewill Baptist Printing Establishment, 1861.

Carey, William. *An Enquiry into the Obligations of Christians to Use Means for the Conversion of the Heathen*. Leicester, England: Ann Ireland, 1792.

Cauthen, W. Kenneth. *The Rise of American Religious Liberalism*. New York: Harper and Row, 1962.

———. *Systematic Theology: A Modern Protestant Approach*. Lewiston, N.Y.: Edward Mellen Press, 1986.

Clarke, William N. *An Outline of Christian Theology*. New York: Charles Scribner's, 1909.

Clements, Keith W. *Lovers of Discord: Twentieth Century Theological Controversies in England*. London: SPCK, 1988.

Connor, Walter T. *Christian Doctrine*. Nashville, Tenn.: Broadman Press, 1937.

Cook, Henry. *What Baptists Stand For*. London: Carey Kingsgate Press, 1947.

Cox, Harvey. *Religion in the Secular City: Toward a Post-Modern Theology*. New York: Simon and Schuster, 1984.

Crabtree, Arthur B. *The Restored Relationship: A Study in Justification and Reconciliation*. Valley Forge, Pa.: Judson Press, 1963.

Dagg, J. L. *A Manual of Theology*. Charleston, S.C.: Southern Baptist Publication Society, 1857.

Dockery, David S., and George, Timothy, editors. *Baptist Theologians*. Nashville, Tenn.: Broadman Press, 1990.

Erickson, Millard J. *Christian Theology*. Grand Rapids, Mich.: Baker Book House, 1983.

Foster, George B. *The Finality of the Christian Religion*. Chicago, Ill.: University of Chicago Press, 1906.

Fuller, Andrew. *The Gospel of Christ Worthy of All Acceptation*. Northampton: T. Dicey, 1785.

Garrett, James Leo. *Systematic Theology: Biblical, Historical, & Evangelical*. 2 vols. Grand Rapids, Mich.: Wm. B. Eerdmans, 1990.

Gill, John. *A Complete Body of Doctrinal and Practical Divinity*. London: Author, 1769.

Grantham, Thomas. *Christianismus Primitivus*. London: Francis Smith, 1678.

Grenz, Stanley J. *Theology for the Community of God*. Nashville, Tenn.: Broadman and Holman, 1994.

Hall, Robert. *Help to Zion's Travellers; Being an Attempt to Remove Various Stumblingblocks Out of the Way, Relating to Doctrinal, Experimental, and Practical Religion*. Alexandria, Va.: John Par, 1814.

Hamilton, William. *The New Essence of Christianity*. New York: Association Press, 1966.

Hayden, Roger. *Continuity and Change: Evangelical Calvinism among Eighteenth Century Baptist Ministers Trained at Bristol Academy, 1690–1791*. Didcot: Baptist Historical Society, 2006.

Helwys, Thomas. *A Short and Plaine Proofe by the Word and Workes of God That God's Decree Is the Cause of Anye Mans Sinne or Condemnation; and That All Men Are Redeemed by Christ; as Also That No Infants Are Condemned*. London: n.p., 1611(?).

Henry, Carl F. H. *God, Revelation, and Authority*. 6 vols. Waco, Tex.: Word Books, 1976–1983.

Hill, Christopher. *The English Bible and the Seventeenth Century Revolution*. London: Allen Lane, 1993.

Hovey, Alvah. *Christian Theology*. Newton Center, Mass.: Newton Theological Institution, 1896.

Jenkins, Charles A. *Baptist Doctrines*. St. Louis, Mo.: Chancy R. Barns, 1881.

Johnson, Elias H. *Outline of Systematic Theology*. Philadelphia, Pa.: American Baptist Publication Society, 1891.

Judson, Edward. *The Institutional Church: A Primer in Pastoral Theology*. New York: Lentilhon, 1899.

King, Martin Luther, Jr. *Strength to Love*. New York: Walker and Co., 1963.

Ladd, George E. *Theology of the New Testament*. Guildford: Lutterworth Press, 1975.

Lagergran, Carl G. *Bibelus grundlaror, systematisk teologi*. Minneapolis, Minn.: Veckobladets boktrycker, 1922.

Land, Richard D. "Doctrinal Controversies of English Particular Baptists (1644–1691), as Illustrated in the Career and Writings of Thomas Collier." D.Phil. thesis, University of Oxford, 1979.

Lewis, Gordon R., and Demarest, Bruce A. *Integrative Theology*. 3 vols. Grand Rapids, Mich.: Zondervan, 1987–1994.

Lorenzen, Thorwald. *Resurrection and Discipleship*. Maryknoll, N.Y.: Orbis Books, 1995.

Lumpkin, William L. *Baptist Confessions of Faith*. Valley Forge, Pa.: Judson Press, 1959.

Macintosh, Douglas C. *Theology as an Empirical Science*. New York: Macmillan, 1919.

Mathews, Shailer. *The Faith of Modernism*. New York: Macmillan, 1924.

McClendon, James W., Jr. *Systematic Theology: Ethics, Doctrine*. 3 vols. Nashville, Tenn.: Abingdon Press, 1986, 1994, 2002.

McGlothlin, William J. *Baptist Confessions of Faith*. Philadelphia, Pa.: American Baptist Publication Society, 1910.

Moody, Dale. *The Word of Truth: A Summary of Christian Doctrine Based on Biblical Revelation*. Grand Rapids, Mich.: Wm. B. Eerdmans, 1981.

Mullins, Edgar Y. *The Christian Religion in Its Doctrinal Expression*. Philadelphia, Pa.: Judson Press, 1917.

Peden, Creighton, and Stone, Jerome A., editors. *The Chicago School of Theology: Pioneers in Religious Inquiry. 2 vols.* Lewiston, N.Y.: Edwin Mellen Press, 1996.

Pendleton, James M. *Christian Doctrines: A Compendium of Theology*. Philadelphia, Pa.: American Baptist Publication Society, 1878.

Pepper, George D. B. *Outlines of Systematic Theology*. Philadelphia, Pa.: J. B. Rodgers, 1873.

Pinnock, Clark H. *The Scripture Principle*. New York: Harper and Row, 1984.

Rauschenbusch, Walter. *A Theology for the Social Gospel*. New York: Macmillan, 1917.

Robinson, Ezekiel G. *Christian Theology*. Rochester, N.Y.: E. R. Andrews, 1894.

Smith, Gerald B. *Social Idealism and the Changing Theology*. New York: Macmillan, 1913.

Smyth, John. *Differences in the Churches of the Separation*. Amsterdam: 1608.

Strong, Augustus H. *Systematic Theology: A Compendium*. Philadelphia, Pa.: American Baptist Publication Society, 1907.

Taylor, Dan. *Fundamentals of Religion in Faith and Practice*. London: 1775.

Timpany, Americus V. *Compendium of Theology*. Madras: Foster, 1879.

Walton, Robert C. *The Gathered Community*. London: Carey Press, 1946.

Wayland, Francis. *Elements of Moral Science*. Boston, Mass.: Gould, Kendall and Lincoln, 1835.

BAPTIST POLITY, PRACTICE, AND WORSHIP

The primary topic in this area has always been baptism and there continues to be a steady flow of books on the subject. Next are the studies of the Lord's Supper and church manuals, beginning with Samuel Jones. George R. Beasley-Murray on baptism, Michael Walker on the Lord's Supper, and Norman Maring and Winthrop Hudson's polity manual are outstanding resources.

Aldwinckle, Russell F. *Of Water and the Spirit: A Baptist View of Church Membership*. Brantford, Ont.: Baptist Federation of Canada, 1964.

Ayer, William W. "The Independent Tabernacle Movement and the Organized Denominational Church." *Watchman-Examiner*, March 7, 1935: 242–243.

Baldwin, Thomas. *The Baptism of Believers Only, and the Particular Communion of the Baptist Churches, Explained and Vindicated in Three Parts*. Boston, Mass.: Manning and Loring, 1806.

Beasley-Murray, George R. *Baptism in the New Testament*. London: Macmillan, 1963.

Belzile, Michel. "Canadian Baptists at Worship." D.Min. thesis, McMaster University, 1998.

Bogard, Ben M. *The Baptist Way Book: Manual Designed for Use in Baptist Churches*. Texarkana, Tex.: Baptist Sunday School Committee, 1927.

Briggs, John H. Y. "English Baptists and Their Hymnody: An Introduction." In *Baptist Faith and Witness*, edited by William H. Brackney and L.A. Cupit, pp. 152–159. McLean, Va.: Samford University Press and Baptist World Alliance, 1995.

Buffington, W. L. "Clerical Titles among Baptists." *Chronicle*, 1942, 97.

Davies, Horton. *Worship and Theology in England: From Cranmer to Baxter and Fox, 1534–1690*. 2 vols. Princeton, N.J.: Princeton University Press, 1970–1975.

Deweese, Charles W. *Baptist Church Covenants*. Nashville, Tenn.: Broadman Press, 1990.

Dorgan, Howard. *Giving Glory to God in Appalachia: Worship Practices of Six Baptist Subdenominations*. Knoxville, Tenn.: University of Tennessee Press, 1987.

Ellis, Christopher J. *Gathering: A Theology and Spirituality of Worship in the Free Church Tradition*. London: SCM Press, 2004.

Farnsley, Arthur E. *Southern Baptist Politics: Authority and Power in the Restructuring of an American Denomination*. University Park, Pa.: Pennsylvania State University Press, 1994.

Ford, Murray J. S., editor. *Canadian Baptist History and Polity: The McMaster Conference*. Brantford, Ont.: Hurley Publishing Co., 1982.

Gilmore, Alec, editor. *Christian Baptism*. London: Lutterworth Press, 1959.

Graves, James R. *Old Landmarkism: What Is It?* Texarkana, Ark.: Baptist Sunday School Committee, 1880, 1928.

Griffiths, Benjamin. "Essay on the Association." In *Minutes of the Philadelphia Baptist Association A.D. 1707– A.D. 1807*, edited by Abraham D. Gillette, pp. 60–63. Philadelphia, Pa.: American Baptist Publication Society, 1851.

Hall, Robert, Jr. *On Terms of Communion, with a Particular View to the Case of the Baptists and the Paedobaptists*. Leicester, England: Thomas Combe, 1815.

Handy, Robert T. "American Baptist Polity: What's Happening and Why?" *Baptist History and Heritage* 14:3 (July 1979): 12–21.

Harkness, R. E. E. "Origin of the Prayer-Meeting among English and American Baptists." *Chronicle* 1:4 (October 1938): 149–161.

Harrison, Paul M. *Authority and Power in the Free Church Tradition*. Princeton, N.J.: Princeton University Press, 1959.

Hiscox, Edward T. *The Standard Manual for Baptist Churches*. Philadelphia, Pa.: American Baptist Publication Society, 1890.

Holmes, Elkanah. *A Church Covenant, Including a Summary of the Fundamental Doctrines of the Gospel*. Baltimore, Md.: 1818.

Hudson, Winthrop S., editor. *Baptist Concepts of the Church*. Valley Forge, Pa.: Judson Press, 1959.

Jones, Samuel. *A Treatise on Church Discipline*. Philadelphia, Pa.: S. C. Ustick, 1798.

Lord, F. Townley. *Baptist World Fellowship: A Short History of the Baptist World Alliance*. Nashville, Tenn.: Broadman Press, 1955.

Maring, Norman H. *A Baptist Manual of Polity and Practice*. Valley Forge, Pa.: Judson Press, 1993.

McNutt, William R. *Polity and Practice in Baptist Churches*. Philadelphia, Pa.: Judson Press, 1935.

Pendleton, James M. *Church Manual, Designed for the Use of Baptist Churches*. Philadelphia, Pa.: American Baptist Publication Society, 1867.

Robinson, H. Wheeler. *The Life and Faith of the Baptists*. London: Methuen, 1927.

Sacks, Francis. *The Philadelphia Tradition of Church and Church Authority: An Ecumenical Analysis and Theological Interpretation*. Lewiston, N.Y.: Edwin Mellen Press, 1990.

Shurden, Walter. *Associationalism among Baptists in America: 1707–1814*. New York: Arno Press, 1980.

Stoffer, Dale R., editor. *The Lord's Supper: Believers Church Perspectives*. Scottdale, Pa.: Herald Press, 1997.

Sullivan, James L. *Baptist Polity as I See It*. Nashville, Tenn.: Broadman Press, 1983.

Torbet, Robert G. *The Baptist Ministry: Then and Now*. Philadelphia, Pa.: Judson Press, 1953.

———. *A Social History of the Philadelphia Baptist Association 1707–1940*. Philadelphia, Pa.: Western Book Publishing Company, 1944.

Walker, Michael. *Baptists at the Table: The Theology of the Lord's Supper amongst English Baptists in the Nineteenth Century*. Didcot: Baptist Historical Society, 1992.

Wilkinson, William C. *The Baptist Principle, in Application to Baptism and the Lord's Supper*. Philadelphia, Pa.: American Baptist Publication Society, 1897.

BAPTISTS AND OTHER CHRISTIANS

Works defining Baptists in conversation and relationships with other Christians are a continuing area of scholarly interest. William Estep's work on Christian unity and Paul Toews' report and analysis on Baptist-Mennonite relations are most useful.

Boney, W. J., and Iglehart, Glenn A. *Baptists and Ecumenism*. Valley Forge, Pa.: Judson Press, 1980.

Brackney, William H., editor. *The Believers Church, a Voluntary Church*. Kitchener, Ont.: Pandora Press, 1998.

Champion, Leonard G. *Baptists and Unity*. London: A. R. Mowbray, 1962.

Child, Robert L. *Baptists and Christian Unity*. London: Carey Kingsgate Press, 1948.

Estep, William R. *Baptists and Christian Unity*. Nashville, Tenn.: Broadman Press, 1966.

Garrett, James L., editor. *Baptist Relations with Other Christians*. Valley Forge, Pa.: Judson Press, 1974.

———. *Baptists and Roman Catholicism*. Nashville, Tenn.: Broadman Press, 1965.

Gates, Erret. *The Early Relation and Separation of Baptists and Disciples*. Chicago, Ill.: R. R. Donnelly, 1904.

Gilmore, Alec. *Baptism and Christian Unity*. Valley Forge, Pa.: Judson Press, 1966.

Goadby, Joseph. *Baptists and Quakers in Northamptonshire, 1650–1700*. Northampton: n.p., 1882.

Hinson, E. Glenn. "Southern Baptists and Ecumenism: Some Contemporary Patterns." *Review and Expositor*, Summer 1969, 274.

Hughey, John D. "Baptists and the Ecumenical Movement." *Ecumenical Review* 10:4 (July 1958): 401–410.

Jackson, Joseph H. *Many but One: The Ecumenics of Charity*. New York: Sheed and Ward, 1964.

Payne, Ernest A. *The Fellowship of Believers*. London: Carey Kingsgate, 1954.

Pestana, Carla. *Quakers and Baptists in Colonial Massachusetts*. New York: Cambridge University Press, 1991.

Roberts-Thompson, E. *Baptists and Disciples of Christ*. London: Carey Kingsgate, 1951.

——. *With Hands Outstretched: Baptists and the Ecumenical Movement*. London: Marshall, Morgan, and Scott, 1962.

Russell, David S. *Baptists and Some Contemporary Issues*. London: Baptist Union, 1968.

Stubblefield, Jerry M. "The Attitude and Relationship of the Southern Baptist Convention to Certain Other Baptist and Interdenominational Bodies." Th.D. dissertation, Southern Baptist Theological Seminary, 1967.

Swain, Anna C. "Baptists and Ecumenicity." *Chronicle* 18:2 (April 1955): 70–78.

Toews, Paul, editor. *Mennonites and Baptists: A Continuing Conversation*. Winnipeg, Man.: Kindred Press, 1993.

Torbet, Robert G. *Ecumenism: Free Church Dilemma*. Valley Forge, Pa.: Judson Press, 1958.

Underwood, T. L. *Primitivism, Radicalism, and the Lamb's War: The Baptist-Quaker Conflict in Seventeenth Century England*. New York: Oxford University Press, 1997.

West, W. M. S. *Baptists Together*. Didcot: Baptist Historical Society, 2000.

THEMES IN BAPTIST HISTORY

Themes emerge in Baptist studies according to trends in the academy and the religious culture. As the scholar-historians investigate religious fundamentalism, peace and justice, feminist and racial/ethnic issues, those in the churches follow the lead of women, education, music, officers, polity, and the ordinances.

Ammerman, Nancy. *Baptist Battles: Social Change and Religious Conflict in the Southern Baptist Convention*. New Brunswick, N.J.: Rutgers University Press, 1990.

Barnhart, Joe E. *The Southern Baptist Holy War*. Austin, Tex.: Texas Monthly Press, 1986.

Beale, David O. *SBC: House on the Sand*. Greenville, S.C.: Unusual Publications, 1985.

Boone, Isley. *Elements in Baptist Development: A Study of Denominational Contributions to National Life, Christian Ideals, and World Movements*. Boston, Mass.: Backus Historical Society, 1913.

Boylan, Anne M. *Sunday School: The Formation of an American Institution*. New Haven, Conn.: Yale University Press, 1988.

Brown, J. Newton. *Baptist Martyrs*. Philadelphia, Pa.: American Baptist Publication Society, 1854.

Brown, Louise F. *The Political Activities of the Baptists and Fifth Monarchy Men in England during the Interregnum*. Washington, D.C.: American Historical Association, 1912.

Carwardine, Richard. *Trans-Atlantic Revivalism: Popular Evagelicalism in Britain and America, 1790–1865*. Westport, Conn.: Greenwood Press, 1978.

Cothen, Grady. *What Happened to the Southern Baptist Convention?* Macon, Ga.: Mercer University Press, 1993.

Davis, Lawrence B. *Immigrants, Baptists, and the Protestant Mind in America*. Urbana, Ill.: University of Illinois Press, 1973.

Dekar, Paul R. *Baptist Peacemakers*. Macon, Ga.: Smyth and Helwys, 1993.

Dollar, George W. *A History of Fundamentalism in America*. Greenville, S.C.: Bob Jones University Press, 1973.

Durso, Keith R. *No Armour for the Back: Baptist Prison Writings, 1600s–1700s*. Macon, Ga.: Baptist History and Heritage Society, 2007.

Eighmy, John Lee. *Churches in Cultural Captivity: A History of Social Attitudes of Southern Baptists*. Knoxville, Tenn.: University of Tennessee Press, 1972.

Garrett, James Leo, Hinson, E. Glenn, and Tull, James E. *Are Southern Baptist Evangelicals?* Macon, Ga.: Mercer University Press, 1983.

Goodwin, Everett, editor. *Baptists in the Balance: The Tension between Freedom and Responsibility*. Valley Forge, Pa.: Judson Press, 1997.

Heyrman, Christine L. *Southern Cross: The Beginnings of the Bible Belt*. New York: Alfred Knopf, 1997.

Hindmarsh, Bruce. *John Newton and the English Evangelical Tradition: Between the Conversions of Wesley and Whitefield*. Oxford: The Clarendon Press, 1996.

Hudson, Winthrop S. *Baptists in Transition: Individualism and Christian Responsibility*. Valley Forge, Pa.: Judson Press, 1979.

Lappin, Maitland M. *Baptists in the Protestant Tradition*. Toronto, Ont.: Ryerson, 1947.

McBeth, H. Leon. *English Baptist Literature on Religious Liberty to 1689*. New York: Arno Press, 1980.

McLoughlin, William G. *Champions of the Cherokees: Evan and John B. Jones*. Princeton, N.J.: Princeton University Press, 1990.

Moss, Lemuel. *The Baptists and the National Centenary: A Record of Christian Work: 1776–1876*. Philadelphia, Pa.: American Baptist Publication Society, 1876.

Music, David W., and Richardson, Paul A. *I Will Sing the Wondrous Story: A History of Baptist Hymnody in North America*. Macon, Ga.: Mercer University Press, 2008.

Newman, Albert H. *A Century of Baptist Achievement*. Philadelphia, Pa.: American Baptist Publication Society, 1901.

Patterson, W. Morgan. *Baptist Successionism*. Valley Forge, Pa.: Judson Press, 1969.

Peacock, James, and Tyson, Ruel W. *Pilgrims of Paradox: Calvinism and Experience among the Primitive Baptists of Blue Ridge*. Washington, D.C.: Smithsonian Institution Press, 1989.

Putnam, Mary G. *The Baptists and Slavery, 1840–45*. Ann Arbor, Mich.: G. Wahr, 1913.

Shurden, Walter B. *Proclaiming the Baptist Vision: Religious Liberty*. Macon, Ga.: Smyth and Helwys, 1997.

——, editor. *The Struggle for the Soul of the SBC*. Macon, Ga.: Mercer University Press, 1993.

Stewart, Howard R. *Baptists and Local Autonomy*. Hicksville, N.Y.: Exposition Press, 1974.

Storey, John W. *Texas Baptist Leadership and Social Christianity. 1900–1980*. College Station, Tex.: Texas A&M University, 1986.

Thompson, James J. *Tried as by Fire: Southern Baptists and the Religious Controversies of the 1920s*. Macon, Ga.: Mercer University Press, 1982.

Vedder, Henry C. *Baptists and the Liberty of Conscience*. Cincinnati, Ohio: J. Bauimes, 1884.

WOMEN IN BAPTIST LIFE

Formerly a category with other themes, investigation of Baptist women has become a category in itself. Of particular interest are missionary women and persons of color, along with the proverbial interest in the ordination of women.

Anderson, O. "Women Preachers in Mid-Victorian Britain: Some Reflections on Feminism, Popular Religion and Social Change." *Historical Journal* 12:3 (1969): 467–484.

Bailey, Faith C., and Wenger, Margaret N. *Two Directions*. Rochester, N.Y.: Baptist Missionary Training School, 1964.

Bellinger, Elizabeth, editor. *A Costly Ordeal: Sermons by Women of Steadfast Spirit*. Valley Forge, Pa.: Judson Press, 1994.

Blevins, Carolyn D. "Women in Baptist History." *Review and Expositor* 83:1 (January 1986): 51–62.

Briggs, John. "She-Preachers, Widows and Other Women: The Feminine Dimension in Baptist Life since 1600." *Baptist Quarterly* 31:7 (July 1986): 337–352.

Brooks, Evelyn. "The Woman's Movement in the Black Baptist Church, 1880–1920." Ph.D. dissertation, University of Rochester, 1984.

Chatterjee, Sunil K. *Hannah Marshman: The First Woman Missionary in India*. Calcutta: People's Little Press, 1987.

Daniel, Sadie I. *Women Builders*. Washington, D.C.: Association Publishers, 1931.

Dowling, John, editor. *The Judson Offering, Intended as a Token of Christian Sympathy with the Living, and a Memento of Christian Affection for the Dead*. New York: L. Colby, 1846.

Durso, Pamela R. "Baptists and the Turn toward Women in Ministry." In *Turning Points in Baptist History: A Festschrift in Honor of Harry Leon McBeth*, edited by Michael E. Williams, Sr., and Walter B. Shurden, pp. 275–287. Macon, Ga.; Mercer Universitry Press, 2008.

Gouldbourne, Ruth M. B. *Reinventing the Wheel: Women and Ministry in English Baptist Life*. Oxford: Whitley Publications, 1997.

Greaves, Richard L. *Triumph over Silence: Women in Protestant History*. Westport, Conn.: Greenwood Press, 1985.

McBeth, H. Leon. *Women in Baptist Life*. Nashville, Tenn.: Broadman Press, 1979.

Mitchell, Ella P. *Those Preachin' Women*. 3 vols. Valley Forge, Pa.: Judson Press, 1985, 1996.

Moore, Joanna P. *In Christ's Stead*. Chicago, Ill.: Woman's Baptist Home Mission Society, 1902.

Porter, M. *Women in the Church: The Great Ordination Debate in Australia*. Ringwood: Penguin Books, 1989.

Smith, Karen E. "Beyond Public and Private Spheres: Another Look at Women in Baptist History and Historiography." *Baptist Quarterly* 34:1 (January 1991): 79–87.

Vail, Albert L. *Mary Webb and the Mother Society*. Philadelphia, Pa.: American Baptist Publication Society, 1914.

Van Broekhoven, Deborah B. *Abolitionists Were Female: Rhode Island Women and the Antislavery Network*. Urbana: University of Illinois Press, 1999.

Vose, Heather M. "The Ministry of Women in the Baptist Churches of the U.S.S.R." In *Faith, Life and Witness*, edited by William H. Brackney, pp. 129–137. Birmingham, Ala.: Samford University Press, 1990.

SELECT BIOGRAPHIES

Biographies occupy a large segment of Baptist historical resources. Some are richer in detail than others. Among the best scholarship are the works on Harvey Cox, James Manning, Obadiah Holmes, Lottie Moon, Walter Rauschenbusch, Harry Emerson Fosdick, Isaac T. Tichenor, and Howard Thurman.

Abernathy, Ralph David. *And the Walls Came Tumbling Down*. New York: Harper and Row, 1989.

Allen, Catherine B. *The New Lottie Moon Story*. Nashville, Tenn.: Broadman Press, 1980.

Babcock, Rufus, editor. *Memoirs of John Mason Peck, D.D.* Carbondale: Southern Illinois University Press, 1965.

Balders, Gunter. *Theurer Bruder Oncken: Das Leben Johann Gerhard Onckens in Bildern und Dokumenten*. Kassel: Oncken Verlag, 1978.

Beck, James R. *Dorothy Carey: The Tragic and Untold Story of Mrs. William Carey*. Grand Rapids, Mich.: Baker Book House, 1992.

Benedict, David. *Fifty Years among the Baptists*. New York: Sheldon, 1860.

Buckingham, William, and Ross, George W. *The Hon. Alexander Mackenzie: His Life and Times.* Toronto, Ont.: Rose Publishing Co., 1892.

Burgess, Walter H. *John Smyth the Se-Baptist, Thomas Helwys and the First Baptist Church in England.* London: James Clarke, 1911.

Burton, Joe W. *Road to Augusta: R.B.C. Howell and the Formation of the Southern Baptist Convention.* Nashville, Tenn.: Broadman Press, 1976.

Byrt, G. W. *John Clifford: A Fighting Free Churchman.* London: Carey Kingsgate Press, 1947.

Camp, L. Raymond. *Roger Williams: God's Apostle of Advocacy: Biography and Rhetoric.* Lewiston, N.Y.: Edwin Mellen Press, 1993.

Carey, John J. *Carlyle Marney: A Pilgrim's Progress.* Macon, Ga.: Mercer University Press, 1980.

Carlton, John W. *The World in His Heart: The Life and Legacy of Theodore F. Adams.* Nashville, Tenn.: Broadman Press, 1985.

Carter, Joseph R. *The "Acres of Diamond Man": A Memorial Archive of Russell H. Conwell.* 3 vols. Philadelphia, Pa.: Temple University, 1981.

Chaplin, Jeremiah. *Life of Henry Dunster: First President of Harvard College.* Boston, Mass.: J. R. Osgood, 1872.

Clark, Robert W. "The Contribution of Shailer Mathews to the Social Movement in American Protestantism." Th.D. dissertation, Southern Baptist Theological Seminary, 1959.

Cox, Harvey Gallagher. *Just as I Am.* New York: Harper and Row, 1975.

Cuthbert, James H. *Life of Richard Fuller D.D.* New York: Sheldon, 1879.

Davies, David. *Vavasor Powell: The Baptist Evangelist of Wales in the Seventeenth Century.* London: Alexander and Shephard, 1896.

Davis, John W. "George Leile and Andrew Bryan, Pioneer Negro Baptist Preachers." *Journal of Negro History* 3:2 (April 1918): 119–127.

Day, Richard E. *Rhapsody in Black: The Life Story of John Jasper.* Philadelphia, Pa.: Judson Press, 1953.

Dill, Jacob S. *Isaac Taylor Tichenor: The Home Mission Statesman.* Nashville, Tenn.: Sunday School Board, 1897.

Douglas, Crerar, editor. *Autobiography of Augustus Hopkins Strong.* Valley Forge, Pa.: Judson Press, 1981.

Elliott, David R., and Miller, Iris. *Bible Bill: A Biography of William Aberhart.* Edmonton, Alb.: Reidmore Books, 1987.

Elliott, Ralph H. *The Genesis Controversy and Continuity in Southern Baptist Chaos—A Eulogy for a Great Tradition.* Macon, Ga.: Mercer University Press, 1992.

Fletcher, Jesse. *Baker James Cauthen—A Man for All Nations*. Nashville, Tenn.: Broadman Press, 1977.

Fosdick, Harry Emerson. *The Living of These Days: An Autobiography*. New York: Harper and Brothers, 1956.

Franklin, John Hope. *George Washington Williams: A Biography*. Chicago, Ill.: University of Chicago Press, 1985.

Gano, John. *Biographical Memoirs of the Late John Gano of Frankfort, Kentucky, Formerly of the City of New York*. New York: Southwick and Hardcastle, 1806.

Gaustad, Edwin S., editor. *Baptist Piety: The Last Will and Testament of Obadiah Holmes*. New York: Arno Press, 1980.

———. *Liberty of Conscience: Roger Williams in America*. Grand Rapids, Mich.: Wm. B. Eerdmans, 1991.

Gayle, Clement. *George Leile: Pioneer Missionary to Jamaica*. Kingston, Jamaica: Baptist Union of Jamaica, 1982.

Gibson, Theo T. *Beyond the Granite Curtain: The Story of Alexander McDonald: Pioneer Baptist Missionary to the Canadian North-West*. Ancaster, Ont.: Author, 1975.

———. *Robert A. Fyfe: His Contemporaries and His Influence*. Burlington, Ont.: G. R. Welch, 1988.

Gilpin, W. Clark. *The Millennarian Piety of Roger Williams*. Chicago, Ill.: University of Chicago Press, 1979.

Greaves, Richard L., editor. *Biographical Dictionary of British Radicals in the 17th Century*. Brighton-Sussex: Harvester Press, 1982–1984.

Green, Bernard. *Tomorrow's Man: A Biography of James Henry Rushbrooke*. Didcot, England: Baptist Historical Society, 1997.

Greene, Louise F. *The Writings of John Leland*. New York: Arno Press, 1969.

Guild, Reuben *Chaplain Smith and the Baptists*. Philadelphia, Pa.: American Baptist Publication Society, 1885.

———. *Life, Times, and Correspondence of James Manning*. Boston, Mass.: Gould and Lincoln, 1864.

Hardin, Shields T. *The Colgate Story*. New York: Vantage Press, 1959.

Harlan, Louis R. *Booker T. Washington: The Making of a Black Leader 1856–1915*. 2 vols. New York: Oxford University Press, 1972, 1983.

Hatcher, William E. *Life of J.B. Jeter, D.D.* Baltimore, Md.: H. M. Wharton, 1887.

Haykin, Michael A. G. *One Heart and One Soul: John Sutcliff of Olney, His Friends and His Times*. Durham, U.K.: Evangelical Press, 1994.

Hines, Herbert W. *Clough: The Kingdom-Builder in South India*. Philadelphia, Pa.: Judson Press, 1929.

Hinton, John H. *Memoir of William Knibb, Missionary in Jamaica*. London: Houlston and Stoneman, 1847.

Hovey, George Rice. *Alvah Hovey: His Life and Letters*. Philadelphia, Pa.: Judson Press, 1928.

Hynes, William J. *Shirley Jackson Case and the Chicago School: The Socio-Historical Method*. Chico, Calif.: Scholars Press, 1981.

James, Powhatan W. *George W. Truett: A Biography*. New York: The Macmillan Co., 1939.

Jeffrey, R. *Autobiography of Elder Jacob Knapp*. New York: Sheldon, 1868.

Jeter, Jeremiah Bell. *Recollections of a Long Life*. Richmond, Va.: Religious Herald Publishing Co., 1880.

King, Martin Luther, Sr. *Daddy King: An Autobiography*. New York: William Morrow, 1980.

Kruppa, Patricia S. *Charles Haddon Spurgeon: A Preacher's Progress*. New York: Garland Press, 1982.

Luckey, Hans. *Gottfried Wilhelm Lehmann und die Entstehung einer deutschen Freikirche*. Kassel, Germany: Verlag Oncken, 1959.

Lynd, S. W. Lynd. *Memoir of the Rev. William Staughton D.D.* Boston, Mass.: Lincoln and Edmands, 1834.

Mallary, Charles D. *Memoirs of Elder Jesse Mercer*. New York: J. Gray, 1844.

Marchant, James. *Dr. John Clifford: Life, Letters, and Reminiscences*. London: Cassell and Co., 1924.

Marks, Marilla. *Memoirs of the Life of David Marks*. Dover, N.H.: Freewill Baptist Printing Establishment, 1846.

Marshman, John C. *The Life and Labors of Carey, Marshman & Ward, The Serampore Missionaries*. New York: U. D. Ward, 1867.

McDormand, Thomas B. *A Diversified Ministry: An Autobiography of Thomas B. McDormand*. Hantsport, N.S.: Lancelot Press, 1987.

Mellette, Peter. "Alexander Mackenzie: An Example of Christian Statesmanship." *Chronicle* 7:4 (October 1944): 171–181.

Mild, Warren P. *Howard Malcolm and the Great Mission Advance*. Valley Forge, Pa.: Board of International Ministries, 1988.

Miller, Robert M. *Harry Emerson Fosdick: Preacher, Pastor, Prophet*. New York: Oxford University Press, 1985.

Minus, Paul M. *Walter Rauschenbusch: American Reformer*. New York: Macmillan, 1988.

Murray, James O. *Francis Wayland*. Boston, Mass.: Houghton Mifflin, 1891.

Nelson, Wilbur. *The Hero of Aquidneck: A Life of John Clarke*. New York: Fleming H. Revell, 1983.

Oates, Stephen B. *Let the Trumpet Sound: The Life of Martin Luther King, Jr*. London: Search Press, 1982.

Owens, Loulie L. *Oliver Hart, 1723–1795: A Biography*. Greenville, S.C.: 1966.

Parker, F. Calvin. *Jonathan Goble of Japan: Marine, Missionary, Maverick*. Lanham, Md.: University Press of America, 1990.

Perkin, J. R. C. *Morning in His Heart: A Biographical Sketch of Watson Kirkconnell, 1895–1977*. Hantsport, N.S.: Lancelot Press, 1986.

Pidwell, Harold. *A Gentle Bunyip: The Athol Gill Story*. South Australia: Seaview Press, 2007.

Pipkin, H. Wayne, and Yoder, John H., editors. *Balthasar Hubmaier: Theologian of Anabaptism*. Scottdale, Pa.: Herald Press, 1989.

Powell, Adam Clayton, Jr. *Against the Tide*. New York: Arno Press, 1980.

Prestridge, J. N. *Modern Baptist Heroes and Martyrs*. Louisville, Ky.: World Press, 1911.

Reid, C. S. *Samuel Sharpe: From Slave to National Hero*. Montego Bay, Jamaica: Bustamente Institute of Public Affairs, 1988.

Robertson, Archibald T. *Life and Letters of John Albert Broadus*. Philadelphia, Pa.: American Baptist Publication Society.

Rogers, James A. *Richard Furman: Life and Legacy*. Macon, Ga.: Mercer University Press, 1985.

Russell, C. Allyn. *Voices of American Fundamentalism: Seven Biographical Studies*. Philadelphia, Pa.: Westminster Press, 1976.

Saker, Emily H. *Alfred Saker, the Pioneer of the Cameroons*. London: Religious Tract Society, 1908.

Sears, Charles H. *Edward Judson: Interpreter of God*. Philadelphia, Pa.: American Baptist Publication Society, 1917.

Smith, Elias. *The Life, Conversion, Preaching, Travels and Suffering of Elias Smith*. Portsmouth, N.H.: Beck and Foster, 1816.

Smith, Luther E., Jr. *Howard Thurman: The Mystic as Prophet*. Lanham, Md.: University Press of America, 1981.

Sorrill, Bobbie. *Annie Armstrong: Dreamer in Action*. Nashville, Tenn.: Broadman Press, 1984.

Steadman, Thomas. *Memoir of the Rev. William Steadman D.D.* London: Thomas Ward, 1838.

Stearns, W. O. *William Newton Clarke: A Biography*. New York: Charles Scribner's, 1916.

Sweeny, Joseph R. "Elhanan Winchester and the Universal Baptists." Ph.D. dissertation, University of Pennsylvania, 1969.

Tarr, Leslie K. *Shields of Canada: T. T. Shields (1873–1955)*. Grand Rapids, Mich.: Baker Book House, 1967.

Taylor, George B. *Life and Times of James B. Taylor*. Philadelphia, Pa.: Bible and Publication Society, 1872.

Thompson, Helen W. *Luther Rice: Believer in Tomorrow*. Nashville, Tenn.: Broadman Press, 1967.

Thurman, Howard. *With Head and Heart: Autobiography of Howard Thurman*. New York: Harcourt, Brace, Jovanovich, 1979.

Tull, James E. *Shapers of Baptist Thought*. Valley Forge, Pa.: Judson Press, 1972.

Vick, Joyce. *From Victory to Victory: A Biography of Dr. G. B. Vick*. Akron, Ohio: n.p., n.d.

Wacker, Grant. *Augustus H. Strong and the Dilemma of Historical Consciousness*. Macon, Ga.: Mercer University Press, 1985.

Walden, Viola. *John R. Rice: The Captain of Our Team*. Murfreesboro, Tenn.: Sword of the Lord Press, 1990.

Washington, James M., editor. *A Testament of Hope: The Essential Writings of Martin Luther King, Jr*. San Francisco, Ca.: Harper and Row, 1991.

West, W. M. S. *To Be a Pilgrim: A Memoir of Ernest A. Payne*. Guildford, England: Lutterworth Press, 1983.

Williams, A. D. *Benoni Stinson and the General Baptists*. Owensville, Ind.: General Baptist Press, 1880.

Williams, Michael E., Sr. *Isaac Taylor Tichenor: The Creation of the Baptist New South*. Tuscaloosa: University of Alabama Press, 2005.

Wood, H. G. *Terrot Reaveley Glover: A Biography*. Cambridge: Cambridge University Press, 1953.

Woodson, Hortense. *Giant in the Land: A Biography of William Bullein Johnson, First President of the Southern Baptist Convention*. Nashville, Tenn.: Broadman Press, 1950.

LIBRARIES AND ARCHIVAL REPOSITORIES

The outstanding collection of Baptist historical resources is the Samuel Colgate Baptist Historical Collection of the American Baptist Historical

Society, followed by the Angus Library of Regent's Park College, Oxford. There are first-rate European collections in Elstal, Germany; Uppsala, Sweden; and Prague, Czech Republic. In the North American scene, Brown University, Acadia University, Southwestern Baptist Seminary, and Southern Baptist Seminary have significant holdings of original material. The Southern Baptist Library and Archives, and Furman, Richmond, and Mercer universities likewise are custodians of important Southern Baptist heritage.

American Baptist Historical Society. Atlanta, Georgia.
Anabaptist and Baptist Collection, Baptist Theological Seminary. Prague, Czech Republic.
Angus Library, Regent's Park College. Oxford, England.
Atlantic Baptist Archives, Acadia University. Wolfville, Nova Scotia.
Baptist Union of Queensland Archives. Gaythorne, Queensland.
Baptist Union of Sweden Archives, Betelseminariat. Stockholm, Sweden.
Baptist Union of Victoria. Camberwell, Victoria.
Burleigh College. Unley, South Australia.
Canadian Baptist Archives, McMaster University. Hamilton, Ontario.
Dr. Williams' Library. Gordon Square, London, England.
Franklin Trask Library, Andover Newton Theological School. Newton Centre, Massachusetts.
Free Baptist Collection, Bates College. Lewiston, Maine.
Freewill Baptist Collection, Mt. Olive College. Mt. Olive, North Carolina.
Georgia Baptist Historical Collection. Mercer University, Macon, Georgia.
German Union Archives, Theological Seminary. Elstal, Germany.
Hungarian Baptist Archives, Baptista Teological Szeminarium. Budapest, Hungary.
Irish Baptist Historical Society. Belfast, Northern Ireland.
Italian Baptist Archives, Centro Filadelfia. Turin, Italy.
John Hay Library, Brown University. Providence, Rhode Island.
John Rylands Library of Manchester University. Manchester, England.
Morling College Archives. Eastwood, New South Wales.
North American Baptist Archives (German), North American Baptist Seminary. Sioux Falls, South Dakota.
Norwegian Baptist Archives, Theological Seminary. Stabbek, Norway.
Polish Baptist Historical Archives, Church House. Warsaw, Poland.

Scottish Baptist Archives, Baptist Theological College. Glasgow, Scotland.
Southern Baptist Historical Collection. Nashville, Tennessee.
Swedish Baptist Archives, Betelseminariat. Stockholm, Sweden.
Swedish Baptist Collection, Bethel College. St. Paul, Minnesota.
University of Tasmania. Hobart, Tasmania.
Virginia Baptist Historical Collection, University of Richmond. Richmond, Virginia.
Vose Theological College. Bentley, Western Austraila.
Welsh Baptist Historical Collection, Ilston House. Swansea, Wales.

USEFUL BAPTIST INTERNET WEBSITES

American Baptist Historical Society
abc-usa.org/abhs
Angus Library, Regents Park College (U.K.)
rpc.ox.uk.ResourceCentres
Baptist Center for Ethics
ethicsdaily.com
Baptist Distinctives (Private Site)
baptistdistinctives.org
Baptist General Convention of Texas Archives
www.bgct.org
Baptist Heritage Council (Corporate Site)
www.baptistheritage.com
Baptist Historical Society (U.K.)
www.baptisthistory.org.uk
Baptist World Alliance
bwanet.org
German Baptist Archives
baptisten.org.
Mercer University Archives Special Collections
mercer.edu
Seventh Day Baptist Archives
seventhdaybaptist.org
Southern Baptist Historical Library and Archives
sbhla.org

Southern Baptist Theological Seminary Archives
  archives.sbts.edu
Spurgeon Library, Midwestern Baptist Seminary
  mbts.edu.library.spurgeon-collection
Strict Baptist Historical Society (U.K.)
  strictbaptisthistory.org.uk
The Baptist Page (Private Site)
  thebaptistpage.com

About the Author

William H. Brackney is the Dr. Millard R. Cherry Distinguished Professor of Christian Theology and Ethics at Acadia University in Wolfville, Nova Scotia, Canada (2006–). Formerly, he was principal of McMaster Divinity College and professor of historical theology at McMaster University in Hamilton, Ontario (1989–2000) and then professor of religion and chair of the Department of Religion, Baylor University in Waco, Texas. Dr. Brackney holds degrees from the University of Maryland (B.A., with honors), the Eastern Baptist Theological Seminary (M.A.R.), and Temple University (M.A., Ph.D.), and has taught religion and history at Houghton College, Colgate Rochester Divinity School, and the Eastern Baptist Theological Seminary. He has served as executive director and archivist for the American Baptist Historical Society and chair of the Division of Study and Research of the Baptist World Alliance. Dr. Brackney's previously published books include *Baptist Life and Thought* (1983, 1998), *The Baptists* (1988), *Christian Voluntarism: Theology and Praxis* (1997), *A Genetic History of Baptist Thought* (2005), *Human Rights and the World's Major Religions* (5 vols., 2004), *Baptists in North America*: *An Analytical History* (2006), and *Congregation and Campus: A History of Baptists in Higher Education* (2008).